MICROSOFT
ACCESS 95
HOW-TO

A compendium of indispensable tips from master developers who reveal their best techniques

Ken Getz and Paul Litwin

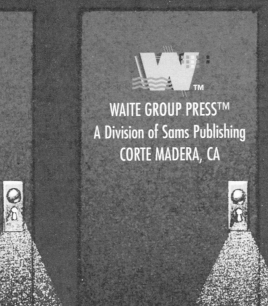

WAITE GROUP PRESS™
A Division of Sams Publishing
CORTE MADERA, CA

PUBLISHER Mitchell Waite
EDITOR-IN-CHIEF Charles Drucker

ACQUISITIONS EDITOR Jill Pisoni

EDITORIAL DIRECTOR John Crudo
MANAGING EDITOR Kurt Stephan
COPY EDITOR Deirdre McDonald Greene, Deborah Anker
TECHNICAL REVIEWER Michael S. Kaplan

PRODUCTION DIRECTOR Julianne Ososke
PRODUCTION MANAGER Cecile Kaufman
COVER DESIGN Karen Johnston
COVER ILLUSTRATION David Tillinghast
DESIGN Sestina Quarequio
PRODUCTION Michele Cuneo, Deborah Anker

Library of Congress Cataloging-in-Publication Data

Getz, Ken.
    Microsoft Access 95 how to / Ken Getz, Paul Litwin.
        p.   cm.
    Includes index.
    ISBN 1-57169-052-2
    1. Microsoft Access. 2. Database management. I. Litwin, Paul.
  II. Title.
QA76.9.D3G485 1996
005.75′65--dc20
                                                    96-5167
                                                    CIP

DEDICATION

To my parents, Chutie and Gerry. They always told me I could accomplish whatever I wanted. Not completely true, but it's a great place to start.

—KNG

To my parents, Joan and Tom, who have always supported me from day one.

—PEL

Message from the
Publisher

WELCOME TO OUR NERVOUS SYSTEM

Some people say that the World Wide Web is a graphical extension of the information superhighway, just a network of humans and machines sending each other long lists of the equivalent of digital junk mail.

I think it is much more than that. To me the Web is nothing less than the nervous system of the entire planet—not just a collection of computer brains connected together, but more like a billion silicon neurons entangled and recirculating electro-chemical signals of information and data, each contributing to the birth of another CPU and another Web site.

Think of each person's hard disk connected at once to every other hard disk on earth, driven by human navigators searching like Columbus for the New World. Seen this way the Web is more of a super entity, a growing, living thing, controlled by the universal human will to expand, to be more. Yet, unlike a purposeful business plan with rigid rules, the Web expands in a nonlinear, unpredictable, creative way that echoes natural evolution.

We created our Web site not just to extend the reach of our computer book products but to be part of this synaptic neural network, to experience, like a nerve in the body, the flow of ideas and then to pass those ideas up the food chain of the mind. Your mind. Even more, we wanted to pump some of our own creative juices into this rich wine of technology.

TASTE OUR DIGITAL WINE

And so we ask you to taste our wine by visiting the body of our business. Begin by understanding the metaphor we have created for our Web site—a universal learning center, situated in outer space in the form of a space station. A place where you can journey to study any topic from the convenience of your own screen. Right now we are focusing on computer topics, but the stars are the limit on the Web.

If you are interested in discussing this Web site or finding out more about the Waite Group, please send me email with your comments and I will be happy to respond. Being a programmer myself, I love to talk about technology and find out what our readers are looking for.

Sincerely,

Mitchell Waite

Mitchell Waite, C.E.O. and Publisher

200 Tamal Plaza
Corte Madera CA 94925
415 924 2575
415 924 2576 fax

Internet e-mail:
support@waite.com

Website:
http://www.waite.com/waite

CREATING THE HIGHEST QUALITY COMPUTER BOOKS IN THE INDUSTRY

Waite Group Press
Waite Group New Media

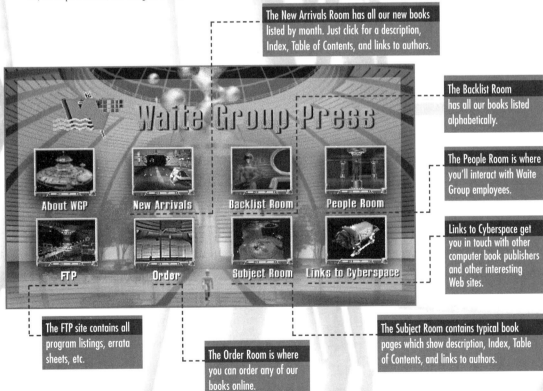

ABOUT THE AUTHORS

Ken Getz is an independent consultant, focusing on the Microsoft suite of products. He has received Microsoft's MVP award for each of the past three years and has written two books on developing applications using Microsoft Access. He and coauthor Paul Litwin (with Mike Gilbert and Greg Reddick) also collaborated on *Microsoft Access 95 Developer's Handbook* (Sybex, 1996). Currently, Ken spends a great deal of time traveling around the country presenting training classes aimed at Access developers for Application Developers Training Company. He also speaks at many conferences and trade shows throughout the world and is a contributing editor of Smart Access. When taking a break from the computer, he turns the chair around and handles the other keyboard: the grand piano that fills the other half of his office.

Paul Litwin is an independent developer focusing on Microsoft Access and SQL Server solutions. He's also the editor of Smart Access, a monthly newsletter for Access developers, and has written articles and reviews for various publications, including Smart Access, PC World, and Visual Basic Programmer's Journal. Paul authored the Microsoft Jet Engine White Paper and also worked with Ken Getz on *Microsoft Access 95 Developer's Handbook*. He also travels around North America for Application Developers Training Company, providing training to Access developers, and has been a featured speaker at many conferences, including Tech*Ed, Windows Solutions, PC Database Summit, Microsoft Developer Days, and VB Teach. When he has a spare moment, Paul enjoys running, as well as coaching his 9-year-old son's soccer team.

TABLE OF CONTENTS

CONTENTS

ACKNOWLEDGMENTS

No book gets written without some help from outside sources, and this one is no exception. We'd like to thank Kurt Stephan and Jill Pisoni at Waite Group Press for being so patient about our "rolling deadline." Due to unplanned extensions in the ship date of Microsoft Access for Windows 95, our original estimate of the book's completion date slid a bit. In addition, we'd like to thank Helen Feddema, Mike Gunderloy, and Dan Haught for their contributions to the first edition of this book, some of which remain (though altered for Access 95) in this edition.

We'd also like to thank the Microsoft Product Support and Services team, especially those that worked on the Access 95 beta program, for their patience and help. In particular, we'd like to thank Steve Alboucq, MariEsther Burnham, Jim Hance, Roger Harui, Tad Orman, Monte Slichter, and Sterling Smith. In addition, we'd like to thank Dan Frumin, Scott Horn, Debbie Johnson, David Lazar, Michael Risse, James Sturms, David Risher, and the many others in the Access product group who made sure we got the information we needed to make this book possible.

Special thanks to those that contributed suggestions and read chapters in their early stages, including Joe Maki, Sue Hogemeier, and Jim Newman.

Most of all, we'd like to thank Michael Kaplan, our technical editor, who reviewed every word of this book and every byte on the CD with loving care. He made many, many suggestions to make this book better (some of which we regretfully had to pass on, due to space and time limitations). The success of this book will be, in part, due to Michael's diligence and care.

FOREWORD

Since its introduction three years ago, Microsoft Access has become a gigantic success in the desktop database market. The product's success has generated an enormous demand for answers to questions on Access database development and design. For example, Access Support Engineers at Microsoft respond to well over 4,500 phone calls per day, the Microsoft Access forums on CompuServe and the Microsoft Network handle more than 1,000 messages per day, and downloads of technical articles from our online services number in the tens of thousands per month. People are putting Access to good use, and they are demanding answers to questions that arise as they develop their database applications.

Microsoft Access 95 How-To is the kind of book that Microsoft Access Support engineers enjoy seeing on bookstore shelves because it answers the frequently asked questions that cause customers to reach for their phone to call our support lines.

Microsoft Access makes it easier than any other desktop database to solve tough database management challenges. However, because of the complexity and variety of our data management requirements, we all encounter involved problems as we develop our applications—and nothing brightens our day like finding a quick answer to a problem that is holding up progress. The authors of this book, Ken Getz and Paul Litwin, are well known in the Access community for their creative ideas in solving the trickiest challenges of using Access. They have accumulated expansive knowledge of Access and have kept in close touch with the common problems and pitfalls that beset Access application developers. *Microsoft Access 95 How-To* represents many of their best ideas compiled in one convenient place. It is an ideal resource for an idea that will get us over a design hurdle, or when we want to add ease-of-use features to our applications.

There are numerous reference books on the market for Access, most focused on the lower- or mid-range user. The authors of this book have accomplished something significant—they've created a reference that is useful for the complete range of Access users. It is a resource that belongs on the desk of the novice user as well as the Access Basic guru; in other words, it is the book for anyone who wants to find smart solutions to common database development challenges.

The goal at Microsoft Access Product Support is to deliver the right answer right now. This book supports our goal by providing easy-to-understand explanations of how to solve frequently encountered problems. Our thanks go out to Ken, Paul, and Waite Group Press for once again creating an outstanding Access book.

Steve Alboucq
Microsoft Access Product Support Team Manager

INTRODUCTION

What This Book Is About

This is an "idea" book. It's a compendium of solutions, suggestions, and just "neat stuff"—all devoted to making your work with Microsoft Access more productive. If you're using Access, and aspire to database applications that are more than Wizard-created clones of every other database application, this is the book for you.

If, on the other hand, you're looking for a book that shows you how to create a form, or how to write your first Visual Basic for Applications function, or how to use the Crosstab Query Wizard, this may *not* be the book you need. For those kinds of things we recommend one of the many Access books geared toward the first-time user.

Promotes Creative Use of the Product

Rather than rehash the manuals, *Microsoft Access 95 How-To* offers you solutions to problems you may have already encountered, have yet to encounter, or perhaps have never even considered. Some of the issues discussed in this book are in direct response to questions posted in the Microsoft Access forum on CompuServe; others are problems we've encountered while developing our own applications. In any case, our goal is to show you how to push the edges of the product, making it do things you might not have thought possible.

For example, you'll learn how to create a query that joins tables based on some condition besides equality; how to size a form's controls to match the form's size; how to store and retrieve the location and sizes of forms from session to session; and how to create a page range indicator on every report page. You'll see how to use some of the Windows common dialog boxes from your Access application; how to internationalize your messages; how to *really* control your printer; and how to store the user name and date last edited for each row. There are How-To's for creating a runtime execution profiler, filling list boxes a number of different ways, and for optimizing your applications. You'll find details on using Access in multiuser environments, creating transaction logs, adjusting database options depending on who's logged in, and keeping track of users and groups programmatically. There are instructions for using the Windows API to restrict mouse movement to a specific area of a form, exiting Windows under program control, and checking the status of and shutting down another Windows application. Finally, you'll see how, with OLE (and a little DDE), you can use Access together with other applications such as the Windows shell, Microsoft Graph, Excel, and Word.

Uses the Tools at Hand

This book focuses on using the right tool for the right problem. If at all possible, the solutions provided here use macros. (Given that the majority of Access users don't already use program code, we wanted to make as many of these How-To's accessible to as many readers as possible.) On the other hand, some tasks just aren't well suited for macros and must be handled with code. Sometimes even plain VBA (Visual Basic for Applications) code isn't sufficient, and we needed to use the Windows API or other libraries that all users have. In each case, we've tried to make the implementation of the technique as simple as possible, yet as generic as possible.

> **NOTE**
>
> Old habits are hard to break. Previous to this version of Microsoft Access, the programming language built into the product was "Access Basic," and Visual Basic was a different development environment altogether. With the release of Microsoft Access for Windows 95, Microsoft has merged their cross-application programming language, Visual Basic for Applications (VBA), into Access. And we've tried to make sure that everywhere we would have said "Access Basic," we've used "VBA" or "Visual Basic" instead. When we say "Access Basic," "VBA," "Visual Basic," or "Basic" in this book, we mean "the implementation of VBA included in Microsoft Access for Windows 95." That would have been a mouthful.

Question-and-Answer Format

The structure of this book is simple: Each How-To consists of a single question and its solution. The chapters of questions and answers are arranged by categories: queries, forms, reports, application design, printing, data manipulation, VBA, optimization, user interface, multiuser, Windows API, and OLE/DDE. Each How-To contains a database with complete construction details, indicating which modules you'll need to import, what controls you'll need to create, and what events you'll need to react to. All the code, bitmaps, sample data, and necessary tools are included on the CD-ROM that accompanies the book.

Expected Level of Reader

No, you don't have to be a VBA whiz to use this book. It's been designed for all levels of readers: end users, power users, and developers. We've assigned each How-To a level of difficulty (Easy, Intermediate, or Advanced) based on the "complexity" of the solution. Problems that can be solved with a macro or two, or simple VBA code, are Easy. If a solution requires substantial code, or even a little code that's nontrivial, it's Intermediate. Solutions that rely on advanced VBA techniques or on Windows API calls are generally Advanced.

In every case, we've made the steps to implement the solution as simple as possible. When VBA is involved, we've recommended the modules to import from the sample database, with a discussion of the important features of the code within the text. You shouldn't have to retype any of the code unless you care to. What's more, you don't actually have to understand the solution to any of the problems covered in this book in order to make use of them. In each case, you'll find a sample database that demonstrates the technique, and explicit instructions on how to implement the same technique in your own applications. Of course, you'll learn the most by "digging in" to the samples to see how they work.

What You Need to Use This Book

In order to use this book you'll need a computer capable of running Windows 95 (or higher) or Windows NT 3.51 (or higher) and Microsoft Access for Windows 95. All of the example databases were prepared for display on a 640 x 480 (VGA) display. They'll work fine at a higher resolution, but you'll need at least standard VGA to run the examples well. A pointing device (mouse, pen, etc.) is highly recommended.

To demonstrate the topics in Chapter 12, you'll need to have copies of Microsoft Excel, Microsoft Word, PowerPoint, and Schedule Plus, all in 32-bit versions (such as the versions included in Microsoft Office for Windows 95). These items aren't necessary, of course, but will allow you to try out the example databases.

How This Book Is Organized

This book is organized into twelve chapters.

Chapter 1: Using the Power of Queries

This chapter covers the many types of queries and the power you have over the Access environment through the use of queries. From simple select queries through parameter, crosstab, totals, and Data Definition Language (DDL) queries, this chapter will show many different ways to use queries in your applications. Queries are the real "heart" of Access, and learning to use them intelligently will make your work in Access go much smoother.

Chapter 2: Designing Creative and Useful Forms

Most database applications require some sort of user interface, and in Access, that user interface is almost always centered around forms. This chapter will demonstrate some new and useful ways to make forms do your bidding, whether it be in terms of controlling data or making forms do things you didn't think were possible. We demonstrate how to create multipaged forms and how to create an incremental search list box. We also show how to create your own pop-up forms with a technique you can use in many situations. Forms can do much more than you might have imagined, and this chapter is a good place to look for some new ideas.

Chapter 3: Reporting as an Art Form

It seems like reports ought to be simple: Just place some data on the design surface and "let her rip!" That's true for simple reports, but Access' report writer is incredibly flexible and allows a great deal of customization. In addition, it's quite subtle in its use of properties and events. The topics in this chapter will advance your understanding of Access' report writer, from creating snaking column reports to printing alternating gray bars. Some of the How-To's in the chapter will require programming, but many don't. If you need to create attractive reports (and everyone working with Access does, sooner or later), the topics in this chapter will make your work a lot easier.

Chapter 4: Developing and Distributing Applications

This chapter is a compendium of tips and suggestions on making your application development go more smoothly, more professionally, and more internationally. Rather than focus on specific topics, this chapter brings up a number of issues that many developers run across as they ready their applications for distribution. How do you build a list of objects? How do you make sure all your objects' settings are similar? How do you translate text in your application? How do you use the Windows common dialog boxes? How do you install an add-in you've written? All these questions, and more, make up this group of tips for the application developer.

Chapter 5: Taming Your Printer

Many developers need to gain tight control over printed output, and Access doesn't make this easy. This chapter focuses on the three printer-related properties of forms and reports that are just barely documented: prtMip, prtDevMode, and prtDevNames. We'll cover these properties in detail and show examples of their use. You'll be able to retrieve a list of all the installed printers and make a choice from that list, setting the new default Windows printer. You'll learn how to modify margin settings in forms and reports, thereby avoiding the use of Access's Print|Page Setup dialog box in your applications. You'll get help on changing printer options, such as the number of copies to print, page orientation, and printer resolution. This chapter is full of somewhat daunting code, but the tools are useful even if you don't take the time to dig and decipher all the details.

Chapter 6: Managing Data

This chapter concentrates on working with data in ways that traditional database operations don't support. You'll learn how to filter your data, back it up, locate it on the file system, how to calculate a median, perform sound-alike searches, save housekeeping information, and more. Most examples in this chapter use some form of VBA, but don't worry. They are clearly explained, and "testbed" applications are supplied to show you how each technique works.

Chapter 7: Exploring VBA in Microsoft Access

The How-To's in this chapter cover some of the details of VBA that you might not find in the Access manuals. We've included topics on several issues that plague many Access developers, from handling embedded quotes in strings and creating a procedure stack and code profiler, to filling list boxes programmatically, to working with objects and properties. We've included code to sort an array, and How-To's that combine together several of the previous topics, such as filling a list box with a sorted list of file names. If you're an intermediate VBA programmer, this chapter is a good place to expand your skills. If you're already an expert, this chapter can add some new tools to your toolbox.

Chapter 8: Optimizing Your Application

Access is a big application, and you have a number of choices to make when designing applications, each of which can affect the application's performance. Unless you're creating only the most trivial of applications, you'll have to spend some time optimizing your applications. This chapter's topics work through eight different areas of optimization—steps you can take to make your databases work as smoothly as possible. The topics range from optimizing queries, forms and VBA, to testing the speed of various optimization techniques, to accelerating client/server applications. If you want your applications to run as fast as possible, this chapter would be a good place to look for tips.

Chapter 9: Making the Most of Your User Interface

This chapter presents a compendium of various user interface tips and techniques. By implementing the ideas and techniques in this chapter, you'll be able to create a user interface that stands out and works well. You'll find some simple, but not obvious, techniques for controlling the Access environment—such as altering your global key mappings as you move from one component of your application to another, and creating forms that hide the menu bar when they're active. The chapter shows how to create combo boxes that accept new entries, and how to provide animated images on buttons. You'll also find useful tips on working with data on your forms, using an OLE custom control to improve your interface, and providing your own solution-style message boxes, just like Access does.

Chapter 10: Addressing Multiuser Application Concerns

Very few database applications these days run on a stand-alone machine; most must be able to coordinate with multiple users. This chapter offers solutions to some of the common problems of networking and coordinating multiple simultaneous users. The most important issues are security and locking, and this chapter has examples that cover each. In addition, the topics in this chapter focus on replication, transaction logging, password aging, and automatic updates of shared objects. If you're working in a shared environment, you won't want to miss the ideas in this chapter!

Chapter 11: Making the Most of the Windows API

No matter how much you've avoided using the Windows API in Access applications, in this chapter you'll discover that it's really not a major hurdle. We'll present some interesting uses of the Windows API, with example forms and modules for each How-To. In most cases, using these examples in your own applications takes little more work than importing a module or two and calling some functions. You'll learn how to restrict the mouse movement to a specific area on the screen, how to run another program from your Access Basic code, and to wait until that program is done before continuing. We'll demonstrate a method for exiting Windows under program control, and how to retrieve information about your Access installation and the current Windows environment. The possibilities are endless, once you start diving into the Windows API, and this chapter is an excellent place to start.

Chapter 12: Using OLE (and DDE) to Extend Your Applications

This chapter gives you examples of using OLE in each of the ways it interacts with Access, and an example of using DDE with applications that don't offer OLE Automation. You'll examine how to activate an embedded OLE object (a sound file, for example). One How-To uses the statistical, analytical, and financial prowess of the Excel function libraries directly from Access, and another uses Word for Windows to retrieve document summary information for any selected document. Using DDE, you'll control the Windows shell. Finally, you'll dig into OLE Automation, with examples demonstrating how to use Access to control Microsoft Graph, PowerPoint, and Schedule+.

What We Left Out

In order to keep this book to a reasonable length, we have made some assumptions about your skills. First and foremost, we take it for granted that you are interested in using Microsoft Access and are willing to research the basics in other resources. This isn't a reference manual or a "Getting Started" book, so we assume you have access to that information elsewhere. We expect that you've dabbled in creating the Access objects (tables, queries, forms, and reports), and that you've at least considered working with macros and perhaps VBA (Visual Basic for Applications, the programming language included with Access). We encourage you to look in other resources for answers to routine questions, such as "What does this 'Option Explicit' statement do?"

To get you started, though, the following are basic instructions for what you'll need in order to use the How-To's in this book. For example, you'll encounter requests to "create a new event procedure." Rather than including specific steps for doing this in each and every case, the most common techniques you'll need have been gathered into this section. For each, we've included a help topic name from the Access online help, so you can get more information. By the way, none of the procedures here are the *only* way to get the desired results, but rather a single method for achieving the required goal.

How Do I Create a New Macro?

To create a new macro object, which can contain a single macro or a group of related macros, follow these steps:

1. Make the Database Explorer the active window, if it's not already, by pressing the F11 key.

2. Click on the Macro tab.

3. Click on the New button. Access will create a new, unnamed macro for you.

4. If you want to display (or turn off) the Macro Names column or the Conditions column, use the View|Macro Names and View|Conditions commands to toggle their state.

5. To add an action to your macro, choose it from the drop-down list in the Action column. Add one item per row, as shown in Figure I-1. Fill in the necessary information in the bottom pane (press [F6] to jump from pane to pane).

NOTE

For more information, see *macros; creating; Create a Macro* in Access online help.

How Do I Set Control Properties?

In the steps for many of the How-To's in this book, you'll be asked to assign properties to objects on forms or reports. This is a basic concept in creating any Access application, and you should thoroughly understand it. To assign properties to a control (or group of controls), follow these steps:

1. In design mode, select the control or group of controls. You can use any of the following methods. (Each of the items here refers to form controls but works just as well with reports.)

Single Control: Click on a single control. Access will mark it with up to eight sizing handles—one in each corner, and one in the middle of each side of the control, if possible.

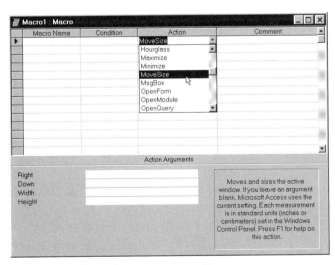

Figure I-1 Choosing a macro action

Multiple Controls: Click on a single control. Then `SHIFT`-`CLICK` on each of the other controls you also want to select. Access will mark them each with sizing handles.

Multiple Controls: Drag the mouse through the ruler (either horizontal or vertical). Access will select each of the controls in the path you dragged over. If partially selected controls don't become part of the selection and you'd like them to, open Tools|Options|Forms/Reports and look at the Selection Behavior option. It should be set to Partially Enclosed.

Multiple Controls: If you need to select all but a few controls, select them all and then remove the ones you don't want. To do this, first select the form (choose Edit|Select Form, or just click on the gray rectangle in the upper left corner of the form, if rulers are visible). Then choose Edit|Select All. Finally `SHIFT`-`CLICK` on the controls you don't want included.

2. Make sure the Properties Sheet is visible. If it's not, use View|Properties (or the corresponding toolbar button).

3. If you've selected a single control, all the properties will be available in the Properties Sheet. If you've selected multiple controls, only the intersection of the selected controls' properties will be available in the Properties Sheet. That is, only the properties all the selected controls have in common will appear in the list. As shown in Figure I-2, select a property group and then assign the

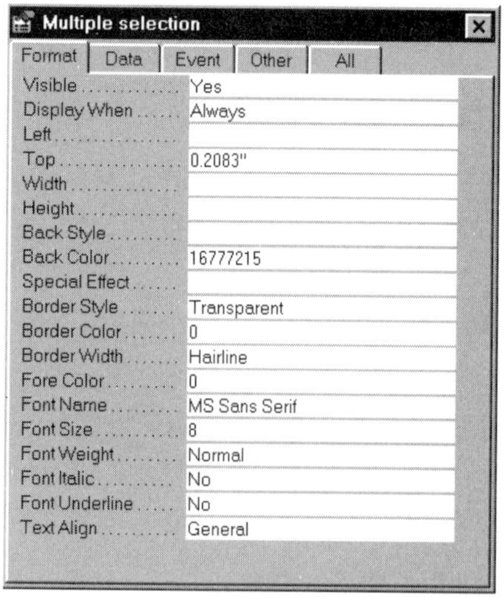

Figure I-2 The properties sheet shows the intersection of available properties when you've selected multiple controls

value you need to the selected property. Repeat this process for any other properties you'd like to set for the same control or group of controls.

> **NOTE**
>
> For more information, browse the various topics under *Properties; Setting* in Access online help.

How Do I Create a New Module?

Visual Basic for Applications (VBA) code is stored in containers called modules, each consisting of a single Declarations area, perhaps followed by one or more procedures. There are two kinds of modules in Access: global modules and form or report modules. Global modules are the ones you see in the Database Explorer, once you choose the Modules tab. Form or report modules (often referred to as CBF, or Code Behind Forms) are stored with the form or report itself and never appear in the Database Explorer. There are various reasons to use one or the other of the two module types, but the major factor of concern is the availability of procedures and variables. Procedures that exist in global modules can, for the most part, be called from any place in Access. Procedures that exist in a form or report's module can only be called from that particular form or report, and never from anywhere else in Access.

You'll never have to create a form or report module because Access creates that kind of module for you when you create the object to which it's attached. To create a global module, follow these steps:

1. From the Database Explorer, click on the Modules tab to select the collection of modules, and then click on the New button, or just choose the Insert|Module menu item.

2. When Access first creates the module, it places you in the Declarations area. All the possible items in the Declarations area are beyond the scope of this introduction, but you should always take one particular step at this point: Insert the Option Explicit instruction after the Option Compare Database instruction that Access has inserted. If you don't insert this statement, and Access encounters a reference to an unknown variable, Access will create the variable for you. With the Option Explicit statement, Access forces you to declare each variable before you use it. (You can skip this step if you've checked the Require Variable Declaration setting on the Module page of the Tools|Options dialog box. In that case, Access will insert the statement for you.)

> **Don't skip this step!**
>
> Although this may seem like an unnecessary burden for a beginner, it's not. It's an incredible time saver for all levels of users. With the Option Explicit statement in place, you can let Access check your code for misspellings. Without it, if you misspell a variable name, Access will just create a new one with the new name and go on about its business.

3. If you are asked to create a new function or subroutine, the simplest way to do that is to use Insert|Procedure. For example, if the How-To instructs you to enter this new procedure:

```
Function SomeFunc(intX as Integer, varY as Variant)
```

you can use Insert|Procedure, as shown in Figure I-3, to help you create the function.

4. Click OK in the Insert Procedure dialog box, and Access creates the new procedure and places the cursor in it, ready to go. For the example in step 3, you must also supply some function parameters, so you'll need to move back up to the first line and enter the "intX as Integer, varY as Variant" between the two parentheses.

> **NOTE**
>
> For more information on creating new modules and functions, see the online help topic *Modules; Creating.*

How Do I Import an Object?

In this book's How-To's, you'll often be asked to import an object from one of the sample databases. Follow these steps:

1. With your database open on the Access desktop, select the Database Explorer by pressing F11.

2. Choose File|Get External Data|Import, or right-click on the Database Explorer window and Choose Import.

3. Find the database from which you want to import a module, and click Import.

4. In the Import Objects dialog box, select all of the objects you'd like to import, moving from object type to object type. When you've selected all the objects you want to import, click on OK.

Figure I-3 The Insert Procedure dialog box helps you create a new function or subroutine

When importing modules, there's one possible problem to be concerned with: Access only allows one instance of a particular function or subroutine name throughout all the loaded modules, unless you've prefaced the procedure name with the "Private" keyword. If you attempt to load a module with duplicate procedure names, Access will complain and you'll need to rename the conflicting procedures in one or the other of the databases. You should also be aware that public Windows API declarations can only appear once in all your global modules. A collision between API declarations won't cause trouble until you attempt to compile your Access Basic code. If Access complains about duplicate definitions at that point, find the offending declaration and comment it out.

If a How-To instructs you to import a module from one of the sample databases that you've already imported (for a different How-To), you can ignore the instruction. Any modules with matching names in the sample database contain the exact same code, so you needn't worry about trying to import it again.

> **NOTE**
>
> For more information on importing objects, see *importing data; import or link* in Access online help.

How Do I Create an Event Macro?

Programming in Access often depends on having macros or VBA procedures reacting to events that occur as you interact with forms. To create a macro that will react to a user event, follow these steps:

1. Select the appropriate object (report, form or control) and make sure the Properties Sheet is displayed.

2. Either choose the Event Properties page on the Properties Sheet, or just scroll down the list until you find the event property you need.

> **Property Names vs. Event Names**
>
> The naming of event properties as opposed to the events themselves is rather ambiguous in Access. The event properties, in general, have an "On" prefix, as in "On Click", or "On Activate". The events themselves, however, are named without the "On" prefix, as in "the Click event" or "the Activate event". We've tried to be consistent throughout the book, but there are some places where the context just doesn't indicate which is the correct usage. You'll need to be aware that with or without the "On" prefix, when the event occurs, it activates the macro or procedure whose name is listed in the property sheet for that event.

3. Click on the "…" button to the right of the event name, as shown in Figure I-4. This is the Build button, and it appears next to Properties Sheet items that have associated builders. In this case, clicking the Build button displays the Choose Builder dialog box, as shown in Figure I-5. Choose the Macro Builder item to create a new macro.

4. Give the macro a name, so Access can save it and place its name in the Properties Sheet. You can always delete it later if you change your mind. Give your new macro the name suggested in the How-To, and fill in the rows as directed. When you're done, save the macro and put it away.

5. Once you're done, you'll see the name of the macro in the Properties Sheet, as shown in Figure I-6. Whenever the event occurs (the Change event, in this case), Access will run the associated macro (mcrHandleChange).

6. If you want to call an existing macro from a given event property, click on the drop-down arrow next to the event name, rather than the Build button. Choose from the displayed list of available macros (including macros that exist as part of a macro group).

> **NOTE**
>
> For more information on attaching macros to events, see *macros; creating* in Access online help.

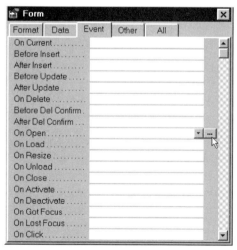

Figure I-4 Choose the Build button to invoke the Choose Builder dialog box

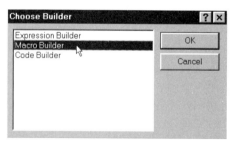

Figure I-5 The Choose Builder dialog box—choose Macro Builder for macros, and Code Builder for VBA

How Do I Create an Event Procedure?

To create an event procedure, follow steps 1, 2, and 3 above, for creating an event macro. In step 3, when you see the Choose Builder dialog box, choose Code Builder instead of Macro Builder.

When you create a new event procedure, Access creates the subroutine name, fills in the parameters that it passes, and places the subroutine into the form or report's private module (also known as CBF, or Code Behind Forms). The name of the procedure is always the name of the object, followed by an underscore and the name of the event. For example, had you created the Click event procedure for the cmdClose command button, you'd see a code skeleton like this:

```
Sub cmdClose_Click()

End Sub
```

Now follow these steps to complete the process:

1. If the How-To asks you to enter code into the event procedure, enter it between the lines of code that Access has created for you. Usually, the code example in the How-To will include the Sub and End Sub statements, so don't enter them again. When you're done, close the module window and save the form. By saving the form, you also save the form's module.

2. Another way to create an event procedure is to select an event property, pull down the list of choices for the property, and choose [Event Procedure]. When you click on the Build button, Access takes you directly to the correct event procedure for the selected event, for the current object.

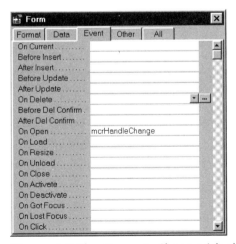

Figure I-6 The Property Sheet with the selected macro assigned to the OnChange event property

> **NOTE**
>
> For more information, see *event procedures; creating* in Access online help.

How Do I Place Code in a Form or Report's Module?

When a How-To asks you to place a procedure in a form or report's module that isn't directly called from an event, follow these simple steps:

1. With the form or report open in design mode, choose View|Code (or click on the Code button on the toolbar, as shown in Figure I-7).

2. To create a new procedure, follow the steps for "How Do I Create a New Module?", starting at step 3.

3. Choose File|Save, close the module and then save the form, or click on the Save icon on the toolbar.

How Do I Know What to Do with Code Examples?

In most cases, the How-To's suggest that you import a module (or multiple modules) from the sample database for the particular How-To, rather than type in code yourself. In fact, code that isn't referenced as part of the discussion doesn't show up at all in the body of the How-To. Therefore, you should count on importing modules as directed. Then follow the instructions in the "Steps" and "How It Works" sections of each How-To to finish working with and studying the code.

If the How-To tells you to place some code in a form's module, follow the steps in "How Do I Place Code in a Form or Report's Module?" If you are instructed to place code in a global module, follow the steps in "How Do I Create a New Module?" In most cases, you'll just import an existing module and not type anything at all.

Figure I-7 Click on the Code toolbar button to view a form or report's module

ABOUT THE CD-ROM

Please note this important information before using the included CD-ROM.

What's on the CD?

The CD-ROM bundled with *Microsoft Access 95 How-To* includes every sample database, icon, bitmap, and external file needed to build and use the example projects in this book. All of these files are debugged and ready to run. The CD also includes several powerful utilities, add-ins, and help files that will enrich your use of Microsoft Access. On the CD, you'll find:

- Shareware custom controls (fully operational) and demonstration versions of OLE controls (partially operational)

- The Microsoft Road Map to Developer Products and Services and Microsoft white papers on Jet locking and replication

- Access 95 add-ins

- A demo of Transcender's certification test preparation tool demo

Figure CD-1 shows the layout of the directory structure on the CD. You can use this figure as a guide while reading the following descriptions of the items.

How to Install the Files

The following paragraphs describe each of the items on the CD, and how to install each of the different databases, utilities, and files you'll find. Please note that you will need to remove the Read-only attributes to run any items copied from the CD to your hard drive.

Chapter Databases (\CHAPTERS\CH01 - \CH12)

All of the examples for each chapter are stored together in their own directory on the disk. For example, all the files for Chapter 2 are in directory \CHAPTERS\CH02. Within each directory the database samples are numbered to match a specific How-To. For example, the database for How-To 11.8 is named 11-08.MDB on the disk.

To use any of the sample databases, you'll need to copy all of the files from the specific directory on the CD to any directory you like on your hard disk. Since some of the examples require external files (bitmaps, icons, etc.), you'll find it simplest if you copy all of the files in the directory to your hard disk. If the given directory contains only MDB files, you can be relatively sure that they're all independent (unless they're marked as a group, as in 10-01BE.MDB and 10-01FE.MDB, where the BE stands for "back-end" and the FE stands for "front-end").

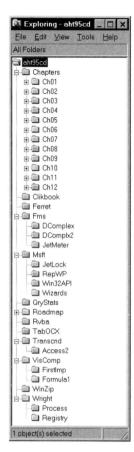

Figure CD-1 Directory structure for the companion CD

NOTE

In general, you cannot run the sample databases directly from the CD-ROM. You'll need to copy them to a writable medium before you'll be able to use them.

ClickBook: Surf 'n' Print (\CLIKBOOK)

Bookmaker Corporation has provided a full, retail copy of its Surf 'n' Print product. This fully functional product, ClickBook, allows you to print documents from any Windows application, folded, reduced, double-sided, rotated, and clipped to fit various page layouts. This version of the ClickBook product allows you to print in only one layout: a folded double-sided booklet, but that layout is not only the company's most popular but one of its most useful. This is a working product, not a demo, and if you want, you can upgrade to the full ClickBook version at a later date.

To install Surf 'n' Print, run SETUP.EXE from the CD-ROM.

Speed Ferret (\FERRET)

Speed Ferret, from Black Moshannon Systems, allows you to search and replace object names (or any other text) throughout your application. (If you've worked with Access for a while, you know how important this tool can be!) The version provided here is a limited but working version of the full program. Run the provided setup program (SETUP.EXE) to install the demonstration add-in on your system.

FMS, Inc.: Complexity Meter (\FMS\DCOMPLEX and \FMS\DCOMPLX2)

FMS, Inc., has provided Access 95 (Dcomplex) and Access 2 (Dcomplx2) versions of this freeware add-in, which calculates an arbitrary "complexity score" for your applications. You can use this score to rate the complexity of various applications, based on a scale that's described in the add-in.

To install the Access 95 version of the add-in, choose the Tools|Add-Ins|Add-In Manager menu (you must have a database open to do this). Click the Add New button, select the file DCOMPLEX.MDA on the CD, and then click the Close button. Once you've done this, you can run the add-in immediately by choosing it from the Tools|Add-Ins menu. Look at DCOMPLEX.WRI for more information about the add-in.

To install the Access 2 version of the add-in, choose the File|Add-Ins|Add-In Manager (you must have a database open to do this). Click the Add New button, select the file DCOMPLX2.MDA on the CD, and then click the Close button. You'll need to restart Access before you can use this add-in. Look at DCOMPLX2.WRI for more information about the add-in.

FMS, Inc.: Jet Statistics Meter (\FMS\JETMETER)

This add-in from FMS, Inc., monitors statistics of the Jet database engine as it does its work and reports the statistics to you. You'll find this tool useful if you're attempting to optimize your queries, or just want to know what your queries are doing internally. To install the add-in (Access 95 only), choose the Tools|Add-Ins|Add-In Manager (with a database open). Click the Add New button, select the file JETMETER.MDA on the disk, and then click the Close button. You can then run the add-in immediately. Look at JETMETER.WRI for more information about the add-in.

Microsoft: Jet Locking White Paper and DLL (\MSFT\JETLOCK)

If you've wondered how the Jet engine performs its locking, the information in this folder will tell you all you need to know: how Jet locks data, how to view locking information, and how to determine which users have a database open, among other details. Microsoft has provided a white paper, a DLL, a utility program, a sample database, and a sample VB4 application to demonstrate how Jet locking works. To use the information provided here, copy MSLDBUSR.DLL file to your Windows\System folder and the remaining files to a new folder on your hard disk. Open JETLOCK.DOC with Word for Windows or Windows 95 WordPad for more details.

Microsoft: Replication White Paper (\MSFT\REPWP)

If you're interested in the Jet engine's support for replication, you'll want to read this white paper from Microsoft. It includes all the basic details about how to use replication, what it does, and how it works. Open REPLICAT.DOC with Word for Windows or Windows 95 WordPad for more details.

Microsoft: Win32API Text File(\MSFT\WIN32API)

If you're using the Windows API, you won't want to be typing Declare statements into your code. This text file allows you to cut and paste the declarations without having to type them. You can either copy it to your hard disk or use it directly from the CD. Open it in any text editor (it's too large for Windows 95 Notepad, however). If you have the Access Developer's Toolkit for Windows 95, you already have this file—it's included with that product.

Microsoft: Unsecured Wizards (\MSFT\WIZARDS)

The wizards that are included with Access 95 have been secured. If you want to study their source code, a treasure trove of trips and tricks, you'll need these unsecured versions (actually, some portions are still secured). The Wizards included here are not supported in any way by Microsoft and are just provided for educational purposes. You can replace the secured wizards with these on your own machine, so you can debug through them, but do not distribute these or use them in a production environment. See WIZREAD.TXT for installation information.

Trigeminal Software: Query Statistics Add-In (\QRYSTATS)

Michael Kaplan provided this free add-in, which (like JETMETER.MDA, though very different) provides information about how your queries (or functions calling queries) interact with Access, Windows, and your hardware. This add-in can give you useful information about exactly what your query is doing as it retrieves information from your data.

To install the add-in, follow the same steps as were described previously for FMS' JETMETER.MDA. For more information and instructions, read QRYSTATS.TXT.

Microsoft Developer Roadmap (\ROADMAP)

This informational piece from Microsoft helps you find information you need, as a developer. It includes marketing materials about operating systems, visual tools, the Office development platform, databases, standards and specifications, and various Microsoft programs and services. The Road Map includes white papers, marketing materials, and articles from various magazines. You can run this directly from the CD (recommended), or you can install it to your hard disk. Either way, run the SETUP.EXE program in the directory, and follow the prompts.

Reddick VBA Naming Conventions (\RVBA)

Throughout this book, we've used a standard naming convention on all objects and variables. This document, RVBA.DOC, from Gregory Reddick & Associates, is the blueprint for the naming style we've adopted. We believe that every developer should adopt some naming standard, and we, along with many other Access developers, have adopted this style. Open RVBA.DOC in Word for Windows or Windows 95 WordPad for more information.

Tab OCX (\TABOCX)

Use this freeware custom control from Andrew Miller (at Microsoft) to create tabbed forms that match the Windows 95 look. There's a similar control in the Access Developer's Toolkit, but this one is simpler to use, and if you used the Access 2 version of the control (also included on this CD), it'll be a simple migration to this new Access 95 version.

To install the Access 2 version of the control, follow these steps:

1. Copy OC25.DLL, TAB.OCX, and TAB.LIC to your \WINDOWS\SYSTEM directory.

2. Execute these command lines:

```
REGSVR.EXE C:\WINDOWS\SYSTEM\OC25.DLL
REGSVR.EXE C:\WINDOWS\SYSTEM\TAB.OCX
```

To install the Windows 95 version of the control, follow these steps:

1. Copy OC30.DLL, TAB32.OCX, and TAB.LIC to your \WINDOWS\SYSTEM directory.

2. Execute these command lines:

```
REGSVR32.EXE C:\WINDOWS\SYSTEM\OC30.DLL
REGSVR32.EXE C:\WINDOWS\SYSTEM\TAB32.OCX
```

NOTE

Although Andrew Miller works for Microsoft, these OLE controls are not provided nor supported by Microsoft Corporation. This is true for any of the add-ins provided in this book, of course, but it's important to understand that these particular tools, though provided by a Microsoft employee, are not Microsoft products and cannot be treated as such.

For more information about the controls, double-click on the TAB.HLP help file located in the \TABOCX directory. This help file describes how to use the controls. In addition, look at TAB.MDB (in Access 2) for examples of using the Tab control.

Access 2 Certification Test Demo (\TRANSCND\ACCESS2)

Transcender Corporation has provided a demonstration of its test preparation tools for the Microsoft Access 2 certification exam (the Access 95 version was not ready at the time we went to print). The demo provides a small sampling of the kinds of questions the preparation tool (and real exam) might include. Run the SETUP.EXE program from the CD to install the demonstration on your hard disk.

Visual Components: First Impression (\VISCOMP\FIRSTIMP)

First Impression provides graphs, charts, and other visual presentations of your data, and provides far more control than Microsoft Graph ever even considered. This demonstration version does not allow you to distribute applications with the control, but it lets you get started and allows you to experiment some. It also includes some sample VB applications, demonstrating the power of the control. For detailed information, double-click to load VCFLU.HLP from the directory where the control has been installed.

To install the demonstration control, run SETUP.EXE from the CD.

Visual Components: Formula One (\VISCOMP\FORMULA1)

Formula One is a spreadsheet-like OLE control, emulating Excel's layout, formulas, and expressions. This demonstration version does not allow you to distribute applications with the control, but it does let you get a feeling for how it looks and feels. Once you install it, you'll find several compiled executables that show off the control. You can also embed the control on a form inside Access and play with it yourself. For more information, see the documentation files (*.WRI) in the directory where you installed the control. For detailed information, load the help file by double-clicking on VCF132.HLP in that same directory.

To install the demonstration control, run SETUP.EXE from the CD.

WinZip(\WINZIP)

WinZip is an extremely popular shell that allows you to compress and decompress files for transfer or storage. This shareware utility, from Nico Mak, makes it easy to archive and compress files. To install the application, run the WinZip95.EXE program from the directory on the CD.

Wright Process Control (\WRIGHT\PROCESS)

This shareware control allows you to run and manipulate external processes from within Access. You can think of it as "Shell( ) on steroids." It can provide more useful information about processes under Windows NT, but much of its power is still available under Windows 95. For complete information, look at WPROC.HLP, which its installation program places in your WINDOWS\SYSTEM directory.

Run SETUP.EXE from the CD to install the control.

Wright Registry Control (\WRIGHT\REGISTRY)

Though there are many methods you can use to read and write values in the Registry, none are as flexible or as simple as using this control. This shareware OLE control makes it easy to work with the Registry. Its use requires some VBA code, however, so you'll want to peruse the help file (WREG.HLP) that its installation program places in your WINDOWS\SYSTEM directory.

To install the control, run SETUP.EXE from the CD.

CHAPTER 1
HARNESSING THE POWER OF QUERIES

HARNESSING THE POWER OF QUERIES

How do I...

1.12   Use a query to show the relationship between employees and their supervisors?

1.13   Create a query that uses case-sensitive criteria?

1.14   Use a query to create a new table complete with indexes?

1.15   Save my queries in a table for better programmatic access and security?

1.16   Create a recordset based on a parameter query from VBA code?

Access queries—the six types that can be created on the easy-to-use query by example (QBE) grid, plus the three SQL-specific queries—give you a tremendous amount of power and flexibility in selecting, sorting, summarizing, modifying, and formatting the data stored in your tables before presenting it to the user on forms or printing it on reports. Access queries may be intimidating at first, especially if you are familiar with the more limited queries available in other database programs, but mastering queries will give you complete control over the appearance and functionality of your forms and reports. And Access queries are flexible—once you learn how to control them, you can use them in places where you might have written program code in other applications.

In this chapter, you'll learn to create parameter queries, allowing you to control selected rows of a report at runtime rather than at design time. You'll use this same technique to control the available values in one combo box based on the choice in another. You'll study the ways to control the output of crosstab queries, and learn a handy technique for mailing labels that lets you group labels by residence to avoid sending duplicate mailings to family members. You'll learn to take advantage of update queries to alter the values in one table based on the values from another, and you'll learn a trick that can be used to filter a query based on the value of a VBA variable. In case you need to pull random sets of data from a data source, you'll see how to use a query to create a random set of rows. You'll also examine a query that uses the Partition function to perform an aging analysis.

You'll also find a group of How-To's dealing with more advanced uses of queries. You'll learn how to create a join that's based on a nonequality comparison. You'll learn how to use union queries to horizontally splice together the data from two tables, and how to take advantage of union queries to add an extra choice to a combo box. You'll learn how to create self-join queries to model powerful recursive relationships and how to perform case-sensitive searches using a query. You'll learn how to use data definition language (DDL) queries to create or alter the structure of tables. You'll also examine a suggested method for storing query information in a table, which can be protected and made invisible in applications, giving you complete control over which queries get run and when. Finally, you'll learn a technique for creating recordsets in VBA code based on parameter queries.

Many of the examples in this chapter are based on a fictional music collection database that you could use to keep track of your favorite musicians and your album collection.

1.1   Specify Query Criteria When the Query Runs

Instead of creating several queries, each with the same basic design but slightly different criteria, you can create one parameter query that allows you to vary one or more parameters when you run the query. This How-To will show you how to create both simple parameter queries that use default prompts and more advanced parameter queries based on controls on a form.

1.2   Limit the Items in One Combo Box Based on the Selected Item in Another

Sometimes it would be nice to limit the values in one combo box based on the value selected in another combo box. This How-To will demonstrate how you can use a parameter query tied to one combo box on a form as the row source for a second combo box, to limit the second combo box's drop-down list to items appropriate to the user's selection in the first combo box.

1.3   Make Formatted Date Columns Sort Correctly in a Crosstab Query

If you have a crosstab query that uses the built-in Format function to convert dates into text for column headings, Access sorts them alphabetically (Apr, Aug, and so on) rather than chronologically. This How-To will demonstrate the use of fixed column headings to specify the headings you want in the correct order for your query.

1.4   Group Mailing Labels by Address

To avoid sending duplicate mailings to members of a family, you can use a totals query to group label data so that people with the same last name who live at the same address will only make up one row in the output query. Additionally, this How-To will demonstrate the creation of a mailing label with different text for mailings to a family.

1.5   Use the Values in a Field in One Table to Update the Values in a Field in Another Table

You probably already know that you can use an update query to update the values of fields in a table, but did you know that you can use an update query to update the values in one table with the values from another? This How-To will show you how to do just that.

1.6   Use a VBA Variable to Filter a Query

Access queries won't accept VBA variables in criteria expressions, but this How-To will show you how to employ variables in query criteria by using a function.

1.7   Use a Query to Retrieve a Random Set of Rows

This How-To will show you how to build a query to return a specified number of rows, randomly chosen from an existing data set.

1.8   Create a Query that Will Show Aging of Receivables

When you're working with sales figures or any other dated values, you may need to perform an aging analysis on the values. To gather information about transactions that occurred, for example, 1–30, 31–60, 61–90, or 91–120 days ago, this How-To will demonstrate the use of the Partition function, which will do the work for you.

1.9   Create a Join that's Based on a Comparison Other than Equality

In Access, relationships among tables are normally based on equality, matching values in one table with those in another. Sometimes, though, you need to join two tables on some other relationship; perhaps the value from one table needs to be between two values in another table. This How-To will demonstrate how you can join two tables based on a condition other than equality.

1.10   Create a Query to Combine Data from Two Tables with Similar Structures

If you have two tables with the same (or similar) structure, you may wish to combine their rows into a single dataset. This How-To will demonstrate how to splice together the data from two tables using a union query.

1.11   Create a Combo Box that Allows a User to Select N/A when None of the Choices is Applicable

If you've ever created a combo box that draws its values from a lookup table, you might have wished there was a simple way to include a "not applicable" row in the combo box without having to store this extra row in the lookup table. This How-To will show you how to create a smarter combo box that includes a N/A choice using a union query.

1.12   Use a Query to Show the Relationship Between Employees and their Supervisors

If you've ever needed to create a database that included information on the hierarchical relationships between employees and supervisors (or a similar hierarchical relationship), you've probably grappled with the difficulty of representing this information in a relational database. This How-To will show how you can store the information on employees and their supervisors in a single table and how to use a self-join query to display the employee–supervisor hierarchy.

1.13   Create a Query that Uses Case-Sensitive Criteria

Access normally disregards case when making string comparisons. This can be frustrating when you need to distinguish between lower- and uppercase. This How-To will demonstrate a technique that employs a simple VBA function to make case-sensitive comparisons in the criteria of a query.

1.14   Use a Query to Create a New Table Complete with Indexes

Sometimes you need to create a table and indexes on the fly without using an existing table and a make-table query. This How-To will show you how to use data definition language (DDL) queries to create and alter the structure of tables.

1.15   Save My Queries in a Table for Better Programmatic Access and Security

Some queries exist only for their use in your applications, not for user examination. You don't want users to be able to modify, or often even to see, these queries. This How-To will propose a solution to this problem that involves storing the SQL string for each query in a table that your application controls and maintains.

1.16   Create a Recordset Based on a Parameter Query from VBA Code

If you've ever attempted to create a recordset in VBA that's based on a parameter query, you may have been surprised to find that the Jet Engine can't seem to find your previously satisfied parameters. This How-To will show you how to help the Jet Engine see your parameters and thus make it possible to create your recordset.

COMPLEXITY:
EASY

1.1   How do I...
Specify query criteria when the query runs?

Problem

When designing my queries, I don't always know which subset of records I would like to see when I run the query. I'd like to be able to create one query that could be used to return the same fields, but a different set of records each time it's run.

Technique

Access lets you create a query with one or more replaceable parameters that it will prompt for at runtime (when you run the query). This How-To demonstrates how you can create and run parameter queries using both the default parameter prompt and more sophisticated form-based parameters.

Steps

Open 01-01.MDB and run the qryAlbumsPrm1 query. You will be prompted for the type of music (see Figure 1-1). Enter a music type such as rock, alternative rock, or

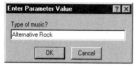

Figure 1-1 The Enter Parameter Value dialog box for the query qryAlbumsPrm1

Figure 1-2 The datasheet for qryAlbumsPrm1

jazz. The query will then execute, returning only the records of the specified music type. For example, if you enter "Alternative Rock" at the prompt, the datasheet shown in Figure 1-2 will be returned.

Now open the frmAlbumsPrm2 form (see Figure 1-3). This form collects three parameters for the parameter query qryAlbumsPrm2. Choose the type of music from the combo box and the range of years to include in the two text boxes. Click on the OK command button to execute the parameter query using the parameters collected on the form.

Creating a Parameter Query Using Default Prompts

Here are the steps to create a parameter query using default prompts:

1. Create any type of query.

2. Choose a field for which you wish to define a parameter. Create a parameter for that field by entering the prompt you would like see when the query is executed surrounded by square brackets ("[]"). For the example query qryAlbumsPrm1, you would create a parameter for the MusicType field by typing

`[Type of Music?]`

in the criteria row under MusicType.

3. Select Query|Parameters to declare the parameter. For this example, enter

`Type of Music?`

in the Parameter column of the Query Parameters dialog box, and choose

`Text`

from the data type combo box to tell Access that this is a text parameter. Steps 2 and 3 are shown in Figure 1-4.

4. Save the query and run it. Access will prompt you with a parameter dialog box to enter the type of music (see Figure 1-1).

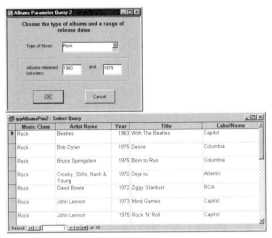

Figure 1-3 The form-based parameter query, qryAlbumsPrm2

Using a Form-Based Parameter Query

The default type of parameter query is useful, but has several drawbacks.

- You get one Enter Parameter Value dialog box for each parameter.

- You can't select the value from a combo box or another control that helps with data entry or use a format or input mask.

- The default parameter dialog boxes are not very user friendly.

If you use a form-based parameter query, you can create a more user-friendly form that collects the parameters.

Here are the steps to create a parameter query using a form-based prompt:

1. Decide how many parameters you will define for the query, in what order you would like them to be requested from the user, and what type of form control

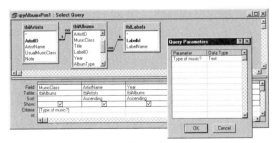

Figure 1-4 The qryAlbumsPrm1 parameter query in design view

you would like to use for each parameter. For the qryAlbumsPrm2 query shown in Figure 1-3, we defined three parameters, as shown in Table 1-1. (Don't worry about the last column in the table yet—we will discuss it shortly.) Note that we included two parameters for the Year field so we could select rows based on a range of years, such as "Between 1970 and 1975."

QUERY FIELD	DATA TYPE	CONTROL TYPE	PARAMETER REFERENCE
MusicType	Text	Combo box	Forms!frmAlbumsPrm2!cboMusicType
Year	Integer	Text box	Forms!frmAlbumsPrm2!txtYear1
Year	Integer	Text box	Forms!frmAlbumsPrm2!txtYear2

Table 1-1 The parameters for qryAlbumsPrm2

2. Create an unbound form with controls that will be used to collect the query's parameters. For qryAlbumsPrm2, we created a form named frmAlbumsPrm2 with three controls that will be used to collect the parameters from Table 1-1. All three controls are unbound; that is, they have no entry for the ControlSource property. We named the text boxes txtYear1 and txtYear2. We also created a combo box called cboMusicType to allow the user to select the type of music from a list of music types. You can use the combo box control wizard to assist you in creating this control or you can create it by hand. If you decide to create it by hand, select Table/Query for the RowSourceType property and tblMusicType for the RowSource (*not* the ControlSource). Leave all of the other properties at their default settings.

3. Add one command button to the form that will be used to execute the query and another that will be used to close the form. For frmAlbumsPrm2, we created two buttons with the captions OK and Cancel. To do this, do one of the following.

Use the Command Button Wizard, which will write the VBA code for you.

Create a macro. Create a new macro sheet (named mfrmAlbumsPrm2 in the example) and make sure the macro names column is showing. If it is not, select View|Macro Names to unhide this column. Create your macros as shown in Table 1-2.

MACRO NAME	ACTION	PARAMETER	VALUE
OK	OpenQuery	QueryName	qryAlbumsPrm2
Cancel	Close		

Table 1-2 Settings for the sample macros (leave all other settings at their default values) in the mfrmAlbumsPrm2 macro sheet

4. Link the macros you just created to the two command buttons by setting properties as shown in Table 1-3.

CONTROL	PROPERTY	VALUE
cmdOK	OnClick	mfrmAlbumsPrm2.OK
cmdCancel	OnClick	mfrmAlbumsPrm2.Cancel

Table 1-3 Property settings for the buttons on the sample form

5. Create the query. You will now create the parameters that reference the controls on the form created in steps 2 through 4. You create form-based parameters a little differently than default parameters. Instead of creating a prompt surrounded by square brackets, you will enter references to the form control for each parameter. For qryAlbumsPrm2, create the parameters shown in Table 1-1. Under the MusicType field, enter

```
Forms![frmAlbumsPrm2]![cboMusicType]
```

Don't enter brackets around the entire parameter, only around each form and control reference. For the Year field, enter

```
Between Forms![frmAlbumsPrm2]![txtYear1] And
  Forms![frmAlbumsPrm2]![txtYear2]
```

6. Select Query|Parameters to declare the data types of the parameters. Use the same parameter names you used in step 5. For qryAlbumsPrm2, choose the data types shown in Table 1-1.

7. Save the query and close it.

8. Open the parameter form in form view. Select or enter each of the parameters. Click on the OK button to execute the parameter query, returning only the rows selected using the parameter form.

How It Works

When you add a parameter to the criteria of a query, Access knows that it needs to resolve that parameter at runtime. You must either reference a control on a form or enter a prompt surrounded by square brackets to let Access know you wish to use a parameter. If you don't use the brackets, Access will interpret the entry as a text string.

When Access runs a query, it checks to see if there are any parameters it needs to resolve. It first attempts to obtain the value from the underlying tables. If it doesn't find it there, it then looks for any other reference it can use, such as a form reference. Finally, if there is no form reference (or if you created a form-based parameter and the form is not open), Access prompts the user for the parameter. This means that you must open the form *prior* to running any parameter queries that contain references to forms.

For queries with simple text parameters, you can get away with not declaring the parameter using the Query|Parameters command. If you use nontext parameters or if you create parameters for Crosstab queries, however, you *must* declare the parameter. We recommend that you get in the habit of always declaring all parameters to eliminate any chance of ambiguity.

Comments

The result of a parameter query needn't be a query's datasheet. You can base reports, forms, and even other queries on a parameter query. When you run the object that is based on the parameter query—for example, a report—Access knows enough to resolve the parameters prior to running the report.

You can use parameters in any type of query, including Select, Totals, Crosstab, Action, and union queries.

Programming Tip

Parameter dialog boxes can sometimes be a symptom of an error in the design of one or more objects in your database. If you ever run a query, form, or report and are prompted for a parameter when you shouldn't be, you probably misspelled the name of a field or renamed a field in a table without changing the reference in the query.

COMPLEXITY:
EASY

1.2 How do I...
Limit the items in one combo box based on the selected item in another?

Problem

I have a form with two combo boxes, one for the type of music and the other for artists. When I select the type of music in the first combo box, I'd like the list of artists in the second combo box to be limited to artists of the selected music type. But no matter which type of music I select, I always get all the artists in the second combo box. Is there any way to link the two combo boxes so I can filter the second combo box based on the selected item in the first?

Technique

When you place two combo boxes on a form, Access by default doesn't link them together. But *you* can link them by basing the second combo box on a parameter query whose criteria points to the value of the first combo box. This How-To shows you how to create a parameter query to use for the RowSource of the second combo box and a simple macro to keep the two combo boxes synchronized.

Steps

Open and run frmAlbumBrowse1 from 01-02.MDB. This form has been designed to allow you to select albums by music type and artist using combo boxes in the form's header, with the selected records displayed in the detail section of the form. If you select a type of music using the first combo box, for example Jazz, a filter is applied to the form and the records in the detail section of the form change to reveal the three Jazz selections from tblAlbums. But when you pull down the second combo box, you'll note that the list of artists is *not* limited to Jazz musicians.

Now open and run frmAlbumBrowse2. This form is identical to frmAlbumBrowse1 except for one difference. When you select Jazz albums using the first combo box, the list of artists in the second combo box is filtered to show only jazz musicians (see Figure 1-5).

Follow these steps to create linked combo boxes:

1. Create a form bound to a table or query. Make it a continuous form by setting the DefaultView property of the form to Continuous Forms.

2. In the header of the form, add two unbound combo boxes. In the frmAlbumBrowse2 example, we named the combo boxes cboMusicType and cboArtistID.

3. Create the query that will supply rows for the first combo box. The query that's the source of rows for cboMusicType is a simple one-column query based on tblMusicType and sorted alphabetically by MusicType.

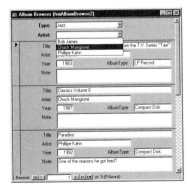

Figure 1-5 Because Jazz was selected for the cboMusicType combo box, the choices in the cboArtistID combo box are filtered to show only jazz artists

4. Create the query that will supply rows to the second combo box. The query that provides rows for the cboArtistID combo box, qryFilteredArtist, contains three columns—ArtistID, ArtistName, and MusicType—and is sorted by ArtistName.

5. Create the parameter that links this query to the first combo box. For qryFilteredArtist, enter the following under the MusicType field.

```
Forms![frmAlbumBrowse2]![cboMusicType]
```

6. Select Query|Parameters to declare the data type of the parameter. Use the exact same parameter name you used in step 5. For qryFilteredArtist, choose Text for the data type. This query is shown in Figure 1-6.

7. Adjust the properties of the two combo box controls so they now obtain their rows from the queries created in steps 3 through 6. In the frmAlbumBrowse2 example, set the properties of the combo boxes as shown in Table 1-4.

NAME	ROWSOURCE TYPE	ROWSOURCE	COLUMN COUNT	COLUMN WIDTHS	BOUND COLUMN
cboMusicType	Table/Query	qryMusicType	1	\<blank\>	1
cboArtistID	Table/Query	qryFilteredArtists	2	0 in; 2 in	1

Table 1-4 The key properties for the combo boxes on frmAlbumBrowse2

8. Attach a macro to the first combo box to force the second combo box to be requeried when the value selected for the first combo box changes. For the frmAlbumBrowse2 example, create the macro in Table 1-5 and attach it to cboMusicType's AfterUpdate property.

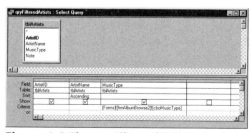

Figure 1-6 The qryFilteredArtist parameter query is used to link the two combo boxes on frmAlbumBrowse2

MACRO NAME	ACTION	PARAMETER	VALUE
FilterByType	ApplyFilter	Where Condition	[MusicType]=[Forms]![frmAlbumBrowse2]![cboMusicType]
	Requery	Control Name	cboArtistID

 Table 1-5 This macro is attached to the AfterUpdate event of cboMusicType

Save this macro as mfrmAlbumBrowse2. The second action, Requery, is the one that keeps the two combo boxes synchronized.

9. Create another macro for the second combo box that applies a filter based on the selection in the combo box. For the frmAlbumBrowse2 example, create the macro shown in Table 1-6 and attach it to cboArtistID's AfterUpdate property.

MACRO NAME	ACTION	PARAMETER	VALUE
FilterByArtist	ApplyFilter	Where Condition	[ArtistID]=[Forms]![frmAlbumBrowse2]![cboArtistID]

Table 1-6 This macro is attached to the AfterUpdate event of cboArtistID

We placed this macro in the same macro sheet, mfrmAlbumBrowse2, as used in step 8.

How It Works

The parameter query (in this example, qryFilteredArtists) causes the second combo box's values to be dependent on the choice made in the first combo box. This works because the criteria for the MusicType field in qryFilteredArtists points directly to the value of the first combo box.

This works without any macro or VBA code until you change the value in the first combo box. To keep the two combo boxes synchronized, however, you must create a macro or event procedure to force a requery of the second combo box's row source whenever the first combo box's value changes. This is accomplished by a simple macro using the Requery action that you attach to the AfterUpdate event of the first combo box.

Comments

The macro attached to cboMusicType also contains an ApplyFilter action that filters the records in the detail section of the form (see Table 1-5). Similarly, we attached another macro to the AfterUpdate event of cboArtistID. Although these two macro actions cause the detail section of the form to be filtered, they have no effect on the synchronization of the two combo boxes.

The example shown here uses two unbound combo boxes in the header of the form that filters a continuous form. Your use of this technique, however, needn't depend on this specific style of form. You can also use this technique with bound combo boxes located in the detail section of a form. For example, you might use the frmSurvey form (also found in the 01-02.MDB database) to record critiques of albums. It contains two linked combo boxes in the detail section: cboArtistID and cboAlbumID. When you select an artist using the first combo box, the second combo box is filtered to display only albums for that artist.

To create a form similar to frmSurvey, follow the steps described in this How-To, placing the combo boxes in the detail section of the form instead of the header. Create a macro sheet similar to mfrmSurvey, which is shown in Table 1-7. Attach the SychAlbum macro from mfrmSurvey to the AfterUpdate event of cboArtistID. In addition, because the cboAlbumID combo box is bound to fields in tblSurvey, you need to force Access to requery cboAlbumID when you navigate to a different record. This can be accomplished by attaching the same macro (mfrmSurvey.SynchAlbum) to the Current event of the form.

MACRO NAME	ACTION	PARAMETER	VALUE
SynchAlbum	Requery	Control Name	cboAlbumID

 Table 1-7 This macro is attached to both cboArtistID's AfterUpdate event and the form's Current event

1.3 How do I...
Make formatted date columns sort correctly in a crosstab query?

Problem

I have a crosstab query that has a column heading based on the Format function that converts the date/time field into month names like Jan, Feb, and so forth. But when I look at this query in datasheet view, the months are sorted alphabetically instead of by date. Is there some way to tell Access to sort the columns by date rather than alphabetically?

Technique

The query property sheet allows you to specify fixed column headings for a crosstab query. This How-To illustrates how to use the ColumnHeadings property to specify column headings so that formatted dates sort chronologically.

Steps

Open 01-03.MDB and run the qryAlbumTypeByMonth1 crosstab query (see Figure 1-7). This query shows the cross-tabulation of the number of albums purchased by album type and the month the album was purchased. The month columns are sorted alphabetically instead of chronologically.

Now run qryAlbumTypeByMonth2, which can also be found in 01-03.MDB. In this query, the months are ordered chronologically (see Figure 1-8).

Follow these steps to create a crosstab query with correctly sorted formatted-date columns:

1. Create a select query. Select Query|Crosstab to convert the query into a crosstab query.
2. Add the columns you want to the crosstab query. Use a calculation for the Column Heading field. This calculation should use the built-in Format function to take a normal date and convert it into an alphabetic string for summarization purposes. This might be the day of week or the month of year. In the example shown in Figure 1-8, we took the date field, DateAcquired, and formatted it as a three-letter month string. Add the remaining fields to qryAlbumTypeByMonth2, as shown in Table 1-8.

FIELD	TABLE	TOTAL	CROSSTAB
AlbumType	tblAlbums	Group By	Row Heading
Month: Format([DateAcquired], "mmm")		Group By	Column Heading
Album ID	tblAlbums	Count	Value

Table 1-8 Field settings for the qryAlbumTypeByMonth2 crosstab query

All crosstab queries must have at least three fields: Row Heading, Column Heading, and Value.

3. Select View|Properties if the property sheet is not already showing. Using the mouse cursor, click on any part of the background of the upper-half of the query screen. This will select the properties for the query itself (as opposed to the Field or Field List properties). Enter the values of the formatted date, in

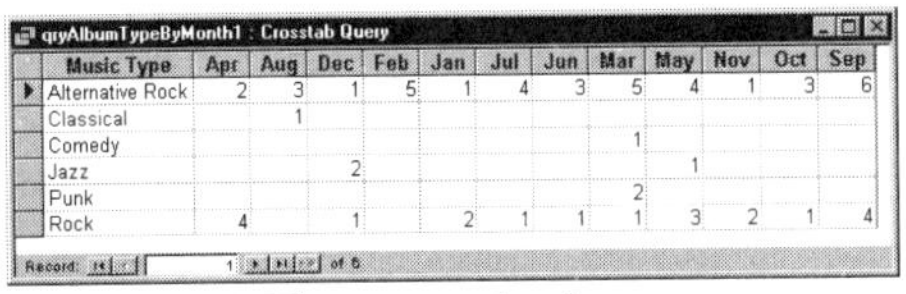
qryAlbumTypeByMonth1 : Crosstab Query

Music Type	Apr	Aug	Dec	Feb	Jan	Jul	Jun	Mar	May	Nov	Oct	Sep
Alternative Rock	2	3	1	5	1	4	3	5	4	1	3	6
Classical		1										
Comedy								1				
Jazz			2						1			
Punk								2				
Rock	4		1		2	1	1	1	3	2	1	4

Record: 1 of 6

Figure 1-7 The months in qryAlbumTypeByMonth1 sort alphabetically

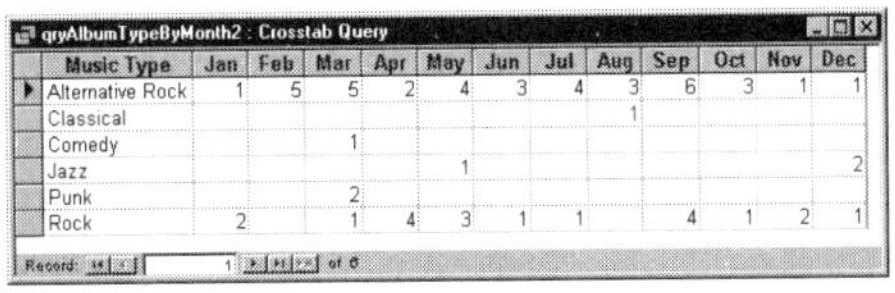
qryAlbumTypeByMonth2 : Crosstab Query

Music Type	Jan	Feb	Mar	Apr	May	Jun	Jul	Aug	Sep	Oct	Nov	Dec
Alternative Rock	1	5	5	2	4	3	4	3	6	3	1	1
Classical								1				
Comedy			1									
Jazz					1							2
Punk			2									
Rock	2		1	4	3	1	1		4	1	2	1

Record: 1 of 6

Figure 1-8 The months in qryAlbumTypeByMonth2 sort chronologically

the order in which you wish for them to appear, into the ColumnHeadings property. For the qryAlbumTypeByMonth2 query, add three-letter strings for each month of the year (see Figure 1-9). Separate each entry with a comma.

4. Save and run the query. The date columns should be ordered chronologically.

How It Works

When you convert a date/time field to a formatted date using the Format function, Access converts the date into a string. This means that the formatted date will sort like any other string—alphabetically. Access includes a special query property, the ColumnHeadings property, to make it easy to work around this unpleasant side effect of using the Format function.

Comments

You aren't limited to using fixed column headings with formatted date strings. This crosstab query property comes in handy for several other situations. You might use the ColumnHeadings property to:

- Force a crosstab to contain a column heading always, even if no values exist for that column. For example, you could use the ColumnHeadings property to include all employee names in a crosstab report, even if one of the employees has no sales for the reporting period.

- Force a unique ordering for the columns of a crosstab query. For example, if your column heading field is made up of the names of regions, you could use the ColumnHeadings property to ensure that the home region always appears as the left-most column.

- Eliminate a column value. If the ColumnHeadings property contains *any* values, then any values not included will be left out of the crosstab query. Of course, this can also be accomplished by using query criteria.

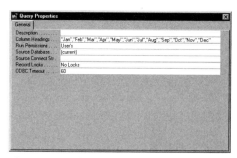

Figure 1-9 The query property sheet for qryAlbumByMonth2

> **Caution**
>
> When you use the ColumnHeadings property, you must spell the column heading values exactly as they appear in your data. If you misspell a column heading value, that value will not appear in the crosstab query. For example, if you use Format(datefield, "ddd") as the column heading field and create fixed column headings of Mon, Tue, Wed, Thr, Fri, Sat, Sun, the Thr column would be completely blank because the Format function returns Thu (not Thr) for day of week.

COMPLEXITY:
EASY

1.4 How do I... Group mailing labels by address?

Problem

I need to print mailing labels intended for the general public. If my mailing list contains multiple occurrences of the same last name at the same address, I only want to print one label, addressed to the entire family. Otherwise, I need to print one label for each person in the table. How can I accomplish this?

Technique

Using a totals query, you can group your label data so that people with the same last name who live at the same address will only make up one row in the output query. If you count the number of occurrences of combinations of last name, address, and zip code, you can create the mailing label text based on that count.

Steps

In 01-04.MDB, open table tblNames. The raw data appears as in Figure 1-10. Note that there are several examples of family members living at the same address—we want to create only one label for each of these families. There's also an example of two people

ID	LastName	FirstName	Address	City	State	Zip
1	Diller	Clark	4567 Planet Road	Kansas City	KS	19284
2	Stevens	Martha	Kent Lane	Smallville	AK	87623
3	Stevens	Jonathon	Kent Lane	Smallville	AK	87623
4	Diller	Lois	4567 Planet Road	Kansas City	KS	19284
5	Diller	Lex	Luthor Towers	Anytown	KS	19000
6	Jones	Alexis	Luthor Towers	Anytown	KS	19000

Figure 1-10 Sample data from tblNames that includes multiple people per address

Figure 1-11 Mailing labels, grouped by last name, address, and zip code

with different last names at the same address—we *don't* want to combine these names into one label. Open the report rptLabels (shown in Figure 1-11). This mailing label report groups the people with common last names and addresses onto single labels, using the family name instead of individual names.

To create this grouping in your own data, follow these steps:

1. Create a new query (qryCountNames in the sample), based on your table. Turn this query into a totals query by choosing View|Totals or by clicking on the Sigma button on the toolbar. This query will group the data using one row for each unique combination of the grouping fields.

2. Add a column to the query grid for each column in your table on which you want to group rows. The example uses [LastName], [Address], and [Zip]. For each column, set the Total field to be Group By. If you want to specify column names, place those names preceding the field names, separated with a colon, as shown in Figure 1-12.

3. Add a column to the query grid in which Access will count the number of rows that it groups together to make a single row in the output. Choose any field that won't have null values, place it in the query grid, and set its Total

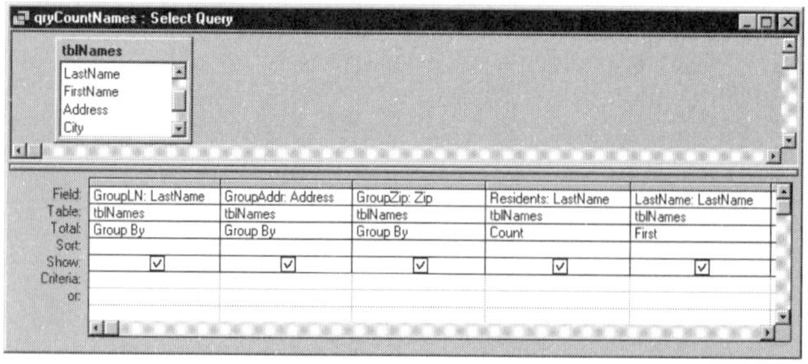

Figure 1-12 The grouping query, qryCountNames, with new column headings

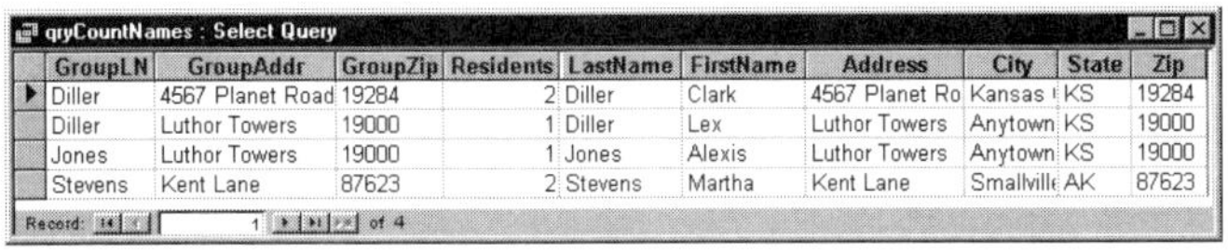

qryCountNames : Select Query

GroupLN	GroupAddr	GroupZip	Residents	LastName	FirstName	Address	City	State	Zip
Diller	4567 Planet Road	19284	2	Diller	Clark	4567 Planet Ro	Kansas	KS	19284
Diller	Luthor Towers	19000	1	Diller	Lex	Luthor Towers	Anytown	KS	19000
Jones	Luthor Towers	19000	1	Jones	Alexis	Luthor Towers	Anytown	KS	19000
Stevens	Kent Lane	87623	2	Stevens	Martha	Kent Lane	Smallvill	AK	87623

Record: 1 of 4

Figure 1-13 The output of the grouping query, qryCountNames

row to be Count. (This field is called [Residents] in the example.) This instructs Access to count the number of rows in the same grouping. (See Figure 1-12.)

4. Add any other fields that you want to show on your labels to the query grid. For each, set the Total field to be First. For each column, add a specific title; otherwise, Access will change each title to FirstOf*Column*. When you run this query, its output will look something like that shown in Figure 1-13. Note that there's only one row in the output for each unique grouping of last name, address, and zip code.
5. To create the text for your labels, create a new query (qryLabels in the example) based on the previous query (qryCountNames). You'll base the mailing label name on the field in which you counted rows ([Residents], in the example), along with the [FirstName] and the [LastName] fields. Pull in whatever columns you want in your label, and add one more for the label name. For the example, the expression for this column ([LabelName]) is

```
LabelName: IIf([Residents] > 1,"The " & [LastName] & " Family",
 [FirstName] & " " & [LastName])
```

6. On the mailing label itself, use the [LabelName] field instead of the [FirstName] and [LastName] fields. This field (shown in Figure 1-14) shows either the family name or the single individual's first and last name, depending on the value in the [Residents] column.

How It Works

By creating a totals query that groups on a combination of fields, you're instructing Access to output a single row for each group of rows that have identical values in those columns. Because you're grouping on last name and address (zip was thrown in to ensure that you wouldn't group two families with the same name at the same address in different

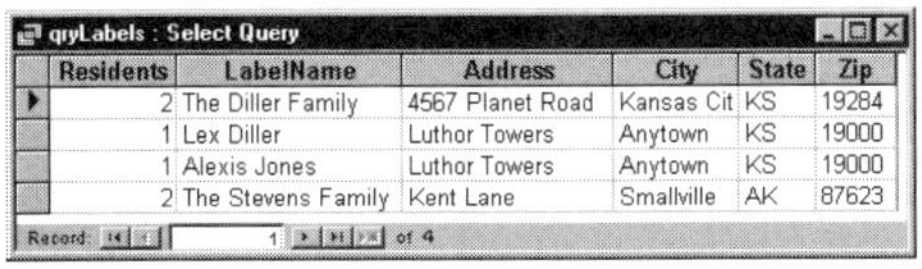

qryLabels : Select Query

Residents	LabelName	Address	City	State	Zip
2	The Diller Family	4567 Planet Road	Kansas Cit	KS	19284
1	Lex Diller	Luthor Towers	Anytown	KS	19000
1	Alexis Jones	Luthor Towers	Anytown	KS	19000
2	The Stevens Family	Kent Lane	Smallville	AK	87623

Record: 1 of 4

Figure 1-14 The LabelName field showing the family name or the individual's name cities), you should end up with one output row for each household. You included one column for counting (the [Residents] field in the example), so Access will tell you how many rows collapsed down into the single output row. This way, the query can decide whether to print an individual's name or the family name on the label.

If the value in the counted field is greater than 1, the query builds an expression that includes just the family name.

```
"The " & [LastName] & " Family"
```

If the count is exactly 1, the query uses the first and last names.

```
[FirstName] & " " & [LastName]
```

The immediate If function, IIf, does this for you, as shown in step 5. It looks at the value in the [Residents] field and decides which format to use based on that value.

Comments

Access does its best to optimize nested queries, so don't feel shy about resorting to basing one query on another. In this case, it simplifies the work. The first-level query groups the rows, and the second one creates the calculated expression based on the first. Though it might be possible to accomplish this same task in a single query, splitting the tasks makes this so much easier to conceptualize that it's worth the extra effort to use two separate queries.

This problem could have also been solved by changing the design of the database so that instead of having a single table, tblNames, with repeating address information for multiple family members, you had two tables, perhaps called tblFamilies and tblFamilyMembers, related in a one-to-many relationship.

COMPLEXITY:
EASY

1.5 How do I...
Use the values in a field in one table to update the values in a field in another table?

Problem

I've imported a table that contains updated prices for some of the records in a table in my database. But the data in all of the other fields for the existing table *is* correct. Is there any way—short of using a complex VBA procedure—to update the price data in the existing table based on the updated prices from the imported table without overwriting any of the other fields in the existing table?

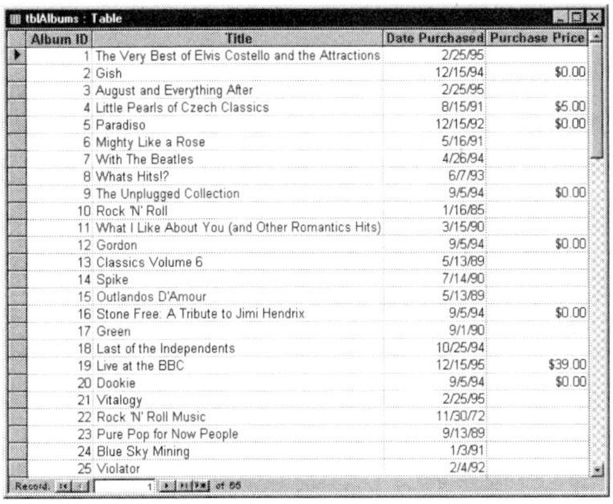

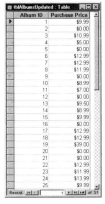

Figure 1-16
tblAlbumsUpdated
contains updated
purchase prices for
many of the same
albums in tblAlbums

Figure 1-15 Many of the purchase values
in tblAlbums are Null

Technique

If you can join the two tables on some common field, you can use an update query
to update a field in one table based on the values found in a second table. This How-
To shows you how to create an update query that does just this.

Steps

Open the tblAlbums table found in the 01-05.MDB database. Note that most of the purchase prices are Null (see Figure 1-15). Open tblAlbumsUpdated and you will see that
many of the purchase prices for the same albums have been entered (see Figure 1-16).

Now run the qryUpdateAlbumPrices query found in the same database (see
Figure 1-17). This action query will take the PurchasePrice values from tblAlbumsUpdated
and copy it into the PurchasePrice field in tblAlbums for each record where the two
AlbumID fields match and the value in tblAlbums is currently Null. When the query
is finished, open tblAlbums again and you should see that PurchasePrice in this table
has been updated based on the values in tblAlbumsUpdated (see Figure 1-18).

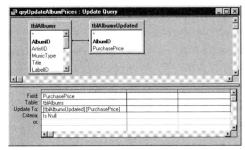

Figure 1-17 The qryUpdateAlbumPrices
update query in design view

23

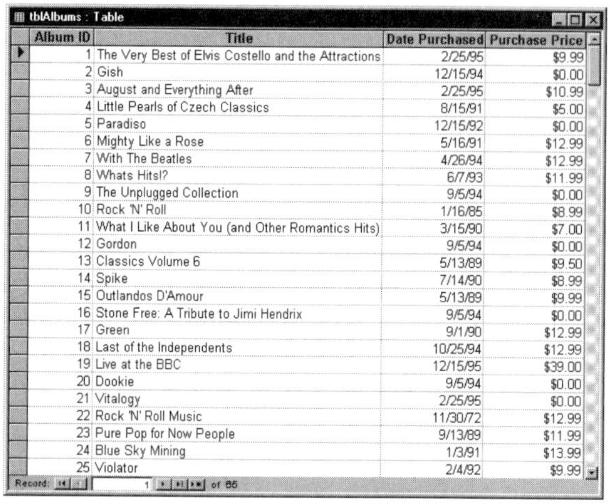

tblAlbums : Table

Album ID	Title	Date Purchased	Purchase Price
1	The Very Best of Elvis Costello and the Attractions	2/25/95	$9.99
2	Gish	12/15/94	$0.00
3	August and Everything After	2/25/95	$10.99
4	Little Pearls of Czech Classics	8/15/91	$5.00
5	Paradiso	12/15/92	$0.00
6	Mighty Like a Rose	5/16/91	$12.99
7	With The Beatles	4/26/94	$12.99
8	Whats Hits!?	6/7/93	$11.99
9	The Unplugged Collection	9/5/94	$0.00
10	Rock 'N' Roll	1/16/85	$8.99
11	What I Like About You (and Other Romantics Hits)	3/15/90	$7.00
12	Gordon	9/5/94	$0.00
13	Classics Volume 6	5/13/89	$9.50
14	Spike	7/14/90	$8.99
15	Outlandos D'Amour	5/13/89	$9.99
16	Stone Free: A Tribute to Jimi Hendrix	9/5/94	$0.00
17	Green	9/1/90	$12.99
18	Last of the Independents	10/25/94	$12.99
19	Live at the BBC	12/15/95	$39.00
20	Dookie	9/5/94	$0.00
21	Vitalogy	2/25/95	$0.00
22	Rock 'N' Roll Music	11/30/72	$12.99
23	Pure Pop for Now People	9/13/89	$11.99
24	Blue Sky Mining	1/3/91	$13.99
25	Violator	2/4/92	$9.99

Record: 1 of 65

Figure 1-18 The updated purchase prices for albums in tblAlbums

Here are the steps to create an update query that updates values across tables:

1. Create a standard Select query. Add the two tables to the query and join them on the common field. In the sample database, we added the tblAlbums and tblAlbumsUpdated tables to the query. We will refer to tblAlbumsUpdated as the *source* table because it will supply the values to be used to update the other table; tblAlbums is the *target* table because it will be the target of the updates. Access has automatically joined the two tables on AlbumID. If the name of the common field is not the same, you will have to join the two tables by dragging the common field from one table to the other.
2. Select Query|Update to change the type of query to an update action query.
3. Drag the field to be updated in the target table to the query grid. In the Update To cell for the field that will be updated, specify the fully qualified name of the field in the source table that will be the source of the updated values. This field name should include the name of the table surrounded by square brackets, a period, and the name of the field surrounded by brackets. For qryUpdateAlbumPrices, drag the AlbumID field from tblAlbums to the query grid. The field settings for AlbumID are shown in Table 1-9.

FIELD	TABLE	UPDATE TO	CRITERIA
AlbumID	tblAlbums	[tblAlbumsUpdated].[PurchasePrice]	Is Null

Table 1-9 The field settings for qryUpdateAlbumPrices

> **Warning**
>
> Be careful when specifying the Update To value. If you misspell the source field name, you run the risk of changing the values to the misspelled string rather than the values in the source field. If Access surrounds the Update To value with quotes or prompts you for a strange parameter when you attempt to execute the update query, it's likely you made a mistake in spelling.

4. Optionally specify criteria to limit the rows to be updated. In the qryUpdateAlbumPrices example, we used criteria to limit the updated rows to those with null (missing) prices (see Table 1-9). This will prevent Access from overwriting any existing nonnull values in tblAlbums.

5. Execute the query by selecting Query|Run or by clicking on the exclamation point icon.

> **Tip**
>
> You can preview the affected records of an action query by choosing View|Datasheet or by clicking on the Datasheet icon. The query will not be run, but you'll be able to see which records would be updated had you run the query.

How It Works

You can use update queries in Access to update the values in a single target table. But even though you can only update the values for one table at a time, you can use another table to supply the values for the update. The trick is to join the two tables using a common field and to specify the name of the field from the source table in the Update To cell properly.

Comments

You can update more than one field at a time in an update query. You can also include additional fields in the query grid to limit the rows to be updated further. Drag these additional fields to the query grid and specify criteria for them. As long as you leave the Update To cell blank, these fields will be used for their criteria only and will not be updated.

COMPLEXITY:
INTERMEDIATE

1.6 How do I... Use a VBA variable to filter a query?

Problem

I'd like to be able to return rows in a query that have a test score greater than a specified value, which is stored in an Visual Basic for Applications (VBA) variable. When I try to use the variable in the query design grid, Access thinks it's a literal value. Is there some way to get queries to understand VBA variables?

Technique

To use a VBA variable in a query, you need to write a VBA function that returns the value of the variable as its return value and reference the VBA function as either part of a calculation or in the criteria of a field. This How-To shows you how to do that.

Steps

In the sample database, 01-06.MDB, you'll find tblScores, a table of names and test scores. The goal of the sample is to allow you to specify a cutoff value and list everyone whose scores are greater than the cutoff value.

Open the frmScores form. This form allows you to choose between a randomly chosen cutoff value and a user-specified cutoff value. If you choose the user-specified cutoff value, a text box is made visible to allow you to enter the cutoff value. When you click on the Show the results command button, an event procedure runs that saves the cutoff value—either the randomly chosen cutoff or the user-specified cutoff—to a module-global variable and then runs the qryScores query.

The qryScores query references the module-global variable using a function, GetCutoff, and then returns the rows in tblScores where the score is greater than the cutoff value (see Figure 1-19).

Follow these steps to use a VBA variable in a query:

1. Create a select query, adding the tables and fields you wish to include in the query. The sample query, qryScores, is based on the tblScores table and contains two fields: Name and Score.

2. Create a VBA function or subprocedure for which you wish to pass a variable to the query from step 1. The sample database includes the frmScores form. The following event procedure is attached to the cmdRunQuery command button.

```
Private Sub cmdRunQuery_Click()

    Dim intCutOff As Integer
```

```
    If Me!grpCriteria = 1 Then
        ' Use a random cutoff.
        ' You generate a random number between x and y
        ' by using the formula Int((y-x+1)*Rnd+x).
        ' This example generates a number between 0 and 100.
        intCutOff = Int(101 * Rnd)
        MsgBox "The random cutoff value is " & intCutOff, _
           vbOKOnly + vbInformation, "Random Cutoff"
        Call SetCutoff(intCutOff)
    Else
        ' Use a user-specified cutoff.
        Call SetCutoff(Me!txtCutOff)
    End If
    DoCmd.OpenQuery "qryScores"

End Sub
```

Based on the user choice made using the grpCriteria option group, the procedure will either generate its own randomly chosen cutoff or grab the cutoff value from the txtCutoff text box. Once the value is generated, the event procedure calls the global subprocedure SetCutoff, which stores the value in a module-level global variable. The SetCutoff subprocedure and the module-level global variable declaration are shown here.

```
Dim mintCutoff As Integer

Sub SetCutoff(pintCutoff As Integer)
    ' Set the module variable to be
    ' the value passed in.
    mintCutoff = pintCutoff
End Sub
```

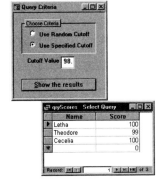

Figure 1-19 The sample form, frmScores, and its output, qryScores

3. Reference the module-global variable using a wrapper function that returns the value currently stored in the variable. For the sample query, qryScores, enter the following criteria for the Score field.

```
>GetCutoff()
```

Design view for this query is shown in Figure 1-20. The GetCutoff function is shown here.

```
Function GetCutoff()
    ' Return the value of the module variable.
    GetCutoff = mintCutoff
End Function
```

4. Execute the VBA procedure from step 2. This will cause the variable to be set, and the query will then run. When the query is executed, it will reference a function that returns the value stored in the VBA variable.

How It Works

A query cannot reference a VBA variable directly. It can, however, call a VBA function that returns the value stored in the VBA variable.

Write a VBA wrapper function for each variable you wish to pass to a query. Because functions on form and report modules are normally local to that form or report (although you can make these functions public), you'll usually want to call a function stored in a global module—a module you can see in the database container.

Comments

In the example, we used a form to collect the values to pass to the VBA variable, mintCutoff. Another way we could solve this problem would be to use a parameter query that directly references the text box on frmScores. (We would have to store the random number in a control on the form, but that would be easy enough to do.) In fact, this solution would have been far simpler than the one demonstrated in this How-To.

Using a form to feed the values to a query will not always be so convenient. There will be times where you need to use a variable without a form. For example, you might

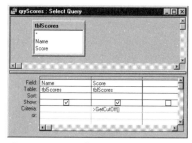

Figure 1-20 The sample query, qryScores, in design view

use global variables to store settings that are read from an options table upon application startup. This options table, for example, might store the complete name of the user, his or her address, and other preferences. You may decide to store these values in a set of global variables to minimize the number of times you have to reread the values from the options table. In this case, these variables would *not* be stored on any form. As another example, you may need to base the query on some value obtained from another application using Dynamic Data Exchange (DDE) or OLE Automation.

COMPLEXITY:
INTERMEDIATE

1.7 How do I... Use a query to retrieve a random set of rows?

Problem

I need to be able to retrieve a random set of rows from a table or a query so I can identify a random sample for a research study. I can't find a way to make this happen in the normal query design grid. What's the trick to getting a random sample of a certain number of rows?

Technique

The solution to this problem is not quite as simple as it might first appear because of the way Access attempts to optimize the use of function calls in queries. This How-To has the answer: Call a VBA function that's tied to a field in the query, using a top values query to retrieve a proportion of the randomly ordered rows.

Steps

In 01-07.MDB, open tblRandom. This table includes 50 rows of data. Your goal is to pull five randomly selected rows for this set of data. To do this, follow these steps:

1. Import the module basRandom from 01-07.MDB or create your own, including this single function:

```
Function ahtGetRandom (varFld As Variant)

    ' Though varFld isn't used, it's the only
    ' way to force the query to call this function
    ' for each and every row.

    Randomize
    ahtGetRandom = Rnd
End Function
```

2. Create a new select query or use an existing one. Add any fields you're interested in.

3. Add an extra column, with the following expression replacing the reference to the State field with a single field in your query's underlying table or query. (This query won't run correctly unless you pass one of *your* field names to the function.)

```
ahtGetRandom([State])
```

4. Most likely, you'll want to clear this field's Show check box, because there's not much point in viewing a continually changing random number as part of your query output.

5. Set the Sort value for the new calculated field to Ascending (see Figure 1-21).

6. Open the query's property sheet (make sure the View|Properties menu item is checked, and click on the upper area of the query design surface so the property sheet says Query Properties in its title bar). Fill in the number of rows you'd like to return in the Top Values property. Figure 1-21 shows the sample query, qryRandom, in design view with the property filled in.

7. Run the query. Your query grid should show you as many rows as you specified in the property sheet. If you press SHIFT-F9, asking Access to requery the data, you will see a different set of rows. Repeating the process will return a different set of rows each time.

How It Works

The general concept behind this How-To is simple: You add a new column to your query, fill it with a list of random numbers, sort on those random numbers, and retrieve the top *n* rows, where *n* is a number between 1 and the number of rows in your underlying data. There's only one complicating factor: To create the random number, you need to call a function for each row. Access tries to optimize such a function call, and

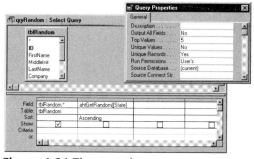

Figure 1-21 The sample query, qryRandom, set up to retrieve five random rows

will only call it once for the entire set of data—unless the function call involves a field in the data. That is, if you replace the call to ahtGetRandom (in step 3) with a simpler call directly to Access' random number function (Rnd), you might be surprised to find that every value in every row will be exactly the same. Access' query engine thinks that the function has nothing to do with data in the query, so it only calls the function once. This will make the random number meaningless, as the whole point of using a random number is to generate a different number for each row.

The workaround, though, is simple: Pass a field, any field, as a parameter to the function you call. That way, Access believes that the return value from the function is dependent on the data in each row, and will call the function once per row, passing to it the field you specify in the expression. The ahtGetRandom function doesn't really care about the value you pass it, because its only goal is to get a random number and return that back to the query. Once you have successfully placed a random number in each row, Access will sort the data based on that number, because you specified Ascending for the column's sorting.

Finally, by specifying the Top Values property for the query, you're asking Access to return only that many rows as the result set of the query. If you want a certain percentage of the total rows, change it by adding the % sign after the Top value.

Comments

The ahtGetRandom function includes a call to the VBA Randomize subroutine. By calling Randomize, you're asking Access to give you a truly random result every time you call the function. If you omit this, Access gives you the same series of random numbers each time you start it up and run this query. If you want a repeatable series of random rows, remove the call to Randomize. If you want a different set of rows each time you run the query, leave the Randomize statement where it is.

Because Access will be passing a field value to the ahtGetRandom function for each and every row of data in your data source, you'll want to optimize this function call as much as you can. If at all possible, use either a very short text field (zip code, for example) or, even better, an integer. You must pass some value, but you want it to be as small as possible to minimize the amount of information that must get moved around for each row of the data.

COMPLEXITY:
INTERMEDIATE

1.8 How do I...
Create a query that will show aging of receivables?

Problem

I need to age my transactions, grouped by Account ID, using a crosstab query into ranges of 1–30 days, 31–60 days, 61–90 days, and greater than 120 days. I know that I can group transactions by month using the standard query tools, but I can't find a way to group them by 30-day increments. How do I do this?

Technique

Access provides the Partition function, which allows you to take a range of values and partition it into even-sized chunks. By specifying a 30-day partition size, you can create a crosstab query that will give you the information you need.

Steps

Load the sample database, 01-08.MDB. This database includes a simple table, tblAccounts (see Figure 1-22), containing information about accounts and their activity. The query qryAging, shown in Figure 1-23, shows the final outcome: a crosstab query including the aging information.

To create a comparable query in your own application, follow these steps:

1. Create a new query based on a table or query containing the appropriate account, date, and amount information.

2. Convert this query to a crosstab query by choosing the Query|Crosstab menu item or by clicking on the Crosstab button on the Query Design toolbar.

Figure 1-22 tblAccounts contains sample data to be used in an aging query

Figure 1-23 qryAgings shows the aging data grouped in 30-day increments

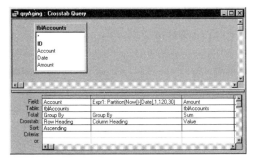

Figure 1-24 The sample query, qryAging, in design mode

3. As when you create any crosstab query, specify at least three columns in the query grid: one for the column headings, one for the row headings, and one for the values that make up the crosstab. In this case, choose the account number (or account name, depending on your data) as the Row Heading, and the amount (summed) as the Value. Figure 1-24 shows the sample query, qryAging, in design mode.

4. For the column headings, group the dates in 30-day increments, using the built-in Partition function. For this specific example, use the value

```
Expr1:Partition(Now()-[Date],1,120,30)
```

for the column's expression. This tells the query to break the information into groups based on the difference between today and the field named Date, starting with one day old, ending with 120 days old, breaking every 30 days. Set the Total item to Group By and the Crosstab item to Column Heading.

5. When you execute the query, you will see output similar to that shown in Figure 1-23. Normally, you'd create a report based on this query, but you can use this raw output to get an overview of the aging of your receivables.

How It Works

Except for the use of the Partition function, this crosstab is no different than any other. It summarizes rows of data, summing the amount column, grouped on a range of values in various columns. The only innovation is the use of the Partition function.

The Partition function returns a string indicating where a value occurs within a calculated series of ranges. That string (in the format *start:end*) becomes the column heading in your query and is based on the starting value, the ending value, and range size. You tell Access each of these values when you call the Partition function. Table 1-10 shows the four parameters you'll use.

ARGUMENT	DESCRIPTION
number	Long integer to evaluate against specified ranges.
start	Long integer, the start of the specified ranges. Can't be less than 0.
stop	Long integer, the end of the specified ranges. Can't be less than the value specified in *start*.
interval	Long integer, the interval spanned by each range in the series from *start* to *stop*. Can't be less than 1.

 Table 1-10 Parameters for the Partition function

For example, the expression

```
Partition( 42, 1, 120, 30)
```

would return the value " 31: 60". This function call asks, Where does the number 42 occur within the range of 1 to 120, broken into 30-day ranges? Clearly, it falls in the 31- to 60-day range. That's what's indicated by the return value

```
" 31: 60"
```

from the previous example. In doing its calculation, Access formats the result for you, in the format you see in the column headings in Figure 1-23.

If a value falls outside the requested range, Access returns an open-ended result. For example, the previous case will return

```
"121:    "
```

if the value is greater than 120, or

```
"    : 0"
```

if the value is less than 1. Access always includes enough space in the two halves of the result string for the largest possible value. This way, the result strings will sort correctly.

To see the Partition function doing its work, open the query qryShowAging from 01-08.MDB in design mode (see Figure 1-25). This simple select query will show the account number, amount due, date on which the transaction occurred, and the age range

Figure 1-25 A simple select query, qryShowAging, using the Partition function

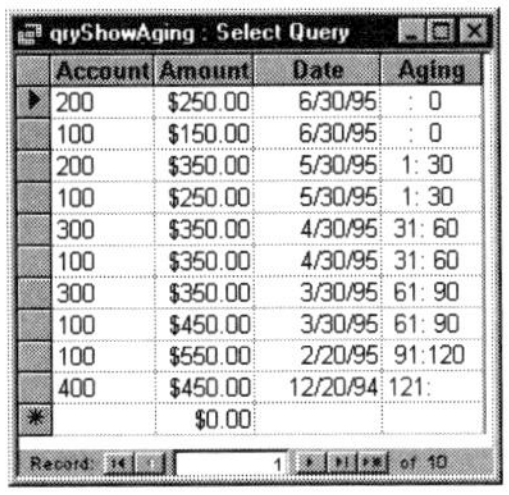

Figure 1-26 The
rows returned by
qryShowAging

the transaction fits into, using the Partition function to calculate the ranges. Figure 1-26 shows the same query in datasheet view, using the data as shown in Figure 1-22. The last column of the datasheet shows the output from the Partition function. When you group the rows on the values in this column, you end up with the crosstab query you created in the Steps section.

Comments

There are some limitations to the Partition function. If you want uneven partitions, you'll need to write your own VBA function to do the work. For example, if you want your partitions to be 0–30 days, 31–60 days, 61–90 days, and 91–120 days, you'd be out of luck with the Partition function: All the partitions specified are 30 days except the first, which is 31. In addition, using Partition in a crosstab query will omit ranges for which no values exist. For example, if no account had transactions between 31 and 60 days ago, there would be no column for this range in the output query. This can be remedied, however, by using fixed column headings (see How-To 1-3).

COMPLEXITY:
INTERMEDIATE

1.9 How do I...
Create a join that's based on a comparison other than equality?

Problem

I need to join together two tables in a query on the Between operator. That is, I have a table of students and their grades, and a table of grade ranges and the matching letter grade. Though there are lots of ways to solve this problem with complex expressions and VBA, I *know* there must be a solution involving just queries. I need a way to join these two tables, finding matches when a value in the first table is between two values in the second table. Can I create an Access query to solve this problem?

Technique

Two tables in an Access query are normally joined in the upper-half of the query design screen—the table pane—by dragging the join field from one table to the other. You can join tables this way for joins based on equality—"equijoins"—that can be inner or outer in nature, but Access doesn't graphically support joins between tables that are joined on an operator other than "=". You can perform these types of joins, however, by specifying the join in the criteria of the linking field.

Steps

From 01-09.MDB, open the tables tblGrades and tblLookup, both shown in Figure 1-27. The first table, tblGrades, includes a row for each student and the students' numeric grades. The lookup table, tblLookup, contains two columns for the range of numeric grades, and a third for the corresponding letter grade. Your goal is to create a query listing each student along with his or her letter grade. To accomplish this goal, follow these steps:

1. Create a new query including both the sample tables. Don't attempt to use the standard Access methods to create a join between the tables, because there's no mechanism for creating the kind of join you need.

2. Drag the fields you'd like to include in your query to the query grid. Make sure to include the field that will link the two tables together (Grade, from tblGrades, in this case).

3. In the criteria cell for the linking field, enter the expression that you'll use to link the two tables, using the syntax

`TableName.FieldName`

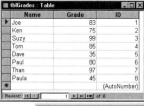

Figure 1-27 The two sample tables, tblGrades and tblLookup

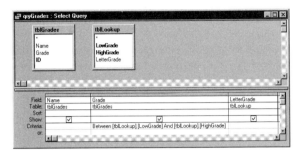

Figure 1-28 The sample query, qryGrades, in design mode

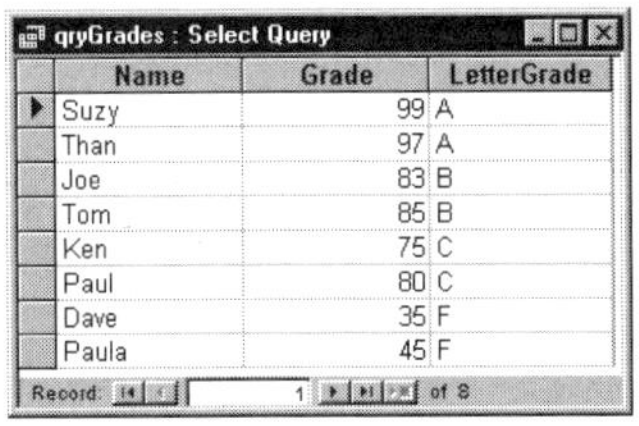

Figure 1-29 The data returned from running qryGrades

for any fields in the second table. Because you have not related the two tables, Access needs the table name to know what you're referring to. In the sample, the expression is

```
Between [tblLookup].[LowGrade] And [tblLookup].[HighGrade]
```

Figure 1-28 shows the sample query in design mode.

4. Run the query. The output should look something like Figure 1-29. For each numeric grade, you have related the data in tblGrades to the values in tblLookup, matching one row in tblLookup to each numeric grade.

How It Works

In a normal join relating two tables, Access takes each value in the "left-hand" table (imagine the two tables laid out in the query design, one on the left and one on the right), finds the first matching value in the related field in the "right-hand" table, and creates a new row in the output set of rows containing information from the two joined rows. In this case, however, you don't care to match the two tables on equality, but rather on "betweenness." Because Access doesn't graphically support this type of join in query design view, you can get the same result by specifying that you only want values for the linking field in the left-hand table where they are between the two comparison values in the right-hand table, and not specifying a standard join. As it builds the output set of rows, Access looks up each value of the linking field in the right-hand table, searching for the first match. It joins the rows in the two tables based on the value from the left-hand table being between the two values in the right-hand table.

Comments

All queries in Access get converted to SQL. If you select View|SQL or use the SQL icon on the toolbar, you can view the SQL for the qryGrades query. When you do, you'll see the following SQL.

```
SELECT DISTINCTROW tblGrades.Name, tblGrades.Grade,
tblLookup.LetterGrade
FROM tblGrades, tblLookup
WHERE (((tblGrades.Grade) Between [tblLookup].[LowGrade]
And [tblLookup].[HighGrade]));
```

The inequality join has been translated into the WHERE clause of Access SQL. If you're familiar with Access SQL, however, you may notice that the placement of the join information is different from where Access normally places it. For example, if we had created a "normal" equijoin between these two tables, joining Grade from tblGrades to LowGrade in tblLookup, the SQL would look like this:

```
SELECT DISTINCTROW tblGrades.Name, tblGrades.Grade,
tblLookup.LetterGrade
FROM tblGrades INNER JOIN tblLookup
ON tblGrades.Grade = tblLookup.LowGrade;
```

(This query would not give us the desired result.) Notice that Access has placed the join information in the FROM clause. (The joining of tables in the FROM clause was introduced in the ANSI 92 SQL standard, but Access also supports joins in the WHERE clause, which is ANSI 89 SQL compatible.) It's interesting to note that you *can* specify nonequijoins using the FROM clause syntax, but you can't do this using query design view. Instead, you must specify the nonequijoin using SQL view. The following SQL will return the same rows as qryScores.

```
SELECT DISTINCTROW tblGrades.Name, tblGrades.Grade,
tblLookup.LetterGrade
FROM tblGrades INNER JOIN tblLookup
ON tblGrades.Grade BETWEEN tblLookup.LowGrade
AND tblLookup.HighGrade;
```

Once you create this type of join using SQL view, Access will refuse to switch to query design view for this query. It does this because it's incapable of representing this type of join in QBE. This version of the scores query, qryScoresSQL, can also be found in the 01-09 database.

This technique isn't limited to the Between operator. You can use any comparison operator (Between, In, >, <. >=, <=, <>) to perform a search in the second table, finding the first row that meets the required criterion. You can even link two tables using the InStr function (which indicates if and where one string occurs within another) to match words in a column of the first table with messages that contain that word in the second table.

As with any relationship between two tables, you'll get the best performance if the values in the matching fields in the right-hand table are indexed. This won't always help (in the InStr example above, for instance, there's really no way for an index to help Access find matches within a string), but in many cases it will. Consider indexing any fields used in the matching condition in either of the tables involved in your relationships, whether you build them yourself or use Access' primary key indexes.

Note

The recordset produced by a query containing a nonequijoin will be read-only.

COMPLEXITY:
INTERMEDIATE

1.10 How do I...
Create a query to combine data from two tables with similar structures?

Problem

I have two tables of addresses, one for clients and one for leads. Generally I send different mailings to these two groups, but sometimes I need to send the same letter to both. I can always create a third table and append to it the data from each of the two tables, but there must be an easier way that doesn't involve the use of temporary tables. Is there a way to combine the data from these two tables into a single recordset, including only the U.S. addresses and sorted by zip code?

Technique

As you may have discovered, if two tables lack fields with matching data, you can't link them by any of the standard join types. However, Access provides a special type of query that can be used to horizontally splice together the data from two or more tables providing they have similar structures. This is the union query, and it can only be constructed using SQL view.

Steps

The following steps show you how to construct a union query to combine data from two tables into a single recordset, limited to addresses in the U.S. and sorted by zip code:

1. Open 01-10.MDB. Open the two tables (tblClients and tblLeads) and examine their structure and data.

2. Create a new select query. Click on Close when you are prompted to add a table.

3. Select Query|SQL Specific|Union. Access will present a blank SQL view.

4. If you'd like, open tblClients in design view so you can see the field names while typing. Then type in the first part of the query.

```
SELECT Company, Address1, Address2, Address3, City, StateProvince,
ZipPostalCode, Country
FROM tblClients
WHERE Country = "U.S.A."
```

(Yes, you must type it—there is no QBE equivalent to a union query.)

5. Type UNION and then the matching fields from tblClients entered in the same order they were entered in step 4.

```
UNION SELECT LeadName, Address1, Address2, "", City, State, Zip, Country
FROM tblLeads
WHERE Country = "U.S.A."
```

6. To sort the query's output by zip code, add an Order By statement using the name of the field as it appears in the first table.

```
ORDER BY ZipPostalCode;
```

Figure 1-30 shows the completed union query.

7. Switch to datasheet view to see the output of the query, as shown in Figure 1-31. Notice that the Canadian addresses are excluded and that all the addresses are sorted by zip code.

8. Save the new query with a name of your choice; in the sample database, it is called qryBothLists.

How It Works

The Union SQL statement joins together the output of two or more Select statements into a single recordset. The field names from the tables need not match, but they must be entered in the same order. If matching fields in the tables appear in different positions but have the same name, you must reorder them in the Select statements because Access uses the order of the fields—not their names—to determine which fields' data to combine together.

If a matching field is absent from one of the tables, as is the case for tblLeads, which lacks an Address3 field, you can include a constant. In the qryCombinedLists example, we used a zero-length string constant (""), but we could have used another constant such as None or N/A.

Comments

While typing in the text of the union query, you may find it helpful to keep the source tables open in Design View so you can be sure you are entering the field names correctly.

```
qryCombinedLists : Union Query                          [_][□][×]
SELECT Company, Address1, Address2, Address3, City, StateProvince, ZipPostalCode,
Country
FROM tblClients
WHERE Country = "U.S.A."

UNION

SELECT LeadName, Address1, Address2, '"', City, State, Zip, Country
FROM tblLeads
WHERE Country = "U.S.A."
ORDER BY ZipPostalCode;
```

Figure 1-30 The completed union query

Figure 1-31 The output of the union query

Some dialects of SQL require the SQL statement to end with a semicolon. Access does not, but it doesn't hurt to use the standard syntax, especially if you program in other languages as well as Access.

A union query is a snapshot of the data in the underlying tables, and therefore it cannot be updated.

To sort a union query, add one Order By clause at the end of the last Select statement, referring to a name of the field from the *first* Select clause (as in the sample query). You can't sort each Select clause individually, just the whole union query.

A union query automatically screens out duplicate records (if any); if you want to include duplicates in the query's dynaset, use UNION ALL in place of the word UNION.

COMPLEXITY:
INTERMEDIATE

1.11 How do I...
Create a combo box that allows a user to select N/A when none of the choices is applicable?

Problem

I'd like to be able to create a combo box that looks up items in a table and is limited to this list of items, but with the additional choice of N/A, which could be used to enter a null value for the field. I tried setting the LimitToList property for the control to Yes, but this won't work because I'm using a bound column that is hidden. Besides, I don't want my users to be able to enter all sorts of "garbage" entries, just N/A (or some other special code). Is there any way to accomplish this?

Technique

You can set the LimitToList property for the combo box to Yes and use a sorted union query to add an additional <N/A> row to the row source for the combo box. We suggest using <N/A> rather than simply N/A to force the entry to sort to the top of the combo box list. When the user selects <N/A> from the combo box, a Null is used for the hidden bound column.

Steps

Open the frmAlbums form in the 01-11.MDB database. This form can be used to edit or add new record albums to tblAlbums. Add a new album that has no single artist. For example, enter a record for Woodstock, which is a compilation of multiple artists. When you pull down the Artist combo box you will see, at the top of the list, the choice <N/A> (see Figure 1-32). Select this item from the list and Access converts your choice to a null value.

To create a combo box with a not applicable entry on a form of your own, follow these steps:

1. Create a normal bound combo box that draws its records from a table. In the sample database, we created a combo box called cboArtistID on the form frmAlbums. To duplicate the combo box in the sample database, create a combo box with the properties shown in Table 1-11.

PROPERTY	VALUE
Name	cboArtistID
ControlSource	ArtistID
RowSourceType	Table/Query
RowSource	
ColumnCount	2
ColumnHeads	No
ColumnWidths	0 in;2 in
BoundColumn	1
ListRows	8
ListWidth	2 in
LimitToList	Yes

Table 1-11 The properties for the cboArtistID combo box on frmAlbums

The other properties for this control don't matter. We purposely left RowSource blank; you will fill this in after you create the union query. The ColumnWidths entries of "0 in;2 in" will make the first column hidden from the user.

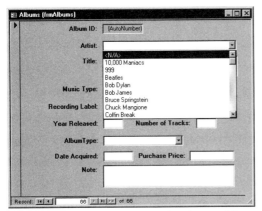

Figure 1-32 The Artist combo box with an <N/A> item

2. Create a new query that will supply the values for the combo box control. Click on Close when you are prompted to add a table. Switch to SQL view by selecting Query|SQL Specific|Union. For the frmAlbums sample form, enter

```
SELECT  ArtistID, ArtistName
FROM tblArtists
UNION SELECT "","<N/A>"
FROM tblArtists
ORDER BY ArtistName;
```

3. Save the query and close it. In the example, we saved the query as qryArtists.

4. Open the form again in design view, and select the name of the query you created in steps 2 through 3 in the RowSource property of the combo box.

5. Run the form and you should now be able to select <N/A> from the list of values for the combo box.

How It Works

The key to this How-To is using a union query. You use a union query—which was discussed in How-To 1-10—to splice together the data from two tables horizontally. This union query is different from the usual variety because it combines the values in one table with values that were literally pulled out of the air. This is accomplished by the union query's second Select statement, show here.

```
UNION SELECT "","<N/A>"
FROM tblArtists
```

Notice that this Select statement selects two constants from a table. These constants aren't actually stored in the tblArtists table (or anywhere else for that matter), but you need to refer to some existing table in the Select statement, so we used tblArtists. This part of the query creates a single row that consists of the constant values "" and "<N/A>" and combines it with the first half of the union query. Finally, the Order By clause for

Figure 1-33 The union query, with a row made up of two constants and combined with the rows from tblArtists

the query tells Access to sort the entries by ArtistName, but because < comes before any letter in the alphabet, the <N/A> entry will sort to the top. If you run this query outside of the form, it will return a datasheet like the one shown in Figure 1-33.

When this query is used as the row source for cboArtists, the <N/A> is displayed because you hid the first column, ArtistID, by setting its column width to 0. When you select <N/A>, Access passes the null value to the hidden bound column (ArtistID). Normally, after you make your choice in a combo box, Access will display the first visible column, which in this case would be ArtistName. But because the <N/A> entry was created on the fly by the union query and doesn't really exist in the combo box's row source, the combo box converts the entry to a Null.

Comments

You can use any value for the "special" row. For example, you may wish to have an entry for <None>, <Missing>, <Unknown>, <Unsure>, or some other string. In fact, you can use additional Select statements in the union query to create multiple special rows, as long as they all point to a null value.

This technique works only if Nulls *are* allowed in the underlying field that's bound to the combo box control. Thus, the bound field—in the example ArtistId—can't have its Required property set to True and can't be the foreign key in an enforced relationship.

Union queries are discussed in more detail in How-To 1.10.

COMPLEXITY:
INTERMEDIATE

1.12 How do I...
Use a query to show the relationship between employees and their supervisors?

Problem

I have a table that includes information on every employee in the company, including management. I'd like to be able to store information on who supervises whom in this same table and then be able to create a query to show this hierarchical relationship. Is there any way to do this in Access?

Technique

You can display an employee-supervisor hierarchical relationship, also known as a recursive relationship, in Access with a select query that uses a *self-join* to join a copy of a table to itself. This How-To shows how to create the table that will store the necessary recursive information, and then how to create the self-join query to list each employee and his or her supervisor.

Steps

Open tblEmployees in 01-12.MDB. This table, which is shown in Figure 1-34, contains a primary key, EmployeeID, and the usual name and address fields. In addition, it contains a field, SupervisorID, that stores the EmployeeID of the employee's immediate supervisor. Now run the query qryEmployeeSupervisors1. This query's datasheet will display each employee and his or her immediate supervisor (see Figure 1-35).

To create the employee table and a query that displays the recursive employee-supervisor relationship, follow these steps:

1. Create the employee table. This table should contain both an EmployeeID field and a SupervisorID field. These fields must have the same field size. In the sample database, tblEmployees contains the EmployeeID and SupervisorID fields. Because EmployeeID is an AutoNumber field with the FieldSize property set to Long Integer, SupervisorID must be a Number field with FieldSize = Long Integer.
2. Enter data into the employee table, making sure that the SupervisorID field is equal to the EmployeeID field of that employee's immediate supervisor.
3. Create a new select query. Add two copies of the employee table. The second copy of the table should have a _1 appended to the end of the table name. Now join the two tables together by dragging the SupervisorID field from the

tblEmployees : Table

EmployeeID	FirstName	LastName	Address	City	State	SupervisorID
1	Shannon	Dodd	9283 Skyline Blvd.	Millers Falls	ID	
2	Anselmo	Bettencourt	2252 63rd Cir.	Indian Mound	AK	1
3	Laura	Ferris	13706 Pine Way	Lost Bridge	NH	10
4	Clifford	Fields	3504 Oak St.	Newport	VI	10
5	Melvin	Knecht	14958 43rd Blvd.	Rockwood	MN	1
6	Max	Powell	7927 Oceanside Ln.	Millers Falls	IL	10
7	Sam	Reid	2481 Luna Terr.	Oakview	SC	10
8	Kirk	Gularte	12350 57th St.	Lost Lake	NJ	10
9	William	Marx	6905 Johnson Blvd.	Moss Hill	CT	8
10	Geoffrey	Litwin	13602 93rd Ln.	Rockwood	MS	1
(AutoNumber)						

Record: 1 of 10

Figure 1-34 The SupervisorID is used to store information on each employee's supervisor

qryEmployeeSupervisors1 : Select Query

EmployeeID	FirstName	LastName	Supervisor
1	Shannon	Dodd	
2	Anselmo	Bettencourt	Shannon Dodd
3	Laura	Ferris	Geoffrey Litwin
4	Clifford	Fields	Geoffrey Litwin
5	Melvin	Knecht	Shannon Dodd
6	Max	Powell	Geoffrey Litwin
7	Sam	Reid	Geoffrey Litwin
8	Kirk	Gularte	Geoffrey Litwin
9	William	Marx	Kirk Gularte
10	Geoffrey	Litwin	Shannon Dodd
(AutoNumber)			

Record: 1 of 10

Figure 1-35 This query uses a self-join to display a recursive relationship between employee and supervisor first copy of the table (the one *without* the _1 suffix) to the EmployeeID field in the second copy of the table (the one *with* the _1 suffix).

4. Drag any fields you wish to include in the query to the query grid. The fields from the first copy of the table describe the employee; the fields from the second copy of the table describe the supervisor. Because the fields of the two tables have the same names—remember they're really two copies of the same table—you need to *alias* (rename) any fields from the second table to avoid confusion. For example, in the qryEmployeeSupervisors1 query, we included the following calculated field, naming it Supervisor, which will display the name of the employee's immediate supervisor.

```
Supervisor: [tblEmployees_1].[FirstName] & " " &
[tblEmployees_1].[LastName]
```

   Notice that the fields that make up the calculation both come from the second copy of the employee table.

5. If you run the query at this point, you will get only employees with supervisors (see Figure 1-36). That's because the query—in the sample database this version of the query is named qryEmployeeSupervisors—uses an inner join. To see all employees, even those without a supervisor (in the example, this would include Shannon Dodd, the company's president), you must change the type of join between the two tables to a left outer join. Double-click on the join line you created in step 3. At the Join Properties dialog box, select choice #2 (see Figure 1-37).

6. Run the query and the datasheet will display the employee-supervisor relationship (see Figure 1-35).

How It Works

You can always model an employee-supervisor relationship as two tables in the database. Put all supervised employees in one table and supervisors in a second table. Then create a regular select query to list out all employees and their supervisors. This

EmployeeID	FirstName	LastName	Supervisor
2	Anselmo	Bettencourt	Shannon Dodd
3	Laura	Ferris	Geoffrey Litwin
4	Clifford	Fields	Geoffrey Litwin
5	Melvin	Knecht	Shannon Dodd
6	Max	Powell	Geoffrey Litwin
7	Sam	Reid	Geoffrey Litwin
8	Kirk	Gularte	Geoffrey Litwin
9	William	Marx	Kirk Gularte
10	Geoffrey	Litwin	Shannon Dodd
(AutoNumber)			

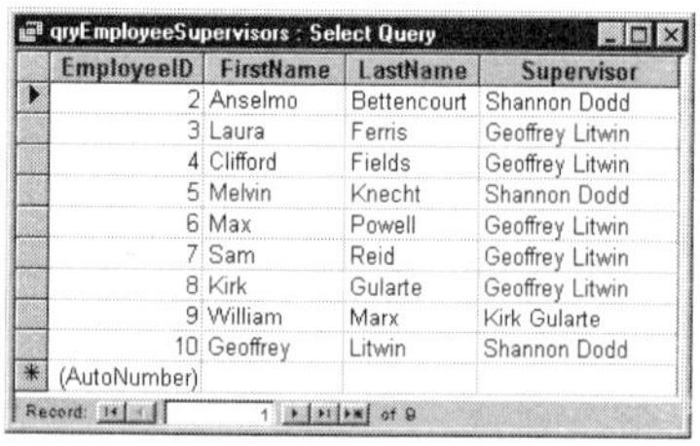

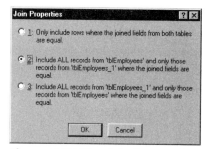

Figure 1-36 This self-join query uses an inner join

Figure 1-37 The Join Properties dialog box allows you to create left or right outer joins

design, however, forces you to duplicate the structure of the employee table. It also means that you must pull data from two tables to create a list of all employees in the company. Finally, this design makes it difficult to model a situation where employee A supervises employee B, who supervises employee C.

A better solution is to store both the descriptive employee information and the information that defines the employee-supervisor hierarchy in one table. You can view the employee-supervisor relationship using a self-join query. In QBE, create a self-join query by adding a table to the query twice and joining a field in the first copy of the table to a different field in the second copy of a table. The key to a self-join query lies in first having a table that is designed to store the information for the recursive relationship.

Comments

The sample query qryEmployeeSupervisors1 displays the employee-supervisor relationship to one level. That is, it shows each employee and his or her immediate supervisor. But you aren't limited to displaying one level of the hierarchy. The sample query qryEmployeeSupervisors3 displays three levels of the employee-supervisor relationship using four copies of tblEmployees and three left outer joins. The design of qryEmployeeSupervisors3 is shown in Figure 1-38; the output is shown in Figure 1-39.

You can use the Access Relationships dialog box to enforce referential integrity for recursive relationships. Select Tools|Relationships to display the Relationships dialog box and add two copies of the table with the recursive relationship. Join the two copies of the table together as if you were creating a self-join query. Choose to establish referential integrity, optionally checking the cascading updates and deleting check boxes. Click on Create to create the new relationship. Now when you enter a value for SupervisorID, Access will prevent you from entering any reference to an EmployeeID that doesn't already exist.

Although the sample database uses an employee-supervisor relationship example, you can use the techniques discussed in this How-To to model other types of hierarchical relationships.

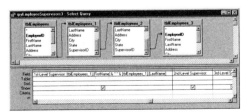

Figure 1-38 This query uses four copies of the same table and three left outer joins to show three levels of the employee-supervisor relationship

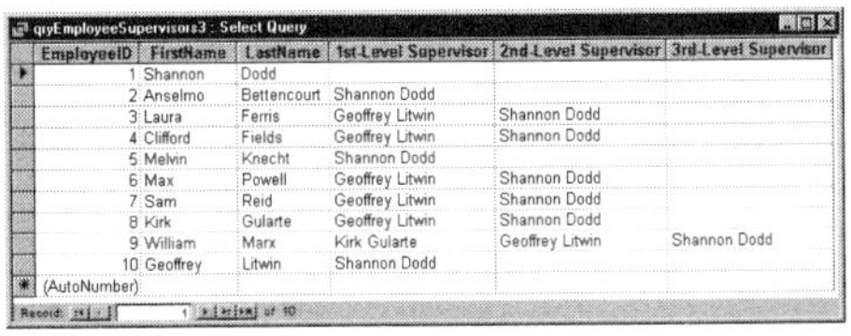

Figure 1-39 The output of qryEmployeeSupervisors3

COMPLEXITY:
INTERMEDIATE

1.13 How do I...
Create a query that uses case-sensitive criteria?

Problem

I have a table of words with some words entered multiple times, each instance spelled using a different combination of upper and lowercase. I'd like to create a query that returns records finding exact matches using case-sensitive criteria; but no matter what I type into the criteria for the query, Access always returns all instances of the same word, disregarding each instance's case. Is there any way to create a query that can select records based on case-sensitive criteria?

Technique

Normally, Access is case insensitive when performing any comparisons of strings. You can use the Option Compare Binary statement in the Declarations section of a module to force VBA to make string comparisons that are case sensitive within the bounds of that module, but this only affects string comparisons made *in* a VBA module, *not* comparisons made by the Jet Engine. Thus, even when you run the query from a VBA Option Compare Binary procedure, any comparisons made in the query are case insensitive. The problem is that the Jet Engine doesn't know how to make case-sensitive string comparisons using any of the standard query operators. Fortunately, you can create your own case-sensitive string comparison function in an Option Compare Binary module and call this function from the query. This How-To shows you how to create the VBA function and how to use it to perform case-sensitive searches.

Steps

Open the tblWords table in 01-13.MDB (see Figure 1-40). Notice that the word swordfish appears in four records, each spelled using a different combination of upper and lowercase letters. Run the qryWordsCI parameter query and enter SwordFish at the prompt. When the query executes, it returns all four swordfish records, not the specific version you typed at the prompt. Now run the qryWordsCS query, entering the same string at the prompt. This time the query returns only one swordfish record, the one that's spelled exactly as you typed.

To use this technique in your own database, follow these steps:

1. Import the basExactMatch module from 01-13.MDB into your database.

2. Create a query for which you wish to perform a case-sensitive search. Add all the desired fields in the query grid.

Figure 1-40 tblWords contains four swordfish records spelled using different combinations of upper and lowercase letters

3. Create a computed field in the query grid that references the ahtExactMatch function found in basExactMatch. For example, if you wish to compare the Word field with a user-entered parameter, create a field like that shown in Table 1-12.

ATTRIBUTE	VALUE
Field	ahtExactMatch([Word], [Enter word])
Table	(blank)
Sort	(blank)
Show	(unchecked)
Criteria	−1

Table 1-12 The settings for the ahtExactMatch field

You can also use a hard-coded string instead of a parameter. We used a parameter in the qryWordCS query, shown in design view in Figure 1-41.

4. Execute the query and it will return only exact, case-sensitive matches. If you run qryWordCS in the 01-13.MDB database and enter SwordFish at the parameter prompt, you should get the datasheet shown in Figure 1-42.

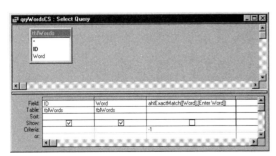

Figure 1-41 qryWordCS uses the ahtExactMatch function to filter records using case-sensitive criteria

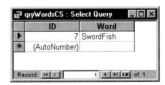

Figure 1-42 qryWordCS uses a case-sensitive comparison function, so it only returns one matching record

49

How It Works

This How-To uses a simple VBA function to perform the comparison of strings. Because this function resides in a module that contains the Option Compare Binary statement, any string comparisons made using procedures in this module are case sensitive. The ahtExactMatch function is very simple.

```
Option Compare Binary
Function ahtExactMatch(var1 As Variant, var2 As Variant) As Boolean
    If var1 = var2 Then
        ahtExactMatch = True
    Else
        ahtExactMatch = False
    End If
End Function
```

This function only returns True when the strings are spelled exactly the same.

Another alternative, which provides slightly less flexibility, is to use the StrComp VBA function. This function can compare two strings on a binary basis (that is, it compares each character in the strings, taking case into account), and will return 0 if the two strings are exact matches. The syntax for calling StrComp in qryWordsCS would look like this:

```
StrComp([Word], [Enter Word], 0)
```

and the Criteria would be 0 (not −1, as shown above).

Comments

You can also use this function when creating a recordset in VBA or when using one of the Find methods on an existing recordset. For example, the sample subprocedure FindString, which can be found in basExactFindSample, finds records using case-sensitive criteria.

```
Sub FindString(strWord As String)

    ' Demonstrates how to find a record using
    ' case-sensitive criteria.
    ' Call this function like so:
    '     Call FindString("SwordFish")

    Dim db As Database
    Dim rst As Recordset
    Dim varCriteria As Variant

    Const ahtcQuote = """"

    Set db = CurrentDb()

    ' Create recordset on tblWords
    Set rst = db.OpenRecordset("tblWords", dbOpenDynaset)
```

```
' Build up the criteria to be used with the Find methods
' strWord was passed in as a parameter
varCriteria = "(ahtExactMatch([Word]," & ahtcQuote & _
 strWord & ahtcQuote & ")0)"

' If you want to use StrComp(), and not carry around
' the extra module containing ahtExactMatch, use the
' following expression:
' varCriteria = "StrComp([Word]," & ahtcQuote & _
'   strWord & ahtcQuote & ", 0) = 0"

Debug.Print "ID", "Word"

With rst
    ' Do initial find
    .FindFirst varCriteria

    ' Print values from record to debug window.
    ' Continue to find additional matches until
    ' there are no more.
        Do While Not .NoMatch
            Debug.Print ![ID], ![Word]

        .FindNext varCriteria
    Loop
    .Close
End With

End Sub
```

When you run this procedure from the Debug Window using

```
Call FindString("SwordFish")
```

this subroutine will only print the one record with the SwordFish spelling to the Debug Window.

You *can't* use StrComp or ahtExactMatch with a recordset's Seek method because seeks can only be performed using the built-in Access operators.

COMPLEXITY:
ADVANCED

1.14 How do I...
Use a query to create a new table complete with indexes?

Problem

I know how to create a table from a make-table query, but when I create a table in this way, it has no primary key or any other indexes. Furthermore, I can only create a new table with a structure based on an existing table. I'd like a way, without using VBA code, to create a table on the fly with the data types and field sizes I want and with appropriate indexes.

Technique

Access provides the data definition language (DDL) query, which is used to create or modify tables programmatically. It is one of the SQL-specific queries, which can only be created using SQL View. This How-To shows you how to create and modify table definitions using DDL queries.

Steps

Open 01-14.MDB. Open the sample data definition language query, qryCreateClients (see Figure 1-43). Select Query|Run or click on the exclamation point icon on the toolbar to execute the DDL query. The tblClients table will be created, complete with a primary key and two other indexes.

Follow these steps to create a table using a DDL query:

1. Design your table, preferably on paper, deciding which fields and indexes you wish to create. For example, before creating qryCreateClients, we came up with the design for tblClients shown in Table 1-13.

FIELDNAME	DATATYPE	FIELDSIZE	INDEX
ClientID	AutoNumber	Long Integer/Increment	Yes, primary key
FirstName	Text	30	Yes, part of ClientName index
LastName	Text	30	Yes, part of ClientName index
CompanyName	Text	60	Yes
Address	Text	80	No
City	Text	40	No
State	Text	2	No
ZipCode	Text	5	No

 Table 1-13 The design for tblClients

2. Create a new query. Click on Close at the Add Table dialog box. Select Query|SQL Specific|Data Definition. This will place you in SQL view.

3. Enter a Create Table SQL statement. To create the sample table, tblClients, enter the following SQL.

```
CREATE TABLE tblClients
(ClientID AutoIncrement CONSTRAINT PrimaryKey PRIMARY KEY,
FirstName TEXT (30),
LastName TEXT (30),
CompanyName TEXT (60) CONSTRAINT CompanyName UNIQUE,
Address TEXT (80),
City TEXT (40),
```

```
State TEXT (2),
ZipCode TEXT (5),
CONSTRAINT ClientName UNIQUE (LastName, FirstName) );
```

4. Save your query and run it by selecting Query|Run or clicking on the exclamation point icon on the toolbar. Look in the database container and you should see the newly created table.

How It Works

When you run a data-definition query, Access reads through the query's clauses and creates a table according to your specifications. This allows you to control the structure of the table and its indexes precisely.

A data-definition query can only contain one data-definition statement. The five types of data-definition statements are listed below.

- CREATE TABLE creates a table.

- ALTER TABLE adds a new field or constraint to an existing table (a constraint creates an index on a field or group of fields).

- DROP TABLE deletes a table from a database.

- CREATE INDEX creates an index for a field or group of fields.

- DROP INDEX removes an index from a field or group of fields.

Note that most of the text fields in the sample query have their lengths specified to save space. If you don't specify a length for a text field in a data-definition query, Access will assign it the maximum length of 255 characters.

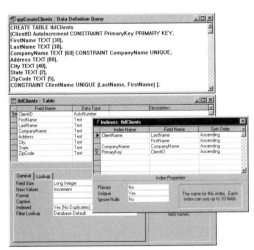

Figure 1-43 A sample data-definition query and the table it creates

If you wish to create field names with embedded spaces, you'll need to surround the names with brackets; otherwise the brackets are optional.

Comments

Like make-table queries, data-definition queries do not automatically overwrite an existing table. However, unlike make-table queries, you aren't offered the option of overwriting the existing table if you want to. If you need to overwrite an existing table when running a data-definition query, execute another DDL query containing a DROP TABLE statement first.

After creating or deleting a table with a data-definition query, the new table won't immediately appear (nor will a deleted one disappear) in the database window. To refresh the display and see the change you made, click on another tab in the database window (for example, the Query tab) and then on the Table tab again.

Warning

As with other SQL-specific queries, be careful not to switch a data-definition query to another query type, such as a select query. If you do, your SQL statement will be discarded, because SQL-specific queries don't have a QBE equivalent.

You can also create tables complete with indexes using data access objects (DAO).

COMPLEXITY:
ADVANCED

1.15 How do I...
Save my queries in a table for better programmatic access and security?

Problem

My application uses a lot of queries, and I don't want these queries available or even visible to the users of my application. Also, I call my queries from VBA code. How can I hide the queries from users, as well as make them easier to retrieve, modify, and execute?

Technique

You can create a query management table that stores the SQL string of your queries in a memo field. Each query is named and includes a description. This technique allows you to store your queries in a table rather than in the collection of queries. This table can be placed in a library database, making the queries accessible only to your VBA code. You can also create a simple VBA function that you can use to retrieve the SQL string of any of your saved queries quickly.

Steps

Open and run frmSavedQueries from 01-15.MDB. After a few moments of processing, the form shown in Figure 1-44 appears. This form is based on the tblQueryDefs table, which stores a record for each query you save. To add a new query to the table, add a new record and enter the SQL statement in the SQL Text control. You may find it easier to copy the SQL from an existing query (see step 2 below for more details). Type in a name and description. Notice that creation and modification times are automatically updated.

To use a saved query in your code, search the tblQueryDefs table for the name of a query and get the value from the SQLText field. To use this technique in your application, follow these steps:

1. Import the tblQueryDefs table, the frmSavedQueries form, and the basSavedQueries module from 01-15.MDB into your database.

2. To add a query to the tblQueryDefs table using the frmSavedQueries form, design and test the query using the Access query designer. Then, from query design view, select View|SQL. When the query's SQL string is displayed, highlight it and copy it to the clipboard. Next, add a new record in the frmSavedQueries form and paste the SQL string into the SQLText text box. Type in a name and description.

3. To get the SQL string of a saved query, use the ahtGetSavedQuerySQL function, located in the basSavedQueries module. The syntax for this function is

```
strSQL = ahtGetSavedQuerySQL ("queryname")
```

where strSQL is the string variable you want to store the query's SQL string in and *queryname* is the name of the saved query you want to retrieve.

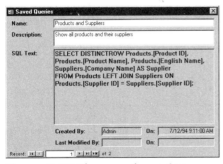

Figure 1-44 The saved queries
form, frmSavedQueries

How It Works

The core of this technique is a simple function that retrieves a value from the tblQueryDefs table. The function uses the Seek method to find the supplied value and, if it finds a match, returns the record's SQLText field value.

```
Function ahtGetSavedQuerySQL (strName As String) As String

    ' Returns a SQL string from a saved query
    ' In  : strName - name of query to retrieve
    ' Out : SQL string

    Dim dbCurrent As Database
    Dim rstQueries As Recordset

    Set dbCurrent = CurrentDB()
    Set rstQueries = dbCurrent.OpenRecordset("tblQueryDefs")
    rstQueries.Index = "PrimaryKey"
    rstQueries.Seek "=", strName
    If Not rstQueries.NoMatch Then
        ahtGetSavedQuerySQL = rstQueries![SQLText]
    End If

    rstQueries.Close
End Function
```

Comments

By extending this technique, you can create a replacement for saved queries in Access. Because you have full programmatic access to each query, you can load, modify, execute, and save queries at will without having to open Querydef objects. Additionally, because you can store the queries table in a library database, you can completely remove a user's access to saved queries except through your code. One drawback of this technique is that you cannot base forms or reports on queries saved in tblQueryDefs without using some VBA code. But this is easily overcome by writing a function that retrieves a saved query's SQL string from tblQueryDefs and assigns the value to the form or report's RecordSource property before the form or report is run.

An obvious enhancement to this technique would be a conversion routine that reads each of your database's saved queries and converts them to records in the tblQueryDefs table. Once this conversion is complete, you can delete the queries from the database window.

1 . 1 6

CREATE A RECORDSET BASED ON A PARAMETER QUERY FROM VBA CODE?

COMPLEXITY:
ADVANCED

1.16 How do I... Create a recordset based on a parameter query from VBA code?

Problem

I have a parameter query that is linked to a form by three parameters. When I open the form, enter the information into the form's controls to satisfy the parameters, and then run the query interactively, everything is fine. But when I open the form, satisfy the parameters, and create a recordset from VBA code based on the same query, I get an error message complaining that no parameters were supplied. This doesn't make sense, as I already supplied the parameters on the form. Is there any way to create a recordset from VBA based on a parameter query?

Technique

When you run a parameter query from the user interface, Access is able to find the parameters if they have already been satisfied using a form and run the query. When you create a recordset from VBA, however, the Jet Engine isn't able to locate the parameter references. Fortunately, you can help the Jet Engine find the parameters by opening the Querydef prior to creating the recordset and telling Jet where to look for the parameters.

Steps

Open the frmAlbumsPrm form found in 01-16.MDB. This form, which is similar to a form used in How-To 1.1, is used to collect parameters for a query, qryAlbumsPrm. Select a music type from the combo box, enter a range of years in the text boxes, and click on OK. An event procedure attached to the cmdOK command button will run, making the form invisible but leaving it open. Now run qryAlbumsPrm from the database container. This query, which has three parameters linked to the now-hidden frmAlbumsPrm, will produce a datasheet limited to the records you specified on the form.

Now open the basCreateRst module from 01-16.MDB. Select the function CreatePrmRst1 from the Proc drop-down list, which is shown here.

```
Sub CreatePrmRst1()

    ' Example of creating a recordset
    ' based on a parameter query
    ' This example fails!

    Dim db As Database
```

continued on next page

continued from previous page

```
Dim rst As Recordset

Set db = CurrentDb()

' Open form to collect parameters
DoCmd.OpenForm "frmAlbumsPrm", , , , , acDialog

' OK was pressed, so create the recordset
If IsFormOpen("frmAlbumsPrm") Then

    ' Attempt to create the recordset
    Set rst = db.OpenRecordset("qryAlbumsPrm")

    rst.MoveLast

    MsgBox "Recordset created with " & rst.RecordCount & _
        " records.", vbOKOnly + vbInformation, "CreatePrmRst"

    rst.Close
Else
    ' Cancel was pressed.
    MsgBox "Query cancelled!", vbOKOnly + vbCritical, _
        "CreatePrmRst"
End If

DoCmd.Close acForm, "frmAlbumsPrm"

End Sub
```

As you can see, this routine starts by opening the form in dialog box mode to collect the three parameters. When the user satisfies the parameters and clicks on OK, the form is hidden by an event procedure, and control passes back to CreatePrmRst1. The subprocedure then attempts to create a recordset based on the parameter query and display a message box with the number of records found. To test this subprocedure, select View|Debug Window and enter the following in the Debug Window.

```
Call CreatePrmRst1
```

The subprocedure will fail with error 3061—"Too few parameters. Expected 3"—at this line:

```
Set rst = db.OpenRecordset("qryAlbumsPrm")
```

Now select the function CreatePrmRst2 from the Proc drop-down list. This subprocedure is the same as CreatePrmRst1, except for some additional code that satisfies the query's parameters prior to creating the recordset. Run this version of the subprocedure by entering the following in the Debug Window.

```
Call CreatePrmRst2
```

You should be rewarded with a dialog box reporting the number of records in the recordset.

How It Works

The VBA code for the second version of the routine, CreatePrmRst2, is shown here.

```
Sub CreatePrmRst2()

    ' Example of creating a recordset
    ' based on a parameter query
    ' This example succeeds!

    Dim db As Database
    Dim qdf As QueryDef
    Dim rst As Recordset

    Set db = CurrentDb()

    ' Open form to collect parameters
    DoCmd.OpenForm "frmAlbumsPrm", , , , , acDialog

    ' OK was pressed, so create the recordset
    If IsFormOpen("frmAlbumsPrm") Then

        ' Satisfy the three parameters before
        ' attempting to create a recordset
        Set qdf = db.QueryDefs("qryAlbumsPrm")

        qdf("Forms!frmAlbumsPrm!cboMusicType") = _
          Forms!frmAlbumsPrm!cboMusicType
        qdf("Forms!frmAlbumsPrm!txtYear1") = _
          Forms!frmAlbumsPrm!txtYear1
        qdf("Forms!frmAlbumsPrm!txtYear2") = _
          Forms!frmAlbumsPrm!txtYear2

        ' Attempt to create the recordset
        Set rst = qdf.OpenRecordset()

        rst.MoveLast

        MsgBox "Recordset created with " & rst.RecordCount & _
          " records.", vbOKOnly + vbInformation, "CreatePrmRst"

        qdf.Close
        rst.Close
    Else
        ' Cancel was pressed.
        MsgBox "Query cancelled!", vbOKOnly + vbCritical, _
          "CreatePrmRst"
    End If

    DoCmd.Close acForm, "frmAlbumsPrm"

End Sub
```

The main difference between the two subprocedures is the inclusion of the following lines of code prior to the line that creates the recordset.

```
Set qdf = db.QueryDefs("qryAlbumsPrm")

qdf("Forms!frmAlbumsPrm!cboMusicType") = _
  Forms!frmAlbumsPrm!cboMusicType
qdf("Forms!frmAlbumsPrm!txtYear1") = _
  Forms!frmAlbumsPrm!txtYear1
qdf("Forms!frmAlbumsPrm!txtYear2") = _
  Forms!frmAlbumsPrm!txtYear2
```

The extra code opens the parameter querydef and then sets each of its parameters equal to its current value. You do this using the following syntax.

```
qdf("Parameter") = Parameter
```

Then the recordset is created based on the opened querydef.

```
Set rst = qdf.OpenRecordset()
```

This time the recordset is created without problem because you supplied the parameters prior to executing the OpenRecordset method.

Comments

You can also use this technique to satisfy parameters using VBA variables. For example, if you collected the parameters for qryAlbumPrm and stored them in three variables, varMusicType, varYear1, and varYear2, you could open the querydef and create the recordset using the following code.

```
Set qdf = db.QueryDefs("qryAlbumsPrm")

qdf("Forms!frmAlbumsPrm!cboMusicType") = varMusicType
qdf("Forms!frmAlbumsPrm!txtYear1") = varYear1
qdf("Forms!frmAlbumsPrm!txtYear2") = varYear2

Set rst = qdf.OpenRecordset()
```

The advantage of using this approach over the one demonstrated in How-To 1-6, which uses a function to satisfy a parameter, is that this technique allows you to use the *same* parameter query and run it either interactively or from VBA code.

CHAPTER 2

DESIGNING CREATIVE AND USEFUL FORMS

2

DESIGNING CREATIVE AND USEFUL FORMS

How do I...

As far as users of your applications are concerned, your forms *are* the application. The forms are the windows into the data that make Access applications work. Access forms are incredibly flexible, and can take on as many different personalities as there are Access developers. The tricks and techniques covered in this chapter are not as complex as ones you might find in other chapters of this book, but they will help form the foundation of your entire application. You'll want to use these tips to help prepare a consistent "look" to your forms and to help users find exactly which control currently has the focus. You'll also learn how to control where users go on your forms by restricting their movement, so they can't move to a new row until you allow them. Plus, you'll learn how to give your forms custom navigation controls. Your understanding of controls will grow, too, as you learn to use option groups to collect and display non-numeric information and to control the display of multipage forms. You'll also learn how to resize the controls inside your forms to match the size of the form. You'll see how to combine controls to create new "hybrid" controls by linking a text box and a list box to create a combination that works like a permanently opened combo box, and how to create your own pop-up forms, such as a replacement for Access' InputBox. You'll learn how to save and restore program settings or application variables to the system registry and how to save and restore the size of your forms from one session to another. Finally, you'll learn how to control multiple instances of a form, allowing you to view multiple rows simultaneously.

2.1   Make Custom Templates for Forms and Reports

When you've decided upon a standard "look" for your forms and reports, you need not spend a lot of time setting the properties for each control. Access allows you to specify a particular form or report to be used as a template for all new forms or reports that you create. This How-To will examine the steps to create your own templates for form and report design.

2.2   Highlight the Current Field in Data Entry Forms

As they move from field to field in data entry forms, users may want some visual clue as to which field has the cursor in it. This simple How-To will demonstrate some methods you can use to make sure the user can tell exactly which control on the form currently has the focus.

2.3   Restrict the User to a Single Row on a Form

As you press the TAB and SHIFT-TAB keys to move about on a form, Access moves from row to row as you move past the first and last controls on a form. If you want to have the cursor move from the last control back to the first, keeping the row current, you'll have to do a little work. This How-To will show how to use the new Cycle property to control tab cycling on a form. In addition, it'll use the new KeyPreview property of a form to trap the PGUP and PGDN keystrokes.

2.4   Use an Option Group to Collect and Display Text Information

In Access, you can use option groups on a form to display numeric data only. Sometimes, though, you'll want to read and write data from a text field through an option group instead. This How-To will show straightforward expressions you can use to read and write text data using an option group.

2.5 Display Multiple Pages of Information on One Form

Many applications need to gather a large amount of information from the user, divided into distinct categories. Using a tabbed dialog format, you can supply a group of tabs (or buttons) that choose a page of data for the user to fill out. Users can choose the order in which they go through the data and which pages they visit. This How-To will suggest a method for creating these useful forms without using an OLE control.

2.6 Provide Record Navigation Buttons on a Form

Access provides navigation buttons for you to use on forms, allowing you to move easily from row to row. However, you can neither move nor resize these buttons, and you can't change anything about their appearance. This How-To will demonstrate the creation of customized navigation buttons. Using the information in this section, you should be able to place your own navigation buttons anywhere on any form.

2.7 Size a Form's Controls to Match the Form's Size

Windows users have become accustomed to resizing forms on their screen. A professional-looking application will resize the controls on a form proportionally when you stretch or reduce the size of a form. This How-To will demonstrate how to base the width and height of the controls in your form on the width and height of the form itself.

2.8 Make a Simple "Searching" List Box

Combo boxes allow you to find matches as you type characters into the text box portion, but they roll up as soon as you leave them. List boxes stay open, but you can only match a single character as you type. By combining a text box and a list box, you can create a hybrid control that gives you the best of both worlds: You'll be able to enter as much text as you need to find a match, and the control will stay open. This How-To will show you how to link the two controls together so that they act as one single control.

2.9 Create a Replacement for Access' InputBox

Although it's useful for gathering information from users, Access' InputBox will never win any awards for aesthetics. This How-To will show how to create your own replacement for the InputBox and how to create pop-up information-gathering forms.

2.10 Store the Sizes and Locations of Forms

This How-To will show how to write particular characteristics about your form to the system registry. It will use built-in functions to save and restore the information and Windows API calls to discern the exact size and location of the form in question. You'll be able to use the code in this How-To to preserve information about any form in your application. By attaching the code to the appropriate event procedure, you can save and restore the necessary information when you close, and later reopen, the forms.

2.11   Open Multiple Instances of a Form

Users often want to be able to view two rows of data so they can compare or copy values, but also want to use single-row forms. This How-To will show how you can use Access' ability to open multiple instances of a form to show as many copies of your form as you like on the screen, each with its own current row and its own set of properties.

COMPLEXITY:
EASY

2.1   How do I...
Make custom templates for forms and reports?

Problem

When I make a new blank form, the form properties and the properties of any control I place on it use the Access defaults. I've decided upon a standard "look" for my forms and reports that is significantly different from these defaults, and I spend too much time changing control properties on every new form I create to make them match my look. I'd like some way to change the standard default values. Can I do this?

Technique

Access allows you to specify a particular form or report to use as a template for new forms or reports that you create. This How-To lists the steps you'll need to take to create your own template for form design. The technique is the same for form templates and report templates.

Steps

Load 02-01.MDB and create a new form. Add controls of various types to the form. Notice that some of them look different than the normal Access defaults. To see where the properties are coming from, load the form named Normal from 02-01.MDB in design mode. Each of the controls on this form will act as a template for any new controls on any forms you create in this database. In addition, any new form you create will inherit its own properties from this template form.

To create your own template form, follow the steps below:

1. Create a new blank form.

2. Make any general changes you want in the form properties, such as changing the GridX and GridY properties to different settings—many users may prefer 24 x 24, the smallest grid that will show dots. To do this, first display the properties sheet: Click on the gray area in the upper-left corner of the form or select the Edit|Select Form menu item. If you don't want a record selector, navigation buttons, minimize or maximize buttons, a control box, and/or scroll bars on your form template, turn them off too, in the Layout section of the form's properties sheet. In addition, you can choose to center the form automatically when it is opened by changing the AutoCenter property to Yes.

3. You may also wish to change the form's background color by changing the background color for the form's Detail section (click on the Detail section bar in form design to select the section). If you want your forms to have page headers/footers or form headers/footers, activate them by checking Format|Page Header/Footer or Form Header/Footer and set their colors as well.

4. Once you have finished setting up the form's general properties, repeat the process to change the default settings for each control that you care to modify. There are two ways you can do this:

🗝 Click on the tool for that control in the toolbox and change the properties in the control's properties sheet. Note that when you do this, the properties sheet's title bar says "Default Label" (or whatever control you have selected), as shown in Figure 2-1.

🗝 Change the controls directly on your form. Add each control type that you care to change to your form, and set the properties visibly. Once you're done, select the Format|Set Control Defaults menu item, with all the controls selected.

5. Save your form with any name you like.

6. Finally, open the Tools|Options|Forms/Reports dialog box, as shown in Figure 2-2. Enter your form's name in the Form Template textbox.

Figure 2-1 The Default
Label properties sheet

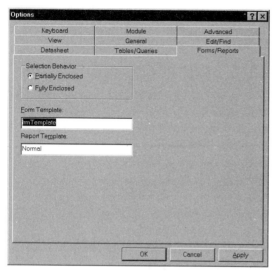

Figure 2-2 The Form & Report Design
Options dialog box

How It Works

Access normally uses a hidden form named Normal for its form template (and a report of the same name for its report template). If you don't specify your own default properties, all your new forms will use Access' built-in form, report, and control properties. If you create a form named Normal and set the default control and form properties for that form, Access will use that form as a template (that's how the example database has been configured). If you name your form something besides Normal, you can instruct Access to use that form (or report) as the template by changing the values in the Tools|Options dialog box.

Comments

You might want to use different background colors for labels attached to text boxes or combo boxes or for unattached labels, but Access won't let you save specific settings for different types of labels. There is just one type of label, as far as Access is concerned. The default label will have one background color, and you will have to change it as needed depending on its attachment.

To make a report template, follow the same procedure as for a form template, though you can omit controls that aren't useful on reports, such as combo boxes and command buttons.

A form or report template only supplies styles, such as color, presence of headers and/or footers, and grid granularity, to new forms and doesn't supply the controls themselves. If you would like all your forms to contain standard controls at fixed locations, you'll need to make a copy of a standard form and work from that copy. If you copy the entire form, any code attached to the control's event procedures (in the form's module) will be copied also—that's not true if you use templates to create your new forms and reports.

The template form (or report) only affects *new* objects. If you create a form based on the template, and then change the template, any forms based on that template will not be affected.

You can maintain several form or report templates in your database. If you want a specific template for dialogs forms, and a different one for data entry forms, keep them both in the database, and change the option when you want to create a new form based on a specific template.

COMPLEXITY:
EASY

2.2 How do I... Highlight the current field in data entry forms?

Problem

The text cursor is too small in Access, and I can't always tell which text box on a form has the cursor. I need some way to *really* highlight the current field.

Technique

There are many visual cues you can use to tell the user which text box has the cursor in it. You could change the color of the text or the background, change the appearance of the text box, or change the appearance of the text box's label.

The simplest solution, which works quite well, is to change both the BackColor and the SpecialEffect properties of the active control. This solution uses two simple macros, attached to each control's Enter and Exit events, to do the work. Figure 2-3 shows the sample form, frmEffects, in use with the City field currently selected.

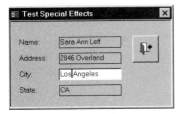

Figure 2-3 frmEffects in use, showing the active field

Steps

Open 02-02.MDB and load frmEffects. As you move from field to field on the form, note that the special effect and background color of each control changes when you enter and again when you leave the control.

Follow these steps to create a form with this same sort of functionality:

1. Create a new macro (named mcrSpecialEffect in 02-02.MDB). Within the macro, turn on the macro names column (choose Macro Names from the View menu). Figure 2-4 shows the macro editing window as it should appear once you've followed all the steps outlined here. This macro will contain all the commands necessary to change the look of each control upon entry and exit.

2. Within the macro, enter the four commands shown in Table 2-1. You can leave a blank row between the two macros (as in Figure 2-4) if you like. You can also enter the comments, as shown in Figure 2-4, if you care to. They don't affect the workings of the macro, but they do make it easier to interpret later on. Once you're done, save this macro as mcrSpecialEffect.

MACRO NAME	ACTION	ITEM	EXPRESSION
Enter	SetValue	Screen.ActiveControl.SpecialEffect	2
	SetValue	Screen.ActiveControl.BackColor	16777215
Exit	SetValue	Screen.ActiveControl.SpecialEffect	0
	SetValue	Screen.ActiveControl.BackColor	12632256

Table 2-1 Contents of mcrSpecialEffect

3. Create your input form, if you haven't already. In design mode, select all of the text boxes to which you'd like to attach this effect. (SHIFT-CLICK) with the mouse allows you to select multiple controls. By selecting a group of controls, you can set properties for all of them at once. Set the properties of this group of controls as shown in Table 2-2. Figure 2-5 shows the design surface with all the text boxes selected. (Note that once you select multiple controls, the

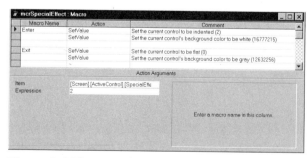

Figure 2-4 The completed mcrSpecialEffect macro

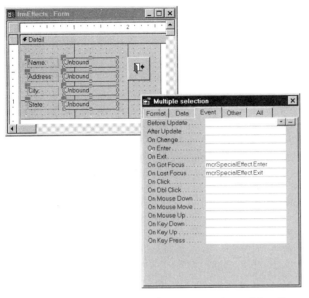

Figure 2-5 frmEffects in design mode, with all
the text boxes selected

properties sheet's title can no longer display the name of the selected control
and it will only show "Multiple selection" as shown in Figure 2-5.)

PROPERTY	VALUE
BackColor	12632256
OnEnter	mcrSpecialEffect.Enter
OnExit	mcrSpecialEffect.Exit

Table 2-2 Property settings for the selected controls on frmEffects

4. Add the following code to the form's Load event procedure (see this book's
Introduction for information on creating event procedures):

```
Sub Form_Open (Cancel As Integer)
    Me.SetFocus
End Sub
```

How It Works

These macros do their work by reacting to the events that occur when you enter or
leave a control on the form. Every time you enter one of the text boxes to which you've
attached a macro, Access executes that macro. Therefore, whenever you enter one of
these special text boxes, Access will cause the text box to appear sunken and will change

its background color to white. When you leave the control (by tab or mouse click), Access will set it back to being flat and will reset its background color to gray.

The pair of macros do their work for any control by using the built-in object Screen.ActiveControl. This object always provides a reference to the currently active control. Therefore, when you enter a control, the macro acts on that particular control, setting the SpecialEffect and BackColor properties.

The only problem with this mechanism is that, when Access first opens a form, there *isn't* a current control. Attempting to refer to Screen.ActiveControl before the form is fully loaded will result in an Access error. Because Access will attempt to enter the first control on your form when it first opens the form and there isn't yet a current control, the macro you've attached to that first text box's Enter event will fail. To work around this problem, you need to use the code attached to the Open event, as shown in step 4. This tiny bit of code will force the form to load completely before it attempts to enter the first text box on your form. You may find this technique useful in other applications you create that use Screen.ActiveControl.

Comments

The macros used in this How-To could be extended to include many other changes to the controls as you enter and leave them. You could change the font or its size, or the foreground color. It would also be nice to change the color of the label attached to the text box, but that is quite difficult. Because Access provides no mechanism for linking a text box (or any other control) to its attached label, you have no programmatic way of referring to a control's label. Access does provide a label's Parent property, which tells you which control a label is linked to; but it doesn't provide the appropriate alternate property, which would tell you which label is attached to the control. You could accomplish the task with a careful naming convention (that way, you know a control's label name because you know the control name), but that method's not reliable and certainly can't be generalized.

COMPLEXITY:
EASY

2.3 How do I...
Restrict the user to a single row on a form?

Problem

When I press the [TAB] or [SHIFT]-[TAB] key, I can't keep Access from moving to the next or previous row of data if I happen to be on the first or last control in a form's tab order. The same thing happens when I press the [PGUP] or [PGDN] key. This often isn't what I want; I want the cursor to stay on the same row and I want complete control over when the user moves to a different row. Is there some way to keep Access from moving to the next or previous row?

Technique

To gain complete control over row movement, you'll need to incorporate two different techniques. You can use the Cycle property of your form to decide whether leaving the first or last control on the row moves you to a different row. If you want to ensure that [PGUP] and [PGDN] don't move to a different row, you'll need to write a bit of code that will trap these particular keystrokes in the KeyDown event for the form and disregard them. This How-To uses both techniques to limit row movement.

Steps

Open and run frmRestricted from 02-03.MDB. Press [TAB] to move from field to field. When you get to the final field on the form, press [TAB] once more, and your cursor will move back up to the first control, rather than moving on to the next row, as it normally would. The same thing occurs when you use [SHIFT]-[TAB] to move backwards through the controls. When you reach the first control, the cursor will wrap around and go to the final control on the same row, rather than moving to the previous row. Try pressing the [PGUP] or [PGDN] keys: They're completely disregarded. The only way to move from row to row is to use the navigation buttons on the form. Try unchecking the Control Movement checkbox, and see how the default behavior differs.

Follow these steps to add this functionality to your own form:

1. Create your form. Set its Cycle property (on the Other properties page) to Current Record. This causes the [TAB] and [SHIFT]-[TAB] keys to work correctly.

2. Set the form's KeyPreview property (on the Event properties page) to Yes. This causes the form to intercept keystrokes before any controls on the form can react to them.

3. Enter the following code for the form's KeyDown event (see the Introduction to this book for information on creating event procedures). Figure 2-6 shows the form, its properties sheet, and the module window.

```
Private Sub Form_KeyDown(KeyCode As Integer, Shift As Integer)


    Select Case KeyCode
        Case vbKeyPageUp, vbKeyPageDown
            KeyCode = 0
        Case Else
            ' Do nothing
    End Select
End Sub
```

How It Works

There are actually two techniques at work in this sample form. The first technique, using the form's Cycle property, forces the cursor to wrap around from bottom to top if moving forwards, or top to bottom if moving backwards, through controls on the form. You can set the property to All Records (the default), Current Record, or

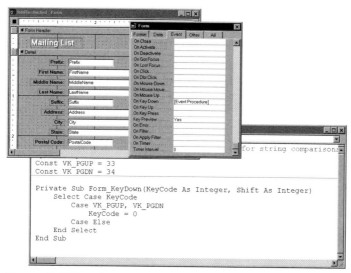

Figure 2-6 Use the KeyDown event to trap keystrokes and control form movement

Current Page. This example uses the Current Record setting, which wraps around for each full record. How-To 2.5 uses the Current Page setting, so that the cursor wraps around on the current page of a multipage form.

The second technique involves trapping keystrokes and convincing Access to disregard specific ones. A form's KeyDown event occurs every time you press any key, and Access informs the event procedure exactly which key was pressed by passing to it the KeyCode and Shift parameters. If you press the PGUP or PGDN key, you would like Access to ignore the keystroke. To make that happen, you can modify the value of the KeyCode parameter, setting it to 0. In that case, Access knows you want the keystroke to be ignored. Step 3 includes the code that performs this transformation. (Think what fun you could have intercepting each keystroke and converting it to something else behind the scenes, just to amuse your users!)

Comments

Most likely, if you're going to use the techniques presented in this How-To, you'll want to provide some method of navigating through the rows on your form. You could use the built-in navigation buttons, but you probably wouldn't have gone to this much effort if you didn't want a bit more control. How-To 2.6 provides a method you can use for placing your own navigation buttons on a form, giving you complete control over the look and placement of the controls. Using those controls, you can ensure that users can't move to a different row until they've satisfied your needs in the current one.

COMPLEXITY:
EASY

2.4 How do I...
Use an option group to collect and display text information?

Problem

Option groups work great for collecting and displaying numeric values. But sometimes I need to use an option group bound to a column of values that isn't numeric. For instance, in each row I have a field that contains just one of four different alphabetic codes. I want some way to let the user choose from those four codes on a form. How can I do that?

Technique

Most often, when you want a control on a form bound to a column in a table that contains a few alphabetic items, you can use a list or combo box to display and collect the information. Other times, though, you want to be able to use an option group, where you can have option buttons or even toggle buttons containing pictures. Option groups, though, as Access implements them, can only be bound to a numeric column.

The solution is to use an unbound option group. Rather than moving the data directly from the form to the underlying data, you'll make a pit stop along the way.

Steps

Open and run frmOptionExample in 02-04.MDB. This form, shown in Figure 2-7, pulls in two columns from the underlying table, tblShipments. Each row contains a Contents field and a Shipper field. The Shipper field can be just one of four values: UPS, Fed Ex, US Mail, or Airborne. The form displays the Contents field in a text box and the Shipper field in an option group. In addition, it shows another text box control: the pit stop mentioned earlier. This (normally hidden) text box is the bound control, not the option group.

To create a minimal sample form that works with the same data, follow these steps:

1. In 02-04.MDB, create a new form. Choose tblShipments for the form's RecordSource property.

2. On your new form, create controls, as shown in Table 2-3. Make sure that you've created the option group before you attempt to place any option buttons inside it. You should see the option group turn dark when you attempt to place an option button in it.

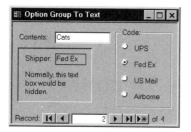

Figure 2-7 Example form
using an option group to
store character data

CONTROL TYPE	PROPERTY	VALUE
Option Group	Name	grpCode
Option Button (UPS)	Name	optUPS
	Option Value	1
Option Button (Fed Ex)	Name	optFedEx
	Option Value	2
Option Button (US Mail)	Name	optUSMail
	Option Value	3
Option Button (Airborne)	Name	optAirborne
	Option Value	4
Text Box	Name	txtShipper
	Control Source	Shipper

Table 2-3 Control properties for the new sample form

3. Create a new macro. Turn on its Macro Name column (choose View|Macro
Names or select the Macro Names button on the toolbar). Add actions as
shown in Table 2-4, and then save it as mcrEvents.

MACRO NAME	ACTION	PARAMETER	VALUE
AfterUpdate	SetValue	Item	[txtShipper]
		Value	Choose([grpCode],"UPS", "Fed Ex", "US Mail", "Airborne")
Current	SetValue	Item	[grpCode]
		Value	Switch([txtShipper] = "UPS", 1,
			[txtShipper] = "Fed Ex", 2,
			[txtShipper] = "US Mail", 3,
			[txtShipper] = "Airborne", 4, Null, Null)

Table 2-4 Macro actions for the sample form

4. For the form's OnCurrent event property, choose mcrEvents.Current from the drop-down list of macros. This macro will set the correct value of the option group as you move from row to row.

5. For the option group's AfterUpdate event property, choose mcrEvents.AfterUpdate from the drop-down list of macros. This macro will set the value in the bound text box, based on your choice in the option group.

How It Works

Using just two simple macros, you've managed to make the sample form store the data as required. The example works because of two distinct events and two distinct functions that you call from those events.

The Events

The form's Current event occurs every time you move from one row to another in the underlying data. In this case, you'll need to convert the data from its raw form (as the shipper's code text strings) into a format that the option group on the form can display for each row as you move to that row.

The option group's AfterUpdate event occurs whenever you change its value. For this control, choosing any of the option buttons within it will trigger the event. Use this event to place a new value into the text box on the form, which is directly bound to the correct column in the underlying data.

The Functions

When you want to convert the raw data into an integer representation (so the option group can display the value), use the Switch function. Its syntax is

```
returnValue = Switch(expr1, value1 [,expr2, value2][, expr3, value3]...)
```

Access will evaluate *each* of the expressions, but will return the value corresponding to the first one that returns a True value. In this example, the macro assigns the value of this expression:

```
Switch([txtShipper] = "UPS", 1, [txtShipper] = "Fed Ex", 2, _
  [txtShipper] = "US Mail", 3, [txtShipper] = "Airborne", 4, Null, Null)
```

to the option group. If the value in [txtShipper] is "UPS", then the option group gets the value 1. If [txtShipper] is "Fed Ex", then the option group is 2, and so on. The final pair (the two null values) ensures that if the value of [txtShipper] is Null, the option group will also be Null. Access calls this function from the form's Current event, so that every time you move from row to row, Access assigns the appropriate value to the option group based on what it finds in the bound text box.

To convert a choice made in the option group into its appropriate text value to be stored in the table, use the Choose function. Its syntax is

```
returnValue = Choose(index, value1 [, value2][, value3]...)
```

Based on the value in *index,* the function will return the matching value from its list of values. In your example, the macro assigns the value of this expression:

```
Choose([grpCode], "UPS", "Fed Ex", "US Mail", "Airborne")
```

to the bound text box once you've made a selection in the option group. If you choose item 1 from the option group, it'll assign "UPS" to the text box. If you choose option 2, it'll assign "Fed Ex", and so forth.

Comments

You can use the two events (AfterUpdate and Current) and the two functions described here to handle your conversions from integers (option group values) to text (as stored in the table). Be aware of a few limitations that apply to the Switch and Choose functions.

> Both functions support only a limited number of options. Switch can support up to seven pairs of expressions/values. Choose can support up to 13 expressions. If you need more than that, you'll need to convert your event handlers to VBA. Of course, you should avoid putting more than seven items in an option group, anyway.

> Both functions evaluate *all* of the expressions they contain before they return a value. This can lead to serious errors unless you plan ahead. The following expression details the worst possible case.

```
returnVal = Choose(index, MsgBox("Item1"), MsgBox("Item2"),⇒
MsgBox("Item3"), _
MsgBox("Item4"), MsgBox("Item5"), MsgBox("Item6"), _
MsgBox("Item7"), MsgBox("Item8"), MsgBox("Item9"), MsgBox("Item10"), _
MsgBox("Item11"), MsgBox("Item12"), MsgBox("Item13"))
```

You might assume that this expression would display the message box corresponding only to the value of *index.* You would be wrong. This expression will always display 13 message boxes, no matter what the value of *index* might be. Because Switch and Choose both evaluate all of their internal expressions before they return a value, they both execute any and all functions that exist as parameters. This could lead to unexpected results as Access runs each and every function used as a parameter to Switch or Choose.

In most cases, you'd be better off using a list or combo box with a separate lookup table, allowing your users to choose from a fixed list. If you have a small number of fixed values and you need to store those values in your table (as opposed to an index value from a small lookup table), then the technique presented here should work fine.

To use the techniques outlined here in your own applications, you'll need to modify the screen display and the two macros. Once you've done that, you should be able to use an option group to gather text information.

COMPLEXITY:
INTERMEDIATE

2.5 How do I...
Display multiple pages of information on one form?

Problem

I have a large number of fields that I need to display on a form. If I place them all on the form at once, it looks too complicated. I need some way to group them by category and display only the ones that correspond to each category as the user works through all the groups. Is there some easy way to make this happen?

Technique

Because Access handles multipage forms so well, this is actually a trivial task. Just divide your fields into categories, creating one page on your form for each category. In the form header, create an option group. The option group's value will control which of the form's pages is visible at any given time. Use the form's GotoPage method to display the page corresponding to the button you've pushed.

Steps

Load 02-05.MDB and open frmMain. This sample form (shown in Figure 2-8) contains a text box and an option group in the form header. By selecting a button in the option group, you cause one of the four possible pages of the form to be displayed in the detail section.

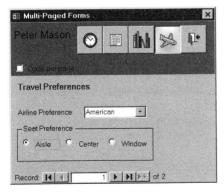

Figure 2-8 The sample form, frmMain

To create your own version of a multipage form, follow these steps:

1. Create the table and/or query on which you want to base your form (tblSample in 02-05.MDB). Make sure your data includes a primary key (ID in tblSample).

2. Open your form (frmMain in 02-05.MDB) in design view. Turn on the form header and footer by choosing View|Form Header/Footer.

3. Set at least the properties shown in Table 2-5 for the form itself. By setting the form's AllowAdditions property value to No, you won't be able to add new rows using this particular form, but the whole package will be much simpler to handle. If you need to use the form to add new rows, you can add an option (perhaps a new command button) later to add the new rows.

PROPERTY	VALUE
RecordSource	tblSample (or the name of your table or query)
AllowAdditions	No
ViewsAllowed	Form
BorderStyle	Dialog

Table 2-5 Form property values for the main form, frmMain

4. In the form's header section, create an option group (grpOptions) and place within it enough toggle buttons to handle all your categories. In addition, add one command button (cmdExit) to close the form. Figure 2-9 shows the option group on the sample form in design view, "exploded" so you can see how the form's header has been laid out. Set the DefaultValue property to 1 (corresponding to the toggle button/subform that you'll want visible when your form first loads). Once you've got everything placed correctly, you can collapse the size of the option group to fit the buttons inside it exactly by pulling its upper-left and lower-right bottom corners in toward the option

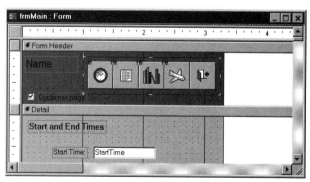

Figure 2-9 The sample form in design mode, "exploded" to show the option group

group as far as possible. Access will size the option group to fit the buttons inside it.

5. Ensure that the OptionValue property for each of the toggle buttons has been set to a unique value. In the sample form, these range from 1 through 4. You'll want these values to be simple increasing values, starting at 1, corresponding to the page number you want displayed when you press each of the buttons.

6. Add code such as the following to the option group's AfterUpdate event procedure. This will select the appropriate page of the form based on your choice from the option group (named grpOptions in the example).

```
Private Sub grpOptions_AfterUpdate()
    Me.GoToPage Me!grpOptions
End Sub
```

7. Add the following code to the OnClick event procedure for the command button (named cmdExit in the sample form).

```
Sub cmdExit_Click ()
    DoCmd.Close
End Sub
```

8. In the form's header section, place controls containing any data that you'd like to have appear no matter which page you've selected. In this example, the Name field appears in the form header.

9. Add the fields to the detail section of the form, and place PageBreak controls evenly spaced on the form indicating where you want the page breaks. The sample form uses 1.5-inch pages. Figure 2-10 shows the four subsidiary pages for the sample.

10. Set the form's Cycle property to Current Page, so that you won't move from page to page by tabbing around the form. (See How-To 2.3 for more information on the Cycle property.)

11. Set the form's KeyPreview property to Yes and enter the following code into the form's KeyDown event procedure. (See How-To 2.3 for more information on trapping keystrokes using this technique.)

```
Private Sub Form_KeyDown(KeyCode As Integer, Shift As Integer)

    Select Case KeyCode
        Case vbKeyPageUp, vbKeyPageDown
            KeyCode = 0
        Case Else
            ' Do Nothing
    End Select
End Sub
```

12. Use the View|Tab Order dialog box, shown in Figure 2-11, to correct the tab order for your form. It is essential that the first control in the tab order is the first control on the page you've designated as the default page in step 4.

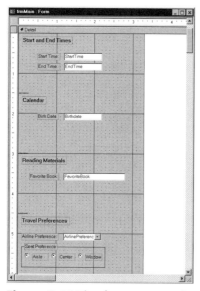

Figure 2-10 The four pages of frmMain

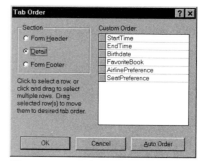

Figure 2-11 The View|Tab Order dialog box sets the tab order for the form's controls

Otherwise, when you first open the form, Access will find that first control and show it, whether or not it's on the page you want shown. It's not a pretty sight.

How It Works

When you make a choice from the option group in the form's header, you trigger the control's AfterUpdate event. This causes the code listed in step 6 to request the form to move to a specific page. The GotoPage method for the form requires you to specify which page to move to; because you've numbered the options in the option group carefully, using

```
Me.GotoPage Me!grpOptions
```

moves the form to the correct page, depending on the button you chose.

This How-To relies on the fact that each member of an option group, whether it's a toggle button, option button, or check box, represents a unique value (the OptionValue property of each control). By choosing one of these internal controls, you supply the option group with a value. That value indicates which page you want to have displayed.

The check box on the sample form turns the form's Cycle property on and off. Normally, you wouldn't include such a mechanism on your own forms, but it's interesting to turn off the Cycle property and see what happens as you use the TAB key to move around. You'll find that the form gets very ugly when you jump from page to page.

The code in step 11 ensures that you can't move from page to page with the PGUP and PGDN keys. Because it's important in most multipage forms that you know what page is currently visible, you'll want to make sure that the only way to move from page to page is under your own control. That way, you'll always know the number of the current page, because your own code put the user there.

Comments

You can use several other methods to create multipage forms, similar to what you saw in this How-To.

> You can use multiple subforms, placing each of the subforms on the main form and setting all of them to be invisible except one. In the AfterUpdate event of the option group, you can make the current subform invisible and the new one visible. This method is somewhat easier to set up than what is shown here, because working with long multipage forms can be awkward. This method also consumes more system resources than the method shown in this How-To.

> You can create one subform control, and in reaction to pressing buttons in the option group, change the SourceObject property of the subform control. This is a very "neat" solution, because there's only one subform on the main form (as opposed to four in the previous alternative). The drawback here is that changing the SourceObject property is quite slow.

> If you own the Access Developer's Toolkit, you can use the TabStrip OLE control that's available there. OLE controls normally provide an excellent solution, though using custom controls can be unwieldy. They require distributing and installing another file or two with your applications, and must be registered with the registry in order to work at all.

COMPLEXITY:
INTERMEDIATE

2.6 How do I...
Provide record navigation buttons on a form?

Problem

I'd like to provide some mechanism for allowing users to move from row to row on my forms, but I think the navigation buttons Access provides are too small and unattractive. Also, I can't control when the user can or can't move to another row. Can I replace these with my own buttons?

Technique

You can create your own buttons, place them on a form, and have each button use the GotoRecord macro action. Unfortunately, this has two drawbacks.

> 🔑 If you attempt to move to the previous or next row and you're already at the end of the recordset, the macro will fail. The GotoRecord macro action just isn't smart enough to work in this case.

> 🔑 Your buttons will always be available, giving no indication as to when you can use them.

To avoid errors, you *must* use VBA. This How-To demonstrates the steps you can take to add the appropriate code to your application so that navigation buttons will move you safely from row to row, and how to disable the navigation buttons when they are unavailable. The form frmNav in 02-06.MDB (see Figure 2-12) works this way. You can load it and give it a try before attempting to build your own. In Figure 2-12, note that the Next button is disabled; the form is currently displaying the last row in the table, and there *is* no next row.

Steps

Open and run frmNav from 02-06.MDB. Use the navigation buttons to move from row to row (there are only a few rows in the table so far). Note that, as you move around in the table, the appropriate buttons become enabled and disabled. Also try using the PGUP and PGDN keys. You'll see that the appropriate buttons still become disabled as necessary. Try entering a row number into the text box in the navigation controls; when you leave the text box, you will move to the selected row number.

Follow the steps below to include this functionality in your own applications:

1. Set your form's properties, as shown in Table 2-6, removing the form's scroll bars and built-in navigation buttons. (Because this method only works for scrolling through rows of data, your form must also have its RecordSource property set so that the form displays rows of data.)

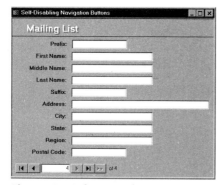

Figure 2-12 frmNav from
02-06.MDB

PROPERTY	VALUE
ScrollBars	Neither
NavigationButtons	No

 Table 2-6 Property settings for forms to remove the built-in navigation buttons

2. Either copy the buttons from frmNav or create your own five buttons on your form. *Do not* use the Access Button Wizard to create your buttons, because that will add inappropriate code to the buttons; you want to be able to supply the code yourself. By creating your own buttons, you can add pictures from Access' selection of pictures. Click on the builder button to the right of the Picture property on the properties sheet for each button. Also, create a text box named txtCurrentRow that will display the current row number and a label named lblTotalRows to display the total number of rows. (Normally, in these How-To's, the exact name of the controls you create doesn't matter. In this one, however, the names *do* matter; make sure your names match ours exactly.)

3. Set the Name property for each of the command buttons, based on the following list. The code you'll use later depends on these particular names.

```
cmdFirst
cmdPrev
cmdNew
cmdNext
cmdLast
```

4. Add the following code to cmdFirst's Click event. (For information on adding code to a form event, see this book's Introduction.)

```
Sub cmdFirst_Click ()
    ahtMoveFirst Me
End Sub
```

5. Add the following code to cmdPrev's Click event.

```
Sub cmdPrev_Click ()
    ahtMovePrevious Me
End Sub
```

6. Add the following code to cmdNew's Click event.

```
Sub cmdNew_Click ()
    ahtMoveNew Me
End Sub
```

7. Add the following code to cmdNext's Click event.

```
Sub cmdNext_Click ()
    ahtMoveNext Me
End Sub
```

85

8. Add the following code to cmdLast's Click event.

```
Sub cmdLast_Click ()
    ahtMoveLast Me
End Sub
```

9. Add the following code to your form's Current event.

```
Sub Form_Current ()
    ahtHandleCurrent Me
End Sub
```

10. Add the following code to your form's KeyPress event.

```
Private Sub Form_KeyPress(KeyAscii As Integer)
    ahtHandleKeys Me
End Sub
```

11. Set the form's KeyPreview property to True.

12. Add the following code to txtCurrentRow's AfterUpdate event.

```
Private Sub txtCurrentRow_AfterUpdate()
    ahtMove Me, Me!txtCurrentRow
End Sub
```

13. Import the basMovement module from 02-06.MDB into your own application.

How It Works

This How-To actually has three parts. The first deals with the record navigation (steps 1 through 8), the second handles disabling the unavailable buttons (steps 9 through 11), and the third controls the direct movement to a specific row (steps 12 and 13).

Handling Record Navigation

For each of the five buttons, you've attached code that will call a common procedure whenever you press the button, thus reacting to the Click event. For each button, the subroutine you call calls a procedure that handles all the motion. Clicking on the First button calls this code:

```
Sub ahtMoveFirst (frm As Form)
    HandleMovement frm, acFirst
End Sub
```

which calls the HandleMovement procedure.

```
Private Sub HandleMovement(frm As Form, intWhere As Integer)
    ' It's quite possible that this'll fail.
    ' Knowing that, just disregard any errors.
    On Error Resume Next
    DoCmd.GoToRecord , , intWhere
    On Error GoTo 0
End Sub
```

Every subroutine that calls HandleMovement passes to it a reference to a form and an Access constant that indicates to what row it wants to move (acFirst, acPrevious, acNewRec, etc.). HandleMovement disables error handling, so Access won't complain if you try to move beyond the edges of the recordset. HandleMovement then uses the GotoRecord macro action to go to the requested row.

Disabling Buttons Depending on Your Location

The second, and most complex, part of this How-To handles the enabling/disabling of the buttons, depending on the current row. In step 9, you attached a subroutine call to the Current event of the form. This tells Access that every time you attempt to move from one row to another, Access should call this procedure before it displays the new row of data. This procedure can then do the work of deciding where in the recordset the current row is and, based on that information, disable or enable each of the five navigation buttons. It also fills in the current row number and updates the display of the total number of rows.

A discussion of the full ahtHandleCurrent code is beyond the scope of this How-To (you can find the fully commented code in basMovement). The code must, however, as part of its work, determine whether or not the current row is the "new" row. That is, if you press the PGDN key until you're on the last row of data and then press the key once more (if your data set allows you to add rows), you'll be on the new row. Access provides the NewRecord property of the form, which tells you if you're on the new row or not. (See How-To 6.2 for more information on using this property.)

In order to enable cmdNew once you've entered some data on the new row, the form's KeyPress event calls ahtHandleKeys, as shown below. This code checks each keystroke, and if cmdNew isn't enabled, and the form is dirty, then the code enables the cmdNew.

```
Sub ahtHandleKeys(frm As Form)

    Dim fEnabled As Boolean
    fEnabled = frm!cmdNew.Enabled
    If Not fEnabled And frm.Dirty Then
        frm!cmdNew.Enabled = True
    End If
End Sub
```

Moving Directly to a Specific Row

To match the functionality of the standard Access navigation controls, the sample form reacts to the AfterUpdate event of the txtCurrentRow text box by moving to the row you've specified. The event procedure calls the ahtMove subroutine, which does all the work. This procedure, shown below, has three parts.

1. Retrieve a pointer to the form's recordset, using the recordset retrieved with the RecordsetClone property of the form.

2. Move to the first row (rst.MoveFirst) and then move the specified number of rows from there (rst.Move).

3. Make the form display the same row that's current in the recordset.

By equating the form's bookmark (a binary value, indicating the current row, whose exact contents are of no interest) and the recordset's bookmark, you make the form display the same row as is current in the underlying recordset. If there is no current row (that is, you've asked to go beyond the final row of data), an error occurs, and the code moves you directly to the new row on the form.

```
Sub ahtMove(frm As Form, ByVal lngRow As Long)

    ' Move to a specified row.
    On Error GoTo ahtMove_Err
    Dim rst As Recordset

    ' Get a pointer to the form's recordset.
    Set rst = frm.RecordsetClone

    ' Move to the first row, and then hop to
    ' the selected row, using the Move method.
    rst.MoveFirst
    If lngRow > 0 Then
        rst.Move lngRow - 1
    End If
    ' Finally, make the form show the
    ' same row as the underlying recordset.
    frm.Bookmark = rst.Bookmark

ahtMove_Exit:
    Exit Sub

ahtMove_Err:
    ' If an error occurs, it's most likely that
    ' you requested to move to the row past the
    ' last row, the New row, and there's no bookmark
    ' there. If that's the error, just move
    ' to the New row programmatically.
    Select Case Err
        Case ahtcErrNoCurrentRow
            DoCmd.GoToRecord , , acNewRec
            Resume Next
        Case Else
            MsgBox Error & " (" & Err & ")"
            Resume ahtMove_Exit
    End Select
End Sub
```

Comments

The code provided in basMovement makes it easy for you to move this functionality from one application to another just by hooking the correct form and control events. On the other hand, you can get similar results by creating your own toolbar and using the record navigation buttons that Access provides. A toolbar you create will control whatever form happens to be the current form. Figure 2-13 shows a form/toolbar combination in action. You'll need to decide for yourself which technique you like best. Certainly, the toolbar approach is simpler, but it is difficult to move toolbars from one

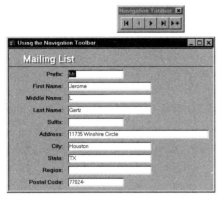

Figure 2-13 A record navigation toolbar can replace navigation buttons on the form

database to another, and they do clutter up the work area. You also have no programmatic control over the toolbars (except their visibility).

The sample form updates the display of the total number of rows, in lblTotalRows, every time you move from row to row. When you first open the form, Access may not yet know how many rows will finally be in the form's recordset, and the value returned in the form's recordset's RecordCount property may be inaccurate. You could move to the last row when you first open the form, forcing Access to find out how many rows there will be, but this can be slow if your form's recordset contains a large number of rows. Access continues to calculate as you use the form, and sooner or later it'll supply the correct value in the RecordCount property of the form's recordset. The compromise used here is that the total number of rows may be incorrect until you use the form for a few seconds. If this bothers you, you can add code to the form's Open event that works like this:

```
Dim rst As Recordset

Set rst = Me.RecordsetClone
rst.MoveLast
```

For small recordsets, this will be very fast, but unnecessary, because the RecordCount property will already be accurate. For large recordsets, this might take a few seconds to calculate, and will make your form's opening seem much slower.

COMPLEXITY:
INTERMEDIATE

2.7 How do I...
Size a form's controls to match the form's size?

Problem

I'd like to be able to resize my forms while the application is running and have the controls on the form react appropriately. For example, the Database Explorer window's list box expands when you expand the window. How can I do this on my own forms?

Technique

Because Access can notify your application when the user resizes a form, you can attach code to that particular form event (Resize) and react to the change in size. Access also triggers this event when it first draws the form, so you can place your controls correctly during that event, as well. You'll want to base your calculations on the form's InsideWidth and InsideHeight properties.

Steps

Load and run the form frmExpando in 02-07.MDB. Resize the form and watch the size of the large text box. Also, notice the positions of the two command buttons. Figure 2-14 shows the form in design mode, and Figure 2-15 shows two copies of the form sized to different proportions. Though it's perfectly reasonable to change the size of all the controls, this form does not. It uses three different techniques.

 Do nothing. The label above the text box doesn't change at all as you resize the form.

Figure 2-14 frmExpando in design mode

Figure 2-15 Two copies of frmExpando with different proportions

Change position only. The two command buttons move with the right edge of the form, but they don't change size.

Change size. The large text box changes its size to match the size of the form.

The code that does the work in this case is specific to the particular form. Follow the steps below to create a form similar to frmExpando. Once you've gone through these steps, you should be able to expand on the concepts (pun intended) and create your own self-sizing forms.

1. Create a new form and create controls and properties as shown in Table 2-7.

CONTROL TYPE	PROPERTY	VALUE
Label	Name	lblSample
	Left	0.1 in
	Top	0.0833 in
	Width	1.7917 in
	Height	0.1667 in
	Caption	Enter some text:
TextBox	Name	txtEntry
	Left	0.1 in
	Top	0.3333 in
	Width	1.8 in
	Height	0.8333 in
Command Button (OK)	Name	cmdOK
	Caption	&OK
	Left	2 in.
	Top	0.3333 in
	Width	0.6979 in
	Height	0.25 in
Command Button (Cancel)	Name	cmdCancel
	Caption	&Cancel
	Left	2 in.
	Top	0.6667 in
	Width	0.6979 in
	Height	0.25 in

Table 2-7 Controls and their properties for frmExpando

2. Place the following code in the form's Resize event procedure (see this book's Introduction for more information on creating event procedures). You can copy this code from frmExpando's.

```
Private Sub Form_Resize()
    Dim intHeight As Integer
    Dim intWidth As Integer
    Dim ctl As Control
    Static fInHere As Integer

    Const ahtcMinHeight = 2000
    Const ahtcMinWidth = 4000

    ' Optimize a bit. If you're already executing
    ' the code in here, just get out. This can
    ' happen if you're in here because of an auto-
    ' resize (if you try and size the form too small).
    If fInHere Then Exit Sub
    fInHere = True

    On Error GoTo Form_Resize_Err

    ' Get the current screen coordinates.
    intHeight = Me.InsideHeight
    intWidth = Me.InsideWidth

    ' Make sure the width and height aren't too small.
    ' If they are, resize the form accordingly.
    ' This could force Access to call this sub again,
    ' so use fInHere to avoid that extra overhead.
    If intWidth < ahtcMinWidth Then
       DoCmd.MoveSize , , ahtcMinWidth
       intWidth = Me.InsideWidth
    End If
    If intHeight < ahtcMinHeight Then
       DoCmd.MoveSize , , , ahtcMinHeight
       intHeight = Me.InsideHeight
    End If

    ' Set the detail section's height to be the same
    ' as the form's. Change this if you want to include
    ' header and footer sections.
    Me.Section(0).Height = intHeight

    ' Align all the other controls, based on the
    ' left margin of the text box.
    Set ctl = Me!txtEntry
    With ctl
       ' Make the left and bottom margins equal.
       .Height = intHeight - (.Left + .Top)

       ' The new width is the width of the form,
       ' minus the width of the buttons, minus 3 times
       ' the gap (the left margin). Two gaps are for the
       ' buttons, and one more is for the left margin
       ' itself.
```

```
        .Width = intWidth - Me!cmdOK.Width - (3 * .Left)
    End With
    ' Set the positions of the two buttons.
    With Me!cmdOK
        .Left = intWidth - .Width - ctl.Left
    End With
    With Me!cmdClose
        .Left = intWidth - .Width - ctl.Left
    End With

Form_Resize_Err:
    fInHere = False
    Exit Sub
End Sub
```

How It Works

The code used in this How-To reacts to the Resize event that will occur when you resize a form in Run mode (as well as when you open the form). The code will retrieve the form's current size (its InsideWidth and InsideHeight properties) and resize controls accordingly.

This example starts out by checking a flag, fInHere, and causes the subroutine to exit if the variable's value is True. It's possible that the procedure itself might cause another Resize event (if you've sized the form smaller than the preset minimum size); this flag ensures that the routine doesn't do more work than it needs to do.

Using the Static Keyword

The flag, fInHere, was declared with the Static keyword. This keyword indicates that Access will maintain the value of the variable between calls to the function. You could accomplish the same effect by making fInHere global, but making the variable static makes it exist as long as the form is loaded, maintains its value from one call to another, and is local to the current procedure. The variable performs its task (as a sentry) without possible intervention from any other procedure.

The code next retrieves the current form size and stores it into local variables. By placing these values into variables, Access doesn't need to retrieve the value of the properties every time you need to use them. This speeds up the operation, because retrieving property values is an "expensive" operation in terms of operating speed.

```
' Get the current screen coordinates.
intHeight = Me.InsideHeight
intWidth = Me.InsideWidth
```

Once it has retrieved the sizes, the procedure next verifies that the form hasn't been sized too small by the user. If so, it forces the form to be at least as large as the preset values of ahtcMinWidth and ahtcMinHeight.

```
If intWidth < ahtcMinWidth Then
    DoCmd.MoveSize , , ahtcMinWidth
    intWidth = Me.InsideWidth
End If
If intHeight < ahtcMinHeight Then
    DoCmd.MoveSize , , , ahtcMinHeight
    intHeight = Me.InsideHeight
End If
```

Finally, the procedure sets the sizes and locations of each of the controls based on the new width and height of the form. First, it sets the height of the form's detail section, Section(0), so there'll be room for all of the controls at the new height. It then sets the width and height of the text box and sets the left coordinate of the command buttons. This will preserve their sizes but reset their positions.

```
Set ctl = Me!txtEntry
With ctl
    .Height = intHeight - (.Left + .Top)
    .Width = intWidth - Me!cmdOK.Width - (3 * .Left)
End With
' Set the positions of the two buttons.
With Me!cmdOK
    .Left = intWidth - .Width - ctl.Left
End With
With Me!cmdClose
    .Left = intWidth - .Width - ctl.Left
End With
```

Comments

The values used as offsets in this example were all chosen arbitrarily. They work for this particular example, but you'll need to vary them for your own forms. Remember, also, that this example was quite simple. You'll be doing many more calculations if you want to resize a multicolumn list box, for example. In any case, the concepts are the same: Resize each of the controls based on the current size of the form. The tricky part is finding some "reference" on which you can base your sizing decisions; in this example, we used the offset of the expanding text box from the left edge of the form.

COMPLEXITY:
ADVANCED

2.8 How do I...
Make a simple "searching" list box?

Problem

I'd like to create a text box/list box combination like the one in Windows Help. As I type in the text box portion of the control, I want the list box to scroll to match whatever's been typed so far. I know I could use a combo box for this, but the combo box keeps closing up. I want something that's permanently open.

Technique

Entering a portion of the value they're looking for and seeing the matches displayed as users type is an excellent way to find specific values in a list. You get the best of both worlds: the functionality of a combo box and the "permanently open" look of a list box.

The key to implementing this functionality is the text box's Change event. Every time the text in the text box changes, the code you'll use will automatically find the matching value in the associated list box. You'll be able to call a function that will handle all the work for you. In addition, because searching through indexed tables is so much faster than walking through dynasets (the results of running a query or an SQL expression), this How-To offers two solutions to this problem: one for list boxes that are bound to tables and another for list boxes that are bound to queries or SQL expressions. Figure 2-16 shows frmSearchFind in action.

The methods you'll find in this How-To apply only to bound list boxes.

Steps

To test out the functionality, open the database 02-08.MDB and then open either frmSearchFind or frmSearchSeek. As you type into the text box, you'll see the associated list box scroll to match what you've typed. If you backspace to delete some

Figure 2-16 Using Incremental Search on frmSearchFind

characters, the list box will still match the characters that appear in the text box. When you leave the text box or click on an item in the list box, you'll see the full text of the chosen item in the text box. The functionality is the same no matter which form you use. The form frmSearchSeek will look up items faster, though, because it's guaranteed to use an index to do its work.

Follow these steps to build a form like frmSearchFind, which will use a query or SQL expression as the row source for the list box:

1. In your own database, create a new form that contains at least a text box and a list box. For the sake of this example, name the text box txtCompany and the list box lstCompany.

2. Set properties, as shown in Table 2-8.

CONTROL TYPE	PROPERTY	SETTING
TextBox	Name	txtCompany
	OnExit	[Event Procedure]
	OnChange	[Event Procedure]
ListBox	Name	lstCompany
	AfterUpdate	[Event Procedure]
	RowSource	qryCustomers
	ColumnCount	2
	ColumnWidths	0

Table 2-8 Controls and properties for search project form

3. Import the table Customers and the query qryCustomers from 02-08.MDB.

4. Put the following code in the lstCompany_AfterUpdate event procedure. (See this book's Introduction for more information on creating event procedures.)

```
Sub lstCompany_AfterUpdate ()
    ahtUpdateSearch Me!txtCompany, Me!lstCompany
End Sub
```

5. Put the following code in the txtCompany_Change event procedure.

```
Sub txtCompany_Change ()
    Dim varRetval As Variant

    varRetval = ahtDoSearchDynaset(Me!txtCompany, _
Me!lstCompany, "Company Name")
End Sub
```

6. Put the following code in the txtCompany_Exit event procedure.

```
Sub txtCompany_Exit (Cancel As Integer)
    ahtUpdateSearch Me!txtCompany, Me!lstCompany
End Sub
```

7. Import the module basSearch from 02-08.MDB. This module contains the code that does all the work.

How It Works

Every time you change the value in txtCompany, Access triggers txtCompany's Change event. The code attached to that event calls down into the common function, ahtDoSearchDynaset. In general, the syntax for calling ahtDoSearchDynaset is as follows:

```
varRetval = ahtDoSearchDynaset(textbox, listbox, "Field to search")
```

where *textbox* is a reference to the text box you're typing in, *listbox* is the list box you're searching in, and *"Field to search"* is the field in the list box's underlying record source through which you're going to search.

The function ahtDoSearchDynaset creates a dynaset-type recordset object, searching through it for the current value of the text box and then sets the value of the list box to match the value the code found in the underlying record source.

```
Function ahtDoSearchDynaset(ctlText As Control, _
 ctlList As Control, strBoundField As String) As Variant

    ' Search through a bound list box, given text to find from a text box.
    ' Move the list box to the appropriate row.
    ' The list box can have either a table or a dynaset
    ' (a query or an SQL statement) as its row source.

    Dim db As Database
    Dim rst As Recordset
    Dim varRetval As Variant

    On Error GoTo ahtDoSearchDynaset_Err

    Set db = CurrentDb()
    Set rst = db.OpenRecordset(ctlList.RowSource, dbOpenDynaset)
    ' Use the .Text property, because you've not yet left the
    ' control. Its value (or its .Value property) aren't
    ' set until you leave the control.
    rst.FindFirst "[" & strBoundField & "] >= " & QUOTE & ctlText.⇒
     Text & QUOTE
    If Not rst.NoMatch Then
        ctlList = rst(strBoundField)
    End If
    varRetval = ahtcErrNoError

ahtDoSearchDynaset_Exit:
    On Error Resume Next
    rst.Close
    On Error GoTo 0
    ahtDoSearchDynaset = varRetval
    Exit Function

ahtDoSearchDynaset_Err:
    varRetval = CVErr(Err)
    Resume ahtDoSearchDynaset_Exit
End Function
```

The example in this How-To is also set up so that if you leave the text box, it pulls in the currently selected item from the list box. That means that you can use TAB to leave the text box and the code will place the value that matches as much as you've typed so far in the text box.

You'll also notice that the list box's ColumnCount property is 2 and the ColumnWidths property is 0 in this example. This occurs because the query used, qryCustomers, contains two columns, with the first column hidden in the list box. Because you're searching for the second column, that must be the bound column.

Comments

This example, as shown so far, uses a query as the data source for the list box. For large data sets, this method can really slow things down, as it's not guaranteed that it'll be able to use an index. If at all possible, you'll want to base your list box directly on a table, instead, especially if your data set is much larger than a few hundred rows. In that case, you can use the Seek method, which is generally much faster than the FindFirst method used in this example. On the other hand, because it only works with a single table as its data source, it's a lot more limiting.

To make this happen, you'll need to change a few properties. To test it out, make a copy of your frmSearchFind and call the new form frmSearchSeek. Change the RowSource property of your list box to be Customers, rather than qryCustomers. In addition, change the function that txtCompany calls from its Change event procedure:

```
Sub txtCompany_Change ()
    Dim varRetval As Variant

    varRetval = ahtDoSearchTable(Me!txtCompany, _
    Me!lstCompany, "Company Name", "Company Name")

End Sub
```

In this case, you'll be calling the ahtDoSearchTable function, which searches through an indexed table instead of through an unindexed dynaset. In general, you'll call ahtDoSearchTable with the following syntax:

```
intRetval = ahtDoSearchTable(textBox, listBox, "BoundField", "IndexName")
```

where *textBox* is a reference to the text box you're typing in, *listBox* is the list box you're searching in, "*BoundField*" is the field in the list box's underlying record source through which you're going to search, and "*IndexName*" is the name of the index you're going to use. (Usually, it'll just be "PrimaryKey", but in this example, use "Company Name". This table is indexed both on the Customer ID field (the primary key) and the Company Name field (you're using the Company Name index).)

The code for ahtDoSearchTable is almost identical to that in ahtDoSearchDynaset, except that the table search uses the Seek method to search through an indexed record-set, instead of the FindFirst method that ahtDoSearchDynaset uses. Because it can use the index, it should be able to find matches much more rapidly than ahtDoSearchDynaset.

> **Note**
>
> Because ahtDoSearchTable requires that the list box's record source be a table, it will trap for that error and return a nonzero value as an error variant if you try to use it with some other data source. In addition, the function will not work correctly if you mismatch the bound field and the index. That is, the bound field must be the only field in the selected index.

The code for ahtDoSearchDynaset, ahtDoSearchTable, and ahtUpdateSearch is in the module basSearch. If you want to use this functionality in other applications, import that single module into your application and follow the steps outlined above to set the properties for your text and list boxes.

COMPLEXITY:
ADVANCED

2.9 How do I...
Create a replacement for Access' InputBox?

Problem

I'd like to be able to use Access' InputBox function in my applications, but it's so *ugly!* There doesn't appear to be any way to modify the way it looks, so I'd like to replace it with a standardized input form of my own. I'd also like to be able to call into my help file with a Help button on the InputBox. How can I do all that?

Technique

The dialog box you see when you run Access' InputBox function is just a form, like any other form, except that it's built into Access. You can create your own form, open it as a dialog form, and have it look any way you like. This How-To demonstrates a technique you can use in many situations: creating a pop-up form that waits for input and, once it's done, allows the caller to retrieve the information gathered on the form. In this case, you'll call the ahtInputBox function instead of InputBox, but the results will be the same.

Steps

Load and run frmTestInputBox from 02-09.MDB. This sample form gathers information and then calls the ahtInputBox function to display the replacement input form. Once you're done with the input form, choose OK (to return the text you've entered)

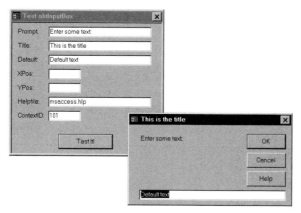

Figure 2-17 Use the frmTestInputBox to test
the replacement input box

or Cancel (to discard it). The sample form will pop up a message box with the text you entered. Figure 2-17 shows the two forms at work.

Follow the simple steps below to include this functionality in your own applications:

1. Import frmInputBox from 02-09.MDB into your database. Modify its appearance any way you like: Change its size, colors, fonts, or any other layout property. Because the form includes a module that handles its set up, you'll want to use the form we've supplied rather than creating your own.

2. Import the module basInputBox from 02-09.MDB. If you modified the form's name in step 1, you'll need to modify the code in basInputBox, making the ahtcInputForm constant match the actual name of the form.

3. To use the new input box, call the ahtInputBox function that's in basInputBox. It requires one parameter and accepts a number of optional parameters, as shown in Table 2-9. These parameters exactly match the parameters used by Access' own InputBox function. The general syntax for ahtInputBox is this:

```
varRetval = ahtInputBox(Prompt[, Title][, Default][, Xpos][, Ypos] _
[, Helpfile, Context])
```

For example, to match the function call in Figure 2-17, you could use code like this:

```
varRetval = ahtInputBox(Prompt:="Enter some text:", _
  Title:="This is the title", Default:="Default Text", _
  HelpFile:="msaccess.hlp", ContextID:=101)
```

4. Once you've called the ahtInputBox function, type a value into the text box on the form, and either press the OK button (or the [RETURN] key), or the Cancel button (or the [ESCAPE] key). Choosing OK returns the text you've typed, and choosing Cancel returns Null.

ARGUMENT	OPTIONAL?	DESCRIPTION
Prompt	No	String expression to be displayed as the prompt in the input box.
Title	Yes	String expression for the caption of the input box. If you omit this parameter, the caption will be empty.
Default	Yes	String expression displayed in the text box when the input box first pops up. If you omit this parameter, the text box will be empty.
XPos	Yes	Numeric expression that specifies, in twips, the distance between the left edge of the screen and the left edge of the input box. If you omit this parameter, the input box will be centered horizontally within the Access work area.
YPos	Yes	Numeric expression that specifies, in twips, the distance between the top edge of the screen and the top edge of the input box. If you omit this parameter, the input box will be centered vertically within the Access work area.
Helpfile	Yes	String expression that identifies the Help file to use to provide context-sensitive Help for the dialog box. If Helpfile is provided, Context must also be provided.
Context	Yes	Numeric expression that is the Help context number the Help author assigned to the appropriate Help topic. If Context is provided, Helpfile must also be provided.

 Table 2-9 Parameters for ahtInputBox

How It Works

This How-To presents several useful techniques: how to use optional parameters, how to pop up a form and wait for user response before returning a value back to the caller, how to initialize a pop-up form with values before presenting it to the user, and how to access online help programmatically.

Using Optional Parameters

Access allows you to declare and pass optional parameters to procedures that you create. That way, you can decide not to pass certain parameters and to use built-in defaults instead. For the ahtInputBox function, only one parameter is required: the prompt. You can leave off all the rest, and the function will assign logical defaults for you. Here are a few comments on using optional parameters in your own procedures.

 Once you use the Optional keyword in your procedure's declaration, all the subsequent parameters must also be optional.

All optional parameters must be Variants.

 If a parameter is optional, use the IsMissing function in your code to determine whether or not the caller supplied a value for the parameter.

The code in ahtInputBox checks each parameter to see if the caller supplied a value; if not, it uses its own built-in default values, as shown in the code below.

```
Function ahtInputBox(Prompt As Variant, Optional Title As Variant, _
  Optional Default As Variant, Optional XPos As Variant, _
  Optional YPos As Variant, Optional HelpFile As Variant, _
  Optional Context As Variant)

  ' This parameter is not optional.
  varPrompt = Prompt

  ' Use a blank title if the caller didn't supply one.
  varTitle = IIf(IsMissing(Title), " ", Title)

  ' Put text into the text box to start with.
  varDefault = IIf(IsMissing(Default), Null, Default)

  ' Specify the screen coordinates, in twips.
  varXPos = IIf(IsMissing(XPos), Null, XPos)
  varYPos = IIf(IsMissing(YPos), Null, YPos)

  ' Specify the help file and context ID.
  varHelpFile = IIf(IsMissing(HelpFile), Null, HelpFile)
  varContext = IIf(IsMissing(Context), Null, Context)

  ' Open the form in dialog mode. The code will
  ' stop processing, and wait for you to either close
  ' the form, or hide it.

  ' See the next section for the rest of the function.
```

Creating Pop-Up Forms

The concept here is that you want to be able to call a function (ahtInputBox) that will gather information and then pop up a form. That form will retain the focus until you are done with it, and then the function will return back to you the information it gathered on that form. The key to this process is in using the acDialog WindowMode parameter when opening the form. That way, the code processing in the original function waits, and the form doesn't relinquish the focus until you've either hidden it (which is what pressing the OK button does) or closed it (which is what pressing the Cancel button does). Once back in the original function, it can check to see if the form is still loaded (indicating that you pressed the OK button) and, if so, retrieve the information it needs directly from the form and then close the pop-up form. Here's the code from ahtInputBox that does all that work.

```
' Open the form in dialog mode. The code will
' stop processing, and wait for you to either close
' the form, or hide it.
DoCmd.OpenForm ahtcInputFormahtcInputForm, WindowMode:=acDialog

' If you get here and the form is open, you pressed
' the OK button. That means you want to handle the
' text in the text box, which you can get as the
' Response property of the form.
If IsFormOpen(ahtcInputForm) Then
    ahtInputBox = Forms(ahtcInputForm).Response
    DoCmd.Close acForm, ahtcInputForm
Else
    ahtInputBox = Null
End If
```

How do you know if the form is still open or not? This code uses the IsFormOpen function, shown below. That function relies on the Access SysCmd function, which, among other things, can tell you the current state of any object. In this case, if there is any state for the object (that is, if SysCmd returns anything besides 0), the form must be open.

```
Private Function IsFormOpen(strName As String) As Boolean
    ' Is the requested form open?
    IsFormOpen = (SysCmd(acSysCmdGetObjectState, acForm, strName) <> 0)
End Function
```

Finally, to retrieve the return value from the pop-up form, you can use a user-defined property of the form. In this case, we set up Response to be a property of the form that returns the value that you typed into the text box on the form. You could, of course, retrieve that value directly, but this means that the caller has to know about the controls on the pop-up form. This way, by exposing a defined interface between the caller and the form, it doesn't matter how you rename or change controls on the form; as long as it continues to provide the Response property, your code will still work.

To provide the read-only Response property, frmInputBox's module includes a Property Get procedure. This procedure, shown below, allows outsiders to retrieve what appear to be properties of the form itself. With this Property Get procedure in place, you can use syntax like this to retrieve the property:

```
ahtInputBox = Forms(ahtcInputForm).Response
```

Access supports Property Let, Get, and Set procedures. Peruse the Access online help for more information.

```
Property Get Response()
    ' Create a user-defined property: Reponse
    ' This property returns the value from
    ' the text box on the form.
    Response = Me!txtResponse
End Property
```

Initializing Pop-Up Forms

You've handled the input parameters and opened the dialog form. How do you tell that form what those parameters were? Just as forms can expose properties, modules can expose public variables that other modules and forms can view and modify. In this case, ahtInputBox placed the appropriate parameters into various module public variables (varPrompt, varDefault, varXPos, etc.). Code attached to the pop-up form's Open event retrieves the values of those public variables and uses them to initialize itself. As shown in the code below, these variables can be accessed as properties of the module (*basInputBox.varDefault*, for example).

```
Private Sub Form_Open(Cancel As Integer)

    On Error GoTo Form_OpenErr

    Me!txtResponse = basInputBox.varDefault
    Me.Caption = basInputBox.varTitle
    Me!lblPrompt.Caption = basInputBox.varPrompt
    If Not IsNull(basInputBox.varHelpFile) And _
      Not IsNull(basInputBox.varContext) Then
        Me!cmdHelp.Visible = True
        ' Set things up for the Help button.
        mvarContext = basInputBox.varContext
        mvarHelpFile = basInputBox.varHelpFile
    Else
        Me!cmdHelp.Visible = False
    End If
    If Not IsNull(basInputBox.varXPos) Then
        DoCmd.MoveSize basInputBox.varXPos
    End If
    If Not IsNull(basInputBox.varYPos) Then
        DoCmd.MoveSize , basInputBox.varYPos
    End If

Form_OpenExit:
    Exit Sub

Form_OpenErr:
    ' No error can occur here, I don't think, that
    ' would make the form open invalid.
    Resume Next
End Sub
```

Accessing Online Help Programmatically

If you specify a help file and a context ID when you call ahtInputBox, the code will enable a Help button on the form. When you click on that button, Access will load the help file, opened to the appropriate page. How did that all happen? The code attached to the Help button's Click event, shown below, calls the WinHelp API function, giving it a help file name, an action (ahtcHELP_CONTEXT, indicating that the code wants to supply a context ID and have that page visible when the file opens), and the context ID you supplied.

```
Const ahtcHELP_CONTEXT = &H1&

Private Declare Function WinHelp Lib "user32" Alias "WinHelpA" _
  (ByVal hWnd As Long, ByVal lpHelpFile As String, _
  ByVal wCommand As Long, ByVal dwData As Any) As Long

Private Sub cmdHelp_Click()
    ' Really, you don't care if this call fails!
    WinHelp Me.hWnd, mvarHelpFile, ahtcHELP_CONTEXT, CLng(mvarContext)
End Sub
```

Every page of a Windows help file can be accessed via its unique context ID that's assigned when you build the help file. Unfortunately, this is only of use if you've built the help file yourself or have a list of the context IDs for the various pages. No such list is available for the Access help file; even if it was, you cannot distribute the Access help file with your own applications. If you provide your own help file with your Access application, however, this technique makes it easy to have a help topic available at the click of a button.

Comments

The techniques presented here are far from limited to this particular How-To. You can use them any time you need to provide a modal dialog box that gathers information and then returns that information once you're done with it. Once you've mastered the concepts in the Creating Pop-Up Forms section, you will have a technique you can use over and over. Use it to provide a pop-up calendar form or a password input form, for example.

The method we chose for initializing the pop-up form (using module Public variables) is not the only method we could have used. Another popular method is to pass information to the form in its OpenArgs property: By adding a OpenArgs parameter to the OpenForm macro action, you can pass information directly to the opening form. In this case, because there were many pieces of information to pass over (and the OpenArgs property is limited to a single string value), we would have had to write treacherous code to parse the string out to retrieve the values. Using the technique we chose, it's just a matter of reading the values from the module where they were declared. Though this may seem a little "messy," it's a lot simpler in the long run.

The Access built-in InputBox function, though documented as supporting the Helpfile and ContextID parameters, does not. The help file includes those parameters for compability with Visual Basic, but they don't work from Access. This replacement for the InputBox function includes the parameters, and implements their functionality.

COMPLEXITY:
ADVANCED

2.10 How do I...
Store the sizes and locations of forms?

Problem

My application uses a number of forms that I can move around the screen. I'd like it if the last location could be stored away somewhere so that the forms will appear in the same location the next time I start the application.

Technique

Some Windows applications are "smart" and can save the locations of their windows when they exit. Your application can do this, too, using the system Registry. You can store settings when you close a form, and read them back the next time you open it.

Steps

Open and run the form frmSavePos in 02-10.MDB. Move it around the screen, and perhaps resize it. When you close the form, code attached to the Close event will save its coordinates in the system registry database. When you reopen the form, if the form can find the keys in the registry, it'll reload the last set of coordinates and resize/position itself accordingly.

To use this technique with your own forms, follow these steps:

1. Import the module basSaveSize from 02-10.MDB into your own application. This module contains the functions necessary to save and restore a form's size and location in the registry.

2. Add the following code to your form's Load event procedure. (See this book's Introduction for more information on creating event procedures.) This will *restore* the size and location when you load the form.

```
Sub Form_Load ()
    ahtRestoreSize Me
End Sub
```

3. Add the following code to your form's Unload event procedure. This will *save* the size and location when you close the form.

```
Sub Form_Unload (Cancel As Integer)
    ahtSaveSize Me
End Sub
```

How It Works

Clearly, judging by the brief number of steps above, most of the work involved in saving and restoring the form size and location must happen in the imported module, basSaveSize. The two event procedures, called from the form's Load and Unload events, do nothing more than call procedures in the imported module, passing a reference to the current form. You'll need to investigate that module to see what's going on!

This How-To relies heavily on two built-in functions: SaveSetting and GetSetting. These two functions store and retrieve values from the registry database that's a part of both Windows 95 and Windows NT. The sample code uses SaveSetting to save each of the four coordinates for a form and GetSetting to retrieve the same information.

SaveSetting and GetSetting make it easy to get and put values in the registry, but they're very limited. They can only work with the path HKEY_CURRENT_USER\Software\VB and VBA Program Settings (see Figure 2-18). They create a new key for each value you save (rather than storing multiple values in one key). We hope that future versions of Access will expand the functionality of these functions. If you're interested, investigate their coverage in online help, along with their companion functions, DeleteSetting and GetAllSettings.

The procedures in basSaveSize also hinge on two Windows API functions. GetWindowRect, aliased as aht_apiGetWindowRect, gets the coordinates of a screen window. MoveWindow, aliased as aht_apiMoveWindow, moves and sizes a window on screen.

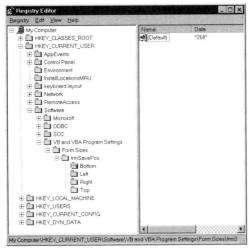

Figure 2-18 The registry holds the information about saved form locations

Why Use MoveWindow Rather than MoveSize?

You might be wondering why you shouldn't use the Access built-in MoveSize macro action: It requires that you select a form first, and this causes the form to display at that point. This looks ugly on screen, and makes the procedure less generic. In addition, it requires some work to convert from screen coordinates (pixels), which GetWindowRect uses, to twips, which MoveSize uses.

The subroutine GetRelativeCoords, in basSaveSize, retrieves the coordinates of a given form. Because the MoveWindow function requires a position relative to that of the window's parent to move a window, GetRelativeCoords must find the coordinates of both the requested window and its parent window. It calls the Windows API function GetParent, aliased as aht_apiGetParent, to find the parent and retrieves the coordinates of both. It fills in a user-defined structure with the relative coordinates.

```
' Store rectangle coordinates.
Type ahtTypeRect
    LngX1 As Long
    LngY1 As Long
    LngX2 As Long
    LngY2 As Long
End Type

Private Sub GetRelativeCoords(frm As Form, rct As ahtTypeRect)

    ' Fill in rct with the coordinates of the window.
    ' Deal with the conversion from screen coordinates (pixels)
    ' to twips.

    Dim hwndParent As Integer
    Dim rctParent As ahtTypeRect
    ' Find the position of the window in question, in
    ' relation to its parent window (the Access desktop, most
    ' likely, unless the form is modal).
    hwndParent = aht_apiGetParent(frm.hWnd)

    ' Get the coordinates of the current window and its parent.
    aht_apiGetWindowRect frm.hWnd, rct
    ' If the form is a pop-up window, its parent won't
    ' be the Access main window. If so, don't
    ' bother subtracting off the coordinates of the
    ' main Access window.
    If hwndParent <> Application.hWndAccessApp Then
        aht_apiGetWindowRect hwndParent, rctParent

        ' Subtract off the left and top parent coordinates, since you
        ' need coordinates relative to the parent for the aht_apiMoveWindow()
        ' function call.
```

```
      With rct
          .lngX1 = (.lngX1 - rctParent.lngX1)
          .lngY1 = (.lngY1 - rctParent.lngY1)
          .lngX2 = (.lngX2 - rctParent.lngX1)
          .lngY2 = (.lngY2 - rctParent.lngY1)
      End With
   End If
End Sub
```

The ahtSaveSize procedure first retrieves the current coordinates for the requested form, and then saves those values to the registry. Figure 2-18 shows the registry after saving the settings for the sample form. The function creates a group in the registry named Form Sizes, with a group inside it for each form whose coordinates you save. Within each subgroup, the procedure creates a single key for each of the four coordinates.

```
Const ahtcRegTag = "Form Sizes"
Const ahtcRegLeft = "Left"
Const ahtcRegRight = "Right"
Const ahtcRegTop = "Top"
Const ahtcRegBottom = "Bottom"

Sub ahtSaveSize(frm As Form)
   Dim rct As ahtTypeRect

   GetRelativeCoords frm, rct
   With rct
      SaveSetting ahtcRegTag, frm.Name, ahtcRegLeft, .lngX1
      SaveSetting ahtcRegTag, frm.Name, ahtcRegRight, .lngX2
      SaveSetting ahtcRegTag, frm.Name, ahtcRegTop, .lngY1
      SaveSetting ahtcRegTag, frm.Name, ahtcRegBottom, .lngY2
   End With
End Sub
```

When it comes time to retrieve the saved coordinates, the ahtRestoreSize procedure retrieves the four coordinates from the registry and then, if the width and the height of the new form would be greater than 0, resizes the form.

```
Sub ahtRestoreSize(frm As Form)
   Dim rct As ahtTypeRect
   Dim lngWidth As Integer
   Dim lngHeight As Integer

   With rct
      .lngX1 = GetSetting(ahtcRegTag, frm.Name, ahtcRegLeft, 0)
      .lngX2 = GetSetting(ahtcRegTag, frm.Name, ahtcRegRight, 0)
      .lngY1 = GetSetting(ahtcRegTag, frm.Name, ahtcRegTop, 0)
      .lngY2 = GetSetting(ahtcRegTag, frm.Name, ahtcRegBottom, 0)

      lngWidth = .lngX2 - .lngX1
      lngHeight = .lngY2 - .lngY1

      ' No sense even trying if both aren't greater than 0.
      If (lngWidth > 0) And (lngHeight > 0) Then
```

continued on next page

109

continued from previous page

```
                    ' You would think the MoveSize action would work here, but that
                    ' requires actually SELECTING the window first. That seemed like
                    ' too much work, when this procedure will move/size ANY window.
                    ' Also, MoveSize must DISPLAY the window before it can move it.
                    ' It looked quite ugly.
                    aht_apiMoveWindow frm.hWnd, .lngX1, .lngY1, _
                        lngWidth, lngHeight, True
                End If
            End With
        End Sub
```

Comments

You might want to store other properties besides the size and location of the form, for instance, the current record number for a bound form or which control was last selected. In any case, the example in 02-10.MDB stores information in such a way that you can store as many properties as you would like to by adding to the group describing each form in the registry.

COMPLEXITY:
ADVANCED

2.11 How do I...
Open multiple instances of a form?

Problem

In an application, I have a form showing information about a customer. I would like it if I could open another copy of the form so I could move to a different row, compare values, perhaps copy from one row to another, or just look at more than one customer's record at once. As far as I can tell, I can only have one open copy of a form at a time.

Technique

In previous versions of Access, you were limited to a single copy of a form open at any time. In Access 95, you have the capability of opening multiple instances of a form, under complete program control. There's no user interface for this functionality, however, so you must write code to make it happen. This How-To demonstrates how to create, handle, and delete multiple instances of a form using the New keyword and user-defined collections.

Steps

To see this functionality in action, load and run frmCustomers from 02-11.MDB. Once it's open, click View Another Customer. This will create a new instance of the original form, with its own set of properties and current row. You can create as many new forms as you like and move from row to row on any or all of them. When you're done, click Close All Extra Copies, which will run code to delete all the extra forms. Figure 2-19 shows the original form, along with five extras.

Follow these steps to convert your own forms to allow for multiple instances:

1. Add two buttons to your form, with captions like Create New Instance (named cmdViewAnother in the example) and Delete all Extra Instances (named cmdCloseAll in the example).

2. Add the following code to the Click event procedure of the Create New Instance button.

```
Private Sub cmdViewAnother_Click()
    Call ahtAddForm
End Sub
```

3. Add the following code to the Click event procedure of the Delete all Extra Instances button.

```
Private Sub cmdCloseAll_Click()
    Call ahtRemoveAllForms
End Sub
```

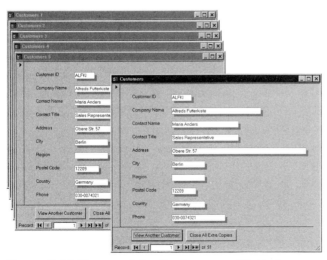

Figure 2-19 Clones of frmCustomers with their own current row

4. Add the following code to the Close event procedure for the form.

```
Private Sub Form_Close()
    Call ahtRemoveForm(Me)
End Sub
```

5. Import the module basMultiInstance from 02-11.MDB.

How It Works

Working with multiple instances of forms requires three skills: creating the new forms, storing their references, and deleting them. All three topics center around user-defined collections: These collections allow you to add and delete items at will, based on either their position in the collection or a string value that uniquely identifies each element. This example uses each form's hWnd property to identify the form in the collection.

Creating New Forms

In Access 95, each form stored in the database can be viewed as its own "class" of form: It's an object that you can replicate in memory, using the New keyword. The following statement will create a new instance of the form named frmCustomers.

```
Set frm = New Form_frmCustomers
```

Form_frmCustomers is the object type, and its name originates from its type (Form) concatenated with the actual class name (frmCustomers). Once you've executed this line of code, frm refers to a new, invisible form. You can set its properties, if you like, or make it visible with the statement

```
frm.Visible = True
```

Storing Form References

If you want to refer to your new form later, you'll need to store a reference to it somewhere. In the example code, we used a user-defined collection. When you create a new instance of the form, the code adds that form reference to the collection so you can find the form, under progam control, when you need to refer to it again.

Lifespan of a Form

The variables that refer to the newly created forms must have a lifespan longer than the procedure that creates the form. In this case, the form references are stored in a module-level collection, so their lifetime is the same as the database itself. When you create a new instance of a form, if the variable referring to that form goes out of scope, Access destroys the new form instance. Because you'll want your forms to hang around longer than that, make sure your form variables have a static, module, or global scope.

In this example, the ahtAddForm subroutine creates and stores the new form references. As it creates a new form (when requested to do so by a button click on frmCustomers), it adds the form reference to the collection of forms. The Add method of a collection allows you to add the item and optionally store a unique string value describing the value at the same time. In this case, the code stores the form's hWnd, converted to a string, as its unique identifier. The code also increments a variable that keeps track of the number of instances, and places the new form at a convenient location before making it visible. This is the ahtAddForm subroutine:

```
Sub ahtAddForm()
    Dim frm As Form

    Set frm = New Form_frmCustomers

    ' You have to convert the Key to a string,
    ' so tack a "" onto the hWnd (which uniquely
    ' identifies each form instance) to convert
    ' it to a string.
    colForms.Add Item:=frm, Key:=frm.hWnd & ""

    ' Build up the caption for each new instance.
    mintForm = mintForm + 1
    frm.Caption = frm.Caption & " " & mintForm

    ' The numbers used below are arbitrary, and are
    ' really only useful for this simple example.
    frm.SetFocus
    DoCmd.MoveSize mintForm * ahtcOffsetHoriz, _
     mintForm * ahtcOffsetVert
    ' Finally, set this form to be visible.
    frm.Visible = True
End Sub
```

Deleting Form Instances

Sooner or later, you're going to want to close down all the extra instances of your form. This is quite simple: Once you delete the form reference, Access will close the form for you. Therefore, in reaction to the Close All Instances button you created on your form, Access runs this subroutine:

```
Sub ahtRemoveAllForms()
    Dim varForm As Variant

    ' Reset the static variables
    mintForm = 0
    For Each varForm In colForms
        colForms.Remove 1
    Next varForm
End Sub
```

This subroutine first resets the total number of instances back to 0, then walks through the collection of form instances, one at a time, removing the first item each time. Because

Access renumbers the collection each time you remove an item, this is the simplest way to remove all the items.

To keep things neat, we instructed you to attach code to the form's Close event that removes the specific form from the collection of forms when you close the form. Though this example doesn't need that, you may find, in other situations, that you do need your collection to reflect accurately the forms that are currently loaded (if you wanted to list all the open forms, for example). There is one wrinkle here, however: When you ask the application to close all extra instances, Access closes each form, one by one. This, in turn, triggers the Close event for each of those forms. The Close event, of course, calls code attached to that event that attempts to remove the form from the collection of forms. But that form has already been removed from the collection. Therefore, the ahtRemoveForm subroutine, shown below, disables error handling; attempting to remove an already removed form won't trigger an error.

```
Sub ahtRemoveForm(frm As Form)
    ' All the forms call this from their
    ' Close event. Since the main form isn't
    ' in the collection at all, it'll
    ' cause an error. Just disregard that.
    On Error Resume Next
    colForms.Remove frm.hWnd & ""
    On Error GoTo 0
End Sub
```

Comments

Extra instances of forms aren't really treated exactly the same as their originals. For example, all the copies of a form share the same name as the original, so if you attempt to use the syntax

```
Forms!frmCustomers
```

or

```
Forms("frmCustomers")
```

to refer to an instance of a form, you'll only be able to access the original form. Access does add each instance to the Forms collection, but you can only access them by their ordinal position in the collection. You could loop through the Forms collection to close all open forms, and the code would close the instances, too.

Form instances have their own properties and their own current row, but any changes you make to a form instance will not be saved. That is, all instances of a form besides the original are read only. That's not to say that the data on the form is read only: It's the *design* of the form instance that's read only.

You'll find multiple instances of forms to be a very useful addition to your programming arsenal. It allows users to view multiple rows with their forms in Form View (the proverbial "have their cake and eat it, too" situation), and from there they can copy/cut/paste data from one row to another. Your responsibility as the developer is to manage the creation, storage, and deletion of these forms carefully, because the Access user interface provides no help.

CHAPTER 3
REPORTING AS AN ART FORM

3

REPORTING AS AN ART FORM

How do I...

3.14 Keep a report from breaking at an inappropriate place?

3.15 Customize a report's grouping and sorting at runtime?

You may devote days, weeks, or even months of work to designing tables and queries, and writing the macros and code to put the application together, but along with your application's forms, its reports *are* the application. Because of this you'll want to make them as clear and attractive as possible.

The first How-To will show how to do something that should be (and is) easy: print a report with line numbers. Next, you'll learn how to print the value of query parameters on a report based on a parameter query and how to create an attractive multiple-column report.

The next group of How-To's will teach you how to use Visual Basic for Applications (VBA) code and macros to print a message on a report only if certain conditions are met, how to create telephone-book-style page-range indicators, how to print a bar graph on a report using rectangle controls, and how to calculate page totals.

Then you'll employ more challenging VBA code to work around the limitations of the CanGrow/CanShrink properties and prevent blank rows on reports by combining an entire address into a single expression for a mailing labels report. You'll see how to suppress printing a report if there are no records to print. Using an event procedure run from the report's Format event, you'll learn how to print one set of headers and footers on odd pages and another (mirror-image) set on even pages. Then you will learn how to use the Line method to draw lines or rectangles on a report, in this case to make a line the same height as a variable-height text box. Next, you'll learn how to alternate gray bars on every other row of the report.

The final three How-To's show you how to tie a report's recordset to the filtered recordset of a form; how to prevent your report from breaking at an inappropriate place, such as right after a group header; and finally, in the most complex How-To in this chapter, how to modify a report's grouping and sorting fields on the fly.

3.1 Create a Report with Line Numbers

There's no line number property of a report, but this How-To will show how to use the Running Sum property of a control to print line numbers on your reports.

3.2 Print the Value of a Parameter on a Report

Access allows you to create reports based on queries, but it's not obvious how to print the value of parameters on the reports. This How-To will show how you can reference query parameters as if they were fields in the underlying query's recordset.

3.3 Create a Report with Multiple Columns

This How-To will show how to set up a report in a multiple-column format and group its data by the first letter of a grouping field.

3.4 Print a Message on a Report If Certain Conditions Are Met

This How-To will demonstrate the use of code attached to the OnFormat event property to make a control or an entire report section visible only if the current record meets conditions you specify.

3.5 Create a Page-range Indicator on Each Page

This How-To will suggest a macro to display the first and last items on each page in the page footer, as in a telephone book.

3.6 Create a Simple Bar Graph on a Report

Microsoft Graph is nice, but sometimes you might like to print a graph without incurring the resource drain of this overstuffed applet. This How-To will show how to create a simple bar graph and a macro.

3.7 Create a Page Total

Access does not have a built-in page total, but you can construct one using two simple macros. This How-To will show you how.

3.8 Avoid Unwanted Blank Rows on Mailing Labels

Mailing label reports have special features that induce problems with the CanGrow and CanShrink properties of text boxes, resulting in blank rows in the addresses. This How-To will illustrate how to combine the entire text of an address into a single expression to prevent these unwanted blank rows.

3.9 Suppress Printing a Report If There Are No Records to Print

Have you ever tried to print a report containing no records? Access prints *#Error* all over the detail section of the report. This How-To will show how to use a simple VBA event procedure, attached to the new NoData event of Access 95, to suppress printing of the report when no records are found.

3.10 Print Different Headers or Footers on Odd and Even Pages

Double-sided printing requires different headers on odd and even pages for a symmetrical look, but Access lacks explicit Odd and Even footer properties. This How-To will show how to use VBA code called from the header or footer section's Format event to print one of two sets of mirror-image header (or footer) controls, depending on whether the current page is odd or even.

3.11 Make a Vertical Line the Same Height as a CanGrow/CanShrink Control

Graphic lines on reports won't grow or shrink to match the size of a text box with CanGrow and CanShrink set to Yes; this How-To will show you how to use VBA's Line method to create a line that will grow or shrink to match the varying height of a text box.

3.12 Alternate Gray Bars on My Reports

Gray bars on alternate rows make a long report more readable. This How-To will illustrate how to change the background color of the report's detail section to create a gray bar report.

3.13 Print Only Records Matching a Form's Filter

Prior versions of Access had no way to link a report's recordset to the filtered recordset of a form. This How-To will show how to take advantage of the new Filter and FilterOn properties of forms and reports to print report records that match the filtered recordset of a form.

3.14 Keep a Report from Breaking at an Inappropriate Place

Sometimes the built-in KeepTogether properties aren't enough to keep a report from breaking at inappropriate places, particularly when you want a group header to be followed by at least one line of detail text. This How-To will demonstrate how to attach a function to the OnFormat event property of a report's group header to ensure that a new page will start unless there is enough room to print a line of text under a group heading.

3.15 Customize a Report's Grouping and Sorting at Runtime

This How-To will illustrate how you can create a single report that can be customized at runtime to use different grouping and sorting fields.

COMPLEXITY:
EASY

3.1 How do I...
Create a report with line numbers?

Problem

I have a legal report that has a list of items in the detail section. I'm required to number each item in the list on the report sequentially. I thought about using an AutoNumber field, but this won't work because I want the number to reset itself for

each group, plus I often want to print the items in a different order than I entered them. Is there an easy way to create report line numbers on the fly that pertain only to the data printed on the report?

Technique

Yes, there is an easy way to do this that makes use of an underused property of a text box: Running Sum. This How-To shows you how to add line numbers to your report by creating an unbound text box based on a simple calculation and adjusting the Running Sum property of this control.

Steps

Open 03-01.MDB. Run the rptEvidenceByCase report in preview view (see Figure 3-1). This report prints out a list of all evidence items, grouped by CaseId. Notice the line number field on the left side of the report that resets to zero at the start of each group.

To create line numbers on your own reports, follow these steps:

1. Create a new report or open an existing report in design mode. Add an unbound text box control to the detail section with the following Control Source setting.

=1

For the sample report, we named the control txtLineNo.

2. Change the Running Sum property for the control from the default of No to either Over Group or Over All. We chose Over Group for the sample report (see Figure 3-2).

3. Save the report and preview it to confirm that it now includes sequential line numbers.

Evidence Report

Case: 1   Liar, Jamba

Line#	Evidence	Evidence #	Collected	Weight
1	34 caliber revolver	ex4345a	12/13/95	12 lbs.
2	Belt	fy9800a	12/13/95	1 lbs.
3	Blood-stained plastic green lizard	gt1003w	12/14/95	1 lbs.
4	Left sock, size 9	pq3458x	12/14/95	1 lbs.
5	Starbricks coffee mug, white	pl345667	12/15/95	2 lbs.
6	Starbricks mocha java coffee, 1 lb.	po9000u	12/15/96	1 lbs.

Figure 3-1 The rptEvidenceByCase report includes line numbers

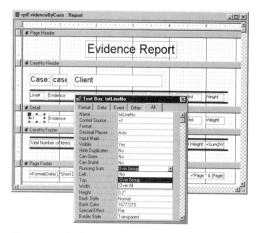

Figure 3-2 The Running Sum property can be set to No, Over Group, or Over All

How It Works

By setting the Control Source of the line number control to a constant of "=1", you are telling Access to print a constant of 1 for all records. And this is what would happen if you didn't also adjust the Running Sum property of the control.

By setting the Running Sum property of a control to Over Group or Over All, you are telling Access to print the value of the first record as it would normally (in this case, 1) but, for the second record, to take the value of the first record and add it to the value of the second record, printing the cumulative total instead of the value it would normally print (in this case, 2). For the third record, Access adds the value from the second record (which is really a sum of the first and second records' values) to the value from the third record (in this case, 3). This accumulation of values continues until the end of the report (if you set Running Sum = Over All) or until the beginning of the next group (if you set Running Sum = Over Group).

Comments

You can use Running Sum to accumulate nonconstant values, too. For example, if you want a running total of the weight of evidence items in the rptEvidenceByCase report for each record, you might add a second weight text box control to the right of the existing weight control that was identical to the first, except that Running Sum was set to Over Group. You'll also find the Running Sum property useful for financial reports for which you'd like to include a cumulative year-to-date column.

COMPLEXITY:
EASY

3.2 How do I... Print the value of a parameter on a report?

Problem

I've created a report based on a parameter query that prompts the user for one or more parameters when the query is run. The report works just fine, but I'd like to be able to document somewhere on the report what parameter values were entered by the user. That way, I'll know, for example, which years' records are included in the report. Is there any way to do this with Access?

Technique

Although it is not well documented, you can print the value of query parameters on a report by referring to the parameters as if they were fields in the underlying query. This How-To shows you how to create controls on a report that document the user-entered runtime parameters.

Steps

Load the 03-02.MDB database and open the qryAlbumsPrm query in design mode to verify that this query has three parameters (see Figure 3-3). Now open the rptAlbumsPrm in preview view. Because this report is based on qryAlbumsPrm, you will be prompted for the three parameters.

Enter values at the parameter prompt. If you enter the parameter values from Table 3-1, you should see a report that looks similar to the one shown in Figure 3-4.

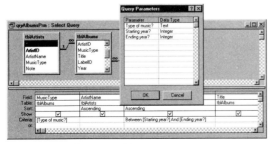

Figure 3-3 The qryAlbumsPrm parameter query includes three parameters

Bingo's Music Shop Album Report

Music Type: Rock

Years: 1960 to 1979

Artist Name	Year	Title	Label Name
Beatles	1963	With The Beatles	Capitol
Crosby, Stills, Nash & Young	1970	Deja vu	Atlantic
Pink Floyd	1971	Meddle	Capitol
David Bowie	1972	Ziggy Stardust	RCA
John Lennon	1973	Mind Games	Capitol
Pink Floyd	1973	Dark Side of the Moon	Capitol
Bob Dylan	1975	Desire	Columbia
Bruce Springstein	1975	Born to Run	Columbia
John Lennon	1975	Rock 'N' Roll	Capitol

Figure 3-4 The rptAlbumsPrm report includes the parameter values in the header

Notice that the selected parameters are included in the page header of the report. Run the report again, entering different parameters, and verify that the new parameters are printed correctly on the report.

PARAMETER	SAMPLE VALUE
Type of music?	Rock
Starting year?	1960
Ending year?	1979

Table 3-1 Parameters and sample values for qryAlbumsPrm

Follow these steps to print the value of query parameters on your own report:

1. Create a query with one or more parameters. If you aren't sure how to do this, read How-To 1.1. Don't forget to declare your parameters using the Query|Parameters command (see Figure 3-3). In the sample database, we created a parameter query named qryAlbumsPrm with three parameters.

2. Create a report based on the parameter query from step 1. In the page header of the report (or any other section you'd like), create text boxes that reference the parameters as if they were fields in the underlying query. Surround each parameter reference with square brackets. Note: These parameter fields will not be listed in the either the field list window or the drop-down list of fields in the Control Source property of controls. For example, we used two text boxes in the rptAlbumsPrm sample report, as summarized in Table 3-2.

TEXT BOX NAME	CONTROL SOURCE
txtMusic	="Music Type: " & [Type of music?]
txtYears	="Years: " & [Starting year?] & " to " & [Ending year?]

Table 3-2 These two text boxes reference three parameters from the underlying query

How It Works

During report design, you are free to reference any "unknown" you'd like as long as you put brackets around it. (If you don't put brackets around it and it's not a field in the underlying record source, then Access thinks you entered a string constant and forgot to surround it with quotes—so it puts the quotes in for you.) When you run the report, Access tries to locate the unknown references. If it locates a query parameter or form control that satisfies the reference, it copies the value into the control and continues running the report. If it can't locate the unknown reference, however, it puts up a parameter dialog box, requesting help in locating that unknown piece of data.

> **Note**
>
> If you run a report and get a parameter dialog box when you didn't expect one, it's likely you misspelled either a field or a reference to a query's parameter.

Comments

You can also create parameters directly on reports that are independent of query parameters. For example, you might use this type of "report parameter" if you create a report that requires a person's name and signature at the bottom of the page, but the name will vary every time you run the report (and cannot be obtained from the report's record source). Simply add a text box that references the new parameter—for example, [Enter signature name:]. Access will prompt you for this report parameter when you run the report just as if you had defined the parameter in the report's underlying query.

COMPLEXITY:
EASY

3.3   How do I...
Create a report with multiple columns?

Problem

I want to print a two-column phone-book-style report with large initial capital letters to set off each alphabetical grouping. There is no Report Wizard for creating such a report and I don't see any Column property to set up the number of columns I want. How can I make a multiple-column report in Access?

Technique

There is a way to format a report for multiple columns, but it's not where you might look for it, on a report's properties sheet or the report design menu. Instead, you'll find it on the Layout tab of the Page Setup dialog box. This How-To guides you through setting up a multiple-column phone-book-style report that includes a large drop cap for each letter of the alphabet.

Steps

Load 03-03.MDB. The tblCompanyAddresses table contains a list of businesses and their addresses and phone numbers. Open rptPhoneBook in preview view. As you can see in Figure 3-5, this report prints the data in two snaking (newspaper-style) columns.

Follow these steps to create your own multiple-column report:

1. Open the report you want to format for multiple columns in design view and select File|Page Setup. The Page Setup dialog box appears. Click the Layout tab of the Page Setup dialog box (see Figure 3-6).

2. Enter the appropriate settings for your report. A brief description of these settings and the settings used for the sample report can be found in Table 3-3. Press OK when done.

SETTING	PURPOSE	SAMPLE
Items Across	The number of columns.	2
Row Spacing	Extra space in inches between rows.	0
Column Spacing	Extra space in inches between columns.	0.25"
Width	Width of each column.	3"
Height	Height of each column.	1.0625"
Same as Detail	When you check this, Access will copy the width and height of the report's detail section into the Width and Height controls.	unchecked
Layout Items	Select "Down, then Across" for snaking columns, or "Across, then Down" for mailing label style columns.	Down, then Across

Table 3-3 The Page Setup dialog box Layout settings

3. Leave the report and page headers and footers as they are (if your report has these sections); they will still print across the entire report width.

4. To keep each name, phone number, and address from breaking inappropriately, set the detail section's KeepTogether property to Yes.

5. Preview the report; it should now display in two columns.

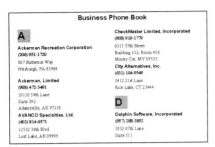

Figure 3-5 The two-column rptPhoneBook report

Figure 3-6 The layout tab of the Page Setup dialog box

Follow these additional steps to create the first letter grouping shown in Figure 3-5:

1. Select View|Sorting and Grouping to display the Sorting and Grouping window. Add the grouping field (in rptPhoneBook, we grouped on Company) twice to the Sorting and Grouping grid. Adjust the settings of each grouping field as shown in Table 3-4 for the sample report.

SETTING	FIRST COMPANY FIELD	SECOND COMPANY FIELD
Field/Expression	Company	Company
Sort Order	Ascending	Ascending
Group Header	Yes	No
Group Footer	No	No
Group On	Prefix Characters	Each Value
Group Interval	1	1
Keep Together	No	No

Table 3-4 Sorting and Grouping settings for rptPhoneBook

2. Add a text box to the header section of the grouping field. In the rptPhoneBook report, we used the property settings in Table 3-5. The completed rptPhoneBook report is shown in design view, with the Sorting and Grouping and properties sheets visible in Figure 3-7.

PROPERTY	SETTING
Name	txtFirstLetter
Control Source	=Left([Company],1)
Width	0.4375"

continued on next page

continued from previous page

PROPERTY	SETTING
Height	0.4375"
Back Color	12632256 (gray)
Fore Color	0 (black)
Font Name	Arial
Font Size	24
Font Weight	Bold

Table 3-5 The property settings for txtFirstLetter

3. Save the report. Switch to print preview mode to preview how it will look when you print it.

How It Works

When you create a report, Access assumes you want only one column unless you specify otherwise. If you want more than one column, you must adjust the layout properties of the page using the Layout tab of the Page Setup dialog box. The key settings are Items Across (the number of columns), Column Spacing (the extra margin between columns), Width (the width of each column), and Layout Items (whether Access first prints an entire column or an entire row). If you want to produce snaking column (newspaper style) reports, select "Down, then Across" for Layout Items; for mailing label type reports, choose "Across, then Down". For most purposes you can ignore the other settings.

Most of the time, you'll create groups in reports that break on the value of a field itself. For example, grouping on Company will trigger a new group for each new unique value of the Company field. Access, however, includes two properties of a group that

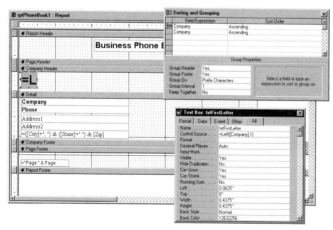

Figure 3-7 The completed rptPhoneBook report in design view

allow you to alter the frequency of groupings: Group On and Group Interval. Depending on the data type of the grouping field (see Table 3-6), Group On can be used to group on some subset of a characters (text), a range of numbers (number, currency), or a period of time (date/time). Using the Group Interval property, you can adjust the grouping further so that, for example, you could break on the first two characters of a name, every $10, or every two months.

DATA TYPE OF FIELD	GROUP ON CHOICES
Text	Each Value (default)
	Prefix Characters
Number, Currency	Each Value (default)
	Interval
Date/Time	Each Value (default)
	Year
	Qtr
	Month
	Week
	Day
	Hour
	Minute

Table 3-6 The Group On property choices depend on the data type of the grouping field

When you use the Group On property to group on anything other than Each Value, it's important you realize that the records within a grouping will not be sorted. This means that in most cases you'll also need to include a second sorted copy of the field with Group On = Each Value. This is what we did in the rptPhoneBook example.

Sorting or Grouping?

When you add a field or expression to the Sorting and Grouping window, you may ask yourself what determines whether a field is a group or merely a sort. There isn't any single property that determines this. Rather, a field becomes a group field if you set either Group Header or Group Footer (or both) to Yes. You can convert an existing group field to a sort field by setting both of these properties to No.

Comments

There are several section, report, and group properties you can adjust to control whether a group is kept together on the same column or page and whether a new column or page is started before or after a group. See the Comments section of How-To 3.14 for more details on controlling page and column breaks.

COMPLEXITY:
EASY

3.4   How do I...
Print a message on a report if certain conditions are met?

Problem

On a letter that I mail to all the customers on my mailing list, I want to print a message on only some customers' letters depending on, for example, the customer's zip code, credit status, or past orders. How do I make a text box print only when certain conditions are met?

Technique

You can create an event procedure that's called from the Format event of a report section to make a single control—or an entire section—visible or invisible depending on a condition you specify. This How-To shows you how to create a simple event procedure that checks each report record for a certain condition and then prints a message only if the condition is met.

Steps

Load the rptMailingByZip report from 03-04.MDB. This sample report, which is bound to the tblCompanyAddresses table, is used to print a letter to customers, sorted by zip code. It includes a message in the page header that announces the company's booth in an upcoming conference. The message prints for all customers, even those outside the Seattle area. Now load rptMailingByZipWithCondition. Notice that this version of the report only prints the message for zip codes beginning with 98 (see Figures 3-8 and 3-9).

Follow these steps to add an event procedure to your report that prints a message only for certain rows:

1. Create a new report or open an existing report in design view. Add any controls to the page header section that you wish to show for only selected records. In the rptMailingByZipWithCondition sample, we included three labels and a rectangle control in the page header section.

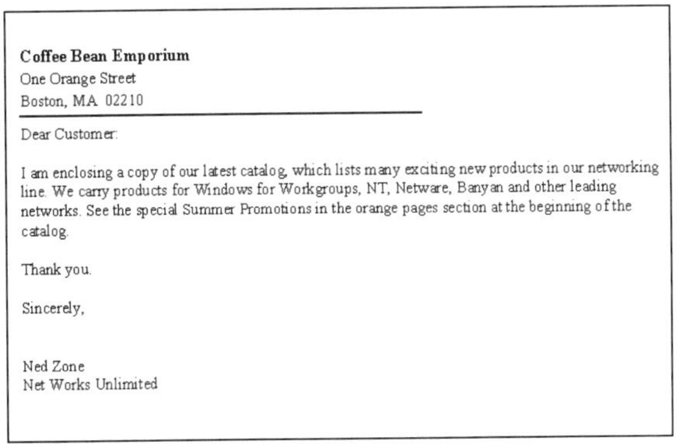

Coffee Bean Emporium
One Orange Street
Boston, MA 02210

Dear Customer:

I am enclosing a copy of our latest catalog, which lists many exciting new products in our networking line. We carry products for Windows for Workgroups, NT, Netware, Banyan and other leading networks. See the special Summer Promotions in the orange pages section at the beginning of the catalog.

Thank you.

Sincerely,

Ned Zone
Net Works Unlimited

Figure 3-8 An address whose zip code does not start with 98, with no message

2. While the cursor is still located in the page header section, select View|Properties to view the section's properties sheet if it's not already open.

3. Create a new event procedure for the section's Format event. (If you're unsure how to do this, see the "How Do I Create an Event Procedure" section in the Introduction of this book.)

4. Add an If...Then statement to the Format event procedure with the following basic structure.

```
If (some condition) Then
    Me.Section(acPageHeader).Visible = True
Else
    Me.Section(acPageHeader).Visible = False
End If
```

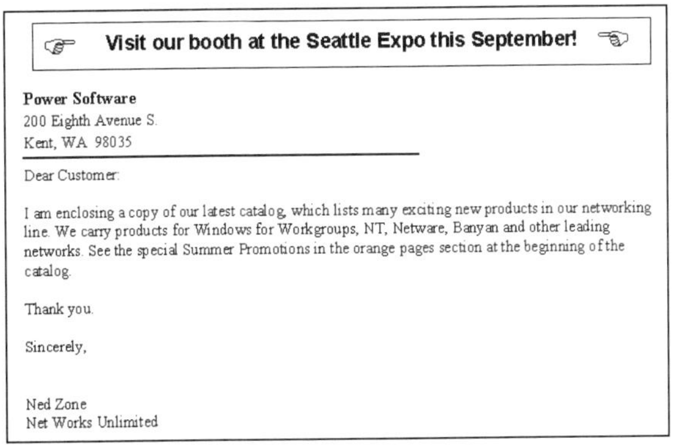

☞ **Visit our booth at the Seattle Expo this September!** ☜

Power Software
200 Eighth Avenue S.
Kent, WA 98035

Dear Customer:

I am enclosing a copy of our latest catalog, which lists many exciting new products in our networking line. We carry products for Windows for Workgroups, NT, Netware, Banyan and other leading networks. See the special Summer Promotions in the orange pages section at the beginning of the catalog.

Thank you.

Sincerely,

Ned Zone
Net Works Unlimited

Figure 3-9 An address whose zip code starts with 98, with the message

For example, in the rptMailingByZipWithCondition, we added an event procedure that tests if the first two characters of the zip code field are equal to 98. The complete event procedure is shown here.

```
Private Sub PageHeader0_Format(Cancel As Integer, _
    FormatCount As Integer)

    ' Set the visibility of the page header section,
    ' depending on whether or not the current
    ' zip code starts with "98".

    If Left(Me![ZipPostalCode], 2) = "98" Then
        Me.Section(acPageHeader).Visible = True
    Else
        Me.Section(acPageHeader).Visible = False
    End If

End Sub
```

5. Save the report and preview it to check that the event procedure is working properly.

How It Works

The event procedure uses the report's Section property and the section's Visible property to make an entire section visible or invisible when the report is formatted. Whether or not the section is visible depends on its meeting the condition in the If...Then expression. Only zip/postal codes starting with 98 meet this condition, so the message about the Seattle Expo will print only on pages for customers located in or near Seattle.

Comments

Table 3-7 lists the values and constants you can use in expressions to refer to the various sections on a form or report. Group levels 3 through 10 (reports only) continue the numbering scheme shown here, but have no corresponding VBA constants.

SETTING	VBA CONSTANT	DESCRIPTION
0	acDetail	Detail section.
1	acHeader	Form or report header section.
2	acFooter	Form or report footer section.
3	acPageHeader	Form or report page header section.
4	acPageFooter	Form or report page footer section.
5	acGroupLevel1Header	Group-level 1 header section (reports only).
6	acGroupLevel1Footer	Group-level 1 footer section (reports only).
7	acGroupLevel2Header	Group-level 2 header section (reports only).
8	acGroupLevel2Footer	Group-level 2 footer section (reports only).

Table 3-7 Values used to identify form and report sections in expressions

In the sample report, which prints one record per page, four controls need to be turned on or off together: the label with the message, two labels with Wingdings pointing-hand graphics, and a rectangle surrounding the other controls. Placing all of these controls in one section and making the whole section visible or invisible together is more efficient than making each control visible or invisible. Often, however, you'll need to print a message on a report that contains multiple records per page. For example, you might print the word "Outstanding" alongside a sales report when a salesperson has had more than $1 million in sales for a year. In this case, you'll have to use code that works with the Visible property of individual controls, such as that shown here.

```
If Me!Sales >= 1000000 Then
    Me!txtOutstanding.Visible = True
Else
    Me!txtOutstanding.Visible = False
End If
```

If you look at rptMailingByZip or rptMailingByZipWithCondition in design view, you may notice an odd expression as the ControlSource for the txtCityStateZip control in both reports.

```
=([City]+", ") & ([StateProvince]+" ") & [ZipPostalCode]
```

Note that we have used both the + and & concatenation operators in this expression. These two operators have a subtle difference: When you use + and one of the concatenated strings is Null, the whole expression becomes Null; when you use &, the null part of the expression is ignored. The effect caused by the + operator is termed *null propagation,* which you can short-circuit by surrounding that part of the expression in parentheses. The net effect of all this is that in the above expression, if City is Null, then City *and* the comma and space following it will drop out of the entire expression. Likewise, if StateProvince is Null, then it *and* the two spaces that it is concatenated to will drop out of the expression. Selective use of the + concatenation operator is both easier to read and more efficient than using one or more IIf() functions.

COMPLEXITY:
INTERMEDIATE

3.5 How do I...
Create a page-range indicator on each page?

Problem

I'm creating a report that contains a large number of items. To make it easier to see the range of items on each page, I'd like to create a page-range indicator. This would show the first and last items on the page, as in a telephone book. Is there a way to do this?

Technique

The answer to your question is a qualified Yes. You can create such a page-range indicator, but placing it anywhere but in the page footer is difficult. Although you *can* place it in the page header, the method to do so is quite complex and is the subject of a topic in the Microsoft Access Solutions database (SOLUTIONS.MDB), which ships with Access 95.

Because Access prints documents from top to bottom, by the time you know the last item on the page, it's too late to print it at the top of the page. The Solutions database workaround involves forcing the report to format itself twice, capturing the page ranges for all the pages during the first pass and storing the values in an array. When it makes the second pass, you supply the values from the array. That solution requires VBA and is cumbersome. This How-To focuses on a simpler method, placing the information you need in the page footer. If you can live with this placement, then the solution is straightforward.

Steps

Load the rptPageRange report from 03-05.MDB in preview view (see Figure 3-10). You'll see, at the bottom of each page, a listing of the items printed on that page.

To create a page-range indicator on your own reports, follow these steps:

1. Create a new macro named mcrPageRange. In it, create a single action, as shown in Table 3-8. Replace the [Product Name] reference with the name of the table field you'd like to keep track of.

ACTION	PARAMETER	VALUE
SetValue	Item	[txtFirstItem]
	Value	[Product Name]

Table 3-8 Macro information for tracking page ranges

Figure 3-10 The sample report, rptPageRange, includes a page-range indicator in the page footer

2. Create a new report or open an existing one in design view. Make sure that the report includes page header and footer sections (if it doesn't, choose Format|Page Header/Footer to add them). In the Page Header section, add a text box and set its properties, as shown in Table 3-9. This text box will hold the first row's value when you print the page.

PROPERTY	VALUE
Name	txtFirstItem
Visible	No

Table 3-9 Property values for the hidden text box in the report's page header

3. In the report's Page Footer section, add a text box. None of its properties are important to this technique except one, its ControlSource property. Set the text box's ControlSource property to be the expression

```
=[txtFirstItem] & " -- " & [Product Name]
```

replacing the [Product Name] reference with the name of the field you'd like to track in the page-range indicator. This must match the field name you used in step 1.

4. Set the OnFormat event property for the report's page header section to be mcrPageRange. This tells Access to call the macro every time it formats the page header (once per page). To set the property, place the cursor anywhere in the page header section and choose the OnFormat event property from the properties sheet. Finally, enter the correct macro name. Figure 3-11 shows the report and the properties sheet as they will look after you've assigned the property.

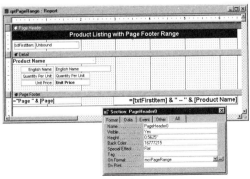

Figure 3-11 The sample report, rptPageRange, after setting the OnFormat event property

5. Save and run your report. You should see the page-range indicator as in the sample report, rptPageRange.

How It Works

The technique presented in this How-To is based on the fact that when Access prints the page header (or the report header or a group header), it gives you access to the row of data it's about to print. The same goes for footers, in reverse—there you have access to the row of data that's just been printed.

When you call mcrPageRange from the Format event of the page header, you place the data from the page's first row into the hidden text box, txtFirstItem. The data in that text box doesn't change until you again format the page. When Access gets to the bottom of the page and attempts to print the page footer, it calculates the value of the text box you've placed there. That text box retrieves the value you previously stored in txtFirstItem and combines it with the data from the last row that printed on the page to create the page-range indicator.

Comments

Though simple, this method does have its limitations.

- The page-range indicator must go in the page footer. If you attempt to place it in the page header, the data it prints will always be off by a page in one direction or another, depending on how you're viewing the report. If you need to have the page range in the page header, check out the method proposed in the Access Solutions database.

- For this method to work, you must include the page header section on every page. (The PageHeader property for the report must be set to All Pages.) Because you must fill in the hidden text box once for each page, the only place you can do that is in the page header.

COMPLEXITY:
INTERMEDIATE

3.6 How do I...
Create a simple bar graph on a report?

Problem

I need to create a simple bar graph on a report. Microsoft Graph works, but it's far too complex and slow for my purposes. I need a bar for each row showing the relative score for each student. Can I do this with the standard Access controls?

Technique

You can place a rectangle control in the detail section of your report and set its width during the Format event that occurs as Access lays out each row of data. This How-To shows how you can create a simple bar graph, setting the width of the rectangle control to be based on a numeric value in your data.

Steps

Open and run the report rptGraph in 03-06.MDB (see Figure 3-12). This report shows a list of students and their scores, along with a bar whose width represents the value of the score.

To create a bar graph like this one in your own applications, follow these steps:

1. Create your report, including the text data you'd like to show for each row. The sample report shows the Name and Score fields from tblScores, using controls named txtName and txtScore.

2. Add a rectangle control from the report toolbox and place it next to the data in the detail section. In the sample report, the rectangle's control name is rctBar. The control's width isn't important, because you'll be adjusting that programmatically (the example report sets the width of the rectangle to be the maximum width for the report, 4 inches). For appearance purposes, you'll probably want to set its height to be the same as the height of the text boxes you've already placed on the report. Figure 3-13 shows the report in design view.

3. If you want, you can place vertical lines at regular intervals along the maximum length of the bar. In the sample report, the vertical lines are placed at the 25 percent, 50 percent, and 75 percent locations. You can place these wherever you like; if they're the same height as the detail section, they'll appear as continuous lines on the printed report. If you've used group headers and/or footers in your report, you'll need to place the vertical lines in those sections as well to make them appear continuous.

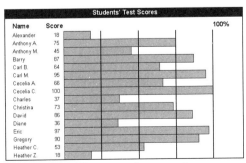

Figure 3-12 The sample report, rptGraph (partial)

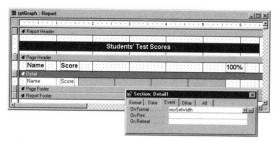

Figure 3-13 The sample report, rptGraph, in design view

4. To set the width of the rectangle for each row, create a macro. (This could also be done in VBA, but because it's so simple, a macro seems reasonable for this task.) Create a new macro named mcrSetWidth and enter the single action shown in Table 3-10. (The final 4 in the macro indicates the maximum width of the rectangle; the 100 indicates the maximum value for the numeric field. You'll need to alter these values to match your own circumstances.)

ACTION	PARAMETER	VALUE
SetValue	Item	[rctBar].[Width]
	Value	([txtScore]/100)*(1440*4)

Table 3-10 The mcrSetWidth macro sets the width of the rectangle for each row of data

5. Tell Access to run your new macro each time it formats a row of data. To do this, place the name of your macro in the OnFormat event property for the report's detail section. Figure 3-13 shows the properties sheet for the detail section.

6. Save and run the report. It should look similar to the report shown in Figure 3-12.

How It Works

As Access lays out the report and prepares to print it, it formats each row of data for presentation. As it does this, it runs any macro or VBA code attached to the OnFormat event property. In this case, for each row of data, you've told Access to set the width of the rectangle control based on the value in a numeric field. When it prints that row, the rectangle has a width proportional to the value in that numeric field.

In the sample report, the maximum width of the rectangle is four inches. If a student has a score of 100 percent, you want the printed bar to be four inches wide. Therefore, the expression

```
[txtScore]/100 * 4
```

will evaluate to be the number of inches wide you'd like the bar to be. To set the width of the bar from the Format event, however, you'll need to specify the width in twips, not inches, because that's what Access expects. There are 20 twips in a point, and 72 points in an inch, so there are 1440 twips in an inch. To convert the number of inches to twips, then, you must multiply the calculated value by 1440. The final expression in the sample report is

```
([txtScore]/100) * (1440 * 4)
```

This expression will evaluate to be the width of the bar in twips, which is exactly what you need. If your report needs a scaling factor other than 100 or a maximum width other than 4, you'll need to adjust the expression accordingly.

Comments

Though the method presented in this How-To will only work for the simplest of cases, when it does work, it does a great job. It's quick, it's simple, and it produces very nice output. To achieve the effect you want, experiment with different shadings, border colors, and gaps between the rows.

COMPLEXITY:
INTERMEDIATE

3.7 How do I...
Create a page total?

Problem

Access allows me to create a group total in the group footer on a report or a report total on the report footer, but I can't find a way to create a page total in the page footer. I understand that this doesn't come up too often, but for my report, I really could use this element. Is there a way to sum up values over a single page?

Technique

It's true that Access only allows aggregate calculations in group or report footers. You can, however, easily create page totals using two simple macros. This How-To demonstrates this technique and shows how to add this capability to any of your own reports.

Steps

Load rptPageTotals from 03-07.MDB in preview view (see Figure 3-14). This report is used to track orders and their freight costs. The items are grouped by month, and each group has a total in the group footer. At the bottom of each page, you'll see the total for all items on the current page. Figure 3-15 shows the sample report in design mode.

B's Beverages	Fauntleroy Circus	London	$22.77
Berglunds snabbköp	Berguvsvägen 8	Luleå	$92.69
Berglunds snabbköp	Berguvsvägen 8	Luleå	$8.98
Blondel père et fils	24, place Kléber	Strasbourg	$5.74
			$130.18

Ordered: August 1992

| Ana Trujillo Emparedados y | Avda. de la Constitución 2222 | México D.F. | $1.61 |
| | | | $1.61 |

Ordered: September 1992

Bólido Comidas preparadas	C/ Araquil, 67	Madrid	$77.92
Bon app'	12, rue des Bouchers	Marseille	$10.19
Bon app'	12, rue des Bouchers	Marseille	$166.31
			$254.42

| | | Page Total: | $898.42 |

Figure 3-14 Page 2 of the rptPageTotals report with page totals

To create page totals for your own reports, follow these steps:

1. Create a new macro group; save it as mcrTotals. Within the macro group, create two macros, as described in Table 3-11. Where the example refers to a field named [Freight], use any numeric field you would like to sum up in the page footer. Figure 3-16 shows the macro in design mode.

MACRO NAME	ACTION	PARAMETER	VALUE
Accumulate	SetValue	Item	[txtPageTotal]
		Value	[txtPageTotal] + [Freight]
Reset	SetValue	Item	[txtPageTotal]
		Value	0

 Table 3-11 Macro information for calculating page totals in mcrTotals

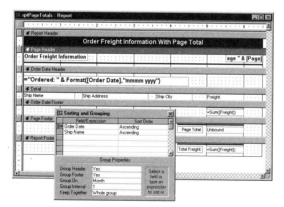

Figure 3-15 The rptPageTotals report in design mode

Figure 3-16 The macro group, mcrTotals, in design mode

2. Create your report. Sort and group the data in any fashion you like. In the report's Page Footer section, include at least a text box. The macros you created in step 1 expect the name of the text box to be txtPageTotal. If you changed the name in the macro, make name of the text box control matches.

3. Attach the macros to the appropriate report events, as shown in Table 3-12.

ITEM	EVENT PROPERTY	MACRO
Report Header	OnFormat	mcrTotals.Reset
Page Header	OnFormat	mcrTotals.Reset
Detail	OnPrint	mcrTotals.Accumulate

Table 3-12 Event property assignments to create page totals.

4. Save your report. When you run it, you will see the total of the field you set in the Accumulate macro (in step 1) in the page footer.

How It Works

Access makes it simple to sum values in group or report footers: Use the Sum() function in the ControlSource property for a text box. For example, to sum the Freight costs in either a group footer or a report footer, you could use an expression like this:

```
=Sum([Freight])
```

and Access would perform the sum over the range included in the footer section (either the group or the entire report). To create a page total, however, you must dig a bit deeper into the way Access prints reports.

The Access Report Engine and Printing Events

The report printing engine in Access works as a forward-marching machine: The engine formats and then prints each section as it comes to the section. Each section is handled in the order it appears on the page. The report printing engine deals first with the report header, then any page header, then any group header, then each row of the

141

detail section, and so forth. At each point, Access allows you to "hook" into various events, doing work alongside its work.

The two events described in this How-To are the Format event and the Print event. Access formats each section before it prints the section. Normally, you'll attach a macro or VBA procedure to the Format event of a section if you want to affect the section's layout on the page. You'll use the Print event to make calculations based on the data as you know it's going to print. When Access calls your macro or Basic code from the Print event, you are guaranteed that the current row is going to be printed. From the Format event, you can't assume this, because Access calls the code attached to the Format event before it decides whether or not the current row will fit on the current page. From either event, you have access to the current row of data that's about to be printed, and you can use that as part of your macro or procedure.

Using Events to Calculate the Page Total

In this case, calculating a page total requires two steps: You must reset the page total for each page (and before you start printing the report) and you must accumulate the value in each row as you print the row.

The accumulation part is simple: Every time you print a row, the macro attached to the detail section's Print event adds the current row's Freight amount (or whatever field you're tracking on your own report) to the current value in txtPageTotal. When Access needs to print the page footer, that value is filled in and ready to print. You should call this macro from the Print event, not the Format event, to ensure that you never add a value to the page footer unless you're sure the row will be printed on the current page. Calling the macro from the Print event guarantees this.

You can reset the page total so it starts from 0 from the Format event of the page header section. Because this is the first section that will print on every page, resetting the total in the page header should work. You *could* use the Print event here, but because you're guaranteed that the page header section will fit on its page, you might as well do the work as early as possible. The problem here arises from the fact that, in some reports, you may tell Access to print the page header only on pages where there isn't a report header (see the report's PageHeader property). If you do this, Access won't format the page header on the first page, and it therefore won't call the necessary macro. To make up for this, the example report (rptPageTotals in 03-07.MDB) also calls the macro from the report header's Format event. Because this event only occurs when Access prints the first page, there's no redundancy here. You may not need to reset the page total from the report header, but it can't hurt.

Comments

Be wary of performing any calculations during a section's Format event. Because you aren't guaranteed that the section will actually print on the current page, you could be calculating based on a value that won't be a part of the page. Making this mistake in the sample report, for example, would be a major error. Because this report is set up so that Access will print a group only if the entire group can fit on a page, it might format a number of rows and then decide that the whole group can't fit. Each time it attempts to format a row, it will call the code attached to the Format event, which will add the value to the total. To avoid this problem, perform calculations from a section's Print event only. Use the Format event to change the layout of a section—perhaps to make a specific control visible or invisible, depending on the data you find in the current row (see How-To 3.4 for an example of this).

COMPLEXITY:
INTERMEDIATE

3.8   How do I...
Avoid unwanted blank rows on mailing labels?

Problem

When I print mailing labels, especially when I use a small font size and place the address text boxes close together, sometimes I get unwanted blank rows in the addresses when the labels print. I also can't seem to use lines or graphics on my labels without causing blank rows. How can I get my labels to print correctly—without blank rows—in these situations?

Technique

The CanGrow and CanShrink text box properties for reports allow text boxes to grow or shrink vertically as needed. These properties normally work well, but sometimes overlapping text boxes or graphics can interfere with text boxes' ability to shrink or grow. This How-To shows how you can avoid these problems by combining the output of several fields into a single expression and using that expression as the row source of a single text box.

Steps

Open the tblCompanyAddresses table from 03-08.MDB in datasheet view. You can see that this table contains typical address data, with three address fields (Address1, Address2, and POBox). Some of the sample records have blanks in at least one of these address fields.

Close the table and open the rptLabels report in preview mode. This is a typical mailing labels report, as might have been produced by the Mailing Label Report Wizard. Notice that there are no blank rows in the addresses. Now open the rptLabelsWithImageBroken in preview view (see Figure 3-17). We added an Image control to the left side of each label that causes unwanted blank lines. Finally, open the rptLabelsWithImageFixed report in preview view (see Figure 3-18). Notice that this version of the report doesn't have any unwanted blank lines, even though the same image appears on the left of each label.

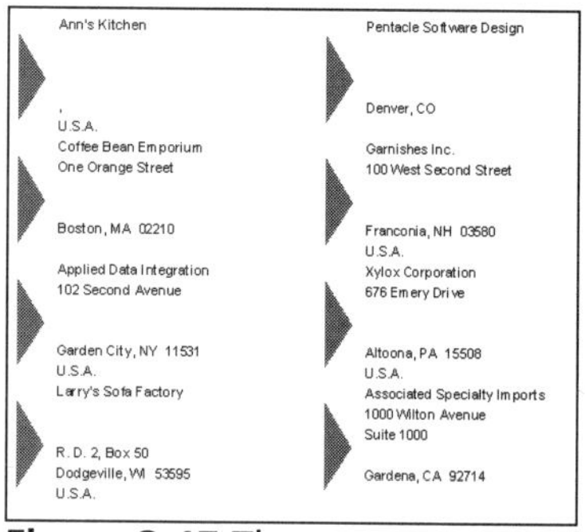

Figure 3-17 The rptLabelsWithImageBroken report prints labels with unwanted blank rows

Figure 3-18 A modified version of the report, rptLabelsWithImageFixed, prints fine

Follow these steps to create a mailing labels report, complete with a graphic on each label but without any unwanted blank lines:

1. Create a new mailing label report. The easiest way to do this is to use the Mailing Label Report Wizard. The rptLabels sample report was created using this wizard. Its record source is tblCompanyAddresses.

2. Add a line, unbound object frame, or Image control to the label. In the sample database, rptLabelsWithImageBroken includes an Image control containing a gray triangle (a Paintbrush image) to the left of the addresses. Here, the Image control prevents the text boxes' CanShrink property from working, resulting in numerous blank rows in the addresses (see Figure 3-17).

3. Import the basCrLf module from 03-08.MDB into your database.

4. Delete the multiple address line controls (five in rptLabelsWithImageBroken) and replace them with a single text box that concatenates each of the address lines together. For each text box that may be missing data, create an expression to wrap the field in the ahtMakeLine function (discussed in the How It Works section below). The final control source expression should look something like the control source for the txtWholeAddress control in rptLabelsWithImageFixed, which is shown here.

```
=ahtMakeLine([Address1]) & ahtMakeLine([Address2]) & ahtMakeLine([POBox]) &
ahtMakeLine(([City]+", ") & ([StateProvince]+" ") & [ZipPostalCode]) &
ahtMakeLine([Country])
```

> **Tip**
>
> Press SHIFT-F2 when your cursor is in the text box's Control Source property (or any other property) to open up the Zoom box, which lets you see the whole expression as you work with it.

5. Save the report and run it to make sure it produces the desired output (like that shown in Figure 3-18). The completed report is shown in design view in Figure 3-19.

How It Works

When you combine several address fields into a single expression and use that expression as the row source of a single text box, you have only one text box to grow or shrink as needed. The elimination of multiple text boxes prevents problems with CanGrow/CanShrink that occur when a text box that needs to shrink is placed on the same row as a text box or other control (such as an Image control) that can't shrink.

We have used the ahtMakeLine function to check for nulls in a text field and return a null value for the line if the varValue argument is Null; otherwise, ahtMakeLine adds carriage return and line feed characters after the field. Thus, a new line is created only if the address line is non-null, giving us essentially the same effect as using the CanShrink property. The ahtMakeLine function is shown here.

```
Function ahtMakeLine(varValue as Variant)
    If IsNull(varValue) Then
        ahtMakeLine = Null
    Else
        ahtMakeLine = varValue & vbCrLf
    End If
End Function
```

The function ahtMakeLine uses the built-in vbCrLf constant, which is equivalent to typing Chr$(13) & Chr$(10).

Comments

If you use a concatenated expression for an address, you can accommodate more fields on a label than you could if you placed each address text box on a separate line. This method works fine as long as you know that each address will be missing at least one row of address data. If your labels only have room for four lines of data, for example, you could put five lines of data into a concatenated expression if you know that no address will use all five lines.

Figure 3-19 The rptLabelsWithImageFixed report in design view

Unlike specialized label-printing programs, Access does not lock the report size to the label's dimensions to prevent you from accidentally changing the size of labels after you have created them with the Mailing Labels Report Wizard. It is very easy to nudge the right edge or bottom edge of a mailing label report accidentally (by moving a control, for example) so that the report contents overprint the labels.

We could have used a series of IIf functions instead of using the ahtMakeLine function, but using ahtMakeLine is simpler and less confusing.

Tip

When you first create a mailing labels report, write down its width and detail section height, so you can quickly recover from any accidental resizing of the report, which could result in label text printing outside of the label's boundaries.

3.9 How do I...
Suppress printing a report if there are no records to print?

Problem

I have a report that prints records I select from a criteria form. Sometimes there aren't any records that match the criteria and the report opens with *#Error* in the detail section, which is unattractive and confusing. Is there any way I can prevent the report from printing when it has no records to print?

Technique

Access 95 includes a new event, NoData, that fires when no records are present in the report's underlying recordset. This How-To shows you how to use this new event to suppress printing of the report when no records match the specified criteria.

Steps

Load the 03-09.MDB database. Open the frmCriteria1 pop-up criteria form. This form allows you to enter criteria for the rptSelect1 report (see Figure 3-20). When you press the traffic light button, a simple event procedure will execute that opens the report in print preview mode. The rptSelect1 report is based on the qryCriteria1 parameter query, which derives its parameter values from the controls on the frmCriteria1

Figure 3-20 The frmCriteria1 pop-up criteria form with default values

form. If you accept the default values, the parameter query will return a recordset with no records. This will produce the report shown in Figure 3-21.

Now open the frmCriteria2 pop-up criteria form. This form is identical to the first, except that the event procedure attached to its command button runs the rptSelect2 report instead. If you accept the default values, then the rptSelect2 report will attempt to run, again with no records. But this version of the report has an event procedure attached to its NoData event that suppresses printing and instead displays the message box shown in Figure 3-22.

To create a report that suppresses printing when there are no records, follow these steps:

1. Create a new report or open an existing report in design view.

2. Create an event procedure attached to the NoData property of the report. (If you're unsure how to do this, see the How Do I Create an Event Procedure section in the Introduction of this book.) In the event procedure, enter the following VBA code.

```
Private Sub Report_NoData(Cancel As Integer)
    MsgBox "Sorry, no records match these criteria!", _
        vbExclamation, "No Records to Print"
    Cancel = True
End Sub
```

Figure 3-22 The rptCriteria2 report displays this message and cancels printing when there are no records

Figure 3-21 The rptCriteria1 report prints a page of errors when no records are selected

3. Save and run the report. If you enter criteria that do not match any records, you will get a message box telling you that no records meet the criteria (like that shown in Figure 3-22).

How It Works

The NoData event is triggered whenever a report attempts to print with no records. If you attach an event procedure to the NoData event, then your code will run whenever the report prints without any records. While the MsgBox statement informs the user what has happened, the key line of code is

```
Cancel = True
```

This line of code tells Access to cancel printing of the report (by setting the passed Cancel parameter equal to a True value).

Comments

The report header contains controls to display the selection criteria, which are picked up from the criteria form, using expressions like this one:

```
=[Forms]![frmCriteria1]![txtLastOrderAfter]
```

For more information on printing query criteria on reports, see How-To 3.2.

The form disappears from view when the report opens in print preview because the event procedure attached to the traffic light button sets the form's Visible property to False before opening the report. Making the form invisible (rather than closing it) ensures that the selection criteria are still available for the report's data source.

Get a Performance Boost by Converting Old Report Code

Prior to Access 95, you had to use a DCount function in an event procedure attached to the report's OnOpen event to solve the "no data" problem. This workaround, however, had the negative side effect of forcing Access to execute the report's query an extra time when there *were* records in the report's recordset. If you have used this workaround (which still works in Access 95), you will realize a significant performance boost in your report by instead using the solution presented in this How-To.

3.10 How do I...
Print different headers or footers on odd and even pages?

Problem

Some of my reports are printed double-sided and I would like to have mirror-image headers and footers on odd and even pages. How do I do this in Access?

Technique

This technique makes use of two sets of header and footer controls, one for odd pages and one for even pages. An event procedure run from the section's Format event that uses the Page property and the Mod operator to determine whether the page is odd or even and makes the appropriate controls visible or invisible.

Steps

Load 03-10.MDB. Open rptEvenOdd in print preview mode and you should get a report that has one header and footer for odd pages and a different header and footer for even pages (see Figures 3-23 and 3-24).

The following steps show you how to create your own report that prints different headers and footers on odd and even pages:

1. Open the report you want to print double-sided (or even single-sided with different odd and even headers and footers).

2. Make a copy of the header control and place one of the copies of the control on the left of the header and the other on the right. Make the left-hand control

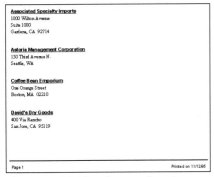

Figure 3-23 The footer for the odd pages of rptEvenOdd

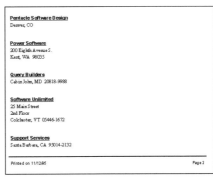

Figure 3-24 The footer for the even pages of rptEvenOdd

left-aligned (to print on even-numbered pages) and the right-hand control right-aligned (to print on odd-numbered pages).

3. Create an event procedure attached to the OnFormat property of the report's page header section. (If you're unsure how to do this, see the How Do I Create an Event Procedure section in the Introduction of this book.) In the event procedure, enter code similar to the following.

```
Private Sub PageHeader_Format(Cancel As Integer, FormatCount As Integer)
    On Error GoTo PageHeader_FormatError

    Dim fIsEven As Boolean

    fIsEven = ahtIsEven(Me.Page)

    Me![lblTitleLeft].Visible = Not fIsEven
    Me![lblTitleRight].Visible = fIsEven

End Sub
```

You'll need to replace the controls in the event procedure with the names of your controls.

4. Make copies of the footer controls as well, and make a similar event procedure for the footer's OnFormat event property, referencing its left and right controls. In the event procedure, enter code similar to the following.

```
Private Sub PageFooter_Format(Cancel As Integer, FormatCount As Integer)

    Dim fIsEven As Boolean

    fIsEven = ahtIsEven(Me.Page)

    Me![txtPageLeft].Visible = Not fIsEven
    Me![txtPageRight].Visible = fIsEven
    Me![txtPrintedOnLeft].Visible = fIsEven
    Me![txtPrintedOnRight].Visible = Not fIsEven

End Sub
```

Again, you'll need to replace the controls in the event procedure with the names of your controls.

5. Without closing the module, add the following function to the form's module.

```
Private Function ahtIsEven(ByVal intValue As Integer) As Boolean
    ' Return True if intValue is even, False otherwise.
    ahtIsEven = ((intValue Mod 2) = 0)
End Function
```

6. Save and execute the report to confirm it performs as desired. The completed report is shown in Design View in Figure 3-25.

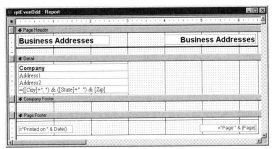

Figure 3-25 The rptEvenOdd report in Design View

How It Works

The two event procedures call the ahtIsEven function to determine whether the current page is even or odd, passing the function the current page number. The current page number is determined by referencing the Page property of the report: Me.Page. ahtIsEven uses the Mod operator, which returns the remainder when the page number is divided by 2, yielding 0 for even pages or 1 for odd pages. The statement

```
ahtIsEven = ((intValue Mod 2) = 0)
```

returns True to the calling procedure if the page Mod 2 is 0, that is, if the page is even; otherwise it returns False.

By setting fIsOdd to the return value of ahtIsEven, you can then set the visibility of the rest of the controls based on its value.

Comments

You can't see them in Figure 3-25, but there are four text boxes in the footer section of the report. On the left side of the footer, the txtPrintedOnLeft control has been placed on top of the txtPageLeft control. On the right side of the footer, the txtPageRight control has been placed on top of the txtPrintedOnRight control. This works just fine because only one set of controls (txtPrintedOnLeft *and* txtPageRight or txtPrintedOnRight *and* txtPageLeft) are visible at the same time.

As an alternative to using two controls in the header of the report, you could use just one control that is as wide as the report and alternately set its TextAlign property to Left or Right based on the return value of ahtIsEven. (You can't do this in the footer because of the need for two sets of controls with different alignments.)

COMPLEXITY:
ADVANCED

3.11 How do I...
Make a vertical line the same height as a CanGrow/CanShrink control?

Problem

I have a control on a report that has its CanGrow and CanShrink properties set to Yes so it can grow or shrink to accommodate different amounts of text. I placed a vertical line to the left of the control, and I want it to be the same height as the control. Is there a way I can synchronize the height of the two controls?

Technique

If you place a line on a report using the Line tool, it will always be the same size. To make a line change its height to match the height of another control (or group of controls), you need to use the Line method in a procedure attached to the Print event of a report section. This How-To uses the Line method to make a line whose height varies to accommodate the changing height of a text box that displays a memo field.

Steps

Load 03-11.MDB. Open rptBusinessAddresses1 in preview view (Figure 3-26). This report lists business addresses and contract conditions. Notice that the line in the company footer section is of fixed height and does not vary to match the height of this section. Now open rptBusinessAddresses2 in preview view (Figure 3-27). This version of

Amberley Enterprises Ltd.
50 First Street
Suite 150
Ottawa, Ontario A1Z 8R7

  | **Contract Conditions:**

  | INSTALLATION: The contractor shall furnish and install at the premises of the subscriber located at
  | the following alarm system and/or equipment:

- -

Ann's Kitchen
28 South Street
Boston, MA 02211

  | **Contract Conditions:**

  | PRICE: The price for the purchase and installation is $_____. Payment shall be made as
  | follows: Subscriber shall make a one-time down payment at the time of purchase of $_____
  | and _____ subsequent payments of $_____ on a monthly basis. There shall be a 2% per
  | month penalty for late payment. The subscriber agrees that it will not remove the alarm system and/or
  | equipment.

- -

Figure 3-26 This report contains a fixed-height line next to a variable-height text box

3.11

MAKE VERTICAL LINES THE SAME HEIGHT AS CANGROW/CANSHRINK CONTROLS?

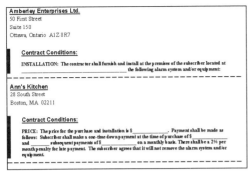

Figure 3-27 A report with a programmatically created variable-length line

the report contains a line whose height matches the height of the entire company footer section.

Follow these steps to add a vertical line to your own report that grows or shrinks to match one or more CanGrow/CanShrink controls in a section:

1. Create a report or open an existing report in design view. Don't use the line control to create a vertical line in the report. If you've already created such a line, remove it now.

2. Create an event procedure for the Print event of the group footer section (or the section on your report where you'd like the line to appear). (For more information on creating event procedures, see the book's Introduction.) In the event procedure, add code similar to this:

```
Private Sub GroupFooter0_Print(Cancel As Integer, PrintCount As Integer)

    Dim sngLineTop As Single
    Dim sngLineLeft As Single
    Dim sngLineWidth As Single
    Dim sngLineHeight As Single

    Const ahtcSMTwips = 1
    Const ahtcDSSolid = 0

    Me.ScaleMode = ahtcSMTwips
    Me.DrawStyle = ahtcDSSolid

    'Set coordinates for line
    sngLineTop = Me![lblConditions].Top
    sngLineLeft = 0
    sngLineWidth = 100
    With Me![txtConditions]
        sngLineHeight = .Top + .Height
    End With
```

continued on next page

continued from previous page

```
          ' Draw the line
          Me.Line (sngLineLeft, sngLineTop)-Step(sngLineWidth, sngLineHeight), , BF

End Sub
```

Replace the references to [lblConditions] and [txtConditions] with the names of the controls in your own report.

3. Save and preview the report to verify that the line alongside the CanGrow/CanShrink changes, as in Figure 3-27. The completed sample report is shown in design view in Figure 3-28.

How It Works

The event procedure uses the Line method to create a line that starts at the top of the lblConditions label and extends to the bottom of the txtConditions text box, growing and shrinking in proportion to the text box. You can use the Line method to draw lines or rectangles on reports using the coordinates you specify (sngLineHeight through sngLineWidth in the sample procedure). The event procedure sets the sngLineTop argument to the top of the [lblConditions] label, sngLineLeft to 0, sngLineWidth to 100, and sngLineHeight to the bottom of the [txtConditions] text box. Because Access does not provide an Access Basic Bottom property for controls, this value is calculated by adding the text box's Height property to its Top property using the following piece of code that makes use of the new With...End With construct of VBA.

```
With Me![txtConditions]
    sngLineHeight = .Top + .Height
End With
```

The line itself (actually, a rectangle) is drawn by the following line of code:

```
Me.Line (sngLineLeft, sngLineTop)-Step(sngLineWidth, sngLineHeight), , BF
```

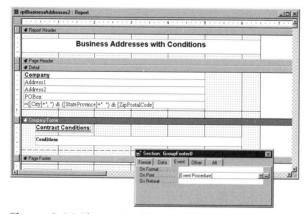

Figure 3-28 The rptBusinessAddresses2 in design view

where the variables in the first set of parentheses define the upper-left corner of the rectangle and those in the second set of parentheses define its width and height. The reserved word Step allows you to use height and width values for the rectangle instead of specifying the lower-right corner. The last argument, BF, indicates that the line will be a rectangle (B) instead of a line and that it will be filled with the same color as its border (F).

Comments

The ScaleMode property specifies the unit of measurement. Because Access uses twips as its measurement unit, this property is generally set to twips, as in the ahtcSMTwips constant in the sample code. The available settings are listed in Table 3-13.

SETTING	DESCRIPTION
0	Custom values for ScaleHeight, ScaleWidth, ScaleLeft and ScaleTop
1	(Default) Twip
2	Point
3	Pixel
4	Character
5	Inch
6	Millimeter
7	Centimeter

Table 3-13 Available ScaleMode property settings

The DrawStyle property specifies the line type; it is set to Solid in the sample code using the ahtcDSSolid constant. The available settings are listed in Table 3-14.

SETTING	DESCRIPTION
0	(Default) Solid
1	Dash
2	Dot
3	Dash-dot
4	Dash-dot-dot
5	Invisible
6	Inside solid

Table 3-14 Available DrawStyle property settings

COMPLEXITY:
ADVANCED

3.12 How do I... Alternate gray bars on my reports?

Problem

I have some reports on which I'd like to print alternate rows with gray bars in the background. It makes the reports easier to read, especially when there's lots of data or the report is very wide. Is there a way to create these bars in Access?

Technique

There are a number of ways to print alternate rows with gray and white backgrounds. The simplest method is to alternate the background color of the detail section for each new record. This How-To shows you how to use this method to achieve the desired effect on your reports.

Steps

Load 03-12.MDB and open the rptGrayBar report in preview view. If you view this report in preview view, it may not look very good on your screen (it depends on the screen resolution and color depth of your screen driver). Printed, however, it looks something like the report shown in Figure 3-29. (The exact output will depend on your printer; you may need to modify the color setting for the gray bar to optimize it.)

Company	City	Last Order
Amberley Enterprises Ltd.	Ottawa	1/12/92
Ann's Kitchen	Boston	2/25/93
Applied Data Integration	Garden City	6/15/94
Associated Specialty Imports	Gardena	8/22/93
Astoria Management Corporation	Seattle	2/4/93
Coffee Bean Emporium	Boston	9/19/93
David's Dry Goods	San Jose	5/17/94
Garnishes Inc.	Franconia	5/22/94
Holography Inc.	Beaconsfield	4/7/93
Larry's Sofa Factory	Dodgeville	7/22/93
Mabel's Old Fashioned Soda Fountai	Redmond	7/1/94
Pentacle Software Design	Denver	7/14/93
Power Software	Kent	2/2/93
Query Builders	Cabin John	4/3/94
Software Unlimited	Colchester	4/14/94
Support Services	Santa Barbara	8/16/93
Xylox Corporation	Altoona	8/2/92

Figure 3-29 A report with gray bars on alternate rows

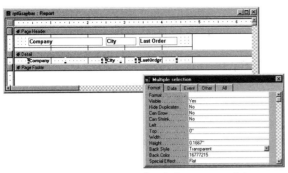

Figure 3-30 Changing all of the controls'
BackStyle property in one operation

To create your own reports with alternating gray bars in the detail section, follow these steps:

1. Create your report. Because this method will fill the entire detail section with gray shading, the effect will work best if your detail section is one line high. (It will work with taller detail sections, but it won't look as good.)

2. Make sure that every control in the detail section has its BackStyle property set to Transparent. You can quickly change this property for all of the controls in the section by marquee-selecting all of the controls and then changing the BackStyle property in the properties sheet, which will now have the title Multiple Selection (see Figure 3-30).

3. Edit the report's module (click on the Code button on the report design toolbar or choose the View|Code menu option) and enter the following lines of code in the module's Declarations area.

```
' Shade this row or not?
Dim fShade As Boolean
```

4. Create an event procedure attached to the OnPrint event property of your report's detail section and add the code that follows. This code must be attached to the OnPrint event property because the Line method for reports will not work when called during the Format event. (For more information on creating event procedures, see this book's Introduction.)

```
Private Sub Detail1_Print(Cancel As Integer, PrintCount As Integer)

    Const ahtcColorGray = &HC0C0C0
    Const ahtcColorWhite = &HFFFFFF

    If fShade Then
        Me.Detail1.BackColor = ahtcColorGray
    Else
        Me.Detail1.BackColor = ahtcColorWhite
    End If
```

continued on next page

continued from previous page

```
      ' Alternate the value of fShade
      fShade = Not fShade
End Sub
```

5. If it matters whether the first row on a page is specifically shaded or not, create an event procedure attached to the OnPrint property of the report's page header. Replace the False value with True if you want the first row on each page to be shaded.

```
Sub PageHeader0_Print (Cancel As Integer, PrintCount As Integer)
      ' Make sure the first row on the page isn't shaded.
      ' Use True if you want the first row on each page shaded.
      fShade = False
End Sub
```

6. Save and print the report. Every other row in the detail section will be printed with a gray background, the same size as the detail section.

How It Works

The code shown in step 4 relies on a module global variable, fShade, that alternates between True and False. If you followed the instructions for step 5, you set the value of fShade to a particular value every time you print the page header (before any rows are printed on that page). From then on, every time Access prints the detail section, it decides what to do based on the value in fShade. What's more, every time it prints the detail section, it alternates the value of fShade using this line of code:

```
fShade = Not fShade
```

That is, if fShade was False, now it'll be True and vice versa.

Once the code has decided whether or not to shade the section, it sets the background color to the color value of gray or white, based on the value of fShade using the following If...Then...Else statement.

```
If fShade Then
    Me.Detail1.BackColor = ahtcColorGray
  Else
    Me.Detail1.BackColor = ahtcColorWhite
End If
```

We used constants to make the code easier to read. We determined the values for the constants by using the color palette in the Access UI to set the desired color and then reading the color value off of the properties sheet.

Comments

If you have a color printer, you might consider altering the value of the ahtcColorGray constant so that it prints out a green shading.

The settings you choose for your printer driver can affect the output of the gray bars. For example, with the HP LaserJet 4 driver, the bars looked better after choosing the Line Art Images value for the Dithering option in the Graphics tab of the Properties dialog

Figure 3-31 The Graphics tab of the
HP LaserJet 4 Properties dialog box

box for the printer (see Figure 3-31). You may find settings like this for your own printer driver can make a marked difference in the appearance of gray-scale colors.

COMPLEXITY:
ADVANCED

3.13 How do I...
Print only records matching a form's filter?

Problem

I have a form I use to view and edit my collection of record and CD albums. On the form, I've placed a command button I use to print the records contained in the form's recordset. This works fine, but I'd like to enhance the functionality of the form so that when I filter records on the form and then print the report, only the filtered records will print. Is there any way to do this in Access?

Technique

Access 95 includes new properties (Filter and FilterOn) of forms and reports that can be used to manipulate form and report filters programmatically. This How-To shows you how to make use of these new properties to print records on a report that includes only those records filtered by a form.

Steps

Load 03-13.MDB and open the frmAlbums form. Press the Print Records button and you should see the preview of a report, rptAlbums, that includes all 65 records from qryAlbums. Close the report and go back to frmAlbums, which should still be open. Now create a filter of the form's records using one of the filter toolbar buttons or the Records|Filter command. For example, you might create a filter by using the new Filter By Form facility (see Figure 3-32). When you are finished creating the filter, apply it. You should see a filtered subset of the records (Figure 3-33). Now press the Print Records button and you should see a preview of the same report, rptAlbums, this time filtered to match the same records you filtered using frmAlbums. If you print the filtered report, you should see a report similar to the one shown in Figure 3-34.

To create your own report that synchronizes its records with those of a form's, follow these steps:

1. Create a new form or edit an existing one. The sample form, frmAlbums, is an unbound main form with an embedded subform bound to the qryAlbums query, but you can use any style of form you like.

2. Create a new report or edit an existing one that's based on the same record source as the form (or, if you are using an embedded subform, that's based on the same record source as the subform) from step 1. Save the report and give it a name. The sample report is named rptAlbums.

3. Switch back to the form. Add a command button to the form with an event procedure that uses the DoCmd.OpenReport method to open the report from step 2 in preview view. (For more information on creating event procedures, see this book's Introduction.) The code for the cmdPrint button on frmAlbums is shown here.

```
Private Sub cmdPrint_Click()
    DoCmd.OpenReport "rptAlbums", View:=acPreview
End Sub
```

Figure 3-32 The Filter By Form facility is used to filter records on frmAlbums

Figure 3-33 The records have been filtered, resulting in 10 records

Bingo's Music Shop Album Report

Artist Name	Year	Title	Label Name
Graham Parker	1982	Another Grey Area	Arista
Bruce Springstein	1984	Born in the U.S.A.	Columbia
Julian Lennon	1984	Valotte	Atlantic
Elvis Costello	1989	Spike	Warner Brothers
Elvis Costello	1991	Mighty Like a Rose	Warner Brothers
Paul McCartney	1991	Unplugged (The Official Bootleg)	Capitol
Compilation	1993	Stone Free: A Tribute to Jimi Hendrix	Reprise
Beatles	1994	Live at the BBC	Capitol
Compilation	1994	The Unplugged Collection	Warner Brothers
Elvis Costello	1994	The Very Best of Elvis Costello and the Attractions	Ryodisc

Total Number of Albums: 10

Figure 3-34 The report includes only those records from the filtered form

Change "rptAlbums" to the name of the report created in step 2. Save the form and close it.

4. Switch back to the report and create an event procedure attached to the report's Open event. Add code similar to that shown here for rptAlbums.

```
Private Sub Report_Open(Cancel As Integer)

    Dim frmFilter As Form

    Const ahtcFilterFrm = "frmAlbums"
    Const ahtcFilterSubFrmCtl = "subAlbums"

    ' Is the report's filtering form open?
    If SysCmd(acSysCmdGetObjectState, acForm, ahtcFilterFrm)  0 Then

        Set frmFilter = Forms(ahtcFilterFrm)

        ' Is form currently filtered?
        If frmFilter.FilterOn Then
            ' Set report's filter to subform's filter
            Me.Filter = frmFilter(ahtcFilterSubFrmCtl).Form.Filter
            ' If the filter form didn't include a subform,
            ' we'd use this (simpler) syntax instead:
            ' Me.Filter = frmFilter.Filter
            Me.FilterOn = True
            Me.Caption = Me.Caption & " (filtered)"
        End If

    End If

End Sub
```

Change the value of the ahtcFilterFrm constant to the name of the form and the ahtcFilterSubFrmCtl constant to the name of the subform control created in step 1. If your form *doesn't* include an embedded subform, then delete "(ahtcFilterSubFrmCtl).Form" from the line of code or completely delete this line of code and the two comment lines that follow and uncomment (remove the leading single quote from) the following line of code.

```
' Me.Filter = frmFilter.Filter
```

You should also delete the following line of code if you *aren't* using a subform (although leaving it in won't hurt anything).

```
Const ahtcFilterSubFrmCtl = "subAlbums"
```

5. If you wish to display the filter value on the report whenever the report is based on a filtered subset of records, then add a text box control to the page footer (or any other section you'd prefer) and name this control txtFilter. Next, add the following code to an event procedure attached to the section's Format event.

```
Private Sub ReportFooter_Format(Cancel As Integer, FormatCount As Integer)

    ' If this report is filtered, then make the
    ' txtFilter control visible and set its value
    ' to the filter property of the report
    If Me.FilterOn Then
        Me!txtFilter = Me.Filter
        Me!txtFilter.Visible = True
    Else
        Me!txtFilter.Visible = False
    End If
End Sub
```

6. Save the report and close it. You can test the report by opening the filtering form, choosing various filters, and then pressing the Print Records button on the form.

How It Works

This How-To works by setting the report's Filter property to the value of the Filter property of the form. The form and report's Filter properties contain the last filter created for the object. Because the last filter hangs around even after you've turned it off (by using the Records|Remove Filter/Sort command or the equivalent toolbar button), the code in step 4 first checks the status of the FilterOn property. This property is set to True when a filter is active and False when there is no filter or there *is* one but it isn't currently active.

At the beginning of the report's Open event procedure, the code first checks to see if the form associated with this report is open, using the following code.

```
If SysCmd(acSysCmdGetObjectState, acForm, ahtcFilterFrm) <> 0 Then
```

The SysCmd function, is a potpourri function, which allows you to:

    display a progress meter or text in the status bar;

return status information about Access (such as the Access directory, whether the runtime or retail product is running, and so on); and

return the state of a database object to indicate whether it is open, is a new object, or has been changed but not saved.

You indicate to Access which flavor of SysCmd you want by passing it a constant as the first parameter. (You can find each of the SysCmd constants in the online help.) The code in the Open event procedure passes SysCmd the acSysCmdGetObjectState constant, which tells SysCmd that you would like information on the open status of the frmAlbums form. SysCmd obliges by returning one of the values listed in Table 3-15 (yes, the value 3 is skipped for some reason).

SYSCMD RETURN VALUE	ACCESS CONSTANT	MEANING
0	(none)	The object either doesn't exist or is closed.
1	acObjStateOpen	The object is open, but not new or dirty.
2	acObjStateDirty	The object is in an unsaved state.
4	acObjStateNew	The object is new and in an unsaved state.

Table 3-15 The SysCmd object state return values

In this case, you only care if the SysCmd return value is nonzero.

The next stretch of code does all the work.

```
Set frmFilter = Forms(ahtcFilterFrm)

' Is form currently filtered?
If frmFilter.FilterOn Then
    ' Set report's filter to subform's filter
    Me.Filter = frmFilter(ahtcFilterSubFrmCtl).Form.Filter
    ' If the filter form didn't include a subform,
    ' you use this (simpler) syntax instead:
    ' Me.Filter = frmFilter.Filter
    Me.FilterOn = True
    Me.Caption = Me.Caption & " (filtered)"
End If
```

If the form is currently filtered (frmFilter.FilterOn = True, which is the same in VBA as just saying frmFilterOn), then the report's filter is set to the form's filter. Because the subform control on the form is actually being filtered, we set the report's filter equal to the subform's filter.

Notice that we used "frmFilter(ahtcFilterSubFrmCtl).Form.Filter" rather than "frmFilter(ahtcFilterSubFrmCtl).Filter". This odd-looking syntax must be used to tell Access that you want the Filter property of the subform that the subform control contains, not the Filter property of the subform control itself (which doesn't have such a property).

163

If no subform is used on the form, then you can simplify the statement to this:

```
Me.Filter = frmFilter.Filter
```

Next, the code sets the report's FilterOn property to True, which causes the report to be filtered using the previously set Filter property. Finally, the code changes the caption of the report so that "(filtered)" appears in the title bar when you preview the report. This last statement is optional—it provides a nice added touch.

The optional code in step 5—in the sample report, this code was added to the page footer's Format event—documents the filter by displaying it in a text box on the report. The syntax of the filter is the same as a SQL Where clause (without the WHERE keyword).

Comments

You may also wish to set the report's OrderBy property to the form's OrderBy property. If you do this, you must also check the status of the OrderByOn property, which is analogous to the FilterOn property. The syntax of the OrderBy property is similar to the SQL Order By clause (without the ORDER BY keyword).

COMPLEXITY:
ADVANCED

3.14 How do I...
Keep a report from breaking at an inappropriate place?

Problem

On some of my reports, I use the KeepTogether property to keep a whole group together or to ensure that a group header won't print without at least one detail item. However, when detail items are long, I may not want to keep an entire detail item together but I do want to have a reasonable number of lines under the header so that a header won't be the last line on a report page. How do I make a report start a new page instead of printing the group header with just a single detail line at the bottom of a page?

Technique

You can use an event procedure called from a report's Format event to evaluate the length of a report page before it actually prints and take an action only if certain criteria are met (in this case, the action is activating a page break control). This technique makes use of the ahtConditionalBreak function and a page break control. This How-To demonstrates how to use ahtConditionalBreak to force a page break if there is not enough room to print at least one line of text from the detail section under a group header.

Steps

Open 03-14.MDB and print the report rptBadBreaks. This typical business address report, which has its detail section's KeepTogether property set to Yes, occasionally prints a page with the Category group header as the last line of the page, as is shown in Figure 3-35. Now print the rptConditionalBreaks report. Notice that it has avoided the bad break by moving the New World Communications record to the top of page 3 (see Figure 3-36).

Follow these steps to avoid bad breaks in your own reports:

1. Import the basConditionalPageBreak module from 03-14.MDB into your database.

2. Create a new report or open an existing one in design view. Select the group header you want to keep together with some text. Insert a page break control above any other controls in this group section (you may need to move some controls down a bit). You can see the page break control above the txtCompany text box in the Company header section of the sample report, rptConditionalBreaks, in design view in Figure 3-37.

3. If it's not already open, open the group header properties sheet (View|Properties) and set ForceNewPage to None and KeepTogether to Yes (this ensures that the group section itself won't be broken up).

4. Enter the following expression in the OnFormat property (substituting the name of your page break control for "PageBreak1" if it is different).

```
=ahtConditionalBreak ([Report],12600,[PageBreak1])
```

We used 12,600 in the previous function call to indicate that we want a break at 8.75 inches (8.75 * 1,440 = 12,600). Adjust this argument as necessary until the report breaks appropriately (see the How It Works section).

5. Set the detail section's KeepTogether property to No to allow it to break.

6. Save and print the report, which should look like the sample report shown in Figure 3-37.

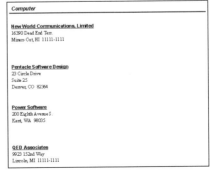

Atlantic Software, Inc.
12322 Arlington Ave.
Room 112
Monroe, IA 11111-1111

Foothill Communications, Limited
1535 Vista Ave.
Dept. 905
Maple Lake, MN 11111-1111

GWA Software, Ltd.
11863 24th Way
Oceanside, NH 11111-1111

New World Communications, Limited

Page 2   Printed on 11/12/95

Figure 3-35 Page 2 of rptBadBreaks shows an inappropriate break for New World Communications

Computer

New World Communications, Limited
16390 Dead End Terr.
Miners Cut, HI 11111-1111

Pentacle Software Design
23 Circle Drive
Suite 25
Denver, CO 82364

Power Software
200 Eighth Avenue S.
Kent, WA 98035

QED Associates
9923 152nd Way
Lincoln, MI 11111-1111

Figure 3-36 rptConditionalBreaks moves New World Communications to the top of page 3

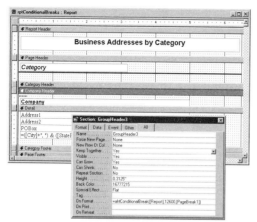

Figure 3-37 The sample report, rptConditionalBreaks, in design view

How It Works

The ahtConditionalBreak function forces a page break if the section will print at or below the specified location on the page. This function takes three arguments: a report object variable, the point at which to force a new page in twips, and an object variable pointing to the page break control that you wish to make visible if the section's location is at or below the specified position.

Here is the ahtConditionalBreak function.

```
Function ahtConditionalBreak(rpt As Report, intBreak As Integer, _
    ctl As Control)

    ctl.Visible = (rpt.Top >= intBreak)

End Function
```

Access evaluates the expression to the right of the equals sign (rpt.Top >= intBreak) as either True or False and then assigns that value to the expression to the left of the equals sign. Thus, the code makes the page break control visible or invisible, depending on whether or not the current page top value has gone beyond the value in intBreak. When the control is made visible, a page break is forced before the section is printed.

You may need to experiment with different numbers for the intBreak argument until you get it working right for your report. Start by measuring the amount of vertical space needed to print a group header, together with the minimum number of detail lines you want to print with it. Add to this amount the height of the page footer. If you are measuring in inches, multiply this sum by 1,440 to convert it to twips; if you are measuring in centimeters, multiply the sum by 567. Subtract the resulting amount from the total height of the page in twips (15,840 = 1,440 * 11 for a standard letter-sized sheet in portrait orientation). This will give you a starting point; adjust as necessary until the report starts a new page unless there is enough room to print the number of lines you want under a group heading.

The following calculations were used for the sample report.

Header + 1 address line = 1-1/4"

footer = $\dfrac{1"}{2\text{-}1/4"}$ = 3,240 twips

Page height = $\dfrac{\begin{array}{r}15{,}840 \text{ twips}\\ -3{,}240 \text{ twips}\end{array}}{12{,}500 \text{ twips}}$

You can determine the amount of blank space to leave between the bottom of the last address on a page and the footer by changing the twips value in the ahtConditionalBreak function. The current value allows a generous amount; to save space, you can reduce the twips argument by a few hundred twips.

Comments

Several properties of reports affect how a page (or column in a multiple-column report) breaks. For many reports, you may be able to use some combination of these properties instead of the technique used in this How-To. The properties are listed in Table 3-16.

PROPERTY SET	PROPERTY NAME	EFFECT
Report	Grp Keep Together	Controls whether groups in a report that have their Keep Together property set to "Whole Group" or "with First Detail" will be kept together by page or by column.
Group	Keep Together	When set to "Whole Group" or "With First Detail", Access attempts to keep all of the sections of a group (header, footer, and detail) on the same page (or column).
Section	Keep Together	When set to "Whole Group" or "With First Detail", Access attempts to keep the whole section on the same page (or column).
	Force New Page	Tells Access to force a new page never, before, after, or before *and* after the section.
	New Row or Col	Similar to Force New Page except this property tells Access to force a new row or column never, before, after, or before *and* after the section. If you select "Across, Then Down" in the Layout Items option in the Layout tab of the Page Setup dialog box, then a new row is started; if you select "Down, Then Across", a new column is started.
	Repeat Section	When set to Yes, Access will repeat this section at the top of the next page (or column) when the group spans more than one page or column.

Table 3-16 The many different properties that affect where a page or column breaks

3.15 How do I...
Customize a report's grouping and sorting at runtime?

Problem

I have a report that has several different grouping and sorting fields I wish to rearrange every time I run the report. To do this, I've created five or six different versions of the same report, changing only the order of the fields and which fields are sorted or grouped. This is a maintenance nightmare, especially when I want to change some aspect of the report, which means having to change all the variants of this same report. Is there any easier way to do this in Access?

Technique

You can manipulate most aspects of the design of a report using VBA code. This How-To shows you how to open a report in design mode programmatically and manipulate several properties of controls and groups. Using this technique and a driving form, you can create a single report that can be customized using different sorting and grouping fields every time it is run.

Steps

Load 03-15.MDB and open frm_rptCompaniesSetup, which is shown in Figure 3-38. Select a grouping field and zero, one, two, or three other fields for the report (any or all of which can be sorted). When done, press the Preview or Print button and a report matching the chosen sorting/grouping fields will be previewed or printed for you. A sample report using the settings from Figure 3-38 is shown in Figure 3-39.

To create a customizable report of your own, follow these steps:

1. Identify the table or query the report will be based on. In the example, the report is based on the tblCompanies table. Decide which of the fields in this table or query you wish to allow to be selected, grouped, or sorted. In the sample database, we decided to use all of the fields from tblCompanies.

2. Create a table with one field, ReportFieldName, with a data type of text. Make this field the primary key of the table. Save the table—in the example, we named it zstbl_rptCompaniesFields—and switch to datasheet view, adding a record for each field identified in step 1.

3. Create a new unbound form. Add one unbound combo box per field you wish to be able to customize at runtime. For example, in the frm_rptCompaniesSetup

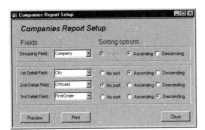

Figure 3-38 The frm_rptCompaniesSetup form is used to set up the rptCompanies report

Figure 3-39 The rptCompanies report is customized every time it is run

form, we allow for one grouping field and up to three sorting fields (see Figure 3-38). The names of the combo box fields and their Row Source properties are listed in Table 3-17. All other properties are set to the default values.

NAME	ROW SOURCE
cboField0	zstbl_rptCompaniesFields
cboField1	SELECT ReportFieldName FROM zstbl_rptCompaniesFields
	WHERE ReportFieldName <> Forms!frm_rptCompaniesSetup!cboField0;
cboField2	SELECT ReportFieldName FROM zstbl_rptCompaniesFields
	WHERE ReportFieldName <> Forms!frm_rptCompaniesSetup!cboField0
	And ReportFieldName <> Forms!frm_rptCompaniesSetup!cboField1
cboField3	SELECT ReportFieldName FROM zstbl_rptCompaniesFields;
	WHERE ReportFieldName <> Forms!frm_rptCompaniesSetup!cboField0
	And ReportFieldName <> Forms!frm_rptCompaniesSetup!cboField1
	And ReportFieldName <> Forms!frm_rptCompaniesSetup!cboField2;

Table 3-17 The combo box field settings on the sample form

Change "zstbl_rptCompaniesFields" to the name of the table from step 2. Change "frm_rptCompaniesSetup" to the name of your form. Create additional combo boxes as needed, following the pattern of Name and Row Source properties from Table 3-17.

4. For all but the last combo box created in step 3, create an event procedure attached to the AfterUpdate event of the control containing code similar to the following.

```
Private Sub cboField1_AfterUpdate()
    Me!cboField2.Requery
```

continued on next page

continued from previous page

```
        Call FixUpCombos(Me!cboField1)
    End Sub
```

Replace cboField1 with the name of the combo box and cboField2 with the name of next combo box after this one.

Add the following code to the end of the first combo box's (cboField0's) event procedure.

```
' Enable the buttons once you've chosen
' the group field
If Not IsNull(Me!cboField0) Then
    Me!cmdPrint.Enabled = True
    Me!cmdPreview.Enabled = True
End If
```

Don't create an AfterUpdate event procedure for the last combo box.

5. Add one option group control alongside each combo box, as listed in Table 3-18. If you have more than four fields, then add additional option groups following the same naming pattern and assigning default values of 1 to each additional option group.

NAME	DEFAULT VALUE
grpSort0	0
grpSort1	1
grpSort2	1
grpSort3	1

Table 3-18 The option groups for the sample form

For each option group, add three option buttons, as listed in Table 3-19. The names of the option buttons don't matter.

LABEL	OPTION VALUE
No sort	1
Ascending	0
Descending	−1

Table 3-19 The option buttons

6. Add a command button named cmdPreview with the caption "Preview" to the form. Attach the following code to its AfterUpdate event.

```
Private Sub cmdPreview_Click()
    Call HandlePrinting(ahtcReport, acPreview)
End Sub
```

7. Add a command button named cmdPrint with the caption "Print" to the form. Attach the following code to its AfterUpdate event.

```
Private Sub cmdPrint_Click()
    Call HandlePrinting(ahtcReport, acNormal)
End Sub
```

8. Add a command button named cmdClose with the caption "Close" to the form. Attach the following code to its AfterUpdate event.

```
Private Sub cmdClose_Click()
    DoCmd.Close acForm, Me.Name
End Sub
```

9. Edit the form's module (click on the code button on the report design toolbar or choose the View|Code menu option) and enter the following lines of code in the module's Declarations section.

```
Const ahtcReport = "rptCompanies"
Const ahtcNoSort = 1
Const ahtcMaxGroupFields = 1
Const ahtcMaxSortFields = 3
```

10. With the form's module still open, add the following two subprocedures to the module (or copy them into your form's module from the sample database).

```
Private Sub FixUpCombos(ctlCalling As Control)

    Dim bytIndex As Byte
    Dim intI As Integer

    ' Grab the last character of the calling
    ' control's name and convert to a byte
    bytIndex = CByte(Right$(ctlCalling.Name, 1))

    ' Enable the next control if and only if the
    ' value of the calling control is non-null
    If bytIndex < ahtcMaxSortFields Then
        With Me("cboField" & bytIndex + 1)
            .Value = Null
            .Enabled = (Not IsNull(ctlCalling))
        End With
        Me("grpSort" & bytIndex + 1).Enabled = (Not IsNull(ctlCalling))
    End If

    ' Disable all controls after the next one
    If bytIndex < ahtcMaxSortFields - 1 Then
        For intI = bytIndex + 2 To ahtcMaxSortFields
            With Me("cboField" & intI)
                .Value = Null
                .Enabled = False
            End With
            With Me("grpSort" & intI)
                .Value = ahtcNoSort
                .Enabled = False
```

continued on next page

continued from previous page

```
                    End With
            Next intI
        End If

    End Sub

    Sub HandlePrinting(strReport As String, ByVal intPrintOption As Integer)

        Dim intI As Integer
        Dim intFieldCnt As Integer
        Dim avarFields(0 To ahtcMaxSortFields) As Variant
        Dim aintSorts(0 To ahtcMaxSortFields) As Integer
        Dim rpt As Report
        Dim varGroupLevel As Variant

        On Error GoTo HandlePrinting_Err

        DoCmd.Hourglass True

        ' Count up the non-null grouping/sorting fields
        ' and the sort property fields and store them in
        ' two arrays
        intFieldCnt = -1
        For intI = 0 To ahtcMaxSortFields
            If Not IsNull(Me("cboField" & intI)) Then
                intFieldCnt = intFieldCnt + 1
                avarFields(intFieldCnt) = Me("cboField" & intI)
                aintSorts(intFieldCnt) = Me("grpSort" & intI)
            End If
        Next intI

        ' Delete old temp copy of report
        On Error Resume Next
        DoCmd.DeleteObject acReport, "rptTemp"
        On Error GoTo 0

        ' Turn off screen updating and open the report in
        ' design mode where it will be manipulated
        Application.Echo False
        DoCmd.OpenReport strReport, View:=acDesign

        ' Set up a report object to point to the report
        Set rpt = Reports(strReport)

        ' Always have a single grouping field.
        ' First set the properties of the group
        rpt.GroupLevel(0).ControlSource = avarFields(0)
        rpt.GroupLevel(0).SortOrder = aintSorts(0)
        ' Set the first label and text box to match
        ' the grouping properties
        rpt("txtField0").ControlSource = avarFields(0)
        rpt("lblField0").Caption = avarFields(0)

        ' Already used GroupLevel(0) for the grouping field,
        ' so now work through the remaining fields
        For intI = 1 To intFieldCnt
```

```
                    ' Set the text box to be visible
                    ' and bind to the chosen field
                    With rpt("txtField" & intI)
                        .Visible = True
                        .ControlSource = avarFields(intI)
                    End With

                    ' Set the label to be visible with its caption
                    ' equal to the name of the field
                    With rpt("lblField" & intI)
                        .Visible = True
                        .Caption = avarFields(intI)
                    End With

                    ' Now create each sorting field group
                    If aintSorts(intI) <> ahtcNoSort Then
                        varGroupLevel = CreateGroupLevel(rpt.Name, _
                         avarFields(intI), False, False)
                        rpt.GroupLevel(varGroupLevel).SortOrder = aintSorts(intI)
                    End If
                Next intI

            ' Make any unneeded fields invisible
            For intI = intFieldCnt + 1 To ahtcMaxSortFields
                rpt("txtField" & intI).Visible = False
                rpt("lblField" & intI).Visible = False
            Next intI

            ' Now make a temp copy of the report and save
            ' changes in the temp copy.
            ' This is done to avoid the user getting the
            ' "Do you want to save your changes?" prompt
            ' and saving this version of the report, which
            ' might mess things up for the next time it is run.
            ' Warning: only do this in a local copy of the database;
            ' never in a shared copy.
            DoCmd.SelectObject acReport, ahtcReport
            SendKeys "rptTemp{Enter}", False
            DoCmd.DoMenuItem 7, 0, 5, 0, acMenuVer70

HandlePrinting_Err:
    DoCmd.Hourglass False
    DoCmd.OpenReport "rptTemp", View:=intPrintOption
    Application.Echo True
End Sub
```

11. Save the form. The complete frm_rptCompaniesSetup sample form is shown, in design view, in Figure 3-40. Close the form.

12. Create a new report. Add one sorting/grouping field to the report. The actual field you choose doesn't matter because the code behind frm_rptCompaniesSetup will change the field name. What is important is that you set the Group Header and Group Footer properties to Yes (which makes it a grouping field). Don't add any additional sorting fields.

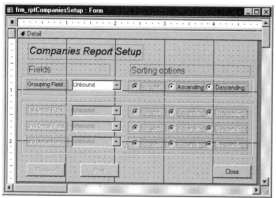

Figure 3-40 The sample form in design view

13. Add a label control for each combo box field from frm_rptCompaniesSetup to the group header section of the report. Make all the labels the same size and give them names in the following style: lblField0, lblField1, and so on.

14. Add an unbound text box control for each combo box field from frm_rptCompaniesSetup to the detail section of the report. These fields should line up under the labels added in step 13, should all be the same dimensions, and should have names like txtField0, txtField1, and so on.

15. Add any page and report headers and footers. Save the report and close it. The completed sample report is shown in Figure 3-41 in design view.

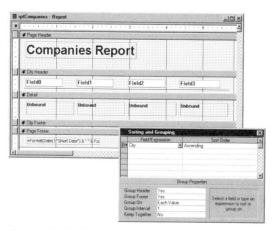

Figure 3-41 The rptCompanies report in design view

How It Works

The zstbl_rptCompaniesFields table holds the names of all the possible fields in the report. This table is used to supply the Row Source for the combo boxes on the driving form. Each record in this table corresponds to one field that may be selected, sorted, or grouped. In the sample database, we used all five fields from tblCompanies.

Most of the work in this How-To is done by the *driving form*. This is the form, frm_rptCompaniesSetup in the sample database, that drives the report customization process. For the person running the report to be able to customize it, you must provide some user interface (UI) mechanism for picking and choosing fields. The combo boxes and option groups provide this mechanism.

Many of the How-To steps (steps 3 through 5 and the FixUpCombos subroutine in step 10) are used to make the UI for the driving form as easy to use and as foolproof as possible. For example, we created Row Source properties (listed in Table 3-17) that make it difficult for the user to select the same grouping/sorting field twice by refining the combo box list for each field that eliminates any fields already chosen from the list.

Whereas the Row Source properties make it difficult to select the same field twice, the code in the FixUpCombos subprocedure makes it next to impossible to select the same field twice. When the form first opens, all of the controls except the first combo box and the first option group are disabled. After you have selected a field from a combo box, the code enables the next combo box/option group while keeping controls that come after the next combo box/option group disabled. Although this takes care of forward movement, the user can always back up and change a combo box field out of order so, in addition to disabling the controls, the code also nulls out any values that may have been entered into subsequent combo boxes.

When the cmdPrint or cmdPreview buttons are pressed, the HandlePrinting subroutine is called. This subroutine takes all of the data entered on the form, opens the report in design mode, and customizes it prior to printing the form to the screen or printer.

HandlePrinting begins by counting up the non-null combo box controls on the form, storing their values and the values of the associated option groups into two arrays.

```
intFieldCnt = -1
For intI = 0 To ahtcMaxSortFields
    If Not IsNull(Me("cboField" & intI)) Then
        intFieldCnt = intFieldCnt + 1
        avarFields(intFieldCnt) = Me("cboField" & intI)
        aintSorts(intFieldCnt) = Me("grpSort" & intI)
    End If
Next intI
```

Next, the code opens the report in design view (after suspending most, but not all screen updating) and adjusts the properties of the first field which makes up the one and only grouping field:

```
' Always have a single grouping field.
' First set the properties of the group
```

continued on next page

continued from previous page

```
rpt.GroupLevel(0).ControlSource = avarFields(0)
rpt.GroupLevel(0).SortOrder = aintSorts(0)
' Set the first label and text box to match
' the grouping properties
rpt("txtField0").ControlSource = avarFields(0)
rpt("lblField0").Caption = avarFields(0)
```

The next stretch of code iterates through the remaining fields, which are all sorting (or nonsorting detail) fields. First, the unbound text box controls are made visible and their control sources are set to the names of the fields selected from the form. Next, the labels are made visible and their captions are set to match the text boxes. The CreateGroupLevel function is then called to create any and all sorting fields based on the selection from the option groups on the form. (The last two parameters of this function tell Access whether you want a header or a footer. Because this code is creating sorting fields only, both of these parameters are set to False.) This chunk of HandlePrinting is shown here.

```
For intI = 1 To intFieldCnt
    ' Set the text box to be visible
    ' and bind to the chosen field
    With rpt("txtField" & intI)
        .Visible = True
        .ControlSource = avarFields(intI)
    End With

    ' Set the label to be visible with its caption
    ' equal to the name of the field
    With rpt("lblField" & intI)
        .Visible = True
        .Caption = avarFields(intI)
    End With

    ' Now create each sorting field group
    If aintSorts(intI)  ahtcNoSort Then
        varGroupLevel = CreateGroupLevel(rpt.Name, _
         avarFields(intI), False, False)
        rpt.GroupLevel(varGroupLevel).SortOrder = aintSorts(intI)
    End If
Next intI
```

Next, any unneeded fields are made invisible.

```
For intI = intFieldCnt + 1 To ahtcMaxSortFields
    rpt("txtField" & intI).Visible = False
    rpt("lblField" & intI).Visible = False
Next intI
```

A temporary copy of the report is then made. This is necessary because design-time changes have been made to the report. This eliminates the chance that the user saves the modified report over the original, which could mess things up the next time the report is run.

```
DoCmd.SelectObject acReport, ahtcReport
SendKeys "rptTemp{Enter}", False
DoCmd.DoMenuItem 7, 0, 5, 0, acMenuVer70
```

Finally, the temporary copy of report is opened and screen updating is turned back on.

```
DoCmd.Hourglass False
DoCmd.OpenReport "rptTemp", View:=intPrintOption
Application.Echo True
```

Comments

By making a temporary copy of the report, you are eliminating the possibility that the original report is left in a state that makes it unusable the next time the report is run. This is important because there is no programmatic way to remove sort fields, meaning that you can't make a report that has been saved with two sort fields into a report with one sort field. But if the user is allowed to save the modified version of the report, this is exactly what might happen. Therefore, we made the decision to use a temporary copy of the report (but only after trying numerous other workarounds). A caveat with this approach is that it won't work if you are sharing the database over a network. However, if you split your database into "application" and "data" databases, either manually or by using the Database Splitter Wizard (Tools|Add-ins|Database Splitter), and share only the "data" database with other users, then the temp tables will be local and thus will not be a problem, even in a networked environment.

The sample report and accompanying code assume you want only one grouping field. This was done to simplify the example, but you could extend it by including code to make additional grouping fields (just like the code that now makes the sorting fields). If you do this, you'll have to deal with creating controls and placing them in the header of the groups. You can create controls using the CreateReportControl function, which is described in Access online help.

CHAPTER 4
DEVELOPING AND DISTRIBUTING APPLICATIONS

DEVELOPING
AND DISTRIBUTING
APPLICATIONS

How do I...

4.10 Clean test data out of a database when I'm ready to ship it?

4.11 Package an add-in for distribution?

This chapter is a compendium of tips and suggestions on making your application development go more smoothly and your applications more professional. You'll learn how to convert queries into embedded SQL strings providing data for forms or reports. You'll learn how to build an object inventory so you can document your applications better, and how to ensure that properties for objects that should match up actually do. You'll learn how to disable screen output more effectively than the methods Access provides internally can. You'll find tips on discerning the current language version of Access and modifying text in error messages and on forms and reports to accommodate the current language. You'll see how to set and restore the Access caption, and how to set startup options for your application. You'll also see how to use some of the common Windows dialogs: the File Open/Save dialogs and the common color-choosing dialog. The final two topics concern application distribution: clearing out test data before shipping your application, and packaging an add-in for distribution.

Some of the techniques in this chapter use Windows API calls, and some use a library that's not part of Windows but actually part of Access itself. This library, MSAU7032.DLL, was written by the Access development team to help the Access Wizards perform some of their wizardry. The Wizards are written using VBA code, just like your applications, so nothing's keeping you from using this library yourself (except, of course, the fact that Microsoft didn't document it). Topics 4.5 and 4.9 use this library, and the sample databases for these topics include the necessary declarations for calling the functions included in the MSAU7032.DLL library.

4.1 Convert Queries into Embedded SQL Statements

In many situations in Access, you have a choice whether to use a query or an embedded SQL statement to retrieve the data you need. This How-To will show how you can convert from stored queries to embedded SQL and the trade-offs in making that conversion.

4.2 Build an Object Inventory

As a developer, you often need to build an inventory of objects in your database. This How-To will show how to scan Access object collections and build a table containing information about each of the objects in your database.

4.3 Verify That Objects Use Consistent Settings

Your application is finished and it's time to deliver it, but you want to make sure that all similar controls use the same font, or that all command buttons have their ControlTipText properties set. Access makes this possible, but not very easy: You'd have to visit every control on every form to verify that you've used consistent settings on all your objects. This How-To will help you create a query that lists all the objects on any forms or reports you specify. Given that query, you can sort and group to convince yourself that all your objects have their properties set the way you intended.

4.4   *Really* Hide Access Screen Activity

Sometimes you need more control over screen repainting than what you get with either Application.Echo or Form.Repaint. You can instruct Windows to stop updating a certain window and all its children. This How-To will demonstrate the use of the LockWindowUpdate API call, which almost always provides a clean way of disabling screen updates in Access.

4.5   Find Out What Language Version of Access Is Installed

If you distribute applications to international users, certain parts of your code may depend on the specific version of Access that's installed at a site. If you're using SendKeys, for example, you may need to alter the strings you're using to accommodate a particular language. This How-To will show how you can determine which language version of Access is currently running, using a function in MSAU7032.DLL.

4.6   Internationalize Text in My Applications

This How-To will present some issues and some solutions to the problems involved in internationalizing your applications. This complex topic could take up several chapters, so we'll cover just some of the most important aspects, including message tables and altering forms and message boxes.

4.7   Change and Reset the Access Caption Bar

As part of your application, you may need to change the Access caption bar (which normally contains the text *Microsoft Access)* to something more appropriate for your application. This How-To will show how you can store the current caption, change it to match your preferences, and then put the caption back the way it was once you're done.

4.8   Use the Windows File Open/Save Common Dialog Boxes

Windows provides common File Open and Save dialog boxes used by most applications. Access doesn't make these available to you directly, but you can get to them easily by using the wrapper function that calls into the Windows API. This How-To will show you how to use this function and the meaning of the options that are available when you call the function.

4.9   Use the Windows Color-Choosing Common Dialog Box

When you want to choose colors from within your applications, you'll probably want to use the standard Windows common color-choosing dialog box. Though Access doesn't make the common dialog boxes available to you directly, MSAU7032.DLL again comes to your aid. This How-To will show how you can use this library to provide color-choosing capabilities for your applications.

4.10 Clean Test Data out of a Database When I'm Ready to Ship It

In the process of designing and testing a database, you'll normally put in some simple test data to verify that everything is working right. When it's time to ship the database to a client, you'll need to remove this data. This How-To will demonstrate a method of automatically removing test data without worrying about referential integrity or losing permanent lookup table data.

4.11 Package an Add-in for Distribution

Access 95 makes it easier to load add-ins (Wizards, Builders, and other extensions to the core Access functionality). When your add-in is working correctly, you can add that polish by packaging it for automatic Access installation. This How-To will show you how to make your add-in available via the Add-In Manager and explain some underdocumented information on getting it set up correctly.

COMPLEXITY:
EASY

4.1 How do I...
Convert queries into embedded SQL statements?

Problem

Access' Query Builder makes it easy to create SQL statements as row sources for combo boxes or as record sources for forms and reports. I'd prefer to use SQL statements for row and record sources because they reduce the number of unnecessary objects in my databases. Is there an easy way to make these conversions? What's the trade-off of using embedded SQL statements instead of query objects to provide my data?

Technique

There is no automatic conversion utility to transform queries into SQL statements, but you can use the View SQL button on the Query Design toolbar to display a query's SQL statement, copy it to the Windows Clipboard, and then paste it into the RecordSource or RowSource property of a form or combo box.

Steps

Open 04-01.MDB and look at the form frmCompanyInfoQuery. This form has a simple query as its record source; the combo box in its header also has a query as its row source. Neither of these queries is needed elsewhere, so they are prime candidates for conversion into SQL statements.

Take the following steps to convert a query, using the form's record source query as an example. These steps have already been taken for the form frmCompanyInfoSQL, both for the form's RecordSource property and for the combo box's RowSource property.

1. Open the form whose RecordSource you want to convert to a single SQL statement in design view, and make sure that the properties sheet is open (Figure 4-1).

2. Click on the Build button (...) next to the RecordSource property to open the Query Builder for the record source query.

3. With the Query Builder open, click on the View SQL button on the toolbar or select View|SQL.

4. The SQL window opens, displaying the query as a SQL statement, as shown in Figure 4-2.

5. Highlight the entire SQL statement and press CTRL-C or select Edit|Copy to copy it to the Clipboard.

6. Close the SQL window.

7. Highlight the query name in the RecordSource properties sheet and press CTRL-V or select Edit|Paste to replace the query name with the SQL statement. Figure 4-3 shows the form's RecordSource property with the SQL statement in place.

8. Delete the original RecordSource query from the Database Container.

How It Works

Most Access queries can be converted back and forth between the graphical representation shown in the Query Builder window and the SQL representation of the query. The SQL window makes it easy to extract a query's SQL statement and use it directly as a record source or row source or in VBA code. Because all queries in Access can be represented as an SQL statement, you have a choice—you can base a form or report on a query, or you can supply the SQL string directly in the properties sheet.

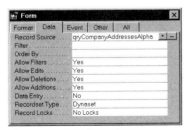

Figure 4-1 A form's properties sheet, with a query as its RecordSource property

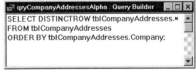

Figure 4-2 The SQL window for a simple query

Figure 4-3 A form's Properties Sheet
with a SQL statement as its
RecordSource property

Comments

Converting row source queries into SQL statements lets you eliminate many trivial queries that have no purpose other than filling forms or combo boxes. If you have an SQL statement as a record or row source, you can open the Query Builder window to view or modify it, which makes it easy to use SQL statements in place of queries.

Three caveats: If you use the same complex query as a row source for several different database objects, and especially if you anticipate changing the query, it may be best to leave the query as a query object rather than converting it into an SQL statement. If you use one query as a record source for several forms or reports, when you change the query, the changes will be picked up by all the forms or reports that use it. Also, Access can precompile queries. Once you've set up a query in the Query Builder, Access compiles it and stores the compiled version with the query itself. This can help speed query load times. When you base a form or report on an SQL string instead of a query, you're forfeiting the option of precompiling the query. Finally, there are some query properties that only apply to saved queries, such as the Run Permissions property. If you need to use these properties in a secured database, you need to leave the queries as query objects.

In some cases, you may need to convert an SQL statement into a query (for example, if you need to use it as a record source for several forms or reports). In that case, simply reverse the above steps: Open the SQL statement in the Query Builder window and then save it as a named query, which you can use as a record source for other database objects.

In addition, you can use the query builder to help create a row source or control source from scratch. Simply click on the builder button and build an SQL statement as if you were building a query. Rather than saving a query object in the database container, Access will save the SQL string you've created into the appropriate property.

COMPLEXITY:
INTERMEDIATE

4.2   How do I...
Build an object inventory?

Problem

To document my application, I'd like to be able to create a list of all the objects in my databases, including their owners, date of creation, and date of last update. I'm sure I can do it manually, but is there a better way to create a table containing all this information?

Technique

Access' data access objects (DAO) can give you the information you need. By programmatically working your way through each of Access' container collections, you can add a row to an inventory table for each object in your application, storing information about that object. You should be able to use the techniques for this operation to write your own code for enumerating other collections in Access. There are a few tricks along the way, and this How-To discusses those, but in general this is a straightforward project.

Steps

To create an object inventory for your applications, take only two steps:

1. Import the form zsfrmInventory from 04-02.MDB into your own application.

2. Load and run the form. As it opens, it builds the object inventory, saving the data in zstblInventory. If you want to rebuild the inventory once the form's up, click the Rebuild Object Inventory button. This recreates the inventory table and fills it with information about all the objects in your database. Figure 4-4 shows the form once it's been run on a sample database.

> **Note**
>
> This example form includes the Access system tables, which you may never have encountered. These tables are part of every Access database, and are not cause for alarm. You can view them in the Database Explorer by choosing the Tools|Options menu, and turning on the Show System Objects option.

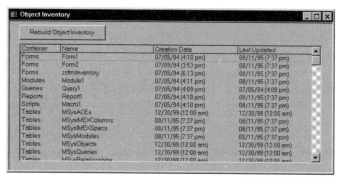

Figure 4-4 The inventory-creating form once it's done its work on a sample database

How It Works

In this topic, How It Works is a lot more interesting than the final product. The object inventory itself can be useful, but the steps in creating the inventory may be more useful to you in the long run. All the code examples used in this section come from the form module attached to zsfrmInventory (in 04-02.MDB).

Starting the Process

When the form loads, or when you click the Rebuild Object Inventory button on zsfrmInventory, you execute the following code. (The *zs* prefix, by the way, reminds you that zsfrmInventory is a "system" form, used only by your application. The z forces this form to sort to the bottom of the database container so you won't get it confused with your "real" forms.)

```
Private Sub RebuildInventory()
    On Error GoTo Rebuild_Err
    DoCmd.Hourglass True

    Me!lstInventory.RowSource = Null
    Call CreateInventory
    Me!lstInventory.RowSource = "SELECT DISTINCTROW ID, Container, Name, " & _
        "Format([DateCreated],'mm/dd/yy (h:nn am/pm)') AS [Creation Date], " & _
        "Format([LastUpdated],'mm/dd/yy (h:nn am/pm)') AS [Last Updated], " & _
        "Owner FROM zstblInventory ORDER BY Container, Name;"
    Me!cmdDocumentSelected.Enabled = False

Rebuild_Exit:
    DoCmd.Hourglass False
    Exit Sub

Rebuild_Err:
    Resume Rebuild_Exit
End Sub
```

This code turns on the hourglass cursor and sets the main list box's RowSource property to be Null. (It must do this, because it's about to call the CreateInventory procedure, which attempts to delete the table holding the data. If the list box were still bound to that table, the code couldn't delete the table—it would be locked!) It then calls the CreateInventory subroutine. This procedure fills zstblInventory with the object inventory, and can take a few seconds to run. When it's done, the code resets the list box's RowSource, resets the cursor, and exits.

Documenting All the Containers

The CreateInventory subroutine first creates the zstblInventory table. If CreateTable succeeds, CreateInventory then calls the AddInventory procedure for each of the useful Access containers (Tables, Relationships, Forms, Reports, Scripts, and Modules) that represent user objects. (Tables and Queries are lumped together in one container. As you'll see, it'll take a bit of extra effort to distinguish them.) Because each of the AddInventory procedure calls writes to the status bar, CreateInventory clears out the status bar once it's done, using the Access SysCmd function. The following code fragment shows the CreateInventory subroutine.

```
Private Sub CreateInventory()
    If (CreateTable()) Then
        ' These routines use the status line,
        ' so clear it once everyone's done.
        Call AddInventory("Tables")
        Call AddInventory("Relationships")
        Call AddInventory("Forms")
        Call AddInventory("Reports")
        Call AddInventory("Scripts")
        Call AddInventory("Modules")

        ' Clear out the status bar.
        Call SysCmd(acSysCmdClearStatus)
    Else
        MsgBox "Unable to create zstblInventory."
    End If
End Sub
```

Creating the Inventory Table

The CreateTable function prepares the table zstblInventory to hold the current database's inventory. The code in CreateTable first attempts to delete zstblInventory (using the Drop Table SQL statement). If the table exists, the code will succeed. If it doesn't exist, the code will trigger a runtime error, but the error-handling code will allow the procedure to continue anyway. CreateTable then recreates the table from scratch. The following code fragment, the function CreateTable, does the work: It uses a data definition language (DDL) Query to create the table. (See How-To 1.14 for more information on DDL queries.) CreateTable returns True if it succeeds, False if it fails.

```
Private Function CreateTable()

    ' Return True on success, False otherwise
```

continued on next page

continued from previous page

```
        Dim qdf As QueryDef
        Dim db As Database
        Dim strSQL As String

        On Error GoTo CreateTableError
        Set db = CurrentDb()

        DoCmd.SetWarnings False
        DoCmd.RunSQL "Drop Table zstblInventory"

        ' Create zstblInventory
        strSQL = "CREATE TABLE zstblInventory (Name Text (255), " & _
         "Container Text (50), DateCreated DateTime, " & _
         "LastUpdated DateTime, Owner Text (50), " & _
         "ID AutoIncrement Constraint PrimaryKey PRIMARY KEY)"
        DoCmd.RunSQL strSQL

        ' If you got here, you succeeded!
        db.TableDefs.Refresh
        CreateTable = True

CreateTableExit:
    DoCmd.SetWarnings True
    Exit Function

CreateTableError:
    Select Case Err
        Case ahtcErrTableNotFound, ahtcErrObjectNotFound
            Resume Next
        Case Else
            CreateTable = False
            Resume CreateTableExit
    End Select
    Resume CreateTableExit
End Function
```

Documenting Each Container

The AddInventory subroutine is the heart of the inventory-creating operation. In Access, each database maintains a group of container objects, each of which contains a number of documents. These documents are the saved objects of the container's type, such as tables, relationships, forms, reports, scripts (macros), or modules. For each container, AddInventory looks at each document, adds a new row to zstblInventory for each, and copies the information into the new row of the table. (All the code examples in this subsection come from AddInventory, in zsfrmInventory's module.)

The first step is to set up the necessary object variables.

```
Set wrk = DBEngine.Workspaces(0)
Set db = wrk.Databases(0)
Set con = db.Containers(strContainer)
Set rst = db.OpenRecordset("zstblInventory")
```

The code then loops through each document in the given container, gathering information about each document.

```
For Each doc In con.Documents
...
Next doc
```

For each document, the code must first determine, if it is the Tables container, whether the given document is a table or query. To do this, it calls the isTable function. This function attempts to retrieve a reference to the requested object from the database's TableDefs collection. If this doesn't trigger a runtime error, then that table must exist. Because attempting to retrieve a query's name from the TableDefs collection will certainly fail, you can use the isTable function to determine whether or not an element of the Tables container (which contains both tables and queries) is a table.

```
Private Function isTable(ByVal strName As String)
    Dim db As Database
    Dim tdf As TableDef

    On Error Resume Next

    Set db = CurrentDb()

    ' See comment below for information why this
    ' is commented out.
    'db.Tabledefs.Refresh

    Set tdf = db.TableDefs(strName)
    isTable = (Err = 0)
    On Error GoTo 0
End Function
```

> ### Using the Refresh Method
>
> Normally, before retrieving information about any Access persistent object collection (TableDefs, QueryDefs, etc.), you must refresh the collection. Because Access doesn't keep these collections up to date unless necessary, it's possible that a table recently added by a user in the user interface might not yet be added to the TableDefs collection. In this case, you'd be calling isTable repeatedly. To speed the operation of zsfrmInventory, the isTable function used here does not use the Refresh method each time it's called. It counts on the caller to have refreshed the collection. In almost any other use besides this one, you'd want to "uncomment" the call to the Refresh method in the code example and allow the code to refresh the collection before checking for the existence of a particular table.

The result of this code fragment is to fill a string variable, *strType,* with the type of the current document (Tables, Relationships, Queries, Forms, Reports, Scripts, or Modules).

This value will be written to zstblInventory along with the document information, as shown here.

```
If strContainer = "Tables" Then
    strType = IIf(isTable(doc.Name), "Tables", "Queries")
Else
    strType = strContainer
End If
```

Caching Object References

Note that the previous code sample uses an object variable, *doc*, to refer to the current document. The For Each...Next statement sets up this reference for you. This construct, new in Access 95 (it's actually VBA that provides this), loops through every item in a collection, assigning a reference to each object as it loops. We could have used a simple For...Next loop, as would have been necessary in Access 2, but it would have been less efficient. Because later code will refer to this particular document a number of times, it's more efficient to set up this direct reference than to ask Access to parse the general reference, con.Documents(intl), each time it needs to refer to the document. In general, any time you need to refer to an object more than once, you can make your code run a little better by setting an object variable to refer to that object. This will save Access from having to look up the object each time.

Once AddInventory has determined the correct value for strType, it can add the information to zstblInventory. AddInventory retrieves the various properties of the document referred to by *doc* and copies them to the current row in zstblInventory, referred to by *rst*. Once it's done, it uses the recordset's Update method to commit the new row.

```
With rst
    .AddNew
        !Container = strType
        !Owner = doc.Owner
        !Name = doc.Name
        !DateCreated = doc.DateCreated
        !LastUpdated = doc.LastUpdated
    .Update
End With
```

Using Transactions

If you look at the code in zsfrmInventory, you'll notice that entire loop that was just discussed is surrounded by statements that begin and commit a transaction.

```
wrk.BeginTrans
```
.

.
.
.
```
wrk.CommitTrans
```

These methods of the workspace object are normally used to allow for rollbacks of failed transactions. In this case, however, they're being used to accelerate the operation. Because file activities inside a transaction are cached (stored in memory if possible) and aren't actually written to disk until the code executes the CommitTrans method, wrapping disk-intensive activity inside a BeginTrans/CommitTrans pair can make a big difference in speed. For small applications, this speed difference won't be visible. For large applications that include many hundreds of objects, you should be able to notice the difference.

Note

Access 95's version of the Jet database engine supposedly performs its own internal caching better than previous versions did, so you may find that using transactions doesn't help as much as it used to. In addition, if you're working with very large sets of data inside a transaction, it can actually slow you down! Because the transaction needs to buffer all the changes made until you commit the transaction, when it runs out of physical memory that it can use for buffering, it will start buffering to your disk. When it does that, your data access becomes much slower than it would have been otherwise, because Access is now writing your data to disk twice (once for buffering and once when you commit the transaction). If you're using transactions to speed up your data access, you'll need to ensure that you're working with small data sets (less than 10,000 rows or so) or that you commit and then restart your transaction every time you process a fixed number of rows. See Chapter 8 for more information on testing whether transactions will speed operations in your own environment.

Avoiding Errors

The list box on zsfrmInventory has the following expression as its RowSource property.

```
SELECT DISTINCTROW ID, Container, Name,
 Format([DateCreated],"mm/dd/yy (h:nn am/pm)") AS [Creation Date],
 Format([LastUpdated],"mm/dd/yy (h:nn am/pm)") AS [Last Updated],
 Owner FROM zstblInventory ORDER BY Container, Name;"
```

There are two issues here. First, the SQL string used as the RowSource pulls data from zstblInventory. It's quite possible, though, that when you load the form, zstblInventory doesn't exist. To avoid this problem, the form has been saved with the list box's RowSource set to a null value. When the form loads, it doesn't attempt to retrieve the data until the code has had time to create the table, as you can see in the RebuildInventory procedure, shown above.

The second thing to bear in mind is that Access doesn't always keep the collections completely up to date: You may find deleted objects in the collections. (These deleted objects have names starting with "~TMPCLP".) You'll most likely not want to include these objects in the inventory, so the code that loops through the collections specifically excludes objects with names that start with "~TMPCLP". To know which objects are deleted, the code calls the isTemp function. It would be great if there was a less "low-tech" solution, but for now, this is how you can detect deleted objects in the collections of objects.

```
For Each doc In con.Documents
    If Not IsTemp(doc.Name) Then
    ...
    End If
Next doc

Private Function isTemp(ByVal strName As String)
    isTemp = Left(strName, 7) = "~TMPCLP"
End Function
```

Comments

A complete discussion of Access' Data Access Objects is far beyond the scope of this book. It could (and does) fill many more pages in manuals and online help than this book can incorporate. For more information, start with the diagram in the *Access Building Applications* manual. That diagram shows the relationships between various collections and the objects they contain. From there, work through examples like this one (and others in this book that use DAO to do their work), and the examples in Access' online help. Once you get the hang of it, DAO is really straightforward.

If you want to remove system objects from your inventory, you'll need to check each object and, if it's a system object, skip it in the display. To check an object to see if it's a system object, you can use its Attributes property. See Access' online help for more information.

You might wonder why this application uses the Access containers to retrieve information about Tables and Queries; this requires more effort than if the code had just used the TableDefs and QueryDefs collections. This example uses the Tables collection instead because the TableDefs/QueryDefs collections don't contain information about the owner of the objects. Because that's the information this application is attempting to track, it makes sense to use the containers. That's the only way to gather the necessary information.

COMPLEXITY:
INTERMEDIATE

4.3 How do I...
Verify that objects use consistent settings?

Problem

I've finished my application and I'm ready to deliver it, but I notice that my use of color, fonts, alignment, and other layout properties aren't consistent across all my forms or reports. I know I can manually check the values of all the properties of all the controls on my forms and reports, but there's got to be a faster way. Is there some method I can use to compare similar properties for all the objects in my application?

Technique

Access doesn't provide a "cross-section" of your properties, which is really what you need—some way to look at properties not listed by item, but by property name, across all objects. Building on the technology introduced in How-To 4.2, this How-To creates a group of tables containing information about all the properties on whichever forms and/or reports you select. Once it builds those tables, it constructs a query that will allow you, using the Quick Sort menu items (new in Access 95), to view all the property settings for various objects, sorted any way you'd like. Once you've sorted the output on property name, for example, you'll quickly be able to see which objects have incorrect settings for that particular property.

Steps

The sample database, 04-03.MDB, includes a single form, zsfrmVerifySettings. Figure 4-5 shows the form after it has done its cataloging in NWIND.MDB, ready to present property information on three different forms. Figure 4-6 shows the output data, sorted by property name, showing that several controls have different background colors.

To use zsfrmVerifySettings to catalog properties in your own applications, follow these steps:

1. Import zsfrmVerifySettings from 04-03.MDB into your own database.

2. Load zsfrmVerifySettings in Form view. As it loads, it will build the object property inventory, creating tables and queries as necessary.

3. Once the form has presented the list of forms and reports, click on the items you want documented. Click again on an item to remove it from the list of selected items. You can also use the Select All, Select All Forms, and Select All Reports buttons to select groups of items.

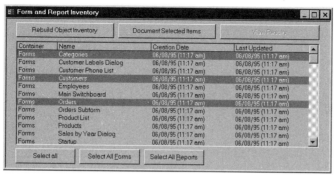

Figure 4-5 zsfrmVerifySettings is ready to catalog all controls on three selected forms

4. When you've selected all the forms or reports you'd like to work with, click the Document Selected Items button. This will work its way through the list of items you've selected and will document all the properties of each control on each of those items.

5. When the documentation process is finished (it may take some time to work through all the items you've selected), click the View Results button. This will open zsqryProperties, listing all the properties of all the objects and the sections and controls on those objects.

6. Use the toolbar buttons to control sorting and filtering so that you can view only the properties you want for the objects you care about. For example, you might want to ensure that all command buttons on all your forms have their ControlTipText properties set. To do that, follow these steps (assuming you've followed the steps above):

7. Open zsfrmVerifySettings and select all the forms in your application from the list of objects.

Figure 4-6 zsqryProperties allows you to sort by any categories to view your property settings

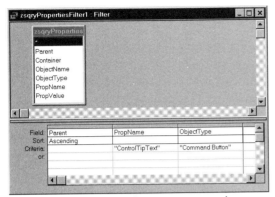

Figure 4-7 This filter limits rows to the ControlTipText property of command buttons

8. Click on the Document Selected button. Go out for lunch while it does its work.

9. Once it's finished, click on the View Results button, which brings up zsqryProperties, showing one row for each property of each object you selected. For a large set of forms or reports, this query could return tens of thousands of rows.

10. Choose Records|Filter|Advanced Filter/Sort and build a filter that sorts on Parent and limits the output to rows with "ControlTipText" in the PropName field, and "Command Button" in the ObjectType field. Figure 4-7 shows this filter.

11. Apply the filter by clicking on the "funnel" button on the toolbar, or by right-clicking on the filter design area, and choosing Apply Filter/Sort. You will see only the rows for the command buttons' ControlTipText property. Look for the rows where there's no value in the PropValue column. Those are the buttons that don't yet have a value set. Figure 4-8 shows the output of the sample

Parent	Container	ObjectName	ObjectType	PropName	PropValue
Customer Label	Forms	Preview	Command butto	ControlTipText	
Customer Label	Forms	Print	Command butto	ControlTipText	
Customer Label	Forms	Cancel	Command butto	ControlTipText	
Employees	Forms	PersonalInfo	Command butto	ControlTipText	
Employees	Forms	CompanyInfo	Command butto	ControlTipText	
Main Switchboa	Forms	Suppliers	Command butto	ControlTipText	Open the Suppli
Main Switchboa	Forms	ExitMicrosoftAccess	Command butto	ControlTipText	Close the North
Main Switchboa	Forms	DisplayDatabaseWindow	Command butto	ControlTipText	Close this switc
Main Switchboa	Forms	PrintSalesReports	Command butto	ControlTipText	Open the Print S
Main Switchboa	Forms	Products	Command butto	ControlTipText	Open the Produ
Main Switchboa	Forms	Orders	Command butto	ControlTipText	Open the Orders
Main Switchboa	Forms	Categories	Command butto	ControlTipText	Open the Categ
Orders	Forms	PrintInvoice	Command butto	ControlTipText	
Orders	Forms	PrintInvoice	Command butto	ControlTipText	

Record: 7 of 22 (Filtered)

Figure 4-8 The result query makes it clear which buttons don't have their ControlTipText property set

query. It's quite clear which buttons don't yet have their ControlTipText properties set.

How It Works

To build the list of forms and reports, zsfrmVerifySettings borrows code from the example in How-To 4.2. Instead of looping through all the collections, however, it works only with the Forms and Reports collections. Otherwise, the mechanics of creating the list of objects are the same as in How-To 4.2; investigate that topic if you'd like more information on building the object inventory.

Creating the Temporary Tables and Query

How-To 4.2 created a single table, zstblInventory, to hold the list of objects. In this case, however, you need three tables (zstblInventory for main objects, zstblSubObjects for objects on those forms or reports, and zstblProperties for property information). You also need a query (zsqryProperties) to join the three tables and display the output. The function CreateTables, shown below, uses data-definition language (DDL) queries to create each of the necessary tables (see How-To 1.14 for more information on DDL queries) and data access objects (DAO) to create the query (see Chapter 6 for more information on using DAO).

```
Private Function CreateTables()

    ' Return True on success, False otherwise

    Dim qdf As QueryDef
    Dim strSQL As String

    On Error GoTo CreateTableError

    DoCmd.SetWarnings False

    DoCmd.RunSQL "Drop Table zstblInventory"
    DoCmd.RunSQL "Drop Table zstblSubObjects"
    DoCmd.RunSQL "Drop Table zstblProperties"

    ' Create zstblInventory
    strSQL = "CREATE TABLE zstblInventory (Name Text (255), " & _
     "Container Text (50), DateCreated DateTime, " & _
     "LastUpdated DateTime, Owner Text (50), " & _
     "ID AutoIncrement Constraint PrimaryKey PRIMARY KEY)"
    DoCmd.RunSQL strSQL

    ' Create zstblSubObjects
    strSQL = "CREATE TABLE zstblSubObjects (ParentID Long, " & _
     "ObjectName Text (50), ObjectType Text (50), " & _
     "ObjectID AutoIncrement Constraint PrimaryKey PRIMARY KEY)"
    DoCmd.RunSQL strSQL

    ' Create zstblProperties
    strSQL = "CREATE TABLE zstblProperties (ObjectID Long, " & _
```

```
    "PropName Text (50), PropType Short, " & _
    "PropValue Text (255), " & _
    "PropertyID AutoIncrement Constraint PrimaryKey PRIMARY KEY)"
    DoCmd.RunSQL strSQL

    ' Create zsqryProperties
    strSQL = "SELECT DISTINCTROW zstblInventory.Name AS Parent, " & _
      "zstblInventory.Container, zstblSubObjects.ObjectName, " & _
      "zstblSubObjects.ObjectType, zstblProperties.PropName, " & _
      "zstblProperties.PropValue FROM zstblInventory " & _
      "INNER JOIN (zstblSubObjects INNER JOIN zstblProperties " & _
      "ON zstblSubObjects.ObjectID = zstblProperties.ObjectID) " & _
      "ON zstblInventory.ID = zstblSubObjects.ParentID;"

    DoCmd.DeleteObject acQuery, "zsqryProperties"
    CurrentDb.CreateQueryDef "zsqryProperties", strSQL

    ' If you got here, you succeeded!
    CurrentDb.TableDefs.Refresh
    CreateTables = True

CreateTableExit:
    DoCmd.SetWarnings True
    Exit Function

CreateTableError:
    Select Case Err
        Case ahtcErrTableNotFound, ahtcErrObjectNotFound
            Resume Next
        Case Else
            CreateTables = False
            Resume CreateTableExit
    End Select
End Function
```

Getting Ready to Document Items

When you click on the Document Selected Items button, the form must walk through the list of selected items and then document the object. The code in cmdDocumentSelected_Click does the work: It looks through the ItemsSelected collection of the list box, and for each selected item, calls either DocumentForm or DocumentReport, depending on the value in the first column of the list box. Each of those procedures requires the ID of the parent object (the form or report in question) and the name of the object.

```
Private Sub cmdDocumentSelected_Click()

    ' In the list box:
    ' ParentID == Column(0)
    ' Container == Column(1)
    ' Name == Column(2)

    Dim varItem As Variant
    Dim wrk As Workspace
    Static fInHere As Boolean
```

continued on next page

continued from previous page

```
Dim strName As String
Dim lngParentID As Long

' Don't allow recursive entry. If this routine
' is doing its thing, don't allow more button
' clicks to get you in again, until the first
' pass has finished its work.
If fInHere Then Exit Sub
fInHere = True

DoCmd.Hourglass True
Set wrk = DBEngine.Workspaces(0)
wrk.BeginTrans
With Me!lstInventory
    For Each varItem In .ItemsSelected
        strName = .Column(2, varItem)
        lngParentID = .Column(0, varItem)
        Select Case .Column(1, varItem)
            ' This will only handle forms and reports.
            Case "Forms"
                Call DocumentForm(strName, lngParentID)
            Case "Reports"
                Call DocumentReport(strName, lngParentID)
        End Select
    Next varItem
End With

Call SysCmd(acSysCmdClearStatus)
Me!cmdViewResults.Enabled = True

DocumentSelected_Exit:
    wrk.CommitTrans
    DoCmd.Hourglass False
    fInHere = False
    Exit Sub

DocumentSelected_Err:
    MsgBox "Error: " & Error & " (" & Err & ")", _
        vbExclamation, "DocumentSelected"
    Resume DocumentSelected_Exit
End Sub
```

Visiting All the Objects

Both procedures, DocumentForm and DocumentReport, do the same things, though in slightly different ways. They both document the properties of the main object itself, then the properties of each of the sections (forms can have up to five sections, reports up to 25). Finally, both procedures walk through the collection of controls on the main object, documenting all the properties of each control. The code below shows DocumentForm, but DocumentReport is almost identical.

```
Private Sub DocumentForm(ByVal strName As String, ByVal lngParentID As Long)
    ' You must first open the form in design mode, and then
    ' retrieve the information. With forms, you can open the
    ' form in hidden mode, at least.
```

VERIFY THAT OBJECTS USE CONSISTENT SETTINGS?

```
On Error GoTo DocumentForm_Err
Dim rstObj As Recordset
Dim rstProps As Recordset
Dim lngObjectID As Long
Dim frm As Form
Dim ctl As Control
Dim intI As Integer
Dim obj As Object
Dim db As Database

Call SysCmd(acSysCmdSetStatus, "Getting information on form " & _
  strName & ".")

Set db = CurrentDb()
' No need to open the form if it's THIS form.
If strName <> Me.Name Then
    DoCmd.OpenForm strName, View:=acDesign, WindowMode:=acHidden
End If
Set rstObj = db.OpenRecordset("zstblSubObjects", _
  dbOpenTable, dbAppendOnly)
Set rstProps = db.OpenRecordset("zstblProperties", _
  dbOpenTable, dbAppendOnly)

' Handle the form properties first.
Set frm = Forms(strName)
AddProps rstObj, rstProps, frm, "Form", lngParentID

' Handle the 5 possible form sections.
For intI = 0 To 4
    Set obj = frm.Section(intI)
    AddProps rstObj, rstProps, obj, "Section", lngParentID
Form_Next_Section:
  Next intI

' Handle all the controls.
For Each ctl In frm.Controls
    AddProps rstObj, rstProps, ctl, GetControlType(ctl), lngParentID
Next ctl

' Don't close the form that's running all this.
If Me.Name <> strName Then
    DoCmd.Close acForm, strName
End If

DocumentForm_Exit:
  Exit Sub

DocumentForm_Err:
  Select Case Err
      Case ahtcErrInvalidSection
          Resume Form_Next_Section
      Case Else
          MsgBox "Error: " & Error & " (" & Err & ")", _
            vbExclamation, "DocumentForm"
  End Select
  Resume Next
End Sub
```

The procedure starts by opening the requested object in design mode so it can get the information it needs. It cannot open the objects in normal view mode, because that would run the objects' event procedures, which might have unpleasant side-effects. Also, it's interesting to notice that OpenForm supports the WindowMode parameter, allowing you to open your hidden forms. OpenReport does not allow this, so DocumentReport also turns the screen display off and back on again, to avoid unsightly screen updates.

As shown in the example, if the code tries to open the current form, it simply skips the step. (This means, of course, that your documentation on the current form will be different than other forms: It's already open in Form view, and the rest will be opened in design view.) Skipping the current form isn't an issue if you're documenting reports. When it's complete, DocumentForm/Report also closes the object (as long as it wasn't the current form).

```
' No need to open the form if it's THIS form.
If strName <> Me.Name Then
    DoCmd.OpenForm strName, View:=acDesign, WindowMode:=acHidden
End If
.
. ' All the real work happens here...
.
' Don't close the form that's running all this.
If Me.Name <> strName Then
    DoCmd.Close acForm, strName
End If
```

As its next step, DocumentForm opens two recordsets, to which it adds rows as it documents your objects. These are specified as append-only recordsets in order to speed the processing.

```
Set rstObj = db.OpenRecordset("zstblSubObjects", _
  dbOpenTable, dbAppendOnly)
Set rstProps = db.OpenRecordset("zstblProperties", _
  dbOpenTable, dbAppendOnly)
```

Next, the procedure documents all the properties of the main object itself. As it will do when documenting all the objects, it calls the AddProps procedure, which expects to receive references to the two recordsets, a reference to the object to be documented, the text to appear in the list box for the object's type, and the ID value for the main, parent object.

```
' Handle the form properties first.
Set frm = Forms(strName)
AddProps rstObj, rstProps, frm, "Form", lngParentID
```

The procedure then documents the properties of the sections. For forms, there can be at most five sections (Detail, Form Header/Footer, Page Header/Footer). For reports, there can be up to 25: the same five as for forms, plus a header and footer for up to ten report grouping sections. Note that any section may or may not exist. Therefore, the code traps for this error and jumps on to the next numbered section if the current one doesn't exist.

```
' Handle the 5 possible form sections.
For intI = 0 To 4
    Set obj = frm.Section(intI)
    AddProps rstObj, rstProps, obj, "Section", lngParentID
Form_Next_Section:
  Next intI
```

Finally, DocumentForm/Report visits each of the controls on the form or report, calling AddProps with information about each control.

```
' Handle all the controls.
For Each ctl In frm.Controls
    AddProps rstObj, rstProps, ctl, GetControlType(ctl), lngParentID
Next ctl
```

Recording Property Information

The AddProps procedure, shown below, does the work of recording information about the selected object into zstblSubObject and about all its properties into zstblProperties. Note the large error-handling section; several properties of forms, reports, sections, and controls are not available in design mode, and attempting to retrieve those property values triggers a number of different error messages.

```
Private Sub AddProps(rstObj As Recordset, rstProps As Recordset, _
  obj As Object, ByVal strType As String, ByVal lngParentID As Long)
    Dim lngObjectID As Long
    Dim prp As Property

    On Error GoTo AddPropsErr

    With rstObj
        .AddNew
            !ParentID = lngParentID
            !ObjectName = obj.Name
            !ObjectType = strType
        .Update
        ' Make the newly modified row be the current row.
        .Move 0, .LastModified
        lngObjectID = !ObjectID
    End With
    With rstProps
        For Each prp In obj.Properties
            .AddNew
                !ObjectID = lngObjectID
                !PropName = prp.Name
                !PropType = prp.Type
                !PropValue = Left(prp.Value & "", 255)
            .Update
        Next prp
    End With

AddPropsExit:
    Exit Sub
```

continued on next page

continued from previous page

```
AddPropsErr:
    Select Case Err
        ' Some property values just aren't available in the design view.
        Case ahtcErrInvalidView, ahtcErrNotInThisView, _
            ahtcErrCantRetrieveProp, ahtcErrCantGetProp
            Resume Next
        Case Else
            MsgBox "Error: " & Error & " (" & Err & ")", _
                vbExclamation, "AddProps"
    End Select
    Resume AddPropsExit

End Sub
```

To add a row about the object to zstblSubObjects, the AddProps uses the AddNew method of the recordset, and then fills in the appropriate fields. When it's done, it uses the Update method to save the new row. Because the Update method does not make the new row the current row, AddProps also uses the Move method to make the last modified row the new current row, so the code can grab the counter value from the new row to be used as the object ID in the properties table.

```
With rstObj
    .AddNew
        !ParentID = lngParentID
        !ObjectName = obj.Name
        !ObjectType = strType
    .Update
    ' Make the newly modified row be the current row.
    .Move 0, .LastModified
    lngObjectID = !ObjectID
End With
```

Next, AddProps loops through all the properties in the object's Properties collection, adding a row for each to zstblProperties. Note that because tables don't support Variant fields, we've set the PropValue field to be a 255-character text field; the code converts the property value to be text and truncates it to no more than 255 characters.

```
With rstProps
    For Each prp In obj.Properties
        .AddNew
            !ObjectID = lngObjectID
            !PropName = prp.Name
            !PropType = prp.Type
            !PropValue = Left(prp.Value & "", 255)
        .Update
    Next prp
End With
```

All the Rest

The rest of the code in zsfrmVerifySettings' module deals with selecting items in the list box. You're welcome to peruse that code, if you need to, but it's not crucial to understanding the object/property inventory.

Getting the Results You Need

The final step in getting the information you need is manipulating the output data from zsqryProperties. As shown in the second example above, where you found all the command buttons that hadn't yet had their ControlTipText properties set, it's simply a matter of sorting and filtering until you get the objects and properties that you care about. The Records|Filter|Advanced Filter/Sort will make it easy to get the rows you need. You might also use Access 95's new Filter By Selection to help you out: Select the property you care about and click on the Filter By Selection toolbar button (the funnel with a lightning bolt) to limit the rows to just that property. You could then repeat this to limit the selection even further, choosing specific control types, and the like.

Comments

If you're interested in working with multiselect list boxes in your applications, take the time to work through the code that manipulates the list box in this example. The code uses the Selected property of the list box, setting various rows to be selected or not by setting the value of the property. It also makes heavy use of the Column property, allowing random access to any item stored in the list box.

More than most of the How-To's in this book, effective use of the techniques covered here requires some of your own imagination. Not only are the techniques for providing the object and property inventory interesting, but the output itself can be useful as well. Since we developed this example, we've used it in several applications to verify that all the controls used the same fonts, that all command buttons had their ControlTipText set, and that all detail sections used the same background color. You should strive for design consistency in your applications; this tool can help you achieve that.

COMPLEXITY:
INTERMEDIATE

4.4 How do I...
Really hide Access screen activity?

Problem

I can use a form's Painting property to disable updates to that form and the Application.Echo method to disable updates to the Access window, but some activities still seem to show through. For example, when I need to open up reports in design mode to alter print settings, the screen flashes a lot. Is there any way to *really* hide screen activity?

Technique

You've already exhausted the alternatives that Access provides for controlling the screen display. But there is one more alternative: Windows itself allows you to disable screen updates for a window and all its children. Because Access 95 makes it simple to retrieve the handle for the main Access window, you can disable all updates to that (or any other) window. This How-To demonstrates a method of truly shutting off screen updates to the Access window. (Before you try it, however, be sure to read the cautions in the Comments section.)

Steps

Load and run frmLockScreen (Figure 4-9) from 04-04.MDB. This sample form does nothing more than open three reports in design mode and then close them. (This is just the sort of thing you might do when changing the prtDevMode or prtMip property of a report; see Chapter 5.) The form includes a check box that allows you to run the test with screen updates enabled or disabled. Try it both ways; you should see a clear difference between the two ways of running the test. With the check box set, the underlying code disables screen updates, so you shouldn't see the reports' icons pop up. Without the check box set, you will see the icons.

To use the Windows API to disable screen updates in your own applications, follow these steps:

1. Include the module basLockScreen from 04-04.MDB. This module includes the API declarations and code to disable updates to the Access main window.

2. When you want to disable screen updates, call the ahtShowUpdates subroutine, passing a False value. To re-enable screen updates, call the subroutine again, passing it a True value.

```
Call ahtShowUpdates(False)
' Do your work in here...
Call ahtShowUpdates(True)
```

How It Works

The ahtShowUpdates subroutine (in basLockScreen) does its work by calling the Windows API function LockWindowUpdate (aliased as aht_apiLockWindowUpdate). This

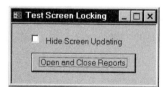

Figure 4-9 The sample form, frmLockScreen, ready to run its tests

function takes as its only parameter a window handle. If that handle is nonzero, Windows simply stops updating the contents of that window on screen. If the handle is 0, Windows re-enables screen updates to the locked window.

Because the only window you care about locking in Access is the main Access window itself, the ahtShowUpdates routine shields you from any of the details. If you pass it a False value, it blocks window updates. If you pass it a True value, it re-enables updates. It finds the Access window handle for you, if necessary, and then calls LockWindowUpdate.

```
Sub ahtShowUpdates (fShow As Integer)
   If fShow Then
      aht_apiLockWindowUpdate 0
   Else
      aht_apiLockWindowUpdate Application.hWndAccessApp
   End If
End Sub
```

Note

In previous versions of Access, finding the window handle (the unique integer that identifies every window) for the Access window was quite difficult. It required a good deal of work with multiple Windows API functions. In Access 95, the Application object exposes the hWndAccessApp property, which returns the window handle of the main Access window.

Comments

Though effective, this method of disabling screen updates isn't perfect. Because Access has no idea that you've "turned it off," Access itself occasionally turns screen updates on. For example, depending on how you open forms and reports in design mode, hiding the properties sheet completely may be very difficult. In the sample application, 04-04.MDB, the reports' properties sheet isn't showing. If you open one of the reports, open the properties sheet, and then save the report, no combination of Application.Echo and calls to LockWindowUpdate will completely remove that properties sheet form the screen when you open the report in design mode.

Hiding the Properties Sheet

If you really care about the visual problems caused by the properties sheet, you can make sure, from your application, that it's not displayed when your code opens a form or report. Be warned, however, that this method is totally undocumented, and is unsupported by Microsoft.

The Application object in Access supports the GetOption and SetOption methods, which allow you to get and set global options. Most of these options are documented (see the Online help topics for GetOption/SetOption). A few items are not documented but do useful work. One such option allows you to retrieve and set the coordinates for the form or report properties sheet, and to set whether or not you want the property sheet to be visible when you open a form or report in design mode.

To retrieve the information about the report properties sheet, use a call like this:

```
strInfo = Application.GetOption("_26")
```

This will retrieve a string containing information on the report properties sheet's location and whether or not to display it when you open a report in design mode. The string will be in this format:

```
open?;left;top;width;height;
```

For example, it might look like this:

```
1;510;433;835;683;
```

indicating that the property sheet will be visible when you load a report, and when it does show up, it'll be at 510, 433 with a width of 835 and a height of 683.

To make sure that your application doesn't show the properties sheet while it does its work, you can retrieve this property, set the first character to 0, and then save it. The code might look like this:

```
Dim strInfo As String
strInfo = Application.GetOption("_26")
strInfo = "0" & Mid(strInfo, 2)
Application.SetOption "_26", strInfo
```

The only way this will have any influence is if you call this code before you've loaded any reports in design mode. Access only looks at this information once, when it loads the properties sheet for the first time. Once it has loaded the properties sheet, it doesn't look at these values again. Every time you leave design mode, Access stores information about the properties sheet, so if you're going to try to set these values for the next time you start Access, make sure you do it when there's no report open in design mode. Otherwise, Access will override your settings when it saves them itself.

To use this technique for forms, use option "_24" instead. It's not nearly as useful with forms as it is with reports, however, because you can open hidden forms, but you cannot open hidden reports.

Beware the Pitfalls!

Be aware that, although setting Application.Echo to False does disable updates to the Access MDI Client window (the window that contains all the Access objects), setting it back to True causes a repaint of the entire Access MDI Client window. This is why, when you run the sample in 04-04.MDB with screen updates showing, you see the report icons appear at the bottom of the screen. Each time the code in ahtOpenReport opens a report, it sets Application.Echo back to True. As a generic routine, it must do this—any routine that turns off a screen display should turn it back on. The subroutine that calls ahtOpenReport, then, must surround the code with calls to ahtShowUpdates, turning off the entire display before opening the three reports, and turning it back on once all three reports are closed.

```
If Me!chkHideUpdates Then
    Call ahtShowUpdates(False)
End If
For intI = 1 To 3
    intSuccess = ahtOpenReport("rptReport" & intI, acDesign)
Next intI
' You could modify your reports in design mode here
' if you needed to.
For intI = 1 To 3
    DoCmd.Close acReport, "rptReport" & intI
Next intI
```

Throughout this book, we warn you of potential pitfalls involved in the techniques presented. Few actions have as much potential for disaster as turning off screen updates, and here's the advice.

Never Turn Off the Screen without an Error Handler!

Though this same advice goes for using Application.Echo or Form.Painting, it's especially true for using LockWindowUpdate. Any time you turn off the screen display, you absolutely must include an error handler in your routine that will immediately re-enable screen updates if an error occurs. Sooner or later, a runtime error *will* occur, and your code must react to this and clean up. Users tend to do unpleasant things, such as rebooting their computer when their screen stops dead (that's what would happen if an error occurred while you had screen updates turned off). This can be detrimental to their data and to your application, so never consider turning off the screen unless you also include an error handler to turn it back on.

As an example of an error handler that resets screen updates, the code executed by frmLockScreen handles errors by using the normal exit route from the routine.

```
Private Sub cmdOpenReports_Click()
    Dim intI As Integer
    Dim intSuccess As Integer

    On Error GoTo OpenReportsError
    If Me!chkHideUpdates Then
        Call ahtShowUpdates(False)
    End If
    For intI = 1 To 3
        intSuccess = ahtOpenReport("rptReport" & intI, acDesign)
    Next intI
    For intI = 1 To 3
        DoCmd.Close acReport, "rptReport" & intI
    Next intI
```

continued on next page

continued from previous page

```
OpenReportsExit:
    If Me!chkHideUpdates Then
        Call ahtShowUpdates(True)
    End If
    Exit Sub

OpenReportsError:
    Resume OpenReportsExit
End Sub
```

If an error occurs while this subroutine is active, the code will jump to the OpenReportsError label, and from there will resume at the OpenReportsExit label. The code will re-enable screen updates and then exit the routine. Your own code may not look exactly like this, but you must handle errors so that the screen never locks up when an error occurs.

COMPLEXITY:
INTERMEDIATE

4.5 How do I... Find out what language version of Access is installed?

Problem

I distribute my applications in several countries, and my users have different internationalized versions of Access installed. I'd like my applications to be able to make decisions based on the installed version of Access. How can I find out which language version of Access is currently running?

Technique

It would be very helpful if Access' SysCmd function returned information about the national language version, but it does not. You can use SysCmd to tell you which version *number* is running and whether it's a runtime version or not, but you'll need to go outside of Access to find the national language version. Luckily, the Access Wizards need this information, and there's a convenient entry point in the MSAU7032.DLL library (which ships with Access) that you can use to retrieve the information you need. This How-To demonstrates how you can gather the language information you need.

Steps

Load and run the form frmLanguage in 04-05.MDB. As it loads, it calls the necessary functions to determine the currently running version of Access. Figure 4-10 shows the form after it's been loaded into a retail German version of Microsoft Access for Windows 95, version 7.0.

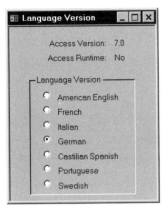

Figure 4-10 frmLanguage indicates the national language version of Access that's running

To include this functionality in your own applications, follow these steps:

1. Import the module basFileLanguage from 04-05.MDB into your own application. This module includes constants representing the seven most likely languages and the related function definitions you'll need.

2. Create a module or global variable, intLanguage, somewhere in your code. When your application starts up, make a call to ahtAccessLanguage, which will return a constant representing the current running version of Access. You can use the value of that variable throughout your application to make decisions based on the current language version of Access.

```
intLanguage = ahtAccessLanguage()
```

How It Works

Retrieving language information directly from Windows requires calling a Windows API function that is both difficult to call and returns a great deal more information than you need. The function mentioned in step 2, ahtAccessLanguage, calls directly into the Access-supplied library, MSAU7032.DLL, which calls the Windows API to retrieve the information it needs. Though this library is not documented, several How-To's in this chapter use it, and the Access Wizards use it to do their work. You have the right to distribute this DLL along with any runtime applications you create.

The DLL function, aliased in the declaration as aht_apiGetLanguage, does most of the work for you, and retrieves language version information that's stored with most Windows applications' executable files or DLLs. In this case, you use it to ask MSAIN300.DLL (one of the portions of Access itself that gets translated for national language versions) what it thinks the current version is.

Calling aht_apiGetLanguage

The call to aht_apiGetLanguage requires four parameters: two provide information about what you want, and two are filled in during the function call. The general syntax is as follows; Table 4-1 lists the parameters and their uses.

```
intRetval = aht_apiGetLanguage(strModuleOrFile, fFileOrModule, _
    intLang, intCharSet)
```

PARAMETER NAME	DATA TYPE	USAGE	INPUT/OUTPUT
strFileOrMod	String	Name of disk file or loaded module. Specify the disk file (MSAIN300.DLL) or loaded module (MSAIN300).	Input
fFileOrMod	Long	True if strFileOrMod is a disk file name, False if it's a loaded module name.	Input
intLang	Integer	Filled in with the current language value.	Output
intCodePage	Integer	Filled in with the current character set.	Output

Table 4-1 Parameters for aht_apiGetLanguage and their usage

The following two uses are functionally equivalent.

```
Const ahtcLangModule = False
Const ahtcLangFile = True

intRetval = aht_apiGetLanguage("MSAIN300.DLL", ahtcLangFile, _
    intLang, intCharSet)
intRetval = aht_apiGetLanguage("MSAIN300", ahtcLangModule, _
    intLang, intCharSet)
```

In the first case, the function looks for MSAIN300.DLL wherever Windows normally looks for DLLs (the current directory, the Windows directory, the Windows/System directory, the DOS path, etc.). In the second case, the function looks through all the running application modules for a loaded library with the specified name. Either version will work, though the first version requires that MSAIN300.DLL be available on disk in a place Windows can find it. You could use this same mechanism to investigate the language version of any Windows executable or DLL.

Return Values from aht_apiGetLanguage

The function fills in the values for both intLang, which tells you which language version the function found, and intCharSet, which tells you the Windows character set the application will use. Table 4-2 lists a few of the Windows languages and the ID values associated with them, though Access is generally available in only a few of these. If you need information about a language that's not listed here, you'll find a full list in many of the Windows 95 and Windows NT resource documents.

LANGUAGE	ID
American	1033
French (Standard)	1036
German (Standard)	1031
Italian (Standard)	1040
Spanish (Modern Sort)	3082
Spanish (Traditional Sort)	1034
Portuguese (Brazilian)	1046
Portuguese (Standard)	2070
Swedish	1053
Zulu	1078

Table 4-2 Windows languages and ID values

Table 4-3 lists some of the Windows character sets and their associated ID values. (The U.S. version of Access uses character set 1252, Windows Multilingual.) For more information, see the Windows 95 or Windows resource documentation,

DESCRIPTION	CHARACTER SET
737	Greek (formerly 437G)
855	IBM Cyrillic (primarily Russian)
857	IBM Turkish
862	Hebrew
864	Arabic
869	IBM Modern Greek
874	Thai
932	Japan
936	Chinese (PRC, Singapore)
949	Korean
950	Chinese (Taiwan, Hong Kong)
1026	EBCDIC
1200	Unicode (BMP of ISO 10646)
1250	Windows 3.1 Eastern European
1251	Windows 3.1 Cyrillic
1252	Windows 3.1 US (ANSI)
1253	Windows 3.1 Greek
1254	Windows 3.1 Turkish

continued on next page

continued from previous page

DESCRIPTION	CHARACTER SET
1255	Hebrew
1256	Arabic
1257	Baltic
1361	Korean (Johab)

 Table 4-3 Windows character sets and ID values

The simple function in basFileLanguage, ahtAccessLanguage, returns only the national language ID number (from Table 4-2) for the running copy of MSAIN300.DLL and disregards the character set value. Because you're likely to need only the language ID, that's all the function returns, for the sake of simplicity.

```
Function ahtAccessLanguage ()

Dim intRetval As Integer
    Dim intLang As Integer
    Dim intCharSet As Integer

    ' Fill in intLang and intCharSet
    intRetval = aht_apiGetLanguage("MSAIN300.DLL", ahtcLangFile, _
     intLang, intCharSet)
    ahtAccessLanguage = intLang
End Function
```

If you find that you need the character set also, you can modify this function, or write your own, that calls aht_apiGetLanguage directly.

Comments

Once you know the ID for the national language, you can make choices in your application. As shown in the next two How-To's, you can modify labels on forms and reports and modify the error messages that you display. However, you'll need to be acutely cautious of the use of the SendKeys action in your applications. Because the Access menus are different in every version of Access (the position and action of each menu stays constant, but the text and the menu hot keys change), you can't always count on your SendKeys statements to work. Most professional programmers using Access do anything they can to avoid using SendKeys. It makes VBA code difficult to read and maintain, and is prone to the troubles that can occur when you're running more than one application. If you find that you just can't avoid using SendKeys, at least make sure that you check the language and react accordingly. (Using the wrong keystrokes will, at best, do nothing. At worst, the keystrokes might do something completely different than what you intended, and could be potentially dangerous.) For example, you could use code like this to handle your SendKeys:

```
Dim strKeys as String
Select Case ahtAccessLanguage()
    Case conAmerican
        strKeys = "%vo"
```

```
        Case conFrench
            strKeys = "%ao"
        ' You fill in the rest...
    End Select
    SendKeys strKeys
```

If you find that you have several SendKeys instances in your application, consider storing the key strings in a table and using the lookup mechanism suggested in the next How-To to retrieve the strings, rather than using a Select Case statement each time.

The example form uses two functions from basAccessInfo in 04-05.MDB, ahtGetVersion and ahtIsRuntime. Both are quite simple, and each requires only a single call to the built-in SysCmd function. The first, ahtGetVersion, returns the version number of the currently running copy of Access. The second, ahtIsRuntime, returns True if your application is running in the runtime version of Access, or False if it's in the retail version. You may find these functions useful if your application needs to react differently to different environments.

```
Function ahtGetVersion()
    ' Retrieve the Access version for places
    ' that can't use symbolic constants.

    ahtGetVersion = SysCmd(acSysCmdAccessVer)
End Function

Function ahtIsRuntime()
    ' Use SysCmd() to gather the information.

    ahtIsRunTime = SysCmd(acSysCmdRuntime)
End Function
```

COMPLEXITY:
INTERMEDIATE

4.6 How do I...
Internationalize text in my applications?

Problem

I'd like to be able to pop up translated error messages in my applications, based on the currently running national language version of Access. I'd also like other text on my forms and reports to adjust automatically based on the current language version. I know there are a number of ways to do this, but I can't decide which is best. How should I store and retrieve messages in multiple languages?

Technique

The translated version of Access handles its own error messages (in the German version, for example, the Access error messages appear in German). But you do need to translate your own messages if you want your application to run smoothly in other languages. Though there are several methods for handling text, the most reasonable solution uses a table of messages, which you can look up by ID number.

Steps

Load and run the form frmTestMessage from 04-06.MDB. This form, shown in Figure 4-11, allows you to choose from three different languages (English, French, and Spanish) in an option group. As you choose each language, code attached to the option group's AfterUpdate event changes the captions for labels on the form and the status bar text for text boxes accordingly. To try a sample error message in the chosen language, click the Test Message button.

In each case, the messages are coming from the table tblMessages. This table includes a column for the message identifier (the primary key) and one column for each of the languages your application supports. Figure 4-12 shows the table, filled in for the sample application.

To include similar functionality in your own applications, follow these steps:

1. From 04-06.MDB, import the modules basFileLanguage (which includes the procedures from How-To 4.5 for obtaining the current language version of Access) and basGetMessages (which looks up particular messages in tblMessages).

2. From 04-06.MDB, import the table tblMessages. This is the table you'll use to hold your messages. Delete the existing rows, if you care to. Also, you can modify the structure and add more languages if you need to.

Figure 4-11 The sample form, frmTestMessage, showing the French test error message

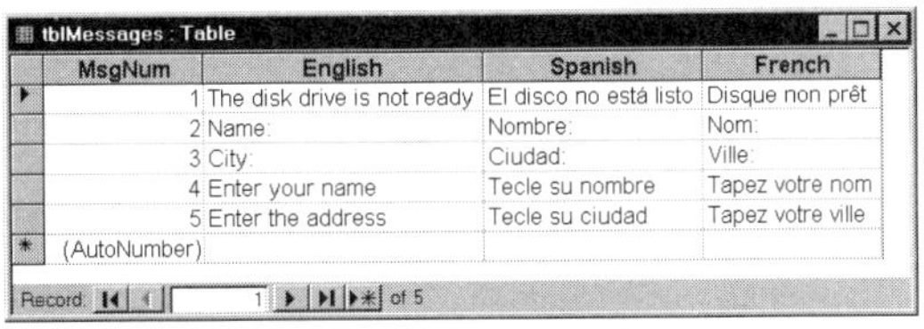
tblMessages : Table

MsgNum	English	Spanish	French
1	The disk drive is not ready	El disco no está listo	Disque non prêt
2	Name:	Nombre:	Nom:
3	City:	Ciudad:	Ville:
4	Enter your name	Tecle su nombre	Tapez votre nom
5	Enter the address	Tecle su ciudad	Tapez votre ville
(AutoNumber)			

Record: 1 of 5

Figure 4-12 The message table, tblMessages, filled in for the sample application 04-06.MDB

3. Add the necessary rows to tblMessages, filling in each column with the translated text, as shown in Figure 4-12.
4. On any form for which you'd like to have language-sensitive captions and status bar text, place the message ID (the MsgNum column from tblMessages) in the Tag property for the control whose text you'd like to change. For labels, the code you'll call is set up to change the Caption property; and for text boxes, the code is set up to change the StatusBarText property. (If you want to include other control types, you can modify the code in the subroutine GetInfo, as described in the How It Works section.)
5. To set the captions for labels and the status bar text for text boxes when your form loads, place the following code in the Open event procedure for your form.

```
Private Sub grpLanguage_AfterUpdate()
   ahtSetText Me, Me!grpLanguage.Value
End Sub
```

The ahtSetText subroutine walks through all the controls on your form, searching for ones with a numeric value in the Tag property. For any such controls, it looks up the appropriate message and assigns it to the Caption or StatusBarText property.

How It Works

The technique presented in this How-To includes two basic pieces of functionality: retrieving the correct messages from the table of messages and replacing all the required property values on your form or report. Together, these two operations accomplish the goals of changing labels and status bar text in addition to providing translated error messages.

The ahtGetMessage function retrieves the messages you need from tblMessages. You pass to it, as parameters, a long integer specifying the message number you want and an integer specifying the correct language.

```
Function ahtGetMessage(ByVal lngMessage As Long, _
 ByVal intLanguage As Integer) As Variant
```

continued on next page

continued from previous page

```
Dim rst As Recordset
Dim varLanguage As Variant
Dim varResult As Variant
Dim db As Database

On Error GoTo GetMessageError

Set db = CurrentDb()
varResult = Null
Set rst = db.OpenRecordset(ahtcMsgTable, dbOpenTable)
With rst
    If Not .EOF Then
        ' Set the index, which is the message number
        .Index = "PrimaryKey"
        .Seek "=", lngMessage
        If .NoMatch Then
            ' We're in BIG trouble!
            varResult = Null
        Else
            varLanguage = GetLanguageName(intLanguage)
            If Not IsNull(varLanguage) Then
                varResult = rst(varLanguage)
            Else
                varResult = Null
            End If
        End If
    End If
End With
GetMessageExit:
    If Not rst Is Nothing Then rst.Close
    ahtGetMessage = varResult
    Exit Function

GetMessageError:
    varResult = Null
    Resume GetMessageExit
End Function
```

This function starts by creating a table-type recordset based on tblMessages.

```
Set rst = db.OpenRecordset(ahtcMsgTable, dbOpenTable)
```

If there are any rows in tblMessages, the function attempts to seek the row you've requested. If it doesn't find a match, you must have requested a message number that's not in the table, so the function returns a null value.

```
With rst
    If Not .EOF Then
        ' Set the index, which is the message number
        .Index = "PrimaryKey"
        .Seek "=", lngMessage
        If .NoMatch Then
            ' We're in BIG trouble!
            varResult = Null
```

If it does find a match, it converts the language number into the table's column name for the language (using the GetLanguageName function). If it finds a language name, it retrieves the appropriate message from tblMessages.

```
    Else
        varLanguage = GetLanguageName(intLanguage)
        If Not IsNull(varLanguage) Then
            varResult = rst(varLanguage)
        Else
            varResult = Null
        End If
    End If
End With
```

If any error occurs along the way, ahtGetMessage returns a null value. If things work out, it returns the message it found in tblMessages.

You can call ahtGetMessage directly, perhaps to fill the text for a message box or to build up a more complex error string. In addition, the function that replaces the form text at load time calls it multiple times, once for each message. The ahtSetText subroutine does the work of replacing text when you load a form or report, and it uses ahtGetMessage to do its work.

The ahtSetText procedure takes two parameters, as shown in Table 4-4.

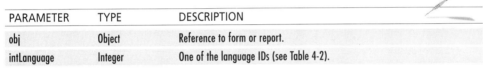

PARAMETER	TYPE	DESCRIPTION
obj	Object	Reference to form or report.
intLanguage	Integer	One of the language IDs (see Table 4-2).

 Table 4-4 The parameters for ahtSetText

This procedure will walk through all the controls on the requested form or report, calling the GetInfo function for each.

```
Dim ctl As Control

For Each ctl In obj.Controls
    GetInfo ctl, intLanguage
Next ctl
```

The GetInfo subroutine does the actual work; this is the procedure you'll need to change if you want to handle more than just labels' Caption properties and text boxes' StatusBarText properties. It checks the Tag property and, if it's numeric, looks up the associated text string in the appropriate language. Once it has the string, it checks the control type and places the string in the correct property for the given control type.

```
With ctl
    If IsNumeric(.Tag) Then
        varCaption = ahtGetMessage(.Tag, intLanguage)
        If Not IsNull(varCaption) Then
            Select Case .ControlType
                Case acLabel
                    .Caption = varCaption
```

continued on next page

continued from previous page

```
            Case acTextBox
                .StatusBarText = varCaption
          End Select
        End If
      End If
  End With
```

If you want to support more languages than just the three used in this example, you'll need to modify the structure of tblMessages, adding a new column for each new language, as well as modify the GetLanguageName procedure in the basGetMessage module. As it is now, GetLanguageName looks like this:

```
Private Function GetLanguageName(ByVal intLanguage As Integer) As
Variant
    ' Given a language identifier, get the
    ' column name in tblMessages that corresponds.

    ' This application only understands
    ' English, French and Spanish.

    Dim varLang As Variant

    Select Case intLanguage
       Case ahtcAmerican
          varLang = "English"
       Case ahtcFrench
          varLang = "French"
       Case ahtcCastilianSpanish
          varLang = "Spanish"
    End Select
    GetLanguageName = varLang
End Function
```

Add more Cases to the Select Case statement, matching the new columns in your messages table. The constants (ahtcAmerican, ahtcFrench, etc.) come from the module basFileLanguage. You can add more, from Table 4-2, if you need to.

Comments

The method suggested here will only work for forms that do not contain a large number of controls needing dynamic translation. Attempting to modify the properties of several hundred controls would prohibitively increase load time for a form. For forms that contain more than just a few controls, you might be better off creating multiple versions of the form, one per language, and distributing translated versions of your application.

Another problem you should consider when attempting to modify captions "on the fly" is that most non-English languages take more space to present the same information. You'll find that some languages require twice as much space (or more) for a given text string. This may mean that dynamic translation isn't feasible due to real-estate problems. Again, the best solution is to plan the translated versions carefully and prepare a different set of forms and reports for each language.

Message boxes don't present such a problem, of course, because Access resizes them automatically to fit the data you send to them. The same goes for ControlTipText. Call the ahtGetMessage function to provide the text for any text box you wish to fill, as in this example.

```
varRetval = MsgBox(ahtGetText(intLanguage, 1), _
  vbExclamation, ahtGetText(intLanguage, 2))
```

You can use this same technique to alter any messages within your application at runtime. If you want to provide different levels of help for different users, you could keep all your messages in a table, and retrieve the correct help messages depending on the current user. Rather than looking up language names, in this case, you'd be looking up user or group names.

COMPLEXITY:
INTERMEDIATE

4.7 How do I... Change and reset the Access caption bar?

Problem

I'd like to be able to change the caption of the main Access window as part of my application. Of course, I need to be able to reset it back to its original value when I'm done. I've found the AppTitle property in Access, but I just can't get it to work. Is there some simple way to retrieve and set the Access caption, as I can with any of the windows within Access?

Technique

It's funny: This is one situation where it's simpler to use the Windows API than it is to use the built-in functionality. Although Access does provide a property of the current database, AppTitle, that you can use to set and retrieve the Access title bar, it's clumsy to use because AppTitle is a user-defined property. With the Windows API, retrieving and setting the Access caption both require a few steps, but neither process is terribly difficult. This How-To demonstrates the steps to set and retrieve the Access caption.

Steps

To try changing the Access caption, load and run frmSetCaption from 04-07.MDB. The form displays the current Access caption. By filling in a new value in the New Access Caption text box and selecting the Set New Caption button, you can change the caption on the main Access window. Figure 4-13 shows the form once it's already done its work. Press the Reset Caption button when you're done to reset the Access caption.

Figure 4-13 The sample form, frmSetCaption, after it's set the new Access caption

To include this functionality in your own applications, follow these steps:

1. Import the module basCaption (which supplies the necessary Windows API declarations and the interface routines) from 04-07.MDB.

2. To retrieve the current Access caption, call the ahtGetAccessCaption function. For example:

```
strOldCaption = ahtGetAccessCaption()
```

3. To set a new Access caption, call the ahtSetAccessCaption subroutine, passing to it a string that holds your new caption.

```
ahtSetAccessCaption "Peter's Pet Palace"
```

4. To set the caption of any window, given its window handle, call aht_apiSetWindowText directly.

```
aht_apiSetWindowText hWnd, "Your New Caption"
```

How It Works

To retrieve the Access window caption, call the ahtGetAccessCaption function, which passes the Access window handle (Application.hWndAccessApp) to the more generalized ahtGetWindowCaption function, which does its work in three steps.

1. It sizes a string buffer large enough to hold all the characters, using the built-in Space function.

2. It calls the Windows API function GetWindowText (aliased as aht_apiGetWindowText) to fill the buffer with the actual window caption. GetWindowText returns the number of characters it filled in.

3. It uses the built-in Left function to remove extra characters.

```
Function ahtGetWindowCaption (ByVal hWnd As Integer) As Variant

    ' Get any window's caption, given its hWnd.
```

```
Dim intLen As Integer
Dim strBuffer As String

Const ahtcMaxLen = 255

If hWnd <> 0 Then
    strBuffer = Space(ahtcMaxLen)
    intLen = aht_apiGetWindowText(hWnd, strBuffer, ahtcMaxLen)
    ahtGetWindowCaption = Left(strBuffer, intLen)
End If
End Function
```

To set the Access caption, you call the ahtSetAccessCaption subroutine, passing to it the new caption you'd like to use. This procedure is much simpler than the previous one: It passes the Access window handle and the caption to the SetWindowText API procedure (aliased as aht_apiSetWindowText).

```
Sub ahtSetAccessCaption (ByVal strCaption As String)

    ' Set the Access caption to be the value in strCaption.
    Call aht_apiSetWindowText(Application.hWndAccessApp, strCaption)
End Sub
```

Comments

Access does provide a built-in mechanism for setting the caption to be used while a specific database is loaded: the Tools|Startup dialog box, shown in Figure 4-14. Using this dialog box, you can set many of the startup options you'll need to deliver any application: the startup form, titlebar, icon, shortcut menu bar, and global menu bar. You can set environment settings as well, such as displaying the database window at startup, displaying the status bar, using built-in toolbars or allowing toolbar changes.

The AppTitle property allows you to set the database's title bar, and the AppIcon property allows you to set an icon for the application. Both are really intended to be set using the user-interface, but you can modify them programmatically, as long as you remember that they're not built-in properties of the database. You must first create the properties and append them to the collection of properties; then you'll be able to use them. (For more information on creating user-defined properties, see How-To 7.9.)

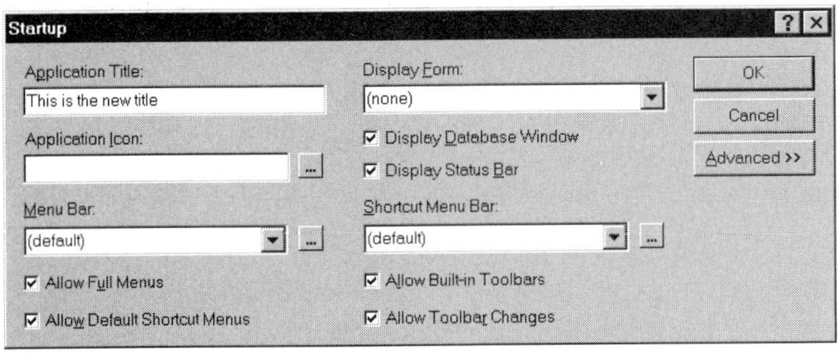

Figure 4-14 Use the Tools|Startup dialog box to set application startup options

For example, you could use code like this to set the title bar (you must use a procedure like this if you want to set the database's AppTitle property, which using the Windows API methods discussed earlier will not):

```
Sub ahtSetTitlebar(strTitle As String)
    Dim prp As Property
    Dim db As Database

    On Error Resume Next
    Set db = CurrentDB()
    db.Properties!AppTitle = strTitle
    If Err <> 0 Then
        Set prp = db.CreateProperty("AppTitle", dbText, strTitle)
        db.Properties.Append prp
    End If
    ' If you want the titlebar to change right now,
    ' refresh it.
    Application.RefreshTitleBar
    On Error Goto 0
End Sub
```

To retrieve the title bar, use a procedure like this:

```
Function ahtGetTitlebar()
    Dim strTitle as String

    On Error Resume Next
    Dim db As Database
    Set db = CurrentDb()
    strTitle = db.Properties!AppTitle
    If Err <> 0 Then
        ahtGetTitleBar = "Microsoft Access"
    Else
        ahtGetTitleBar = strTitle
    End if
    On Error Goto 0
End Function
```

What are the trade-offs? The Windows API requires less code, runs faster, and works with applications besides Access (if you can get a window handle, you can set the caption). The AppTitle property actually sets the database's property persistently, so the next time you load the database, that title is set for you. It takes a bit more work to use the non-API Access method, but it does allow you to preserve the setting for your next session.

One final note: The Windows API allows you to set the caption to be an empty string. You cannot set the Access AppTitle property to be an empty string; Access will reject it. If you want to remove the text from the title bar altogether, use the API method.

Create Your Own Splash Screen

The Tools|Startup menu does not provide a method by which you can supply your own startup bitmap image. If you want to supply your own bitmap splash screen to use rather than Access' built-in image, you can place a bitmap file (*.BMP) in the same directory as your application with the same name as your application. When you double-click on your MDB file to start it, or create a shortcut that starts it, Access will find your bitmap and use that as your startup splash screen. If you want no splash screen at all, simply create a single-pixel bitmap (use a light color for that single pixel) so small that no one will notice it as Access displays it.

COMPLEXITY:
ADVANCED

4.8 How do I...
Use the Windows File Open/Save common dialog boxes?

Problem

I need to allow users to choose file names for opening and saving files. I know that Windows supports a common way to get these names. How can I use this mechanism from within Access?

Technique

Not only can you use the common File Open/Save dialog boxes, but you have three choices. You can use the OLE control, COMMDLG.OCX, that ships with the Access Developer's Toolkit (ADT); you can call a function in MSAU7032.DLL, which is how the Wizards show the dialog boxes; or you can call the Windows API directly. If you don't have the ADT, the first suggestion won't help. MSAU7032.DLL's interface for using these dialog boxes is a bit simpler than doing the work from scratch, but it's also quite limiting (you only get a few options). Thus, this How-To shows how to call the Windows API directly and lists all the options you have when using these common dialog boxes.

Steps

Open and run the form frmTestOpenSave from 04-08.MDB. This sample form allows you to set various flags (described later in this How-To) and try out the settings. You can try both the File Save and File Open common dialog boxes. Try changing some of the settings and see what happens. Figure 4-15 shows the File Open dialog box with

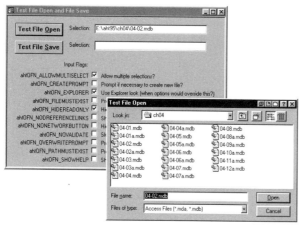

Figure 4-15 The sample form, frmTestOpenSave,
showing the File Open dialog box in use

the Read-Only check box hidden, and allowing for multiple selections, displayed in Explorer mode (as opposed to the older Program Manager look, which is what Windows will use if you specify the multiselect option by itself).

To use this functionality within your own applications, follow these steps:

1. Import the module basCommonFile from 04-08.MDB into your own application. This module provides the type and API function declarations you'll need and the wrapper functions that make it easy for you to use the common dialog boxes.

2. To use the File Open or File Save dialog boxes, call the ahtCommonFileOpenSave function, passing to it information indicating what you want it to do. Table 4-5 lists the options available when you call the function. None of the parameters is required; the table lists the default values the function will use if you leave off each of the parameters. As a simple example, the following function call will ask for the name of the file you'd like to save to, suggesting FOO.TXT, returning the full path of the file you choose.

```
varFileName = ahtCommonFileOpenSave(FileName:="FOO.TXT", OpenFile:=False)
```

Note

Because the ahtCommonFileOpenSave function accepts so many optional parameters, and you'll generally only care to set a few of them, you may find VBA's support for named parameters useful. That is, rather than depending on the exact order of the parameters you send to ahtCommonFileOpenSave, use the name of the parameter, a ":=" and then the value, as we've done in the example. This will make your code easier to read and far less error prone.

PARAMETER NAME	DESCRIPTION	DEFAULT VALUE
Flags	A combination of 0 or more flags from Table 4-6 that control the operation of the dialog box. Combine them using the OR operator.	0
InitialDir	The initial directory that the dialog box should use.	""
Filter	A string listing the available file filters. Use ahtAddFilter, as shown in the examples, to build this parameter. The format of this item is very important, so make sure to use the function, rather than just setting the value by hand.	""
FilterIndex	The number of the filter item to use when the dialog box first opens. The first filter is numbered 1.	1
DefaultExt	A default file extension to be appended to the file name if the user doesn't supply one. Don't include a period.	""
FileName	The file name to use when the dialog box is first displayed.	""
DialogTitle	Title for the dialog box. Usually you won't specify this parameter.	Open/Save As
hWnd	Window handle for the parent window of the dialog box. This value controls where the dialog box will be placed.	Application.hWndAccessApp
OpenFile	Open or Save dialog box? (True = Open, False = Save).	True

Table 4-5 Parameters for the ahtCommonFileOpenSave function (all optional)

3. If you want to also specify filter choices that show up in the Files of type: combo box on the dialog box, call the ahtAddFilterItem function. This function accepts three parameters: the string of filters to which you want to add items, the description for your filter ("Databases (*.mdb, *.mda)", for example), and the actual filter file specifications, delimited with a semicolon ("*.mda;*.mda", to match the previous example). The function returns the new filter string. You can call ahtAddFilterItem as many times as you need to build up your list of filters. For example, the following example (similar to the example in basCommonFile) sets up four filter expressions. You can call TestIt from the Debug Window in Access to test out the filters.

```
Function TestIt()
    Dim strFilter As String
```

continued on next page

continued from previous page

```
    strFilter = ahtAddFilterItem(strFilter, "Access Files (*.mda, *.mdb)", _
      "*.MDA;*.MDB")
    strFilter = ahtAddFilterItem(strFilter, "dBASE Files (*.dbf)", "*.DBF")
    strFilter = ahtAddFilterItem(strFilter, "Text Files (*.txt)", "*.TXT")
    strFilter = ahtAddFilterItem(strFilter, "All Files (*.*)", "*.*")

    MsgBox "You selected: " & ahtCommonFileOpenSave(InitialDir:="C:\", _
      Filter:=strFilter, FilterIndex:=3, DialogTitle:="Hello! Open Me!")
End Function
```

4. You may want to specify some of the available options for controlling the common dialog boxes, as shown in frmTestOpenSave. You can specify any of the options shown there, and more, when you call the function. To specify your selected options, choose values from the items in Table 4-6, combine them together with the OR operator, and send this value to the ahtCommonFileOpenSave function as the Flags parameter. For example, the following statement will build up a flags value that tells Windows to hide the Read Only check box and the Network button and that the output path must already exist.

```
lngFlags = ahtOFN_HIDEREADONLY Or ahtOFN_NONETWORKBUTTON Or _
  ahtOFN_PATHMUSTEXIST
```

How It Works

When you call ahtCommonFileOpenSave, you're actually calling the GetOpenFileName or GetSaveFileName Windows API functions. The ahtCommonFileOpenSave function just takes the parameters you send it, replacing missing ones with the default values shown in Table 4-5, and fills in a user-defined data structure that both API functions expect to receive. The API functions actually do the work, and ahtCommonFileOpenSave returns to you the chosen file name. Although you may find it interesting to dig into the details of calling the API functions directly, that's beyond the scope of this How-To. The wrapper function, ahtCommonFileOpenSave, handles a large majority of the cases where you'll need to use common File Open/Save dialog boxes.

Table 4-6 lists all the values you can use in the Flags parameter of the call to ahtCommonFileOpenSave. You can skip the parameter altogether, or you can use one or more of these values, combined with the OR operator. For example, to hide the Read Only check box and allow multiple files to be selected, use this code:

```
lngFlags = ahtOFN_HIDEREADONLY Or ahtOFN_ALLOWMULTISELECT
```

Not all of the flags make sense for both File Open and File Save operations, of course. Your best bet is to experiment with the flags, using the sample form frmTestOpenSave from 04-08.MDB or in your own code.

Some of the flags are only useful on return from the function call. For example, if you select the Read-Only check box on the common dialog box, Windows passes that fact back to you in the Flags parameter. To retrieve that information from your call to ahtCommonFileOpenSave, make sure to pass the Flags parameter in a variable, not directly as a literal value. Because ahtCommonFileOpenSave accepts the Flags parameter by reference, it can return to your calling procedure the value after you've selected a file name. To check to see if a particular flag value was set during the call to ahtCommonFileOpenSave, use the AND operator with the return value, as in this example fragment (see How-To 11.1 for more information on using the AND and OR operators).

```
Dim lngFlags As Long
Dim varFileName As Variant

lngFlags = 0
varFileName = ahtCommonFileOpenSave(Flags:=lngFlags)
If lngFlags AND ahtOFN_READONLY  0 Then
    ' The user checked the Read-Only check box.
End if
```

CONSTANT NAME	ON INPUT	ON OUTPUT
ahtOFN_ALLOWMULTISELECT	Allow you to select more than one file name (File Open only).	The strFile member will contain the chosen path followed by all the files within that path that were chosen, separated with spaces, as in C:\ File1.TXT File2.TXT.
ahtOFN_CREATEPROMPT	Prompts you if the selected file doesn't exist, allowing you to go on or make a different choice.	
ahtOFN_EXPLORER	Creates an Open or Save As dialog box that uses user-interface features similar to the Windows Explorer.	
ahtOFN_EXTENSIONDIFFERENT		Set if the chosen file name has a different extension than that supplied in the DefaultExt parameter.
ahtOFN_FILEMUSTEXIST	Forces you to supply only existing file names.	
ahtOFN_HIDEREADONLY	Hides the Read-Only check box.	
ahtOFN_LONGNAMES	Causes the Open or Save As dialog box to display long file names. If this flag is not specified, the dialog box displays file names in 8.3 format. This value is ignored if OFN_EXPLORER is set.	
ahtOFN_NOCHANGEDIR		Restores the current directory to its original value if the user changed the directory while searching for files.

continued on next page

continued from previous page

CONSTANT NAME	ON INPUT	ON OUTPUT
ahtOFN_NODEREFERENCELINKS		Returns the path and file name of the selected shortcut (.LNK) file. If you don't use this flag, the dialog box returns the path and file name of the file referenced by the shortcut.
ahtOFN_NOLONGNAMES	Specifies that long file names are not displayed in the File Name list box. This value is ignored if OFN_EXPLORER is set.	
ahtOFN_NONETWORKBUTTON	Don't show the Network button on the dialog box.	
ahtOFN_NOREADONLYRETURN		Specifies that the returned file does not have the Read-Only check box checked and is not in a write-protected directory.
ahtOFN_NOTESTFILECREATE	Normally, COMMDLG.DLL tests to make sure that you'll be able to create the file when you choose a file name for saving. If set, it doesn't test, providing no protection against common disk errors.	
ahtOFN_NOVALIDATE	Disables file name validation. Normally, Windows checks the chosen file name to make sure it's a valid name.	
ahtOFN_OVERWRITEPROMPT	Issues a warning if you select an existing file for a File Save As operation.	
ahtOFN_PATHMUSTEXIST	Forces you to supply only valid path names.	
ahtOFN_READONLY	Forces the Read-Only check box to be checked.	Set if the user checked the Read-Only check box.
ahtOFN_SHAREAWARE	Ignores sharing violations. Because Access code cannot handle the errors that occur when sharing violations occur in this code, you should not set this flag.	
ahtOFN_SHOWHELP	Shows a Help button on the dialog box. Though this option works, the button will not, so its use in Access is limited.	

Table 4-6 Values that can be combined in the Flags member of the tagOPENFILENAME structure

If you pass a variable to ahtCommonFileOpenSave containing the Flags information (rather than not sending the parameter, or sending a literal value), the function will return, to the caller, information about what happened while the dialog box was in use. Several of the flags listed in Table 4-6 provide information on output. That is, you can check the state of the Flags variable, and if it contains the flags from Table 4-6, you know that the tested condition was true. For example, to open a file and then check to see if the selected file is to be opened read-only, you could use code like this:

```
Dim lngFlags As Long
Dim varRetval As Variant

varRetval = ahtCommonFileOpenSave(Flags:=lngFlags)
If Not IsNull(varRetval) Then
    If lngFlags AND ahtOFN_READONLY Then
        MsgBox "You opened the file read-only!"
    End If
End If
```

As you can see in the example, use the AND operator to check to see if the flags contain the specific flag you care about.

Comments

The file filter (the Filter parameter to ahtCommonFileOpenSave) has a unique format: It consists of pairs of strings. Each item is terminated with vbNullChar (Chr$(0)). The first item in the pair supplies the text portion, which appears in the combo box in the lower-left of the dialog box. The second item supplies the file specifications that Windows uses to filter the list of files. Though it doesn't matter what you use in the first item, by convention, most applications use something like this:

```
Oogly Files (*.oog)
```

listing the file description. The conventional file specification looks something like this:

```
*.oog
```

To make it easier to build these filter strings, use the ahtAddFilterItem function from basCommonFile. See step 3 for an example.

Take the time to study all the parameters in Table 4-5 and all the options in Table 4-6. There's not room here to go into detail for each one, so your best bet is to try them all out. You can play with frmTestOpenSave to try out the effects of some of the flag values. See what happens when you place a value into one of them, and then experiment from there.

Although you have no direct control over the placement of the common dialog boxes, when they pop up, the choice of the parent window can affect the location. If you use pass 0, Application.hWndAccessApp, or a normal form's hWnd property for the hWnd parameter to ahtCommonFileOpenSave (or just don't send a value, so it uses the default value), the dialog box will appear in the upper-left corner of the Access MDI client window. If, on the other hand, you pass it the hWnd property of a pop-up form, Windows will place the dialog box in the upper-left corner of that pop-up form *even if the form's not visible.* Therefore, for complete control over the placement of the dialog box, create a form, set its Pop-up property to True, and use that form to place the dialog box.

Finally, remember that these dialog boxes don't actually *do* anything. They just supply you with the names of files: It's up to your application code to open or save the requested files.

COMPLEXITY:
ADVANCED

4.9   How do I...
Use the Windows color-choosing common dialog box?

Problem

I'd like to be able to select colors for objects in my applications while the application is running. I know that Windows provides a standard interface for choosing colors. How can I use this standard interface from within my applications? I'd also like to find a way that I can use the standard Windows system colors in my applications; that is, if the user changes the standard background color, I'd like my forms to use that same color.

Technique

Once again, the Access Wizard developers have made your life simpler. The MSAU7032.DLL library includes a simple interface for you to use, allowing quick access to the standard Windows color-choosing dialog box. This How-To demonstrates the use of this dialog box and explains all the options available to your application.

Color values, in Windows, are stored as the combination of their red, green, and blue (RGB) color values, ranging from 0 to 255 (&hFF in hexadecimal) for each. For example, &hFF0000 (16711680) is solid blue, &h00FF00 (65280) is solid green, and &h0000FF (255) is solid red. Combining full red and blue, &hFF00FF (16711935), gives you bright purple. To try these out, enter either the hexadecimal values (preceded by the characters &h) or the decimal values given in the examples above into the BackColor property of a label control. When you call the common dialog box, it returns the long integer representing the color you've chosen and an array of 16 long integers representing the custom colors you've created.

Steps

To test the color-choosing dialog box, load and run frmChooseColors in 04-09.MDB. This form, shown in Figure 4-16, allows you to choose the foreground and background colors for a test label, as well as the background color for the form. In addition, it shows

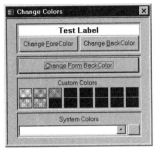

Figure 4-16
frmChooseColors allows
you to test the color-
choosing common
dialog box

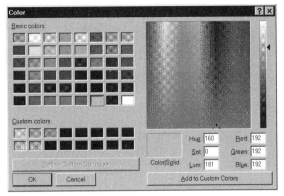

Figure 4-17 The Windows common color-
choosing dialog box

you the custom colors you might have created and demonstrates the use of the standard Windows system colors. The following steps separate the use of color into three topics: retrieving colors using the dialog box, using the custom colors, and setting colors to match the Windows system colors.

Retrieving Colors Using the Common Dialog Box

The Windows common color-choosing dialog box allows you to select a color from 48 basic colors or from up to 16 custom colors. Once you've opened the dialog box, select the Define Custom Colors button. From these options, select the hue, saturation, and luminosity (HSL) of a custom color, and then add the color to your selected list of up to 16 colors. (As you'll see in How It Works, you can disable the creation of custom colors when you call the common dialog.) Figure 4-17 shows the dialog box in action.

To use the Windows common color-choosing dialog box to retrieve color selections in your applications, follow these steps:

1. Import the module basPickColors from 04-09.MDB. This module includes the constant declarations and functions you'll need to access the code in MSAU7032.DLL.

2. At the point in your application where you want to pop up the common dialog, call the ahtPickColor function, passing to it the color you'd like to have chosen when the dialog first appears. For example, to call the dialog box with the color of the current controls text selected, use this code:

```
Dim ctl as Control
Set ctl = Screen.ActiveControl
ctl.ForeColor = ahtPickColor(ctl.ForeColor)
```

If you need more control over options, or if you want to use a different window as the owner of the dialog box, you can call the function aht_apiGetColor

233

yourself, rather than calling the ahtPickColor function. See the How It Works section for more information.

Using the Custom Colors

When you create custom colors in the common dialog box, Windows sends those color values back to you as part of the data structure you passed in to the dialog box. They're stored as an array of long integers, one for each of the 16 colors (with 0 representing black, or no choice at all).

If you call ahtPickColor to select a color value, you can retrieve the custom color values by calling the ahtGetCustom subroutine in basPickColors. (If you call aht_apiGetColor, see How It Works for information on the data structure and the array of custom colors it contains.)

To retrieve the custom colors after you call ahtPickColor, follow these steps:

1. Create an array of long integers in your own code.

```
Dim alngCustom(16) As Long
```

2. Call the ahtGetCustom subroutine, passing to it your array.

```
Call ahtGetCustom(alngCustom())
```

3. On return from the subroutine call, use the values in alngCustom as you need. The sample form displays them in the 16 text boxes, using this subroutine in the form's module to place their values in the correct control's properties.

```
Private Sub FillInCustom()
   ReDim alngColors(1 To 16) As Long
   Dim intI As Integer

   ahtGetCustom alngColors()
   For intI = LBound(alngColors) To UBound(alngColors)
      Me("txtCustom" & intI).BackColor = alngColors(intI)
   Next intI
End Sub
```

Setting Colors to Match the Windows System Colors

Windows supports 25 system colors (the active window colors, desktop colors, button colors, etc.) that you can set by choosing the Appearance tab of the Display Properties dialog box for the Windows desktop. Sometimes you may want to have your application match those standard Windows colors. To allow this, Access supports special color numbers, one for each of the standard Windows colors.

To see these colors on an Access form, choose a color from the System Colors box at the bottom of frmChooseColors (see Figure 4-16). The code attached to this combo box's AfterUpdate event will place the appropriate color in the text box to the right of the combo box.

To use a Windows system color in your own applications, choose a value from the list shown in Table 4-7, filling in either the ForeColor or BackColor property of any form or report section or any control. You can use either the decimal or the hexadecimal value to set the property.

DESCRIPTION	HEX VALUE	COLOR SETTING
3D Dark Shadow	&H80000015&	−2147483627
3D Light Shadow	&H80000016&	−2147483626
Active border	&H8000000A&	−2147483638
Active title bar	&H80000002&	−2147483646
Active title bar text	&H80000009&	−2147483639
Application workspace	&H8000000C&	−2147483636
Button face	&H8000000F&	−2147483633
Button highlight	&H80000014&	−2147483628
Button shadow	&H80000010&	−2147483632
Button text	&H80000012&	−2147483630
Desktops	&H80000001&	−2147483647
Disabled text	&H80000011&	−2147483631
Highlight	&H8000000D&	−2147483635
Highlighted text	&H8000000E&	−2147483634
Inactive border	&H8000000B&	−2147483637
Inactive title bar	&H80000003&	−2147483645
Inactive title bar text	&H80000013&	−2147483629
Info Background	&H80000018&	−2147483624
Info Text	&H80000017&	−2147483625
Menu bar	&H80000004&	−2147483644
Menu text	&H80000007&	−2147483641
Scroll bars	&H80000000&	−2147483648
Window background	&H80000005&	−2147483643
Window frame	&H80000006&	−2147483642
Window text	&H80000008&	−2147483640

Table 4-7 Windows system colors and the properties sheet settings to use them in Access

How It Works

Your applications can call ahtPickColor to use the color-choosing common dialog box. If you're interested in how it works, though, you'll have to dig a bit deeper. Though you can call directly into the Windows API to use the color-choosing dialog box, the interface in MSAU7032.DLL is a lot easier. Using this simplified interface is just a matter of filling values into a user-defined data structure and calling the aht_apiGetColor function. This causes the dialog box to pop up. When you're done with the dialog box, the function returns the chosen value to you (along with some other information in the data structure).

The data structure itself (the type name is aht_tagGetColorInfo) has several fields that you can fill in and retrieve values from. Table 4-8 describes all the members of the structure.

FIELD NAME	DATA TYPE	DESCRIPTION
hWndOwner	Long	The handle of the dialog box's owner (parent). Either the value returned from Application.hWndAccessApp or 0 (or blank) to have Windows use 0 (the dialog box will be owned by the screen, and you will be able to switch freely from this dialog box to any other window in any application). Using the Access window handle will keep you from switching to any other Access window while the dialog box is up.
rgbResult	Long	Color selection after the dialog box has been dismissed. If the ahtCC_RGBINIT flag is also set in the Flags field, then place the initial color setting in this field.
Flags	Long	A combination of 0 or more flags from Table 4-9 that control the operation of the dialog box. Combine them using the OR operator.
rgCustColors(16)	Long	Storage for 16 custom colors, as defined by the user. To preserve the colors between invocations of your program, store the 16 colors in an INI file and retrieve them at program startup.

Table 4-8 Members of the aht_tagGetColorInfo structure

The Flags member of the aht_tagGetColorInfo structure can contain combinations of different values from Table 4-9, controlling how the color-choosing dialog box operates.

CONSTANT NAME	DESCRIPTION
ahtCC_RGBINIT	Use the color in the rgbResult field to initialize the dialog box.
ahtCC_FULLOPEN	The full dialog box, including the custom color portion, should be open when the dialog box first appears.
ahtCC_PREVENTFULLOPEN	Only the left side of the dialog box will be available (you won't be able to create custom colors).

Table 4-9 Values that can be combined in the Flags member of the aht_tagGetColorInfo structure

Retrieving Colors Using the Common Dialog Box

The function mentioned in the Steps section above, ahtPickColor, calls the DLL function aht_apiGetColor to do its work. First ahtPickColor fills in the default color field, then it sets the owner's window handle and the flags field; finally it calls aht_apiGetColor.

On return from the function call, the rgbResult field of the aht_tagGetColorInfo structure will hold the color you chose.

```
Function ahtPickColor(ByVal lngCurrentColor As Long) As Long

    ' Pick a color, and return its value, along with
    ' the current set of 16 custom colors.
    '
    Dim lngRetval As Long

    gci.rgbResult = lngCurrentColor
    gci.hwndOwner = Application.hWndAccessApp
    gci.Flags = ahtCC_RGBINIT
    lngRetval = aht_apiGetColor(gci)
    ahtPickColor = IIf(lngRetval = 0, gci.rgbResult, -1)
End Function
```

If you need more control over the Flags field, or would like to use a different parent for the dialog box (rather than the Access main window), you can rewrite this function for your own needs.

Using the Custom Colors

On return from the call to aht_apiGetColor, the aht_tagGetColorInfo's array of custom colors, the rgCustColors member, will hold a value for each of the 16 possible custom colors. The basPickColors module defines a module global variable, gci, of type aht_tagGetColorInfo, that it uses when it pops up the color-choosing dialog box. Because the variable is global only in its module, however, it's not available from outside the module. To make the array of custom colors available to outside procedures, the module includes a subroutine, ahtGetCustom, that will copy the values from the global variable, gci, to an array you pass to the subroutine. (See Using the Custom Colors, step 3.)

```
Sub ahtGetCustom(aCustomColors() As Long)

    ' Retrieve the custom color array from the module
    ' global variable, gci.

    Dim intI As Integer

    For intI = LBound(aCustomColors) To UBound(aCustomColors)
        aCustomColors(intI) = gci.rgCustColors(intI)
    Next intI
End Sub
```

Comments

If you want to preserve the custom-color choices for future sessions of your application, you can write them out to the Registry, using the techniques shown in Chapter 2. One solution might be to loop through them all, building up a single string, separating the values with a single space, and then storing that long string as a single item in your Registry.

You can control the placement of this dialog box, when it first pops up, by sending in an appropriate value in the hWndOwner field. See the information in the Comments section of the previous How-To for more information.

Changes made to controls' colors (as in the sample form, frmChooseColors) while the form is in any mode besides design mode won't be saved with the form. Access keeps two sets of control properties: one that's permanently set, at design time, and a temporary set, copied from the permanent values every time you run the form. If you want to save settings to your forms between sessions, you'll need to place the values in your Registry and load them when you restart your application. See How-To 2.10 for more information on saving and restoring program settings.

COMPLEXITY:
INTERMEDIATE

4.10 How do I...
Clean test data out of a database when I'm ready to ship it?

Problem

I'm finished designing and building a database; it's ready to ship to my client. Before they can use it, I need to remove the artificial data I've put in, without destroying permanent lookup tables. Is there a simple way to do this without running into referential integrity problems?

Technique

One solution is to open every data table in datasheet view, select all records, press the DELETE key, and confirm the deletion. However, there are three problems with this simple method.

- You have to open tables in a particular order (tables on the many side of a relationship before their related one-side tables).

- You have to remember which tables contain test data and which ones contain production data.

- The task is tedious and repetitive.

Instead of clearing out your test data by hand, you can write a general-purpose routine that uses a table of tables and a simple SQL statement to remove only the test data in the correct order.

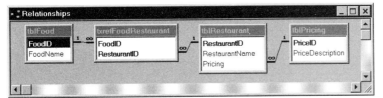

Figure 4-18 Relationships in the sample database

Steps

Open 04-10.MDB and view the tables in the database container. Open the tblFood table and try to delete some records. You'll get a referential integrity error, because there are related records in txrefFoodRestaurant. Figure 4-18 shows the relationships set up for the sample database. Now open frmDemo and click on the Clear button to remove all of the test data from the database without any manual intervention.

To implement this technique in your own database, follow these steps:

1. Import the table zstblDeleteOrder (structure only, without data) into your own database, or create a new table with the fields shown in Table 4-10.

FIELD NAME	DATA TYPE	FIELD SIZE	PROPERTIES
Order	Number	Integer	Primary Key
TableName	Text		

Table 4-10 Structure of zstblDeleteOrder

2. Import the module zsbasMaintain into your database, or create a new module with the single function shown here.

```
Function ahtClearData()
    ' Remove all data from tables specified in
    ' zstblDeleteOrder. Data is removed in the
    ' order specified to avoid referential integrity
    ' violations.

    On Error GoTo ahtClearData_Err

    Dim db As Database
    Dim rst As Recordset

    Set db = CurrentDb()
    Set rst = db.OpenRecordset( _
      "zstblDeleteOrder", dbOpenSnapshot)

    DoCmd.SetWarnings False

    Do While Not rst.EOF
        DoCmd.RunSQL "DELETE * FROM " & rst![TableName]
```

continued on next page

continued from previous page

```
            rst.MoveNext
    Loop

    DoCmd.SetWarnings True

    rst.Close

ahtClearData_Exit:
    On Error GoTo 0
    Exit Function

ahtClearData_Err:
    MsgBox "Error " & Err & ": " & Error$, vbExclamation, _
      "ahtClearData()"
    Resume ahtClearData_Exit
End Function
```

3. Open zstblDeleteOrder in datasheet view and add one record for each table you want to clear out before shipping. These tables must be listed in the order in which you want them cleared. Assign each table a unique order number, with the lowest number belonging to the first table to be cleared. Tables on the many side of a one-to-many relationship should be listed before tables on the one side of the relationship. Tables that you don't want to clear (including zstblDeleteOrder) should not be entered at all. Figure 4-19 shows the sample version of zstblDeleteOrder.

4. If you'd like a form to control the deletion process, create a new, blank form. Place one command button on the form and set the command button's OnClick property to:

```
=ahtClearData()
```

If you'd rather reset your data from a procedure, add the line

```
Call ahtClearData
```

to your procedure.

How It Works

The ahtClearData function automates the tedium of selecting the order of your tables and then deleting the data table by table. You select the order when you build the zstblDeleteOrder table. The function works by opening a snapshot of this table and

Figure 4-19 Sample zstblDeleteOrder

looping through the snapshot one line at a time. The line in the function that does the actual work is

```
DoCmd RunSQL "DELETE * FROM " & rstTables![TableName]
```

This line concatenates the table name found in rstTables, using SQL keywords to form a complete SQL statement. If you specify tblFood as one of the tables to delete, for example, Access builds the SQL statement:

```
DELETE * FROM tblFood;
```

This is the SQL equivalent of a delete query that selects all rows from the table and deletes them. The DoCmd RunSQL statement turns this query over to the Jet engine for execution.

Comments

The sample database has a second button, Restock, on the demo form. This button runs a macro that in turn runs four append queries to take backup copies of the data and return them to the main data tables. This lets you test the function in the sample database more than once.

When you use this technique in your own database, be sure to compact the database before you distribute it to your users. To do this, select Tools|Database Utilities|Compact Database when no database is currently open. There are two reasons to compact your database at this point.

> Until you compact, the Access file won't shrink at all. When you delete data from tables, Access marks the data pages as empty, but it doesn't give them back to your hard drive as free file space. This only occurs when you compact.

> When you compact a database, Access resets the next counter values for all counter fields. If you remove all the data from a table with a counter in it and compact the database, the next record added will have a counter value of 1.

COMPLEXITY:
ADVANCED

4.11 How do I... Package an add-in for distribution?

Problem

I've written an Access add-in that I'd like to distribute. I want it to install just as the built-in add-ins do. How can I accomplish this?

Technique

There are many reasons why you might write an Access add-in: to automate a task, to provide common code you can use in multiple applications, or perhaps you've written your own Wizard, or, as in this example, a code fragment builder. When it comes time to distribute your add-in, you'll need to use the standard Access Add-In Manager to install it. To do that, you must both set your database's properties and create a special table named USysRegInfo, which the Access Add-In Manager uses to install your add-in. This table contains information that the Add-In Manager uses to add settings to the system Registry. Access, then, will find the necessary information in the Registry to be able to use the Add-In.

Steps

The steps that follow show you how to install and use the example builder, in 04-11.MDA, how to open the builder so you can see how it works, and how to add similar features to your own add-ins. The sample add-in attaches itself to the Build button when you're editing a module and allows you to insert "canned" code fragments into your module.

To Install and Use the Sample Builder

1. Copy 04-11.MDA to your Access directory.

2. Start Access and load any database.

3. Select Add-Ins from the Tools Menu, and then select Add-In Manager.

4. Scroll down the list of available add-ins until you find the entry for the Code Fragment Builder (your list will probably be different than that shown in Figure 4-20). Note the display of the add-in name, company, and description in the dialog box. These come from the add-in database's properties. Select the Code Fragment Builder, then click on Install and then Close.

5. Open a module and create a new function.

6. Click the Build button on the Module toolbar and select Code Fragment Builder from the list. Choose a fragment from the combo box and click the

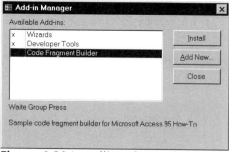

Figure 4-20 Installing the Code Fragment Builder

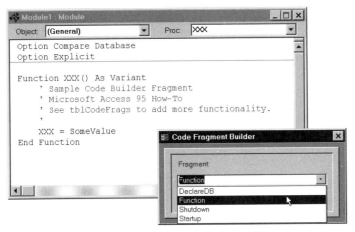

Figure 4-21 Using the Code Fragment Builder

OK button to insert that fragment of code into your module. Figure 4-21 shows the Code Fragment Builder in use.

7. If you'd like to investigate the workings of the code fragment builder, you'll first need to uninstall it as a library. To do that, execute steps 3 and 4 again, but choose the Uninstall option this time. Now you'll be able to load 04-11.MDA just like any other Access database.

Note

In previous versions of Access, you were forced to quit and restart Access for library databases (which is what add-ins are) to take effect. VBA allows Access to load libraries at any time. Therefore, in this version of Access, you can start using your add-in as soon as you've finished installing it. No more starting and restarting Access over and over as you debug your add-ins! Access is not so good about *unloading* libraries, however, if you decide to uninstall one. That will require you to restart Access.

To Add These Features to Your Own Add-In

1. To create an installation table for your add-in, import the USysRegInfo table from 04-11.MDA or any of the Microsoft Wizards. This will ensure that you get the right definition for each field in the table. You will need to choose Tools|Options|View and set Show Hidden Objects to Yes before this table will appear in the list of available tables to import.

USysRegInfo : Table

Subkey	Type	ValName	Value
HKEY_CURRENT_ACCESS_PROFILE\Wizards\Property Wizards\Module\MSModuleBuilder	4	Can Edit	1
HKEY_CURRENT_ACCESS_PROFILE\Wizards\Property Wizards\Module\MSModuleBuilder	1	Description	Access How-To Code Builder
HKEY_CURRENT_ACCESS_PROFILE\Wizards\Property Wizards\Module\MSModuleBuilder	1	Function	cf_BuildCodeFragment
HKEY_CURRENT_ACCESS_PROFILE\Wizards\Property Wizards\Module\MSModuleBuilder	1	Library	04-11.mda
HKEY_CURRENT_ACCESS_PROFILE\Wizards\Property Wizards\Module\MSModuleBuilder	0		

Record: 1 of 5

Figure 4-22 USysRegInfo table for the Code Fragment Builder

2. Change the values in the imported installation table to the appropriate ones for your add-in. For the sample builder, which builds a code property, Figure 4-22 shows the necessary settings. See the How It Works section below for information on the option settings.
3. Save the USysRegInfo table and close your database. Give it an MDA extension and it will install like any other add-in as soon as it's copied into an Access directory. (You don't actually have to place it into the Access directory yourself; the Add-In Manager will copy it from wherever it is, as long as you choose the Add New button rather than the Install button.)
4. Set the appropriate database properties. Select the File|Database Properties menu and fill in at least the Title, Company, and Description fields. The Add-In Manager uses these properties to display information about your add-in.

How It Works

The Add-In Manager works by opening each file in your Access directory with the .MDA extension and looking in it for the three database properties: Title, Company, and Description. It displays that information as you scroll through the list of add-ins. When you choose to install the add-in, it looks for a USysRegInfo table in your database. If it finds one, it uses the entries in this table to control the changes it makes to your system Registry. By installing a USysRegInfo table in your own add-in, you can make use of this custom installation procedure.

Even though you may have imported a copy of USysRegInfo from an existing add-in, you'll still need to modify all of the entries to match your situation. The rest of this section discusses each of the items in USysRegInfo, with an explanation and your options for each. You'll find it most useful if you follow this discussion with either the USysRegInfo table from your copy of 04-11.MDA open in datasheet view or with Figure 4-22.

Where's All This Going?

When you add an add-in to your Access environment, Access stores information about the add-in in the system Registry. (If you've never delved into the Registry, this is as good a time to start as any, but beware about making manual changes: Unless you know what you're doing, don't delete any items or change any values!) To find all the Access add-ins, work your way down through the hierarchy of Registry subkeys, starting with HKEY_LOCAL_MACHINE, and working down to:

```
HKEY_LOCAL_MACHINE\SOFTWARE\Microsoft\Access\7.0\Wizards
```

At each level, double-click on the "+" sign to open the level, working your way in deeper and deeper. One step below the Wizards subkey, you'll find the Property Wizards information, as shown in Figure 4-23. Unless you've already installed the Code Fragment Builder, you won't see the items shown in the figure, of course.

The goal of placing information in USysRegInfo is to get that information placed into the Registry, as shown in Figure 4-23. Different types of add-ins use different information, so if you're building an add-in that's not a builder, you'll want to investigate the information stored for that kind of builder by rummaging around in other Registry subkeys. (How do you think we found out how to install the Code Fragment Builder? This isn't documented anywhere!)

HKEY_CURRENT_ACCESS_PROFILE

The Subkey column in USysRegInfo tells the Add-In Manager where to place the various pieces of information in the other columns. In the example USysRegInfo, all the Subkey values begin with HKEY_CURRENT_ACCESS_PROFILE. Normally, when working with the Registry, you work with subkeys based on one of the built-in root keys (HKEY_CURRENT_USER, HKEY_LOCAL_MACHINE, etc.). HKEY_CURRENT_ACCESS_PROFILE is not one of the standard root keys, but one that the Access Add-In Manager recognizes and converts into a real Registry subkey. Access allows multiple users each to maintain their own profile of user settings; you'll want to install your add-in in that particular user's profile. By choosing the HKEY_CURRENT_ACCESS_PROFILE root key, the Add-In Manager knows to find the correct user profile under the HKEY_LOCAL_MACHINE root key. You could specify a *real* root key, of course, if you wanted to bypass the profile mechanism, but it's not a good idea if you want to allow different users to have different settings. Of course, if you want the Add-In Manager to add a specific value to the registry that holds for all users, by all means specify the exact Registry path to get to that subkey.

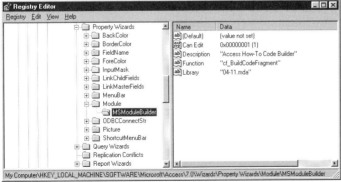

Figure 4-23 Deep in the registry, you'll find information about the Code Fragment Builder

Getting Your Add-In Loaded

You may or may not want your add-in loaded automatically when Access starts up. For menu add-ins (add-ins called from the Tools|Add-In menu), for example, you may decide to delay loading the library until someone actually tries to use your add-in. This will cause Access to load slightly faster (because it won't need to load your library at startup), but will cause your add-in to start significantly slower the first time someone uses it.

If you decide to load your library at startup (as we've done for the Code Fragment Builder), you'll need an entry in USysRegInfo to cause this to happen. The first entry in Figure 4-22 contains the information the Add-In Manager uses to load your add-in when Access starts up. The value in the Subkey column tells it which subkey to find (\Wizards\LoadOnStartup). The Type column tells the Add-In Manager what to do with the ValName and Value columns, as shown in Table 4-11.

TYPE	DESCRIPTION
0	Create a new key item at the location specified in the Subkey column. You must create the subkey before you can place any values inside it. The \Wizards\LoadOnStartup subkey will already exist, but if you're paranoid, add an item to USysRegInfo to create that subkey as well. Leave the ValName and Value columns empty when you're creating a subkey.
1	Create a text value under the subkey specified in the Subkey column. The ValName column should contain the name of the item ("Description", for example), and the Value column should hold the value associated with that item ("Access How-To Code Builder").
4	Create a numeric value under the subkey specified in the Subkey column. The ValName column should contain the name of the item ("Can Edit", for example), and the Value column should hold the value associated with that item (1).

Table 4-11 Options for USysRegInfo's Type column

As you can see in Figure 4-23, based on information in Table 4-11, the second row creates the necessary subkey in the Registry and the rest of the table creates items underneath that subkey. (How did we know what values to create? We looked at other examples in the Registry, of course!)

Sometimes, you may need to include references to the Access directory in your Value setting. Because you can't know where the Access directory is on your target system when you create your rows in USysRegInfo, the Add-In Manager recognizes the special token "|ACCDIR" to mean the directory where Access is installed on the target machine. There's no reason not to include settings in the Registry that aren't used by Access at all, but only by your add-in, which can retrieve them directly from the Registry while it's running. That is, you can add as many rows to USysRegInfo as you like: Access will disregard items that it doesn't care about once they're in the Registry.

Comments

Make sure you create a backup of your Registry before you start playing with installing an add-in on your test system. We managed to lose a lot of important settings by not making a backup first! To do this, select the topmost My Computer icon in the Registry's left window, then choose the Registry|Export Registry File menu item. That'll create an image, on disk, of your entire Registry. That way, if something goes wrong, you can always restore to your last "good" state.

This How-To topic discussed how to create an add-in, in general, but really didn't touch on how this particular add-in works. If you're interested, you'll find it worthwhile to dig through the small amount of code included in 04-11.MDA. It's a good start, but would require a great deal of effort to turn into a useful add-in. (That's left as an exercise for you!)

If your add-in contains proprietary code or data, you'll also want to investigate Access security. Too large a topic to be covered here, security gets more coverage in Chapter 10. Take a look there if you'd like to delve into that topic.

CHAPTER 5
TAMING
YOUR PRINTER

TAMING YOUR PRINTER

How do I...

Printing output is a major component of any database product, and Access gives you a great deal of control over the "look" of your forms and reports. Programmatic control over the printer itself, however, is somewhat complex in Access. Windows provides very rich and intricate support for output devices, and Access attempts to shield you from most of that intricacy. Sometimes, however, you do need to take control over your output devices: You may need to change the particular device, or change a setting pertaining to a particular device. Access makes this possible, but not easy. The topics in this chapter will make some of the details of handling your output devices more reasonable.

This chapter focuses on the three printer-related properties of forms and reports that are just barely documented: prtMip, prtDevMode, and prtDevNames. We'll cover these properties in detail, and show examples of their use. You'll be able to retrieve a list of all the installed printers and make a choice from that list, setting the new default Windows printer. You'll learn how to modify margin settings in forms and reports, thereby avoiding the use of Access's File|Page Setup dialog box in your applications. You'll get help on changing printer options, such as the number of copies to print, the page orientation, and the printer resolution. In particular, How-To 5.5 will demonstrate how you can print to paper sizes that your printer doesn't regularly support (if your printer supports variable size pages, of course). How-To 5.6 shows how to print the first page of a document from one paper tray and the rest of the pages from a different paper tray programmatically. This allows you to print the first page on letterhead paper and the rest on normal paper. Finally, you'll learn how to determine which device has been selected to print a report or form and whether it's the default device. If it is, you can change the destination from your application, provide users with a choice of output devices, and print the object to a particular device. You'll also find a development tool that will run through all your reports and let you know which aren't set up to print to the default printer. By ensuring that all your reports print to the default printer, you will be able to send them to any output device simply by changing what Windows thinks is the default printer.

5.1   Retrieve a List of All the Installed Output Devices

Windows stores the list of available output devices in WIN.INI. This How-To will describe how to retrieve that list and make it available on a form. The steps involve reading the information from WIN.INI a number of times; this is a good exercise in using the Windows API functions that read from INI files. Though Microsoft suggests not using INI files for storing data, they break their own rules in this case.

5.2   Set and Retrieve the Name of the Default Output Device

Windows stores information about the default output device in WIN.INI. This How-To will demonstrate steps for retrieving and setting the identity of the default output device.

5.3   Programmatically Change Margin and Column Settings for Reports

Access provides a programmatic method for retrieving and setting margin and column settings for reports and forms: the prtMip property. Like the prtDevMode and prtDevNames properties explained in upcoming How-To's, the prtMip property is unusual in that it's not a distinct value, but an entire data structure stored as a stream of bytes. This How-To will show how to move that unreadable stream of information into an editable data structure, and how to move it back. In addition, it will describe the prtMip property in detail.

5.4 Programmatically Change Printer Options

Though you could use SendKeys to manipulate settings in File|Page Setup dialog boxes, every printer works a bit differently, and sooner or later SendKeys will fail to perform the specific action you need. Access externalizes information about the print settings of each document that can be printed in the prtDevMode property. This How-To will show you how to change various print settings, such as the orientation and the number of copies, for any document you want to print from Access.

5.5 Print on Odd-Sized Paper

Once you know how to analyze the printer settings stored in the prtDevMode property, you'll be able to change many of the printer settings. This How-To will demonstrate the use of this property to print on paper sizes your printer might otherwise not support. (This How-To will only work if your printer supports custom paper sizes. Although most dot-matrix printers do, many laser printers, except the most recent, do not.)

5.6 Programmatically Control the Paper Source

Using the same techniques shown in How-To 5.5, you'll learn how to control the paper source for your print jobs in this section. This will allow your applications to print the first page of a report on letterhead paper in one paper tray and the rest of the report on normal paper from a different tray without human intervention. This method can be expanded to allow any page of a report to go to a specific printer tray.

5.7 Retrieve Information About a Report's or Form's Selected Printer

Using the prtDevNames property, you can retrieve information about a form or report's selected output device. Access provides this property as a stream of bytes, such as prtMip and prtDevMode, and you must take some care in "picking it apart." This How-To will provide the tools you need to crack the prtDevNames property, and will tell you the device, the driver, and the output port for any form or report. In addition, you'll find out if an object is set to print to the default output device—crucial information if you want to change the output device in your applications.

5.8 Choose an Output Device at Runtime

This How-To will demonstrate how, given a list of available printers, you can store information about the currently chosen printer, set the default printer to be the chosen device, print your document, and then set the default printer back to its original setting. This method is particularly useful for sending documents to various fax drivers or other devices.

5.9 Find the Reports That Are Not Set to Print to the Default Printer

To use the technique shown in How-To 5.7, the object you're trying to print must be configured to print to the default output device. If you have a large number of reports in your application, it can be difficult to track which ones may be configured to print to a specific printer. This How-To will provide a simple form and report that walks through all the reports in your application and lists each report and whether it's been configured to print to the default output device. You'll recognize concepts from several earlier How-To's, and find some additional methods involving Data Access Objects to do the looping.

COMPLEXITY:
ADVANCED

5.1 How do I...
Retrieve a list of all the installed output devices?

Problem

I'd like to be able to present my users with a list of all the installed printers, but I can't find a way to retrieve this information from within Access. Is there some API call that will give me this list?

Technique

Windows stores a complete list of all the installed printing devices in WIN.INI. Though Microsoft has suggested that applications not use INI files for storing information (they should use the registry instead), WIN.INI is still the only place to retrieve the name of the default printer, and is the simplest way to retrieve the list of installed printers. Retrieving this list is just a matter of using the standard INI-reading API functions. Windows provides a special feature that allows you to retrieve an entire section of an INI file in one function call. This How-To uses this technique to read in the entire list of printers in one step. From there, it's a simple matter to break the resulting string into the various pieces that you need to provide the list of devices.

The steps involved in creating the list of printers and their output ports is, however, much more difficult, because of the way Windows stores the information. This How-To presents data structures and techniques to retrieve the information that will be used throughout this chapter.

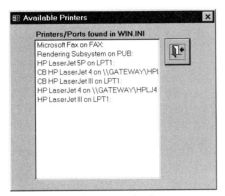

Figure 5-1 The sample form, frmPrinterList, showing the list of installed devices

Steps

Load and run the form frmPrinterList from 05-01.MDB. Figure 5-1 shows the form displaying all the installed printers on a test machine. The How It Works section below describes, in detail, the techniques used in building the list in Figure 5-1.

To create your own list of installed printers, follow these steps:

1. Import the four modules from 05-01.MDB listed in Table 5-1.

MODULE NAME	PURPOSE	CONTAINS
basGetPrinters	Create an array of printers, fill a list box with the array.	ahtGetPrinterList, ahtFillPrinterList
basINIFile	Read/write information in INI files.	ahtGetINIInt, ahtGetINIString, ahtGetPrivateINIInt, ahtGetPrivateINIString, ahtGetProfileSection, ahtGetPrivateProfileSection
basPrintTypes	Define data types and constants for all examples in this chapter.	
basToken	Retrieve pieces of a string: a utility module.	ahtGetToken

Table 5-1 Modules to import from 05-01.MDB

2. On a new or existing form, place a list or combo box. Set its properties as shown in Table 5-2, and set any other properties however you like.

PROPERTY	VALUE
RowSourceType	ahtFillPrinterList
ColumnCount	1
BoundColumn	1

Table 5-2 List/combo box property settings for displaying a list of output devices

How It Works

Though it's simple to use the example code we've provided to create your list of output devices (Table 5-1), a lot of action is going on underneath. This section is divided into subtopics, making it easier to follow the steps that ahtFillPrinterList goes through to fill that list or combo box with the list of installed devices. These subtopics focus on the code in the ahtGetPrinterList function, which ahtFillPrinterList must call to retrieve the list of devices, along with their drivers and output ports.

What's the Goal?

The goal of the code in basGetPrinters is to fill an array with information about all the installed output devices. For each device, there are three bits of information that you're interested in: the device name, its device driver name, and the output port to which it will send its information. Because these three items are used so often as a group, basPrintTypes contains a structure definition that almost every How-To in this chapter will use to hold the information:

```
Type aht_tagDeviceRec
    drDeviceName As String
    drDriverName As String
    drPort As String
End Type
```

The first element, drDeviceName, holds the device name. The second, drDriverName, holds the name of the device driver (without its file name extension); drPort holds the output port. Given an array of aht_tagDeviceRec structures, you can easily fill a list box (as in the sample form) or do anything else you'd like with the list.

What's in WIN.INI and How Do I Retrieve the Information?

The first step, then, is to retrieve the information from WIN.INI. Windows stores the entire list of installed devices in a section of WIN.INI, titled [devices]. In the WIN.INI that produced Figure 5-1, the section looked like this (most likely, you'll never run across a WIN.INI that contains this many different devices):

```
[devices]
Microsoft Fax=WPSUNI,FAX:
Rendering Subsystem=WPSUNI,PUB:
HP LaserJet 5P=HPPCL5MS,LPT1:
CB HP LaserJet 4=ClikBook,\\GATEWAY\HPLJ4
CB HP LaserJet III=ClikBook,LPT1:
HP LaserJet 4=HPPCL5MS,\\GATEWAY\HPLJ4
HP LaserJet III=HPPCL5MS,LPT1:
```

Every line in the section is in this format:

DeviceName=DriverName,Port

where *DeviceName* contains the string the user sees as the name of the device, *DriverName* contains the actual device driver name (without its file extension), and *Port* contains the output port to which the device has been connected.

To retrieve the list from WIN.INI, you can call the GetProfileSection API function, which reads directly from WIN.INI. GetProfileSection allows you to retrieve all the items associated with a given topic in an INI file; that's what you need in this case: You want the entire list for the [Devices] topic. Given a buffer to fill, GetProfileSection fills it with a list of all the items in a section, strung together in one string. Each of the three items has a null (Chr$(0), not the digit "0") separating it from the next item, with a final trailing Chr$(0) at the end of the string. The code you could use to retrieve the string might look like this:

```
Dim varPrinters As Variant

' Get complete section labeled "[Devices]" from Win.INI
varPrinters = ahtGetProfileSection("DEVICES")
```

Now That I Have the List of Names, What Do I Do?

Having a null-delimited list of device names doesn't do you much good. You must first find some way to split them apart into an array of strings. The example code uses the GetDevices function in basGetPrinters to take on this job.

```
intCount = GetDevices(varPrinters, atagDevices())
```

GetDevices breaks up the long string containing device names (strPrinters) into an array of device records (atagDevices()). To do its work, it uses an utility function, ahtGetToken (in basToken), which you may find useful for other tasks. The general syntax for calling ahtGetToken is

```
varToken = ahtGetToken (strValue, strDelimiter, intPiece)
```

where *strValue* is the string you want to search through, *strDelimiter* holds the delimiter character, and *intPiece* tells the function which token you want to extract from the list.

For example, to retrieve the third word from the sentence, "Hello, my name is John!", you could use this function call:

```
varWord3 = ahtGetToken("Hello, my name is John!", " ", 3)
```

Because the sentence uses space characters as word delimiters, this example uses a space character in quotes as the second parameter.

When breaking up the list of printers, GetDevices first walks through the list, counting the number of 0s.

```
For intI = 1 To Len(strPrinters)
   If Mid$(strPrinters, intI, 1) = Chr$(0) Then
      intCount = intCount + 1
   End If
Next intI
```

Once GetDevices knows how many pieces there are, it calls ahtGetToken repeatedly, pulling out all the device information. It makes sure the array to hold them contains enough rows, and returns the number of rows as the function's return value.

```
' Reserve enough space in the array for them all.
ReDim atagDevices(1 To intCount)

For intI = 1 To intCount
   ' Split up the entries that look like this:
   ' Device=Driver,Port
   strBuffer = ahtGetToken(strPrinters, Chr$(0), intI)
   '
   ' More stuff here... (see the next code example)
Next intI
```

For each of the items in the list, GetDevices must now pull apart the piece to the left of the equal sign (the device name) and the two pieces of information from the right-hand side of the equal sign (the driver and output port). To do that, GetDevices uses the following code:

```
atagDevices(intI).drDeviceName = ahtGetToken(strBuffer, "=", 1)
' Get all the stuff after the "="
strBuffer = ahtGetToken(strBuffer, "=", 2)

' Now pull out the two pieces.
atagDevices(intI).drDriverName = ahtGetToken(strBuffer, ",", 1)
atagDevices(intI).drPort = ahtGetToken(strBuffer, ",", 2)
```

This fills in the drDeviceName member of the structure with the text to the left of the equal sign, and then uses the comma as the delimiter to pull apart the next two pieces, filling the drDriverName and drPort members.

Once GetDevices has done its work, the atagDevices array is filled in with a list of all the installed devices parsed out into the necessary pieces.

Using the Array of aht_tagDeviceRec Structures

To fill the list box, frmPrinterList uses the ahtFillPrinterList function, a list-filling callback function (for information on using such functions, see How-To 7.5). In its initialization step, ahtFillPrinterList calls ahtGetPrinterList to fill its array of aht_tagDeviceRec structures.

```
Case acLBInitialize
    intCount = ahtGetPrinterList(atagDevices())
```

Then, when Access requests data items from ahtFillPrinterList, it returns a string constructed from two elements of the aht_tagDeviceRec structure.

```
Case acLBGetValue
    varRetval = atagDevices(varRow + 1).drDeviceName & " on " & _
        atagDevices(varRow + 1).drPort
```

Comments

It's true: This seems like an awful lot of work just to retrieve a list of installed output devices. But How-To topics later in the chapter will build on these ideas, allowing you to select a new default printer, for example. Because all the code you need to retrieve the list of printers is so neatly encapsulated in the single function ahtGetPrinterList, you shouldn't need to worry about how the items all got into their array. By calling this function to provide the array, you should be able to use the list any way you'd like.

COMPLEXITY:
INTERMEDIATE

5.2 How do I...
Set and retrieve the name of the default output device?

Problem

Windows allows me to install a number of printer drivers, but one of them must always be denoted as the default printer. I'd like to be able to control which printer Windows thinks is the default printer, perhaps even choosing from a list of all the installed printers. Is there a way to do this from within Access?

Technique

Just as Windows stores the full list of available printers in the WIN.INI file (see How-To 5.1 for information on retrieving the full list of installed devices), it also stores information about the default printer in WIN.INI. This How-To shows how you can retrieve and change the default printer setting.

Figure 5-2 The sample form, frmDefaultPrinterList, from which you can choose a new default printer

Steps

Load and run the form frmDefaultPrinterList from 05-02.MDB. This form, shown in Figure 5-2, includes a combo box from which you can select a new default printer. When you first load the form, the combo box should already have the current default output device selected. If you make a choice, the code attached to the AfterUpdate event for the combo box will write the changed value for the default printer to WIN.INI. This change will affect any program that counts on retrieving the default output device from WIN.INI (and, according to the Win32 SDK, this is the recommended way to get the information, so most do).

To create a combo box in your own application like the one on frmDefaultPrinterList, follow these steps:

1. Import the modules listed in Table 5-3 into your own application. Skip any modules that you've previously imported. These modules supply the support routines you'll need to provide the list of devices and to retrieve and set the default printer in WIN.INI.

MODULE	PURPOSE	CONTAINS
basDefaultPrinter	Retrieve and set default printer setting.	ahtGetDefaultPrinter,
		ahtSetDefaultPrinter
basGetPrinters	Create an array of printers, fill a list box	ahtGetPrinterList,
	with the array.	ahtFillPrinterList
basINIFile	Read/write information in INI files.	ahtGetINIInt,
		ahtGetINIString,
		ahtGetPrivateINIInt,
		ahtGetPrivateINIString,
		ahtGetProfileSection,
		ahtGetPrivateProfileSection
basPrintTypes	Define data types and constants for all	
	examples in this chapter.	
basToken	Retrieve pieces of a string: a utility module.	ahtGetToken

Table 5-3 Modules to import from 05-02.MDB

2. Create a combo box on a new or existing form. Set the properties as shown in Table 5-4 (other properties may be set as you see fit).

PROPERTY	VALUE
Name	cboPrinters
RowSourceType	FillPrinterList
ColumnCount	4
ColumnHeads	No
ColumnWidths	;0 in;0 in;0 in
BoundColumn	1
AfterUpdate	[Event Procedure]

 Table 5-4 Properties to be set for cboPrinters

3. Place the following code in the form's Open event procedure. (For more information on creating event procedures, see this book's Introduction.) This code retrieves the current default printer from WIN.INI and sets cboPrinters to show the name and output port for the default printer.

```
Sub Form_Open (Cancel As Integer)
    Dim dr As aht_tagDeviceRec

    If ahtGetDefaultPrinter(dr) Then
        Me!cboPrinters = BuildName(dr)
    End If
End Sub
```

4. Place the following code in the combo box cboPrinters' AfterUpdate event procedure (in the form's module). This code writes the chosen value back to WIN.INI.

```
Private Sub cboPrinters_AfterUpdate()

    Dim dr As aht_tagDeviceRec
    Dim intRetval As Integer
    Dim ctl As Control

    ' Retrieve the pieces needed by dr from
    ' the combo box.
    Set ctl = Me!cboPrinters
    With dr
        .drDeviceName = ctl.Column(1)
        .drDriverName = ctl.Column(2)
        .drPort = ctl.Column(3)
    End With
    intRetval = ahtSetDefaultPrinter(dr)
End Sub
```

5. Add the following function to the form's module (*not* to a global module). This function fills the combo box.

```
Private Function FillPrinterList(ctl As Control, varID As Variant, _
  varRow As Variant, varCol As Variant, varCode As Variant)    Static
atagDevices() As aht_tagDeviceRec
    Static intCount As Integer
    Dim varRetval As Variant

    Select Case varCode
        Case acLBInitialize
            intCount = ahtGetPrinterList(atagDevices())
            varRetval = True

        Case acLBOpen
            varRetval = Timer

        Case acLBGetRowCount
            varRetval = intCount

        Case acLBGetColumnCount
            varRetval = 4

        Case acLBGetValue
            ' Because you're going to want to be able to retrieve all the
            ' separate pieces later, store them all in the combo box.
            ' Then when you need to retrieve them, you can use the Column()
            ' property to pull them out.
            Select Case varCol
                Case 0
                    varRetval = BuildName(atagDevices(varRow + 1))
                Case 1
                    varRetval = atagDevices(varRow + 1).drDeviceName
                Case 2
                    varRetval = atagDevices(varRow + 1).drDriverName
                Case 3
                    varRetval = atagDevices(varRow + 1).drPort
            End Select

        Case acLBEnd
            Erase atagDevices
    End Select
    FillPrinterList = varRetval
End Function
```

6. Add the following function to the form's module (*not* to a global module). This function builds up the string that appears in the combo box, and is called by several procedures in the form.

```
Private Function BuildName (dr As aht_tagDeviceRec)
    BuildName = dr.drDeviceName & " on " & dr.drPort
End Function
```

How It Works

The important actions of this example take place in the two support functions, ahtSetDefaultPrinter and ahtGetDefaultPrinter (in the basDefaultPrinter module). Each function takes, as a parameter, an aht_tagDeviceRec structure (see How-To 5.1 for details on the aht_tagDeviceRec structure). The ahtGetDefaultPrinter function looks in WIN.INI, in the [Windows] section, for a line with the keyword Device. A sample WIN.INI section might look like this:

```
[Windows]
spooler=yes
load=
run=
Beep=Yes
NullPort=None
CursorBlinkRate=530
DoubleClickSpeed=452
Programs=PIF EXE BAT COM
Documents=doc txt wri xls xlc sam jw jwt tg1 qw qwt
CoolSwitch=1
Device= HP LaserJet III,HPPCL5MS,LPT1:
```

The final line with Device as the keyword indicates the name, driver, and output port of the default output device. The ahtGetDefaultPrinter function uses the ahtGetINIString function to read from WIN.INI, and then uses the ahtGetToken function to separate the comma-delimited pieces. It places the values in the appropriate fields of the aht_tagDeviceRec structure.

```
Function ahtGetDefaultPrinter(dr As aht_tagDeviceRec) As Boolean

    Dim strBuffer As String

    strBuffer = ahtGetINIString("Windows", "Device")
    If Len(strBuffer) > 0 Then
        With dr
            .drDeviceName = ahtGetToken(strBuffer, ",", 1)
            .drDriverName = ahtGetToken(strBuffer, ",", 2)
            .drPort = ahtGetToken(strBuffer, ",", 3)
        End With
        ahtGetDefaultPrinter = True
    Else
        ahtGetDefaultPrinter = False
    End If
End Function
```

The ahtSetDefaultPrinter function performs almost the same set of steps as ahtGetDefaultPrinter, in reverse. It builds up a comma-delimited string, pulling the pieces from the passed-in aht_tagDeviceRec structure. It then calls aht_apiWriteProfileString to write the new value back out to WIN.INI.

```
Function ahtSetDefaultPrinter(dr As aht_tagDeviceRec) As Boolean

    Dim strBuffer As String
```

continued on next page

continued from previous page

```
' Build up the appropriate string.
strBuffer = dr.drDeviceName & ","
strBuffer = strBuffer & dr.drDriverName & ","
strBuffer = strBuffer & dr.drPort

' Now write that string out to WIN.INI.
ahtSetDefaultPrinter = (aht_apiWriteProfileString("Windows", _
   "Device", strBuffer) <> 0)
End Function
```

For information on the mechanisms of providing the list of available printers, see How-To 5.1. The details here are all the same, except for one: In this combo box, there are four columns (instead of just one, as in How-To 5.1). This example shows one column, containing a string with the device name and its output port, but stores all the three pieces from the aht_tagDeviceRec structure in hidden columns in the combo box. Thus it's much easier to retrieve the values for all the fields when you need to set the new default printer. The acLBGetValue case (from step 5) shows the details.

```
Case acLBGetValue
   Select Case varCol
      Case 0
         varRetval = BuildName(atagDevices(varRow + 1))
      Case 1
         varRetval = atagDevices(varRow + 1).drDeviceName
      Case 2
         varRetval = atagDevices(varRow + 1).drDriverName
      Case 3
         varRetval = atagDevices(varRow + 1).drPort
   End Select
```

Now when you need to retrieve the values from the combo box to write out to WIN.INI, you can just pull them from the selected row in the combo box, using the Column property, as shown in this code from step 4:

```
With dr
   .drDeviceName = ctl.Column(1)
   .drDriverName = ctl.Column(2)
   .drPort = ctl.Column(3)
End With
intRetval = ahtSetDefaultPrinter(dr)
```

Comments

Access uses the default output device for printing unless you specify otherwise, using Access' File|Page Setup dialog box. How-To 5.7 will combine methods from this topic and others to show you how to send a report to the printer you choose at runtime. The methods shown there will allow you to direct a report to the printer today and to the fax modem tomorrow.

Though it's possible to remove the default printer name from WIN.INI, you should not do this. Access (and many other Windows programs) will complain and request that you select a default printer if you attempt to print without one. You can, of course, use the code presented here to let users set the default printer if your application determines that none is currently selected.

COMPLEXITY:
ADVANCED

5.3   How do I...
Programmatically change margin and column settings for reports?

Problem

I'd like to give users of my applications some control over report layout, especially in designating column and margin settings. I could just "let them loose" in report design mode, but I'd like to maintain a little control over their actions. Is there some way to modify these layout settings from VBA?

Technique

Access provides three underdocumented properties for forms and reports: prtMip, prtDevMode, and prtDevNames. This How-To will focus on prtMip; How-To 5.4 will focus on prtDevMode; and How-To 5.6 will focus on prtDevNames.

You can use the prtMip property to retrieve and set layout properties of reports and forms, though it's not easy. This How-To provides some wrapper functions to hide the details of the property, which will make the process a bit easier for you. The prtMip property is actually a data structure containing information about the layout of your object. It contains fields representing the left, top, bottom, and right margins; the number of columns; and the size, spacing, and item order of the columns. In addition, it contains the Data Only option in the File|Page Setup dialog box. To use the prtMip property, you'll need to retrieve it, copy it to a user-defined structure, set new values, and then copy it back to the property. The How It Works section of this How-To explains all the details.

Steps

Load and run the form frmPrintSettings from 05-03.MDB. Figure 5-3 shows the form (which emulates Access's File|Page Setup dialog box) after the report rptReport3 has been selected from the list of reports. Choose a report from the drop-down list, and the form will load that report in design mode. By typing new values into the text boxes, you can change the settings for the selected report. Some of the items on the form are only available if you've specified more than one column for the Items Across value, so you'll want to use a number greater than 1 in that field. To save the changes back to the selected report, click on Save Settings. This writes the new prtMip property back to the report. (This doesn't actually save the report, however. If you want to permanently save the report with the new settings, you can choose to save the report when

Figure 5-3 The sample form, frmPrintSettings, was modeled after the Access File|Page Setup dialog box

you close it.) If you view the chosen report in Print Preview mode once you've reset its prtMip property, you will see your changes in effect. The following sections explain both how to use the sample form from 05-03.MDB and how to read and write the prtMip property of your own objects.

Using the Sample Form

To use the sample form in your own applications, follow these steps:

1. Import the modules listed in Table 5-5 from 05-03.MDB into your own application. Skip any modules you have already imported. These modules supply the support routines you'll need to generate the list of reports and to retrieve and set the prtMip property.

MODULE	PURPOSE	CONTAINS
basOpenReport	Open a report in design mode, or do nothing if it's already open.	ahtOpenReport
basPrintTypes	Define data types and constants for all examples in this chapter.	
basPrtMip	Get and set prtMip values.	ahtGetMip, ahtSetMip

Table 5-5 Modules to import from 05-03.MDB in order to use the frmPrintSettings

2. Import the form frmPrintSettings into your application. This form allows you to choose from the existing reports in your database. Once you've chosen the report (which the form will open in design mode), you can alter print layout settings. Once you're done, you'll need to save the report using the Access menus or your own code; the sample form will not save the reports for you.

Using the Routines to Read and Write the prtMip Property

To use the routines that read and write the prtMip property *without* the sample form, follow these steps:

1. Import the modules listed in Table 5-6 from 05-03.MDB into your own application. These modules supply the support routines you'll need to retrieve and set the prtMip property.

MODULE	PURPOSE	CONTAINS
basPrintTypes	Define data types and constants for all examples in this chapter.	
basPrtMip	Get and set prtMip values.	ahtGetMip, ahtSetMip

Table 5-6 Modules to import from 05-03.MDB in order to modify an object's prtMip property

2. To retrieve an object's prtMip property, call the ahtGetMip function. It takes two parameters: a reference to an object and an aht_tagMip structure to hold the values. For example, the following code fills the variable *mip* with the requested report or form's prtMip property information (the report or form must already be open in any view for this code to work).

```
Dim mip As aht_tagMip
Dim fSuccess as Integer

fSuccess = ahtGetMip(Reports!rptYourReport, mip)
' or, for a form:
' fSuccess = ahtGetMip(Forms!frmYourForm, mip)
```

3. To modify the prtMip values, you need to modify values in the aht_tagMip structure. The How It Works section below explains this. Once you're done, you must write the prtMip value back to the original object for it to take effect. To do that, call the ahtSetMip function. It takes the same parameters as the ahtGetMip function: a reference to an object and an aht_tagMip structure that holds the new values. For example, the following code replaces the selected open object's prtMip property with the values stored in *mip*:

```
fSuccess = ahtSetMip(Reports!rptYourReport, mip)
' or, for a form:
' fSuccess = ahtSetMip(Forms!frmYourForm, mip)
```

How It Works

Using the code we've supplied here is quite simple. Underneath, however, a lot of work is going on. The following sections describe the prtMip property in detail, how to retrieve the prtMip setting, how to modify its data, and how to place the changed data into your form or report. In addition, we'll introduce the wrapper functions that shield you from most of this level of detail.

The prtMip Data Structure

The prtMip property, as well as the prtDevMode and prtDevNames properties (discussed in later How-To's), are unique in that they're not directly readable. As stored and retrieved from an object, these properties are just a stream of bytes: To peruse them or modify their values, you need to copy them into a user-defined data structure that's been declared in just the right way. The information's the same either way you look at it, but it's impossible to view or edit it as an unbroken stream of bytes. Once you copy it to a data structure, though, it's easy to access any of the pieces of the property.

To use the prtMip property, copy its value into a data structure (as defined in basPrintTypes) of type aht_tagMip.

```
Type aht_tagMIP
    xLeftMargin As Long
    yTopMargin As Long
    xRightMargin As Long
    yBotMargin As Long
    fDataOnly As Long
    xFormSize As Long
    yFormSize As Long
    fDefaultSize As Long
    cxColumns As Long
    xFormSpacing As Long
    yFormSpacing As Long
    radItemOrder As Long
    fFastPrinting As Long
    fDataSheet As Long
End Type
```

Table 5-7 describes the fields in the aht_tagMip structure.

FIELD	DESCRIPTION	COMMENTS
xLeftMargin	Left margin	Distance between the edge of the paper and the object to be printed (in twips: 1 twip = 1/1440 inch)
yTopMargin	Top margin	Distance between the top edge of the paper and the object to be printed (in twips)
xRightMargin	Right margin	Distance between the right edge of the paper and the object to be printed (in twips)
yBotMargin	Bottom margin	Distance between the bottom edge of the paper and the object to be printed (in twips)

FIELD	DESCRIPTION	COMMENTS
fDataOnly	Print data only?	If True (−1), Access should print just data, not labels, control borders, gridlines and display graphics; if False (0), Access prints all elements
xFormSize	Column width	Width of the detail area; if the fDefaultSize element is False and cxColumns is greater than 1, the width of each column (in twips)
yFormSize	Column height	Returns the height of the detail section (read-only)
fDefaultSize	Use default size?	If True (−1), use the width and height of the design mode detail section when printing; if False (0), use the valuesFormSize and yFormSize members
cxColumns	Items across	Integer that specifies the number of columns across the page for multiple-columned reports
xFormSpacing	Column spacing	Distance between detail section columns (if cxColumns > 1) in twips
yFormSpacing	Row Spacing	Distance between detail sections vertically (in twips)
radItemOrder	Item order	Horizontal (1953) or vertical (1954) layout for multiple-columned reports

 Table 5-7 Members of the aht_tagMip structure and their meanings

Retrieving prtMip Settings

Retrieving prtMip settings is trivial: Copy the value of the property from an open report or form into a string variable.

```
Dim strMip As String
strMip = Reports!rptReport1.prtMip
```

At this point, strMip will contain an unformatted stream of bytes, representing all the information in Table 5-7. You'll need some way of separating all the data into a data structure of type aht_tagMip. Although you could do this by brute force, copying the data 1 byte at a time, VBA provides a method for copying data from one data type to another, converting the individual bytes as necessary. A form of the LSet command lets you move the data from the prtMip property directly into an aht_tagMip data structure. LSet's general syntax is

```
LSet Data1 = Data2
```

where *Data1* and *Data2* are variables of user-defined data types—and there lies the catch. The data types on both sides of the equal sign must be user-defined types. You can't copy the data directly from the prtMip property using the LSet command.

The trick, then, is to use a second user-defined type. You'll find one of these "helper" types defined in basPrintTypes for each of the prtMip, prtDevMode, and prtDevNames properties. The type aht_tagMIPStr is defined as a single 56-byte string (characters in Access strings each take up 2 bytes):

```
Type aht_tagMIPStr
   MIPStr As String * 28
End Type
```

269

This may be a cheap trick to get around a limitation in the LSet command, but it does solve the problem. Therefore, to retrieve a report's prtMip property, you'd use code like this:

```
Dim mipStrTemp As aht_tagMIPStr
Dim mip As aht_tagMIP

mipStrTemp.MIPStr = Reports!rptReport1.prtMip
LSet mip = mipStrTemp
```

After you execute those lines of code, *mip* contains all the data from the report's prtMip property neatly parsed out into the correct fields. The same technique will work for each of the prtMip, prtDevMode, and prtDevNames properties: Using the correct "helper" data structure, you'll copy data from the property into the helper structure, and then use the LSet command to move the data into the appropriate "real" data structure.

Modifying the Data

Once you've got the data into the data structure, you can change the values as you would with any other user-defined structure. For example, given a variable containing prtMip data, you would set the left margin to be 3 inches using code like this:

```
' Don't forget to convert to TWIPS!
mip.xLeftMargin = 3 * 1440
```

Putting Data Back

To place the changed aht_tagMip structure back into a form or report's prtMip property, follow the steps outlined above in Retrieving prtMip Settings, except in reverse.

```
Dim mipStrTemp As aht_tagMIPStr

' mip is the structure containing your changed values
LSet mipStrTemp = mip
Reports!rptReport1.prtMip = mipStrTemp.MIPStr
```

First use the LSet command to copy the data from the aht_tagMIP structure into the helper structure; from there, copy the string in the helper structure directly to the prtMip property.

Making It a Bit Easier

To make things a bit simpler, we've supplied ahtGetMip and ahtSetMip in the module basPrtMip in 05-03.MDB. These two functions, used in the example form for this How-To, make it easy to retrieve and set an object's prtMip property. These functions follow the steps in this How-To, doing all of the work for you. For information on calling these functions, see steps 2 and 3 under Using the Routines to Read and Write the prtMip Property. To see examples of using ahtGetMip and ahtSetMip, look at the cboReportList_AfterUpdate and cmdSaveSettings_Click event procedures in the frmPrintSettings module (in 05-03.MDB).

The ahtGetMip function (from basPrtMip) retrieves the prtMip property for any opened object and places it into the aht_tagMIP structure that you pass to it. It returns True on success, False otherwise.

```
Function ahtGetMip(obj As Object, mip As aht_tagMIP) As Boolean

    ' Retrieve the prtMip property and stick the info
    ' into mip.

    ' The object in question, a form or a report,
    ' needs to be open already, in either design or run mode.

    Dim mipStrTemp As aht_tagMIPStr
    Dim intRetval As Integer

    ' Assume Failure
    intRetval = False

    On Error Resume Next
    mipStrTemp.MIPStr = obj.prtMip
    If Err = 0 Then
        LSet mip = mipStrTemp
        intRetval = True
    End If
    ahtGetMip = intRetval
End Function
```

The ahtSetMip function does exactly the opposite: It places the value that's stored in the aht_tagMIP structure passed to it in the prtMip property of the open object (which must be open in design view) whose reference you've passed to the function.

```
Function ahtSetMip(obj As Object, mip As aht_tagMIP) As Boolean

    ' Set the prtMip property from the info in mip.

    ' The object in question, a form or a report,
    ' needs to be open already, in design mode.

    Dim mipStrTemp As aht_tagMIPStr
    Dim intRetval As Integer

    ' Assume Failure
    intRetval = False

    On Error Resume Next
    LSet mipStrTemp = mip
    obj.prtMip = mipStrTemp.MIPStr
    If Err = 0 Then
        intRetval = True
    End If
    ahtSetMip = intRetval
End Function
```

Comments

The prtMip, prtDevMode, and prtDevNames properties are all read/write in design mode, but they are *read-only* at runtime. This means you must open an object in design mode if you need to change any of these properties. The example database 05-03.MDB contains a function, ahtOpenReport (in basOpenReport), that will ensure that the report whose name you pass is open and in the mode you need. You might find this function useful in your own applications.

Don't forget that all the measurements in the aht_tagMip structure are stored in twips. To convert from inches to twips, multiply by 1,440. (A twip is defined as 1/20 of a point. There are 72 points per inch, and 20 twips per point; therefore, 72 * 20 = 1,440 twips per inch). To convert from twips to inches, divide by 1,440.

The combo box with the list of reports uses a common but undocumented technique. The Access system tables (check Tools|Options|View|System Objects to see the system tables in the database container) contain information about the current database. One table in particular, MSysObjects, contains a row for each object in the database. To fill the combo box with a list of reports, you can use this SQL expression:

```
Select Name from MSysObjects where Type = -32764 Order By Name;
```

The Name column includes the name for each object, and the Type column contains -32764 for reports (it contains -32768 for forms). Microsoft suggests not querying against the system tables to retrieve lists of items, but using Data Access Objects instead; however, our method is much faster and much simpler for filling lists. This method has worked in every version of Access so far; we can only assume it will continue to work.

COMPLEXITY:
ADVANCED

5.4 How do I...
Programmatically change printer options?

Problem

I've tried using SendKeys to change printing options in the File|Setup Page dialog box, but this really isn't satisfactory. Sometimes it works and sometimes it doesn't, depending on the circumstances and the printer driver that's loaded. Is there some way to modify printer options without using SendKeys?

Technique

Windows makes many of the printer driver settings available to applications, including the number of copies, page orientation, and page size. Though Access makes it rather difficult to retrieve and modify these values, you can get at them through the prtDevMode property of forms and reports. This How-To focuses on the prtDevMode property and demonstrates how to read and write values in it.

Steps

Load and run the form frmPrintSettings in 05-04.MDB. Figure 5-4 shows the sample form in action. This form allows you to choose a report from a combo box. Once you've made your choice, the form loads the report in design mode and retrieves the number of copies, page size, and page orientation from the report's prtDevMode property. You can change any of these values; once you press the Save Settings button, and the form will write the values back to the report's prtDevMode property. If you save the report, those settings will still be there the next time you open the report.

To be able to modify prtDevMode settings for reports or forms in your own application, follow these steps:

1. Import the modules from 05-04.MDB listed in Table 5-8 into your own application. Skip any modules you may have previously imported.

MODULE	PURPOSE	CONTAINS
basOpenReport	Open a report in design mode, or do nothing if it's already open.	ahtOpenReport
basPrintTypes	Define data types and constants for all examples in this chapter.	
basPrtDevMode	Get and set prtDevMode values.	ahtGetDevMode, ahtSetDevMode, various constants

Table 5-8 Modules to import from 05-04.MDB in order to access the prtDevMode property

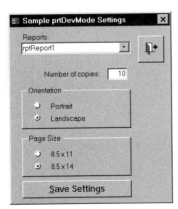

Figure 5-4 The sample form, frmPrintSettings, showing prtDevMode information for rptReport1

2. To retrieve the prtDevMode property values from a given report or form, call
the ahtGetDevMode function, as shown below. If the return value from the
function call is True, then you can use the information that the function filled
in for you in the aht_tagDevMode structure. For example, the following code
fragment retrieves the prtDevMode property for a report whose name is stored
in strReport:

```
Dim DM as aht_tagDevMode
Dim fSuccess as Integer

' Pass ahtGetDevMode a reference to the object, and a structure to
' fill in (type aht_tagDevMode).
fSuccess = ahtGetDevMode(Reports(strReport), DM)
```

3. To change values in the prtDevMode property, manipulate values in the
aht_tagDevMode structure. You must also tell Windows that you've changed
the field, by changing the value in the dmFields member. See the How It
Works section for details on filling in the various fields of the aht_tagDevMode
structure. For example, to set the number of copies to 2, you would use code
like this:

```
' Change the value.
DM.dmCopies = 2
' Make sure to tell Windows that you changed the value!
DM.dmFields = dm.dmFields Or ahtDM_COPIES
```

4. To write the prtDevMode value back to the object, call the ahtSetDevMode
function.

```
fSuccess = ahtSetDevMode(Reports(strReport), DM)
```

How It Works

The following sections discuss the prtDevMode data structure and how to use it in your
code. Just like the prtMip property discussed in How-To 5.3, the prtDevMode property is actually an entire data structure stored as a stream of bytes. To read values from
it, you need to move it into a user-defined data structure. If you've not read the How
It Works section from How-To 5.3, do so now so you understand the LSet command
used there. Unlike the prtMip property, however, the structure stored in the
prtDevMode property is not specific to Access. Windows supplies the DEVMODE data
structure, which contains exactly the same information that is stored in the prtDevMode
property. The settings in the prtDevMode property, then, are not determined by Access,
but by your selected printer driver.

The Data Structure

The module basPrintTypes contains a definition for a data structure, type aht_tagDevMode,
that can contain all the information stored in an object's prtDevMode property.

```
Type aht_tagDEVMODE
    dmDeviceName(1 To 32) As Byte
```

```
        dmSpecVersion As Integer
        dmDriverVersion As Integer
        dmSize As Integer
        dmDriverExtra As Integer
        dmFields As Long
        dmOrientation As Integer
        dmPaperSize As Integer
        dmPaperLength As Integer
        dmPaperWidth As Integer
        dmScale As Integer
        dmCopies As Integer
        dmDefaultSource As Integer
        dmPrintQuality As Integer
        dmColor As Integer
        dmDuplex As Integer
        dmYResolution As Integer
        dmTTOption As Integer
        dmCollate As Integer
        dmFormName(1 To 32) As Byte
        dmLogPixels As Integer
        dmBitsPerPixel As Long
        dmPelsWidth As Long
        dmPelsHeight As Long
        dmDisplayFlags As Long
        dmDisplayFrequency As Long
        dmICMMethod As Long
        dmICMIntent As Long
        dmMediaType As Long
        dmDitherType As Long
        dmICCManufacturer As Long
        dmICCModel As Long
        dmDriverExtraBytes(1 To 1024) As Byte
    End Type
```

Any time you need to work with an object's prtDevMode property settings, move the property into a structure of this type, make your modifications, and then move the structure back into the prtDevMode property, just as in How-To 5.3. Table 5-9 describes most of the items in this structure and their range of values. Notice that some items in this structure cannot be changed by your code.

FIELD NAME	READ-ONLY?	CONTAINS	DATA TYPE	VALUES (FROM basPrtDevMode)
dmDeviceName	Yes	Device supported by the selected driver.	32-byte text	For example, HP LaserJet 4
dmSpecVersion	Yes	Version number of this structure itself.	Integer	
dmDriverVersion	Yes	Version of the driver, as assigned by the driver developer.	Integer	

continued on next page

continued from previous page

FIELD NAME	READ-ONLY?	CONTAINS	DATA TYPE	VALUES (FROM basPrtDevMode)
dmSize	Yes	Size, in bytes, of the DEVMODE structure.	Integer	
dmDriverExtra	Yes	Size, in bytes, of the optional driver-specific data, which can follow this structure.	Integer	
dmFields	No	Indication of fields that have been intialized or changed in the structure; if you modify a value in this structure and then write the structure back to the form or report, this value must reflect the fields you've changed.	Long	None or more of the values in Table 5-10, added together
dmOrientation	No	Paper orientation.	Integer	ahtDMORIENT_PORTRAIT (1), or ahtDMORIENT_LANDSCAPE (2)
dmPaperSize	No	Size of the physical page to print on.	Integer	A value from Table 5-11 (depending on which paper sizes the printer supports). If you choose ahtDMPAPER_USER, the width and length of the paper are specified by the dmPaperWidth and dmPaperLength members of this structure.
dmPaperLength	No	Paper length (measured in tenths of a millimeter); used only if the value ofthe Paper Size member is 256 (user-defined).	Integer	Limited by data storage to 328 centimeters
dmPaperWidth	No	Paper width (measured in tenths of a millimeter); used only if the value of the Paper Size member is 256 (user-defined).	Integer	Limited by data storage to 328 centimeters
dmScale	No	Factor by which the printed output is to be scaled. The apparent page size is scaled from the physical page size by a factor or scale/100.	Integer	

FIELD NAME	READ-ONLY?	CONTAINS	DATA TYPE	VALUES (FROM basPrtDevMode)
dmCopies	No	If the printing device supports multiple copies, the number of copies to be printed.	Integer	
dmDefaultSource	No	Default bin from which paper is to be fed.	Integer	A value from Table 5-12
dmPrintQuality	No	Printer resolution. If you specify a positive value, it's treated as the X-resolution, in dots per inch (DPI), and is device dependent; in this case, the dmYResolution field must contain the Y-resolution in DPI.	Integer	A device-independent value from Table 5-13, or a device-dependent value of your choosing, in dots per inch
dmColor	No	Color usage, if the printer supports color printing.	Integer	ahtDMCOLOR_COLOR (1) or ahtDMCOLOR_MONOCHROME (2)
dmDuplex	No	Duplex usage, if the printer supports duplex printing.	Integer	ahtDMDUP_SIMPLEX (1), ahtDMDUP_HORIZONTAL (2), or ahtDMDUP_VERTICAL (3)
dmYResolution	No	Y-resolution for the printer, in dots per inch (DPI); if this value is specified, you must also specify the X-resolution in the dmPrintQuality member; these values are device specific.	Integer	If the dmPrintQuality field is positive, a device-dependent value in dots per inch
dmTTOptions	No	Specifies how TrueType fonts should be printed.	Integer	A value from Table 5-14

Table 5-9 Members of the aht_tagDevMode structure

Because Access makes all this information available to you through the prtDevMode property, you can retrieve and modify any of the settings in the property that aren't read-only. The prtDevMode property for reports and forms provides the only programmatic access to these aspects of printing.

Table 5-10 shows the flags you need to use when setting or retrieving information from the dmFields member. To see if a specific field has been initialized in the structure, you can use code like this:

```
If DM.dmFields AND ahtDM_COPIES <> 0 Then
    ' Now you know that the dmCopies member
    ' has been initialized.
End If
```

To make sure that Access knows that your code has modified one of the fields in the aht_tagDevMode structure, set the value in the dmFields member like this:

```
' Tell Access that you've changed the dmCopies member.
DM.dmFields = DM.dmFields OR ahtDM_COPIES
```

FLAGS FOR THE dmFields MEMBER	VALUE
ahtDM_ORIENTATION	&H0000001
ahtDM_PAPERSIZE	&H0000002
ahtDM_PAPERLENGTH	&H0000004
ahtDM_PAPERWIDTH	&H0000008
ahtDM_SCALE	&H0000010
ahtDM_COPIES	&H0000100
ahtDM_DEFAULTSOURCE	&H0000200
ahtDM_PRINTQUALITY	&H0000400
ahtDM_COLOR	&H0000800
ahtDM_DUPLEX	&H0001000
ahtDM_YRESOLUTION	&H0002000
ahtDM_TTOPTION	&H0004000

Table 5-10 Constants for the dmFields member flags

Table 5-11 shows a list of all the defined paper sizes. You can use one of these constants in the dmPaperSize member to set a new paper size, or you can use ahtDMPAPER_USER (256). The latter alternative will tell Windows that you want to use the values in the dmPaperLength and dmPaperWidth members to specify the paper size.

CONSTANT	VALUE	DESCRIPTION
ahtDMPAPER_LETTER	1	Letter (8.5 x 11 in.)
ahtDMPAPER_LETTERSMALL	2	Letter Small (8.5 x 11 in.)
ahtDMPAPER_TABLOID	3	Tabloid (11 x 17 in.)
ahtDMPAPER_LEDGER	4	Ledger (17 x 11 in.)
ahtDMPAPER_LEGAL	5	Legal (8.5 x 14 in.)
ahtDMPAPER_STATEMENT	6	Statement (5.5 x 8.5 in.)
ahtDMPAPER_EXECUTIVE	7	Executive (7.25 x 10.5 in.)
ahtDMPAPER_A3	8	A3 (297 x 420 mm)
ahtDMPAPER_A4	9	A4 (210 x 297 mm)

CONSTANT	VALUE	DESCRIPTION
ahtDMPAPER_A4SMALL	10	A4 Small (210 x 297 mm)
ahtDMPAPER_A5	11	A5 (148 x 210 mm)
ahtDMPAPER_B4	12	B4 (250 x 354 mm)
ahtDMPAPER_B5	13	B5 (182 x 257 mm)
ahtDMPAPER_FOLIO	14	Folio (8.5 x 13 in.)
ahtDMPAPER_QUARTO	15	Quarto (215 x 275 mm)
ahtDMPAPER_10X14	16	10 x 14 in.
ahtDMPAPER_11X17	17	11 x 17 in.
ahtDMPAPER_NOTE	18	Note (8.5 x 11 in.)
ahtDMPAPER_ENV_9	19	Envelope #9 (3.875 x 8.875 in.)
ahtDMPAPER_ENV_10	20	Envelope #10 (4.125 x 9.5 in.)
ahtDMPAPER_ENV_11	21	Envelope #11 (4.5 x 10.375 in.)
ahtDMPAPER_ENV_12	22	Envelope #12 (4.25 x 11 in.)
ahtDMPAPER_ENV_14	23	Envelope #14 (5 x 11.5 in.)
ahtDMPAPER_CSHEET	24	C size sheet (17 x 22 in.)
ahtDMPAPER_DSHEET	25	D size sheet (22 x 34 in.)
ahtDMPAPER_ESHEET	26	E size sheet (34 x 44 in.)
ahtDMPAPER_ENV_DL	27	Envelope DL (110 x 220 mm)
ahtDMPAPER_ENV_C5	28	Envelope C5 (162 x 229 mm)
ahtDMPAPER_ENV_C3	29	Envelope C3 (324 x 458 mm)
ahtDMPAPER_ENV_C4	30	Envelope C4 (229 x 324 mm)
ahtDMPAPER_ENV_C6	31	Envelope C6 (114 x 162 mm)
ahtDMPAPER_ENV_C65	32	Envelope C65 (114 x 229 mm)
ahtDMPAPER_ENV_B4	33	Envelope B4 (250 x 353 mm)
ahtDMPAPER_ENV_B5	34	Envelope B5 (176 x 250 mm
ahtDMPAPER_ENV_B6	35	Envelope B6 (176 x 125 mm)
ahtDMPAPER_ENV_ITALY	36	Envelope (110 x 230 mm)
ahtDMPAPER_ENV_MONARCH	37	Envelope Monarch (3.875 x 7.5 in.)
ahtDMPAPER_ENV_PERSONAL	38	6-3/4 Envelope (3.625 x 6.5 in.)
ahtDMPAPER_FANFOLD_US	39	US Std Fanfold (14.875 x 11 in.)
ahtDMPAPER_FANFOLD_STD_GERMAN	40	German Std Fanfold (8.5 x 12 in.)
ahtDMPAPER_FANFOLD_LGL_GERMAN	41	German Legal Fanfold (8.5 x 13 in.)
ahtDMPAPER_USER	256	User-defined

Table 5-11 Constants and descriptions for the dmPaperSize member

Table 5-12 shows possible values for the dmDefaultSource member of the structure.

CONSTANT	VALUE	DESCRIPTION
ahtDMBIN_UPPER	1	Upper bin
ahtDMBIN_ONLYONE	1	Only one bin
ahtDMBIN_LOWER	2	Lower bin
ahtDMBIN_MIDDLE	3	Middle bin
ahtDMBIN_MANUAL	4	Manual bin
ahtDMBIN_ENVELOPE	5	Envelope bin
ahtDMBIN_ENVMANUAL	6	Envelope manual bin
ahtDMBIN_AUTO	7	Automatic bin
ahtDMBIN_TRACTOR	8	Tractor bin
ahtDMBIN_SMALLFMT	9	Small-format bin
ahtDMBIN_LARGEFMT	10	Large-format bin
ahtDMBIN_LARGECAPACITY	11	Large-capacity bin
ahtDMBIN_CASSETTE	14	Cassette bin
ahtDMBIN_USER	256	Device-specific bins start here

Table 5-12 Constants and descriptions for the dmDefaultSource member

Table 5-13 shows the predefined, device-independent choices for the dmPrintQuality field of the aht_tagDevMode structure. You can use a positive value instead, which will then represent a device-dependent X-resolution value, measured in dots per inch (DPI). If you choose this method, then you must also specify a device-dependent positive value in the dmYResolution member.

CONSTANT	VALUE	DESCRIPTION
ahtDMRES_HIGH	−4	High resolution
ahtDMRES_MEDIUM	−3	Medium resolution
ahtDMRES_LOW	−2	Low resolution
ahtDMRES_DRAFT	−1	Draft

Table 5-13 Constants and descriptions for the dmPrintQuality member

Table 5-14 lists the several possible ways that the printer can handle TrueType fonts. The dmTTOption member of the aht_tagDevMode structure will contain one of these values.

CONSTANT	VALUE	DESCRIPTION
ahtDMTT_BITMAP	1	Print TT fonts as graphics
ahtDMTT_DOWNLOAD	2	Download TT fonts as soft fonts
ahtDMTT_SUBDEV	3	Substitute device fonts for TT fonts

 Table 5-14 Constants and descriptions for the dmTTOption member

Using the prtDevMode Property

The Steps section above shows how to use the ahtGetDevMode and ahtSetDevMode functions to retrieve and set the prtDevMode property for a form or report. The two functions work exactly like their counterparts in How-To 5.3: They use the LSet command to move data to and from the raw property value.

In between calls to ahtGetDevMode and ahtSetDevMode, however, you need to do a bit more work with the aht_tagDevMode structure than you did with the aht_tagMip structure. Specifically, you must set the dmFields member of the structure, indicating to Access which fields you've modified. For example, to set the number of copies, the orientation, and the page size, you would need code like this:

```
Sub SetDevMode ()

    ' Set rptReport1 to print 5 copies in landscape mode on
    ' normal letter paper.

    Dim dm As aht_tagDEVMODE
    Dim intSuccess As Integer

    ' rptReport1 must be open in design mode for this to succeed.
    If ahtGetDevMode(Reports!rptReport1, dm) Then
        dm.dmCopies = 5
        dm.dmOrientation = ahtDMORIENT_LANDSCAPE
        dm.dmPaperSize = ahtDMPAPER_LETTER
        ' Tell Access which fields you changed!
        dm.dmFields = dm.dmFields Or ahtDM_COPIES Or ahtDM_ORIENTATION _
          Or ahtDM_PAPERSIZE
        intSuccess = ahtSetDevMode(Reports!rptReport1, dm)
    End If
End Sub
```

Comments

By using the functions supplied here—ahtGetDevMode and ahtSetDevMode—you can be assured that you're getting the data copied in and out of the prtDevMode property correctly. On the other hand, this property is very "raw." If you set it incorrectly, chances are that Access and/or Windows will crash when you try to preview or print the form or report. As when working with the Windows API, you should be careful to save everything before you run any code dealing with the prtDevMode (or prtMip or prtDevNames) property.

5.5 How do I... Print on odd-sized paper?

Problem

My printer driver supports user-defined paper sizes. I can see that option in the list of available paper sizes on the File|Page Setup dialog box. But when I choose it, I can't find a way to tell Access how big the page should be. Is there a way to control this from VBA?

Technique

Some printers support user-defined paper sizes. Most laser printers do not, but the new HP LaserJet 5P/5MP, for example, does. If you're printing an odd-sized report, you must set up your printer so that it knows what paper size to expect. This information is especially crucial on continuous-feed printers, because the printer must eject just enough paper once it's finished printing the current page to get to the top of the next.

To find out if your printer supports custom page sizes, open the Access File|Page Setup dialog box and scroll through the values available in the Paper Size combo box (see Figure 5-5). If you see a User-Defined Size or Custom Size option, then you know your printer supports custom paper sizes. If not, you won't be able to use the technique in this How-To.

This How-To uses the prtDevMode property, presented in detail in How-To 5.4, to allow you to choose custom page sizes for printing. Although Access won't complain if you run this example code with a printer selected that doesn't support custom paper sizes, the code will appear to be broken; it will do nothing at all to your reports.

Steps

This section covers two ways to manipulate page sizes: using the example form frmPrintSettings and in your own applications. Before trying the sample, you'll need to load Access' File|Page Setup dialog box and take note of the supported paper sizes. Then load and run frmPrintSettings in 05-05.MDB (as shown in Figure 5-6).

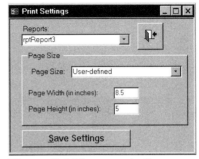

Figure 5-6 The sample form, frmPrintSettings, showing rptReport3's page size settings

Figure 5-5 The Access File|Page Setup dialog box, with a user-defined page size selected

Using the Example Form

1. With frmPrintSettings loaded, choose a report from the Reports combo box. This opens the report in design mode, minimized.

2. If your printer supports user-defined sizes, choose that value from the Page Size combo box. If not, you can choose one of the other paper sizes from the sample form's combo box. (Note: This example provides a list of all the Windows-available paper sizes, no matter which printer driver you've selected. If you select a paper size that your printer doesn't know about, Access will disregard your selection.)

3. If you chose user-defined in step 2, the two text boxes on frmPrintSettings will be available. Enter a reasonable page width and height (in inches) into the text boxes. If you choose a size that makes it impossible for Access to print the report, given the report's margin settings, the driver will substitute a page size based on its own internal calculations.

4. Choose the Save Settings button. The code attached to this button's Click event will write a new aht_tagDevMode structure to the chosen report's prtDevMode property, but will not actually save the report. (See How-To 5.4 for more information on the prtDevMode property.) Unless you click this button, the form will make no changes to the report.

5. Select the report, click on it to open it, and switch it into Print Preview mode. It will be displayed using the page dimensions you've selected. Figure 5-7 shows rptReport3 set up to print on a 5 x 5-inch square of paper.

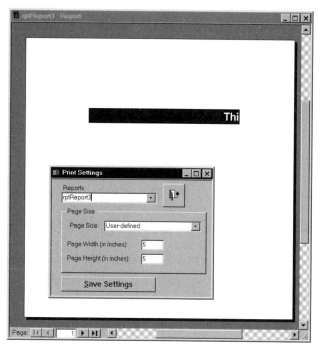

Figure 5-7 The rptReport3 report in Print Preview mode, set up for printing on a 5 x 5-inch square

Using the Code in Your Own Application

To use this technique in your own application, import the objects listed in Table 5-15 from 05-05.MDB into your database.

OBJECT TYPE	OBJECT NAME
Form	frmPrintSettings
Module	basOpenReport
Module	basPrintTypes
Module	basPrtDevMode

Table 5-15 Objects to import from 05-05.MDB, allowing you to change paper sizes

With these objects in your application, you can use code from the module attached to frmPrintSettings, along with the routines in the global modules (as shown in How It Works), to set the paper size for any report or form in your application.

How It Works

As mentioned in How-To 5.4, you can set an object's page size (among many other values) using the object's prtDevMode property. In this case, you're working with the dmPaperSize member of the user-defined aht_tagDevMode structure. The value of this member can be any of the items from the first column in Table 5-11. If its value is ahtDMPAPER_USER (256), for example, then you must supply the exact paper size, in 1/10 millimeters, in the dmPaperWidth and dmPaperLength elements of the structure.

On the frmPrintSettings sample form, once you choose a specific report, the code attached to the Reports combo box's AfterUpdate event executes this fragment:

```
If ahtOpenReport(strReport, acDesign) Then
    If ahtGetDevMode(Reports(strReport), dm) Then
        With Me
            !cboPaperSize = dm.dmPaperSize
            !txtPaperWidth = dm.dmPaperWidth / ahtcInchesToMM
            !txtPaperLength = dm.dmPaperLength / ahtcInchesToMM
        End With
    End If
    ' Enable the two text boxes if the user chose
    ' a user-defined page size.
    EnableItems
End If
```

Once the code succeeds in opening the selected report in design mode, it attempts to retrieve the prtDevMode property for that report, in the aht_tagDevMode structure named *dm*. If it succeeds, it pulls the dmPaperSize, dmPaperWidth, and dmPaperLength values from that structure and places them in controls on the form. Note that the code converts the width and length values to inches from tenths of millimeters by dividing by the ahtcInchesToMM constant (254). Finally, if the report's to be printed on paper with a user-defined size, this code enables the width and length text boxes on the form.

Once you enter the width and height values you want, clicking the Save Settings button executes this code fragment:

```
With dm
    .dmPaperSize = Me!cboPaperSize
    If .dmPaperSize <> ahtDMPAPER_USER Then
        .dmPaperWidth = 0
        .dmPaperLength = 0
    Else
        .dmPaperWidth = Me!txtPaperWidth * ahtcInchesToMM
        .dmPaperLength = Me!txtPaperLength * ahtcInchesToMM
    End If
    .dmFields = dm.dmFields Or ahtDM_PAPERSIZE Or _
    ahtDM_PAPERLENGTH Or ahtDM_PAPERWIDTH
End With
intSuccess = ahtSetDevMode(rpt, dm)
```

This code retrieves the selected paper size from the combo box on the form. If you selected anything besides a user-defined size, the code sets the dmPaperWidth and dmPaperLength members to 0. Otherwise, it converts the values you entered from inches to tenths of millimeters (multiplying by ahtcInchesToMM (254)) and stores the new values in the dmPaperWidth and dmPaperLength members.

Before it replaces the report's prtDevMode property, it must take one final action: setting the dmFields member to reflect the fields that have changed. The code uses the OR operator to add together the three constants from Table 5-10 that indicate which fields have been changed, and places the sum in the dmFields member of the structure. Once this is done, the code can call the ahtSetDevMode function to replace the prtDevMode property.

OR vs. Addition

Programmers normally use the OR operator to add together constants, like the ahtDM_* constants in Table 5-10. The constants in that table tell the dmFields member of the aht_tagDevMode structure which fields have been changed in the structure. Each constant consists of a 32-bit hexadecimal value that has exactly one bit set to 1. All the rest of the bits in the value are 0. Using this technique, you can store up to 32 different pieces of information in one 32-bit number. You can use the + to add the values, but using the OR operator instead makes it clear, in context, that you're not so much adding ordinary values as setting the bits in a flag field.

Comments

The technique presented in this How-To will only work if the object whose prtDevMode property you're modifying is opened in design mode. If you switch the report to Print Preview mode and then select the Save Settings button on frmPrintSettings, you'll see no error message; the code attached to the button will simply fail in its attempt to set the prtDevMode property. In production code, you either want to handle this situation or ensure that the object is open in the correct mode before attempting to set the property.

To help you check the mode, use one of two methods:

 For forms, check the CurrentView property. This will tell you if the form is in Design, Form, or Datasheet view.

For reports, there is no such convenient test. To check to see whether the report's in Design view (which is all that really matters for your purposes here), use the isReportInDesignMode function in the basOpenReport module. You'll find it set up as a private function, but you can easily remove the Private keyword and use it as is, or copy it to your own application. It returns True if the report you specify is open in design mode, False if otherwise.

Paper size is just one of many options you can change using the prtDevMode property. Because it's more involved than most, we chose it as the topic for this How-To. The next How-To will demonstrate using the prtDevMode property to choose the paper source on your printer. You may want to combine the information in these topics with the details in How-To 5.4 to create your own form that will allow your applications to change any or all of the prtDevMode properties for reports or forms.

COMPLEXITY:
ADVANCED

5.6 How do I... Programmatically control the paper source?

Problem

I'd like to be able to print the first page of my reports from a paper tray containing letterhead paper, and then print the rest on normal paper stock. Is there some way to convince Access to switch paper trays programmatically, from within my application?

Technique

The paper source is another of the members of the prtDevMode property (see How-To 5.4 for a description of the prtDevMode property) that you can control programmatically. Given the procedures in How-To 5.4, it's relatively easy to change the paper source for a report so that the first page prints from one paper bin and the rest prints from another.

Steps

This section will show you two ways to control paper sources: using the example form and in your own code. Load and run frmPaperSource in 05-06.MDB (Figure 5-8).

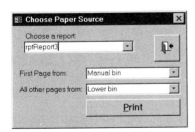

Figure 5-8 The sample form, frmPaperSource, allowing you to print from different paper sources

Using the Example Form

1. With frmPaperSource loaded, choose a report. This will load the report in design mode, minimized.

2. Choose a paper bin for the first page and for the rest of the pages. Note that the lists of paper bins contain all the possible paper sources; your printer may support only one, or perhaps some of the options listed in the combo boxes. You'll need to find the bins that work correctly with your printer driver. (For the HP LaserJet 4, Manual and Lower work once the settings on the printer are changed to allow manual control over the paper source.)

3. Choose the Print button. Access should print the first page of the report from the chosen bin for the first page, and the second page from the other bin you've chosen.

Using the Code in Your Own Application

To use this technique in your own application, import the objects listed in Table 5-16 from 05-06.MDB into your database.

OBJECT TYPE	OBJECT NAME
Form	frmPaperSource
Module	basOpenReport
Module	basPrintTypes
Module	basPrtDevMode

Table 5-16 Objects to import from 05-06.MDB, allowing you to control paper sources

With these objects in your application, you can use code from the module attached to frmPaperSource, along with the routines in the global modules (as shown in How It Works), to control the paper sources for printing any report or form in your application.

How It Works

As you saw in How-To 5.4, you can use a form or report's prtDevMode property to change its paper source. Printing one page of a report from one bin and the rest from another is quite simple. First, use the ahtGetDevMode() function to retrieve the object's prtDevMode property. Once you have that, set the dmDefaultSource member to be one of the values from Table 5-12, set the dmFields member to indicate the value you've changed, and replace the report's prtDevMode property.

```
If ahtGetDevMode(rpt, dm) Then
    ' Handle the first page.
    With dm
        .dmDefaultSource = Me!cboFirstPage
        .dmFields = dm.dmFields Or ahtDM_DEFAULTSOURCE
```

```
        End With
        fSuccess = ahtSetDevMode(rpt, dm)
        ' ...
End If
```

Once you've set up your report with the prtDevMode property telling it what bin to use as its paper source, print the first page:

```
DoCmd.SelectObject acReport, strReport
DoCmd.Print acPages, 1, 1
```

Then revisit the prtDevMode property, setting the paper source to the bin you've chosen for the rest of the pages. After you've set the paper source, use the Print macro action to print all the rest of the pages (2 through the arbitrarily chosen 32,000).

```
With dm
    .dmDefaultSource = Me!cboAllOther
    .dmFields = dm.dmFields Or ahtDM_DEFAULTSOURCE
End With
fSuccess = ahtSetDevMode(rpt, dm)
If Not fSuccess Then
    MsgBox "Unable to set the prtDevMode property!"
Else
    ' Print all the rest (up to page 32000)
    DoCmd.PrintOut acPages, 2, 32000
End If
```

The following listing shows all the code attached to the Click event of the Print button on the sample form.

```
Private Sub cmdPrint_Click()
    Dim dm As aht_tagDEVMODE
    Dim fSuccess As Boolean
    Dim strReport As String
    Dim rpt As Report

    strReport = Me!cboReportList
    Set rpt = Reports(strReport)

    If ahtGetDevMode(rpt, dm) Then
        ' Handle the first page.
        With dm
            .dmDefaultSource = Me!cboFirstPage
            .dmFields = dm.dmFields Or ahtDM_DEFAULTSOURCE
        End With
        fSuccess = ahtSetDevMode(rpt, dm)
        If Not fSuccess Then
            MsgBox "Unable to set the prtDevMode property!"
        Else
            ' Print the first page
            DoCmd.SelectObject acReport, strReport
            DoCmd.PrintOut acPages, 1, 1
        End If

        ' Print all the rest of the pages.
        Set rpt = Reports(strReport)
        With dm
```

continued on next page

289

continued from previous page

```
          .dmDefaultSource = Me!cboAllOther
          .dmFields = dm.dmFields Or ahtDM_DEFAULTSOURCE
      End With
      fSuccess = ahtSetDevMode(rpt, dm)
      If Not fSuccess Then
          MsgBox "Unable to set the prtDevMode property!"
      Else
          ' Print all the rest (up to page 32000)
          DoCmd.PrintOut acPages, 2, 32000
      End If
      DoCmd.Close acReport, strReport, acExit
  Else
      MsgBox "Unable to get the prtDevMode property!"
  End If
End Sub
```

Comments

As mentioned in the Comments section of How-To 5.5, this method requires that the report to be printed is first opened in Design view, as the prtDevMode property is read-only in all other views. How-To 5.5 suggests some ways you can check to make sure the report is in the correct view; otherwise you can, as in this How-To, control that yourself.

If you're going to provide this functionality in an application to be distributed to users who have printers that you've not tested it on, you'll need to make it clear that some of the bins listed in the combo boxes may not work with their printers. It may require some experimentation on their part to determine which are the correct settings.

COMPLEXITY:
ADVANCED

5.7 How do I...
Retrieve information about a report's or form's selected printer?

Problem

Access's File|Page Setup dialog box allows me to specify either the default printer or a specific printer for each printable object. I'd like to be able to find out, programmatically, which printer has been selected for an object and whether or not the object is set to print to the default printer. How can I retrieve that information?

Technique

The Windows DEVNAMES structure keeps track of the three pieces of information Windows must know about an output device: the device name (HP LaserJet 4), the driver name (WINSPOOL), and the output port (LPT1:). In addition, the DEVNAMES structure keeps track of whether the specific printer happens to be the default Windows printer. The DEVNAMES structure is too complex to be very useful to Basic programmers, so Access provides the prtDevNames property, which mirrors the data in the DEVNAMES structure for forms and reports. The goal of this How-To is to get the information from an object's prtDevNames property into an aht_tagDeviceRec structure, which is far simpler to manage but carries the same information.

Steps

Load and run the form frmSelectedPrinters in 05-07.MDB. Figure 5-9 shows the form after rptReport3 is selected and the report's output device, driver, and port are filled in on the form. In addition, because this report was set up to print to the default printer, the Printing to Default Printer check box is selected.

To retrieve printer information about forms or reports in your own applications, follow these steps:

1. Import the modules listed in Table 5-17 from 05-07.MDB into your own application. Skip any modules that you've previously imported.

MODULE	PURPOSE	CONTAINS
basOpenReport	Open a report in design mode, or do nothing if it's already open.	ahtOpenReport
basPrintTypes	Define data types and constants for all examples in this chapter.	
basPrtDevNames	Get and set prtDevName values, copying them into an aht_tagDeviceRec structure.	ahtGetDevNames, ahtSetDevNames

Table 5-17 Modules to import from 05-07.MDB in order to access the prtDevNames property

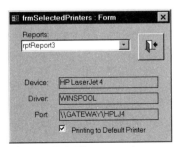

Figure 5-9 The sample form, frmSelectedPrinters, after selecting rptReport3

2. To retrieve prtDevNames information about a particular form or report, call the ahtGetDevNames function with the following syntax. Table 5-18 lists the parameters for ahtGetDevNames and their data types.

```
fSuccess = ahtGetDevNames (obj, dr, fDefault)
```

PARAMETER	DATA TYPE	PURPOSE
obj	Form or Report	The form or report to retrieve information about.
dr	aht_tagDeviceRec	On return, the prtDevNames info.
fDefault	Integer	On return, True if this is the default printer, False otherwise.

Table 5-18 Parameters for the ahtGetDevNames function

For example, the following code fragment, from frmSelectedPrinters, displays the chosen report's device name, driver name, and output port in text boxes on the form. In addition, it sets the value of the chkDefault check box if the selected printer is also the default printer.

```
If ahtGetDevNames(rpt, dr, fDefault) Then
    With Me
        !txtDevice = dr.drDeviceName
        !txtDriver = dr.drDriverName
        !txtPort = dr.drPort
        !chkDefault = fDefault
    End With
End If
```

How It Works

Just like the prtMip and prtDevMode properties discussed in How-To's 5.3 and 5.4, the prtDevNames property consists of a stream of bytes, not distinct values. To retrieve the values, you must use the LSet command to overlay the data from the prtDevNames property onto a user-defined type. The prtDevNames property is a bit more complex, however, than explained in How-To 5.3, because it contains variable-length text. Unlike prtMip and prtDevMode, the prtDevNames property includes two parts: The first part contains integers acting as pointers into the second part. The first part contains three integers that give the offsets, within the second part, of the three null-delimited strings contained in the property (the device name, the driver name, and the output port). The first part contains one extra integer containing either a 1 or a 0, indicating whether or not the object was set up to print to the default printer (1) or to a specific printer (0).

The following paragraphs explain how the ahtGetDevNames extracts the necessary three strings from an object's prtDevNames property. (All the following code fragments are from ahtGetDevNames, in basPrtDevNames.) First, it copies the prtDevNames property of an object to a string variable.

```
Dim strNames As String

strNames = obj.prtDevNames
```

Because *strNames* now holds a stream of bytes containing all the information you need, you must use the LSet command to copy it to a structure where you can break it down into its component pieces. Remember, though, that LSet requires that both operands be user-defined data types. In this case, you just want the first 8 bytes of the prtDevNames property (three offsets plus the default flag), so use a helper structure defined like this:

```
Type aht_tagDEVNAMEStr
    DNStr As String * 4
End Type
```

You'll need to use the LSet command to copy the first 8 bytes from the string (comprising the four integers you need, as each one takes up 2 bytes) into the structure where you really want the four integers, of user-defined type aht_tagDevNames. As usual, basPrintTypes contains all the type definitions you'll need.

```
Type aht_tagDEVNAMES
    dnDriverOffset As Integer
    dnDeviceOffset As Integer
    dnOutputOffset As Integer
    dnDefault As Integer
End Type
```

The code, then, looks like this:

```
Dim dnStrTemp As aht_tagDevNameStr
Dim dn As aht_tagDEVNAMES

dnStrTemp.dnStr = LeftB(strNames, 8)
If Err = 0 Then
    LSet dn = dnStrTemp
    '...
End If
```

Once you've gotten the four integers into the aht_tagDevNames structure, you can pull apart the three strings that follow the integers in the original data. To make this as simple as possible, basPrtDevNames includes a function, GrabDevName, whose purpose it is to pull pieces out of the prtDevNames string, given a starting position. The code in ahtGetDevNames calls GrabDevName like this:

```
With dr
    .drDeviceName = GrabDevName(strNames, dn.dnDeviceOffset)
    .drDriverName = GrabDevName(strNames, dn.dnDriverOffset)
    .drPort = GrabDevName(strNames, dn.dnOutputOffset)
End With
```

This code fills in all three pieces of dr, the aht_tagDeviceRec structure that ahtGetDevNames is attempting to fill in.

To finish up, ahtGetDevNames copies the value from dn.dnDefault into the integer parameter you passed to ahtGetDevNames.

```
fDefault = dn.dnDefault
```

Comments

Notice that basPrtDevNames includes a function named ahtSetDevNames. This function exists only for the sake of completeness; you should be wary about using it. Normally, you can't use it to set the values in the prtDevNames property, because changing the output device in the prtDevNames property also requires changing it in the prtDevMode property. But if you change the output device without also retrieving reasonable data for the rest of the prtDevMode property, you're likely to cause Access to crash, because Windows and Access will be at odds as to the current output device and its characteristics. Though it's possible to make this work using a number of Windows API calls, you're better off just setting up your reports to print to the default printer and changing that value.

If you can't use the prtDevNames property without a lot of extra work to change the selected printer for an object, you might be tempted to believe that prtDevNames doesn't do you any good. That's not true, as you'll see in How-To's 5.8 and 5.9. How-To 5.8 discusses how you can choose a new default printer at runtime so that reports configured to print to the default device will now go to the new default printer. You can (and should) set the default printer back to its original state when you're done. How-To 5.9 shows you how to use the prtDevNames property to create a report listing all the reports in your database and whether or not they're configured to print to the default printer. Using this tool, you can ensure that all your reports are set up correctly before delivering your application. As long as all your reports print to the default printer, you can use the technique from How-To 5.8 to change the default printer, print the report, and then switch the default printer back to its original state.

COMPLEXITY:
INTERMEDIATE

5.8   How do I...
Choose an output device at runtime?

Problem

I'd like to be able to select an output device while my application is running without having to pop up the File|Page Setup dialog box. Is there a way to present a list of available printers and have the chosen report print to the chosen device? For example, I'd like to print my reports to the printer sometimes and to the fax device other times.

Technique

Though this topic sounds complex, its solution is really just a combination of other How-To's in this chapter. How-To 5.2 shows how to retrieve a list of available print devices and retrieve and set the default device. How-To 5.7 shows how to determine if a given report or form is configured to print to the default printer. Given those two techniques, this How-To shows you how to retrieve and store the current default output device, set a new output device, print the Access object (using the new default device), and then restore the original default device. This process will only work for Access objects that print to the default printer, and the sample form takes that into account.

Steps

Load and run frmDefaultPrinterList from 05-08.MDB. Figure 5-10 shows the form in use, with the report rptReport3 selected and ready to print. Because rptReport3 has been configured to print to the default printer (you can open the File|Page Setup dialog box to confirm this), the Default Printer? check box on the sample form is checked. In addition, if the chosen object will print to the default printer, you can choose a different output device from the combo box on the bottom of the form (of course, this will only be interesting if you happen to have more than one output device installed). If the report you choose is set up to print to a specific printer, you won't be able to choose a new output device. (In the sample database, only rptReport3 is configured to print to the default printer.) If you choose a different output device (a fax driver, for example), the sample form will send the selected report to that output device, saving, modifying, and restoring the default print device.

1. To print a report to a specific output device in your own applications, import the objects listed in Table 5-19 from 05-08.MDB.

OBJECT TYPE	OBJECT NAME
Form	frmDefaultPrinterList
Module	basDefaultPrinter
Module	basGetPrinters
Module	basINIFile
Module	basOpenReport
Module	basPrintItem
Module	basPrintTypes
Module	basPrtDevNames
Module	basToken

Table 5-19 Objects to import from 05-08.MDB, allowing you to choose output devices at runtime

2. When you're ready to print, open the form frmDefaultPrinterList. If you select a report that's set up to print to the default printer, you'll be able to specify a new output device.

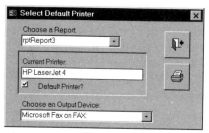

Figure 5-10 The sample form,
frmDefaultPrinterList, ready to
choose a new output device

How It Works

The sample form, frmDefaultPrinterList, consists of three items, all of which have been covered previously. The list of reports was used in How-To's 5.3 through 5.7, and the method for filling the list was discussed in How-To 5.3 in the Comments section. Once you've chosen a report from the combo box, the sample form shows the selected printer for that report and whether or not the report is to be printed on the default printer. The combo box on the bottom of the sample form allows you to choose an output device if the selected report is destined for the default printer.

The only outstanding issue, then, is the code for printing the report: storing away the current default printer, setting the new printer, printing the report to the new printer, and then resetting the original device. These activities are well supported by the routines you'll find in the 05-08.MDB modules.

When you click on the printer button on the sample form, you execute the following code in the form's module.

```
Private Sub cmdPrint_Click()

    Dim dr As aht_tagDeviceRec
    Dim ctl As Control

    ' Retrieve the pieces needed by dr from
    ' the combo box.
    Set ctl = Me!cboPrinters
    With dr
        .drDeviceName = ctl.Column(1)
        .drDriverName = ctl.Column(2)
        .drPort = ctl.Column(3)
    End With
    If Not PrintItem(Me!cboReportList, acReport, dr) Then
        MsgBox "Unable to print " & Me!cboReportList
    End If
End Sub
```

The first step in cmdPrint_Click is to gather up the information about the new printer. Because the combo box showing the list of printers contains all the necessary information (device name, driver name, and output port) in hidden columns, it's simple to fill in the required aht_tagDeviceRec structure using the Column property of the combo box.

```
With dr
    .drDeviceName = ctl.Column(1)
    .drDriverName = ctl.Column(2)
    .drPort = ctl.Column(3)
End With
```

Once you've got the data structure filled, cmdPrint_Click calls the PrintItem function (in the basPrintItem module) to do the work of storing away the current printer, setting the chosen output device, printing the report, and then resetting the output device to its original status.

```
Function PrintItem(ByVal strName As String, intType As Integer, _
  dr As aht_tagDeviceRec) As Boolean

    ' Return True if successful, False otherwise.

    Dim drOld As aht_tagDeviceRec
    Dim intRetval As Integer

    intRetval = False

    ' Store away the previous default printer
    If (ahtGetDefaultPrinter(drOld)) Then
        If ahtSetDefaultPrinter(dr) Then
            ' Turn off error checking, so canceling the
            ' report doesn't trigger a runtime error.
            On Error Resume Next
            With DoCmd
                Select Case intType
                    Case acReport
                        .OpenReport strName, acNormal
                        .Close acReport, strName
                    Case acForm
                        .OpenForm strName
                        .PrintOut
                        .Close acForm, strName
                End Select
            End With
            On Error GoTo 0

            ' Put the original printer information back in
            ' WIN.INI.
            If ahtSetDefaultPrinter(drOld) Then
                ' If you got all the way to here,
                ' you succeeded!
                intRetval = True
            End If
        End If
    End If
    PrintItem = intRetval
End Function
```

This is the procedure that does all the work, and you can call this from any application in which you need this functionality—it's not dependent on the form. Pass it an object reference and a filled-in structure with information about the printing device, and you're all set.

To change the default printer, PrintItem first preserves the original default printer.

```
If (ahtGetDefaultPrinter(drOld)) Then ...
```

Then it sets the new output device.

```
If ahtSetDefaultPrinter(dr) Then ...
```

Then it's time to print. PrintItem opens the object and prints it, using macro actions that depend on the object type.

```
' Turn off error checking, so canceling the
' report doesn't trigger a runtime error.
On Error Resume Next
With DoCmd
    Select Case intType
        Case acReport
            .OpenReport strName, acNormal
            .Close acReport, strName
        Case acForm
            .OpenForm strName
            .PrintOut
            .Close acForm, strName
    End Select
End With
On Error GoTo 0
```

Finally, PrintItem restores the original printer.

```
' Put the original printer information back in WIN.INI.
If ahtSetDefaultPrinter(drOld) Then
    ' If you got all the way to here,
    ' you succeeded!
    intRetval = True
End If
```

Comments

You can make many changes to this sample application. You might, for example, want to supply the report name without providing a combo box for it on the form. In that case, you would use a form like the sample form in How-To 5.2, showing only the list of output devices. You would modify the cmdPrint_Click procedure, above, to take the report name from a variable instead of from the form's combo box.

You might also want to add some error handling. For the sake of simplicity, the routines here include minimal, if any, error handling. Though it's unlikely that your application will be unable to write or read WIN.INI, it certainly could happen. Production code would enable error handling and check the error value any time you read or write disk files, and react accordingly should an error occur.

5.9

FIND THE REPORTS THAT AREN'T SET TO PRINT TO THE DEFAULT PRINTER?

COMPLEXITY:
INTERMEDIATE

5.9 How do I...
Find the reports that are not set to print to the default printer?

Problem

I am about to distribute my application to other Access users. I want to ensure that all my reports are set to Default Printer so they will work with the user's installation of Windows. How do I create a list of all my reports and show whether or not they have been saved with the Default Printer setting?

Technique

Building on the code examples in this chapter, you can use the functionality of the ahtGetDevNames procedure to determine if a report has the Default Printer selected. This How-To uses this function, along with some simple Data Access Object code, to get a list of reports in your database, to check the Default Printer setting, and to save the results to a table. This table feeds a report that you can print, rptReportPrinters. Once you have this list, you can set the output device for each report that has been set to print to a specific printer, rather than to the Windows default printer.

Steps

Open and run frmShowReports from 05-09.MDB. Figure 5-11 shows the form once it's done all its calculations. It will show the name of every report in your database, along with the Default Printer setting for each. You can obtain a printout of this

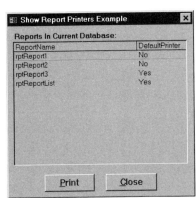

Figure 5-11 The Show Report Printers Example form

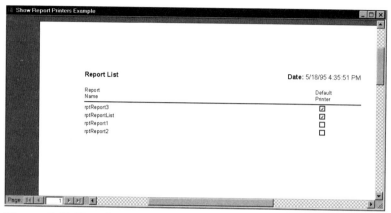

Figure 5-12 The Show Report Printers Example report

information by pressing the Print button that prints the rptReportPrinters report (as shown in Figure 5-12).

To use this form in your own applications, follow these steps:

1. Import the objects listed in Table 5-20 from 05-09.MDB. (Skip any of the modules that you might have imported already.)

OBJECT TYPE	OBJECT NAME
Table	tblReportPrinters
Form	frmShowReports
Report	rptReportPrinters
Module	basOpenReport
Module	basPrintTypes
Module	basPrtDevNames

 Table 5-20 Objects to import from 05-09.MDB, allowing the creation of output status report

2. Once you've imported the objects, open the form frmShowReports to create the list of reports in your application, along with their output status.

How It Works

To see how this technique works, open the frmShowReports form in design view, then open the form's module window and locate Form_Open. This subroutine calls the GetReports subroutine, which does most of the actual work. By iterating through the Documents collection of the Reports container, GetReports has access to each report in your database. Notice that the subroutine calls the Refresh method before it actually uses the collection; this ensures that the collection is up to date.

```
Private Sub GetReports()
    '
    ' Get a list of reports from the current database
    ' and write the name, along with the default printer
    ' status, to the output table
    '
    Dim db As Database
    Dim rst As Recordset
    Dim conReports As Container
    Dim intCounter As Integer
    Dim doc As Document

    On Error GoTo GetReportsError

    Call EmptyTable("tblReportPrinters")
    Set db = CurrentDb()
    Set rst = db.OpenRecordset("tblReportPrinters", dbOpenTable)
    Set conReports = db.Containers("Reports")

    Application.Echo False

    ' Refresh to get latest list
    conReports.Documents.Refresh

    ' Loop through all the reports in the container's
    ' documents collection, opening each report in turn,
    ' and checking to see if that report is formatted to
    ' send its output to the default printer.
    With rst
        For Each doc In conReports.Documents
            .AddNew
                ![ReportName] = doc.Name
                ![DefaultPrinter] = GetDefaultPrinter(doc.Name)
            .Update
        Next
    End With

GetReportsExit:
    Application.Echo True
    If Not rst Is Nothing Then rst.Close
    Exit Sub

GetReportsError:
    Resume GetReportsExit

End Sub
```

The core of this technique is the ahtGetDevNames function, introduced in How-To 5.7. By calling this function and checking the value of the passed fDefault parameter, you can quickly tell if a report is set to print to the Windows default printer. This function only works on an open report, so the technique must first open the report. (In this case, since you won't be writing to the report but just retrieving its prtDevNames property, you can open it in preview mode. This will minimize the screen flashing.) It opens the report by calling ahtOpenReport, obtaining the output status by calling GetDefaultPrinter, and then closing the report. GetDefaultPrinter is the function that determines if a report is set to print to the default printer or not.

```
Private Function GetDefaultPrinter(ByVal strReport As String) As Boolean
    '
    ' Determine if the named report is set to print to the default printer
    '
    ' In  : strReport - name of report to check
    ' Out : True/False
    '
    Dim dr As aht_tagDeviceRec
    Dim fDefault As Boolean
    Dim rpt As Report

    ' Assume the negative
    GetDefaultPrinter = False
    If ahtOpenReport(strReport, acPreview) Then
        Set rpt = Reports(strReport)
        If ahtGetDevNames(rpt, dr, fDefault) Then
            GetDefaultPrinter = fDefault
        End If
    End If

    ' ahtOpenReport() leaves the report open,
    ' so close it now.
    DoCmd.Close acReport, strReport

End Function
```

This routine is passed a report name, which passes it in turn to ahtOpenReport. The ahtOpenReport function, used throughout this chapter, handles opening the report. Next, the routine calls the ahtGetDevNames function to determine whether or not the report has been set to print to the Windows default printer. Finally, the routine closes the report and returns the value stored in fDefault to the GetReports subroutine. GetReports fills in the table named tblReportPrinters that contains a record for each report containing the report name, and a Yes/No field for the Default Printer setting of that report.

Comments

This How-To loads every report, in turn, to retrieve the prtDevNames property of each. When you open a report, there is some screen painting involved. When you open a report in Design View, the toolbars and property sheet associated with report design also open. When you open a report in Print Preview mode (as in this How-To) the screen still flashes a bit as the code loads each report. Even if you turn off the screen display using Application.Echo before opening the report, you will see activity on your monitor. Although this is not a problem in a development process such as the technique shown here, it can be a real eyesore when presented to your users. Unfortunately, Access has no built-in functionality to disable screen painting completely. On the other hand, if you are willing to do a little Windows API programming, you can easily call the LockWindowUpdate function to disable screen painting completely, as shown in How-To 4.4.

CHAPTER 6
MANAGING DATA

6

MANAGING DATA

How do I...

The point of a database program is to manage data. Although Access provides the majority of the tools you'll need, there are many tasks where you have to roll your own solution. This chapter concentrates on working with data in ways that traditional database operations don't support. You'll learn how to search for records phonetically, back up your database objects, perform lightning-fast finds on linked tables, save housekeeping information, and more. All examples in this chapter use some form of Visual Basic for Applications (VBA) code, but don't worry. All examples are clearly explained and "testbed" applications are supplied to show you how each technique works.

6.1 Save Each Record with the Name of the Last Person Who Edited It, the Date, and the Time

Microsoft Access keeps track of when an object is created and last modified. However, it does not track this information at the record level. This How-To will show how to use the CurrentUser and Now functions to retrieve this information and then use form events to write this information to the form's record whenever a record is changed or added.

6.2 Determine If I'm on a New Record in a Form

It's often useful to know if you are in the midst of adding a new record or editing an existing record. This How-To will show how to use the NewRecord property to determine if you are on a new record.

6.3 Find All Records with Names That Sound Alike

Access provides flexible pattern-searching capabilities in queries that let you search, for example, for all names that begin with S, but there's no way to search for all records that sound like Smith. This How-To will demonstrate a Soundex function and will show you how to use it to search for names phonetically.

6.4 Find the Median Value for a Field

There are built-in domain functions for calculating average, sum, standard deviation, and variance, but there's no built-in function for calculating the median of a set of data. This How-To will present a median-calculating function and will show how to use it in your own applications.

6.5 Quickly Find a Record in a Linked Table

The Seek method is the fastest way to find a value in an indexed field of a table. Unfortunately, you can't use the Seek method on linked tables. Or can you? This How-To will show you how to take advantage of the OpenDatabase method to open the source database directly and perform seek operations on your linked tables.

6.6 Get a Complete List of Field Properties from a Table or Query

Through the Data Access Objects (DAO) model, Access maintains a list of each object in your database and its properties. This How-To will show you how to use DAO to distill this valuable property information into a table that you can use elsewhere in your application.

6.7 Create and Use Flexible AutoNumber Fields

Access AutoNumber fields provide an easy way to add unique key values to records. However, the value of an AutoNumber field is often not useful for sorting or identifying a record. This How-To will demonstrate the use of custom AutoNumber fields that are multiuser ready and may contain characters from another identifying field (such as Last Name) to create unique keys that sort intuitively.

6.8 Back Up Selected Objects to Another Database

Because Access saves all database objects in a single MDB file, it can be difficult to save and restore selected objects from backups. This How-To will demonstrate how to create a set of routines to save Access objects selectively to another database.

COMPLEXITY:
EASY

6.1 How do I...
Save each record with the name of the last person who edited it, the date, and the time?

Problem

My application is used in a multiuser environment with users regularly adding and editing records. With each record, I want to log who created the record, who last edited the record, and the date and time associated with each of these actions. Is this possible?

Technique

Access has no built-in feature that records who edited a record and when the edit was made, but it's fairly easy to create your own. You'll need to add four fields to each of your tables to hold this information. In addition, you'll need to create two simple macros and attach them to the BeforeInsert and BeforeUpdate events of your forms.

Steps

Load the frmCustomer1 form from 06-01.MDB. This form, shown in Figure 6-1, allows you to enter and edit data in the tblCustomer table. Make a change to an existing record and the DateModified and UserModified fields are updated with the current date and

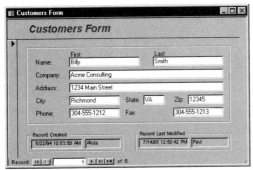

Figure 6-1 The frmCustomer1 form

time and user name. Add a new record and the DateCreated and UserCreated fields are updated.

To add this technique to your application, follow these steps:

1. Modify your table to include four new fields, as shown in Table 6-1.

FIELD NAME	FIELD TYPE
DateCreated	Date/Time
UserCreated	Text (20)
DateModified	Date/Time
UserModified	Text (20)

Table 6-1 New fields for tblCustomer

2. Open your form in design view. Add new text box controls, as shown in Table 6-2. You can place these controls anywhere on the form; they needn't be visible. In the example form, we placed these controls along the bottom of the form (see Figure 6-1).

CONTROL NAME	CONTROL SOURCE
txtDateCreated	DateCreated
txtUserCreated	UserCreated
txtDateModified	DateModified
txtUserModified	UserModified

Table 6-2 New controls for frmCustomer1

3. Set the Enabled property of these controls to No and the Locked property to Yes. This prevents users from modifying the values that will be computed automatically. You may also wish to set the TabStop property of these controls to No to remove these fields from the normal tab sequence of the form.

4. Create a new macro sheet. For the example, we called the macro sheet mfrmCustomer1. Create two macros named SetCreated and SetModified, as shown in Table 6-3.

MACRO NAME	ACTION	PARAMETER	VALUE
SetCreated	SetValue	Item	[Forms]![frmCustomer1]![txtDateCreated]
		Expression	Now()
	SetValue	Item	[Forms]![frmCustomer1]![txtUserCreated]
		Expression	CurrentUser()
SetModified	SetValue	Item	[Forms]![frmCustomer1]![txtDateModified]
		Expression	Now()

MACRO NAME	ACTION	PARAMETER	VALUE
	SetValue	Item	[Forms]![frmCustomer1]![txtUserModified]
		Expression	CurrentUser()

 Table 6-3 Macros used for frmCustomer1

5. Go back to the form in design view. Open the form's property sheet if it's not visible, and reference the macros you just created in the BeforeInsert and BeforeUpdate event properties, as shown in Figure 6-2.

6. Save and close the form. Open the form and run it to test your new code.

How It Works

To keep track of the user name and the date and time a record is created and updated, you must do two things:

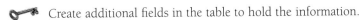 Create additional fields in the table to hold the information.

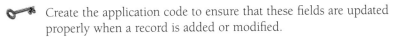 Create the application code to ensure that these fields are updated properly when a record is added or modified.

We added four fields to tblCustomer: two fields to hold the user name and date/time the record was created, and another two fields to hold the user name and date/time the record was last modified. You don't have to create all four fields, only the fields for which you wish to log information.

We also created two macros to update these columns whenever a record is inserted or updated. The first macro in the mfrmCustomer1 macro sheet, SetCreated, uses the SetValue action to update the value of the txtDateCreated and txtUserCreated controls on the form. The macro sets the txtDateCreated control to the current date and time using the built-in Now function; if you'd prefer to record only the date of the change *without* a time, you can use the Date function instead. The macro also saves the name of the current user using the built-in CurrentUser function. To trigger this macro code at the right moment, we attached the macro to the BeforeInsert event property of frmCustomer1. This event is triggered when you dirty (enter any information onto) a new record.

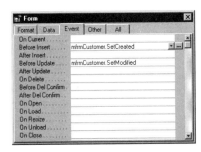

Figure 6-2 Referencing the macros for frmCustomer1

309

The second macro, SetModified, is similar to SetCreated. The only difference is that this macro updates the txtDateModified and txtUserModified controls instead and is attached to the BeforeUpdate event property. This event occurs right before Access saves your record.

Comments

If you prefer to use VBA code instead of macros, you can write two event procedures analogous to the SetUpdated and SetCreated macros. In the 06-01.MDB database, there is an alternate form, frmCustomer2, that uses VBA code to update the values of the controls in Table 6-2. To implement this on a form of your own, create an event procedure for the form's BeforeInsert event and enter the following code.

```
Private Sub Form_BeforeInsert(Cancel As Integer)
    Me!txtDateCreated = Now()
    Me!txtUserCreated = CurrentUser()
End Sub
```

Similarly, enter the following code into the event procedure for the form's BeforeUpdate event.

```
Private Sub Form_BeforeUpdate(Cancel As Integer)
    Me!txtDateModified = Now()
    Me!txtUserModified = CurrentUser()
End Sub
```

Access doesn't support the specification of calculated fields at the table level. Because it doesn't, all of the logic presented in this How-To occurs at the form level. This means that you must recreate this logic for every form that updates the data in this table. It also means that if you add new records or update existing records outside of a form—perhaps by using an update query or by importing records from another database—the fields in Table 6-2 will not be updated.

You can ensure that one of the fields, DateCreated, is updated correctly for every record by adding the following expression to the DefaultValue property of DateCreated.

`=Now()`

Unfortunately, you can't use the DefaultValue property for either of the updated fields because DefaultValue is only evaluated when the record is initially created. Also, you can't use this property to update the UserCreated field, because DefaultValue cannot call built-in or user-defined functions (except for the special Now and Date functions).

You may have noticed that placing the four controls from Table 6-2 on the form takes up a considerable amount of screen space. Fortunately, you don't need controls to make this technique work because Access lets you refer to a form's record-source fields directly. You'll find a third version of the form, frmCustomer3, in the sample database that demonstrates this variation of the technique. Notice that there are no txtDateCreated, txtUserCreated, txtDateModified, or txtUserModified controls on frmCustomer3; yet when you enter or edit a record using this form, the fields in tblCustomer are correctly updated. Here's the BeforeUpdate event procedure for this form:

```
Private Sub Form_BeforeUpdate(Cancel As Integer)
    Me!DateModified = Now()
    Me!UserModified = CurrentUser()
End Sub
```

Note that we have referred to the DateModified and UserModified fields in the form's underlying record source (tblCustomer) as if they were controls on the form, even though they are not. This is possible because Access lets you refer to fields in a form's underlying record source. In fact, because of this, it's a good idea to always name the controls on a form differently than the underlying fields. Then you can be sure you are always referring to the correct object.

COMPLEXITY:
EASY

6.2 How do I...
Determine if I'm on a new record in a form?

Problem

Oftentimes, I need to do different things, depending on whether or not the current row is the "new" row on a form. For example, I might want to display a certain message box only when adding records. How can I do this?

Technique

You can use the NewRecord property of a form (new for Access 95) to determine if you are on a new record by checking its value from an event procedure attached to the OnCurrent event property or some other event property of the form.

Steps

Load and open frmContacts from 06-02.MDB. Notice that the picture in the upper-left corner of the form changes to indicate whether you are editing an existing record (Figure 6-3) or adding a new record (Figure 6-4). In addition, when you save a newly added record, a message box is displayed that reminds you to log the new record (Figure 6-4). The message box does not appear when you save changes to an existing record.

Follow these steps to implement this functionality in your own forms:

1. Create a new form or modify the design of an existing form.

2. Create an event procedure for the form's Current event. In that event procedure, create an If...Then statement that will branch based on the value of the form's NewRecord property. The code of the event procedure should look like this:

311

Figure 6-3 The sample form indicates that you are editing an existing record

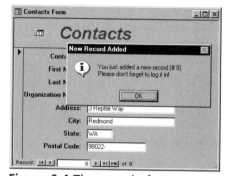

Figure 6-4 The sample form indicates that you are adding a record

```
Private Sub Form_Current()
    If Me.NewRecord Then
        ' Do something for a new record
    Else
        ' Do something for an existing record
    End If
End Sub
```

3. You may wish to alter some visual cue on the form to indicate whether you are on a new record. For example, you might change the text of a label, the text of the title bar of the form, or the picture of an Image control. In the sample form, we changed the picture of an Image control in the header of the form, imgFlag, by copying the picture from one of two hidden Image controls that are also located on the form. The final Current event procedure looks like this:

```
Private Sub Form_Current()

    ' Determine if this is a new record
    ' and change the bitmap of the imgFlag control
    ' to give user visual feedback.

    ' (See How-To 9.8 for an explanation of
    ' using the PictureData property.)

    If Me.NewRecord Then
        Me!imgFlag.PictureData = Me!imgFlagNew.PictureData
    Else
        Me!imgFlag.PictureData = Me!imgFlagEdit.PictureData
    End If
End Sub
```

4. Create any additional code that reacts to the NewRecord property. In the sample form, we decided to remind the user to log in the new record when saving it. Thus, we created the following event procedure attached to the form's BeforeUpdate event.

```
Private Sub Form_BeforeUpdate(Cancel As Integer)

    Dim strMsg As String

    If Me.NewRecord Then
        strMsg = "You just added a new record " & _
        "(# " & Me!ContactID & ")" & vbCrLf & _
        "Please don't forget to log it in!"
        Beep
        MsgBox strMsg, vbOKOnly + vbInformation, "New Record Added"
    End If

End Sub
```

How It Works

The NewRecord property is very simple: Its value is True when adding a new record, False otherwise. This property is True from the moment the record is first inserted (at the time of the BeforeInsert event) until the moment the record is saved (the BeforeUpdate event). NewRecord is reset to False right after the BeforeUpdate event; it is False during both the AfterUpdate and AfterInsert events.

Comments

The Image control used to display the add/edit icon uses a trick to change its picture quickly. Rather than loading a bitmap image from a disk file, which would be slow, it copies the picture from one of two hidden "source" Image controls on the form. You do this by setting the Image control's PictureData property to the value of the PictureData property of another Image control. How-To 9.8 discusses the PictureData property in more detail.

COMPLEXITY:
INTERMEDIATE

6.3 How do I...
Find all records with names that sound alike?

Problem

I enter people's names into a table where misspellings are a common occurrence. I would like a way to search for a person's record disregarding slight differences in spelling. I've tried using the Like operator with the first letter of the person's last name, but that produces too many names to rummage through. Is there any way to search for records that sound alike?

Technique

Access has no built-in sound-alike function, but you can create one that employs a standard algorithm called the Russell Soundex algorithm. Using this algorithm, it's fairly easy to search for a last name phonetically.

Steps

Run the qrySoundex query found in 06-03.MDB. Enter a last name in the query parameter dialog box, and qrySoundex will return all records from tblStaff that sound like the name you entered. For example, if you enter the name "Jahnsin" at the parameter prompt, qrySoundex will return the records shown in Figure 6-5.

To perform Soundex searches in your own applications, follow these steps:

1. Import the basSoundex module from 06-03.MDB into your database.

2. Create a query based on a table that contains a field that holds people's last names. Include the last name field and any additional fields you wish to see in the output of the query.

3. Create a calculated field that calculates the Soundex code for the last name field using the ahtSoundex function. In qrySoundex, we used the following calculation to create a new field called Soundex.

```
Soundex: ahtSoundex([LastName])
```

4. Enter criteria for the calculated field that compares the field against the Soundex code of a user-entered parameter. The Soundex code of the parameter is obtained by again using the ahtSoundex function. We used the following criteria in qrySoundex.

```
ahtSoundex([Enter Last Name])
```

This qrySoundex query is shown in Figure 6-6.

5. Declare the parameter to be of type Text using the Query|Parameters dialog box.

6. Save and run the query.

	EmployeeID	FirstName	LastName	Soundex	Title	BirthDate	HireDate
▶	2	Andrew	Jonsen	J525	Vice President, Sales	19-Feb-42	15-Jul-87
	11	Phil	Johnson	J525	Temp	05-Mar-49	13-Jun-93
	13	Andrew	Jonsen	J525	Vice President, Sales	19-Feb-42	15-Jul-87
	22	Phil	Johnson	J525	Temp	05-Mar-49	13-Jun-93
	149	Nelda	Jamison	J525	Temp		
	304	Janice	Johnson	J525	Temp		
✱	(AutoNumber)						

Figure 6-5 The records returned by searching for "Jahnsin"

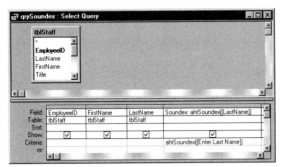

Figure 6-6 The qrySoundex query in design view

How It Works

The ahtSoundex function can be found in basSoundex in 06-03.MDB. This function takes a last name and returns a four-digit Soundex code for the name. If you look at the fourth column in Figure 6-5, you can see that the Soundex code for all rows is the same. In this case—for names sounding like "Jahnsin"—the code is "J525". Soundex codes always begin with the first letter of the name followed by three digits ranging between 0 and 6 that represent the remaining significant consonants in the name.

The ahtSoundex function is shown here.

```
Function ahtSoundex(ByVal varSurName As Variant) As Variant

    ' Takes a surname string and returns a 4-digit
    ' code representing the Russell Soundex code.

    On Error GoTo ahtSoundexErr

    Dim intLength As Integer
    Dim intCharCount As Integer
    Dim intSdxCount As Integer
    Dim intSeparator As Integer
    Dim intSdxCode As Integer
    Dim intPrvCode As Integer
    Dim varChar As Variant
    Dim varSdx As Variant

    Const ahtcSoundexLength = 4

    ' We add "" to take care of a passed Null
    intLength = Len(varSurName & "")

    If intLength > 0 Then
        intSeparator = 0           'Keeps track of vowel separators
        intPrvCode = 0             'The code of the previous char
        intCharCount = 0           'Counts number of input chars
        intSdxCount = 0            'Counts number of output chars
```

continued on next page

continued from previous page

```
'Loop until the soundex code is of ahtcSoundexLength
'or we have run out of characters in the surname
Do Until (intSdxCount = ahtcSoundexLength Or ⇒
    intCharCount = intLength)
    intCharCount = intCharCount + 1
    varChar = Mid(varSurName, intCharCount, 1)

    'Calculate the code for the current character
    Select Case varChar
        Case "B", "F", "P", "V"
            intSdxCode = 1
        Case "C", "G", "J", "K", "Q", "S", "X", "Z"
            intSdxCode = 2
        Case "D", "T"
            intSdxCode = 3
        Case "L"
            intSdxCode = 4
        Case "M", "N"
            intSdxCode = 5
        Case "R"
            intSdxCode = 6
        Case "A", "E", "I", "O", "U", "Y"
            intSdxCode = -1
        Case Else
            intSdxCode = -2
    End Select

    'Special case the first character
    If intCharCount = 1 Then
        varSdx = UCase(varChar)
        intSdxCount = intSdxCount + 1
        intPrvCode = intSdxCode
        intSeparator = 0
    'If a significant constant and not a repeat
    'without a separator then code this character
    ElseIf intSdxCode > 0 And _
      (intSdxCode <> intPrvCode Or intSeparator = 1) Then
        varSdx = varSdx & intSdxCode
        intSdxCount = intSdxCount + 1
        intPrvCode = intSdxCode
        intSeparator = 0
    'If a vowel, this character is not coded,
    'but it will act as a separator
    ElseIf intSdxCode = -1 Then
        intSeparator = 1
    End If
Loop

'If the code is < ahtcSoundexLength chars long, then
'fill the rest of code with zeros
If intSdxCount < ahtcSoundexLength Then
    varSdx = varSdx & String((ahtcSoundexLength - ⇒
    intSdxCount), "0")
End If
```

```
            ahtSoundex = varSdx
        Else
            ahtSoundex = Null
        End If

ahtSoundexDone:
        On Error GoTo 0
        Exit Function

ahtSoundexErr:
        Select Case Err
        Case Else
            MsgBox "Error#" & Err & ": " & Error$, _
            vbOKOnly + vbCritical, "ahtSoundex"
        End Select
        Resume ahtSoundexDone

    End Function
```

Comments

The ahtSoundex function is based on a standard algorithm, the Russell Soundex algorithm. Soundex is the most commonly used sound-alike algorithm in the United States. It works by discarding the most unreliable parts of a name, while retaining much of the name's discriminating power. It works best when used with the English version of names of peoples originating from Europe. Its discriminating power is reduced when used with very short or very long names or names with a high percentage of vowels. Other sound-alike algorithms may work better in these situations.

The Soundex algorithm was created to work with people's last names. It appears to work reasonably well with people's first names also, but not for names of businesses. Soundex does not work well for business names primarily because these names tend to be longer than people's names and Soundex only encodes the first four significant characters. We've found that extending the number of encoded characters to eight works better for business names, although this is a nonstandard implementation of the algorithm. You can easily extend the number of encoded characters by changing the ahtcSoundexLength constant found at the beginning of ahtSoundex. If you decide to do this, however, we suggest you rename the function to something like ahtSoundex8 to distinguish it from the standard function.

Soundex will not work satisfactorily with non-name data.

COMPLEXITY:
INTERMEDIATE

6.4 How do I...
Find the median value for a field?

Problem

Access provides the DAvg function to calculate the mean value for a numeric field, but I can't find the equivalent function for calculating medians. I need to calculate the median for a numeric field. How do I do this?

Technique

Access provides no built-in DMedian function, but one can be crafted using VBA code. This How-To demonstrates a median function that you can use in your own applications.

Steps

Load the frmMedian form from 06-04.MDB. Choose the name of a table and a field in that table using the combo boxes on the form. After choosing a field, the median value will be calculated and displayed in a text box using the ahtDMedian function found in basMedian (see Figure 6-7). An error message will be displayed if you have chosen a field with a non-numeric data type; the string "(Null)" will be displayed if the median value happens to be a Null.

Follow these steps to use ahtDMedian in your own applications:

1. Import the basMedian module from 06-04.MDB into your database.

2. Call the ahtDMedian function using syntax that is similar to the built-in DAvg function. The calling syntax is summarized in Table 6-4.

Figure 6-7 The frmMedian form

PARAMETER	DESCRIPTION	EXAMPLE
Field	Name of field for which to calculate median.	"UnitPrice"
Domain	Name of a table or query.	"Products"
Criteria	Optional where clause to limit the rows considered.	"CategoryID = 1"

Table 6-4 The ahtDMedian parameters

Make sure each parameter is delimited with quotes. The third parameter is optional. For example, you might enter the following statement at the Debug Window.

```
? ahtDMedian("UnitPrice", "tblProducts", "SupplierID = 1")
```

The function would return a median value of 18 (assuming you are using the data in the 06-04.MDB sample database).

3. The return value from the function is the median value.

How It Works

The ahtDMedian function, which you can find in basMedian in 06-04.MDB, is purposely patterned to look and act like the built-in DAvg domain function. The algorithm used to calculate the median, however, is quite a bit more complicated than what you would use to calculate the mean. (See the comments section of this How-To for a discussion of the implications of this difference.) The median of a field is calculated using the following algorithm.

 Sort the dataset on the field.

 Find the middle row of the dataset and return the value of the field. If there are an odd number of rows, this will be the value in a single row. If there are an even number of rows, there is no middle row, so you will need to find the mean of the values in the two rows straddling the middle.

After declaring a few variables, the ahtDMedian function begins by creating a recordset based on the three parameters passed to the function (strField, strDomain, and varCriteria).

```
Set db = CurrentDb()

' Initialize return value
varMedian = Null

' Build SQL string for recordset
strSQL = "Select " & strField
strSQL = strSQL & " FROM " & strDomain
```

continued on next page

continued from previous page

```
' Only use a WHERE clause if one is passed in
If Not IsMissing(varCriteria) Then
    strSQL = strSQL & " WHERE " & CStr(varCriteria)
End If

strSQL = strSQL & " ORDER BY " & strField

Set rstDomain = db.OpenRecordset(strSQL)
```

The process of building the SQL string that defines the recordset is straightforward, except for the construction of the optional WHERE clause. Because varCriteria was defined as an optional parameter (using the Optional keyword), ahtDMedian checks if a value was passed using the IsMissing function.

Once ahtDMedian builds the SQL string, it creates a recordset based on that SQL string.

Next, ahtDMedian checks the data type of the field: It will only calculate the median for numeric and date/time fields. If any other date type has been passed to ahtDMedian, the function forces an error by using the Raise method of the Err object and then uses the special CVErr function in the error handler of ahtDMedian to send the error state back to the calling procedure.

```
' Check the data type of the median field
intFieldType = rstDomain.Fields(strField).Type
Select Case intFieldType
Case dbByte, dbInteger, dbLong, dbCurrency, dbSingle, dbDouble, dbDate
' ... more code follows ...
Case Else
    ' Non-numeric field; so raise an app error
    Err.Raise ahtcErrAppTypeError
End Select

' ... more code follows ...

ahtDMedianDone:
    On Error GoTo 0
    Exit Function

ahtDMedianErr:
    ' Return an error value
    ahtDMedian = CVErr(Err)
    Resume ahtDMedianDone
End Function
```

If the field is numeric, then ahtDMedian checks if there are any rows in the recordset using the following If...Then statement, returning a Null if there are no rows.

```
' Numeric field
If Not rstDomain.EOF Then
    ' ... more code follows ...
Else
    ' No records; return Null
    varMedian = Null
End If
```

If there are rows, however, the function moves to the end of the recordset to get a count of the total number of records. This is necessary because the RecordCount property only returns the number of rows that have been visited.

```
rstDomain.MoveLast
intRecords = rstDomain.RecordCount
```

If the number of records is an even number, ahtDMedian moves to the record just before the middle using the Move method, which allows you to move an arbitrary number of records from the current record. The number of records to move forward is calculated using the following formula.

```
intRecords \ 2 - 1
```

This tells Access to divide the total number of records by 2. You then subtract 1 from the result because you are starting from the first record. For example, if you are on the first record and there are 500 records, you would move $(500 \backslash 2 - 1) = (250 - 1) = 249$ records forward, which would bring you to the 250th record. Once the function has moved that many records, it's a simple matter to grab the value of the 250th and 251st records and divide the result by 2. This part of the function is shown here.

```
' Start from the first record
rstDomain.MoveFirst

If (intRecords Mod 2) = 0 Then
    ' Even number of records

    ' No middle record, so move to the
    ' record right before the middle
    rstDomain.Move ((intRecords \ 2) - 1)
    varMedian = rstDomain.Fields(strField)
    ' Now move to the next record, the
    ' one right after the middle
    rstDomain.MoveNext
    ' And average the two values
    varMedian = (varMedian + rstDomain.Fields(strField)) / 2
```

Because ahtDMedian supports dates, the function needs to make sure a date value is returned when taking the average of two dates.

```
    ' Make sure you return a date, even when
    ' averaging two dates
    If intFieldType = dbDate And Not IsNull(varMedian) Then
        varMedian = CDate(varMedian)
    End If
```

The code for an even number of rows is much simpler.

```
Else
    ' Odd number of records

    ' Move to the middle record and return it's value
    rstDomain.Move ((intRecords \ 2))
    varMedian = rstDomain.Fields(strField)
End If
```

Finally, ahtDMedian returns the median value to the calling procedure.

```
ahtDMedian = varMedian
```

Comments

The median, like the average (or arithmetic mean), is known statistically as a measure of central tendency. In other words, both measures are a way to estimate the middle of a set of data. The mean represents the mathematical average value; the median represents the middle-most value. For many datasets, these two measures are the same or very close to each other. Sometimes, however, depending on how the data is distributed, the mean and median will report widely varying values. In these cases, many people favor the median as a better "average" than the mean.

Calculating the median requires sorting the dataset, so it can be rather slow on large datasets. Calculating the mean, however, doesn't require a sort, so it will always be faster to calculate than the median.

> **Note**
>
> Microsoft Excel includes a Median function that you could call from Access using OLE Automation. How-To 12.3 shows you how to do this. Because using OLE Automation with Excel requires starting a copy of Excel to do the calculation, you'll almost always find it simpler and faster to use the all-Access solution presented in this How-To.

COMPLEXITY:
INTERMEDIATE

6.5 How do I...
Quickly find a record in a linked table?

Problem

I like to use the ultra-fast Seek method to search for data in indexed fields in my table-type recordsets. But the Seek method won't work with linked tables, because you can only open dynaset-type recordsets against linked tables. I can use the Find methods to search for data in these types of recordsets, but Find is much slower at finding data than Seek. Is there any way to use the Seek method on linked tables?

Technique

The Seek method only works on table-type recordsets, so you can't perform seeks on linked tables. However, there's no reason why you can't open the source database that contains the linked table and perform the seek operation there. This How-To shows you how to do this.

Steps

Copy the 06-05.MDB and 06-05Ext.MDB databases to a folder on your hard drive. Make sure that the 06-05Ext.MDB database is in the same folder (subdirectory) as 06-05.MDB. Open the 06-05.MDB database and create a link to the tblCustomer table in 06-05Ext using the File|Get External Data|Link Tables command. Open the frmSeekExternal form from 06-05.MDB. Enter a first and last name to search (you may find it helpful to browse through tblCustomer first) and press the Use Seek command button (see Figure 6-8). Even though this table does not exist in the 06-05.MDB database, the row will be searched using the fast Seek method.

To use the Seek method on external tables, follow these general steps:

1. Use the OpenDatabase method to open the source database that contains the linked table. For example, in the event procedure attached to the cmdSeek command button on frmSeekExternal, you'll find the following code.

```
Const ahtcDbExt = "06-05Ext.Mdb"

Set wrk = DBEngine.Workspaces(0)

' Directly open the external database
' DB will be opened non-exlusively, read-write, and type = Access
Set dbExternal = wrk.OpenDatabase(GetDBDir() & ahtcDbExt, False, False, "")
```

2. Create a table-type recordset based on the source table. If you renamed the table when you linked to it, make sure you use the name used in the source database. The sample form uses this code:

```
' Create a table-type recordset based on the external table
Set rstCustomer = dbExternal.OpenRecordset("tblCustomer", dbOpenTable)
```

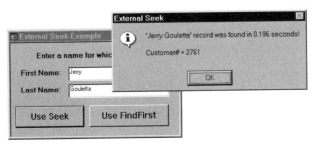

Figure 6-8 The frmSeekExternal form

3. Set an index and perform the seek operation as in this code behind the sample form.

```
' This index consists of last & first names
rstCustomer.Index = "FullName"

' Perform seek and then check if record was found
rstCustomer.Seek "=", ctlLName.Value, ctlFName.Value
```

4. Any time you perform a seek or a find, you must next check to see if the operation was successful. You do this using the NoMatch property of the recordset. For example, on the sample form, you'll find the following code.

```
strMsg = "'" & ctlFName & " " & ctlLName & "' record was"
If Not rstCustomer.NoMatch Then
    strMsg = strMsg & " found!" & vbCrLf & vbCrLf
    strMsg = strMsg & "Customer# = " & rstCustomer![Customer#]
    MsgBox strMsg, vbOKOnly + vbInformation, "External Seek"
Else
    strMsg = strMsg & " not found!"
    MsgBox strMsg, vbOKOnly + vbCritical, "External Seek"
End If
```

5. Close the recordset and the external database. The sample form uses this code:

```
rstCustomer.Close
dbExternal.Close
```

How It Works

The key to this technique is in using the OpenDatabase method on the workspace object to open the external database directly where the linked table physically resides. The OpenDatabase method takes four parameters, which are detailed in Table 6-5.

PARAMETER	DESCRIPTION	FRMSEEKEXTERNAL EXAMPLE
dbname	The name of the database, including path.	GetDBDir() & ahtcDbExt
exclusive	True to open the database exclusively.	False
read-only	True to open the database in read-only mode.	False
source	Connect string for opening database; use "" for Access databases.	""

Table 6-5 The OpenDatabase method

Here's the code that opens the database in the sample form.

```
Set dbExternal = wrk.OpenDatabase(GetDBDir() & ahtcDbExt, False, False, "")
```

In the sample form, we used "GetDBDir( ) & ahtcDbExt" for the name of the database. The constant, ahtcDbExt, is equal to "06-05Ext.MDB", which was defined at the beginning of the subroutine. If we had used ahtcDbExt by itself, Access would look for the database in the default folder (subdirectory), which may not be the same as the folder where 06-05.MDB resides. Instead, we concatenated GetDBDir( ) (which returns the path to the current database) to the database name.

The code for GetDBDir is shown here.

```
Function GetDBDir() As String

    ' Gets the directory of the currently open database.

On Error Resume Next

    Dim strDbName As String

    strDbName = CurrentDb().Name

    Do While Right$(strDbName, 1) <> "\"
        strDbName = Left$(strDbName, Len(strDbName) - 1)
    Loop

    GetDBDir = UCase$(strDbName)

    On Error GoTo 0

End Function
```

The logic behind this function is simple. The function begins by grabbing the name of the current database. Starting from the right end of the name, it searches backwards until it finds a backslash character. The path to the database consists of everything to the left of the right-most backslash.

Comments

You won't notice much difference between the Seek and Find methods with small tables, but with moderately large tables, the difference in speed will be great. Because there is some overhead involved with attaching to an external database, the Find method will be faster on very small tables.

You are not limited to using the Seek method on Access databases. It works with indexed non-native ISAM databases also, and the tables needn't be linked to the current database.

You can't perform a seek on text, spreadsheet, or ODBC data sources.

COMPLEXITY:
ADVANCED

6.6   How do I...
Get a complete list of field properties from a table or query?

Problem

I want to get a list of fields in a table or query and their properties. The ListFields method is fine for certain situations, but it returns only a few of the fields' properties. Plus Microsoft has made it clear that this method will not exist in a future release of Access. How can I create a replacement for ListFields that supplies all the available information on fields?

Technique

In Access 1.x, the ListFields method was the only supported way to return a list of fields and their properties. Its usefulness is marred by the fact that it only returns a few field properties, and always returns a snapshot. Using the more flexible Data Access Objects (DAO) hierarchy, however, you can get all the properties of field objects and create a replacement for the outdated ListFields method that returns all of a field's properties (or as much as you'd like), placing the results in a readily accessible table.

Steps

Open and run the frmListFields form from 06-06.MDB (see Figure 6-9). Choose Tables, Queries, or Both, and whether you wish to include system objects. Select an object from the Object combo box. After a moment, the form will display a list of fields and

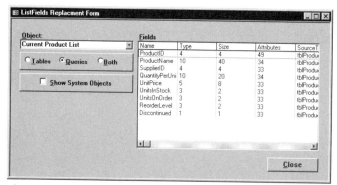

Figure 6-9 The ListFields Replacement Form

their properties in the Fields list box. Scroll left and right to see additional properties; scroll up and down to see additional fields.

To use this technique in your application, follow these steps:

1. Import the basListFields module into your database.

2. Call the ahtListFields subroutine, using the following syntax.

```
Call ahtListFields (strName, fTable, strOutputTable)
```

The parameters are summarized in Table 6-6.

PARAMETER	DESCRIPTION	EXAMPLE
strName	The name of the table or query.	"Customers"
fTable	True if strName is a table, False if it is a query.	True
strOutputTable	The name of the table that will hold the list of field properties.	"tmpOutputFields"

Table 6-6 Syntax for the ahtListFields subroutine

3. The subroutine creates a table with the name specified by strOutputTable and fills it with one record for every field in the specified table or query. The table is similar in structure to the snapshot returned by the ListFields method, except that it has new fields to hold the values of additional field properties. Table 6-7 lists the structure of the resulting table. Note that the first seven fields are identical to those returned by the Access version 1 ListFields method. The remaining fields are additional information supplied only by ahtListFields.

FIELD NAME	DATATYPE	DESCRIPTION
Name	String	The name of the field.
Type	Integer	The datatype of the field as represented by an integer. Search Access help under ListFields to decode this value.
Size	Integer	The size of the field.
Attributes	Long Integer	The field's attributes. Search Access help under Attributes to decode this value.
SourceTable	String	The name of the field's underlying table. If the table is an attached table, this field will contain the name of the table as it exists in the source database.

continued on next page

continued from previous page

FIELD NAME	DATATYPE	DESCRIPTION
SourceField	String	The name of the field.
CollatingOrder	Integer	The collating order of the table. Search Access help under CollatingOrder to decode this value.
AllowZeroLength	Integer	True if zero-length strings are allowed in the field; false otherwise.
DataUpdatable	Integer	True if the field is updatable; false otherwise.
DefaultValue	Text	The field's default value.
OrdinalPosition	Integer	The field's position in the table starting at 0.
Required	Integer	True if the field requires an entry; false otherwise.
ValidationRule	String	The field's Validation Rule property.
ValidationText	String	The field's Validation Text property.
Caption	String	The field's Caption property.
ColumnHidden	Integer	True if the field is hidden in datasheet view; False otherwise.
ColumnOrder	Integer	The order that the field appears in datasheet view.
ColumnWidth	Integer	The width of the field as it appears in datasheet view.
DecimalPlaces	Integer	The field's number of decimal places.
Description	Text	The field's description.
Format	Text	The field's format string.
InputMask	Text	The field's input mask string.

Table 6-7 The ahtListFields output table structure

6.6

GET COMPLETE LISTS OF FIELD PROPERTIES FROM A TABLE OR QUERY?

How It Works

The ahtListFields subroutine uses a table-driven approach to populate the list fields output table with the properties of the fields in the input table or query. Here's the basic algorithm for ahtListFields.

1. Call ahtMakeTables to create the output table. This routine either creates a brand new table or deletes all of its rows if it already exists. If it needs to create the output table, it uses a create table query. The names of the fields in the output table are the same as the properties that ahtListFields will place there.

2. Open a recordset on the table created in step 1.

3. Count the fields in the input table/query.

4. For each field in the input table/query, add a new row in the output table and iterate through the fields in the *output* table, retrieving the properties for the input table/query field with the same name as the output table fields, adding them in turn to the new row in the output table.

The ahtListFields subroutine is shown here.

```
Sub ahtListFields(strName As String, fTable As Boolean, _
strOutputTable As String)

    '       Saves a list of the most common field
    '       properties of a table or query's fields to a
    '       table that is similar to the Snapshot produced by
    '       the version 1 ListFields method.

    On Error GoTo ahtListFieldsErr

    Dim dbCurrent As Database
    Dim rstOutput As Recordset
    Dim tdfInput As TableDef
    Dim qdfInput As QueryDef
    Dim intFieldCount As Integer
    Dim intI As Integer
    Dim intJ As Integer
    Dim fldInput As Field
    Dim strOutputField As String

    Call ahtMakeListTable(strOutputTable)

    Set dbCurrent = CurrentDb()
    Set rstOutput = dbCurrent.OpenRecordset(strOutputTable)

    ' If the input object is a table, use a TableDef.
    ' Otherwise, use a QueryDef.
    If fTable Then
        Set tdfInput = dbCurrent.TableDefs(strName)
        intFieldCount = tdfInput.Fields.Count
    Else
        Set qdfInput = dbCurrent.QueryDefs(strName)
        intFieldCount = qdfInput.Fields.Count
    End If
```

continued on next page

continued from previous page

```
    ' Iterate through the fields in the
    ' TableDef or QueryDef.
    For intI = 0 To intFieldCount - 1
        ' Create a new record for each field
        rstOutput.AddNew
        If fTable Then
            Set fldInput = tdfInput.Fields(intI)
        Else
            Set fldInput = qdfInput.Fields(intI)
        End If
        ' Iterate through the fields in rstOutput.
        ' The field names of these fields are named
        ' exactly the same as the properties we wish
        ' to store there so we take advantage of this fact.
        For intJ = 0 To rstOutput.Fields.Count - 1
            strOutputField = rstOutput.Fields(intJ).Name
            On Error Resume Next
            rstOutput.Fields(strOutputField) = _
             fldInput.Properties(strOutputField)
            On Error GoTo 0
        Next intJ
        rstOutput.Update
    Next intI

ahtListFieldsDone:
    If Not rstOutput Is Nothing Then rstOutput.Close
    If Not qdfInput Is Nothing Then qdfInput.Close
    On Error GoTo 0
    Exit Sub

ahtListFieldsErr:
    Select Case Err
    Case ahtcErrPrpNotFound
        ' Skip the property if it can't be found
        Resume Next
    Case Else
        MsgBox "Error#" & Err & ": " & Error$, _
        vbOKOnly + vbCritical, "ahtListFields"
        Resume ahtListFieldsDone
    End Select

End Sub
```

Notice that in the innermost For…Next loop of ahtMakeListTable, we included an On Error Resume Next statement right before attempting to retrieve each property.

```
On Error Resume Next
rstOutput.Fields(strOutputField) = _
 fldInput.Properties(strOutputField)
On Error GoTo 0
```

This is necessary because some properties do not exist until they are assigned a value. If the error-handling statement was not in effect, a runtime error would occur when the code tried to read the value of one of these nonexistent properties. This isn't necessary for certain core properties that are always present, but many Access properties—such as the Description property—do not exist until they have been assigned a value. See How-To 7-9 for more details on retrieving and setting properties.

Once ahtListFields has completed its work, you can open the output table and use it any way you'd like. The sample frmListFields form displays the output table using a list box control.

Comments

This technique is quite easy to implement and offers more functionality than the built-in ListFields method. Many more field properties are retrieved (although not all of the possible properties are retrieved), and, because ahtListFields returns a table instead of a snapshot, you have added flexibility.

The subroutine ahtListFields doesn't decide which properties to write to the output table. Instead, it drives the process using the names of the fields in the output table. If you wish to collect a different set of properties, all you need to do is modify the code in ahtMakeListTable and delete the output table (which will be recreated the next time you run ahtListFields).

There is useful sample code behind the frmListFields form. Look at the GetTables function for an example of how to get a list of tables and queries and at the FillTables function for an example of a list-filling function (see How-To's 6.8 and 7.8 for more details on list-filling functions).

In your own applications, you may wish to hide the output table in the database container. You can do this either by prefixing its name with "USys" or by checking the Hidden setting in the table's property sheet.

COMPLEXITY:
ADVANCED

6.7 How do I...
Create and use flexible
AutoNumber fields?

Problem

I use AutoNumber fields in my tables to ensure that I have unique values for my key fields. But a key based on the an auto-incrementing Long Integer AutoNumber field doesn't sort my tables in a useful order. Also, auto-incrementing AutoNumber fields always start at 1 and I want my AutoNumber values to start at another number. How can I create a replacement for Access' AutoNumber fields that gets around these limitations?

Technique

Access makes it easy to add unique value key fields to a table using the AutoNumber datatype (referred to as the Counter datatype prior to Access 95). AutoNumbers are

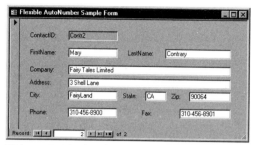

Figure 6-10 The frmFlexAutoNum
sample form

automatically maintained by Access and ensure a unique value for each record.
Auto-incrementing AutoNumber fields always start at 1, with one added for each new
record, limiting their usefulness when your application needs to start from some other
value or use some other increment. This How-To shows how to create your own flexible AutoNumber fields that are multiuser ready. You can also combine these custom
AutoNumber values with other fields in the table to make your data sort more
intuitively.

Steps

Open and run the frmFlexAutoNum form from 06-07.MDB. Add a new record. Type
in some data and be sure to put a value in the LastName field. Save the new record
by pressing SHIFT-ENTER. When you save the record, a new automatically incremented
value will be placed into the ContactID field (see Figure 6-10).

You can add this technique to your own application by following these steps:

1. Import the tblFlexAutoNum table and the basFlexAutoNum module into your
database.

2. Prepare your table by adding a new field to become the key value. If you only
want to store a numeric AutoNumber value, set the field's type to Number,
Long Integer. If you want to add additional information for sorting, set the
new field's type to Text and set its length long enough to accommodate the
numbers returned by the flexible AutoNumber routine plus the length of the
characters you want to concatenate to the field.

3. Open the tblFlexAutoNum table and edit the CounterValue field to start at the
desired value.

4. Open the data entry form for your application in Design View. In the form's
BeforeUpdate event procedure, add code that calls the ahtGetCounter function, writing the returned value to your key field. To call the routine, use the
following syntax.

```
Dim lngCounter As Long
lngCounter = ahtGetCounter()
```

```
If lngCounter > 0 Then
    Me!KeyField = lngCounter
End If
```

This code will run whenever a new record is added to the form, but before the new record is actually written to the form's table. The lngCounter variable is assigned to the value returned by ahtGetCounter. If the value is greater than zero, it is written to the KeyField field. If you want to add information to the key field, use the same technique, but concatenate the AutoNumber value with a value from another field, as shown in this example:

```
Dim lngCounter As Long
lngCounter = ahtGetCounter()
If lngCounter > 0 Then
    Me!KeyField = Left$(Me!LastName,5) & lngCounter
End If
```

If you are basing your key value on another field, your code should ensure that a value exists in that field before attempting to use it. The best way to ensure this is to set the Required property of the field to Yes.

How It Works

The heart of this technique is the ahtGetCounter function. In a nutshell, the function tries to open the tblFlexAutoNum table exclusively and, if it succeeds, get the value in the CounterValue field, incrementing by some fixed number. This value is then returned to the calling procedure. ahtGetCounter is shown here.

```
Function ahtGetCounter() As Long

    ' Get a value from the counters table and
    ' increment it

    Dim dbCurrent As Database
    Dim rstCounter As Recordset
    Dim intLockOptions As Integer
    Dim intLocked As Integer
    Dim intRetries As Integer
    Dim lngTime As Long
    Dim lngCnt As Long

    ' Set number of retries
    Const ahtcMaxRetries = 5
    Const ahtcMinDelay = 1
    Const ahtcMaxDelay = 10

    Const ahtcAutoNumTable = "tblFlexAutoNum"
    Const ahtcAutoNumInc = 1

    DoCmd.Hourglass True

    Set dbCurrent = CurrentDb()
    intLockOptions = dbDenyWrite + dbDenyRead
    intLocked = False
```

continued on next page

continued from previous page

```
        Do While (True)
            For intRetries = 0 To ahtcMaxRetries
                On Error Resume Next
                Set rstCounter = dbCurrent.OpenRecordset(ahtcAutoNumTable, _
                dbOpenTable, intLockOptions)
                If Err = 0 Then
                    intLocked = True
                    Exit For
                Else
                    DBEngine.Idle dbFreeLocks
                    lngTime = intRetries ^ 2 * _
                    Int((ahtcMaxDelay - ahtcMinDelay + 1) * Rnd + ahtcMinDelay)
                    For lngCnt = 1 To lngTime
                        DoEvents
                    Next lngCnt
                End If
            Next intRetries

            If Not intLocked Then
                DoCmd.Hourglass False
                Beep
                If MsgBox("Could not get a counter: " & Error$ & _
                " Try again?", vbQuestion + vbYesNo) = vbYes Then
                    intRetries = 0
                DoCmd.Hourglass True
                Else
                    Exit Do
                End If
            Else
                Exit Do
            End If
        Loop

        On Error GoTo 0
        If intLocked Then
            ahtGetCounter = rstCounter![CounterValue]
            rstCounter.Edit
                rstCounter![CounterValue] = rstCounter![CounterValue] + ⇒
                ahtcAutoNumInc
            rstCounter.Update
            rstCounter.Close
        Else
            ahtGetCounter = -1
        End If

        DoCmd.Hourglass False

    End Function
```

After declaring several variables and turning the Hourglass cursor on, ahtGetCounter attempts to open a recordset object on the table specified by the ahtcAutoNumTable constant (tblFlexAutoNum). By specifying the dbDenyRead and dbDenyWrite constants as the Options argument to the OpenRecordset method, it attempts to lock the table exclusively, preventing other users from reading or writing to this table.

The function attempts to obtain a lock on the ahtcAutoNumTable by using a common multiuser coding construct: a retry loop. The retry loop from ahtGetCounter is shown here.

```
For intRetries = 0 To ahtcMaxRetries
    On Error Resume Next
    Set rstCounter = dbCurrent.OpenRecordset(ahtcAutoNumTable, _
     dbOpenTable, intLockOptions)
    If Err = 0 Then
        intLocked = True
        Exit For
    Else
        DBEngine.Idle dbFreeLocks
        lngTime = intRetries ^ 2 * _
          Int((ahtcMaxDelay - ahtcMinDelay + 1) * Rnd + ahtcMinDelay)
        For lngCnt = 1 To lngTime
            DoEvents
        Next lngCnt
    End If
Next intRetries
```

Note what happens if the lock is not immediately obtained. First, ahtGetCounter issues a DBEngine.Idle dbFreelocks statement that tells the Jet Engine to release any read locks it hadn't bothered to release previously. Next, it calculates a long number that's a function of the number of retries, the ahtcMaxDelay and ahtcMinDelay constants that were set at the beginning of the function, and a random number. This calculated number, lngTime, is then used to waste time using a For…Next loop that simply counts from 1 to lngTime. Because this is wasted time, we placed a DoEvents statement inside the loop so that Access multitasks during this dead time.

The point of the retry loop and the time-wasting code is to wait a little before attempting to obtain the lock. Because this code is meant to work in a multiuser situation, it's important that retries are not attempted repeatedly without waiting for the lock to be released. ahtGetCounter includes a random component to lngTime that gets larger with each retry to separate out multiple users who might be trying to obtain that lock at the same time.

If the function cannot lock the table after the number of retries specified by the ahtcMaxRetries constant, it displays a message box allowing the user to retry or cancel. If the user chooses to cancel, a value of -1 is returned; if the user chooses to retry, the whole retry loop is started over. If the lock succeeds, the value of the AutoNumber field is saved and the AutoNumber field is incremented by the value of the ahtcAutoNumInc constant.

Comments

The tblFlexAutoNum table provides AutoNumber values for one table only. You may wish to extend this technique so that there is some provision for recording multiple AutoNumber values in tblFlexAutoNum. Alternately, you could create a separate AutoNumber table for each flexible AutoNumber value you need in your application. You may wish to hide these tables in the database container either by prefixing the table names with "USys" or by checking the Hidden setting in the tables' property sheets.

The example form transfers the first five letters from the LastName field to the AutoNumber value. While this can be helpful in sorting, this can also have a negative side effect: The AutoNumber field will have to be changed when the LastName field is changed.

You could use an alphanumeric prefix to your AutoNumber field that was site-specific. This would allow you to create AutoNumber values in two different copies of a database that could then be merged together at a later time. Since each copy of the database would use a different site prefix, you wouldn't have duplicate values.

COMPLEXITY:
ADVANCED

6.8   How do I...
Back up selected objects to another database?

Problem

I use a standard backup program to save my databases, but this only works at the database level. This is fine for archival purposes, but I often want to back up individual objects. How can I get Access to display a list of objects and allow me to save selected ones to an output database I specify?

Technique

This How-To shows how to create a form that selectively saves Access objects to another database. It works by using a multiselect list box and the CopyObject action.

Steps

Open frmBackup from 06-08.MDB, which is shown in Figure 6-11. This form can be used to back up selected objects from the current database to another database. Select one or more objects from the list box, using SHIFT or CTRL to extend the selection. When you are finished selecting objects and have specified a backup database (a default database name is created for you), press the Backup button. The backup process will begin, copying objects from the current database to the backup database.

To add this functionality to your own database, follow these steps:

1. Import the frmBackup from 06-08.MDB to your database.

2. Call the backup procedure from anywhere in your application by opening the frmBackup form. For example, you might place a command button on your main switchboard form with the following event procedure attached to the button's Click event.

```
DoCmd.OpenForm "frmBackup"
```

How It Works

To see how it works, open frmBackup in design view. The form consists of a list box, two text boxes (one of which is initially hidden), two command buttons, and several labels. The list box control displays the list of objects. One text box is used to gather the name of the backup database; the other is used to display the progress of the backup operation. The command buttons are used to initiate the backup process and to close the form. All of the VBA code that makes frmBackup work is stored in the form's module.

The MultiSelect Property

The key control on the form is the lboObjects list box. We have taken advantage of the list box's MultiSelect property to allow the user to select more than one item in the list box. This property, which is new for Access 95, can be set to None, Simple, or Extended (see Figure 6-12). If you set MultiSelect to None, which is the default setting, only one item may be selected. If you choose Simple, an item will be selected whenever you click on it, and it will remain selected until it is clicked again. If you choose Extended, the list box will behave like most of Windows' built-in list box controls—you select multiple items by holding down (SHIFT) or (CTRL) while clicking on items.

Filling the lboObjects List Box

Unlike most list boxes, which derive their list of values from either a fixed list of items or the rows from a table or query, lboObjects uses a list-filling callback function to fill the list box with the list of the names of the database container objects. List-filling functions are described in detail in How-To 7.5. We use a list-filling function here because the list of database container objects is not stored in a user-accessible table. (Actually,

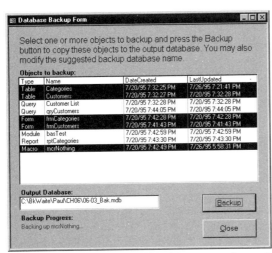

Figure 6-11 frmBackup backing up selected database objects

Figure 6-12 The MultiSelect property set to Extended

you *can* fill a list box with a list of database container objects using a query based on the undocumented MSysObjects system table, but this practice is not supported by Microsoft, and therefore it is not recommended.) The list-filling function for lboObjects, FillObjectList, is shown here.

```
Private Function FillObjectList(ctl As Control, varID As Variant, _
    varRow As Variant, varCol As Variant, varCode As Variant) As Variant

        ' List filling function for lboObjects.
        ' Fills the list box with a list of
        ' the database container objects.

        Dim varRetVal As Variant
        Static sintRows As Integer

        varRetVal = Null

        Select Case varCode
        Case acLBInitialize
            ' Fill mavarObjects array with a list of
            ' database container objects
            sintRows = FillObjArray()
            varRetVal = True
        Case acLBOpen
            varRetVal = Timer
        Case acLBGetRowCount
            varRetVal = sintRows
        Case acLBGetColumnCount
            varRetVal = ahtcMaxCols
        Case acLBGetValue
            ' varRow and varCol are zero-based so add 1
            varRetVal = mavarObjects(varRow + 1, varCol + 1)
        Case acLBEnd
            Erase mavarObjects
        End Select

        FillObjectList = varRetVal

End Function
```

FillObjectList looks like most typical list-filling functions (see How-To 7.8 for more details). Most of the work is done during the initialization step, when the FillObjArray function is called to fill a module-level array with the list of database container objects.

The purpose of FillObjArray is to fill an array with a list of names of each database container object, the type of object, the date and time the object was created, and the date and time the object was last modified. Before the function can place elements in an array, it must first declare the maximum number of elements the array will contain. Thus, the function begins by determining the maximum number of database container objects that exist in the database. This is accomplished by "walking" the Containers collection of the current database and tallying the number of objects in each of the containers. There are eight different containers in the Containers collection, which are summarized in Table 6-8.

CONTAINER	CONTAINS THESE DOCUMENTS	BACKUP DOCUMENTS?
Databases	General information about the database	No
Forms	Saved forms	Yes
Modules	Saved modules	Yes
Relationships	Enforced relationships	No
Reports	Saved reports	Yes
Scripts	Saved macros	Yes
SysRel	Unenforced relationships	No
Tables	Saved tables and queries	Yes

 Table 6-8 The Containers collection

Because you are only interested in backing up the objects that appear in the Access database container, the function should ignore containers in Table 6-8 where "Backup documents" is No, but for now it's easier to include these objects in the count. Later in the function, the size of the array will be adjusted to the actual number of included objects. Once FillObjArray has determined the maximum number of objects, it dimensions the array that will hold the objects.

```
Set db = CurrentDb()

intObjCount = 0
For Each con In db.Containers
    intObjCount = intObjCount + con.Documents.Count
Next con

' Resize the array based on the object count
ReDim mavarObjects(1 To intObjCount, 1 To ahtcMaxCols)
```

Next, FillObjArray places the list box headings in the first item of the array.

```
intItem = 1

' Setup the first row of field names
Call SaveToArray("Type", "Name", "DateCreated", _
    "LastUpdated", intItem)
```

We want this first row to become the headings of the list box, so we set the ColumnHeads property of the list box to Yes. This setting tells Access to freeze the first row of the list box so that it doesn't scroll with the other rows. In addition, you cannot select this special row.

With the array dimensioned, the function needs to walk the collections a second time, this time storing away the information that will appear in the list box. This *should* be relatively simple, but there is one complicating factor: The Tables container includes both tables and queries, mixed together in unsorted order. Fortunately, there's an alternate method for getting separate lists of tables and queries in the database. Instead of using the Tables container, FillObjArray walks the TableDefs and QueryDefs collections to extract the necessary information.

```
' Special case TableDefs
db.TableDefs.Refresh
For Each tdf In db.TableDefs
    ' Only include non-system tables
    If Not (tdf.Attributes And dbSystemObject) <> 0 Then
        intItem = intItem + 1
        Call SaveToArray("Table", tdf.Name, tdf.DateCreated, _
        tdf.LastUpdated, intItem)
    End If
Next tdf

' Special case QueryDefs
db.QueryDefs.Refresh
For Each qdf In db.QueryDefs
    intItem = intItem + 1
    Call SaveToArray("Query", qdf.Name, qdf.DateCreated, _
    qdf.LastUpdated, intItem)
Next qdf
```

The TableDefs collection requires an additional test to exclude the normally hidden system tables from the list.

With the tables and queries taken care of, the function can now walk the remaining container collections for macros, forms, modules, and reports.

```
' Iterate through remaining containers of interest
' and then document each within the container
For Each con In db.Containers
    Select Case con.Name
    Case "Scripts"
        strObjType = "Macro"
    Case "Forms"
        strObjType = "Form"
    Case "Modules"
        strObjType = "Module"
    Case "Reports"
        strObjType = "Report"
    Case Else
        strObjType = ""
    End Select

    ' If this isn't one of the important containers, don't
    ' bother listing documents.
    If strObjType <> "" Then
        con.Documents.Refresh
        For Each doc In con.Documents
            ' You can't back up the current form, since it's open.
            If Not (doc.Name = Me.Name And con.Name = "Forms") Then
                intItem = intItem + 1
                fReturn = SaveToArray(strObjType, doc.Name, ⇒
                doc.DateCreated, _
                doc.LastUpdated, intItem)
                ' If SaveToArray returns False, then this was a deleted
```

```
                            ' object that we don't want to include, so decrement
                            ' the intItem counter.
                            If Not fReturn Then intItem = intItem - 1
                    End If
                Next doc
        End If

Next con
```

Finally, the array is resized to the actual number of objects that were found.

```
' Now redimension the array based on the true
' object count
ReDim Preserve mavarObjects(1 To intItem, 1 To ahtcMaxCols)
FillObjArray = intItem
```

We used the Preserve option of the ReDim statement to ensure that the values are not lost when the array is resized.

The SaveToArray subroutine called by FillObjArray is shown here.

```
Private Sub SaveToArray(ByVal strType As String, ByVal strName As String, _
  ByVal strDateCreated As String, ByVal strLastUpdated As String, _
  ByVal intObjIndex As Integer) As Boolean

    ' Save data to mavarObjects array
    ' Skip deleted objects
    If Left$(strName, 7) <> "~TMPCLP" Then
        mavarObjects(intObjIndex, 1) = strType
        mavarObjects(intObjIndex, 2) = strName
        mavarObjects(intObjIndex, 3) = strDateCreated
        mavarObjects(intObjIndex, 4) = strLastUpdated
        SaveToArray = True
    Else
        SaveToArray = False
    End If
End Sub
```

Access doesn't immediately remove database container objects that you have deleted. Instead, it renames the deleted object to a name that begins with "~TMPCLP". We didn't want these objects to appear in the list of objects to back up, so we included code here to exclude them explicitly from the list box.

The Backup Process

Once you have selected one or more database objects in the lboObjects list box, you initiate the backup process by clicking on the cmdBackup command button. The event procedure attached to this button calls the MakeBackup subroutine. This routine begins by checking to see if the backup database exists. If so, you are warned that it will be overwritten before proceeding. Next, MakeBackup creates the output database using the following code.

```
Set dbOutput = DBEngine.Workspaces(0). _
  CreateDatabase(strOutputDatabase, dbLangGeneral)

dbOutput.Close
```

The output database is immediately closed, because the backup process doesn't require it to be open. MakeBackup then iterates through the selected objects and calls ExportObject, passing it the name of the output database and the name and type of the object to be backed up.

```
intObjCnt = 0
ctlProgress = "Backing up objects..."

For Each varItem In ctlObjects.ItemsSelected
    intObjCnt = intObjCnt + 1
    strType = ctlObjects.Column(0, varItem)
    strName = ctlObjects.Column(1, varItem)
    ctlProgress = "Backing up " & strName & "..."
    DoEvents
    Call ExportObject(strOutputDatabase, strType, strName)
Next varItem
```

The ExportObject subroutine backs up each object using the CopyObject action. ExportObject is shown here.

```
Sub ExportObject(strOutputDatabase As String, _
  strType As String, strName As String)

    Dim intType As Integer

    Select Case strType
        Case "Table"
            intType = acTable
        Case "Query"
            intType = acQuery
        Case "Form"
            intType = acForm
        Case "Report"
            intType = acReport
        Case "Macro"
            intType = acMacro
        Case "Module"
            intType = acModule
    End Select

    ' If export fails, let the user know
    On Error Resume Next

    DoCmd.CopyObject strOutputDatabase, strName, intType, strName
    If Err <> 0 Then
        Beep
        MsgBox "Unable to backup " & strType & ": " & strName, _
          vbOKOnly + vbCritical, "ExportObject"
    End If

End Sub
```

Comments

This technique uses the CopyObject action instead of the more traditional TransferDatabase action. CopyObject, which was added in Access 2.0, provides you with the same functionality as TransferDatabase, but because it only supports Access objects, it requires fewer arguments. The CopyObject action also allows you to specify a new name for the object in the destination database. This is useful if you want give the copy a name that's different from the source object.

CHAPTER 7
EXPLORING VBA IN MICROSOFT ACCESS

EXPLORING VBA IN MICROSOFT ACCESS

How do I...

Most applications that are distributed to users include at least some VBA (Visual Basic for Applications) code. Because VBA provides the only mechanism for performing some tasks (using variables, building SQL strings on the fly, handling errors, and using the

Windows API, among others), most developers sooner or later must delve into its intri-
cacies. The topics in this chapter cover some of the details of VBA that you might not
find in the Access manuals. You'll first find a complete explanation of embedding strings
inside other strings, allowing you to build SQL strings and other expressions that require
embedded values. Two How-To's are devoted to creating a procedure stack, allowing
you to keep track of the current procedure at all times. The second of the two also creates a profiling log file, helping you document where and for how long your code wandered.
You'll learn about the DoEvents statement, which gives Windows time to handle its
own chores while your code is running. A group of four How-To's will cover the details
of creating list-filling functions, passing arrays as parameters, sorting arrays, and filling a list box with the results of a directory search. The final two How-To's cover some
details of working with Data Access Objects: how to set and retrieve object properties, whether or not the properties are built-in, and how to tell if an object exists in
your application or not.

A Note on Conventions

The replacement of Embedded Basic with Visual Basic for
Applications is one of the most significant changes that occurred
in Microsoft Access for Windows 95. Because of this addition,
Access 95 can share a great deal of code with other VBA-
equipped applications (such as Microsoft Excel, Project and
Visual Basic). Access 95 inherits new language constructs, and it
gets a new integrated development environment (IDE) for free.
To avoid confusion, when we refer to Visual Basic, VBA, or Access
Basic in this chapter, we're referring to the version of VBA that
Access 95 supports as its programming language.

7.1 Build Up String References with Embedded Quotes

Many times throughout your work with Access, you'll need to build up string expressions that, in turn, include other strings. When calling the domain functions, or building
SQL expressions, or using the FindFirst or Seek methods, you'll find yourself needing to build expressions. This How-To will go into detail to help you figure out these
complex expressions.

7.2 Create a Global Procedure Stack

Access supplies no function for returning the name of the current procedure. This information can be very useful in error-handling routines. If an error occurs, the user can
be presented with an error message and the name of the procedure that was
executing when the error occurred. This simple How-To will demonstrate a method
you can use to implement your own call stack.

7.3 Create an Execution Time Profiler for My Applications

Many programming languages such as C and Pascal have profilers that allow the developer to see execution times of each component of an application. Using an extension of the procedure stack discussed in How-To 7.2, this How-To will show how to implement a profiler. This profiler creates a log file of each procedure executed and its execution time.

7.4 Multitask My Access Basic Code

Even with Windows 95 and its preemptive multitasking, it's still quite possible for your VBA code to tie Windows up for the duration of your procedure. This How-To will demonstrate how your code can take control over Windows inadvertently and how you can solve the problem using the DoEvents statement.

7.5 Add Items to a List or Combo Box Programmatically

Unlike the other implementations of VBA, Access' version of VBA doesn't support the simple AddItem method for adding new items to a combo or list box. Because of its data-centric viewpoint, Access' controls are geared toward pulling data in from tables or queries. Sometimes, however, you must fill a list or combo box with data that isn't stored in a table. This How-To will provide two methods for dynamically filling a control with data.

7.6 Pass a Variable Number of Parameters to a Procedure

VBA supports a number of ways to pass arrays to functions and subroutines. Unfortunately, the syntax is not clearly documented. This How-To will give examples of how to pass arrays to procedures as parameters. Using these techniques, you'll be able to supply a variable number of parameters to any procedure you write.

7.7 Sort an Array in Access Basic

A glaring omission from Access is support for a method of sorting arrays. This How-To will demonstrate a general-purpose algorithm you can use to sort arrays in your applications.

7.8 Fill a List Box with a List of Files

Using the concepts from the previous three How-To's, this How-To will demonstrate how you can fill a control with a sorted list of file names, given a file specification. In addition, it will demonstrate how to use the built-in Dir function to retrieve the list of names.

7.9 Handle Object Properties, in General

Access supports two kinds of properties: user defined and built in. It's not always clear which properties belong to which type, and attempting to work with user-defined properties as if they are built in will cause a runtime error. This How-To will demonstrate a method for working with all properties in a standardized fashion and will provide code to make setting or retrieving any property a simple task.

7.10   Detect If an Object Exists or Not

As you write more and more complex applications, there undoubtedly will be times when your application can't know until runtime whether or not an object exists. Has tblCustomers been attached yet? Did the user create a new query? In these cases, you'll need some foolproof method of determining whether a specific object, of a specific type, exists in the database. This How-To will use Data Access Objects (DAO) to solve this problem.

COMPLEXITY:
INTERMEDIATE

7.1   How do I...
Build up string references with embedded quotes?

Problem

I need to use the DLookup function, specifying a search criterion based on a variable. No matter what I do, I can't get Access to understand what I'm trying to do. What am I doing wrong?

Technique

In any place in Access that you're required to provide a string expression that contains other strings, you're going to face this problem. That might be in using the domain functions (DLookup, DMax, DMin, etc.), as in the above problem, in building an SQL expression on the fly, or in using the Find methods (FindFirst, FindNext, FindPrevious, and FindLast) on a recordset. Because all strings must be surrounded with quotes, and you can't embed quotes inside a quoted string, you can quickly find yourself in trouble. Many programmers agonize over these constructs, but the situation needn't be that difficult. This How-To explains the problem and shows you a generic solution.

Steps

To see an example of building expressions on the fly, load and run frmQuoteTest in 07-01.MDB. This form, shown in Figure 7-1, allows you to specify criteria. Once you press the Search button, the code attached to the button will build the SQL expression shown in the text box, and will set the RowSource property for the list box at the bottom of the form accordingly.

To try all the features of the form, follow these three steps:

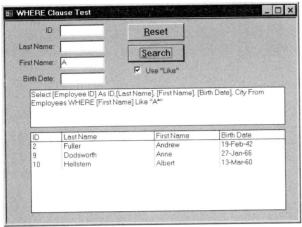

Figure 7-1 The test form, frmQuoteTest, with a subset of the data selected

1. In the First Name text box, enter A. When you press (RETURN), the form builds the appropriate SQL string and filters the list box. In the SQL string, note that the value you entered is surrounded in quotes. (This is the state in which Figure 7-1 was captured.)

2. In the Birth Date text box, enter 3/13/60. Again, the form should filter the data (down to a single row). Note that the SQL expression must have "#" signs around the date value you entered, because all dates must be surrounded by "#" signs.

3. Press the Reset button to delete all the data from the four text boxes. That will fill the list box with all the rows again. Enter the value 8 in the ID text box, and then press (RETURN). Note that the SQL string this time has no delimiter around the value that you entered.

How It Works

The point of the above exercise was to alert you to the fact that different data types require specific delimiters when they become part of an expression. For example, to use DLookup to find the row in which the [LastName] field was Smith, you'd need an expression like this:

```
[LastName] = "Smith"
```

Certainly, leaving those quotes off would confuse Access, because it would be looking for some variable named Smith.

Date values don't require quotes. Instead, they require # delimiters. To find the row in which the [BirthDate] field is May 16, 1956, you'd need an expression like this:

```
[BirthDate] = #5/16/56#
```

If you left off the delimiters, Access would think you were trying to numerically divide 5 by 16, and then by 56.

Numeric values require no delimiters. If you were searching for the row where the ID value was 8, you could use this expression:

```
[ID] = 8
```

and Access would know exactly what you meant.

Building Search Criteria

Many situations in Access require that you create strings that supply a search criteria. Because the Jet database engine has no knowledge of Access Basic or its variables, you must supply the actual values before you apply any search criteria or perform lookups. That is, you must create a string expression that contains the *value* of any variable involved, not the variable name.

Any of the three examples in the previous section could have been used as search criteria, and string values would have needed to be surrounded by quotes. The next few paragraphs cover the steps you need to take in creating these search criteria strings.

To build expressions that involve variables, you must supply any required delimiters. For numeric expressions, there is no required delimiter. If the variable named *intID* contains the value 8, then you could use this expression to create the search string that you need:

```
"[ID] = " & intID
```

As part of an SQL string, or as a parameter to DLookup, this string is unambiguous in its directions to Access.

To create a search criterion that includes a date variable, you'll need to include the # delimiters. For example, if you have a variant variable named *varDate* that contains the date May 22, 1959, and you want to end up with this expression:

```
"[BirthDate] = #5/22/59#"
```

you have to insert the delimiters yourself. The solution might look like this:

```
"[BirthDate] = #" & varDate & "#"
```

The complex case occurs when you must include strings. For those cases, you'll need to build a string expression that contains a string itself, surrounded by quotes, with the whole expression surrounded by quotes. The rules for working with strings in Access are as follows.

- An expression that's delimited with quotes can't itself contain quotes.

- Two quotes ("") inside a string are seen by Access as a single quote.

- You can use apostrophes (') as string delimiters.

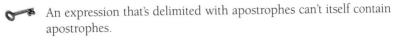 An expression that's delimited with apostrophes can't itself contain apostrophes.

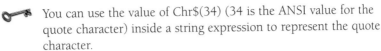 You can use the value of Chr$(34) (34 is the ANSI value for the quote character) inside a string expression to represent the quote character.

Given these rules, you can create a number of solutions to the same problem. For example, if the variable *strLastName* contains "Smith", and you want to create a WHERE clause that will search for that name, you will end up with this expression:

```
"[LastName] = "Smith""
```

That expression, of course, isn't allowed, because it includes internal quotes. An acceptable solution would be the following:

```
"[LastName] = ""Smith"""
```

The problem here is that the literal value "Smith" is still in the expression. You're trying to replace that with the name of the variable, *strLastName*. You might try this expression:

```
"[LastName] = ""strLastName"""
```

but that will search for a row with the last name of "strLastName". You probably won't find a match.

One solution, then, is to break that up into three separate pieces: the portion before the variable, the variable, and the portion after the variable (the final quote).

```
"[LastName] = """ & strLastName & """"
```

Although that may look confusing, it's correct. The first string

```
"[LastName] = """
```

is simply a string containing the name of the field, an equal sign, and two quotes. The rule is that two quotes inside a string are treated as one. The same logic works for the portion of the expression after the variable (""""). That's a string containing two quotes, which Access sees as a one quote. Although this solution works, it's quite confusing.

To make things simpler, you can just use apostrophes inside the string:

```
"[LastName] = '" & strLastName & "'"
```

This is somewhat less confusing, but there's a serious drawback: If the name itself contains an apostrophe ("O'Connor", for example), you'll be in trouble. Access doesn't allow you to nest apostrophes inside apostrophe delimiters, either. So this solution only works when you're assured that the data in the variable can never itself include an apostrophe.

The simplest solution, then, is to use Chr$(34) to embed the quotes. An expression such as the following would do the trick.

```
"[LastName] = " & Chr$(34) & strLastName & Chr$(34)
```

If you don't believe this works, go to the Debug Window in Access and type this:

```
? Chr$(34)
```

Access will return to you by typing the value of Chr$(34)—a quote character.

To make this solution a little simpler, you could create a string variable at the beginning of your procedure and assign to it the value of Chr$(34).

```
Dim strQuote As String
Dim strLookup As String

strQuote = Chr$(34)
strLookup = "[LastName] = " & strQuote & strLastName & strQuote
```

This actually makes the code almost readable!

Finally, if you weary of defining that variable in every procedure you write, you might consider using a constant instead. You might be tempted to try this:

```
Const QUOTE = Chr$(34)
```

But, alas, Access won't allow you to create a constant whose value is an expression. If you want to use a constant, your answer is to rely on the "two-quote" rule:

```
Const QUOTE = """"
```

Although this expression's use is not immediately clear, once you understand the two-quote rule, it works just fine. The constant is two quotes (which Access will see as a single quote) inside a quoted string. Using this constant, the previous expression becomes

```
strLookup = "[LastName] = " & QUOTE & strLastName & QUOTE
```

Comments

To encapsulate all these rules, you might want to use the function named FixUp, in the basFixUpValue module in 07-01.MDB. This function takes as a parameter a variant value and surrounds it with appropriate delimiters.

```
Function ahtFixUp(ByVal varValue As Variant) As Variant

    ' Add the appropriate delimiters, depending on the data type.
    ' Put quotes around text, # around dates, and nothing
    ' around numeric values.
    '
    ' If you're using equality in your expression, you should
    ' use Basic's BuildCriteria function instead of calling
    ' this function.

    Const QUOTE = """"

    Select Case VarType(varValue)
        Case vbInteger, vbSingle, vbDouble, vbLong, vbCurrency
            ahtFixUp = CStr(varValue)
        Case vbString
            ahtFixUp = QUOTE & varValue & QUOTE
        Case vbDate
            ahtFixUp = "#" & varValue & "#"
```

```
      Case Else
           ahtFixUp = Null
    End Select
End Function
```

Once you've included this function in your own application, you can call it, rather than formatting the data yourself. The sample code in frmQuoteTest uses this function. For example, here's how to build the expression you labored over in the above example:

```
"[LastName] = " & FixUp(strLastName)
```

FixUp would do the work of figuring out the data type and surrounding the data with the necessary delimiters.

Access also provides a useful function, BuildCriteria, that will accept a field name, a data type, and a field value, and will create an expression of this sort:

```
FieldName = "FieldValue"
```

with the appropriate delimiters, depending on the data type. We've used this in our example in the case where you uncheck the Use Like check box. It won't help if you want an expression that uses wild cards, but if you're looking for an exact match, it does most of the work of inserting the correct delimiters for you. To study the example, look at the BuildWhere function in frmQuoteTest's module.

COMPLEXITY:
INTERMEDIATE

7.2 How do I...
Create a global procedure stack?

Problem

Often when I'm writing an application, I need to know the name of the current procedure from within my code. For example, if an error occurs, I'd like to be able to have a generic function handle the error and display the name of the procedure in which the error occurred, and all the procedures that have been called on the way to get to here. VBA doesn't include a way to retrieve this information. How can I accomplish this?

Technique

By maintaining a list of active procedures, adding the current name to the list on the way into the procedure and removing it on the way out, you can always keep track of the current procedure and the procedure calls that got you there. There are many other uses for this functionality (see the next How-To, for example), but one simple use is to retrieve the name of the current procedure in a global error-handling procedure.

The kind of data structure that you'll need for maintaining your list is called a stack. As you enter a new procedure, you "push" its name onto the top of the stack. When

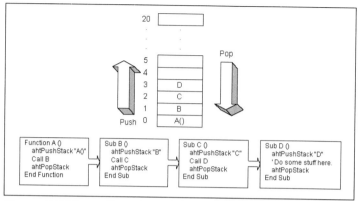

Figure 7-2 The call stack and the sample routines to fill it

you leave the procedure, you "pop" the name off the stack. Figure 7-2 shows a graphical representation of a procedure stack in action. The arrows indicate the direction in which the stack grows and shrinks as you add and remove items.

Steps

To see the procedure stack in action, load 07-02.MDB. Open the module basTestStack in design mode. Open the Debug Window (choose View|Debug Window). In the Debug Window, type

```
? A()
```

which will execute the function named A. Figure 7-2 shows A and the procedures it calls. At each step, the current procedure pushes its name onto the procedure stack and then calls some other procedure. Once the calling procedure gets control again, it pops its name off of the stack. In addition, each procedure prints the name of the current procedure (using the ahtCurrentProc function, discussed later in this How-To) to the Debug Window. Once all execution has finished, you should see output like that shown in Figure 7-3 in the Debug Window.

Follow these steps to incorporate this functionality into your own applications:

1. Import the module basStack into your application. This includes the procedures that initialize and maintain the procedure stack.

2. Insert a call to the ahtInitStack subroutine into code that's executed when your application starts up. Consider adding this procedure call to the code in your main form's Load event procedure. You'll want to call ahtInitStack any time you restart your program during development, so you probably don't want to call it from the Autoexec macro, which only gets executed when you first load

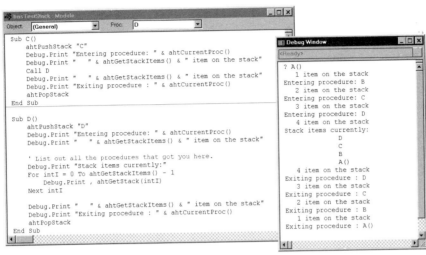

Figure 7-3 The output from running the sample procedure

the database. To call ahtInitStack, either place its name alone on a line of code or use the Call construct:

```
ahtInitStack
```

or

```
Call ahtInitStack
```

3. For each procedure in your application, place a call to ahtPushStack as the first statement. This procedure will place the value it's passed on the top of the stack. As the single argument for each call, pass the name of the current procedure. The example places a pair of parentheses after function names and nothing after subroutine names as a matter of style. As the last line in each procedure, add a call to ahtPopStack, which will remove the current name from the top of the stack.

4. At any time in your application, to retrieve the name of the currently executing procedure, call the ahtCurrentProc function. This function looks at the top of the stack and returns the string it finds there. You can use this as part of an error handler or, as in the next How-To, to help track procedure performance.

How It Works

The module you imported from 07-02.MDB, basStack, includes code for maintaining the procedure stack and a module-local variable that is the stack itself. There are just six entry points (nonprivate procedures) in the module. Table 7-1 lists those procedures.

PROCEDURE NAME	PURPOSE	PARAMETERS
ahtInitStack	Initialize the stack	
ahtPushStack	Add an item to the stack	A string to push
ahtPopStack	Remove an item from the stack	
ahtCurrentProc	Retrieve the name of the current procedure	
ahtGetStack	Retrieve a specific item from the stack	Item number to retrieve
ahtGetStackItems	Retrieve number of items on the stack	

Table 7-1 The six entry points into basStack

By encapsulating all the code for the stack in that one module, you never really have to know how it all works. On the other hand, it's quite simple.

BasStack includes two module-global variables: mastrStack, the array of strings that is the stack itself, and mintStackTop, an integer that holds the array slot into which the next stack item will be placed. When you begin your work with the stack, mintStackTop must be 0, so the first item will go in the slot numbered 0. The ahtInitStack procedure does nothing besides initialize mintStackTop.

```
Sub ahtInitStack ()

    ' Resets the stack top to be 0.
    mintStackTop = 0
End Sub
```

At any time, you can add an item to the stack by calling ahtPushStack. You pass to this subroutine the item you want pushed. To push the item, the code places the item in the array at the location stored in mintStackTop, and then increments the value of mintStackTop.

```
Sub ahtPushStack (strToPush As String)

    ' Handle the error case first.
    If mintStackTop > ahtcMaxStack Then
        MsgBox ahtcMsgStackOverflow
    Else
        ' Store away the string and time.
        mastrStack(mintStackTop) = strToPush

        ' Set mintStackTop to point to the NEXT
        ' item to be filled.
        mintStackTop = mintStackTop + 1
    End If
End Sub
```

The only problem that might occur is that the stack might be full. The constant ahtcMaxStack is originally set to be 20, which ought to be enough levels. (Remember that mintStackTop only goes up one when a procedure calls another procedure. If you have

20 levels of procedure calling, then you might consider rethinking your application, instead of worrying about procedure stacks!) If the stack is full, ahtPushStack will pop up an alert, and will not add the item to the stack.

When leaving a procedure, you'll want to remove an item from the stack. To do so, call the ahtPopStack procedure.

```
Sub ahtPopStack ()

    ' Handle the error case first.
    If mintStackTop = 0 Then
        MsgBox ahtcMsgStackUnderflow
    Else
        ' Because you're removing an item, not adding one,
        ' set the stack top back to the previous row. Next time
        ' you add an item, it'll go right here.
        mintStackTop = mintStackTop - 1
    End If
End Sub
```

Just as in ahtPushStack, this code first checks to make sure that the stack integrity hasn't been violated; you can't remove an item from the stack if there's nothing to remove! If you try, ahtPopStack will pop up an alert and exit. If the stack's intact, then the procedure will decrement the value of mintStackTop. By decrementing that value, you've set up the next call to ahtPushStack so that it'll place the new value where the old one used to be.

To retrieve the value at the top of the stack without pushing or popping anything, call the ahtCurrentProc function.

```
Function ahtCurrentProc () As String
    ahtCurrentProc = IIf(mintStackTop > 0, _
    mastrStack(mintStackTop - 1), "")
End Function
```

This function retrieves the value most recently placed on the stack (at the location one less than mintStackTop, because mintStackTop always points to the next location to be filled). You can't look at mastrStack yourself, because it's local to basStack. And that's the way it *ought* to be. By keeping you from the details of how the stack works, you can replace basStack, using a different architecture for the stack data structure, and the rest of your code won't have to change at all.

To retrieve more information about what's in the stack, you can call ahtGetStackItems to find out how many items there are in the stack and ahtGetStack, which retrieves a specific item from the stack. For example, write code like this to dump out the entire stack (see subroutine D, which does just this, in the basTestStack module):

```
Debug.Print "Stack items currently:"
For intI = 0 To ahtGetStackItems() - 1
    Debug.Print , ahtGetStack(intI)
Next intI
```

The ahtGetStackItems function is very simple: It returns the value of mintStackTop, because that value always contains the number of items.

```
Function ahtGetStackItems() As Integer
   ' Retrieve the number of items in the stack.
   ahtGetStackItems = mintStackTop
End Function
```

The ahtGetStack function is a little more complex. It accepts an item number (requesting item 0 returns the item at the top of the stack), and calculates the position of the item to retrieve.

```
Function ahtGetStack(intItem As Integer) As String
   ' Retrieve the item that's intItems from the top of the
   ' stack. That is,
   ' ? ahtGetStack(0)
   ' would return the same value as ahtCurrentProc.
   ' ? ahtGetStack(3) would return the value 3 from the top.
   ahtGetStack = IIf(mintStackTop >= intItem, _
     mastrStack(mintStackTop - intItem - 1), "")
End Function
```

Comments

For the procedure stack to work, you have to place calls to ahtPushStack and ahtPopStack on entry and exit from *each and every* procedure call. Good coding practice supports the concept of only one exit point from each procedure, but even the best programmer sometimes breaks this rule. To use the call stack, however, you must catch each and every exit point with a call to ahtPopStack. Keep this in mind as you retrofit old code to use this mechanism and when devising new code to use it. You can always code for a single exit point, and you will find code maintenance much more reasonable if you do.

COMPLEXITY:
INTERMEDIATE

7.3   How do I...
Create an execution time profiler for my applications?

Problem

I'd like to optimize my VBA code, but it's almost impossible to tell how long Access is spending inside any one routine, and it's very difficult to track which procedures get called by my code most often. I'd like some way to track which routines get called, in what order, and how much time each takes to run. Can I do this?

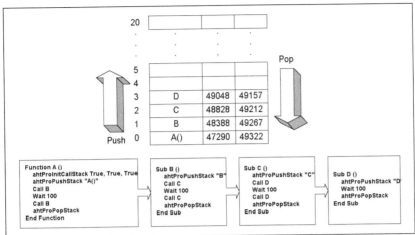

Figure 7-4 The profile stack and the sample routines used to fill it

Technique

As outlined in How-To 7.2, you can create a code profiler using a stack data structure to keep track of the execution order and timing of the procedures in your application. Though the code involved in this situation is a bit more advanced than in How-To 7.2, it's not terribly difficult to create the profiler. Using it is simple, as all the work is wrapped up in a single module.

Steps

Open the database 07-03.MDB and load the module basTestProfiler in design mode. In the Debug Window, type:

```
? A()
```

to run the test procedures. Figure 7-4 shows the profile stack and the code in A. As you can see, A calls B, which calls C, which calls D, which waits 100 milliseconds and then returns to C. C waits 100 milliseconds, and then calls D again. Once D returns, C returns to B, which waits 100 milliseconds and then calls C again. This pattern repeats until the code gets back to A, where it finally quits. The timings in the profile stack in Figure 7-4 are actual timings from one run of the sample.

As the code is set up now, the profiler writes to a text file named LOGFILE.TXT in your Access subdirectory. You can read this file in any text editor. For a sample run of function A, the file contained this text:

```
********************************
Procedure Profiling
6/14/95 4:58:07 PM
********************************
+ Entering procedure: A()
    + Entering procedure: B
```

continued on next page

continued from previous page

```
  + Entering procedure: C
     + Entering procedure: D
     - Exiting  procedure : D              109 msecs.
     + Entering procedure: D
     - Exiting  procedure : D              110 msecs.
  - Exiting procedure : C            329 msecs.
  + Entering procedure: C
     + Entering procedure: D
     - Exiting  procedure : D              110 msecs.
     + Entering procedure: D
     - Exiting  procedure : D              110 msecs.
  - Exiting procedure : C            330 msecs.
- Exiting procedure : B           824 msecs.
+ Entering procedure: B
  + Entering procedure: C
     + Entering procedure: D
     - Exiting  procedure : D              110 msecs.
     + Entering procedure: D
     - Exiting  procedure : D              110 msecs.
  - Exiting procedure : C            330 msecs.
  + Entering procedure: C
     + Entering procedure: D
     - Exiting  procedure : D              110 msecs.
     + Entering procedure: D
     - Exiting  procedure : D              109 msecs.
  - Exiting procedure : C            329 msecs.
- Exiting procedure : B           769 msecs.
- Exiting procedure : A()      1702 msecs.
```

To incorporate this sort of profiling into your own applications, follow these steps:

1. Import the module basProfiler into your application. This module includes all the procedures to initialize and use the profiling stack.

2. Insert a call to ahtProInitCallStack into code that's executed when your application starts up. In How-To 7.2, you might have got by without calling the initialization routine. In this situation, however, you must call ahtProInitCallStack each time you want to profile your code, or the profile stack will not work correctly. To call ahtProInitCallStack, you must pass it three parameters, all of which are logical values (True or False). Table 7-2 lists the question answered by each of the three parameters.

PARAMETER NAME	USAGE
fDisplay	Display message box if an error occurs?
fLog	Write to log file or just track items in the array in memory?
fTimeStamp	If writing to the log file, also write out time values?

Table 7-2 Parameters for ahtProInitCallStack

The procedure initializes some global variables, and, if you're writing to a log file, writes a log header to the file. A typical call to ahtProInitCallStack might look like this:

```
ahtProInitCallStack False,True,True
```

3. For each procedure in your application, place a call to ahtProPushStack as the first statement. This procedure places the value it's passed on the top of the stack, along with the current time. As the single argument for each call, pass the name of the current procedure. The example places a pair of parentheses after function names and nothing after subroutine names as a matter of style. As the last line in each procedure, add a call to ahtProPopStack, which will remove the current name from the top of the stack and record the current time.

4. At any time in your application, to retrieve the name of the currently executing procedure, call the ahtProCurrentProc function. This function looks at the top of the stack and returns the string it finds there.

5. To review the outcome of your logging, view the file LOGFILE.TXT (in your Access directory) in any text editor. If you followed the previous steps carefully, you should see matching entry and exit points for every routine. Nested levels are indented in the printout, and entry and exit points are marked differently (entry with a "+" and exit with a "–").

How It Works

The module you imported from 07-03.MDB, basProfiler, includes all the code that maintains the profiler. There are five public entry points to the module, as shown in Table 7-3.

PROCEDURE NAME	PURPOSE	PARAMETERS
ahtProInitCallStack	Initialize the profile stack.	
ahtProPushStack	Add an item to the profile stack.	A string to push
ahtProPopStack	Remove an item from the profile stack.	
ahtProCurrentProc	Retrieve the name of the current procedure.	
ahtProLogString	Add any string to the log file.	A string to log

Table 7-3 The five entry points into basProfiler

In general, the profiler works almost exactly like the simpler procedure stack shown in How-To 7.2. As a matter of fact, the code for this How-To was written first, and was then stripped down for use in the simpler example. This example includes the code necessary to write to the file on disk, as well as to gather timing information. The next few paragraphs outline the major differences and how they work.

Storing Information

Whereas How-To 7.2 used a simple array of strings to hold the stack information, the profiler also needs to store starting and ending times for each routine. Therefore, it uses an array of a user-defined type, ahtStack, defined as follows, to create the stack.

```
Type ahtStack
    strItem As String
    lngStart As Long
    lngEnd As Long
End Type
Dim maStack(0 To ahtcMaxStack) As ahtStack
```

Gathering Time Information

Access provides the Timer function, which returns the number of seconds since midnight, but for measuring the duration of procedures in Access Basic, this resolution won't give you enough information. Windows provides the GetTickCount function, which returns the number of milliseconds since you started Windows. In addition, GetTickCount (aliased as aht_apiProGetTickCount in the code) resets itself to 0 every 48 days, whereas Timer resets once every day. So if you need to time a lengthy operation, GetTickCount provides a mechanism for measuring time spans longer than a single day (and makes it possible to measure time spans that cross midnight). (Of course, if you're timing an operation that takes more than a day, you're probably not going to care about millisecond accuracy, but that's what you get!) The code in basProfiler calls GetTickCount to retrieve the current "time" whenever you push or pop a value and stores it in the stack array. You can call GetTickCount in any application, once you include this declaration in a global module:

```
Declare Function aht_apiProGetTickCount Lib "Kernel32" _
    Alias "GetTickCount" () As Long
```

The code in basTestProfiler also uses GetTickCount, in the Wait subroutine. This procedure does nothing but wait for the requested number of milliseconds, calling DoEvents inside the loop, giving Windows time to do its work.

```
Sub Wait (intWait As Integer)
    Dim lngStart As Long
    lngStart = aht_apiProGetTickCount()
    Do While aht_apiProGetTickCount() < lngStart + intWait
        DoEvents
    Loop
End Sub
```

Writing to the Log File

The code in basProfiler opens and closes the output file each time it needs to write a piece of information. Although this slows down your application, it ensures that if your machine crashes for some reason, your log file will always be current. Although you'll never actually call this routine directly, you might find it interesting to see how it does its work, if you've never used Access to write directly to a text file.

The procedure, ahtProWriteToLog, first checks to see if an error has ever occurred in the logging mechanism (that is, if mfLogErrorOccurred has been set to True). If so, it doesn't try to write anything to the file, because something may be wrong with the disk. Otherwise, it gets a free file handle, opens the log file for appending, writes the item to the file, and then closes it.

```
Private Sub ahtProWriteToLog (strItem As String)

    On Error GoTo LogIt_Err

    ' If an error has EVER occurred in this session,
    ' then just get out of here.
    If mfLogErrorOccurred Then Exit Sub

    Dim intFile As Integer
    intFile = FreeFile
    Open ahtcLogFile For Append As intFile
    Print #intFile, strItem
    Close #intFile
    Exit Sub

LogIt_Err:
    mfLogErrorOccurred = True
    MsgBox "Error: " & Error & " (" & Err & _
      ") while writing to log."
    Exit Sub
End Sub
```

Comments

As in How-To 7.2, you'll find that you must be conscientious about the placement of your calls to ahtProPushStack and ahtProPopStack for the procedure stack profiler mechanism to be of any value. If you have multiple exit points from routines, this is a good time to try to consolidate them. If you can't, then you'll need to make sure that you've placed a call to ahtProPopStack before every exit point in a procedure.

If you attempt to decipher the log file, you'll notice that the elapsed time for each procedure must also include any procedures it happens to call, as in the example of A calling B, which calls C, which calls D. The elapsed time for function A was 1,702 milliseconds. That's the time that elapsed between the calls to ahtProPushStack and ahtProPopStack in function A, including the time it took to run all the calls to B, C, and D. This isn't necessarily a problem, nor is it wrong, but you should be aware that there's no way to "stop the clock" while in subsidiary procedures.

The code for the profiler includes another public entry point, ahtProLogString. The profiler doesn't actually call this procedure, but your own code can. Pass it a single string, and the profile will send that string to the log file for you. For example, the following code will append "This is a test" to the log file.

```
ahtProLogString "This is a test"
```

COMPLEXITY:
INTERMEDIATE

7.4   How do I...
Multitask my Access Basic code?

Problem

If my VBA code includes a loop that runs for more than just a second or two, Access seems to come to a halt. I can't move the windows on the screen, and mouse-clicks inside Access are disregarded until my code has finished running. Why is this happening? Is there something I can do to relinquish some control?

Technique

You may have noticed that it's quite possible to tie up Access with a simple bit of VBA code. Though 32-bit Windows is multithreaded, this only helps if the applications running under it are also multithreaded. It appears that the executing Basic code ties up Access' processing, so the multithreaded nature of Windows doesn't help. You should make a conscious effort, if your code contains loops that run for a while, to give Windows time to catch up and do its own work. VBA includes the DoEvents statement, which effectively yields time to Windows so that Access can perform whatever other tasks it must. Effective use of DoEvents can make the difference between an Access application that hogs Access' ability to multitask and one that allows Access to run smoothly at the same time as your VBA code is executing.

Steps

To see the problem in action, load and run the form frmMoveTest (in 07-04.MDB). Figure 7-5 shows the form in use. The form includes three command buttons, each of which causes the label with the caption "Watch Me Grow!" to change its width in

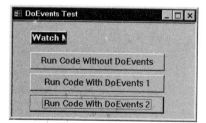

Figure 7-5 The sample DoEvents Test form, frmMoveTest, in action

increments of 5 from 500 to 2,000 twips wide (in Figure 7-5, you can only see a portion of the label), in a loop like this:

```
For intI = 0 To 1500 Step 5
    Me!lblGrow1.Width = Me!lblGrow1.Width + 5
    ' Without this call to Repaint, you'll
    ' never see any changes on the screen.
    Me.Repaint
Next intI
```

To test the effects of DoEvents, try these steps:

1. Press the Run Code Without DoEvents button. The code attached to this button (as seen in Figure 7-5) will change the width of the label inside a loop without yielding time to Access. While the code is running, try to click on another button on the form, or to move or size the active window. You will find that any of these tasks are impossible while the label is expanding. Once the label has finished growing, Access will display any actions you attempted to make during the process.

2. Try the same loop with DoEvents inserted. Click the second button, labeled Run Code With DoEvents 1. This time, as the code executes, you will be able to move or size the active window. In addition, you can click on any of the form's buttons while the code is running. The next step tests this situation.

3. While the label is growing, click on the Run Code With DoEvents 1 button many times in quick succession. Every time you click the button, Access starts up another instance of the Click event procedure, and each instance continues to make the label grow. This is called recursion, in which multiple calls are made into the same routine, each starting before the last instance has completed. In addition, each time you call the Click event, you use a bit of Access' stack space (a memory area set aside for each procedure's entry information and local variables). It's possible that, with many invocations, you could use up that memory. Using Access 95, we've never made this happen. Using Access 2, this was easy to reproduce. The next step offers a solution to this recursion problem.

4. Click the third button, labeled Run Code with DoEvents 2. While the label is expanding, try clicking on the button again. You'll see that this time your clicks won't have any effect. The code attached to this button checks to see if it's already running, and if so, exits the code. This method will solve the problem of recursive calls to DoEvents.

How It Works

The code attached to the first button does its work without any concern for Windows or other running applications. When you press it, it executes this code:

```
Sub cmdNoDoevents_Click ()
    Dim intI As Integer
```

continued on next page

continued from previous page

```
      Me!lblGrow1.Width = 500
      For intI = 0 To 1500 Step 5
         Me!lblGrow1.Width = Me!lblGrow1.Width + 5
         ' Without this call to Repaint, you'll
         ' never see any changes on the screen.
         Me.Repaint
      Next intI
   End Sub
```

Because the code never gives Windows time to "catch up," you must include the call to Me.Repaint to make sure the form repaints itself after each change. To see for yourself how this works, comment out that line and press the first button again. You'll see that the screen won't repaint until the entire operation is done.

The code attached to the second button does the same work, but it calls DoEvents within the loop. With that statement added, you no longer need the call to Me.Repaint, because DoEvents allows Windows to take care of the pending repaints. In addition, it allows you to use the mouse and other applications while this loop is running. The code attached to the second button looks like this:

```
Sub cmdDoEvents1_Click ()
   Dim intI As Integer

   Me!lblGrow1.Width = 500
   For intI = 0 To 1500 Step 5
      Me!lblGrow1.Width = Me!lblGrow1.Width + 5
      DoEvents
   Next intI
End Sub
```

The problem with this code, as mentioned in step 2, is that nothing's keeping you from initiating it again while it's running. That is, if you press the same button while the code is in the middle of the loop, Access will start up the same procedure again. Every time Access starts running a VBA routine, it stores information about the routine and its local variables in a reserved area of memory, called its stack. The size of this area is fixed and limits the number of procedures that can be running concurrently. If you press that button over and over again, in quick succession, it's possible you'll overrun Access' stack space. (It's doubtful you'll ever be able to reproduce the problem with this tiny example. Though the stack space was limited to 40K in Access 2, the stack can grow up to one megabyte in Access 95. You'd have to press that button very fast for a very long time to fill up that much stack space. In more complex situations, if you were passing a large amount of data to a procedure in its list of parameters, this could still be a problem, however.) The third button on the form demonstrates the solution to this problem. It ensures that its code isn't already running before it starts the loop. If it's already in progress, the code just exits. The code attached to the third button looks like this:

```
Sub cmdDoEvents2_Click ()
   Dim intI As Integer
   Static fInHere As Boolean
```

```
    If fInHere Then Exit Sub
    fInHere = True
    cmdDoEvents1_Click
    fInHere = False
End Sub
```

It uses a static variable, fInHere, to keep track of whether the routine is already running. If fInHere is currently True, then it exits. If not, it sets the variable to True and then calls cmdDoEvents1_Click (the previous code fragment). Once cmdDoEvents1_Click returns, cmdDoEvents2_Click sets fInHere back to False, clearing the way for another invocation.

Comments

DoEvents is one of the most misunderstood elements of VBA. No matter what programmers would *like* DoEvents to do, under Access 95 it does nothing more than yield time to Access so it can process all the messages in its message queue. It has no effect on the Access database engine itself, and can't be used to slow things down or help timing issues, other than those involving Windows messages. When used in VBA code, DoEvents will release control to the operating environment, which won't return control until it has processed the events in its queue and handled all the keys in the SendKeys queue. Access will ignore DoEvents in:

- A user-defined procedure that calculates a field in a query, form, or report

- A user-defined procedure that creates a list to fill a combo or list box

As you can see from the second button on the sample form, calling DoEvents recursively can lead to trouble. You should take steps, as in the example of the third button, to make sure that this won't occur in your applications.

COMPLEXITY:
ADVANCED

7.5 How do I...
Add items to a list or combo box programmatically?

Problem

Getting items into a list or combo box from a data source is elementary in Access. Sometimes, though, I need to put things into a list box that I don't have stored in a table. In Visual Basic and other implementations of VBA, this is simple: I just use the AddItem method. But Access list boxes don't support this method. How can I add items to a list box that aren't stored in a table?

Technique

It's true: Access list boxes (and combo boxes) don't support the AddItem method that Visual Basic programmers are used to. To make it easy for you to get bound data into list and combo boxes, the Access developers had to forego a simple method for loading unbound data. To get around this limitation, there are two methods you can use to place data into an Access list or combo box: You can programmatically build the RowSource string yourself, or you can call a list-filling callback function. Providing the RowSource string is easy, but it only works in the simplest of situations. A callback function, though, will work in any situation. This How-To demonstrates both methods.

One important question, of course, is why you would ever need either of these methods for filling your list or combo box. Because you can always pull data from a table, query, or SQL expression directly into the control, why bother with all this work? The answer is simple. Sometimes you don't know ahead of time what data you're going to need, and the data's not stored in a table. Or perhaps you need to load the contents of an array into the control and you don't need to store the data permanently.

Steps

Follow these steps to walk through using both of the methods for modifying the contents of a list or combo box while your application is running. The first example modifies the value of the RowSource property, given that the RowSourceType property is set to Value List. The second example covers list-filling callback functions.

Filling a List Box by Modifying the RowSource Property

1. Open the form frmRowSource in 07-05.MDB.

2. Change the contents of the list box by choosing either Days or Months from the option group on the left. Try both settings and change the number of columns, to get a feel for how this method works. Figure 7-6 shows the form set to display month names in three columns.

Filling a List Box by Creating a List-Filling Callback Function

1. Open the form frmListFill in 07-05.MDB.

2. Select a weekday from the first list box, and you'll see the second list box show you the date of that day this week, plus the next three instances of that weekday. Figure 7-7 shows the form with Wednesday, June 7, 1995, selected.

3. To use this method, set the control's RowSourceType property to the name of a function (without an equal sign and without parentheses). Functions called this way must meet very strict requirements, as is discussed in the next section. Figure 7-8 shows the property sheet for the list box on frmListFill, showing the RowSourceType property with the name of the list-filling function.

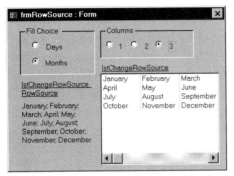

Figure 7-6 The sample form, frmRowSource, displaying months in three columns

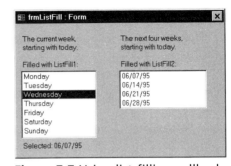

Figure 7-7 Using list-filling callback functions to fill the lists on frmListFill

How It Works

This section explains the two methods for filling list and combo boxes programmatically. The text refers only to filling list boxes, but the same techniques apply to combo boxes as well. You may find it useful to open up the form module for each form as it's being discussed here.

Modifying the RowSource Property

If you set a list box's RowSourceType property to be Value List, then you can supply a list of items, separated with semicolons, that will fill the list. By placing this list in the control's RowSource property, you tell Access to display the items one by one in each row and column that it needs to fill. Because you're placing data directly into the property sheet, you're limited by the amount of space available in the property sheet: 2,048 characters.

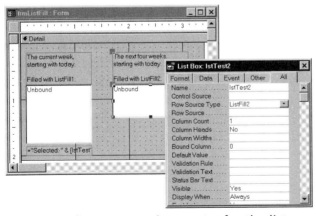

Figure 7-8 The property sheet entry for the list-filling function

At any time, you can modify the RowSource property of a list box, placing into it a semicolon-delimited list of values. The ColumnCount property plays a part, in that Access fills the rows first and then the columns. You can see this for yourself if you modify the ColumnCount property on the sample form (frmRowSource).

The sample form creates a list of either the days in a week or the months in a year, based on the value and option group on the form. The code that performs the work looks like this:

```
Select Case Me!grpChoice
    Case 1   ' Days
        ' Get last Sunday's date.
        varStart = Now - WeekDay(Now)
        ' Loop through all the week days.
        For intI = 1 To 7
            strList = strList & ";" & Format(varStart + intI, "dddd")
        Next intI

    Case 2   ' Months
        For intI = 1 To 12
            strList = strList & ";" & Format(DateSerial(1995, intI, 1), "mmmm")
        Next intI
End Select

' Get rid of the extra "; " at the beginning.
strList = Mid(strList, 2)
Me!txtFillString = strList
```

Depending on the choice in grpChoice, you'll end up with either a string of days:

```
Sunday; Monday; Tuesday; Wednesday; Thursday; Friday; _
  Saturday; Sunday
```

(the extra spaces are included only so the displayed version of this string on the form will wrap correctly—Access disregards the extra space) or a string of months.

```
January; February; March; April; May; June; July; August; _
  September; October; November; December
```

Once you've built the string up, make sure that the RowSourceType property is set correctly, and then insert the new RowSource string.

```
lstChangeRowSource.RowSourceType = "Value List"
lstChangeRowSource.RowSource = strList
```

Creating a List-Filling Callback Function

This technique, which involves creating a special Access Visual Basic function that provides the information Access needs to fill your list box, is not well documented in the Access manuals. List filling using a callback function provides a great deal of flexibility, and it's not very difficult.

The concept is quite simple: You provide Access with a function that, when requested, returns information about the control you're attempting to fill. Access "asks you questions" about the number of rows, number of columns, width of the columns, column formatting, and the actual data itself. Your function must react to these requests and provide the information so Access can fill the control with data. This is the only situation in Access where you provide a function that you never need to call. Access calls your function as it needs information in order to fill the control. The sample form frmFillList uses two of these functions to fill its two list boxes.

To communicate with Access, your function must accept five specific parameters. Table 7-4 lists those parameters and explains their purpose. (The parameter names are arbitrary, and are provided here as examples only.)

ARGUMENT	DATA TYPE	DESCRIPTION
ctl	Control	A reference to the control being filled.
varId	Variant	A unique value that identifies the control that's being filled (you assign this value in your code). Although you could use this value to let you use the same function for multiple controls, this is most often not worth the extraordinary trouble it causes.
lngRow	Long	The row currently being filled (0-based).
lngCol	Long	The column currently being filled (0-based).
intCode	Integer	A code that indicates the kind of information that Access is requesting.

Table 7-4 The required parameters for all list-filling functions

Access uses the final parameter, intCode, to let you know what information it's currently requesting. Access places a particular value in that variable, and it's up to your code to react to that request and supply the necessary information as the return value of your function. Table 7-5 lists the possible values of intCode, the meaning, and the value your function must return to Access in response to each.

CONSTANT	MEANING	RETURN VALUE
acLBInitialize	Initialize data.	Nonzero if the function will be able to fill the list; Null or 0 otherwise.
acLBOpen	Open the control.	Nonzero unique ID if the function will be able to fill the list; Null or 0 otherwise.
acLBGetRowCount	Get number of rows.	Number of rows in the list; −1 if unknown (see the text for information).
acLBGetColumnCount	Get number of columns.	Number of columns in the list (cannot be 0).
acLBGetColumnWidth	Get column widths.	Width (in twips) of the column specified in the lngCol argument (0-based); specify −1 to use the default width.
acLBGetValue	Get a value to display.	Value to be displayed in the row and column specified by the lngRow and lngCol arguments.
acLBGetFormat	Get column formats.	Format string to be used by the column specified in lngCol.
acLBClose	(Unknown)	
acLBEnd	End (when the form is closed).	Nothing.

Table 7-5 The values of intCode, their meanings, and return values

You'll find that almost all of your list-filling functions will be structured the same. Therefore, you may find it useful to always start with the ListFillSkeleton function, listed below. It's set up to receive all the correct parameters and includes a Select Case statement handling each of the useful values of intCode. All you need to do is change its name and make it return some real values.

```
Function ListFillSkeleton (ctl As Control, varId As Variant, _
   lngRow As Long, lngCol As Long, intCode As Integer)

   Dim varRetval As Variant

   Select Case intCode
      Case acLBInitialize
         ' Could you initialize?
         varRetval = True

      Case acLBOpen
         ' What's the unique identifier?
         varRetval = Timer

      Case acLBGetRowCount
         ' How many rows are there to be?

      Case acLBGetColumnCount
         ' How many columns are there to be?

      Case acLBGetValue
         ' What's the value in each row/column to be?

      Case acLBGetColumnWidth
         ' How many twips wide should each column be?
         ' (optional)

      Case acLBGetFormat
         ' What's the format for each column to be?
         ' (optional)

      Case acLBEnd
         ' Just clean up, if necessary.
         ' (optional, unless you use an array whose
         ' memory you want to release)

   End Select
   ListFillSkeleton = varRetval
End Function
```

For example, the following function from frmListFill fills in the first list box on the form. This function fills in a two-column list box, with the second column hidden (its width is set to 0 twips). Each time Access calls the function with acLBGetValue in intCode, the function calculates a new value for the date and returns it as the return value.

```
Private Function ListFill1(ctl As Control, varId As Variant, _
   lngRow As Long, lngCol As Long, intCode As Integer)
```

```
Select Case intCode
    Case acLBInitialize
        ' Could you initialize?
        ListFill1 = True

    Case acLBOpen
        ' What's the unique identifier?
        ListFill1 = Timer

    Case acLBGetRowCount
        ' How many rows are there to be?
        ListFill1 = 7

    Case acLBGetColumnCount
        ' How many columns are there to be?

        ' The first column will hold the day of the week.
        ' The second, hidden, column will hold the actual date.
        ListFill1 = 2

    Case acLBGetColumnWidth
        ' How many twips wide should each column be?

        ' Set the width of the 2nd column to 0.
        ' Remember, they're 0-based.
        If lngCol = 1 Then ListFill1 = 0

    Case acLBGetFormat
        ' What's the format for each column to be?

        ' Set the format for the first column so
        ' that it displays the day of the week.
        If lngCol = 0 Then
            ListFill1 = "dddd"
        Else
            ListFill1 = "mm/dd/yy"
        End If

    Case acLBGetValue
        ' What's the value for each row in each column to be?

        ' No matter which column you're in, return
        ' the date lngRow days from now.
        ListFill1 = Now + lngRow

    Case acLBEnd
        ' Just clean up, if necessary.

    End Select
End Function
```

The next example, which fills the second list box on the sample form, fills an array of values in the initialization step (acLBInitialize) and returns items from the array when requested. This function displays the next four instances of a particular day of the week. That is, if you choose Monday in the first list box, this function will fill the second list box with the date of the Monday in the current week, along with the dates of the next three Mondays.

```
Private Function ListFill2(ctl As Control, varId As Variant, _
  lngRow As Long, lngCol As Long, intCode As Integer)

Const MAXDATES = 4

    Static varStartDate As Variant
    Static avarDates(0 To MAXDATES) As Variant
    Dim intI As Integer
    Dim varRetval As Variant

    Select Case intCode
       Case acLBInitialize
          ' Could you initialize?

          ' Do the initialization. This is code
          ' you only want to execute once.
          varStartDate = Me!lstTest1
          If Not IsNull(varStartDate) Then
             For intI = 0 To MAXDATES - 1
                avarDates(intI) = DateAdd("d", 7 * intI, varStartDate)
             Next intI
             varRetval = True
          Else
             varRetval = False
          End If

       Case acLBOpen
          ' What's the unique identifier?
          varRetval = Timer

       Case acLBGetRowCount
          ' How many rows are there to be?
          varRetval = MAXDATES

       Case acLBGetFormat
          ' What's the format for each column to be?
          varRetval = "mm/dd/yy"

       Case acLBGetValue
          ' What's the value for each row in each column to be?
          varRetval = avarDates(lngRow)

       Case acLBEnd
          ' Just clean up, if necessary.
          Erase avarDates

    End Select
    ListFill2 = varRetval
End Function
```

Note that the array this function fills, avarDates, is declared as a Static variable. Declaring it this way makes it persistent: Its value remains available between calls to the function. Because the code fills the array in the acLBInitialize case, but doesn't use it until the multiple calls in the acLBGetValue case, avarDates must "hang around" between calls to the function. If you fill an array with data for your control, it's imperative that you declare the array as Static.

You should also consider the fact that Access only calls the acLBInitialize case once, but it calls the acLBGetValue case at least once for every data item to be displayed. In this tiny example, that barely makes a difference. If you're doing considerable work to calculate values for display, however, you should put all the time-consuming work in the acLBInitialize case, and have the acLBGetValue case do as little as possible. This optimization can make a big differerence if you have a large number of values to calculate and display.

Three more things to note about this second list box example:

- In the acLBEnd case, the function clears out the memory used by the array. In this small example, this hardly matters. If you are filling a large array with data, you'd want to make sure that the data gets released at this point. For dynamic arrays (where you specify the size at runtime), Erase releases all the memory. For fixed-size arrays, Erase empties out all the elements.

- This example didn't include code for all the possible cases of intCode. If you don't need a specific case, don't bother coding for it. Here there was no need to set the column widths, so there's no code handling acLBGetColumnWidth.

- At the time of this writing, there's a small error in the way Access handles these callback functions. Although it correctly calls the acLBInitialize case only once when you open a form which requires a control to be filled with the function, if you later change the RowSourceType in code, Access will call the acLBInitialize case twice. This doesn't come up often, but you should be aware that there are circumstances under which Access will erroneously call this section of your code more times than you'd intended. To solve this problem, you can use a static or global variable as a flag to keep track of the fact that the initialization has been done, and opt to not execute the code after the first pass through.

Comments

If you intend to use the first method presented in this How-To, modifying the RowSource property, make sure you understand its main limitation: Because it writes the string containing all the values for the control into the control's property sheet, it's limited by the number of characters the property sheet can hold. You can use, at most, 2,048 characters in the RowSource property. If you need more data than that, you'll need to use a different method.

In the list-filling callback function method, when Access requests the number of rows in the control (when it passes acLBGetRowCount in intCode), you'll most often return the number of rows as the return value from your function. Sometimes, however, you won't know the number of rows or can't get the information easily. For example, if you're filling the list box with the results of a query that returns a large number of rows, you won't want to perform the MoveLast method you'd need to find out how many rows the query returned. This requires Access to walk through all the rows returned from the query, and would make the load time for the list box too long. Instead, respond to acLBGetRowCount with a –1. This tells Access that you'll tell it later how many rows there are. Then, in response to the acLBGetValue case, return data until you've reached the end. Once you return a Null in response to the acLBGetValue case, Access understands that there's no more data.

This method has its pitfalls, too. Although it allows you to load the list box with data almost immediately, it means that the vertical scroll bar can't operate correctly until you've scrolled down to the end. If you can tolerate this side effect, returning –1 in response to acLBGetRowCount will significantly speed the loading of massive amounts of data into list and combo box controls.

To provide values for the acLBGetColumnWidth case, you can specify a different width for each column based on the lngCol parameter. To convert from inches to twips, multiply the value by 1,440. For example, to specify a 1/2-inch column, return 0.5 * 1,440.

COMPLEXITY:
INTERMEDIATE

7.6   How do I...
Pass a variable number of parameters to a procedure?

Problem

I need a procedure that will work on a list of items, and I don't know ahead of time how many there will be. I know that VBA will allow me to use optional parameters, but this requires me to know exactly how many items I might ever need to pass, and I can't predict that value. How can I accomplish this?

Technique

You have two choices in solving this problem: You can pass an array as a parameter, or you can pass a comma-delimited list, which Access will convert into an array for you. An array (an ordered list of items) must contain a single data type. By using the variant data type, though, you can pass a list of varying types into your procedure. This How-To demonstrates both these techniques.

Steps

From 07-06.MDB, load the module basArrays in design mode.

1. Open the Debug Window (choose the Debug Window button on the toolbar, or choose the View|Debug Window menu item). In these steps, you will run code from the Debug Window.

2. Perhaps you need a procedure that will take a list of words and convert each to uppercase. The UCaseArray procedure can do this for you. To test it, type in the Debug Window

```
TestUCase 5
```

You can replace the 5 in the command line with any value between 1 and 26 that you like. The procedure will create as many strings as you request, place them into an array, and then call the UCaseArray procedure. This procedure will convert all the strings in the array to uppercase. The test procedure will display the original version, followed by the altered version of the array. As you can see, no matter how many items you specify for the UCaseArray procedure to work on, it'll convert them all to uppercase. Figure 7-9 shows this procedure in use.

3. Here's another case: a procedure that can accept any number of numeric arguments and perform some operation on them. The sample procedure, SumThemUp, accepts an array of integers, calculates their sum, and returns the total. To try it, type

```
TestSum 15
```

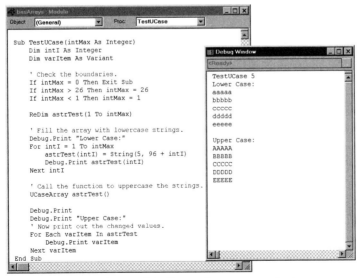

Figure 7-9 TestUCase with five strings converted

in the Debug Window (you can use any number between 1 and 20). The sample routine, TestSum, will generate an array full of random integers between 1 and 9 and will send the array to SumThemUp for processing. Figure 7-10 shows TestSum working with 15 values.

4. You may have a need to write a function that can accept a list of values, not an array. The ParamArray declaration modifier allows you to do this. Try the MinValue function in basArrays: Pass to it a comma-delimited list of values, and it'll return the minimum numeric value from the list you entered. For example:

```
varMin = MinValue(0, -10, 15)
```

will return −10, which is the minimum of the three values you passed it.

How It Works

Both UCaseArray and SumThemUp accept a variant as a parameter. This variant variable can hold either a single value or an array of values. From the calling end, you can pass either a variant or an actual array of values. To send an array as a parameter, you must add the trailing () characters, indicating to Access that the variable represents an array. Therefore, to pass the array named aintValues to SumThemUp, call the function like this, making sure to include the () on the array name:

```
varSum = SumThemUp(aintValues())
```

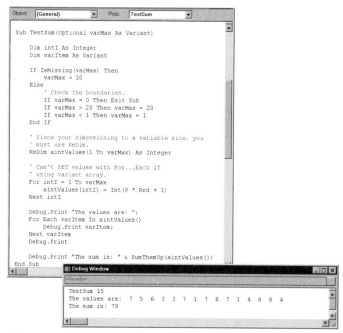

Figure 7-10 TestSum summing 15 values

To receive a parameter that is an array, the procedure declaration can include the parentheses:

```
Function SumThemUp (aintValues() As Integer) As Variant
```

in which case you can only pass an array. You can also declare it like this:

```
Function SumThemUp (varValues As Variant) As Variant
```

in which case you can pass it either a single variant value or an array of values.

Once the procedure has received the array, it needs some way to loop through all the elements of the array. Access provides two methods for walking the array: looping through the items by number with For...Next loop, or with a For Each...Next loop without using the index. UCaseArray uses the first method to loop through all the members of its array, and SumThemUp uses the second.

To loop through the elements of an array by number, you must know the bounds of the array: the lowest and highest element number. Access provides the two functions LBound and UBound to retrieve the lowest and highest element numbers. UCaseArray includes code like this:

```
For intI = LBound(varValues) To UBound(varValues)
    varValues(intI) = UCase(varValues(intI))
Next intI
```

that loops through all the elements in the array, no matter what the starting and ending items are. In Basic, you can declare an array with any positive integer as its start and end points. For example, in

```
Dim avarArray(13 To 97) as Integer
```

you'd need to loop from 13 to 97 to access each element of the array. The LBound and UBound functions make it possible for generic routines to loop through all the elements of an array, even though they don't know ahead of time how many elements there will be.

The UCaseArray procedure is quite simple: Once it determines that the input value is actually an array, using the IsArray function, it loops through all the elements of the passed-in array, converting each to uppercase.

```
Sub UCaseArray(varValues As Variant)

    ' Convert the entire passed-in array to uppercase.
    Dim varItem As Variant
    Dim intI As Integer

    If IsArray(varValues) Then
        For intI = LBound(varValues) To UBound(varValues)
            varValues(intI) = UCase(varValues(intI))
        Next intI
    Else
        varValues = UCase(varValues)
    End If
End Sub
```

The SumThemUp function is no more complex. It uses the For Each…Next syntax to walk through all the elements of the array, maintaining a running sum as it loops. In this case, the variant variable varItem takes on the value of each element of the array as it loops through items, and adds its value to varSum.

```
Function SumThemUp(varValues As Variant) As Variant

    ' Find the sum of the values passed in.

    Dim varItem As Variant
    Dim varSum As Variant

    varSum = 0
    If IsArray(varValues) Then
        For Each varItem In varValues
            varSum = varSum + varItem
        Next varItem
    Else
        varSum = varValues
    End If
    SumThemUp = varSum
End Function
```

Passing a list which Access converts to an array for you is no more diffficult. To use this technique, you must declare your procedure's formal parameters so that the list of values is the last parameter the procedure expects to receive. Use the ParamArray keyword to indicate that you want to treat an incoming list as an array, and declare your array parameter as an array of variants.

```
Function MinValue(ParamArray varValues() As Variant) As Variant
```

Once inside the procedure, you treat the array parameter just as any other array. That is, you can either loop from LBound to UBound for the array, or use a For Each…Next loop to visit each element.

Comments

To use this method effectively, always be aware that Access creates arrays with the first element numbered 0, unless told otherwise. Some programmers insist on starting all arrays with 1, and so they use the Option Base 1 statement in their modules' Declarations area. Others are happy with 0 as their starting point. You must never assume anything about the lower or upper bounds on arrays, or sooner or later generic routines won't work. Some programmers leave the option base setting at 0 (its default) but they disregard the element numbered 0. If you're writing code that will be called by other programmers, you need to be aware of these variations on the normal usage.

If you decide to use the For Each…Next syntax to access all of the elements of an array, both the variable you use to loop through the elements and the array itself must be variants. In addition, note that you cannot set the value of items in an array using the For Each…Next syntax; it only allows you to retrieve the values from the array. If you want to loop through an array to set its values, you must use the standard For Each…Next syntax, using a numeric value as the loop counter.

COMPLEXITY:
ADVANCED

7.7 How do I...
Sort an array in Access Basic?

Problem

Amazingly, though it's a database product, Access doesn't include a way to sort an array. I need to present sorted arrays in an application, and can't find a reasonable way to sort them without saving them to a table first. I know I've seen array-sorting methods in other languages. Can I write a sorting routine that executes quickly?

Technique

It's true. Access doesn't provide a built-in sorting mechanism for arrays. Entire volumes in libraries are devoted to the study of various sorting and searching algorithms, but it's not necessary to dig too deep for Access array sorting. Because you'll most likely place any large data sets into a table, most arrays in Access aren't very large. Therefore, most any sort will do. This How-To uses a variant of the standard QuickSort algorithm. (For more information on various sorting and searching algorithms, consult your computer library. This is a *big* topic!)

Steps

To try out the sorting mechanism, load the module named basSortDemo in 07-07.MDB. From the Debug Window, type:

```
TestSort 6
```

where the 6 can be any integer between 1 and 20, indicating the number of random integers between 1 and 99 that you want the routine to sort. The sample routine, TestSort, will create the array of integers and send it off to VisSortArray, a special version of the sorting routine ahtSortArray that shows what it's doing as it works. Figure 7-11 shows the output from a sample session.

To use this sorting code in your own application, follow these steps:

1. Import the module named basSortArray into your application.

2. Create the array you'd like to have sorted. This must be an array of variants, but those variants can hold any data type; this How-To uses an array of integers and How-To 7.8 uses an array of strings.

3. Call ahtSortArray, passing to it the name of the array you'd like to sort. For example, to sort an array of named avarStates, use the following call.

```
ahtSortArray avarStates()
```

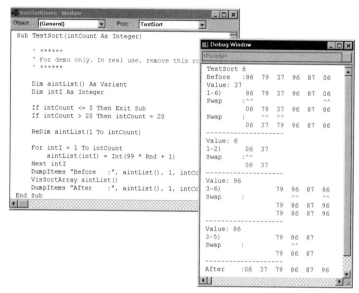

Figure 7-11 The output from a sample run of TestSort

After the call to ahtSortArray, your array will be sorted. Remember that ahtSortArray is sorting your array in place: Once it's sorted, there's no going back! If you don't want to sort your only copy of the array, make a duplicate first.

How It Works

The QuickSort algorithm works by breaking the array into smaller and smaller chunks, sorting each one, until all the chunks are one element in length. The ahtSortArray procedure calls the main sorting routine, QuickSort, passing to it the array and the start and end points for sorting. The QuickSort routine breaks the array into two chunks, then calls itself twice to sort each of the two halves.

You might be grumbling, at this point, about recursive routines and how they use lots of memory. Normally, that's true. This version of the sorting algorithm, however, tries to be conservative about how it uses memory. At each level, it sorts the smaller of the two chunks first. This means that it will have fewer recursive levels: The small chunk will end up containing a single element much more quickly than the large chunk. By always working with the smallest chunk first, this method avoids calling itself more often than it has to.

Following are the basic steps of the QuickSort procedure. These steps use intLeft to refer to the beginning sort item and intRight for the ending item.

```
Private Sub QuickSort (varArray() As Variant, _
   intLeft As Integer, intRight As Integer)
      Dim i As Integer
      Dim j As Integer
```

```
Dim varTestVal As Variant
Dim intMid As Integer

If intLeft < intRight Then
    intMid = (intLeft + intRight) \ 2
    varTestVal = varArray(intMid)
    i = intLeft
    j = intRight
    Do
        Do While varArray(i) < varTestVal
            i = i + 1
        Loop
        Do While varArray(j) > varTestVal
            j = j - 1
        Loop
        If i <= j Then
            SwapElements varArray(), i, j
            i = i + 1
            j = j - 1
        End If
    Loop Until i > j
    ' To optimize the sort, always sort the
    ' smallest segment first.
    If j <= intMid Then
        QuickSort varArray(), intLeft, j
        QuickSort varArray(), i, intRight
    Else
        QuickSort varArray(), i, intRight
        QuickSort varArray(), intLeft, j
    End If
End If
End Sub
```

1. If intLeft isn't less than intRight, the sort's done.

2. The sort takes the value in the middle of the subset of the array that's being sorted as the "comparison" value. Its value is going to be the dividing factor for the two chunks. There are different schools of thought on how to choose the dividing item. This version of the sort uses the item that's physically in the middle of the chosen list of items.

```
intMid = (intLeft + intRight) \ 2
varTestVal = varArray(intMid)
```

3. The sort starts from the left, walking along the array until it finds an item that isn't less than the dividing value. This search is guaranteed to stop at the dividing value, which certainly isn't less than itself.

```
Do While varArray(i) < varTestVal
    i = i + 1
Loop
```

385

4. The sort starts from the right, walking backwards through the array until it finds an item that isn't more than the dividing value. This search is guaranteed to stop at the dividing value, which certainly isn't more than itself.

```
Do While varArray(j) > varTestVal
    j = j - 1
Loop
```

5. If the position from step 3 is less than or equal to the position found in step 4, the sort swaps the elements at the two positions, then increments the pointer for step 3 and decrements the pointer for step 4.

```
If i <= j Then
    SwapElements varArray(), i, j
    i = i + 1
    j = j - 1
End If
```

6. The sort repeats steps 3 through 5 until the pointer from step 3 is greater than the pointer from step 4 (i > j). At this point, every item to the left of the dividing element is less than or equal to it, and everything to the right is greater than or equal to it.

7. Choosing the smaller partition first, the sort repeats all these steps on each of the subsets to either side of the dividing value, until step 1 indicates that it's done.

```
If j <= intMid Then
    QuickSort varArray(), intLeft, j
    QuickSort varArray(), i, intRight
Else
    QuickSort varArray(), i, intRight
    QuickSort varArray(), intLeft, j
End If
```

Comments

There are probably sort algorithms that are simpler than the QuickSort algorithm, but for arrays that aren't already sorted, QuickSort's speed is hard to beat. (For presorted arrays, it doesn't do as well as some other sorts. But most arrays don't come to the QuickSort subroutine in order.) As it is, the QuickSort subroutine is only capable of handling single-column arrays. If you need to sort multicolumn arrays, you'll need to modify the code to handle those cases or you'll need to move the data into a table and let Access do the sorting for you.

See the next How-To for an example of using QuickSort.

COMPLEXITY:
ADVANCED

7.8 How do I...
Fill a list box with a list of files?

Problem

I need to present my users with a sorted list of files in a particular directory, with a specific file name extension. I found the Dir function, but I can't find a way to get this information into a list box. Is there a way to do this?

Technique

The answer to this question is the perfect opportunity to use the past three How-To's. It involves creating a list-filling callback function, passing arrays as parameters, and sorting an array. In addition, you fill that array with a list of files matching a particular criteria, using the Dir function.

Steps

Load the form frmTestFillDirList from 07-08.MDB. Enter a file specification into the text box, perhaps something like C:\WINDOWS*.INI. Once you leave the text box (by pressing either TAB or RETURN), the code attached to the AfterUpdate event will force the list box to requery. When that happens, the list box will fill in with the matching file names. Figure 7-12 shows the results of a search for C:\WINDOWS*.INI.

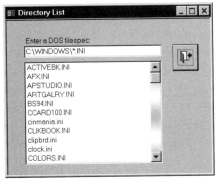

Figure 7-12 frmTestFillDirList, searching for *.INI in the Windows directory

To include this same functionality in your own applications, follow these steps:

1. On a form, create a text box and a list box, with properties set as shown in Table 7-6.

CONTROL	PROPERTY	SETTING
Text Box	Name	txtFileSpec
	AfterUpdate	[Event Procedure]
List Box	Name	lstDirList
	RowSourceType	FillList
	AfterUpdate	[Event Procedure]

 Table 7-6 Property settings for the controls on the directory list form

2. Enter the following code in the text box's AfterUpdate event procedure. (See this book's Introduction for more information on creating event procedures.) This code will force the list box to requery itself when you enter a value in the text box, and then move to some other control.

```
Sub txtFileSpec_AfterUpdate ()
    Me!lstDirList.Requery
End Sub
```

3. Enter the following code in the list box's AfterUpdate event. This is sample code that pops up a message box indicating which file you chose.

```
Sub lstDirList_AfterUpdate ()
    MsgBox "You chose: " & Me!lstDirList.Value
End Sub
```

4. Enter the following code into the form's module. This is the list-filling function for the list box.

```
Private Function FillList(ctl As Control, varID As Variant, lngRow As Long, _
lngCol As Long, intCode As Integer)

    Static avarFiles() As Variant
    Static intFileCount As Integer

    Select Case intCode
        Case acLBInitialize
            If Not IsNull(Me!txtFileSpec) Then
                intFileCount = FillDirList(Me!txtFileSpec, avarFiles())
            End If
            FillList = True

        Case acLBOpen
            FillList = Timer

        Case acLBGetRowCount
            FillList = intFileCount
```

```
        Case acLBGetValue
            FillList = avarFiles(lngRow)

        Case acLBEnd
            Erase avarFiles
    End Select
End Function
```

5. Enter the following code into a global module. (Though this code would work fine in a form's module, it's general enough that it will serve you best as part of a global module that can be copied from one database to another.)

```
Function FillDirList(ByVal strFileSpec As String, _
avarFiles() As Variant) As Integer

    ' Given the file specification in strFileSpec, fill in the
    ' dynamic array passed in avarFiles().

    Dim intNumFiles As Integer
    Dim varTemp As Variant

    On Error GoTo FillDirList_Err
    intNumFiles = 0

    ' Set the filespec for the dir() and get the first file name.
    varTemp = Dir(strFileSpec)
    Do While Len(varTemp) > 0
        intNumFiles = intNumFiles + 1
        ReDim Preserve avarFiles(intNumFiles - 1)
        avarFiles(intNumFiles - 1) = varTemp
        varTemp = Dir
    Loop

FillDirList_Exit:
    If intNumFiles > 0 Then
        ahtSortArray avarFiles()
    End If
    FillDirList = intNumFiles
    Exit Function

FillDirList_Err:
    FillDirList = intNumFiles
    Resume FillDirList_Exit
End Function
```

6. Import basSortArray from 07-08.MDB. This is the same sorting code that was covered in How-To 7.7.

How It Works

The list box in this example uses a list-filling callback function, FillList, to supply its data. (See How-To 7.5 for information on callback functions.) In FillList's acLBInitialize case, it calls the FillDirList function to fill in the avarFiles array, based on the value in the text box, txtFileSpec. FillDirList fills in the array, calling ahtSortArray along the way to sort the list of files, and returns the number of files it found. Given that completed array, FillList can return the value from the array that it needs when requested in the acLBGetValue case. It uses the return value from FillDirList, the number of files found, in response to the acLBGetRowCount case.

There's also an interesting situation you should note in the two routines FillList and FillDirList. FillList declares a dynamic array, avarFiles, but doesn't give a size. It can't, because it doesn't yet know the number of files that will be found. FillList passes the array off to FillDirList, which adds file names to the array, based on the file specification, until FillDirList doesn't find any more matches. FillDirList returns the number of matching file names, but it also has the side effect of having set the array's size and filled it in. Here's the code that does the work. This code fragment uses the ReDim Preserve keywords to resize the array every time it finds a matching file name.

```
' Set the filespec for the dir() and get the first file name.
varTemp = Dir(strFileSpec)
Do While Len(varTemp) > 0
    intNumFiles = intNumFiles + 1
    ReDim Preserve avarFiles(intNumFiles - 1)
    avarFiles(intNumFiles - 1) = varTemp
    varTemp = Dir
Loop
```

To create the list of files, FillDirList uses the Dir function. This function is unusual, in that you call it multiple times. The first time you call it, you send it the file specification you're trying to match, and Dir returns the first matching file name. If it returns a nonempty value, you continue to call it, with no parameters, until it *does* return an empty value. Each time you call Dir, it returns the next matching file name.

Once FillDirList has finished retrieving the list of file names, if there are names in the array, it sorts them. It returns the number of files it found as its return value. The following code shows how this is done.

```
If intNumFiles > 0 Then
    ahtSortArray avarFiles()
End If
FillDirList = intNumFiles
```

Comments

FillDirList declares its first parameter, strFileSpec, by value, using the ByVal keyword. Normally, procedures declare their parameters ByVal if they intend to use the parameter internally and may change its value, but they don't want the calling procedure to know that they've changed the value. In this case, and in many procedures like this one, the parameter might be sent directly from the value of a control. Because Access can only pass control values by value, and never by reference, adding the ByVal keyword here makes it possible to use an expression like this:

```
intFileCount = FillDirList(Me!txtFileSpec, avarFiles())
```

Try this without the ByVal keyword, and Access will complain with a "Parameter Type Mismatch" error.

Note that when Access calls the list-filling callback function, values for the lngRow and lngCol parameters are always zero-based. Therefore, when you use arrays within callback functions, you should consider always using zero-based arrays to hold the data you'll display in the control. If you don't, you'll always be dealing with "off by one" errors. Using a zero-based array will mean that the row values (sent to your code in lngRow) will match your array indices.

COMPLEXITY:
INTERMEDIATE

7.9 How do I... Handle object properties, in general?

Problem

I don't understand how to get and set property values in Access. It seems as if there are different kinds of properties, and what works for one object and property won't work for another. Is there some way to settle this once and for all?

Technique

There really are two kinds of properties for objects in Access. Built-in properties are those that always exist for an object, and user-defined properties are properties that you or Access create for an object when requested. The syntax for referring to each type is different, but this How-To will provide a method that works for either type, all the time. This How-To uses the user-defined Description property, but the techniques will work just as well for any other property. The interesting part of this How-To is that the Description property is not a built-in property, and attempting to set or retrieve this property using the standard *object.property* syntax will fail.

Steps

This How-To provides a sample form, which is useful only for demonstrating the technique. The real power of the How-To comes from the module, basHandleProperties, which provides procedures you can use to set and get any kind of property. To try out the sample form, shown in Figure 7-13, load and run frmTestProperties from 07-09.MDB. Choose a table from the list of tables, and notice the Description property shown in the text box underneath the list. If you choose a field from the list of fields, you'll also see the description for that field in the text box underneath the list. You can enter new text into the two text boxes, and the code attached to the AfterUpdate event of either text box will write the text back to the Description property of the selected table or field.

The sample form uses two functions from basHandleProperties, as shown in Table 7-7. These functions allow you to get or set any property of any object, as long as:

- the object already supports the property you're working with, or

- the object allows you to create new properties to add the property if it doesn't already exist.

The only objects to which you can add properties are databases, tables, queries, fields, indexes, and relations. Attempting to add a new property to any other kind of object will fail.

FUNCTION NAME	USAGE	PARAMETERS	RETURNS
ahtGetProperty	Retrieve the value of the specified property of the specified object.	obj As Object: a reference to any existing object. strProperty As String: the name of the property to retrieve.	The value of the requested property, or Null if that property or object doesn't exist.
ahtSetProperty	Set the value of the specified property of the specified object.	obj As Object: a reference to any existing object. strProperty As String: the name of the property to set. varValue As Variant: the value of the property; varPropType As Variant (Optional): the data type of the new property (if the code has to create it). One of: dbBoolean, dbByte, dbInteger, dbLong, dbCurrency, dbSingle, dbDouble, dbDate, dbText, dbLongBinary, dbMemo, dbGUID. If you skip this, Access will use dbText.	The old value of the property, if it existed. Null otherwise.

Table 7-7 Using the ahtGetProperty and ahtSetProperty functions

To use these new functions in your own applications:

1. Import basHandleProperties into your application.

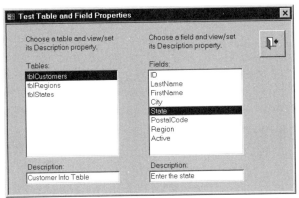

Figure 7-13 The sample form, frmTestProperties, allows you to set and retrieve the Description property of any table or field

2. To set a property, call ahtSetProperty. This function returns the old value of the property. For example:

```
Dim db As Database
Dim varOldDescription As Variant

Set db = CurrentDb()
varOldDescription = ahtSetProperty(db, "Description", _
  "Sample Database")
If Not IsNull(varOldDescription) Then
    MsgBox "The old Description was: " & varOldDescription
End If
```

3. To get the value of a property, call ahtGetProperty. For example:

```
Dim db As Database
Dim varDescription As Variant

Set db = CurrentDb()
varDescription = ahtGetProperty(db, "Description")
If Not IsNull(varDescription) Then
    MsgBox "The database description is: " & varDescription
End If
```

How It Works

Access provides two different types of properties: built-in and user-defined. Built-in properties always exist, and are part of the definition of the object. For example, an object's Name property or its Type property (for most objects) is crucial for its existence. These are built-in properties. On the other hand, the Jet Engine allows you to create new properties and add them to the Properties collection for all the objects it supports, including TableDefs, QueryDefs, Indexes, Fields, Relations, and Containers.

In addition, Access itself, as a client of the Jet Engine, creates several properties for you. For example, when you right-click on an object in the Database Explorer and choose Properties from the floating menu, Access allows you to specify the Description for the object. That Description property doesn't exist until you request that Access create it, using that dialog box or in your own Access Basic code. The same goes for the Caption, ValidationRule, and DefaultValue properties of fields: Those properties don't exist until you request that Access create them for you.

User-Defined vs. Built-In Properties

If you attempt to retrieve or set the value of a property that doesn't yet exist, Access will trigger a runtime error. Your code must be ready to deal with this problem. In addition, you may be used to working with built-in properties, in which case you can refer to the property using the simple *object.property* syntax. This syntax only works for built-in properties. For user-defined (and Access-created user-defined) properties, you must refer to the property using an explicit reference to the Properties collection that contains it. For example, to set the Format property of the City field within tblCustomers, you'll need an expression like this (and this expression will fail with a runtime error if the Format property hasn't yet been set):

```
CurrentDb.TableDefs!tblCustomers.Fields!City.Properties!Format = ">"
```

Because you can always refer to any property using an explicit reference to the Properties collection, you can simplify your code, and ensure that all property references work, by using the same syntax for built-in and user-defined properties. For example, field objects support the AllowZeroLength property as a built-in property. Therefore, this reference will work:

```
CurrentDb.TableDefs!tblCustomers.Fields!City.AllowZeroLength = False
```

If you want to refer to the same property with an explicit reference, you can use this syntax:

```
CurrentDb.TableDefs!tblCustomers.Fields!City.Properties!AllowZeroLength
= False
```

This ability to refer to built-in and user-defined properties using the same syntax is the secret of the code presented in this How-To.

Creating New Properties

To create a new property, you must follow these three steps:

1. Create a new property object, using the CreateProperty method of an existing object.

2. Set the properties of this new property, including its name, type, and default value (you can merge this step with the previous step by supplying the information when you call CreateProperty).

3. Append the new property to the Properties collection of the host object.

For example, to add a Description property to the current database, you might write code like this:

```
Dim db As Database
Dim prp As Property

Set db = CurrentDb()

' Step 1
Set prp = db.CreateProperty()

' Step 2
prp.Name = "Description"
prp.Type = dbText
prp.Value = "Sample Database"

' Step 3
db.Properties.Append prp
```

To combine steps 1 and 2, you could set the properties of the new property at the time you create it.

```
' Steps 1 and 2
Set prp = db.CreateProperty("Description", dbText, "Sample Database")

' Step 3
db.Properties.Append prp
```

Once you've followed these steps, you should be able to retrieve the database's Description property with a statement like this (note that you *must* use the explicit reference to the Properties collection in this case, because Description is a user-defined property):

```
Debug.Print CurrentDb.Properties!Description
```

Making It All a Bit Easier

To relieve you from worrying about the differences between user-defined and built-in properties and whether or not a property already exists for a given object, we've provided the ahtGetProperty and ahtSetProperty functions.

The ahtGetProperty function, shown below, is the simpler of the two. It attempts to retrieve the property you've requested. It may fail for two reasons: The object you care about doesn't really exist, or the property you've tried to retrieve doesn't exist (errors ahtcErrNotInCollection and ahtcErrPropertyNotFound, respectively). If either of these errors occurs, the function returns a null value. If any other error occurs, the function alerts you with a message box before returning a null value. If no error occurs, the function returns the value of the requested property. For an example of calling ahtGetProperty, see the Steps section above and 07-09.MDB.

```
Function ahtGetProperty(obj As Object, strProperty As String) As Variant
    ' Retrieve property for an object
    ' Return the value if found, or Null if not.
```

continued on next page

continued from previous page

```
        On Error GoTo ahtGetProperty_Err

        ahtGetProperty = obj.Properties(strProperty)

    ahtGetProperty_Exit:

        Exit Function

    ahtGetProperty_Err:
        Select Case Err.Number
            Case ahtcErrNotInCollection, ahtcErrPropertyNotFound
                ' Do nothing!
            Case Else
                MsgBox "Error: " & Err.Description & " (" & Err.Number & ")"
        End Select
        ahtGetProperty = Null
        Resume ahtGetProperty_Exit
    End Function
```

The ahtSetProperty function is more interesting. It attempts to set the value of the property you pass to it. The function has several interesting characteristics.

- If you ask it to set a property that doesn't currently exist, it attempts to create that property, and then sets its value.

- The data type is an optional parameter. If you don't tell it what the data type of the new property is to be (you leave that parameter blank), the code will use the IsMissing function to detect this and will use the dbText type by default.

- The function returns the old value of the property, if there was one, so you can store it away and perhaps reset it once you're done with your application.

- To make sure the code will work with either user-defined or built-in properties, the code uses an explicit reference to the Properties collection.

- To know that it needs to try to create the property, the function traps the ahtcErrPropertyNotFound error condition (error 3270), and if that error occurs, it uses the CreateProperty method to try to create the necessary property.

- If you try to assign an invalid property value, Access triggers the ahtcErrDataTypeConversion error condition (error 3421). In that case, there's not much ahtSetProperty can do besides alerting you to that fact and returning a null value.

```
Function ahtSetProperty(obj As Object, strProperty As String, _
    varValue As Variant, Optional varPropType As Variant)

    On Error GoTo ahtSetProperty_Err
```

```
    Dim varOldValue As Variant

    If IsMissing(varPropType) Then varPropType = dbText

    ' This'll fail if the property doesn't exist.
    varOldValue = obj.Properties(strProperty)
    obj.Properties(strProperty) = varValue
    ahtSetProperty = varOldValue

ahtSetProperty_Exit:
    Exit Function

ahtSetProperty_Err:
    Select Case Err.Number
        Case ahtcErrPropertyNotFound
            ' If the property wasn't there, try to create it.
            If ahtCreateProperty(obj, strProperty, _
            varValue, varPropType) Then
                Resume Next
            End If
        Case ahtcErrDataTypeConversion
            MsgBox "Invalid data type!", vbExclamation, "Get Property"
        Case Else
    End Select
    ahtSetProperty = Null
    Resume ahtSetProperty_Exit
End Function
```

Comments

Only objects that are maintained by the Jet engine allow you to create new properties. That is, you can add properties to the Properties collection of database, tabledef, querydef, index, field, relation, and container objects. You won't be able to add new properties to any object that Access is in charge of, such as forms, reports, and controls. If you attempt to use ahtSetProperty to set a user-defined property for an invalid object, the function will return a null value. You can, however, use ahtSetProperty and ahtGetProperty with any Access object, as long as you confine yourself to built-in properties for those objects that don't support user-defined properties. For example, this code fragment will work fine as long as frmTestProperties is currently opened:

```
If IsNull(ahtSetProperty(Forms!frmTestProperties, "Caption", _
  "Test Properties")) Then
    MsgBox "Unable to set the property!"
End If
```

User-defined properties are persistent from session to session. That is, they are saved in the tableDef along with the built-in and Access-defined properties. You can, however, delete a user-defined property using the Delete method on the property's parent collection. For example, you could delete the user-defined property defined earlier using the following statement:

```
CurrentDb.TableDefs!tblSuppliers!Address.Properties.Delete ⇒
"SpecialHandling"
```

COMPLEXITY:
INTERMEDIATE

7.10 How do I...
Detect if an object exists or not?

Problem

I create and delete objects as my application runs. At some point, I need to be able to tell if an object exists or not, and make decisions based on that fact. But I can't find a function in Access that will tell me whether or not a specific object already exists. Am I missing something? This ought to be a basic part of the product!

Technique

You've not missed anything: Access really doesn't supply a simple method of knowing whether or not a specific object already exists. On the other hand, this is really quite simple, as long as you understand two important concepts: Access' support for Data Access Object container objects and the ways you can use error handling to retrieve information. This How-To will use these two subjects to provide a function you can call to check for the existence of any object.

Steps

Load and run frmTestExist from 07-10.MDB. This form, shown in Figure 7-14, lets you specify an object name and its type, and then tells you whether or not that object exists. Certainly, you wouldn't use this form as-is in any application—its purpose is to demonstrate the ahtDoesObjExist function in basExists (07-10.MDB). To make your exploration of frmTestExist easier, Table 7-8 lists the objects that exist in 07-10.MDB. Try entering names that do and don't exist, and get the types right and wrong, to convince yourself that the ahtDoesObjExist function does its job correctly.

OBJECT NAME	OBJECT TYPE
tblTest	Table
qryTest	Query
frmTest	Form
frmTestExist	Form
basExists	Module

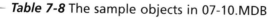
Table 7-8 The sample objects in 07-10.MDB

Follow these steps to use ahtDoesObjExist in your own applications:

1. Import the module basExists from 07-10.MDB. This module contains the ahtDoesObjExist function.

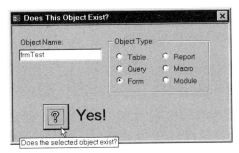

Figure 7-14 frmTestExist allows you
to check for the existence of any
object in the current database

2. To check for the existence of any object, call ahtDoesObjExist, passing to it the
name of the object to check for and an integer indicating the type of the
object. The type parameter must be chosen from the intrinsic Access constants
acTable, acQuery, acForm, acReport, acMacro, or acModule. For example, to
check for the existence of a table named "Customers", call ahtDoesObjExist
like this:

```
If ahtDoesObjExist("Customers", acTable) Then
    ' You know the table exists
Else
    MsgBox "The table 'Customers' doesn't exist!"
End If
```

How It Works

The ahtDoesObjExist function, shown below in full, checks for the existence of an object
by attempting to retrieve that object's Name property. Because every object that
exists exposes a Name property, this action can't fail unless the object doesn't exist. In
skeleton format, the code works like this:

```
    Dim strName As String
    On Error Goto ahtDoesObjExist_Err

    strName = obj.Name
    ahtDoesObjExist = True

ahtDoesObjectExist_Exit:
    Exit Function

ahtDoesObjectExist_Err:
    ahtDoesObjExist = False
    Resume ahtDoesObjectExist_Exit
```

That is, the code sets up an error handler and then attempts to retrieve the Name property of the requested object. If it succeeds, the code falls through, sets the return value

to True, and returns. If it triggers an error, the procedure can be assured that the object doesn't exist, and it returns False.

The only other issue is how to convert from a string containing the name of the object and and integer containing its type to a real object reference. This is where the Jet Engine's Container objects come in handy. The Containers collection, supplied by Access so the Jet Engine can support security for all the Access objects, contain collections of Document objects, one for each saved object in your database. The Containers collection contains collections named "Tables", "Forms", "Reports", "Scripts" (that's *macros* for us users!), and "Modules". Except for tables and queries, the code checks in those collections of documents, looking for the document whose name you've supplied. For tables and queries, it's simpler to use the TableDefs and QueryDefs collections directly. Access lumps tables and queries together in the Tables container, but keeps them separate in the TableDefs and QueryDefs collections. If the code looked in the Tables container, it would have to take an extra step to distinguish tables from queries. Using the collections instead, that decision has already been made.

The code for ahtDoesObjExist is shown below.

```
Function ahtDoesObjExist(strObj As String, intType As Integer)
    Dim strName As String
    Dim db As Database
    Dim strCon As String

    On Error GoTo ahtDoesObjExist_Err

    Set db = CurrentDb()
    Select Case intType
        Case acTable
            strName = db.TableDefs(strObj).Name
        Case acQuery
            strName = db.QueryDefs(strObj).Name
        Case acForm, acReport, acMacro, acModule
            Select Case intType
                Case acForm
                    strCon = "Forms"
                Case acReport
                    strCon = "Reports"
                Case acMacro
                    strCon = "Scripts"
                Case acModule
                    strCon = "Modules"
            End Select
            strName = db.Containers(strCon).Documents(strObj).Name
    End Select
    ahtDoesObjExist = True

ahtDoesObjExist_Exit:
    Exit Function

ahtDoesObjExist_Err:
    ahtDoesObjExist = False
    Resume ahtDoesObjExist_Exit

End Function
```

Note that in the Select Case statement, the code first checks to see if you're asking about a table or a query. If so, it looks in the appropriate collection.

```
Select Case intType
    Case acTable
        strName = db.TableDefs(strObj).Name
    Case acQuery
        strName = db.QueryDefs(strObj).Name
    .
    .
    .
End Select
```

If not, it assigns to *strCon* the name of the container it will need, and then attempts to retrieve the Name property of the particular document within the selected container.

```
Case acForm, acReport, acMacro, acModule
    Select Case intType
        Case acForm
            strCon = "Forms"
        Case acReport
            strCon = "Reports"
        Case acMacro
            strCon = "Scripts"
        Case acModule
            strCon = "Modules"
    End Select
    strName = db.Containers(strCon).Documents(strObj).Name
```

Comments

You may find it useful, if you've not done much investigation of Data Access Objects (DAO) in Access, to study the appropriate chapters in the Building Applications manual that ships with Access. Though a complete coverage of DAO is beyond the scope of this book, there are several examples using DAO in other chapters, especially Chapters 4 and 6.

CHAPTER 8
OPTIMIZING YOUR APPLICATION

OPTIMIZING
YOUR APPLICATION

How do I...

One unavoidable fact of application design is that your application never runs as fast as you'd like. Unless you and your application's users are equipped with the latest and most powerful workstations with huge amounts of memory, you should expect performance that is less than ideal. There are, nevertheless, many techniques you can use to optimize your application, few of which are readily apparent in the Access documentation. Although your Access application may never run like that lean and mean dBASE II application you created 10 years ago, you certainly can make it run at an acceptable speed.

This chapter covers several optimizations you can apply to your applications, including loading forms faster, adding and changing data faster, and making your Visual Basic for Applications (VBA) code run faster. It also covers the optimization of queries and multiuser and client/server optimization techniques. Testing techniques are also described so you can see the speed gains of your own optimizations.

8.1　Accelerate the Load Time of Forms

One of the slowest parts of many Access applications is the time it takes to load forms. This How-To will show how to improve form load time dramatically by preloading forms upon application initialization and keeping the loaded forms hidden instead of closing them.

8.2　Make Slow Forms Run Faster

Access 95 gives you a lot of flexibility to develop dynamite-looking forms. Unfortunately, Access also makes it easy to create forms that run painfully slow. This How-To will discuss how to analyze your forms for various performance bottlenecks and how to fix these bottlenecks. Included is a discussion of the use and misuse of graphic elements and combo and list box controls.

8.3　Use Rushmore to Speedup Queries

Microsoft added Rushmore query optimizations to Access 2.0. But do you know when these optimizations are applied and how to ensure your queries benefit from them? This How-To will give you the lowdown on Rushmore, discussing how it works and showing you how to take advantage of it to give a shot of adrenaline to your queries.

8.4　Accelerate Visual Basic for Applications Code

VBA is an interpreted language and, as such, does not run as fast as compiled languages. This How-To will offer various techniques for accelerating your code execution. Topics include using correct variable types, using object variables, optimizing loops and conditions, and using integer division.

8.5　Accelerate Routines That Add, Edit, and Change Data in Tables

You probably know that Access supports transaction processing to maintain the integrity of a defined set of updates to the database. But did you know that you can take advantage of transactions to speed up data updates even if you don't need the extra integrity support? This How-To will suggest the use of transactions to buffer table writes and enhance the performance of your application.

8.6　Test the Comparative Benefits of Various Optimization Techniques

To find the best optimization technique for a particular operation, you need to compare two or more approaches. In this How-To you will learn how to implement a test-bed utility that shows the comparative timings of two different functions. The utility runs two functions you specify and shows the elapsed time of each function and the difference in times. A discussion of testing accuracy and elimination of outside variables is also provided.

8.7 Accelerate Multiuser Applications

Any performance problems present in your single user applications are magnified greatly when you introduce a local area network and shared database access. This How-To will show how to improve multiuser application performance by limiting the data in your forms' recordsets.

8.8 Accelerate Client/Server Applications

Through open database connectivity (ODBC) Access provides a robust front-end tool for developing client/server applications. Many of the issues involved in working with a back-end database are not obvious. This How-To will cover techniques for improving the performance of applications that attach to server data through ODBC drivers.

COMPLEXITY:
INTERMEDIATE

8.1 How do I...
Accelerate the load time of forms?

Problem

The first time I open a form in my application, it seems to take forever to load. Is there any way to accelerate the time it takes to load forms?

Technique

You can radically improve the time it takes to load a form for the first time by preloading your forms when the database is initially opened. You can also decrease the load time for subsequent loadings of a form by hiding instead of closing forms. This How-To shows you how to improve form load time using these techniques.

Steps

Load the 08-01.MDB database. Note the time it takes for the switchboard form to appear (see Figure 8-1). (Make sure that the "Preload and keep loaded forms" check box is unchecked. If it is checked, then uncheck it, close the database, and start over.) Now press one of the command buttons, for example the Orders button, and record how long it takes Access to initially load the form. Close the form.

Now check the "Preload and keep loaded forms" check box on the switchboard form and close the database. Reload the database and again note the time it takes for the switchboard form to appear. Load the Orders form, again recording the form load time.

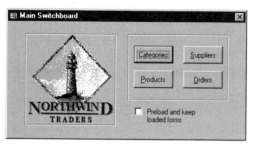

Figure 8-1 The 08-01.MDB switchboard form

Figure 8-2 The list of preloaded forms is stored in zstblPreloadForms

When you checked the "Preload and keep loaded forms" check box on the switchboard form and reloaded the database, you flipped a switch that caused the application to preload its forms (in a hidden state) as the switchboard form was being loaded by Access. This lengthened the time it took for the switchboard form to appear initially. However, because the Orders form was now preloaded, it took much less time for it to appear when you pressed the Orders command button.

> **Note**
>
> A switchboard form is an unbound form that is used for application navigation. Switchboard forms, or menu forms, are usually made up of labels and command buttons with an optional picture.

Follow these steps to set up your application to preload its forms:

1. Create a table for storing the names of the forms you wish to preload. This table (zstblPreloadForms in the sample database) should have a single field, FormName, with a datatype of text. Switch to datasheet view (see Figure 8-2) and add a row for each form in your application that you wish to preload.

2. Create a switchboard form or edit your existing one. Set the form's AutoCenter property to Yes. Create a new event procedure for the form's Open event. (If you're unsure how to do this, see How Do I Create an Event Procedure in the Introduction of this book.) Add the following code to the event procedure.

```
Private Sub Form_Open(Cancel As Integer)

    ' Preload forms

    On Error GoTo Form_OpenErr

    Dim db As Database
    Dim rst As Recordset
    Dim varFormName As Variant
```

```
        DoCmd.OpenForm ahtcSplashForm


        Set db = CurrentDb()

        ' Preload the forms listed in zstblPreloadForms
        Set rst = db.OpenRecordset(ahtcPreloadTable)

        Do While Not rst.EOF
            varFormName = rst!FormName
            If Not IsNull(varFormName) Then
                DoCmd.OpenForm FormName:=varFormName, _
                 WindowMode:=acHidden, OpenArgs:="StayLoaded"
            End If
            rst.MoveNext
        Loop

        DoCmd.Close acForm, ahtcSplashForm

Form_OpenExit:
    If Not rst Is Nothing Then rst.Close
    Exit Sub

Form_OpenErr:
    MsgBox "Error " & Err.Number & ": " & Err.Description, _
     vbOKOnly + vbCritical, "Form Open"
    Resume Form_OpenExit

End Sub
```

If you prefer, you can copy this code from the frmSwitchboard1 form (*not* the frmSwitchboard form) in 08-01.MDB. (The frmSwitchboard1 version of the switchboard form always preloads forms and thus eliminates all of the code associated with the "Preload and keep loaded forms" check box.)

3. Create an event procedure for the switchboard form's close event. Add this code to the event procedure:

```
Private Sub Form_Close()

    ' Unload preloaded forms

    On Error GoTo Form_CloseErr

    Dim db As Database
    Dim rst As Recordset
    Dim varFormName As Variant

    Set db = CurrentDb()

    ' Unload the forms listed in zstblPreloadForms
    Set rst = db.OpenRecordset(ahtcPreloadTable)

    Do While Not rst.EOF
        varFormName = rst!FormName
```

continued on next page

continued from previous page

```
              If Not IsNull(varFormName) Then
                  DoCmd.Close acForm, varFormName
              End If
              rst.MoveNext
        Loop

    Form_CloseExit:
        If Not rst Is Nothing Then rst.Close
        Exit Sub

    Form_CloseErr:
        MsgBox "Error " & Err.Number & ": " & Err.Description, _
          vbOKOnly + vbCritical, "Form Open"
        Resume Form_CloseExit

    End Sub
```

4. Create the following functions in a global module (or import the basStayLoaded module from 08-01.MDB).

```
Function ahtOpenForm(strFormName As String, _
  fStayLoaded As Boolean) As Boolean

    ' Open specified form and pass it
    ' StayLoaded argument

    On Error GoTo ahtOpenFormErr

    If fStayLoaded Then
        DoCmd.OpenForm strFormName, OpenArgs:="StayLoaded"
    Else
        DoCmd.OpenForm strFormName
    End If

ahtOpenFormExit:
    Exit Function

ahtOpenFormErr:
    MsgBox "Error " & Err.Number & ": " & Err.Description, _
      vbOKOnly + vbCritical, "ahtOpenForm"
    Resume ahtOpenFormExit

End Function

Function ahtCloseForm(frmToClose As Form)

    ' If StayLoaded is True, hide the
    ' form instead of closing it

    On Error GoTo ahtCloseFormErr

    If InStr(frmToClose.OpenArgs, "StayLoaded") > 0 Then
        frmToClose.Visible = False
    Else
        DoCmd.Close acForm, frmToClose.Name
    End If
```

```
ahtCloseFormExit:
    Exit Function

ahtCloseFormErr:
    MsgBox "Error " & Err.Number & ": " & Err.Description, _
      vbOKOnly + vbCritical, "ahtCloseForm"
    Resume ahtCloseFormExit

End Function
```

5. Throughout your application, when you create code that opens a form and you wish to load that form only once, call the ahtOpenForm function from step 4. If you wish to open a form from code, you can use this syntax:

```
Call ahtOpenForm("formname", True)
```

You can also call the function directly from an event property. In this case, enter the following in the event property.

```
=ahtOpenForm("formname", True)
```

For those forms that you don't wish to keep loaded, change the second parameter of ahtOpenForm to False.

6. For each form that you are either preloading or loading with the ahtOpenForm function, add a command button with a caption Close. Enter the following in the event property for the button's Click event.

```
=ahtcCloseForm(Form)
```

Don't place any quotes around the Form parameter.

7. Make a copy of the form created in step 2, naming the copy frmSplash. Open frmSplash in design view and remove all of the command button controls. Also remove all of the code behind the form for this copy. In the area where the command buttons used to be, add a label control that contains an initialization message. For example, the label on frmSplash has the attributes shown in Table 8-1. Figure 8-3 shows frmSplash in form view.

PROPERTY	VALUE
Name	lblMessage
Caption	Initializing...
Back Style	Transparent
Border Style	Transparent
Font Name	Arial
Font Size	14
Text Align	Center

Table 8-1 The properties of frmSplash's lblMessage control

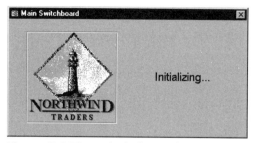

Figure 8-3 The splash form, frmSplash

8. Open the switchboard form created in step 2. Open the form's module and add the following constants to the Declarations section of the module.

```
Const ahtcPreloadTable = "zstblPreloadForms"
Const ahtcSplashForm = "frmSplash"
```

Change "zstblPreloadForms" to the name of the table from step 1. Change "frmSplash" to the name of the form from step 7.

9. Select Tools|Startup to open the database Startup dialog box (see Figure 8-4). Select the switchboard form from step 2 in the Display Form field.

10. Close the database and reload it to test your startup procedure and switchboard form.

How It Works

Access forms are stored as binary data in hidden system tables in your database. When you load a form, Access must recreate that form by reading data from the system tables to display your form. This takes time. This How-To improves the application load time of forms by preloading them when the database is first loaded. This means that the initial application load time will be slower, but users are more tolerant of long application load times, especially because this is a one-time commitment. For example, we tested the sample application on a 40Mhz 486-based machine with 12MB of RAM. The load times of the application and the time it took to load the frmOrders form twice are shown in Table 8-2.

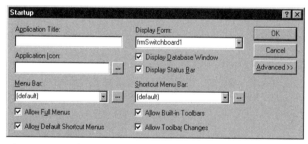

Figure 8-4 The database Startup dialog box

SCENARIO	APPLICATION LOAD TIME	LOAD TIMES OF FRMORDERS
No preloading of forms	30 seconds	16 seconds, 6 seconds
Preloading of 4 forms	60 seconds	3 seconds, 1 second

 Table 8-2 Sample load times for 08-01.MDB

We purposely chose a slow machine because this sample application is rather small. Note that application load time was twice as long when four forms were preloaded. But the time it took to load the form for the first time was very fast. Notice that subsequent form loads were even faster because of caching. On faster machines, form load time is almost instantaneous when forms have been preloaded compared with load times of several seconds when forms have not been preloaded.

Prior to Access 95, you had to use an AutoExec macro to initiate some action upon database startup. With Access 95, you can use the Startup dialog box to specify a form to be opened when the database is loaded. This How-To takes advantage of the Startup properties, but you also could have used an AutoExec macro.

When the switchboard form opens, the Open event is triggered and the code attached to the form's Open form is executed. Unfortunately, when the Open event is called, the form has not had time to paint itself, so users normally see nothing during the lengthy Open event procedure. This is why we created a "splash" form to display during the potentially lengthy process. You don't have to make the splash screen the same size as the switchboard form, but in this case, because the switchboard form was fairly small, we made the two forms very similar in appearance.

The code to preload the forms is shown here.

```
Set rst = db.OpenRecordset(ahtcPreloadTable)

Do While Not rst.EOF
    varFormName = rst!FormName
    If Not IsNull(varFormName) Then
        DoCmd.OpenForm FormName:=varFormName, _
          WindowMode:=acHidden, OpenArgs:="StayLoaded"
    End If
    rst.MoveNext
Loop
```

Each record from the zstblPreloadForms table is read and the named form is loaded in hidden mode. In addition, the form's OpenArgs parameter is passed the string "StayLoaded". You can use the OpenArgs parameter of OpenForm to pass a custom string to a form, much like you pass parameters to a function. This OpenArgs parameter will be used later to decide what to do when the preloaded form is closed.

Once the forms have been loaded in a hidden state, you don't need to do anything special to make them appear. Access is smart enough to make a hidden form visible when you attempt to load it, which makes working with invisible forms easy. We included wrapper functions for opening and closing your application's forms, however, in

413

case you wish for some forms to be treated differently. For example, you may not wish to preload and keep all your forms loaded because they will take up memory and you may not have enough on your machine to preload and keep all forms loaded.

Like the Form_Open event procedure attached to the switchboard form, the ahtOpenForm function passes the string "StayLoaded" to a form via its OpenArgs argument when you pass True as the function's second parameter. The closing of the application form is then handled by ahtCloseForm, which is called by the Click event of each form's Close button. This function determines whether to close or hide the form by checking the OpenArgs property of the form, which was passed to the form when it was opened.

```
If InStr(frmToClose.OpenArgs, "StayLoaded") > 0 Then
    frmToClose.Visible = False
Else
    DoCmd.Close acForm, frmToClose.Name
End If
```

For any forms that you do not wish to preload, don't add them to zstblPreloadForms. For any forms that you wish to close normally when the Close button is pressed, open them using the following syntax.

```
=ahtOpenForm("formname", False)
```

Comments

If you have enough memory, you may wish to preload all forms and not close them until the application is quit. In some situations, however, you may wish to be more selective. By using the preload technique and the ahtOpenForm and ahtCloseForm functions throughout your application, you can easily change your mind or customize form preloading and form hiding for different hardware.

We did not remove the close button and control box from each sample form. This means that you can use one of these alternate mechanisms to bypass the Close button (and the ahtCloseForm function) and close the form instead of hiding it. Thus, you may wish to set the Close Button and Control Box properties of your forms to No to prevent the use of these mechanisms.

The times shown in Table 8-2 are only examples. Your situation will undoubtedly yield different times.

You may wish to make zstblPreloadForms a hidden table. You can adjust the hidden property of an object by selecting View|Properties.

Benchmarking 101

Benchmarking different scenarios is a painstaking process. Because Windows 95 includes a hard disk cache and Access itself caches data, it's very difficult to get fair and accurate timings. Because of caching, the order in which you time things *matters*. The important point is to avoid jumping to conclusions without repeating the timings several times in a different order. Also, there is no reliable programmatic way to measure the time a form takes to load. Although you can set timers at each of the form's events, Access does some things internally after the last loading event has fired. You will find the only accurate way to test a form's loading time is to manually test and average the form load using a stopwatch.

COMPLEXITY:

INTERMEDIATE

8.2 How do I...
Make slow forms run faster?

Problem

I am not happy with the speed at which my forms load and display. How can I change my forms so they will load and display faster?

Technique

How-To 8.1 explains how you can speed up the loading time of all forms by preloading them. This How-To offers advice on how to analyze each form and apply various optimizations to improve form execution performance.

Steps

There are several potential issues to consider when analyzing your forms for performance. We discuss here two common performance bottlenecks and their solutions: controls involving graphic or memo field data along with combo and list box controls.

Graphic and Memo Controls

Load the 08-02a.MDB database. Open the frmCategoriesOriginal form (see Figure 8-5). This form, although attractive, loads fairly slowly and has a noticeable delay on slower machines when moving from record to record. Now open frmCategoriesStep3, which is the final version of the form after various optimizations have been applied to it (see Figure 8-6). Its load and execution time should be noticeably faster.

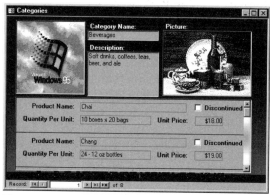

Figure 8-5 The original form,
frmCategoriesOriginal, is slow

Follow these steps to improve the performance of forms that include unbound graphic controls or bound controls that hold OLE or Memo fields:

1. Open the problem form in design view. If you have any unbound object frame controls (also known as unbound OLE controls) that are used to store fixed graphic images, change them to image controls by right-clicking on the object and selecting Change To|Image (see Figure 8-7). The frmCategoriesStep1 form in the 08-02a sample database is identical to frmCategoriesOriginal except we converted ctlLogo from an unbound object frame control to an image control.

2. If you created a watermark for the form, consider removing it. Select the word "bitmap" in the Picture property of the form and press the [DEL] key. Answer yes to the confirming dialog box. The frmCategoriesStep2 form in 08-02a.MDB is identical to frmCategoriesStep1, except we deleted the watermark for the form.

Figure 8-6 The final form,
frmCategoriesStep3, is faster

Figure 8-7 Changing an unbound object control into an image control

3. If your form contains any bound controls that hold either OLE or memo fields, consider moving the controls to a second page of the form. We moved the ctlDescription and ctlPicture controls to a second page in the final version of the Categories form, named frmCategoriesStep3 (see Figure 8-6).

Combo and List Box Controls

Load the 08-02b.MDB database. Open the frmSurveySlow form (see Figure 8-8). This form contains a combo box control, cboPersonId, that has as its row source a SQL Select statement that pulls in 15,000 rows from the tblPeople table. Load time for the form is very slow because Access has to run the query that supplies the 15,000 rows to cboPersonId. Tab to the cboPersonId control and type "th" to search for the name "Thompson, Adrian." Note the long delay before the *th* list of records appears. Now open the frmSurveyFast form (see Figure 8-9). Load time is significantly faster. Press

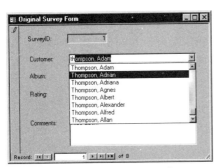

Figure 8-8 The cboPersonId combo box is very slow

417

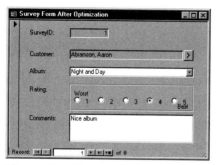

Figure 8-9 The combo box has been replaced with a text box and command button

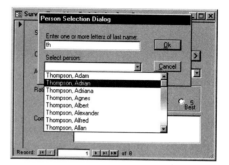

Figure 8-10 Selecting a name from the pop-up list is much faster

the ">" command button to open the frmPersonPopup form. Type "th" in first control and press TAB. After a short delay, you'll be able to select "Thompson, Adrian" from the drop-down list as shown in Figure 8-10. Press the OK button, which will drop the chosen name back into the txtPersonName text box on frmSurveyFast.

Follow these steps to improve the speed of forms that contain combo or list boxes with a large number of rows in their row source:

1. Make a copy of the problem form. Open the copy in design view. Select the slow combo or list box control. Right-click on the control and select Change To|Text Box.

2. Create a new unbound pop-up form with the property settings shown in Table 8-3. Leave the remaining property settings at their defaults. In the sample database, this form is named frmPersonPopup.

PROPERTY	SETTING
Scroll Bars	Neither
Record Selectors	No
Navigation Buttons	No
Auto Resize	Yes
Auto Center	Yes
Pop Up	Yes
Modal	Yes
Min Max Buttons	None

Table 8-3 The property settings for the pop-up form

3. Create four unbound controls on this form: a text box, combo box, and two command buttons. In the sample database, we created the controls shown in

Table 8-4. The text box will be used to limit the number of items in the combo box, using a parameter query created in the next step.

CONTROL TYPE	CONTROL NAME	NOTES
Text box	txtChar	Used to limit the values in the row source of the combo box.
Combo box	cboPersonId	Row source will be parameter query created in next step.
Command button	cmdOK	Hides form.
Command button	cmdCancel	Closes form.

Table 8-4 The controls on frmPersonPopup

4. Create a new query that will serve as the row source for the combo box of the pop-up form. If you used a query as the source for the combo or list box on the original form, you should be able to modify its design. Add the necessary fields to the query. Add a parameter to the form that limits the rows based on a value typed into the text box on the pop-up form. Choose any sort fields. In the sample database, we created the qryPersonComboBox query with the fields shown in Table 8-5. Save and close the query.

QUERY FIELD	SORT	CRITERIA
PersonId	(none)	(none)
FullName: [LastName] & ", " & [FirstName]	(none)	(none)
LastName	Ascending	Like
		[Forms]![frmPersonPopup2]![txtChar]
		& "*"
FirstName	Ascending	

Table 8-5 The fields in qryPersonComboBox

5. Reopen the pop-up form created in steps 2 and 3. Set the Enabled property of the combo box to No. Set the Row Source property to point to the query created in step 4. In the sample database, we set the properties of the cboPersonId combo box to the values in Table 8-6.

PROPERTY	SETTING
Enabled	No
Row Source Type	Table/Query
Row Source	(blank)
Column Count	2
Column Heads	No
Column Widths	0";2.5"

continued on next page

continued from previous page

PROPERTY	SETTING
Bound Column	1
List Rows	8
List Width	2.5"

Table 8-6 The property settings for cboPersonId

6. Create a new event procedure for the text box's Change event. (If you're unsure how to do this, see How Do I Create an Event Procedure in the Introduction of this book.) Add the following code to the event procedure.

```
Private Sub txtChar_Change()

    If Not IsNull(Me!txtChar.Text) Then
        Me!cboPersonID.Enabled = True
    Else
        Me!cboPersonID.Enabled = False
    End If

End Sub
```

Change txtChar to the name of your text box and cboPersonId to the name of your combo box.

7. Create the following new event procedure for the text box's AfterUpdate event.

```
Private Sub txtChar_AfterUpdate()

    Dim ctlPersonId As ComboBox
    Dim ctlChar As TextBox

    Set ctlPersonId = Me!cboPersonID
    Set ctlChar = Me!txtChar

    If Not IsNull(ctlChar) Then
        ctlPersonId.RowSource = "qryPersonComboBox"
        ctlPersonId.SetFocus
        ctlPersonId.Dropdown
    End If

End Sub
```

Change txtChar to the name of your text box and cboPersonId to the name of your combo box. Change qryPersonComboBox to the name of the query you created in step 4.

8. Create the following new event procedure for the OK command button's Click event.

```
Private Sub cmdOK_Click()
    Me.Visible = False
End Sub
```

9. Create the following event procedure for the Cancel command button's Click event.

```
Private Sub cmdCancel_Click()
    DoCmd.Close acForm, Me.Name
End Sub
```

10. Save the pop-up form and close it.

11. Reopen the form from step 1 in design view. Add a button to the right of the text box. Call it cmdPopup. Add the following event procedure to cmdPopup's Click event.

```
Private Sub cmdPopup_Click()

    Const ahtcPopup = "frmPersonPopup"

    ' Open up popup form in dialog mode
    DoCmd.OpenForm ahtcPopup, WindowMode:=acDialog

    ' Check if form is still loaded.
    ' If yes, then OK button was used to close popup.
    If SysCmd(acSysCmdGetObjectState, acForm, ahtcPopup) <> 0 Then
        Me!PersonID = Forms(ahtcPopup)!cboPersonID
        DoCmd.Close acForm, ahtcPopup
    End If

End Sub
```

Change frmPersonPopup to match the name of the pop-up form. Change PersonId and cboPersonId to the names of the appropriate controls.

How It Works

When you have a form that loads and executes slowly, you need to analyze the form and weigh the advantages and disadvantages of the use of graphic features. After a careful analysis of the frmCategoriesOriginal form in the 08-02a database, we made several changes.

First, we changed the unbound object frame control to an image control. The OLE-based object frame control can be used to hold graphic images, sound, and other OLE-based data; but if you only need to display an unbound bitmap, you're better off using the more resource-conservative image control that was introduced in Access 95.

Second, we removed the form watermark. This feature, which is also new in Access 95, will slow down form execution slightly. The improvement in performance will depend on the color-depth of the removed image and the speed of your machine.

Finally, we created a second page and moved the text box bound to the memo field and the bound object frame bound to the OLE field to this second page. These field types (memo and OLE) are stored separately from the rest of fields in a record and thus require additional disk reads to display. Fortunately, Access will not fetch these potentially large fields from the database unless they are visible on the screen. By placing them on the second page, you can quickly navigate from row to row without having to fetch the memo or OLE data. When you need to view the data in the fields, however, you can easily flip to the second page of the form.

The frmSurveySlow form in 08-02b.MDB contains a combo box, cboPersonId, bound to a 15,000-row table. This makes form load and combo box list navigation excruciatingly slow. Combo and list box controls are excellent controls for allowing users to choose from a list of values and work well with a small number of list rows. They are not the right controls, however, when the size of the list exceeds a few thousand rows, even with very fast hardware.

We were able to improve the load time of the survey form significantly by limiting the rows in the person combo box. This was done using a pop-up form containing the same combo box control, but linked to a text box control that filtered the combo box's rows via a parameter query. Using a little VBA code, we were able to disable the combo box control until at least one character was entered into the text box. Thus we reduced a 15,000-row combo box to, on average, 15,000 / 26 = 577 rows. And that's when only the minimum number of characters (one) is typed into the text box.

Besides reducing the large number of rows in the row source for cboPersonId, two other improvements were made to boost combo box performance. On the original frmSurveySlow form, a SQL statement was used as the row source for the combo box. The cboPersonId combo box on the pop-up form uses a saved query instead. Saved queries are always faster than SQL statements because the query optimizer optimizes the query when it is saved (rather than when it is run as with unsaved SQL statements).

In addition, the SQL statement for frmSurverySlow's combo box includes the following OrderBy clause.

```
ORDER BY [LastName] & ", " & [FirstName]
```

In contrast, the SQL for the qryPersonComboBox query that's used as the row source for frmPersonPopup uses the following OrderBy clause.

```
ORDER BY tblPeople.LastName, tblPeople.FirstName
```

Although these two OrderBy clauses look very similar, the first one sorts on an expression, whereas the second sorts on two indexed fields. It's always faster to sort on individual fields rather than expressions.

Comments

There are several other things to consider when looking for ways to speed up your forms. You may wish to try some or all of the following suggestions.

- Preload and keep loaded forms (see How-To 8.1).

- Ensure that fields used to sort or filter rows are indexed in the underlying tables (see How-To 8.3 for more on indexing and Rushmore).

- Use referential integrity throughout your database. Besides the obvious improvements to the quality of your data, when you create enforced relationships, Access creates hidden foreign key indexes that improve the performance of queries, forms, and reports based on the joined tables.

 Create simpler forms with less color, less graphics, and less fonts.

 Limit the number of records in the form's recordset (see How-To 8.7).

The Performance Analyzer

Access 95 includes a wonderful wizard called the Performance Analyzer. You should use this wizard to analyze the performance of all your forms (and other database objects). Although it is somewhat limited in the kinds of suggestions it can make, it's a nice way to check if you've missed any obvious problems. For example, when run against frmSurveySlow, the wizard suggested using a saved query as the row source for the combo box. When run against frmCategoriesOriginal, the wizard suggested changing the unbound object frame to an image control. The Performance Analyzer will also make suggestions regarding indexes and relationships.

COMPLEXITY:
INTERMEDIATE

8.3 How do I...
Use Rushmore to speed up queries?

Problem

I've heard that Rushmore can improve the performance of my queries. How do I create queries that use Rushmore?

Technique

Rushmore query optimizations help the Jet Engine (the database engine built into Access) execute certain types of queries dramatically faster. This How-To explains how Rushmore works and how you can take advantage of it. It also introduces a technique for timing the execution of queries.

Steps

Load the 08-03.MDB database. Open the qryOr1 query in design view. This query, which is shown in Figure 8-11, contains criteria on two fields, Menu# and Quantity.

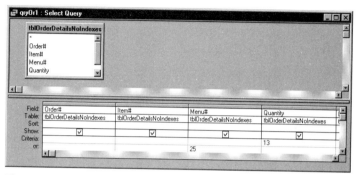

Figure 8-11 The qryOr1 returns rows where Quantity = 13 or Menu# = 25

It returns all records from tblOrderDetailsNoIndexes where Quantity = 13 or where Menu# = 25. If you switch to SQL view, you'll see the following Where clause.

```
WHERE (((tblOrderDetailsNoIndexes.[Quantity])=13)) OR
(((tblOrderDetailsNoIndexes.[Menu#])=25))
```

Close the query and open the tblOrderDetailsNoIndexes table to confirm that this table has no indexes. The qryOr2 and qryOr3 queries are identical to qryOr1 except they are based on different tables. The qryOr2 query is based on tblOrderDetailsPartialIndexed, which contains an index on the Menu# field; and qryOr3 is based on tblOrderDetailsFullyIndexed, which contains indexes for both Menu# and Quantity.

Run the three queries in turn and you should notice that qryOr3 is much faster than qryOr1 or qryOr2, which are of similar speed. To get more accurate timings, open the frmQueryTimer form in form view and create a new test comparing the three queries, as shown in Figure 8-12. Press the Run Test button to begin executing each query the number or times you've specified in the Number of Reps text box. When the test is complete, press the Results button to view a Totals query datasheet that summarizes

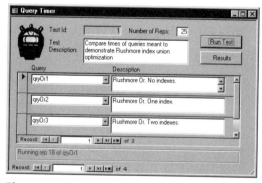

Figure 8-12 A test comparing three queries is run

the results of the test. A datasheet will be displayed (see Figure 8-13). When we ran this particular test on a 90Mhz Pentium machine with 16MB of memory, qryOr3—which takes advantage of Rushmore—was 60 times faster than either qryOr1 or qryOr2, which had virtually identical average execution times.

Follow these steps to take advantage of Rushmore in your own queries:

1. Index all table fields that are referenced in the criteria of your queries.

2. Create queries with:

> two or more criteria on indexed fields in the same underlying table connected with the AND operator, or

> two or more criteria on indexed fields in the same underlying table connected with the OR operator.

In addition, special Rushmore query optimizations will be used whenever you create Totals queries that make use of the Count(*) expression and have either no criteria or criteria on indexed fields only.

How It Works

Most database engines, including the Jet Engine, are quick at executing queries based on a single indexed field. Unfortunately, most database engines slow to a crawl when executing queries involving criteria on two or more indexed fields from the same table connected with the AND or OR operators. That's because most database engines can only use one index when executing a query against a table.

Enter Rushmore, which is Microsoft's name for its ability to combine two or more indexes mathematically and thus execute a query while making use of multiple indexes. The net result is faster execution speed when faced with this class of queries.

Rushmore also comes into play when Jet executes Totals queries involving Count(*). When executing this type of query, Jet is able to execute the query without reading any rows of data. Instead, Jet solves the query by counting the index rows, which is almost always faster than reading pages of data records.

In the sample database, you'll find three tests comparing the various Rushmore optimizations using the three different versions of the tblOrderDetails table. You may wish to run these tests on your own computer to see what results you get. You may also wish to import the query timer form into your own database to time your queries in

zsqryTestAnalysis : Select Query		
QueryName	Reps	AvgTime
qryOr1	25	3.0286
qryOr2	25	3.0690
qryOr3	25	0.0508

Record: 1 of 3

Figure 8-13 The qryOr3 query is 60 times faster than the other two queries

various scenarios. To use the frmQueryTimer form in your own database, import the objects from Table 8-7.

OBJECT TYPE	OBJECT	DESCRIPTION
Table	zstblTests	One row for each test in frmQueryTimer.
Table	zstblQueries	One row for each query compared in a test.
Table	zstblTimes	One row for each time recorded in a test.
Query	zsqryTestAnalysis	Totals query used to analyze the results of a test.
Form	frmQueryTimer	The query timer form.
Form	fsubQueries	Subform used in frmQueryTimer.

Table 8-7 The objects used in the query timer technique

Once you've imported the objects from Table 8-7, you can set up and execute a new test following these steps:

1. Create and save two or more queries you wish to compare.

2. Open frmQueryTimer in form view and enter the number of times to repeat the test in the Number of Reps text box.

3. Enter a description for the test in the Test Description text box.

4. Add a record to the subform for each query you wish to compare for the test. Use the Query combo box control to select the queries created in step 1.

5. Click on the Run Test command button to run the test. When it's done, the status text box will contain the message, "Test completed." Click on the Results command button to view a Totals query comparing the average execution times of the queries.

Comments

The frmQueryTimer form executes each query repeatedly using a For...Next statement that calls the ahtTimeQuery function, which is shown here.

```
Function ahtTimeQuery(ByVal strQry As String, _
    datStart As Date, lngRecs As Long) As Variant

    Dim db As Database
    Dim qdf As QueryDef
    Dim rst As Recordset
    Dim lngStart As Long
    Dim lngEnd As Long

    Set db = CurrentDb()
    Set qdf = db.QueryDefs(strQry)

    lngStart = aht_apiGetTickCount()
    datStart = Now()
```

```
Set rst = qdf.OpenRecordset(dbOpenSnapshot)

If Not rst.EOF Then
    rst.MoveLast
    lngRecs = rst.RecordCount
Else
    lngRecs = 0
End If

lngEnd = aht_apiGetTickCount()

ahtTimeQuery = lngEnd - lngStart

End Function
```

There are two interesting aspects to this function. First, it makes use of the GetTickCount Windows API function to get more accurate measure of time than VBA's built-in Timer function can provide. Second, it executes the query by creating a snapshot recordset, not a dynaset. This forces the query to execute completely rather than returning just the first page of records.

Rushmore can't work if you don't create indexes. In general, it's a good idea to create an index for every field used in:

- query criteria,

- query sorts, and

- ad-hoc joins (when enforced relationships have not been created).

Create Indexes with Care

Don't create indexes on fields that are part of referential integrity relationships because Access already creates indexes to enforce these relationships. Also be aware that Access has a limit of 32 indexes per table. Finally, don't go overboard indexing every field in every table of your database because indexes can slow down operations that add or edit data.

COMPLEXITY:
ADVANCED

8.4 How do I... Accelerate Visual Basic for Applications code?

Problem

I've optimized my forms and queries, but this isn't enough in terms of my entire application. My application contains a lot of Visual Basic for Applications (VBA) code. I'm sure there is something I can do to make it run faster. What optimizations can I perform?

Technique

VBA is an interpreted language that has much in common with any other interpreted language. This How-To demonstrates seven specific programmatic techniques you can apply to accelerate your code. The improvement you will realize can range from modest increases to 30-fold increases in performance.

Steps

To see the seven optimizations in action, open and run frmShowOptimizations from 08-04.MDB, shown in Figure 8-14. Click the Run Tests button and each test will run, one by one, displaying the results in milliseconds. The tests compare two different methods of using VBA to achieve a result.

When these optimizations were performed in Access 2.0, the techniques on the right side of the form were *always* faster; this is no longer true in Access 95. Table 8-8 contrasts the technique timings on the same machine (a 90Mhz Pentium machine with

Test Access Basic Optimizations			
Divide two integers using floating point division (/)	252	Divide two integers using integer division (\)	171
Add two numbers stored in a variant	274	Add two numbers stored in an integer	138
Test for a blank string using string = ""	330	Test for blank string using Len(string) = 0	164
Multiple references to an object without using an object variable	73076	Multiple references to an object using an object variable	2101
Code with comments	769	Code without comments	783
Using IIF() to return a value	4614	Using If..Then..Else to return a value	476
Assign a value to a variable length string	549	Assign a value to a fixed length string	893

[Run Tests]   [Close]

Figure 8-14 The frmShowOptimizations form

16MB of memory), first under Access 2.0 and then under Access 95 (both running under Windows 95).

TECHNIQUE	ACCESS 2.0			ACCESS 95		
	SLOW	FAST	RATIO	SLOW	FAST	RATIO
Integer division	412	192	2.1	252	171	1.5
Integer instead of variant	316	178	1.8	274	138	2.0
Testing for blank string	783	384	2.0	330	164	2.0
Using object variable	4,134	1,895	2.2	73,076	2,101	34.8
Code without comments	2,184	1,334	1.6	769	783	1.0
Using If...Then	1,566	550	2.8	4,614	476	9.7
Using fixed length string	892	646	1.4	549	893	0.6

Table 8-8 Timing results under Access 2.0 and Access 95

Follow these steps for incorporating the results of these comparisons in your applications:

1. When dividing integers, use integer division. A good percentage of the division operations performed by your application are probably done on integer values. Many developers use the / (slash) operator to divide two numbers, without knowing that it is optimized for floating-point division. If you're dividing integers, you should use the \ (backslash) integer division operator instead. With \, Access has to work at the integer level instead of the floating-point level and the computation will be faster. (Of course, this is only useful if you're assigning the results of the division operation to an integer. If you care about the fractional portion of the division, you'll need to use floating-point math, and the / operator, to do your work.) For example, instead of using

```
intX = intY / intZ
```

use

```
intX = intY \ intZ
```

2. Use specific data types instead of variants. Variants offer convenience at the expense of performance. Every time you refer to a variant, Access needs to perform type conversion to ensure the data is in the correct format. By using the data type that matches your variable, you eliminate the need for this type conversion and your code runs faster. In addition, a variant variable is twice as large as an integer (on a 32-bit operating system) and thus takes longer to manipulate.

3. Test for blank strings using the Len function. You probably have code that tests for blank strings by comparing them to an empty string (""). However, because Access stores the length of the string as the first byte in the string, testing for a length of zero using the Len function is always faster. Instead of

```
If strTemp = "" Then
    MsgBox "The string is blank"
End If
```

use

```
If Len(strTemp) = 0 Then
    MsgBox "The string is blank"
End If
```

4. If you refer to an object more than once in a section of code, assign it to an object variable. Every time you reference an object, Access has to perform some work to figure out which object you are referring to. This adds overhead to your code each time the object is referenced. But if you assign the object to an object variable, Access "finds" the object once and caches the reference in memory. In the remainder of the code, you can refer to the object through the object variable and your code will run faster. For example, instead of this code:

```
Dim strTmp As String
Dim lngCount As Long

For lngCount = 0 To ahtcMaxIterations / 2
    strTmp = DBEngine.Workspaces(0).Groups(0).Name
Next lngCount
```

use

```
Dim grp As Group
Dim strTmp As String
Dim lngCount As Long

Set grp = DBEngine.Workspaces(0).Groups(0)

For lngCount = 0 To ahtcMaxIterations / 2
    strTmp = grp.Name
Next lngCount
```

It's interesting to note that the second version of the above code was twice as fast in Access 2.0 but 35 times faster in Access 95. The difference in time will likely depend on the actual object references you use. We created two variations of this test using Access 95. First, we changed the function to refer to a control on an open form instead of a DAO group. The cached reference version of the code was 2.8 times faster—certainly significantly improved, but not of the same magnitude as the DAO group comparison. Second, we compared using an object variable against using the new VBA With…End With construct (without an object reference). With…End With was 6 times slower than using an object variable—slower, but still much faster than using neither an object variable nor With…End With.

5. Don't worry about comments. In the switch from Access Basic to VBA, it appears the use of comments—at least the use of comments of the same magnitude as used in the example—exacts no measurable performance penalty. It's possible, however, that there may be an advantage to using less comments when either your PC is low on memory or your application has a very large memory footprint.

6. Use If…Then…Else instead of the IIf function. By replacing IIf statements with the equivalent If…Then…Else statement, your code will run faster. For example, instead of

```
MsgBox IIf(intX = 1, "One", "Not One")
```

use

```
If intX = 1 Then
    MsgBox "1"
Else
    MsgBox "Not 1"
End If
```

7. Don't use fixed length strings. Although it was faster to use fixed length strings rather than variable length strings in Access 2.0, in Access 95, fixed length strings are almost twice as slow as variable length strings.

How It Works

There are two important things to remember when you are trying to optimize your VBA code. First, VBA is an interpreted language. In most interpreted languages, each line is read and parsed regardless of content, so less verbose code is generally faster code. Keep this in mind as you write code and reduce the number of lines that need to be interpreted. Second, VBA is very similar to other languages, compiled and otherwise, in its interaction with the computer at the lowest level. Many optimizations that apply to other languages could also apply to VBA. For example, the technique of checking for a blank string using the Len function is a common optimization in other languages. Don't be afraid to try new techniques.

Comments

Optimization techniques for programming languages are a vital part of your toolbox. But don't sacrifice other vital elements for the sake of speed. First, make sure your code works correctly before you optimize. Second, write your code so that it's easily understood. It can be very difficult to optimize code you don't understand. Finally, don't break working code when optimizing it. By optimizing code that works correctly (albeit slowly), you may introduce bugs. Follow the three rules of optimization:

Make it right before you make it faster.

Make it clear before you make it faster.

Keep it right as you make it faster.

You may find that there are no easy optimizations for a particular piece of code. No matter what you do, it just won't run fast enough. A favorite saying in software design is, "Don't diddle code to make it faster; find a better algorithm." Often you need to step back from a piece of slow code. Maybe there is a better overall approach or better algorithm you can employ. A good way to get over a hurdle such as this is to ask other programmers how they handle the same situation.

Note

As they say in the auto commercials, "Your mileage may vary." Don't assume anything is faster until you've proven it yourself on the target machine that will be used to run your application!

COMPLEXITY:
INTERMEDIATE

8.5   How do I...
Accelerate routines that add, edit, and change data in tables?

Problem

I have VBA routines that add, edit, and change data in tables using recordset objects. It seems the code I write to edit and delete data in tables runs more slowly than an equivalent Access query. How can I make my table access operations run faster?

Technique

When you programmatically access table data using recordset objects, you will get a modest performance boost by using transactions to buffer database updates. This How-To discusses the advantages of using transactions and explains how the Jet Engine helps you by creating its own transactions even when you don't use explicit ones.

Steps

Open and run frmTestTransactions in 08-05.MDB, as shown in Figure 8-15. This form tests adding, changing, and deleting records in the tblContacts sample table. To see it in action, type in the number of records you wish to add, change, or delete and press the Start Test button. The form runs each of the operations, first without using transactions and then with transactions, and displays the number of milliseconds each method takes. You should notice a slight improvement when using transactions. The operations should be in the range of 1.1 to 1.8 times faster when you use explicit transactions. (In Figure 8-15, the tests were performed on a 90Mhz Pentium machine with 16MB of memory.)

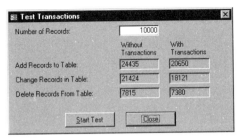

Figure 8-15 The Test Transactions form

To use this technique in your own code, wrap any code that updates data in tables in a transaction. Follow these steps to add explicit transactions to your code:

1. In your code, declare a workspace variable and set the variable to point to the current workspace using code such as this:

```
Dim wrk As Workspace
Set wrk = DBEngine.Workspaces(0)
```

2. Locate a point in your code after the recordset object has been created but *before* you access any data. At that location, start a transaction using the BeginTrans method of the current workspace object. For example:

```
wrk.BeginTrans
```

3. Locate a point in your code *after* all data access is finished but before you close the recordset. At this point, use the CommitTrans method of the current workspace object to commit the changes to disk, like this:

```
wrk.CommitTrans
```

4. You may also wish to include error-handling code in your procedure that rolls back the transaction if an error occurrs while updating the records.

5. A complete example that employs transaction processing along with an error handler is shown here.

```
Sub DeleteLastNames()

    On Error GoTo DeleteLastNamesErr

    Dim db As Database
    Dim rst As Recordset
    Dim wrk As Workspace
    Dim fInTrans As Boolean

    Set wrk = DBEngine.Workspaces(0)
    Set db = wrk.Databases(0)
    Set rst = db.OpenRecordset("tblContacts")

    ' Start Transaction
    wrk.BeginTrans
```

continued on next page

continued from previous page

```
                ' Set flag that says were in a transaction
                fInTrans = True

                With rst
                    Do Until .EOF
                        .Edit
                            !Name = Null
                        .Update
                        .MoveNext
                    Loop
                End With

            ' Commit the transaction
            wrk.CommitTrans
            ' Reset the transaction flag
            fInTrans = False

            MsgBox "Transaction completed."

        DeleteLastNamesExit:
            If Not rst Is Nothing Then rst.Close
            Exit Sub

        DeleteLastNamesErr:
            ' If in the middle of a transaction,
            ' then roll it back
            If fInTrans Then
                wrk.Rollback
                MsgBox "Transaction rolled back."
            End If
            ' Normal error handler
            Select Case Err.Number
            Case Else
                MsgBox "Error#" & Err.Number & ": " & Err.Description, _
                    vbOKOnly + vbCritical, "DeleteLastNames"
            End Select
            Resume DeleteLastNamesExit

        End Sub
```

How It Works

Transactions are crucial in any database product. By using a transaction, you can group a set of operations together as a logical unit. At any point within a transaction, you can commit or roll back the entire transaction. This allows you to save the changes only if all necessary changes were made. Access uses transactions at many levels. When you perform action queries, Access automatically wraps the operation in a transaction, allowing the operation to roll back all changes if an error is encountered.

What does this have to do with performance? A useful side effect of transactions is that changes made to data during a transaction are not actually written to disk. Instead the changes are buffered in memory until a CommitTrans method causes them to be written or a RollBack method causes them to be discarded. Because memory access is much faster than disk access, the result is a faster operation.

Comments

Using explicit transactions in Access 2.0 resulted in great performance improvements. These improvements are mostly negated by a new feature in Access 95: implied transactions. In Access 95, the Jet Engine is able to detect sections of code that could benefit from using transactions; when it does, it creates implicit transactions. Although this is a welcome improvement, timing comparisons reveal that you can still improve performance—although only slightly—by using explicit transactions. As a side benefit, you get the robustness that comes with transactions when you include explicit transaction processing code in your data updating procedures.

If you create very large transactions, it's possible to overflow memory which will cause Windows to overflow the transaction to disk. This can slow down your code instead of speeding it up. In these cases, you should split your single transaction into several smaller transactions that are committed in succession.

COMPLEXITY:
INTERMEDIATE

8.6 How do I...
Test the comparative benefits of various optimization techniques?

Problem

Now that I've tried the optimization techniques in this chapter, I'd like to test some additional optimization ideas. How can I can test various VBA optimization techniques in a standardized fashion?

Technique

By using a Windows API call, some simple math, and a wrapper function, you can easily compare the performance of two optimization techniques with relatively high accuracy. This How-To shows you how to create a form you can use to compare the performance of two functions. It runs the functions and then displays how long each took to execute.

Steps

Open and run frmTestOptimize from 08-06.MDB. The form shown in Figure 8-16 allows you to enter the names of two functions and test their performance relative to each other. The 08-06.MDB database contains two sample functions that show the relative

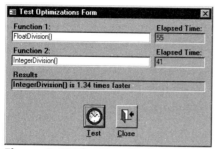

Figure 8-16 The Test Optimizations form

performance of integer division and floating-point division. (This optimization was already discussed in How-To 8-4.) To run the test, enter

```
FloatDivision()
```

into the Function 1 text box; enter

```
IntegerDivision()
```

into the Function 2 text box; and press the Test button. The form will run each function, show the time taken by each function, and display which function is faster and by how much.

To use the frmTestOptimize form to test your own functions, follow these steps:

1. Import frmTestOptimize from 08-06.MDB into your database. This form is completely self-contained and requires no other objects.

2. Open frmTestOptimize in form view and enter the name of the two functions you wish to test along with any required parameters. Type the entries in the Function 1 and Function 2 text boxes exactly as if you were calling the functions in your VBA code, but omit the assignment operator and assignment object. For example, for a function that is called in your VBA code like this:

```
intReturned = MyTestFunction ("MyTable")
```

type the following into the frmTestOptimize text box.

```
MyTestFunction ("MyTable")
```

How It Works

There are two key aspects to this technique. First, we used the Windows API GetTickCount function. GetTickCount returns the number of milliseconds elapsed since Windows was started. This number is useful when employed to compare two points in time. You may wonder if you can use the Timer function built into Access instead, or even the Now function. Both of these functions return time values that are only accurate to within one second. Even though many of your optimization tests will perform operations that run longer than a second, you will lose a great deal of accuracy with these methods. Because GetTickCount returns time measurements in milliseconds, it is more accurate than VBA's Timer function or Now.

Second, this optimization test technique makes use of the Eval function. This function is one of the least understood functions in VBA, yet one of the most powerful. You can use Eval to execute a function that is named in a variable or some other expression. If you have programmed in a lower-level language such as C or Pascal, you probably miss Basic's absence of pointers to functions. You can use the Eval function to simulate this by passing a function name as a parameter to Eval. This technique calls Eval for both functions you type into the form.

Comments

When you are testing optimization techniques, watch out for a couple of things that can yield false results:

Both Access and Windows use caching algorithms to reduce disk writes. Any tests you perform that access objects from the database must take this into account. For example, if you are testing an optimization on form load time, your results can be erroneous if you perform the comparison of the two methods one after the other. The first time you load the form, Access caches it in memory if possible. The second time you load the form, the form will invariably load faster because Access is retrieving it from memory rather than disk, skewing your test results. There are several ways to get around the effects of caching—probably the simplest is to repeat all tests, reversing the order the second time you perform the test.

Windows is a multitasking operating system. Because of this, your test results may be further skewed by the fact that Windows may be performing some other operation in the background while one of your tests is running—for example, a word processing document may be automatically saved in the background in the middle of your test. The best way to minimize this factor is to ensure that no other Windows programs are running when you perform your tests. It is always a good idea to run the test several times and average the results.

COMPLEXITY:
ADVANCED

8.7 How do I...
Accelerate multiuser applications?

Problem

I have a single user application that I just converted to run on a network to be shared by multiple users. My once responsive application is now sluggish. How can I improve the performance of multiuser applications?

Technique

Moving a single user application to a shared environment can make that application much slower for at least three reasons. First, to read or write data from the database, the data must now travel across relatively slow network wires. This will almost always be slower than reading and writing data directly to a local hard disk drive. Second, every time a record is written to disk, Access must spend time obtaining, releasing, and managing locks to make sure that two users do not write to a page of records at the same time. Third, if multiple users are trying to access the same records in the database, they must wait their turn before they can gain access to the records. Because of these factors, you need to make an extra effort to optimize multiuser applications to bring their speed to an acceptable level. This How-To discusses one way to improve performance by limiting the number of records in your form's recordsets.

Steps

This How-To employs two files, 08-07FE.MDB and 08-07BE.MDB. Before you can try it, you'll need to link the data tables from 08-07BE.MDB (the "back-end" or data database) to 08-07FE.MDB (the "front-end" or application database). Linking a data table allows you to use a table from one Access database within another Access database. Start Access and load 08-07FE.MDB. Choose File|Get External Data|Link Tables and select 08-07BE.MDB as the Access link database. At the Link tables dialog box, select tblPeople and click OK. (To appreciate the extra demands made on a multiuser application, you may wish to move the 08-07BE database to a file server on your local area network.)

Splitting Multiuser Databases

This How-To makes use of a common multiuser technique: splitting the application and data into separate databases. Multiuser application performance can be improved considerably if you place the data or back-end database on the file server and a copy of the application or front-end database on each user's desktop. Access 95 includes the Database Splitter wizard, which makes it easy to split an existing database into data and application databases. Select Tools|Add-ins|Database Splitter to run the wizard.

Once you've fixed up the link to tblPeople in the back-end database, open the frmPeopleFindFirst form in form view and note how long it takes to load the form. Enter the value 60000 into the text box in the header of the form. Press the Goto Record button to move to the record with an ID of 60000. Note the time this operation takes, which is displayed to the right of the command button (see Figure 8-17). Now close the form and open the frmPeopleRSChange form in form view. This form is similar to frmPeopleFindFirst except that it initially loads with only one record in its recordset. Because of this, load time should be faster than for frmPeopleFindFirst. This form also differs in how it searches for records. Instead of using the potentially slow FindFirst method to navigate to a different record, it changes the record source of the form on the fly. Enter the value 60000 into the text box in the header of frmPeopleRSChange and press the Goto Record button as you did for the first form. Note the time this operation takes, which should be faster than for frmPeopleFindFirst (see Figure 8-18).

Although the performance difference between these two forms is noticeable with 60,000 records in the sample database, it's not that great. With more records or across a busy network, however, the difference will be much more significant.

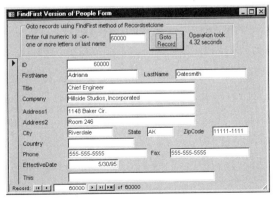

Figure 8-17 The frmPeopleFindFirst form

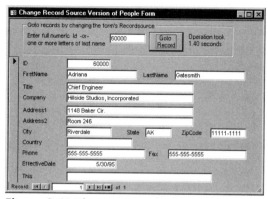

Figure 8-18 The more multiuser-friendly frmPeopleRSChange form

Follow these steps to create a form that uses the record source changing technique of frmPeopleRSChange:

1. Create a new form or edit an existing form in design view. Change the Record Source property of the form so that it initially loads no records. The easiest way to do this is to use a Select statement that restricts the record source by its primary key field to a nonexistent record. For example, we used the following record source for frmPeopleRSChange.

```
SELECT * FROM tblPeople WHERE ID = 0
```

This will cause Access to place you on the new record that's normally at the end of a form's recordset. If you prefer, you can use a Select statement that returns some small subset of the records instead.

2. Add an unbound text box named txtGoto to the form's header. Add a command button control named cmdGoto to the right of the text box.

3. Create a new event procedure for the Change event of the txtGoto text box. (If you're unsure how to do this, see How Do I Create an Event Procedure in the Introduction of this book.) Add the following code to the event procedure.

```
Private Sub txtGoto_Change()

    ' Enable cmdGoto only when a character
    ' has been typed into txtGoto

    Me!cmdGoto.Enabled = (Not IsNull(Me!txtGoto.Text))

End Sub
```

4. Create a new event procedure for the Click event of cmdGoto and add code similar to the following (or copy the cmdGoto_Click event procedure from frmPeopleRSChange; that event procedure has additional code that times the operation, which we eliminated here).

```
Private Sub cmdGoto_Click()

    ' Go to new record by changing
    ' the form's RecordSource property

    On Error GoTo cmdGotoClickErr

    Dim rstClone As Recordset
    Dim ctlGoto As TextBox
    Dim varCriteria As Variant

    Const ahtcQuote = """"

    Set ctlGoto = Me!txtGoto

    ' Create criteria based on type of data
    ' entered into txtGoto
    If IsNumeric(ctlGoto.Value) Then
        varCriteria = "ID = " & CLng(ctlGoto.Value)
    Else
        ' A string, so search LastName
        varCriteria = "LastName Like " & ahtcQuote & _
         ctlGoto.Value & "*" & ahtcQuote
    End If

    ' Change the form's recordset based on criteria
    Me.RecordSource = "SELECT * FROM tblPeople WHERE " & varCriteria

    ' Now clone the new form's recordset to check
    ' if any records are in it
    Set rstClone = Me.RecordsetClone

    With rstClone
        If .EOF And .BOF Then
            MsgBox "No matching record found.", _
             vbOKOnly + vbCritical, "Goto Procedure"
        End If
    End With

cmdGotoClickExit:
    Exit Sub

cmdGotoClickErr:
    Select Case Err.Number
    Case Else
        MsgBox "Error#" & Err.Number & ": " & Err.Description, _
         vbOKOnly + vbCritical, "Goto Procedure"
        Resume cmdGotoClickExit
    End Select

End Sub
```

See the How It Works section for information on how to customize this code for your particular form.

5. Save the form and switch to form view to test it.

How It Works

In a multiuser environment it's always important to limit the amount of data sent across the network to your desktop. By default, however, Access binds forms to all records in the table or query to which your form is bound. This is fine for smaller recordsets of perhaps less than 20,000 records (the exact cutoff figure will vary based on the speed of your PCs, the speed of your network cards and file server, and the average network load), but it can slow things to a crawl for even moderately large recordsets. This How-To improves the performance of the form and reduces network traffic considerably by carefully limiting the records in the form's recordset.

By using an SQL statement for the form's record source that initially returns no records, you can quickly open the form in append mode. When the user enters a value in the txtGoto text box and presses the Goto Record button, code attached to the button's Click event changes the form's RecordSource to the correct record.

The event procedure behind the cmdGoto command button begins by setting up an error handler, declaring a few variables, and setting ctlGoto to point to the txtGoto text box control.

```
On Error GoTo cmdGotoClickErr

Dim rstClone As Recordset
Dim ctlGoto As TextBox
Dim varCriteria As Variant

Const ahtQuote = """"

Set ctlGoto = Me!txtGoto
```

Next, the criteria of the SQL Select statement is constructed using this code:

```
' Create criteria based on type of data
' entered into txtGoto
If IsNumeric(ctlGoto.Value) Then
    varCriteria = "ID = " & CLng(ctlGoto.Value)
Else
    ' A string, so search LastName
    varCriteria = "LastName Like " & ahtQuote & _
    ctlGoto.Value & "*" & ahtQuote
End If
```

In the case of the people form, we decided to be flexible and allow users to search on either last name or ID. You'll want to make sure the fields you allow the user to search are indexed. We determine which field the user wishes to search by using the IsNumeric function to test if the entered value is a number. If so, then we construct criteria using the ID field of tblPeople. If the entered value is non-numeric, then we assume the user wishes to search on LastName. Again, we add a bit of flexibility by allowing the user to enter only partial matches. The criteria is then constructed using the Like operator. Because this is a Text field, we must surround the value with quotes. So we use the ahtcQuote constant that we defined earlier in the subprocedure. Finally, we have added "*" (an asterisk) before the closing quote to perform a pattern match search.

If you wish, you can simplify this code on your own form to use a single field. Even if you decide not to simplify the code, you'll need to change the references to ID and LastName to match the names of the fields (*not* the control names) in your form's record source. If you decide to allow a search on a date/time field, make sure you surround the date/time value with # (pound signs) instead of quotes.

With the criteria built, the SQL statement is easily created.

```
' Change the form's recordset based on criteria
Me.RecordSource = "SELECT * FROM tblPeople WHERE " & varCriteria
```

Of course, you'll need to replace tblPeople with the name of the table or query on which your form is based.

The remaining code determines if any records were found.

```
' Now clone the new form's recordset to check
' if any records are in it
Set rstClone = Me.RecordsetClone

With rstClone
    If .EOF And .BOF Then
        MsgBox "No matching record found.", _
        vbOKOnly + vbCritical, "Goto Procedure"
    End If
End With
```

This portion of code is not absolutely required because Access will pull up the "new" record if no matching records are found. We prefer, however, to notify the user that no records were found. This is accomplished by cloning the form's newly changed recordset to see if it contains any records. If no records are found, Access sets both the end of file (EOF) and beginning of file (BOF) flags to True, so we use this fact to test for the absence of records in the form's recordset.

Comments

A simple error handler is included in this procedure. It's important that you include error-handling code in all multiuser functions and subprocedures to handle the cases where records are locked. See Chapter 10 for more information on developing multiuser applications.

The one negative side to using this technique is that users may find it restrictive because they are used to navigating freely among a multitude of records using the navigation controls at the bottom of the form. The sample form allows users to grab a subset of records from tblPeople by entering a partial match on LastName. If you also need to return groups of records when using numeric primary key field searches, you can use two text boxes to allow users to search for a range of primary key values, perhaps including code that limits the range to some arbitrary number.

The techniques presented in this How-To apply equally to client/server applications. Additional optimization strategies for client/server applications are discussed in the next How-To.

COMPLEXITY:
ADVANCED

8.8 How do I...
Accelerate client/server applications?

Problem

I am using Access as a front-end to tables stored in a client/server database. I'm not satisfied with the response time of my client/server application. What can I do to make it run faster?

Technique

You can apply a variety of optimization techniques when developing client/server applications. If you are attaching remote tables in databases such as SQL Server or Oracle, you are accessing data through open database connectivity (ODBC) drivers. Typically, client/server applications using ODBC require more horsepower on the part of workstations and the network. By knowing how data is retrieved from the server, you can make your application run faster.

Steps

Here are suggestions to consider when optimizing your client/server application:

1. Your forms should retrieve as few records as possible when loading. Fetching data is one of the more significant bottlenecks in client/server applications. Design your form to retrieve few or no records by using the technique demonstrated in How-To 8.7.

2. Optimize the way your application connects to the server. When the user starts your application, log the user into the server using the OpenDatabase method. This establishes a connection and caches it in memory. Subsequent data access is faster because the connection has already been established. Use code that's similar to the following.

```
Sub PreConnectUser (strUser As String, strPass As String)
    Dim wrk As Workspace
    Dim db As Database
    Dim strConnect As Database

    strConnect = "ODBC;DSN=MyServer;DATABASE=dbCustomers;"
    strConnect = strConnect & "UID=" & strUser & ";"
    strConnect = strConnect & "PWD="  & strPass & ";"
    Set wrk = DBEngine.Workspaces(0)
    Set db = wrk.OpenDatabase("", False, False, strConnect)
End Sub
```

3. Reduce connections by limiting dynasets to 100 records or less. Most servers (such as SQL Server) require two connections for dynasets of more than 100 records. By limiting the size of the dynaset, you reduce the number of connections that need to be made, speeding up your application.

4. Offload as much query processing as possible to the server. Generally, your server will search and process data faster than the local Jet Engine (this is probably the reason you moved to client/server in the first place). Design your queries to eliminate expressions or functionality not supported by the server. If an expression or functionality used in the query is not supported by the server, Access will process the query locally and performance will suffer. Read the documentation that comes with your database server to determine which functionality is supported.

5. Use transactions when updating records. In How-To 8.5, you learned how to use Access transactions to optimize updates and inserts of data using VBA code. This becomes even more important in client/server applications. It is usually significantly faster to have Access buffer updates in transaction memory rather than sending all changes across the network. Note that although Access supports five levels of transaction nesting on local tables, it doesn't support nesting on ODBC tables. Only the top-level transaction is passed to the server.

6. Add a time-stamp field to a table to improve update and deletion performance. If a table has a time-stamp field, Access can use it to see if a record has changed. If the table doesn't have this field, Access needs to compare the contents of every field to see if the record has changed. Obviously, checking a single field is a lot faster. To add a time-stamp field to a table on the server, create and execute an SQL-specific query using the ALTER TABLE statement with syntax similar to the following.

```
ALTER TABLE Customers ADD TimeStampCol TIMESTAMP
```

7. Avoid using server data to fill list box and combo box controls. The performance of these controls is generally poor when accessing server data. Consider, instead, storing the data for the list box or combo box in a local database. This approach works if the data does not change frequently and can be easily copied from the server. See How-To 8.2 for more on list box and combo box performance issues and alternatives to their use.

8. Explicitly cache server data in your VBA code. Datasheets and forms automatically cache server data, but recordsets created by your VBA code do not. In addition to using transactions to cache data, use the FillCache method of the recordset object. For example, say you have code that finds all customers with a specific value in a field and updates another field accordingly. You can make

the code run faster by finding the first matching records and starting a cache
at that point in the dynaset, as shown here.

```
Dim wrk As Workspace
Dim db As Database
Dim strConnect As Database
Dim rstCustomers As Recordset

strConnect = "ODBC;DSN=MyServer;DATABASE=dbCustomers;"
strConnect = strConnect & "UID=" & strUser & ";"
strConnect = strConnect & "PWD="  & strPass & ";"
Set wrk = DBEngine.Workspaces(0)
Set db = wrk.OpenDatabase("", False, False, strConnect)
Set rstCustomers = db.OpenRecordset("tblCustomers", _
 dbOpenDynaset)

rstCustomers.FindFirst "[OrdersToDate] > 100000"
If Not rstCustomer.NoMatch Then
   rstCustomers.FillCache rstCustomers.Bookmark, 100
   Do Until rstCustomer.EOF
      If rstCustomers![OrdersToDate] > 100000 Then
         rstCustomers.Edit
            rstCustomers![Status] = "Priority Customer"
         rstCustomers.Update
      End If
      rstCustomers.MoveNext
   Loop
End If
```

In this code, the FillCache method does two things: It initializes a cache to
hold 100 records and it loads 100 records into the cache starting at the first
matching record. Experiment with the cache size to determine the optimal
balance between memory use and performance. Obviously a large setting may
make the code run slower because more records are being retrieved.

9. If you are making a single pass through read-only data, use a forward-scrolling
snapshot recordset. For example:

```
Set rstCustomers = db.OpenRecordset ("tblCustomers", _
_dbOpenSnapshot, dbForwardOnly)
```

By specifying this option, you are telling Access to eliminate the scroll buffer
that is usually created for regular snapshots. This scroll buffer is a mechanism
that stores previously accessed records in a cache.

How It Works

Understanding how client/server applications differ from single-user and file-server
applications is crucial to optimizing their performance. The key is in deciding when
to let Access do the work and when to let the server do the work. With a few excep-
tions, you want the server to perform queries and Access to perform user-interface operations. Concentrate on minimizing the traffic across the network by reducing the data
retrieved from and written to the server. If your application uses VBA code to access

data, remember that automatic optimizations and caching employed by datasheets and forms are not available. You must explicitly write your code to optimize and cache data-access operations.

Comments

A good reference source for additional optimization ideas is the Microsoft Jet Database Engine ODBC Connectivity white paper written by Neil Black and Stephen Hecht. We included a copy of this white paper on the CD that accompanies this book. See the About the CD section in the front of this book for more details.

Microsoft's SQL Server Upsizing Tools

If you're planning on migrating an Access-only application to a client/server front-end application that accesses Microsoft SQL Server 6.0, you should get a copy of the Microsoft Access Upsizing Tools. These tools, which should be available during the first quarter of 1996, will give you a leg-up in upsizing Access applications to Microsoft SQL Server. The tools include the Upsizing Wizard, which eases the upsizing process, and a valuable user guide that includes a chapter on client/server optimization techniques.

CHAPTER 9

MAKING THE MOST OF
YOUR USER INTERFACE

MAKING THE
MOST OF YOUR
USER INTERFACE

How do I...

No matter how much you do behind the scenes to create a solid and robust application, what the users of your application see is your user interface. Certainly, perfecting the database and application design is crucial—but once that's done it pays to devote considerable time to designing a user interface that is workable, aesthetically pleasing, and helps the users get their work done. By implementing the ideas and techniques in this chapter, you'll be on your way to creating an interface that has ease of use and learning written all over it.

You'll learn how to take full advantage of special keystrokes to help users navigate through a complex application. You'll also learn how to create forms—or entire applications—that have no menus and create a map-based interface that lets users navigate by pointing to and clicking on various parts of a map. You'll also discover how to dress up your application with specially formatted message boxes and animated buttons.

You'll learn how to ease data entry pain with forms that let users mark their place while they peruse other records and forms that carry forward data from record to record. You'll see how to hide complexity from your users using a dialog box that expands on request to reveal complex options. You'll also see how to use a combo box not just to select from a list but to maintain that list with new entries as they are needed.

Finally, you'll learn how to create and use two generic, reusable components: a pop-up calendar form for entering dates that makes use of an OLE custom control and a custom-built status meter form complete with an optional Cancel button.

9.1 Create Context-Sensitive Keyboard Shortcuts

The AutoKeys macro allows you to assign keyboard shortcuts to perform specific tasks, but you may run out of special keystrokes and need to reuse some. This How-To will demonstrate how to use a nearly limitless number of AutoKeys macros that are context-sensitive on a form-by-form basis.

9.2 Create a Form with No Menus

The Access built-in menus are nice, but sometimes it would be nicer if you could eliminate menus entirely from a form to reduce user confusion. This How-To will show how to use a simple trick to make Access eliminate menus for either a form or the entire application.

9.3 Create a Geographical Map Interface

Many applications manage large amounts of data organized around states, countries, or regions and users work on records for one geographical region at a time. One way to allow selection of a region is to use a combo box. This How-To will illustrate a more visual, map-based interface in which users click on a section of the map to indicate which geographical region they are interested in working with.

9.4 Create Formatted Message Boxes like the Built-In Ones

You may have noticed that Access creates built-in message boxes that contain specially formatted messages that might include a bolded heading, one or more lines of unbolded text, a bolded Solution heading, and additional unbolded text. In addition, many built-in message boxes include a Help button. This How-To will show how to create message boxes that look and work just like Access' message boxes—with formatted messages and context-sensitive Help buttons.

9.5   Mark a Record on a Form and Return to It Later

A book has a nice familiar user interface: You place a bookmark on a page and then thumb ahead to peruse some other page of the book, returning to the page you marked by using the earlier-deposited bookmark. Why not create a form in Access that lets you mark your place and return to it later? This How-To will demonstrate a technique that lets users press a toggle button to mark a record, navigate to some other record, and then return to the earlier marked record by unpressing the toggle button—much like using a bookmark.

9.6   Carry Forward Data from Record to Record

Much of the motivation for spending time on user interface design is to make your application more usable and to ease the burden placed on the application's users. What can be more of a hassle than to reenter repetitive data on multiple records? This How-To will show how to add a series of tiny toggle buttons to your form along with some VBA code that lets your users determine, on a field-by-field basis, which values should be carried forward to newly added records.

9.7   Create a Combo Box That Accepts New Entries

Combo boxes are often the perfect control to use for choosing from a defined list of values. But what happens when you want to support the addition of new items to the combo box's row source? This How-To will show how to use the NotInList event to trap for a new entry, pop up a form to gather more information, and have the new entry automatically added to the combo box's list.

9.8   Create Animated Buttons

Animated buttons can add pizzazz to your application. This How-To will explain the use of the PictureData property to create animated buttons. You'll learn how to create two-state buttons that look different when you click them and cyclic buttons that run a continuous animation for as long as your form is open.

9.9   Create an Expanding Dialog Box

One way to keep your application easy to use is to hide unnecessary information from your users until it's needed. The Access Startup properties dialog box demonstrates one technique for hiding information: It keeps its advanced options on a section of the form that is hidden until the Advanced button is clicked. This How-To will show how to design a similar expanding dialog box for your own applications and how to manage the switch from the compressed to expanded state and back again.

9.10   Use an OLE Custom Control

Access 95 includes robust support for new 32-bit custom controls. This How-To will show how to use the Calendar custom control that ships in the box with Access to make entry of dates a snap. You'll learn how to use this custom control in both bound and unbound modes and how to use it to create a generic, reusable pop-up calendar form.

9.11 Create a Generic, Reusable Status Meter Form

Users need feedback during long operations. You can use Access' built-in status meter created with the SysCmd function, but this status meter isn't very flexible: You can't move it to a custom position on your screen or change its color or size. This How-To will demonstrate how to create and use a generic, reusable status meter form with an optional Cancel button you can call anytime you need a status meter for giving user feedback during long operations.

COMPLEXITY:
EASY

9.1 How do I...
Create context-sensitive keyboard shortcuts?

Problem

I've used Access' AutoKeys macro to create keyboard shortcuts for my application, but I'd like the shortcut keys to change based on the currently active form. Is there any easy way to create context-sensitive keyboard shortcuts in Access?

Technique

The SetOption method of the Application object allows you to change global database options programmatically. This How-To will show you how to combine this functionality with the Activate and Deactivate event properties of your forms to create custom key shortcut macros for each form of your application.

Steps

Open 09-01.MDB. This sample database contains information on units, assemblies that make up parts, and parts that make up assemblies. Open the frmUnit form in form view. At any time you can press `CTRL`-`D` to "drilldown" to the next level of detail or `CTRL`-`R` to revert to the previous level of detail. When you press `CTRL`-`D` on frmUnit, frmAssembly is loaded. But if you press `CTRL`-`D` from frmAssembly, frmPart is loaded. If you press `CTRL`-`D` a third time while frmPart has the focus, nothing happens. Thus, the behavior of `CTRL`-`D` changes based on its context. The `CTRL`-`R` keyboard macro is similarly context sensitive.

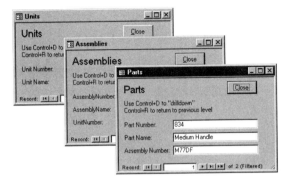

Figure 9-1 The sample database after pressing CTRL-D twice

> **Note**
>
> To keep the example simple, we have not added the additional macro code necessary to keep the forms synchronized. You must manually use CTRL-R to revert, navigate to the desired record, and then CTRL-D to drilldown if you wish to keep the forms synchronzied.

To add context-sensitive AutoKeys macros to your own application, follow these steps:

1. Create a key assignment macro for each form in your application (you can use the same macro for more than one form if you like). Follow all the design rules for an AutoKeys macro, but give your macro a unique name when you are done. In the sample application, for instance, the three key assignment macros are called mcrUnitAutoKeys, mcrAssemblyAutoKeys, and mcrPartAutoKeys, so that the macro name reminds you of its function. Table 9-1 shows the settings for the mcrUnitAutoKeys macro.

MACRO NAME	ACTION	ARGUMENT	VALUE
^D	OpenForm	Form Name	frmAssembly
		View	Form
		Where Condition	[UnitNumber]=[Forms]![frmUnit]![UnitNumber]
		Data Mode	Edit
		Window Mode	Normal
^R	Close	Object Type	Form
		Object Name	frmUnit

Table 9-1 Macro actions for mcrUnitAutoKeys

You'll probably want to add comments to your macro to make it easier to understand and maintain, as illustrated in Figure 9-2.

2. Import the basOptions module from 09-01.MDB into your own database.

3. Add a RunCode action to your AutoExec macro (or create a new macro named AutoExec containing this one action). Set the action's function name argument to:

```
=ahtStoreOriginalAutoKeys()
```

4. In the OnActivate event property of each of your forms, add a call to the function ahtSetAutoKeys. This function takes a single argument: the name of the key assignment macro to use while that form is active. For example, on the frmUnit form in the sample application, this property is set to:

```
=ahtSetAutokeys("mcrUnitAutokeys")
```

5. In the OnClose event of the *last* form to be closed in your application (typically, this is your main switchboard form), add a call to the function ahtRestoreOriginalAutokeys. If there is more than one possible last form in your application, you'll need to add this function call to *every possible* last form. The ahtRestoreOriginalAutokeys function takes no arguments. Figure 9-3 shows these calls in the sample application.

How It Works

The special built-in Application object refers to your entire Access application. The GetOption method of this object lets you read any of the options stored under Tools|Options, Tools|Startup, and additional options that are only available programmatically. The "Key Assignment Macro" option, which was part of the View|Options dialog box in Access 2.0, is no longer available from the Access user interface. Fortunately, it is still available programmatically.

Because the database options are stored in the user's system database, any changes you make to them will affect not only the current database but also any other database the user runs. It's best to always store the original value of any option you change and restore it when your application is closed. The ahtStoreOriginalAutokeys

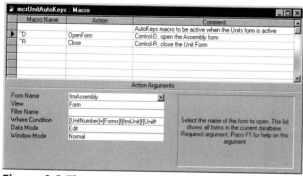

Figure 9-2 The mcrUnitAutoKeys macro

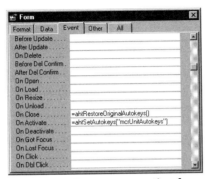

Figure 9-3 Event properties for frmUnit

function uses the GetOption method to read the original key assignment macro name when your application is loaded and store it in the mstrOriginalAutokeys module-level variable. Like the rest of the functions in this How-To, ahtStoreOriginalAutokeys is very simple, consisting of only one statement, a few comments, and an error handler.

```
Dim mstrOriginalAutokeys As String

Function ahtStoreOriginalAutokeys()

    ' Store the user's original Autokeys macro name
    ' so we can restore it when we're done

    On Error GoTo ahtStoreOriginalAutokeys_Err

    mstrOriginalAutokeys = Application.GetOption("Key Assignment Macro")

ahtStoreOriginalAutokeys_Exit:
    Exit Function

ahtStoreOriginalAutokeys_Err:
    MsgBox "Error " & Err.Number & ": " & Err.Description, _
      vbExclamation, "ahtStoreOriginalAutokeys"
    Resume ahtStoreOriginalAutokeys_Exit
End Function
```

The ahtRestoreOriginalAutokeys function resets the option to its original value. This function should be called from the last open form. In the sample database, it is called from the Close event of frmUnit.

```
Function ahtRestoreOriginalAutokeys()

    ' Put the Autokeys macro setting back the way we found it.

    On Error GoTo ahtRestoreOriginalAutokeys_Err

    Application.SetOption "Key Assignment Macro", mstrOriginalAutokeys
```

continued on next page

continued from previous page

```
ahtRestoreOriginalAutokeys_Exit:
    Exit Function

ahtRestoreOriginalAutokeys_Err:
    MsgBox "Error " & Err.Number & ": " & Err.Description, _
    vbExclamation, "ahtRestoreOriginalAutokeys"
    Resume ahtRestoreOriginalAutokeys_Exit
End Function
```

Each form passes the name of its custom key assignment macro to the ahtSetAutokeys function when the form is activated. This is done by calling this function from the Activate event of the form. This function uses the SetOption method to take the passed macro and make it the key assignment macro.

```
Function ahtSetAutokeys(strMacroName As String)

    ' Set a new Autokeys macro. Takes the name of the
    ' macro to use for keyboard reassignment.

    On Error GoTo ahtSetAutokeys_Err

    Application.SetOption "Key Assignment Macro", strMacroName

ahtSetAutokeys_Exit:
    Exit Function

ahtSetAutokeys_Err:
    MsgBox "Error " & Err.Number & ": " & Err.Description, _
    vbExclamation, "ahtSetAutokeys"
    Resume ahtSetAutokeys_Exit

End Function
```

Comments

You can generalize this technique of using GetOption and SetOption to control many properties of your application at runtime; for example, to turn the status bar and toolbars on or off, selectively refuse DDE requests, or allow the user to pick a new font for datasheets from a list you supply. You should always follow the same basic three steps:

1. Use GetOption to read the current option value and save it in a module-level variable.

2. Use SetOption to set your new value. Be sure to use the name of the option exactly as it appears in the Access on-line help.

3. Use SetOption to restore the original value when your application is closed.

Overlapping User Interface (UI) Methods

In a well-designed Windows application, keyboard shortcuts should not be the *only* method a user can employ to accomplish a task. Because they are hard for new users to discover or for infrequent users to remember, keyboard shortcuts should only be used as an alternative method of accomplishing a task. Make the task available from some other UI method, preferably one that is more easily discovered than a keyboard shortcut. Other UI methods include command buttons, toolbar buttons, standard menus, and shortcut menus.

To reduce the time delay in switching key assignment macros, we decided to reset the user's key assignment macro only when the last open form is closed. A safer but perhaps slower alternative would be to reset the key assignment macro in the Deactivate event of each form.

Detecting when a User Closes an Application

There is no built-in way to have Access always run a cleanup routine when the user closes your application. The final event you can trap is the last form's closing. If there are multiple possible last forms, you must make sure you check when any of them closes to see whether it is actually the last form. As an alternative, you can open a hidden form in your AutoExec macro and call your cleanup processing from this form's Close event. Access will automatically close this form when the user exits, and since this was the first form opened, it will be the last form closed.

The individual calls to the ahtSetAutoKeys function are attached to the forms' Activate events rather than their GotFocus events for a very good reason. Unless there are no controls on a form that can get the focus, the form itself will *never* receive the focus. Only forms consisting strictly of graphic objects and disabled controls will ever trigger a form-level GotFocus event.

COMPLEXITY:
EASY

9.2   How do I...
Create a form with no menus?

Problem

I know I can customize the menus displayed on a form using the Menu Bar property of the form, but sometimes I'd like to disable menus for a form completely. Is there any way to remove menus from a form?

Technique

If you set the Menu Bar property of a form to point to a macro in Access that contains no macro actions, you can trick Access into not displaying any menus. This How-To demonstrates this trick and also discusses how you can apply this same trick to the global menus of an application.

Steps

Load the 09-02.MDB sample database. Open the frmCustomerDefaultMenus form in form view and note that the default Access menus are available at the top of the screen (see Figure 9-4). Close this form and open frmCustomerNoMenus. Note the absence of any menus for the form (see Figure 9-5).

To create forms in your database without any menus, follow these steps:

1. Create a new macro sheet without any actions. The mcrNoMenus macro sheet in 09-02.MDB has no macro actions.

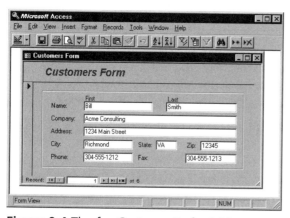

Figure 9-4 The frmCustomerDefaultMenus
form with the default Access menu bar

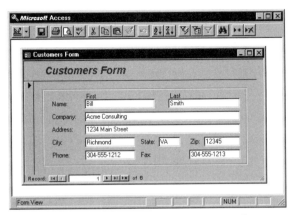

Figure 9-5 The frmCustomerNoMenus form
with no menu bar

2. Create a new form or open an existing form in design view. Select the menu macro from step 1 as the Menu Bar property for the form.

3. Optionally, you may wish to also eliminate right-click shortcut menus for your form. To do this, set the Shortcut Menu Bar property of the form to No.

4. Save the form.

How It Works

You create custom menus in Access by creating menu macros—either manually or, more typically, by using the Menu Builder. The result is a series of macros containing AddMenu, DoMenuItem, RunMacro, and RunCode macro actions. When you open a form with custom menus, Access reconstructs the custom menus from the hierarchy of macros attached to the form's Menu Bar property. But if you attach an empty macro to the Menu Bar property, Access won't create any menus for the form.

Comments

You may want to eliminate menus for a form to reduce the complexity of your application or remove potential chinks in your application's armor. Whenever you remove built-in functionality from forms, however, you must ensure that users of your forms can still perform essential activities. For example, you wouldn't want to remove menus and set the Control Box and Close Button properties of your form to No *unless* you also added either a toolbar button or a command button that could be used to close the form. Another alternative is to use the Menu Builder to create custom menus that contain only a few of the built-in menu items.

In addition to removing menus for a single form, you can set the application's default menu bar to point to an empty macro. Access uses the default menus on all forms on

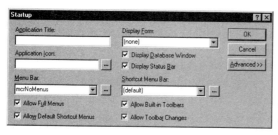

Figure 9-6 You can customize various default properties using the Startup dialog box

which you have not explicitly set a Menu Bar property. Select Tools|Startup to set the default menu bar. In Figure 9-6, we set the default Menu Bar property of the Startup dialog box to mcrNoMenus, thus removing menus for all forms in the application for which custom menus were not created. Another option is to uncheck the Allow Full Menus property. If you uncheck this startup property, Access will remove all menu commands that allow users to switch to design views.

You can also customize the default shortcut menus using the Startup dialog box by changing the Allow Default Shortcut Menus and Shortcut Menu Bar properties.

COMPLEXITY:
EASY

9.3   How do I...
Create a geographical map interface?

Problem

I want to display a map and allow users to click on regions of the map. I want the form to react based on the region clicked on. The regions aren't necessarily rectangular. How can I do this in Access?

Technique

You can accomplish this task using a combination of bitmaps and transparent command buttons. Depending on how far from rectangular your shapes are, this task may be trivial or quite involved. By making the command buttons transparent, you make the application appear to react directly to mouse clicks on the map.

Steps

Open frmWesternUS in 09-03.MDB (Figure 9-7). This form has been created with an imported bitmap file as the background. Above each state's image on the map there's at least one command button with its Transparent property set to Yes. Figure 9-8 shows the form named frmWesternUSDesign, in which the buttons haven't yet had their

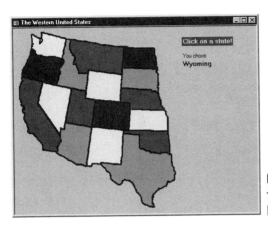

Figure 9-7 The finished map form, frmWesternUS, with transparent buttons

Transparent property set to Yes. Here you can see the actual layout of the command buttons.

To implement similar functionality on your own form, follow these steps:

1. Create a new form, click anywhere in the detail section of the form, and select the Insert|Object (or use the form design toolbox to place an unbound object frame control form on the form). Once you release the mouse button, Access displays a dialog box requesting information about the object. At this point you can create a new object by launching an application such as Microsoft Paint or you can create an object from an existing file. If you choose the latter, a Browse button will appear. Click on the Browse button to select a file (see Figure 9-9.) Choose the appropriate image for the background. For the example form, use USWEST.BMP.

2. Set the bitmap's SizeMode property to Clip. This disallows resizing of the bitmap because you'll be overlaying the bitmap with command buttons.

3. Overlay each defined area of the bitmap with a command button, naming each as desired. Figure 9-8 shows the completed process for the sample form.

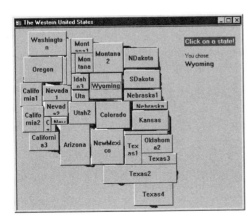

Figure 9-8 The same bitmap form with buttons showing

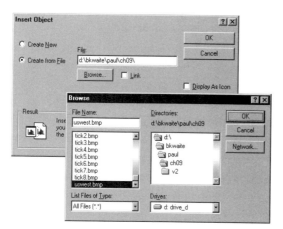

Figure 9-9 Browsing a file from the Insert
Object dialog box

You'll find that for odd-shaped regions, you'll need to use multiple buttons; as
demonstrated for Idaho, Texas, and Nevada on the map.

Use the Keyboard for Exact Placement

The (SHIFT-ARROW) and (CTRL-ARROW) keys are helpful in achieving
exact placement of the command buttons. Use the (SHIFT-ARROW)
keys to expand and contract the size of a control 1 pixel at a time;
use the (CTRL-ARROW) keys to move the control 1 pixel at a time.

---

4. Select all the command buttons (hold the (SHIFT) key down and click on
each.) On the properties sheet, set the Transparent property to Yes, making the
selected controls invisible yet active. Figure 9-10 shows the sample form in
design view; note that in design view you can still see a faint outline of each
button.

5. For each transparent command button, call a function, passing it the name
that describes the defined area (in this example, it's the name of the selected
U.S. state) from the button's OnClick event property. For example, the
OnClick event property for the command button overlaying the state of
Wyoming calls the HandleStateClick function, passing it "Wyoming":

```
=HandleStateClick("Wyoming")
```

6. Create the function called in step 5. This function can be either in the form's
module (as we have created) or in a global module. It's up to you to decide
what to do with the information passed to the function. In the sample form,

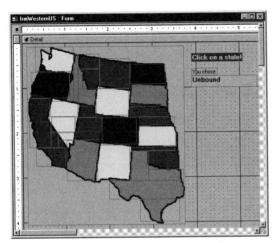

Figure 9-10 The sample map form in design mode

the name of the state is passed to an unbound text box. The HandleStateClick function is shown here.

```
Function HandleStateClick(strState As String)
    Me!txtChosenState = strState
End Function
```

How It Works

Because each button has its Transparent property set to Yes—which is very different from having its Visible property set to No—it's still active. You can click on transparent buttons and they can react to events. Each transparent button corresponds to some physical region on the bitmap, so you can have the buttons' Click event procedures react according to their location on the bitmap. If only Windows supported irregularly shaped command buttons!

Comments

The size of the bitmap is key to the effectiveness of this technique. If you lay out the buttons all over the bitmap and then decide to resize it, your buttons' locations will no longer be correct. Make sure that you've fixed the size of the bitmap before you start laying down buttons. Although you can select all the buttons and resize them as a group, this is not a perfect solution.

Don't spend too much time getting the transparent buttons placed exactly. On the example form, the buttons' placement is fairly concise, but that works only because most of the states in the west are generally rectangular (you'll notice that there's no eastern seaboard on the map). Users will typically click in the center of the region, so covering each pixel on the edge isn't a serious concern.

COMPLEXITY:
EASY

9.4   How do I...
Create formatted message boxes like the built-in ones?

Problem

Access often displays formatted message boxes that include bolded text and a Solution section (see Figure 9-11). I'd like to be able to use this type of message box in my applications, too. Is there any way to create these specially formatted message boxes without creating a separate form for each message box?

Technique

The Access MsgBox macro action and the VBA MsgBox function support a new Access 95 feature that allows you to create formatted message boxes. You use @ characters in the message parameter (which is called the prompt parameter in VBA) to designate various sections of the formatted message. This How-To shows you how to use this undocumented feature to produce formatted message boxes that look similar to Access built-in message boxes. It also shows you how to include an optional Help button in your message box that can call context-sensitive custom help.

Steps

Load the 09-04.MDB database. Run the mcrMBText macro by double-clicking on the macro name in the database explorer. Access displays a message box with simple unbolded text, as shown in Figure 9-12. Now run the mcrMBHeadingTextSolution macro. Access displays a formatted message box with a bolded heading, unbolded text, the bolded Solution heading, and unbolded solution text, as shown in Figure 9-13.

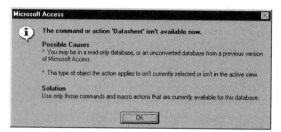

Figure 9-11 A built-in formatted message box

Figure 9-12 A standard message box

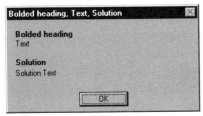

Figure 9-13 A formatted
message box

Follow these steps to produce message boxes using special formatting:

1. Create a new macro sheet or open an existing macro sheet in design view. Add a MsgBox action to the macro sheet.

2. Add text to the Message parameter in the following format.

Heading@Text@Solution text

3. Complete the remaining MsgBox parameters as desired.

4. Save the macro sheet. Call the macro from a form or report's event property.

How It Works

By using two @ characters in the Message parameter of the MsgBox action, you indicate to Access to format your message in a special format. Table 9-2 shows the various combinations that can be used, the result, and the name of the sample macro in 09-04.MDB that demonstrates use of the syntax.

MESSAGE	RESULT	SAMPLE MACRO
text	Simple message box with unbolded *text*.	mcrMBText
heading@text@	Bolded *heading*, new line, unbolded *text*.	mcrMBHeadingText
heading@@solution text	Bolded *heading*, blank line, "Solution" in bold, new line, unbolded *solution text*.	mcrMBHeadingSolution
@text@solution text	Unbolded *text*, blank line, "Solution" in bold, new line, unbolded *solution text*.	mcrMBTextSolution
@@solution text	"Solution" in bold, new line, unbolded *solution text*.	mcrMBSolution
heading@text@solution text	Bolded *heading*, new line, unbolded *text*, blank line, "Solution" in bold, new line, unbolded *solution text*.	mcrMBHeadingTextSolution
@text@	Same as "text".	(none)
text@@	Same as "text".	(none)

Table 9-2 Formatted message box formats

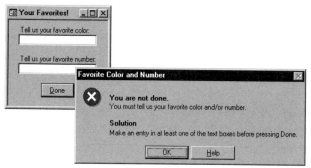

Figure 9-14 frmFavorites displays this message box when no data has been entered

Comments

You can use the same formatting when calling the MsgBox function from VBA code. The frmFavorites form in 09-04.MDB includes code behind the form that displays the formatted message box shown in Figure 9-14 whenever you click on the Done command button with Null entries for both text boxes.

The code behind the cmdDone command button is shown here.

```
Private Sub cmdDone_Click()

    Dim strMsg As String
    Dim strHeading As String
    Dim strExplain As String
    Dim strSolution As String
    Dim intOptions As Integer

    If IsNull(txtFavColor) And IsNull(txtFavNumber) Then
        strHeading = "You are not done."
        strExplain = "You must tell us your favorite color " & _
        "and/or number."
        strSolution = "Make an entry in at least one of the " & _
        "text boxes before pressing Done."
        strMsg = strHeading & "@" & strExplain & "@" & strSolution
        intOptions = vbCritical + vbOKOnly
        MsgBox strMsg, intOptions, "Favorite Color and Number", _
        GetDBDir & "09-04.HLP", 10
    Else
        DoCmd.Close acForm, Me.Name
    End If

End Sub
```

> **MsgBox Help**
>
> The cmdDone_Click event procedure demonstrates another new feature of Access 95. If you've created custom help for your application, you can add a Help button to your message box and hook this button into a context ID of your custom help file using two additional optional MsgBox parameters: helpfile and context. To try this out, copy the 09-04.HLP file to the same directory as the sample database.

COMPLEXITY:
INTERMEDIATE

9.5   How do I...
Mark a record on a form and return to it later?

Problem

Sometimes I get interrupted when I'm in the middle of editing a record on a form and need to move quickly to some other record. I'd like a way to save my place and easily return to it later. Is there any easy way to do this in Access?

Technique

Access forms have a bookmark property that is very similar to the bookmark we use when we want to put a book down but quickly return to it later where we left off. This How-To will show how to use VBA code to store the bookmark value of a particular record and return to it, exposing this functionality to your users using a toggle button.

Steps

Load the 09-05.MDB database, opening the frmCustomer form, which contains 500 customer records. Navigate to a record and begin to make a change to it. For example, in Figure 9-15, we made some edits to Russell Dunham's record. Click on the Save Place toggle button in the form's header to mark the current record and save your place in the recordset. The toggle button will remain depressed and its caption will change to Return to Saved Place (see Figure 9-16). Now navigate to some other record. Click a second time on the toggle button and you will return instantly to the earlier "marked" record.

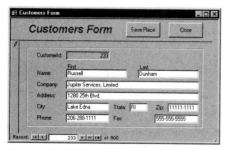

Figure 9-15 The frmCustomer form before marking the current record

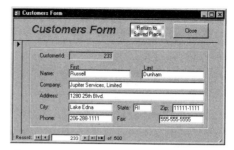

Figure 9-16 The frmCustomer form after marking the current record

Mark the record again and navigate to yet another record. Perhaps this time you have changed your mind and wish to abandon the earlier marked record in favor of the current one. But if you press the toggle button a second time, you will return to the previously marked record, losing your "new" place. You can remedy this situation by right-clicking while the mouse cursor is over the toggle button control. A shortcut menu will appear giving you the option to abandon the previously marked record (see Figure 9-17). Select this option and you'll now be able to mark the current record instead.

Follow these steps to add this capability to your own forms:

1. Create a new bound form or open an existing form in design view. Add a toggle button (*not* a command button) control to the form's header or footer section. In the frmCustomer sample form, we named our button tglMark and added it to the header section.

2. Create an event procedure attached to the Click event of the toggle button. (If you're unsure how to do this, see the How Do I Create an Event Procedure section in the Introduction of this book.) Add the following code to the event procedure.

```
Private Sub tglMark_Click()

    ' If toggle button is depressed, then
    ' mark this record; otherwise return
    ' to previously saved record.
    If Me!tglMark Then
        Call ahtHandleMarkReturn(ahtcMark)
    Else
        Call ahtHandleMarkReturn(ahtcReturn)
    End If

End Sub
```

3. Add the following constants to the Declarations section of the form's module (if the form's module is not currently displayed, select View|Code from design view of the form).

```
Const ahtcMark = 1
Const ahtcReturn = 2
Const ahtcDiscard = 3
```

4. Add the following public function to the form's module.

```
Public Function ahtHandleMarkReturn(intAction As Integer)

    Static svarPlaceHolder As Variant

    With Me!tglMark
        Select Case intAction
        Case ahtcMark
            ' Mark record position
            svarPlaceHolder = Me.Bookmark
            .Caption = "Return to Saved Place"
        Case ahtcReturn
            ' Return to marked position
            Me.Bookmark = svarPlaceHolder
            .Caption = "Save Place"
        Case ahtcDiscard
            ' Reset marked position
            ' and unpress button
            svarPlaceHolder = Empty
            .Caption = "Save Place"
            .Value = False
        Case Else
            ' Shouldn't happen
            MsgBox "Unexpected value for intAction", _
            vbCritical + vbOKOnly, "ahtHandleMarkReturn"
        End Select
    End With

End Function
```

5. Create a macro sheet with a single action, as shown in Table 9-3. In the sample database, we named this macro sheet mcrCustomerShortcutMenu. The value entered as the Menu Macro Name parameter will need to correspond with the name of the macro you create in the next step. Save and close the macro sheet.

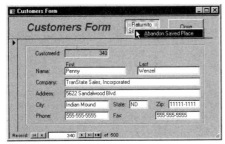

Figure 9-17 The toggle button's shortcut (right-click) menu

MACRO NAME	ACTION	ARGUMENT	VALUE
(blank)	AddMenu	Menu Name	ShortcutMenu
		Menu Macro Name	mcrCustomerShortcutMenu_Bar
		Status Bar Text	*(blank)*

Table 9-3 The mcrCustomerShortcutMenu menu macro

6. Create a second macro sheet, again with a single action, as shown in Table 9-4. The 3 parameter corresponds to the ahtcDiscard constant created in step 3. Save the macro sheet, naming it the same name as the Menu Macro Name parameter you used in step 5.

MACRO NAME	ACTION	ARGUMENT	VALUE
&Abandon Saved Place	RunCode	Function Name	ahtHandleMarkReturn(3)

Table 9-4 The mcrCustomerShortcutMenu_Bar menu macro

7. Reopen the form created earlier. If the properties sheet is not visible, Select View|Properties. Click on the toggle button and select the macro created in step 5 for the Shortcut Menu Bar property of the control. For example, we selected the mcrCustomerShortcutMenu macro for frmCustomer in Figure 9-18.

8. Save the form and verify that it works correctly.

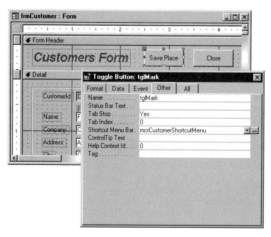

Figure 9-18 The Shortcut Menu Bar property for tglMark

How It Works

The mark and return facility built into the frmCustomer form has several interesting user interface (UI) aspects. First, you use a toggle button as the main user interface element. This control type is ideally suited for this situation because it is able to store binary state information that visually matches the two states you wish to represent (mark and return). Second, the shortcut menu, although a little less discoverable than the toggle button, allows you to offer the extra "abandon" functionality without taking up a lot of screen real estate.

The actual code that implements the mark and return facility is small and basically revolves around grabbing the form's bookmark property and storing it between calls to the ahtHandleMarkReturn function. This is handled by the Select Case statement in ahtHandleMarkReturn.

```
With Me!tglMark
    Select Case intAction
    Case ahtcMark
        ' Mark record position
        svarPlaceHolder = Me.Bookmark
        .Caption = "Return to Saved Place"
    Case ahtcReturn
        ' Return to marked position
        svarPlaceHolder = Empty
        Me.Bookmark = svarPlaceHolder
        .Caption = "Save Place"
    Case ahtcDiscard
        ' Reset marked position
        ' and unpress button
        svarPlaceHolder = Empty
        .Caption = "Save Place"
        .Value = False
    Case Else
        ' Shouldn't happen
        MsgBox "Unexpected value for intAction", _
            vbCritical + vbOKOnly, "ahtHandleMarkReturn"
    End Select
End With
```

The ahtcMark (1) case is executed when the user depresses the toggle button, so the code stores away the bookmark in the svarPlaceHolder static variable and changes the caption to indicate the new state of the button. Notice that we used a static variable rather than a module-level global variable. A static variable is a better choice in this situation because we are changing the value of the variable only within this one function.

When called with the ahtcReturn constant value (2), the code sets the form's bookmark to the previously stored value, clears svarPlaceHolder, and resets the caption to the default.

Bookmarks

A bookmark is an Access-maintained string variable that points to the current record of an open recordset (or in the case of the form's bookmark, the current record of a form's recordset). Bookmarks only make sense within the lifetime of the currently open recordset (or form). If you requery or close and rerun the query or form, the set of bookmarks will be different. A bookmark is not a record number, it's a dynamically created handle (or pointer) to the current record.

Finally, when called with the ahtcDiscard constant value (3), the code clears svarPlaceHolder, resets the caption, and sets the Value property of the toggle button control to False. This causes the toggle button to reset itself to the unpressed state. This last action is necessary, because, in this case, the function is called from the shortcut menu macro without toggling the button.

We made the ahtHandleMarkReturn function public because we needed to call it from the menu macro. If this function were private to the form's module (the default scoping of a procedure in a form's module), we wouldn't have been able to call it from the macro, which lives outside of the context of the form.

Comments

An alternate way to offer this functionality—the ability to browse other records and return to a previous record—is to create multiple instances of the same form. This method is demonstrated in How-To 2.11.

COMPLEXITY:
INTERMEDIATE

9.6 How do I...
Carry forward data from record to record?

Problem

I'd like to reduce some of the tedium of data entry by carrying forward selected values from one record to the next. Ideally, I'd like to have this feature user-selectable at runtime so that each user could indicate, on a control-by-control basis, whether the current value of a control should carry forward onto newly added records. Is there any way to implement this in Access?

Technique

There are two parts to this problem: the mechanics of carrying a value from one record to the next and how best to let a user select which controls should carry forward values. The first part of the problem can be solved with a little VBA code to change the value of a control's Default Value property at runtime, squirreling away the original Default Value, if one exists, in the control's Tag property. The second part of the problem can be handled in a variety of ways—in this How-To, we suggest using a small toggle button paired with each text box or other bound control for which you wish to offer the carry forward feature to users.

Steps

Load the 09-06.MDB database and open the frmCustomer form in form view. Note that many of the text box controls on the form have a small captionless toggle button located just to their right. Navigate to the record of your choice and depress one or more of the toggle buttons to indicate you wish to carry forward that text box's value to newly added records (see Figure 9-19). Now jump to the end of the recordset and add a new record. (A quick way to accomplish this is to click on the right-most navigation button at the bottom of the form.) The values for the "toggled" text boxes carry forward onto the new record (see Figure 9-20). To turn off this feature for a control, click again on its toggle button so it resets to its unpressed state.

To add this feature to your own forms, follow these steps:

1. Open your form in design view. Add a small toggle button control to the right of each bound control for which you wish to add a carry forward feature. On the frmCustomer sample form, we added toggle controls to the right of the Company, Address, City, State, Zip, Phone, and Fax text boxes. Because you can't duplicate an AutoNumber field and you're unlikely to want to carry forward a customer's first or last name, we did not add toggle buttons for these controls.

2. Adjust the toggle buttons' control properties to match those in Table 9-5.

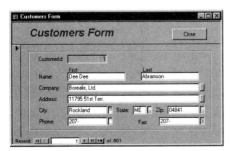

Figure 9-19 The toggle buttons to the right of several text boxes have been depressed

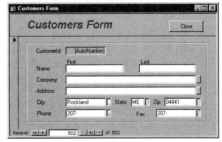

Figure 9-20 The values of the "toggled" text boxes have been carried forward

PROPERTY	VALUE
Width	0.1"
Height	0.1667"
Control Tip	Carry forward *Phone* value to new records
Tag	*txtPhone*
On Click	=ahtCarry([Form], [Screen].[ActiveControl])

Table 9-5 Property settings for tglPhone on frmCustomer

Replace Phone with the label of the bound control to the left of the toggle button; replace txtPhone with the name of the bound control. Replace the Width and Height values to anything that works well on your form without unnecessarily cluttering it. We've found that a width of 0.1" works nicely with a height that matches the height of the bound control (on the sample form, the height of both the text box and the toggle button controls is 0.1667").

3. Add the following function to a global module (or import basCarryForward from 09-06.MDB).

```
Function ahtCarry(frm As Form, ctlToggle As Control)

    Dim ctlData As Control
    Const ahtcQuote = """"

    ' The name of the data control this
    ' toggle control serves is stored in
    ' the toggle control's Tag property
    Set ctlData = frm(ctlToggle.Tag)

    If ctlToggle.Value Then
        ' If the toggle button is depressed
        ' then place current carry field control
        ' into the control's DefaultValue property.
        ' But first, store away existing DefaultValue,
        ' if any, in the control's Tag property
        If Not IsNull(ctlData.DefaultValue) Then
            ctlData.Tag = ctlData.DefaultValue
        End If
        ctlData.DefaultValue = _
         ahtcQuote & ctlData.Value & ahtcQuote
    Else
        ' Toggle button unpressed, so restore
        ' text box's DefaultValue if there is a
        ' non-null Tag property.
        If Not IsNull(ctlData.Tag) Then
            ctlData.DefaultValue = ctlData.Tag
            ctlData.Tag = Null
        Else
            ctlData.DefaultValue = Null
```

```
        End If
    End If

End Function
```

How It Works

Although there are other ways to offer this functionality to users, the toggle button control works well because it stays depressed to indicate that it's in a special state. If we had instead used code attached to the bound control's double-click event or a menu item to indicate that a control should be carried forward, users might find it difficult to remember which fields they had selected to carry forward.

Because the toggle button controls are so small and do not visually call out their purpose, we added control tips to each button to demystify their purpose. Control tips are nice because they don't take up any room on the form until a user leaves the mouse cursor positioned over the control for a few seconds.

The Tag property—which is an extra property that the Access designers have given us for our own use—is used in two ways in this How-To. First, the Tag property of each toggle button is used to indicate which bound control it serves. For example, tglState's Tag property is set to txtState. Second, the Tag property of each bound control is used to store the existing Default Value property so we do not overwrite it when we carry a value forward. In the example form, for instance, txtState contains an existing Default Value of WA.

All the work for this How-To is done by the ahtCarry function. This function is attached to each toggle button's Click event using the following syntax.

```
=ahtCarry([Form], [Screen].[ActiveControl])
```

Rather than passing strings to the function, we pass a reference to the form object and a reference to the active control object. Passing object references instead of the name of the form or control is efficient because back in the function, we will have immediate access to all the object's methods and properties without having to create form and control object variables.

The ahtCarry function does its magic in several steps. First, the function extracts the name of the bound control served by the toggle button from the later control's Tag property.

```
Set ctlData = frm(ctlToggle.Tag)
```

Second, the function checks if the toggle is up or down: If it's depressed, its value will be True which executes the following section of code. This code stores the bound control's DefaultValue property in its Tag property and then sets the DefaultValue equal to the current value of the bound control, adding the necessary quotes along the way.

```
If ctlToggle.Value Then
    ' If the toggle button is depressed
    ' then place current carry field control
    ' into the control's DefaultValue property.
    ' But first, store away existing DefaultValue,
```

continued on next page

continued from previous page

```
' if any, in the control's Tag property
If Not IsNull(ctlData.DefaultValue) Then
    ctlData.Tag = ctlData.DefaultValue
End If
ctlData.DefaultValue = _
 ahtcQuote & ctlData.Value & ahtcQuote
```

Finally, the function resets things to normal if the toggle button has been unpressed.

```
Else
    ' Toggle button unpressed, so restore
    ' text box's DefaultValue if there is a
    ' non-null Tag property.
    If Not IsNull(ctlData.Tag) Then
        ctlData.DefaultValue = ctlData.Tag
        ctlData.Tag = Null
    Else
        ctlData.DefaultValue = Null
    End If
End If
```

Comments

Although the sample form only uses bound text boxes, this technique will work equally well for all bound controls with the exception of bound controls containing AutoNumber or OLE Object fields.

COMPLEXITY:
INTERMEDIATE

9.7 How do I...
Create a combo box that accepts new entries?

Problem

I'm using combo boxes for data entry on my forms. Sometimes I want to allow users to add a new entry to the list of values in the combo box. Can I do this without forcing users to close the data entry form, add the record using a different form, and then return to the original form?

Technique

You can use the NotInList event to trap the error that occurs when a user types a value into a combo box that isn't in the underlying list. You can write an event procedure attached to this event that opens a pop-up form to gather any necessary data for the new entry, adds the new entry to the list, and then continues where the user started. This How-To demonstrates how to create combo boxes that accept new entries by making use of the NotInList event and the OpenArgs property of forms.

Figure 9-21 Adding a new record to
the underlying table

Steps

Load the sample database 09-07.MDB and open the frmDataEntry form in form view.
This form allows you to select a U.S. state from the combo box, but the list is purposely
incomplete for the example. To enter a new state, type its abbreviation in the form and
answer Yes when Access asks whether you want to add a new record. A form will pop
up, as shown in Figure 9-21, to collect the other details (in this case, the state name).
When you close the form, you'll be returned to the original data entry form with your
newly added state already selected in the combo box.

To add this functionality to your own combo boxes, follow these steps:

1. Import the basNotInList module from 09-07.MDB into your application.

2. Open your existing form in design view and create the combo box to which
you wish to add records. Set the combo box properties as shown in Table 9-6.

PROPERTY	SETTING
Row Source Type	Table/Query
Row Source	Any table or query
Limit to List	Yes

Table 9-6 Property settings for combo box

3. Create an event procedure attached to the NotInList event of the combo box
control. (If you're unsure how to do this, see the How Do I Create an Event
Procedure section in the Introduction of this book.) Add the following code to
the event procedure (shown here for a control named cboState).

```
Private Sub cboState_NotInList(NewData As String, Response As Integer)
    Response = ahtAddViaForm("frmState", "txtAbbreviation", NewData)
End Sub
```

Replace the arguments to ahtAddViaForm with the appropriate arguments for
your own database: the name of the data entry form used to add new records
to the combo box and the name of the control on the data entry form that
matches the first displayed column of the combo box.

4. Create the pop-up form that will be used to add new combo box values. Set the form properties as shown in Table 9-7.

PROPERTY	SETTING
Record Source	*The same table or query as the combo box's row source*
Default Editing	*Data Entry*
On Load	*=ahtCheckOpenArgs([Form])*

Table 9-7 Property settings for the pop-up form

5. Add controls to the pop-up form for all table fields that you need the user to fill in. Be sure that one of them is the field that corresponds to the first visible column of the combo box and that this field's name is the one you supplied in step 3.

6. Save the pop-up form, using the name you supplied in step 3. Now open the main form with the combo box on it. Type a new value into the combo box. You should be prompted with a message box asking if you want to add a record (Figure 9-22). Click on Yes, and the pop-up form will appear with the information you typed in the combo box control. Fill in the rest of the required information and close the pop-up form. The new information will be added to the combo box list and the new value will be selected in the combo box.

How It Works

When you have a combo box with its Limit To List property set to Yes, Access generates the NotInList event when the user types in a value that's not in the list. By default, this displays an error message. However, by creating a NotInList event procedure, you can intercept this message before it occurs and add the record to the list yourself.

When you're done processing the event, set the Response argument provided by Access to one of three possible constants:

acDataErrDisplay tells Access to display the default error message.

acDataErrContinue tells Access not to display a message but otherwise continue.

acDataErrAdded tells Access not to display the error message but to requery the underlying list. This is the return value to use when you add the value yourself.

This How-To uses a generic function, ahtAddViaForm, to handle the record addition. To allow for the possibility that the user may not want to enter a new value (perhaps he or she mistyped the entry), the function displays a simple message box and quits if the user selects the No button. You also have to tell the original event procedure what

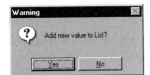

Figure 9-22 Prompt
for new record

to do with the data. The acDataErrContinue constant tells Access to suppress the default error message but not to try to add the new value to the combo box.

```
Function ahtAddViaForm(strAddForm As String, strControlName As String, _
   strNewData As String) As Integer

   On Error GoTo ahtAddviaForm_Err

   Dim varRet As Variant

   ' First, confirm the user really wants to enter a new record
   varRet = MsgBox("Add new value to List?", vbQuestion + vbYesNo, _
   "Warning")
   If varRet = vbNo Then
      ahtAddViaForm = acDataErrContinue
      Exit Function
   End If
```

If the user wants to add the new record, the function opens the pop-up form in dialog box mode. This pauses the function at this point (because a dialog box mode form won't give up the focus until it has been closed or hidden) and lets the user enter the required data to complete the record.

```
' Open up the data add form in dialog mode, feeding it
' the name of the control and data to use
DoCmd.OpenForm FormName:=strAddForm, DataMode:=acAdd, _
 WindowMode:=acDialog, _
 OpenArgs:=strControlName & ";" & strNewData
```

However, this leads to another issue. You can't fill in controls on the form before it's opened and you can't fill them in afterwards because the form is open in dialog box mode. The ahtAddViaForm function gets around this by using the OpenArgs property of the form, which allows you to pass a text string to the form. You'll see later in this How-To how this property is used by the form to fill in its key field.

After the pop-up form is closed, all you have to do is set the appropriate return value. In this case, acDataErrAdded tells Access that you've added the value to the underlying table and it can be used as the value for the combo box.

```
' Before control returns to the calling form,
' tell it we've added the value
ahtAddViaForm = acDataErrAdded
```

When the pop-up form is opened, the Load event is triggered and the ahtCheckOpenArgs function is called, which takes a form variable from the active form as its only parameter. This function is used to process the OpenArgs property of the form (which is where the form places the parameter that was passed to it when it was opened).

```
Function ahtCheckOpenArgs(frm As Form)

    Dim strControlName As String
    Dim strControlValue As String
    Dim intSemi As Integer

    If IsNull(frm.OpenArgs) Then
        Exit Function
    Else
        intSemi = InStr(1, frm.OpenArgs, ";")
        If intSemi = 0 Then
            Exit Function
        End If
        strControlName = Left$(frm.OpenArgs, intSemi - 1)
        strControlValue = Mid$(frm.OpenArgs, intSemi + 1)
        ' Possibly this OpenArgs belongs to someone else
        ' and just looks like ours. Set the error handling
        ' to just ignore any errors on the next line
        On Error Resume Next
        frm.Form(strControlName) = strControlValue
    End If
End Function
```

The ahtCheckOpenArgs has to be careful to avoid errors because it's called every time the form is opened. First, it's possible that no OpenArgs argument was passed in. Second, the OpenArgs argument might be there for another reason. Thus, if OpenArgs doesn't parse out as expected—in the format ControlName;Value—then it's ignored.

If it is determined to be in the correct format, however, then OpenArgs is parsed and the value is placed in the corresponding control on the form.

Comments

The solution presented in this How-To is designed to be generic. You may find that you need a more specific function for some particular combo box. For example, you could allow for users to cancel out of the pop-up form in case they decide against adding a new record, or you could use unbound text boxes on the data entry form to display pertinent information from the main form, adding context for data entry.

COMPLEXITY:
ADVANCED

9.8 How do I...
Create animated buttons?

Problem

I'd like to add some pizzazz to my application. I've seen animated buttons in other applications. How do I create animated buttons on my forms?

Technique

Access command buttons have an underdocumented property called PictureData that stores the bitmap that's displayed on the button face. This How To examines two ways to use this property. First, you will learn how to create "two-state" buttons with pictures that change when you click on them. You will also learn how to create fully animated buttons that cycle through a set of pictures at all times, using the form's Timer event to display a smooth succession of bitmaps.

Steps

Load 09-08.MDB and open frmAnimateDemo (Figure 9-23) in form view. The top two buttons are two-state buttons whose pictures change when you click them. The Copy button (the one on the top left) shows a second document and the Exit button (the one on the top right) shows the door closing just before it closes the form. The bottom two buttons are examples of animated button faces. (Only the Exit button on this form actually does anything when you press it.)

Creating Two-State Buttons

To add a two-state animated button to your form, follow these steps:

1. Open your form in design view. Place a pair of command buttons on the form. The first button should be sized correctly for your pictures and be located

Figure 9-23 The
frmAnimateDemo
form

483

Figure 9-24 The frmAnimateDemo form in design view

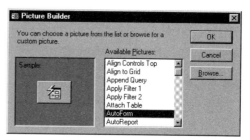

Figure 9-25 The Picture Builder wizard

where you want the button to be displayed. The second button can be located anywhere and be any size. For example, the two-state command button on the top left of frmAnimateDemo was created with cmdCopy and cmdCopy2. The cmdCopy button is shown selected in Figure 9-24; cmdCopy2, which has been reduced in size to save space, is located just to the left of cmdCopy. Set the Visible property of the second command button to No.

2. Click on the first command button of the pair, select the Picture property on its properties sheet, and click the builder button to the right of the property. When the Picture Builder wizard appears, select the face you want your button to have in its unpressed state (see Figure 9-25). You can use the Browse button to select from bitmap files on your disk.

3. Click on the second command button of the pair, select the Picture property, and load the face you want your button to have when it is depressed, again using the builder button.

4. Create an event procedure attached to the MouseDown event of the first button. (If you're unsure how to do this, see the How Do I Create an Event Procedure section in the Introduction of this book.) Add the following code to the event procedure.

```
Private Sub cmdCopy_MouseDown(Button As Integer, _
    Shift As Integer, X As Single, Y As Single)

    Call SwapPictures(Me!cmdCopy, Me!cmdCopy2)

End Sub
```

Replace cmdCopy and cmdCopy2 with the names of your buttons.

5. Create the following event procedure attached to the MouseUp property of the first button.

```
Private Sub cmdCopy_MouseUp(Button As Integer, _
    Shift As Integer, X As Single, Y As Single)
```

```
Call SwapPictures(Me!cmdCopy, Me!cmdCopy2)

End Sub
```

Again, replace cmdCopy and cmdCopy2 with the names of your buttons.

6. Add the following subprocedure to the form's module.

```
Private Sub SwapPictures(cmdButton1 As CommandButton, _
cmdButton2 As CommandButton)

    Dim varTemp As Variant

    varTemp = cmdButton1.PictureData
    cmdButton1.PictureData = cmdButton2.PictureData
    cmdButton2.PictureData = varTemp
    Me.Repaint

End Sub
```

Continuously Animated Buttons

To add a continuously animated button to your form, follow these steps:

1. Import tblButtonAnimation, frmButtonFaceChooser, basAnimate, and basCommonFile from 09-08.MDB into your own database.

2. Open frmButtonFaceChooser (Figure 9-26) and select eight images for use on your animated button. You can either type the file names directly into the text boxes or click on the numbered buttons to select files from the common file dialog box. The pictures will appear on the command buttons as you choose them. The buttons are sized to accept standard 32 x 32-pixel icons or bitmaps, but you may use any size.

3. When you have selected eight bitmaps, enter an animation name to refer to this set of pictures (for example, "clock") and click on the Save button.

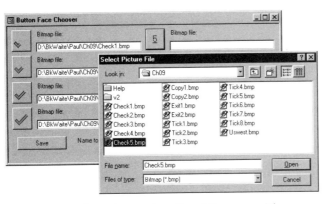

Figure 9-26 Choosing animation bitmaps with frmButtonFaceChooser

4. Create a new blank form and place a command button on it. Set the form's properties as shown in Table 9-8.

PROPERTY	VALUE
On Load	Event Procedure
On Timer	Event Procedure
Timer Interval	250

 Table 9-8 Form properties for animated button form

5. Enter the following code in the Declarations section of the form's module.

```
Const ahtcImages = 8

Dim mintI As Integer
Dim abinAnimation(1 To ahtcImages) As Variant
```

6. Create the following event procedure attached to form's Load event.

```
Private Sub Form_Load()

    Dim dbCurrent As Database
    Dim rstAnimation As Recordset
    Dim intI As Integer

    mintI = 0

    Set dbCurrent = CurrentDb()
    Set rstAnimation = dbCurrent.OpenRecordset("tblButtonAnimation", _
    dbOpenDynaset)

    ' Loop through the table, and load
    ' the animation images
    With rstAnimation
        .MoveFirst
        .FindFirst "AnimationName='checkmark'"
        For intI = LBound(abinAnimation) To UBound(abinAnimation)
            abinAnimation(intI) = .Fields("Face" & intI)
        Next intI
        .Close
    End With

End Sub
```

Replace 'checkmark' with the animation name you used in step 3.

7. Create the following event procedure attached to the form's Timer event.

```
Private Sub Form_Timer()

    ' mintI is 0-based, but the arrays are 1-based, so add 1.
    Me![cmdCheck].PictureData = abinAnimation(mintI + 1)
```

```
' Bump to the next value, wrapping around at
' ahtcImages (8 in this example).
mintI = (mintI + 1) Mod ahtcImages
```

```
End Sub
```

Replace cmdCheck with the name of the command button created in step 4.

8. Save the form and open it in form view. You should see your animation running on the face of the button.

How It Works

Access stores the picture displayed on a command button in the PictureData property. This property is a binary representation of the bitmap displayed and is read/write in all views. To store such a bitmap elsewhere, you have three choices: on another button, in a variable of the Variant data type, or in a table field of the OLE Object data type.

In this How-To you use all three of these techniques. The two-state buttons work by storing the normal image on the button you can see and parking the second image in a small invisible button. You can still read and write the PictureData property of an invisible button. When you click the visible button, its MouseDown event procedure is called, which swaps the pictures on the visible and invisible buttons. The MouseUp event code swaps the pictures again to return the original picture to the button face.

Repainting the Form

To see the effects of the MouseDown event, you must call the form's Repaint method, which tells Access to complete any pending screen updates. On the other hand, you don't need to do this in the MouseUp event (although it doesn't hurt if you do)—for some reason, Access automatically repaints the screen after a MouseUp event.

In the continuously animated button technique, the eight different button faces are stored in a table as Long Binary Data (which is what Access will tell you if you open the table in datasheet view) in OLE Object fields. The form's Load event procedure reads these button faces into an array of variants and its Timer event is used to fetch the next button face every 250 milliseconds in round-robin fashion.

In frmButtonFaceChooser, you'll find an easy way to load bitmaps into the tblButtonAnimation table. You can load a button's PictureData property by setting its Picture property to the name of any bitmap or icon file. The command buttons on this form use the Windows API common dialog box functions to invoke the common file dialog box. If you care to dig into these details, you'll find the common file dialog box code in the basCommonFile module.

Comments

You could extend the animated button technique in several directions.

- By including multiple hidden buttons on your form, you can create three-state buttons that change their picture when they are the currently selected button as well as when they are pushed.

- You can modify the event procedure to allow for animated buttons with more or less than eight frames of animation. To do this, break the table of frames up into two related tables, one holding the name of the animation and the number of frames, the other holding the actual picture data.

- The sample form shows how to use two arrays and some additional code to have two continuously animated buttons on the same form. You might generalize this code as well, but watch out—almost any form will look busy with more buttons animated.

If you open the sample form and hold down any button, you'll see that the animations stop for as long as you keep the button depressed. This prevents the form's Timer events from firing.

COMPLEXITY:
ADVANCED

9.9 How do I...
Create an expanding dialog box?

Problem

I have a dialog box with a lot of options, most of which are needed only in specific situations. I'd like to create this form as an expanding dialog box, similar to the Access Startup options dialog box (Figures 9-27 and 9-28). How can I do this with my own form?

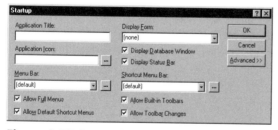

Figure 9-27 Access Startup dialog box in its initial state

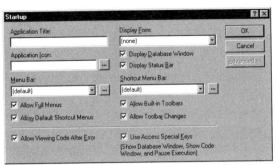

Figure 9-28 Access Startup dialog box in its expanded state

Technique

You can make a hidden section of the form visible at runtime, and use the Window|Size to Fit Form command to force the form to expand to fit its new dimensions. This How-To will show you how to create this type of form using an expanding form footer and how to minimize screen flashing during the resizing of the form by manipulating the Painting property of the form.

Steps

Load the sample database 09-09.MDB and open frmExpandingDialog in form view. The dialog box form will display in its initial contracted state (see Figure 9-29). Click on the Advanced button and the form will expand to reveal additional text boxes (see Figure 9-30). Click again on the button (now labeled Basic) to return to the contracted state. (This sample form is for demonstration purposes only; it doesn't do anything with the data you enter into it.)

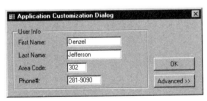

Figure 9-29 The frmExpandingDialog form in its contracted state

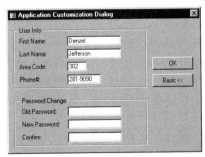

Figure 9-30 The frmExpandingDialog form in its expanded state

Follow these steps to create your own expanding dialog box form:

1. Create a new form. To make the form look like a dialog box, set the properties of the form as shown in Table 9-9. Some of these property settings are optional because the expanding technique will work with nondialog box forms, too. The settings for the Default View and Auto Resize properties are not optional.

FORM PROPERTY	VALUE
Default View	Single Form
Scroll Bars	Neither
Record Selectors	No
Navigation Buttons	No
Auto Resize	Yes
Auto Center	Yes
Pop Up	Yes
Modal	Yes
Border Style	Dialog Box
Min Max Buttons	None

Table 9-9 Form settings to create a dialog box form

2. Select View|Form Header/Footer to add a form footer section to the form. Set the Visible property of the footer section to No. Because you're only interested in the footer section, you may wish grab the bar separating the detail and header sections and drag it up so the header section has zero height.

3. Partition the controls on your form into two groups: those you wish to display at all times and those you wish to display only when the form is in the advanced (expanded) state. Place the first set of controls in the form's detail section; place the second set of controls in the footer section.

4. Add a button named cmdExpand with the caption "Advanced >>" to the detail section of the form. Create an event procedure attached to the Click event of the button. (If you're unsure how to do this, see the How Do I Create an Event Procedure section in the Introduction of this book.) Add the following code to the event procedure (or copy the code from the frmExpandingDialog form's module in 09-09.MDB).

```
Private Sub cmdExpand_Click()

    Dim sct As Section
    Dim fExpanded As Boolean

    Const ahtcFirstBasicCtl = "txtFirstName"
    Const ahtcFirstAdvancedCtl = "txtOldPW"

    Set sct = Me.Section(acFooter)
```

```
        ' Keep track of state of form when first called
        fExpanded = sct.Visible

        ' If form is in non-expanded state, turn off
        ' form painting while expanding form. This
        ' prevents the form from flashing.

        ' If form is in expanded state, however, Access
        ' won't hide the expanded portion unless form
        ' painting is left on.
        If Not fExpanded Then Me.Painting = False

        ' Expand form if currently un-expanded and vice versa
        sct.Visible = Not fExpanded

        ' Size to fit the form to expand or contract form's
        ' borders to match visiblilty of section
        DoCmd.DoMenuItem acFormBar, 7, 6, 0, acMenuVer70

        ' Change button caption and repaint if necessary
        If Not fExpanded Then
            Me!cmdExpand.Caption = "Basic <<"
            Me.Painting = True
            Me(ahtcFirstAdvancedCtl).SetFocus
        Else
            Me!cmdExpand.Caption = "Advanced >>"
            Me(ahtcFirstBasicCtl).SetFocus
        End If

End Sub
```

Change the constant declarations so ahtcFirstBasicCtl holds the name of the first control in the detail section of the form and ahtcFirstAdvancedCtl holds the name of the first control in the footer section of the form.

5. Save and close the form. The final form should look like the one shown in design view in Figure 9-31.

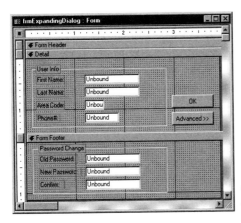

Figure 9-31 The frmExpandingDialog form in design view

How It Works

Because you set the Visible property of the form footer section to No, it will not appear when the form is first opened. In addition, because you set the Auto Resize property to Yes, Access will resize the form to show only the visible areas of the form.

Expansion of the form is handled by the code attached to the cmdExpand button's Click event. This event procedure begins by defining a couple of variables and a couple of constants. The two constants will be used later in the function to shift the focus to the first control of each section.

```
Dim sct As Section
Dim fExpanded As Boolean

Const ahtcFirstBasicCtl = "txtFirstName"
Const ahtcFirstAdvancedCtl = "txtOldPW"
```

Next the procedure sets the section variable to point to the form's footer section using the built-in acFooter constant. In addition, it stores the current state of the Visible property of the section in the Boolean variable fExpanded.

```
Set sct = Me.Section(acFooter)

' Keep track of state of form when first called
fExpanded = sct.Visible
```

If the form is currently contracted, then it needs to be expanded, and vice versa. But before this is done, the code sets the form's Painting property to False if, and only if, the form is being expanded. The technique will work without performing this step, but the form will flash as it expands. On the other hand, if the form is being contracted, you shouldn't turn Painting off; if you do, the form will not properly repaint itself and the nonfunctional advanced section will remain painted on the screen. This step is accomplished with a single line of code and six lines of comments.

```
' If form is in non-expanded state, turn off
' form painting while expanding form. This
' prevents the form from flashing.

' If form is in expanded, state, however, Access
' won't hide the expanded portion unless form
' painting is left on.
If Not fExpanded Then Me.Painting = False
```

The form is then expanded or contracted by setting the Visible property to the Not of its current state.

```
' Expand form if currently un-expanded and vice versa
sct.Visible = Not fExpanded
```

The code then resizes the form using the DoMenuItem method of the DoCmd object to carry out the Window|Size to Fit Form menu command because there's no equivalent Access action or method.

```
' Size to fit the form to expand or contract form's
' borders to match visiblilty of section
DoCmd.DoMenuItem acFormBar, 7, 6, 0, acMenuVer70
```

The function then changes the caption of the button, turns painting back on if it was turned off, and finally moves the focus to the first control of the appropriate section. This last step is not absolutely necessary, but it's a nice touch because the normal tab sequence will not jump across sections.

```
' Change button caption and repaint if necessary
If Not fExpanded Then
    Me!cmdExpand.Caption = "Basic <<"
    Me.Painting = True
    Me(ahtcFirstAdvancedCtl).SetFocus
Else
    Me!cmdExpand.Caption = "Advanced >>"
    Me(ahtcFirstBasicCtl).SetFocus
End If
```

Comments

You can also apply this technique to nondialog box and bound forms. Although it's not commonly done, there's nothing to stop you from placing bound controls in the footer section of a form. On the other hand, it may be more appropriate to use a multipage form instead for bound forms. See How-To 2.5 for more details.

COMPLEXITY:
ADVANCED

9.10 How do I...
Use an OLE custom control?

Problem

Access 95 ships with the Calendar OLE custom control. How can I incorporate this custom control and others into my Access applications?

Technique

Although Access 2.0 supported 16-bit custom controls, the technology running under Windows 3.1 was not quite ready for prime time. Fortunately, the 32-bit OLE custom control support in Access 95 running under Windows 95 or Windows NT is much improved. This How-To will show you how to use the Calendar control in both bound and unbound modes. You'll also learn how to create a general-purpose reusable pop-up calendar form.

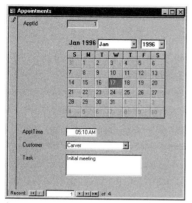

Figure 9-32 The Calendar control is bound to the ApptDate field

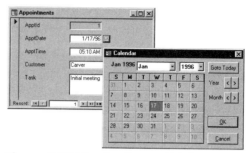

Figure 9-33 The frmPopupCal form can be used to select a date

Steps

Load the 09-10.MDB database and open frmAppointment1 in form view (see Figure 9-32). Create a new record, selecting a date by using the calendar control's Month and Year combo box controls to navigate to the desired month and then clicking on the date on the calendar. Complete the rest of the record and close the form. Now open the tblAppointment table to verify the date you selected was stored in the ApptDate field of that record.

Now open frmAppointment2 in form view and select a date by clicking on the calendar button to the right of the ApptDate text box. A pop-up form will be displayed where you can select a date again using the Calendar control (see Figure 9-33). Double-click on a date to select it and close the calendar pop-up form or click once on a date and use the OK button. You may also wish to experiment with the Goto Today button, the month and year navigation buttons, and the Cancel button.

Adding a Bound Calendar Control to Your Form

Follow these steps to add the calendar control to an existing form to replace a text box for selecting dates:

1. Create a form (or edit an existing one) bound to a table that has a date/time field formatted as a date without time.

2. Select Insert|Custom Control. The Insert OLE Custom Controls dialog box will appear as shown in Figure 9-34. (The list of available controls that appear on your screen will likely differ from the list displayed in Figure 9-34.) Select the Calendar control and click OK to close the dialog box. Move and resize the control as needed. On the frmAppointment1 form, we resized the control to a width of 2.375" and a height of 1.8333".

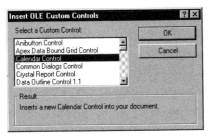

Figure 9-34 The Insert OLE
Custom Controls dialog box

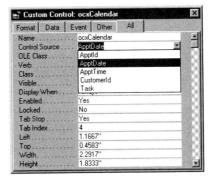

Figure 9-35 The calendar
control can be directly bound
to a field

3. Set the control's Control Source property to point to the date field in the underlying record source for the form. In Figure 9-35, we selected the ApptDate field from tblAppointment.

4. Right-click anywhere on the embedded custom control to display its shortcut menu. Select Calendar Control Object|Properties from the shortcut menu and the Calendar control properties sheet will appear (see Figure 9-36). Using this custom properties sheet, customize the various properties of the control. For example, we changed the properties shown in Table 9-10 to nondefault values to make the calendar look better at a smaller size. Use the Apply button to preview settings while keeping the properties sheet open. You may also wish to use the Help button to view the custom control's Help file at this time. (Not all custom controls support the Apply and Help buttons.) When you're done, click on the OK button to close the custom properties sheet. These special custom control properties are also available from the Other tab of the control's regular properties sheet.

TAB	PROPERTY	VALUE
General	Day Length	Short
	Month Length	Short
Fonts	Title Font	Font: MS Sans Serif, Font Style: Bold, Size: 9.75 points

Table 9-10 Custom property settings for the calendar control

5. Save the form and switch to form view to see it in action.

495

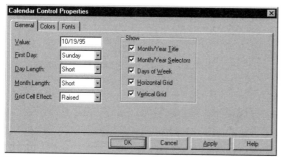

Figure 9-36 Using the custom properties sheet for the Calendar control

Creating a Generic Unbound Pop-Up Calendar Form

Follow these steps to create a generic unbound pop-up calendar form:

1. Create a new form called frmPopupCal with the properties shown in Table 9-11.

FORM PROPERTY	VALUE
Default View	Single Form
Scroll Bars	Neither
Record Selectors	No
Navigation Buttons	No
Auto Resize	Yes
Popup	Yes
Modal	Yes
Border Style	Thin
Min Max Buttons	None

Table 9-11 Form properties for the pop-up calendar form

2. Select Insert|Custom Control. The Insert OLE Custom Controls dialog box will appear, as shown in Figure 9-34. Select the Calendar control and click OK to close the dialog box. Move and resize the control as needed. On the frmPopupCal form, we resized the control to a width of 2.2917" and a height of 1.9167". Name the control ocxCal.

3. Adjust the custom properties of the control as discussed in step 4 of the previous section.

4. Add seven command button controls to the right of the control, as shown in Table 9-12.

CONTROL NAME	CAPTION
cmdToday	Goto Today
cmdPrevYear	<
cmdNextYear	>
cmdPrevMonth	<
cmdNextMonth	>
cmdOK	&OK
cmdCancel	&Cancel

Table 9-12 The command buttons for frmPopupCal

5. Create an event procedure attached to the Click event of each button. (If you're unsure how to do this, see the How Do I Create an Event Procedure section in the Introduction of this book.) Add the following event procedures to the appropriate buttons.

```
Private Sub cmdCancel_Click()
    DoCmd.Close acForm, Me.Name
End Sub

Private Sub cmdNextMonth_Click()
    Me!ocxCal.NextMonth
End Sub

Private Sub cmdNextYear_Click()
    Me!ocxCal.NextYear
End Sub

Private Sub cmdOK_Click()
    Me.Visible = False
End Sub

Private Sub cmdPrevMonth_Click()
    Me!ocxCal.PreviousMonth
End Sub

Private Sub cmdPrevYear_Click()
    Me!ocxCal.PreviousYear
End Sub

Private Sub cmdToday_Click()
    Me!ocxCal.Today
End Sub
```

6. Add the following code to the event procedure attached to the form's Load event.

```
Private Sub Form_Load()
    If Not IsNull(Me.OpenArgs) Then
```

continued on next page

continued from previous page

```
        Me.CalDate = Me.OpenArgs
    End If
End Sub
```

7. Add the following code to the event procedure attached to the Calendar control's DblClick event.

```
Private Sub ocxCal_DblClick()
    Call cmdOK_Click
End Sub
```

Note, this event will be found under the Other tab of the control's properties sheet, *not* the Event tab.

8. Add the following two property procedures to the form's module.

```
Property Let CalDate(datDate As Date)
    Me!ocxCal = datDate
End Property

Property Get CalDate() As Date
    CalDate = Me!ocxCal
End Property
```

9. Save and close frmPopupCal.

10. Import the basCalendar module from 09-10.MDB into your database.

11. Create a new form with a bound date text box control. This form will be used to test the pop-up calendar form created in steps 1–10. Add a command button to the right of the text box control. Name it cmdPopupCal and add the following code to the event procedure attached to the command button's Click event.

```
Private Sub cmdPopupCal_Click()

    Dim ctlDate As TextBox
    Dim varReturn As Variant

    Set ctlDate = Me!txtApptDate

    ' Request date
    varReturn = ahtGetDate(ctlDate.Value)

    ' Only change the value if Null is not
    ' returned; otherwise user cancelled
    ' so preserve existing value.
    If Not IsNull(varReturn) Then
        ctlDate = varReturn
    End If

End Sub
```

Change txtApptDate to the name of the text box created in this step.

12. Save the form, switch to form view, and test out the new pop-up form by clicking on the cmdPopupCal button.

How It Works

You insert a custom control onto an Access form using the Insert|Custom Control command. Once inserted on your form, the control can be moved and resized as necessary. When you insert a custom control onto an Access form, Access merges the properties of the control's container (a bound or unbound OLE frame control) with the properties of the custom control. The custom control's unique properties are placed on the Other tab of the control's regular properties sheet, but you can also manipulate these properties using the custom properties sheet created by the control's creator. You do this by right-clicking on the control and selecting Calendar Control Object|Properties from the shortcut menu.

In step 3 under Adding a Bound Calendar Control to Your Form, you bound the Calendar control directly to a field in the form's underlying record source.

Access 95 and Custom Control Data Binding

Access 95 supports simple custom control data binding. This means you can use controls—like the Calendar control—that are bound to a single field, but you can't use certain types of bound controls—such as Visual Basic 4.0's Data-Bound Grid control—that bind to tables or queries. (You can, however, use controls such as Data-Bound Grid control in Access if they are used in unbound mode.)

In the steps under Creating a Generic Unbound Pop-Up Calendar Form, you created code that manipulated five different methods of the Calendar control: PreviousYear, NextYear, PreviousMonth, NextMonth, and Today. For example, in the event procedure attached to cmdPreviousMonth, you added the following line of code.

```
Me!ocxCal.PreviousMonth
```

Custom Control Documentation

To find additional information on the methods, properties, and events of a particular custom control, you can use the Help button that appears on *some* (but not all) controls' custom properties sheets (see Figure 9-36). Alternately, you may have to load the control's help file separately or consult its printed documentation or electronic readme file.

The frmPopupCal form contains two special procedures, called property procedures, that you may have never seen before. Using property procedures, you can create custom properties for a form that can be called from outside the form. This allows you to expose certain elements of the form to the outer world while keeping all of the form's controls, functions, and subprocedures—the form's inner work-ings—encapsulated within the form. Property procedures are a welcome object-oriented addition to Access 95's forms.

The Let property procedure creates a user-defined property for the form, control-ling what happens when a calling routine sets the value of the form's property. The Get property procedure controls what happens when a calling routine requests the value of the property. The property procedure for frmPopupCal is simple, consisting only of an assignment statement, but you can do anything in a property procedure that you could do in a normal event procedure. For example, you could count the number of text box controls on a form in a Get property procedure or you could set all the labels on a form to a certain color in a Let property procedure. There are examples of more complex property procedures in How-To 9.11.

Get and Let Property Procedure Datatypes

The datatype of the parameter of the Let procedure (or of the last parameter if the Let procedure contains multiple parameters) must match the datatype of the return value of the Get property procedure.

The basCalendar module contains a wrapper function for the frmPopupCal pop-up calendar form. The ahtGetDate wrapper function is shown here.

```
Function ahtGetDate(varDate As Variant) As Variant

    Const ahtcCalForm = "frmPopupCal"

    ' Open calendar form in dialog mode
    ' passing it the current date using OpenArgs
    DoCmd.OpenForm ahtcCalForm, WindowMode:=acDialog, _
     OpenArgs:=Nz(varDate)

    ' Check if the form is open; if so return the date
    ' selected in the Calendar control and close the
    ' popup calendar form and pass the new date back
    ' to the control. Otherwise, just return a Null.
    If IsOpen(ahtcCalForm) Then
        ahtGetDate = Forms(ahtcCalForm).CalDate
        DoCmd.Close acForm, ahtcCalForm
    Else
        ahtGetDate = Null
    End If

End Function
```

The ahtGetDate wrapper function sends the calendar a date by using the OpenArgs property of the form (discussed in How-To 9.7) and requests a date from the form by using the CalDate user-defined property that was created using the Get property procedure. The Load event procedure of frmPopupCal sets the CalDate property to the OpenArgs property. It's necessary, in this case, to use the OpenArgs property because you are opening the form in dialog box mode, which makes it impossible to manipulate properties directly.

By calling the ahtGetDate wrapper function whenever you wish to use the pop-up calendar form to provide a date to your application, you are always going through a single consistent entry point. Thus you never need to bother with opening or closing the form or worrying about the names of the controls on frmPopupCal. Just use the following syntax to get a date using the pop-up form.

```
variable = ahtGetDate(current value)
```

Comments

The pop-up calendar's Auto Center property has been set to Yes so it will always appear in the center of the screen. You may wish to extend ahtGetDate with optional left and top parameters so you can precisely position the pop-up calendar form on the screen when it is first opened.

The techniques presented in this How-To can be applied to other Microsoft and third-party vendor custom controls, including controls that are part of the Access 95 Developer's Toolkit and Visual Basic 4.0.

COMPLEXITY:
ADVANCED

9.11 How do I...
Create a generic, reusable status meter form?

Problem

Access allows me to control the built-in status meter using the SysCmd function, but I have no control over the location or appearance of this status meter. How do I create a status meter that I can control?

Technique

You can create a status meter based on an Access form and control it using VBA routines. The status meter is composed of a Rectangle control and a Label control. By updating the Width property of the rectangle, you can control the meter's progress. Additionally, by updating the Caption property of the label, you can insert messages such as "50% complete." All the internal workings of the control can be encapsulated inside (hidden within) the form using Let and Get property procedures and a global wrapper function.

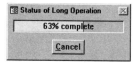

Figure 9-37 The
frmStatusMeter form

Steps

Open and run frmTestStatusMeter from 09-11.MDB (shown in Figure 9-37). To start
the status meter, click the Start button and frmStatusMeter will pop up. If you want
the status meter to include a Cancel button, check the Include Cancel button check
box before clicking the Start button. The status meter will slowly advance to 100%
and then close. If you've included a Cancel button, you can click on it at anytime to
immediately close the status meter and notify the calling form (frmTestStatuMeter) that
cancel has been requested.

Creating a Generic Status Meter

To create a generic status meter for your own application, follow these steps (or skip
these steps entirely and import frmStatusMeter and basStatusMeter from 09-11.MDB
into your database):

1. Create a form and set its properties as shown in Table 9-13.

PROPERTY	VALUE
Default View	Single Form
Record Selectors	No
Scroll Bars	Neither
Navigation Buttons	No
Border Style	Thin
Popup	Yes
Min Max Buttons	None

Table 9-13 Form properties for the status bar form

2. Place a rectangle on the form, name it recStatus, and set its Width property to 0.
Set its background color to the color of your choice.

3. Place a label on the form, name it lblStatus, and set its Width property to the total width you want the status bar to be. Set its Background to Clear. In the Label property, type in "0% Completed".

4. Add a command button control to the form named cmdCancel with a caption of "Cancel". Create an event procedure attached to the Click event of the button. (If you're unsure how to do this, see the How Do I Create an Event Procedure section in the Introduction of this book.) Add the following code to the event procedure.

```
Private Sub cmdCancel_Click()
    mfCancel = True
End Sub
```

5. Add the following global declaration to the Global Declarations section of the form's module.

```
Dim mfCancel As Boolean
```

6. Add the following three property procedures to the form's module.

```
Property Let InitMeter(fIncludeCancel As Boolean, strTitle As String)

    Me!recStatus.Width = 0
    Me!lblStatus.Caption = "0% complete"
    Me.Caption = strTitle
    Me!cmdCancel.Visible = fIncludeCancel

    DoCmd.RepaintObject

    mfCancel = False

End Property

Property Let UpdateMeter(intValue As Integer)

    Me!recStatus.Width = CInt(Me!lblStatus.Width * (intValue / 100))
    Me!lblStatus.Caption = Format$(intValue, "##") & "% complete"

    DoCmd.RepaintObject

End Property

Property Get Cancelled() As Boolean
    Cancelled = mfCancel
End Property
```

7. Save the form as frmStatusMeter and close it.

8. Create a new global module and add the following code (or import the module basStatusMeter from 09-11.MDB).

```
Const ahtcMeterForm = "frmStatusMeter"

Private Function IsOpen(strForm As String)
    IsOpen = (SysCmd(acSysCmdGetObjectState, acForm, strForm) > 0)
End Function
```

continued on next page

continued from previous page

```
Sub ahtCloseMeter()

    On Error GoTo ahtCloseMeterErr

    DoCmd.Close acForm, ahtcMeterForm

ahtCloseMeterExit:
    Exit Sub
ahtCloseMeterErr:
    Select Case Err.Number
    Case Else
        MsgBox "Error#" & Err.Number & ": " & Err.Description, _
            vbOKOnly + vbCritical, "ahtCloseMeter"
    End Select
    Resume ahtCloseMeterExit

End Sub

Sub ahtInitMeter(strTitle As String, fIncludeCancel As Boolean)

    On Error GoTo ahtInitMeterErr

    DoCmd.OpenForm ahtcMeterForm
    Forms(ahtcMeterForm).InitMeter(fIncludeCancel) = strTitle

ahtInitMeterExit:
    Exit Sub
ahtInitMeterErr:
    Select Case Err.Number
    Case Else
        MsgBox "Error#" & Err.Number & ": " & Err.Description, _
            vbOKOnly + vbCritical, "ahtInitMeter"
    End Select
    If IsOpen(ahtcMeterForm) Then Call ahtCloseMeter
    Resume ahtInitMeterExit

End Sub

Function ahtUpdateMeter(intValue As Integer) As Boolean

    On Error GoTo ahtUpdateMeterErr

    Forms(ahtcMeterForm).UpdateMeter = intValue

    ' Return value is False if cancelled
    If Forms(ahtcMeterForm).Cancelled Then
        Call ahtCloseMeter
        ahtUpdateMeter = False
    Else
        ahtUpdateMeter = True
    End If

ahtUpdateMeterExit:
    Exit Function
ahtUpdateMeterErr:
```

```
        Select Case Err.Number
        Case Else
            MsgBox "Error#" & Err.Number & ": " & Err.Description, _
            vbOKOnly + vbCritical, "ahtUpdateMeter"
        End Select
        If IsOpen(ahtcMeterForm) Then Call ahtCloseMeter
        Resume ahtUpdateMeterExit

End Function
```

9. Save and close the global module.

Using the Generic Status Meter in Your Application

To use the generic status meter in your own applications, follow these steps:

1. When you wish to initialize the meter, use the following syntax:

```
Call ahtInitMeter(title, flag)
```

where title is the title you wish for the status meter to assume and flag is True (or −1) to display a Cancel button or False (or 0) to not display a Cancel button. For example, this statement creates a status meter with the title Progress and a Cancel button:

```
Call ahtInitMeter("Progress", True)
```

2. When you wish to update the meter with a new progress value, use the following syntax:

```
variable = ahtUpdateMeter(value)
```

where value is an integer between 0 and 100. The ahtUpdateMeter value will place True or False in the return value. If the return value is False, the user has pressed the Cancel button. (The return value will never be False if you chose not to include the Cancel button when initializing the status meter.) For example, to update the meter with a progress setting of 50%, you might call ahtUpdateMeter like this:

```
fOK = ahtUpdateMeter(50)
```

3. When you wish to close the status meter form, use this syntax:

```
Call ahtCloseMeter
```

How It Works

By manipulating the Width property of the rectangle, you can cause the rectangle to "grow." The rectangle control is placed behind a transparent Label control that defines the boundaries of the status meter and contains the status text. The status meter form is manipulated by three public wrapper functions contained in basStatusMeter: ahtInitMeter, ahtUpdateMeter, and ahtCloseMeter. These functions, in turn, interact with frmStatusMeter through its exposed properties. The wrapper functions know nothing of the inner workings of the form, just the names of the properties and how to call them.

The ahtInitMeter property initializes the status meter by opening the status meter form and setting the InitMeter property to the appropriate string. At the same time, a parameter is passed that determines if the Cancel button is included on the status meter form.

```
DoCmd.OpenForm ahtcMeterForm
Forms(ahtcMeterForm).InitMeter(fIncludeCancel) = strTitle
```

The ahtUpdateMeter property sets the value of the status meter form's UpdateMeter property. It then checks the Cancelled property of the form to determine if the user has clicked on the Cancel button. If so, it closes the status meter form and returns False to the calling procedure; otherwise it returns True.

```
Forms(ahtcMeterForm).UpdateMeter = intValue

' Return value is False if cancelled
If Forms(ahtcMeterForm).Cancelled Then
    Call ahtCloseMeter
    ahtUpdateMeter = False
Else
    ahtUpdateMeter = True
End If
```

The ahtCloseMeter property closes the status meter form using the DoCmd.Close method.

```
DoCmd.Close acForm, ahtcMeterForm
```

Internally, the Let and Get property procedures do all the work. When the InitMeter property is set by some external procedure, the InitMeter Let property procedure runs the following code.

```
Me!recStatus.Width = 0
Me!lblStatus.Caption = "0% complete"
Me.Caption = strTitle
Me!cmdCancel.Visible = fIncludeCancel

DoCmd.RepaintObject

mfCancel = False
```

This code sets the Width property of the of the recStatus control to 0, sets the Caption property of lblStatus to 0% Complete, updates the form's Caption property with the strTitle parameter, and sets the cmdCancel button's Visible property to match the fIncludeCancel parameter. The code then uses the RepaintObject method to force an update of the screen and resets the mfCancel module-level global variable to False.

When the UpdateMeter property of the form is set to a value, the following code is executed by the UpdateMeter Let property procedure.

```
Me!recStatus.Width = CInt(Me!lblStatus.Width * (intValue / 100))
Me!lblStatus.Caption = Format$(intValue, "##") & "% complete"

DoCmd.RepaintObject
```

This code updates the status meter by changing the width of the recStatus control relative to the width of the lblStatus control. This relative change ensures that the status meter rectangle never exceeds the limits as defined by the width of the lblStatus control. The routine then updates the Caption property of the lblStatus control to a formatted percentage value concatenated to the string "% complete". Once again, the code uses the RepaintObject method to force an update of the screen.

The Cancelled property of the status meter form is handled by the Cancelled Get property procedure. When called by an external procedure, this procedure returns the value of the module-level global mfCancel variable. This variable, which was initialized to zero by the InitMeter Let property procedure, is set to False if the user clicks on the cmdCancel button in the cmdCancel_Click event procedure.

Comments

As mentioned in the How It Works section of How-To 9.10, it's a good idea to encapsulate the inner workings of a generic utility form such as frmStatusMeter by keeping all the event procedures private and using the new (for Access 95) Let and Get property procedures to expose a controlled user interface to calling procedures. By getting in the habit of thinking and coding in this object-oriented way, you'll be able to create generic components you can reuse over and over.

The pop-up status meter form's Auto Center property has been set to Yes so it will always appear in the center of the screen. You may wish to extend ahtInitMeter with optional left and top parameters so you can precisely position the pop-up calendar form on the screen when it is first opened.

As an alternative to the form presented in this How-To, you may wish to employ one of the OLE custom controls that offers similar functionality. The Access Developer's Toolkit and Visual Basic both include the Progress Bar control and Visual Basic also includes the Gauge control. Both controls can be used to indicate the progress of long operations.

CHAPTER 10
ADDRESSING MULTIUSER APPLICATION CONCERNS

10

ADDRESSING MULTIUSER APPLICATION CONCERNS

How do I…

Access offers native support, right out of the box, for multiuser applications. But this additional power brings with it some problems, chiefly those of coordinating multiple users who may be spread across a large network. This chapter explores some solutions to problems common to multiuser applications. You'll learn how to use a shared database table to help your users communicate with one another and how to find out which users are logged in at any given time. You'll learn how to implement basic transaction logging, how to determine who has a record locked, and how to prevent a user from locking a record for an excessive amount of time. One of these How-To's tackles the problem of updating a database that exists on multiple workstations. Because multiuser applications often use Access security, these How-To's explore the security system in detail. For instance, you'll learn how to secure your database properly, how to keep track of your users and groups, how to check to see whether users have blank passwords, and how to enforce some additional password requirements beyond those that Access handles itself. Finally, we will explore how to maintain separate but synchronized copies of a database using Access 95's new replication facilities.

10.1   Properly Secure My Database

The Access security system is sophisticated but also complex. It's very easy to think you have secured a database but miss a step or two that leaves your database unsecured. This How-To will walk you through the complex process of securing an Access database so you can rest assured that your database has been properly secured.

10.2   Maintain and Synchronize Multiple Copies of the Same Database

Access 95 includes a powerful new feature called replication. This How-To will show how you can use replication to maintain multiple copies of the same database in different locations while keeping all of the copies synchronized.

10.3   Create a Transaction Log

Server databases offer the ability to record the actions of users and replay them later on a copy of the database. This How-To will help you set up a simple transaction log within Access to track additions, edits, and deletions so you'll have a permanent record of these events.

10.4   Send Messages to Other Users without Using Electronic Mail

If your network uses Microsoft Mail or another MAPI-compliant mailer, Access offers easy connectivity to other users via the SendObject action. But even if you use a different mailer or you don't want the overhead of an e-mail interface, you can still let your users communicate with one another. This How-To will show how to share a data table on a server as a sort of electronic bulletin board and how to check it at regular intervals from each logged-on user.

10.5   Keep Track of Users and Groups Programmatically

If you're in charge of an Access workgroup, you'll need to keep track of your security layout; you can use the tools Access provides to print out such a listing. But if you need to create tables that contain this information so you can use them as part of your applications, you'll need to do a little work. This How-To will demonstrate the steps you need to take to retrieve and store user and group information in tables.

10.6   Adjust My Application Based on Who's Logged In

Using Access security, you can secure your objects easily, but you may need to change your application's look and feel based on the security level of the logged-in user. This How-To will illustrate how to adapt your application to the user's security level.

10.7   List All Users with Blank Passwords

If you're maintaining a workgroup using Access, you have to be aware of potential holes in the security system. One such hole is when users leave their passwords blank. This How-To will show how to use simple VBA code and data access objects (DAO) to retrieve a list of all users and whether or not they've set a password.

10.8   Implement a Password Aging System

Although Access security is good, it isn't perfect. This How-To will help you implement two features that are missing from the built-in security: ensuring that users periodically change their passwords and preventing users from establishing passwords that are too short or easy to guess.

10.9   Track and Limit Users That Have a Shared Database Open

There's no built-in way to find out which users are logged in to a particular shared database. This How-To will work around the problem by initializing and maintaining a table of active users in the shared database. You can also use this method to limit the number of simultaneous logins that your users are allowed.

10.10   Determine If a Record Is Locked and by Whom

In a multiuser application, Access forms simply display a slash icon when another user has the current record locked. There's no built-in mechanism, however, for determining who has the record locked. This How-To will show you how to create a VBA function that reports if a record is locked and, if so, by whom.

10.11   Prevent a User from Locking a Record for an Excessive Period of Time

If you set the RecordLocks property of your forms to Edited Record (pessimistic locking), you've no doubt run into the situation where a user begins to edit a record and then leaves for lunch without releasing the lock. This How-To will show how you can take advantage of the form's Timer event to time-out users who have had a record locked for an excessive time period.

10.12   Automatically Update Objects at Login

When you have multiple copies of an application on a network, it can be a nuisance to update them all. Why not let them update themselves? This How-To will demonstrate how to track version numbers of your application and how to upgrade selected objects automatically whenever an obsolete version of the application logs in to the shared network database.

COMPLEXITY:
INTERMEDIATE

10.1   How do I...
Properly secure my database?

Problem

The database I've developed contains some sensitive data to which I wish to limit access. I'd like to be able to create different classes of users so that some users have no access to this data, others can read the data but can't change it, and still others can read and modify the data. At the same time, I don't want to secure every object in the database in the same way; for example, I don't want non-managerial employees to have access to the sensitive employee data, but these same employees must have read/write access to customer data. Is this all possible with Access?

Technique

Access 95 supports two forms of security: workgroup-based (or user-based) security and database-password security. If you use the simpler database-password security system, you can only assign a single password to the entire database. Fortunately, your needs can be met by using the more sophisticated workgroup-based security system. Securing a database with Access' workgroup-based security system, however, can be a bit tricky. In this How-To, we guide you through the process, starting with a completely unsecured database and finishing with a well-secured database that should meet your needs.

Try to Break In

The sample database 10-01SEC.MDB has been secured using the steps from this How-To. You may wish to try breaking into this database now using either the built-in system database (SYSTEM.MDW) or the system database we have supplied (AHTSYS.MDW). Unless you know the user account names and passwords, you will be unable to read or update any of the objects in this secured database.

Steps

Before you can secure your database properly, you need to come up with a security plan. In this plan, you need to consider who will be using the database and what security permissions they should have for each database object. With a plan in place, you can then secure your database.

Making a Security Plan

The first step in creating a security plan is to make a list of the people who will be using the database. Write out the names of each user, grouping names together into distinct groups. It's okay if a user is a member of more than one group, but you need to assign each user a unique name. Users must type their user name in each time they log into Access, so you may wish to keep the names as short as possible while making the names unique. In a small workgroup, you will be able to use an individual's first name; in larger settings, you may need to include the first name plus the first initial of the last name or some similar scheme to ensure uniqueness. For example, if you were charged with designing a secured database for the How-To company, you might come up with the users and groups found in Table 10-1 and found in the sample workgroup file (AHTSYS.MDW).

GROUP	MEMBERS
Employees	Tom, Pat, Bill
Programmers	Paul, Peter
Managers	Joan, Thomas, Paul
Admins	Paul

Table 10-1 The plan of users and groups

There are several points worthy of mention regarding Table 10-1. First, Paul is a member of three groups: Programmers, Managers, and Admins. Second, two individuals in this company are named Tom; but to ensure uniqueness, we assigned one the user name Thomas. Third, we recommend using the following convention: Make user names singular and group names plural. Finally, you need to identify members of a special built-in group called Admins. This group of users will have full access to all objects and also will be able to administer the security system.

Once you have come up with a plan of users and groups of users, you need to inventory your database objects and determine which groups of users can do what with which objects. Although you *can* assign each user a separate set of permissions, your life will be simpler if you consider permissions for groups of users only. This makes it much simpler to add or subtract users later on. An object inventory for the How-To company database (10-01UNS.MDB) is shown in Table 10-2.

OBJECT	GROUP	ACCESS LEVEL FOR MEMBERS OF GROUP
tblCustomer	Employees	Read, write access to data only
	Programmers	Read, write access to data and design
	Managers	Read, write access to data only
	Admins	Full access
tblEmployee	Employees	No access
	Programmers	Read, write access to data and design
	Managers	Read, write access to data only
	Admins	Full access
frmCustomer	Employees	Run access
	Programmers	Run, read, write access to design
	Managers	Run, read, write access to design
	Admins	Full access
frmEmployee	Employees	No access
	Programmers	Run, read, write access to design
	Managers	Run, read, write access to design
	Admins	Full access

Table 10-2 The object inventory

Securing Your Database

With a plan in hand, you can now begin to secure your database following these steps:

1. Create a new workgroup. Exit Access if you are running it, and run the Access Workgroup Administrator program (WRKGADM.EXE) that was installed in your Access program directory. (Unfortunately, the Access install routine does not add a menu item for this essential program to your Start menu.) Press the Create button to create a new workgroup. At the Workgroup Owner dialog box (shown in Figure 10-1), carefully enter information into all three fields. Write the information down and store it in a safe place in case you ever need to re-create this workgroup. When you press OK, you will be prompted to name your new system database file (which is used to define the

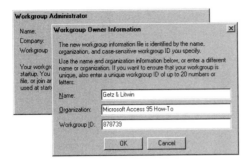

Figure 10-1 The Workgroup Owner
dialog box

workgroup). Choose a name (in the sample, we chose the name
AHTSYS.MDW), and press OK. One more dialog box will ask you to confirm
your choices and give you a final chance to document them. Once you choose
OK in this last dialog box, the program will create the new system database.

2. Change the password for the Admin account. Start Access. By default, you
are logged in as the user Admin with a blank password. You will need to
change the Admin account's password to enable security for this workgroup.
Select Tools|Security|User and Group Accounts. Choose the Change Logon
Password tab in the User and Group Accounts dialog box and enter and confirm a new nonblank password for the Admin account (see Figure 10-2). Store
the password in a safe place. Choose OK to apply the password change.

3. Create a new administrator for the workgroup. Select Tools|Security|User
and Group Accounts. Select the Users tab and create a new user account that
will be used to administer the database. This will most likely be an account
bearing your name. You can't use the built-in Admin account for this purpose
because this account cannot be secured. (This differs from the Admins group
account, which is securable.) When you create a new account, you will be
asked to enter a Name and a Personal ID (see Figure 10-3). Enter your name
under Name and a case-sensitive alphanumeric string between 4 and 20 characters under Personal ID. The Personal ID (or PID) is not your password; it's a
value that makes your account unique. Your password, which you do not set
at this time, is initially blank. Keep the PID secret, but record it somewhere in
case you ever need to re-create your account. By default, you will be made a
member of the built-in Users group; do not remove yourself (or other users)
from this group. At this time, you should also add yourself to the built-in
Admins group. In the sample workgroup, we added Paul to the Admins group
(see Figure 10-4).

**4. Log on as the new administrator and change the password for this
account.** Quit and restart Access. The Logon dialog box will appear (see

Figure 10-3 The New User/Group dialog box

Figure 10-2 Changing the password for the default Admin account

Figure 10-5). Enter the name of your new administrator-level account under Name (in the example, we entered Paul). Leave the Password text box blank because you have not yet set one for this account. When Access has loaded your database, select Tools|Security|User and Group Accounts. Choose the Change Logon Password tab in the User and Group Accounts dialog box and enter and confirm a new nonblank password for the new administrator-level account.

5. **Remove the Admin account from the Admins group.** Select Tools|Security|User and Group Accounts. Select the Users tab and remove the built-in Admin account from the Admins group. (Access will prevent you from doing this if you didn't add another user to the Admins group in step 3).

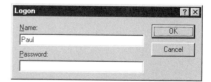

Figure 10-4 Paul is added to the Admins group

Figure 10-5 Logging on to Access

Figure 10-6 The Access Security Wizard

6. **Run the Security Wizard.** Select Tools|Security|User-Level Security Wizard. The Security Wizard dialog box will appear (see Figure 10-6) asking you which objects you wish to secure. Choose all objects and press OK. You will next be asked for a name for the secured version of your database. Choose a name—it can't be the same as the name of the original database (in the example, we chose 10-01SEC.MDB)—and press OK. The Security Wizard will secure all of the objects in your database so that only the user who runs the Wizard (in the example, Paul) and members of the Admins group will be able to view or modify objects in the database. All other users and groups will be able to open the database, but that's about it. When the Security Wizard is finished, you will have both an unsecured and a secured version of the database.

7. **Rename the databases so that the secured version assumes the name of the original database.** Back up the unsecured version of the database and store it away safely offline.

8. **Create the groups.** Select Tools|Security|User and Group Accounts. Select the Groups tab and create the groups from your security plan (except for the Admins account, which is built in). When you create a new group account, you will be asked to enter a Name and a Personal ID (see Figure 10-3). For each group account, enter the name of the group account under Name and a case-sensitive alphanumeric string between 4 and 20 characters under Personal ID. As mentioned earlier, the PID is not the password for the account; it's a value that makes that account unique. Keep it secret, but back it up somewhere in case you ever need to re-create the account.

9. **Create the users.** Select Tools|Security|User and Group Accounts. Select the Users tab and create the users from your security plan, making sure each user is assigned to the correct groups (see Figure 10-4). By default, new users will be members of the built-in Users group; do not remove users from this group.

10. **Give each user a nonblank password.** Log onto each of the new user accounts and select Tools|Security|User and Group Accounts. Choose the Change Logon Password tab and enter and confirm a new nonblank password for each new account.

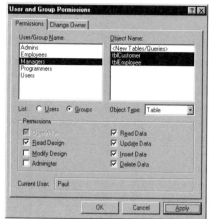

Figure 10-7 Assigning object permissions to the Managers group

11. **Assign permissions to the database objects.** At this time, take the object inventory created earlier (see Table 10-2) and add the desired object permissions for the groups of your security plan. Select Tools|Security|User and Group Permissions. Select the Permissions tab and assign permissions to the groups according to your security plan (see Figure 10-7).

Gaining Access to the AHTSYS.MDW Workgroup

After you've attached to the AHTSYS.MDW using the Access Workgroup Administrator program (WRKGADM.EXE), you'll need to log into Access using one of the user accounts from Table 10-1. With the exception of the Paul and Admin accounts, the passwords for all of the user accounts listed in Table 10-1 are blank. (The passwords for the built-in Admin account and the Paul account are both "password." Note that case *is* significant for passwords.)

How It Works

Access' workgroup-based security model consists of two parts:

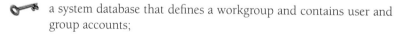 a system database that defines a workgroup and contains user and group accounts;

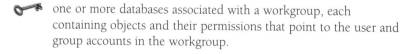 one or more databases associated with a workgroup, each containing objects and their permissions that point to the user and group accounts in the workgroup.

In step 1, you created a new securable workgroup file. Do *not* use the default workgroup file that Access installed on your system. This file (SYSTEM.MDW) contains a

null Workgroup ID (WID) and thus can easily be re-created by someone trying to break into your database.

In steps 2 through 5, you created a new member of the Admins group and then deleted the default Admin user account from the Admins group. Although these two accounts have similar names, they are very different in Access security.

The Admin user account is the default user account for all new workgroups. This account is useful because its presence in every workgroup allows you to ignore security until you need it. This is possible because Access attempts to log you on as Admin with a blank password whenever you start Access. By changing the password for this account, you are unhiding security. Once you assign a password to Admin, however, you must then create a new administrator-level user account (in the example, we used the account Paul), because—by its nature—the Admin account is the same across all Access workgroups and is thus unsecurable.

Unlike the unsecurable Admin user account, the Admins group account *is* securable. In fact, this account is the key account in any secured Access database and derives its PID from the workgroup's WID. Each Admins group account is unique across Access workgroups. Therefore, you can't use the Admins account in one workgroup to try and break into another Access workgroup. Members of this account are able to modify and administer every object in every database associated with that workgroup.

In step 6, you ran the Security Wizard. This wizard secures your database by removing all permissions to objects from all users other than the user who ran the wizard and members of the Admins group. Although it's certainly possible to secure your database without using the Security Wizard, it's very easy to make a mistake and create a database with one or more security holes. Thus it's important to use the wizard!

The Security Wizard gets you to security ground zero. It's then up to you to add the user and group accounts from your security plan (steps 8 through 10) and assign the necessary permissions for each group account to each object in the database (step 11).

Comments

It's best not to assign object permissions to users. You'll find it easier to manage the security for a workgroup by considering only the security of groups, not individual users. Occasionally, however, you may find it useful to give a single user some special set of permissions. The actual level of permissions a user gets for a particular object is the sum of the permissions he or she has been assigned as a user (if any), plus the permissions of each group for which he or she is a member.

When assigning permissions, it's important that you *don't* assign any permissions to either the Admin user account or the Users group account because these accounts are the same in all workgroups and are thus unsecured.

COMPLEXITY:
INTERMEDIATE

10.2 How do I...
Maintain and synchronize multiple copies of the same database?

Problem

I have a database that I'd like to distribute to mobile salespeople. The central copy of the database is updated by multiple users on a daily basis. The salespeople also need to make updates to their copies of the database. Is there any way to let everyone make updates and synchronize these copies when a salesperson returns to the office and plugs into our network?

Technique

Access 95 includes a powerful new feature called replication that allows you to keep multiple copies of the same database synchronized. In this How-To, we discuss how to set up a database for replication, how to synchronize the replicas, and how to deal with synchronization conflicts.

Steps

The next few sections walk you through the process of replicating a database, synchronizing replicas, and managing conflicts.

> **Using the Sample Database**
>
> The 10-02.MDB sample database is an ordinary nonreplicated database that you can use to experiment with replication. Other than that, there's nothing unusual about it.

Replicating a Database

The steps to replicating a database using the Access menus follow:

1. Back up the database and safely store the backup.

2. Select Tools|Replication|Create Replica. A dialog box will appear informing you that *The database must be closed before you can create a replica.* Choose Yes to proceed. A second dialog box will ask you if want Access to make a backup of the database before replicating it. Choose Yes if you failed to make a backup

Figure 10-8 The Create Replica
progress dialog box

in step 1; No if you already made a backup. If you choose Yes, a backup of
your database will be made with the BAK extension. For example, the sample
database 10-02.MDB will be backed up to 10-02.BAK.

3. Access will then create the design master replica, which will take the name of
your original (nonreplicated) database. During this process, Access will display a progress dialog box (see Figure 10-8).

4. Next, Access will prompt you for the name of an additional replica. By default,
it will suggest a name of the form "Replica of xxx.mdb," where xxx is the name
of your original database. For example, using the sample database, the additional replica would be named "Replica of 10-02.mdb." Enter a name or
choose OK to select the default name. Another progress dialog box similar to
the one in Figure 10-8 will appear. The replication process is complete when
you see the database container of the design master replica of the original
database, as shown for the sample database in Figure 10-9.

5. Create additional replicas by opening one of the existing replicas and selecting
Tools|Replication|Create Replica.

6. Distribute the replicas to the salespeople's laptops. Do *not* copy replicas to
multiple machines using DOS or the Windows 95 Explorer. You must create an additional unique replica for each user who will be using the
replicated database.

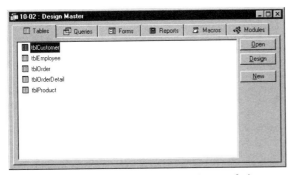

Figure 10-9 The database container of the
replicated 10-02 database

Synchronizing Replicas

Replicas in a replica set remain independent of each other until you choose to synchronize them. You can only synchronize replicas that are members of the same replica set—that is, only copies that have been derived from the same design master. You synchronize replicas one pair at a time. When you are ready to synchronize a pair of replicas—for example, when a salesperson returns to the office and plugs in his or her laptop to the office network—follow these steps:

1. Start Access and open the replica you wish to synchronize.

2. Select Tools|Replication|Synchronize Now.

3. Select the database with which you wish to synchronize using the Synchronize With drop-down box (see Figure 10-10). If you don't see the replica you wish to synchronize with, someone has probably moved it, so you'll need to navigate to it using the Browse button. Once you have located the replica, press OK to start the synchronization process.

4. A progress dialog box will appear. If the synchronization process completed successfully, a dialog box will appear confirming this fact and informing you that you need to close and reopen the database to see all changes. Select Yes to let Access close and reopen the database.

Resolving Conflicts

If multiple users have made updates to the same record in different replicas, one or more users will be informed of conflicts when they close and reopen the database to complete synchronization. See the How It Works section of this How-To for more details on how Access determines which update "wins" a synchronization exchange.

If one or more of your edits "loses" in the exchange, you will receive a dialog box the next time you open the database stating *This member of the replica set has conflicts from synchronizing changes with other members. Do you want to resolve conflicts now?* To resolve the conflicts, follow these steps:

1. Choose Yes at the conflict dialog box to start the resolution process.

2. A second dialog box will appear summarizing the conflicts that have occurred (see Figure 10-11). Select a table in the list box and press the Resolve Conflicts button to resolve the conflicts for that table.

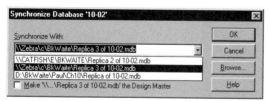

Figure 10-10 The Synchronize Database dialog box

Figure 10-11 The Resolve
Replication Conflicts dialog box

3. After a brief delay, a conflict resolution form will appear for the table. A conflict resolution form for the tblCustomer table is shown in Figure 10-12.

4. For each conflict record, your edits will appear on the left-hand side of the form and the other user's edits will appear on the right. Pick one version of the record that you feel is more "correct." If you like, you can make further edits to this version of the record, combining data from both versions of the record or some third source of information. To resolve the conflicting record, press either the Keep Existing Record button (keeping your edits) or the Overwrite with Conflict Record button (keeping the other user's edits). After a confirming dialog box, the conflict record will be deleted and the next conflict record, if any, will become the current record. Repeat the process for each record in the conflict table.

5. Close the form and repeat steps 2 through 4 for any remaining tables.

How It Works

When you replicate a database in Access, you change the database structure so that Access can track changes made to the database and later synchronize those changes with other copies of the database. Copies of a replicated database are called *replicas;*

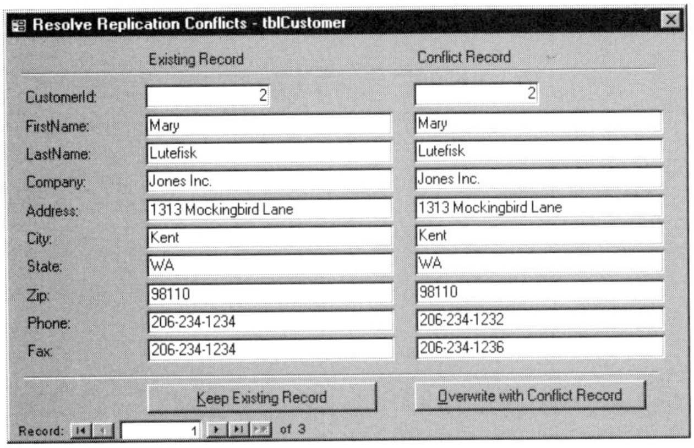

Figure 10-12 A conflict resolution form for
tblCustomer

the original master copy is called the *design master*. You can make design changes only to the design master. The design master and its replicas make up a *replica set*. You can synchronize only members of a replica set.

When converting a nonreplicated database to a replicated one, Access makes the following changes:

- Adds additional tables for tracking changes

- Adds additional fields to each table to ensure uniqueness of records across replicas and to track changes

- Adds new properties to the database

- Changes any sequentially assigned AutoNumber fields to randomly assigned AutoNumber fields to reduce the possibility of AutoNumber conflicts

When you synchronize replicas, Access compares records in each replica using the hidden s_Generation field to determine if records have been updated. During synchronization, only changed rows are exchanged among replicas.

When conflicting edits have been detected during a synchronization exchange, Access determines which edited version of a record "wins" an exchange using the following rules:

- If a record in one replica was changed more times than in the other replica, it wins.

- If all copies of a record were changed an equal number of times, then Access randomly picks a winner.

Only users with "losing" edits will be notified of conflicts.

Comments

Microsoft provides four mechanisms for replicating and managing a replicated database:

- The Access menus

- The Windows 95 Briefcase

- The Access VBA language

- The Replication Manager utility that's part of the Access Developer's Toolkit (ADT)

In this How-To, we discussed replication using the first mechanism only—the Access menus. The Windows 95 Briefcase provides you with an easier-to-use but more limited set of replication features than the Access menus. You can use the Access VBA language for additional control over the replication, synchronization, and conflict management process. The ADT's Replication Manager can be useful when managing many replicas or when replicating databases over a wide area network (WAN). You can use Replication Manager to schedule regular unattended synchronization exchanges.

Replication works best when your replicas are only loosely coupled and it isn't critical that all changes be synchronized as soon as they are made. In addition, Access replication is well suited only when you anticipate a small or moderate number of updates to the same records in different replicas. If you need real-time synchronization or you anticipate a high volume of updates to the records across replicas (that is, a large number of conflicts), then you may wish to consider the replication services built into server databases such as Microsoft SQL Server 6.0 or some other system.

COMPLEXITY:
INTERMEDIATE

10.3 How do I...
Create a transaction log?

Problem

I want to keep a permanent record of activities in my database. With multiple users changing data in my application simultaneously, how can I keep track of who made which changes?

Technique

Client-server databases such as Microsoft SQL Server offer built-in transaction-logging facilities, providing both a permanent record and a way to recover from disasters by replaying the transaction log. This How-To demonstrates a simpler transaction log using Access that tracks users and their edits without saving all the detail necessary to re-create the edits.

Steps

Start Access and load 10-03.MDB. Open frmBook, and add a few records, update some existing records, and delete some records. Then review the information in tblLog; you'll find a record in this table for each change you made, as illustrated in Figure 10-13.

ActionDate	Action	UserName	TableName	RecordPK
9/7/95 4:32:44 PM	Add	Paul	tblBook	11
9/7/95 4:32:44 PM	Update	Paul	tblBook	11
9/7/95 4:32:49 PM	Update	Paul	tblBook	11
9/7/95 4:35:43 PM	Add	Paul	tblBook	12
9/7/95 4:35:43 PM	Update	Paul	tblBook	12
9/18/95 10:28:50 PM	Update	Admin	tblBook	11
9/18/95 10:28:53 PM	Delete	Admin	tblBook	12

Figure 10-13 Logging changes to tblBook

527

To add this simple logging capability to your own database, follow these steps:

1. Create a new table, tblLog, with the fields shown in Table 10-3.

FIELD NAME	DATA TYPE
ActionDate	Date/Time
Action	Number (Byte)
UserName	Text
TableName	Text
RecordPK	Text

Table 10-3 Fields in tblLog

2. Import the module basLogging from 10-03.MDB into your own database.

3. Add three event procedures to each form for which you wish to track changes. In the sample database, these event properties are attached to frmBook; they are listed in Table 10-4. Substitute the name of your own table for "tblBook" and the Primary Key of the table for [BookID].

PROPERTY	VALUE
AfterInsert	=ahtLogAdd("tblBook", [BookID])
AfterUpdate	=ahtLogUpdate("tblBook", [BookID])
OnDelete	=ahtLogDelete("tblBook", [BookID])

Table 10-4 Logging properties for frmBook

How It Works

Changing data through a form triggers a series of events. This technique assigns code to each event that indicates that a change has been executed and uses that code to append a record to a logging table. You can use the CurrentUser function to keep track of who made the change and the Now function to record when it was made.

Because the three types of records in the logging table are similar, the functions are wrappers for a single general-purpose function that actually adds the records. This function depends on symbolic constants that are defined in the Declarations section of the basLogging module.

```
Const ahtcLogAdd = 1
Const ahtcLogUpdate = 2
Const ahtcLogDelete = 3
```

The ahtLog function accepts as arguments all of the information that needs to be stored, opens a recordset on the log table, and then saves the information in a new record of that recordset.

```
Function ahtLog(strTableName As String, varPK As Variant, _
  intAction As Integer) As Integer

   ' Log a user action in the log table

   On Error GoTo ahtLog_Err

   Dim db As Database
   Dim rstLog As Recordset

   Set db = CurrentDb()
   Set rstLog = db.OpenRecordset("tblLog", dbOpenDynaset, _
    dbAppendOnly)

   With rstLog
      .AddNew
         ![UserName] = CurrentUser()
         ![TableName] = strTableName
         ![RecordPK] = varPK
         ![ActionDate] = Now
         ![Action] = intAction
      rstLog.Update
   End With

   rstLog.Close

   ahtLog = True

ahtLog_Exit:
   On Error GoTo 0
   Exit Function

ahtLog_Err:
   MsgBox "Error " & Err.Number & ": " & Err.Description, _
    vbCritical, "ahtLog()"
   ahtLog = False
   Resume ahtLog_Exit

End Function
```

Comments

This technique demonstrates one reason why you should allow users to interact with your application only via Access forms: Forms alone generate events you can trap. If you let users edit data directly via either a table datasheet or a query datasheet, you cannot track the edits.

You could extend this technique to capture additional detail about the records being added, updated, or deleted. You might even add extra fields to the logging table to capture the actual data, rather than just the primary key that identifies the changed record. This could give you the ability to reconstruct the table completely at any point in time by inspecting the log file and making or removing changes. The drawback to this capability is that it requires substantially more storage space because you'll be storing a full copy of the data every time any part of it changes. (This is, in fact, how Access replication works.)

If you wish to log a table with a compound primary key, replace the last parameter when calling the ahtLog functions with a concatenation of each of the fields making up the primary key. For example, to log an addition to the tblOrderDetail table with a primary key made up of OrderId and OrderItem, you would use the following function call in the AfterInsert event property.

```
=ahtLogAdd("tblOrderDetail", [OrderId] & "; " & [OrderItem])
```

The ahtLog function opens a recordset on the logging table with the dbAppendOnly argument. This returns an initially blank recordset ready to receive new records, instead of a full dynaset, where existing records can be edited. This gives you a performance boost when you are only adding new records and therefore do not need to pull in existing records.

COMPLEXITY:
INTERMEDIATE

10.4   How do I...
Send messages to other users without using electronic mail?

Problem

When I have multiple users logged into my application, I'd like them to be able to communicate quickly and easily with one another. I need a simple interface for sending notes back and forth so users can check whether anyone else is editing a particular entry, compare notes on workflow, and so forth. How can I implement this in Access?

Technique

You can keep your notes in a table in a shared database to which all users have access. Whenever someone writes a note to another user, that note is added as another record in this table. By using a form that makes use of the Timer event, you can monitor the status of this table from any Access application and notify users when new messages have arrived.

Steps

This How-To employs two files, 10-04FE.MDB and 10-04BE.MDB. Before you try it, you'll need to link the tblMessage table from 10-04BE.MDB (the "back-end" or data database) to 10-04FE.MDB (the "front-end" or application database). Linking a data table allows you to use a table from one Access database within another Access database. Start Access and load 10-04FE.MDB. Choose File|Get External Data|Link

Figure 10-14 Linking a data table

Tables, and select 10-04BE.MDB as the Access link database. At the Link tables dialog box, select tblMessage and click OK, as shown in Figure 10-14.

Now you can test-drive this How-To by sending a message to yourself. Open both frmSendMail and frmReceiveMail. Minimize the Receive Mail form. Select your user name from the To combo box. If you haven't altered the default Access security settings, your user name will be Admin, which should be confirmed in the From text box. Enter any message and click the Send Message button. In Figure 10-15, Peter has used frmSendMail to compose a message to Joan.

The Send Mail form will clear as soon as the message is sent. Within 10 seconds, the Receive Mail form will pop up with the message. Figure 10-16 shows how Joan would see the message from Peter. Click on the Mark as Read button to clear the Receive Mail form. If there is more than one message waiting, you can navigate through each of them.

To use this technique in your own applications, follow these steps:

1. Identify the shared database you'll be using to hold the messages. This can be an existing shared database or a new one designed expressly for this purpose. Create a new table with the fields shown in Table 10-5. Make MessageID the Primary Key of this table, and save it as tblMessage.

FIELD NAME	DATA TYPE
MessageID	Counter
From	Text
To	Text
DateSent	Date/Time
DateReceived	Date/Time
Message	Memo

Table 10-5 Fields in tblMessage

2. Close the shared database and open the database from which you want to send and receive messages. This is the database where you'll create the

Figure 10-15 A message
from Peter to Joan

Figure 10-16 Joan receives
the message from Peter

remaining objects. Import basMail and basFillUsers from 10-01FE.MDB to
this database.

3. Create a new form with the properties shown in Table 10-6.

PROPERTY	VALUE
Caption	Send Mail
Default View	Single Form
Scroll Bars	Neither
Record Selectors	No
Navigation Buttons	No

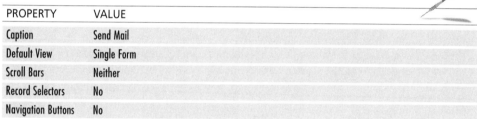

Table 10-6 Properties for frmSendMail

4. Add two unbound text box controls and an unbound combo box control to
the form, as shown in Figure 10-15. Name the first text box txtFrom. Set its
Control Source to:

```
=CurrentUser()
```

Name the second text box txtMessage and size it to hold the text of your message. Set the Enter Key Behavior property for txtMessage to New Line in Field.

5. Name the combo box cboTo and size it the same as txtFrom. Set its combo
box specific properties to match those in Table 10-7.

PROPERTY	VALUE
Row Source Type	ahtFillUserList
Row Source	
Column Count	1
Column Heads	No

PROPERTY	VALUE
Column Widths	
Bound Column	1
List Rows	8
List Width	Auto

 Table 10-7 Properties for the cboTo combo box

6. Add a command button, with the properties shown in Table 10-8, to the form. The &Send Message caption makes the button respond to the [ALT]-[S] accelerator key shortcut.

PROPERTY	VALUE
Name	cmdSend
Caption	&Send Message
On Click	=ahtSendMail()

 Table 10-8 Properties for cmdSend

7. Save this form as frmSendMail.

8. Select File|Get External Data|Link Tables and link the tblMessage table you created in your shared database to this front-end database.

9. Create a new query based on tblMessage. Drag all of the fields from the field list to the query grid. Set query criteria as shown in Table 10-9. Save this query as qryNewMail.

FIELD	CRITERIA
To	CurrentUser()
DateReceived	IsNull

 Table 10-9 Criteria for qryNewMail

10. Create another new form with the properties shown in Table 10-10.

PROPERTY	VALUE
Record Source	qryNewMail
Caption	No mail
Default View	Single Form
Allow Additions	No
Scroll Bars	Neither

continued on next page

continued from previous page

PROPERTY	VALUE
Record Selectors	No
Navigation Buttons	Yes
On Load	=ahtCheckMail()
On Timer	=ahtCheckMail()
Timer Interval	10,000

 Table 10-10 Properties for frmReceiveMail

11. Add three bound text box controls to the form. Name the first one txtFrom, set the Control Source to From, and size it to hold the sender's address. Name the second one txtSent, set the Control Source to DateSent, and size it to hold the date and time the message was sent. Name the third one txtMessage, set the Control Source to Message, and size it to hold the message text.

12. Add a watermark picture to the form using the additional form properties found in Table 10-11.

PROPERTY	VALUE
Picture	*bitmap file*
Picture Type	Embedded
Picture Size Mode	Clip
Picture Alignment	Center
Picture Tiling	No

Table 10-11 Additional properties for frmReceiveMail

In the sample database, we used a simple bitmap created with the Windows 95 Paint program to display a message in the center of the form. This bitmap, NONEW.BMP, is included on the CD. You can add this bitmap to your form or create your own.

13. Place a rectangle control with the same background color as the form's detail section behind all of the controls on the form. After you have positioned and sized it to take up the entire detail section, you can move it behind the other controls by selecting Format|Send to Back.

14. Add a command button, with the properties shown in Table 10-12, to the form.

PROPERTY	VALUE
Name	cmdReceive
Caption	&Mark as Read
On Click	=ahtReceiveMail()

 ***Table 10-12*** Properties for cmdReceive

15. Save this form as frmReceiveMail.

How It Works

This technique works by passing messages back and forth through tblMessage. The sending form is unbound; when you send a message, you don't want to have to flip through all previous messages. The ahtSendMail function takes whatever you type into the form and puts it into this table. It also uses the CurrentUser function to put your name into the From field of the table and the Now function to time-stamp the message. The ahtSendMail function is shown here.

```
Function ahtSendMail() As Integer

    ' Take the message and user from the
    ' frmMailSend form and send it to the mail
    ' backend

    On Error GoTo ahtSendMail_Err

    Dim db As Database
    Dim rstMail As Recordset
    Dim frmMail As Form

    Set db = CurrentDb()
    Set rstMail = db.OpenRecordset("tblMessage", dbOpenDynaset, _
     dbAppendOnly)
    Set frmMail = Forms![frmSendMail]

    With rstMail
       .AddNew
          ![From] = CurrentUser()
          ![To] = frmMail![cboTo]
          ![DateSent] = Now
          ![Message] = frmMail![txtMessage]
       .Update
    End With

    frmMail![cboTo] = Null
    frmMail![txtMessage] = Null

    rstMail.Close

ahtSendMail_Exit:
    On Error GoTo 0
    Exit Function

ahtSendMail_Err:
    MsgBox "Error " & Err.Number & ": " & Err.Description, _
     vbCritical, "ahtSendMail()"
    Resume ahtSendMail_Exit

End Function
```

Opening the recordset with the dbAppendOnly flag accelerates the process of adding a new record because it avoids reading in the existing records that the Send function doesn't care about.

The cboTo combo box uses a list-filling function to fill the combo box with a list of current users in the workgroup. List-filling functions are discussed in How-To 7-5. This particular list-filling function fills its list using security data access objects to iterate through the collection of users in the workgroup. We will defer the discussion of this topic to How-To 10.5.

The Receive Mail form is based on a query that finds all messages directed to the current user with null DateReceived values.

By default, new records added from elsewhere on a network do not show up on an already opened form; you must explicitly requery the form for this to happen. The ahtCheckMail function automatically performs this requery at load time and once every 10 seconds to check for new mail. The ahtCheckMail function is shown here.

```
Declare Function aht_apiIsIconic Lib "user32" _
 Alias "IsIconic" (ByVal Hwnd As Long) As Long

Const ahtcErrNoCurrentRecord = 3021

Function ahtCheckMail() As Integer

    ' Check for new mail, and if there is any,
    ' restore the received mail form

    On Error GoTo ahtCheckMail_Err

    Dim rstClone As Recordset
    Dim frmMail As Form

    Set frmMail = Forms![frmReceiveMail]
    frmMail.Requery

    Set rstClone = frmMail.RecordsetClone
    rstClone.MoveFirst
    If Not rstClone.EOF Then
        frmMail.Caption = "New Mail!"
        If aht_apiIsIconic(frmMail.Hwnd) Then
            frmMail.SetFocus
            DoCmd.Restore
        End If
    Else
        frmMail.Caption = "No mail"
    End If

    rstClone.Close

ahtCheckMail_Exit:
    On Error GoTo 0
    Exit Function
```

```
ahtCheckMail_Err:
    If Err <> ahtcErrNoCurrentRecord Then
        MsgBox "Error " & Err.Number & ": " & Err.Description, _
          vbCritical, "ahtCheckMail()"
    End If
    Resume ahtCheckMail_Exit

End Function
```

After the form is requeried, ahtCheckMail checks for new mail by looking at the RecordsetClone property of the form. This property returns an exact duplicate of the form's underlying recordset. If any new records are found in the clone, EOF (end of file) will not be true; so the function changes the form's caption and, if the form is currently minimized, restores the form to its full size. The function calls the Windows API function IsIconic (aliased as aht_apiIsIconic and declared in the Declarations section of basMail) to determine if the form is minimized.

We have used the form's Picture property, a rectangle, and the form's AllowAdditions property to add one additional effect to the form: When the form's recordset is empty, all of the controls on the form disappear and a bitmap displaying *There are no new mail messages* appears on the form (see Figure 10-17).

This trick is accomplished by setting the form's AllowAdditions property to No, adding a watermark picture to the form, and adding an opaque rectangle that will normally hide the watermark when there are records in the form's recordset. When there are no records in a form's recordset and you have set AllowAdditions to No, Access hides all of the form's controls—including the unbound rectangle control—and prominently displays the form's watermark, if there is one.

Comments

This method uses the Access user name to track mail senders and recipients. To use it in a production environment, you'll need to activate Access security (otherwise, everyone is signed on as the Admin user at all times). See How-To 10.1 for a discussion of how to activate security.

To test this How-To with multiple users, you'll need to have several machines available on a network. Make a copy of 10-04FE.MDB for each computer and use File|Get

Figure 10-17 frmReceiveMail displays a special message when there is no new mail

External Data|Link Tables to link the same copy of tblMessage to each one. Log in as a different user at each computer, and you'll be able to send messages back and forth.

You can adjust the performance impact of this technique by changing the Timer Interval property of frmReceiveMail. This property measures the number of milliseconds between each execution of the On Timer event. In the sample database, the TimerInterval property is set to 10,000 milliseconds, or 10 seconds; its highest possible value is 65,535, or just over a minute.

COMPLEXITY:
ADVANCED

10.5 How do I...
Keep track of users and groups programmatically?

Problem

As the database administrator, I'd like to be able to track users and their groups within my workgroup. I know I can use Tools|Security|Print Security to print a report of users and groups, but I'd like to be able to use that information as part of the applications I write. How can I gather the information I need?

Technique

Using data access objects (DAO), you can retrieve all the information you need about users' names and groups. Once you have that information, you can use it to create lists of users and their groups.

Steps

The sample form frmUserGroups in 10-05.MDB fills tables with the information you need and presents the information to you in a list box. To test it out, open and run frmUserGroups. Figure 10-18 shows the form in use for a sample workgroup.

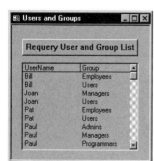

Figure 10-18 frmUserGroups shows users and their groups for a sample workgroup

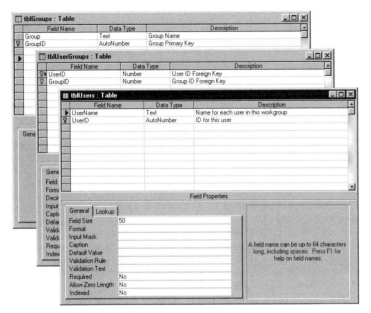

Figure 10-19 The three tables, tblGroups, tblUserGroups, and tblUsers, in design mode

To gather this information in your own applications, follow these steps:

1. Create the tables you'll need to hold the information. Import the three tables from 10-05.MDB or use the information in Table 10-13 to create your own. Figure 10-19 shows the three tables in design mode.

TABLE NAME	FIELD NAME	FIELD TYPE	PRIMARY KEY?
tblGroups	Group	Text	No
	GroupID	Counter	Yes
tblUserGroups	UserID	Number (Long Integer)	Yes
	GroupID	Number (Long Integer)	Yes
tblUsers	UserName	Text	No
	UserID	Counter	Yes

Table 10-13 Table layouts for gathering user/group information

2. If you created your own tables in step 1, you'll also need to add an index to tblGroups. In the Indexes properties sheet (available by choosing View|Indexes when tblGroups is open in design mode), add a row, as described in Table 10-14. Use the default settings for the index properties. Table 10-14 also shows the Primary Key row that should already exist in the Indexes properties sheet.

INDEX NAME	FIELD NAME	SORT ORDER
Group	Group	Ascending
PrimaryKey	GroupID	Ascending

Table 10-14 Index settings for tblGroups

3. Import the module basListUsers from 10-05.MDB or enter the following code into a global module. This is the code you'll use to fill the three tables you just created.

```
Sub ahtListUsers()

    ' Create tables containing all
    ' the users and groups in the current
    ' workgroup.
    '
    ' The results will be in:
    '     tblUsers, tblGroups and
    '     tblUserGroups.
    ' Run qryUserGroups to see sorted list.

    Dim db As Database
    Dim wrk As Workspace

    Dim intI As Integer
    Dim intJ As Integer

    Dim rstUsers As Recordset
    Dim rstGroups As Recordset
    Dim rstUserGroups As Recordset

    Dim usr As User

    ' Clear out the old values.
    DoCmd.SetWarnings False
    DoCmd.RunSQL "Delete * From tblUserGroups"
    DoCmd.RunSQL "Delete * From tblUsers"
    DoCmd.RunSQL "Delete * From tblGroups"
    DoCmd.SetWarnings True

    ' Set up object variables.
    Set wrk = DBEngine.Workspaces(0)
    Set db = wrk.Databases(0)

    Set rstUsers = db.OpenRecordset("tblUsers")
    Set rstGroups = db.OpenRecordset("tblGroups")
    Set rstUserGroups = db.OpenRecordset("tblUserGroups")

    ' Refresh the Users and Groups collections
    ' so you see any recently added members
    wrk.Users.Refresh
    wrk.Groups.Refresh
```

```
' Build up a list of all the groups in tblGroups
For intI = 0 To wrk.Groups.Count - 1
    With rstGroups
        .AddNew
            !Group = wrk.Groups(intI).Name
        .Update
    End With
Next intI

' Loop through all the users, adding
' rows to tblUsers and tblUserGroups.
For intI = 0 To wrk.Users.Count - 1
    ' Add a user to tblUsers.
    Set usr = wrk.Users(intI)
    With rstUsers
        .AddNew
            !UserName = usr.Name
        .Update
        .Move 0, .LastModified
    End With

    ' Now loop through all the groups
    ' that user belongs to, hooking up the rows
    ' in tblUserGroups.
    For intJ = 0 To usr.Groups.Count - 1
        rstGroups.Index = "Group"
        rstGroups.Seek "=", usr.Groups(intJ).Name
        With rstUserGroups
            If Not .NoMatch Then
                .AddNew
                    !UserID = rstUsers!UserID
                    !GroupID = rstGroups!GroupID
                .Update
            End If
        End With
    Next intJ
Next intI

rstUsers.Close
rstGroups.Close
rstUserGroups.Close

End Sub
```

4. Import the query qryUserGroups from 10-05.MDB or create a new query, as
follows: When Access asks you to add a table, close the dialog box. Once in
design mode, click on the SQL button on the toolbar and enter the following
expression.

```
SELECT DISTINCTROW tblUsers.UserName, tblGroups.Group
FROM tblUsers INNER JOIN (tblGroups INNER JOIN tblUserGroups ON
tblGroups.GroupID = tblUserGroups.GroupID) ON tblUsers.UserID =
tblUserGroups.UserID
ORDER BY tblUsers.UserName, tblGroups.Group;
```

Then save the query as qryUserGroups.

5. To produce the current list of users and groups, execute the code in ahtListUsers. You can call it directly, use a button whose Click event calls the procedure, or call it from the Debug Window. (The sample form calls ahtListUsers from the Click event of the cmdRequery button on the form.) Once you've executed that code, you'll have filled in the three tables. You can use qryUserGroups to retrieve the information you need or create your own queries based on the three tables.

How It Works

This How-To relies on DAO to gather its information. The DBEngine object is at the root (or the highest level) of the DAO hierarchy and has a single collection, the Workspaces collection. Each workspace represents a session of the Access database engine. (Unless you're writing sophisticated applications, you'll most likely never see more than a single concurrent workspace.) The default workspace contains information about the collection of open databases (only one is open in the user interface—all others must be opened via VBA code) along with the available Users and Groups collections. These are the collections you'll need for filling tables with the user names and their groups. The code in the ahtListUsers subroutine does all the work.

The ahtListUsers function starts out by deleting all the existing rows in the three tables, using the RunSQL macro action.

```
DoCmd SetWarnings False
DoCmd RunSQL "Delete * From tblUserGroups"
DoCmd RunSQL "Delete * From tblUsers"
DoCmd RunSQL "Delete * From tblGroups"
DoCmd SetWarnings True
```

The SetWarnings macro action is required to disable warnings, or Access would pop up an alert telling you how many rows will be deleted from each table.

The procedure then sets up object variables to refer to several recordset objects and refreshes the Users and Groups collections of the workspace. This is necessary to make sure you see any recent changes to these collections made via the Access user interface or by another Access session.

```
Set wrk = DBEngine.Workspaces(0)
Set db = wrk.Databases(0)

Set rstUsers = db.OpenRecordset("tblUsers")
Set rstGroups = db.OpenRecordset("tblGroups")
Set rstUserGroups = db.OpenRecordset("tblUserGroups")

' Refresh the Users and Groups collections
' so you see any recently added members
wrk.Users.Refresh
wrk.Groups.Refresh
```

The next step is to build a list of all the groups. This is accomplished by looping through all the elements of the workspace's Groups collection. Just like all other collections in Access, the Groups collection has a Count property, indicating how many elements it contains. These items are numbered 0 through Count −1, the code iterates through them all, adding a row to tblGroups for each group in the collection.

```
' Build up a list of all the groups in tblGroups
For intI = 0 To wrk.Groups.Count - 1
    With rstGroups
        .AddNew
            !Group = wrk.Groups(intI).Name
        .Update
    End With
Next intI
```

Once tblGroups is filled in, ahtListUsers does the same for users. Just as the workspace contains a collection of groups, it contains a collection of users. The function walks through the Users collection, adding a row at a time to tblUsers, as shown here.

```
' Loop through all the users, adding
' rows to tblUsers and tblUserGroups.
For intI = 0 To wrk.Users.Count - 1
    ' Add a user to tblUsers.
    Set usr = wrk.Users(intI)
    With rstUsers
        .AddNew
            !UserName = usr.Name
        .Update
        .Move 0, .LastModified
    End With

    ' See the following code example...

Next intI
```

Once a user is added, rows are added to tblUserGroups for each group that contains the current user. This is accomplished by enumerating through the Groups collection for the current user. (There was a choice here: Each member of the workspace's Users collection has its own Groups collection, listing the groups to which it belongs, and each member of the workspace's Groups collection has its own Users collection, listing the member. The code can either walk through the users, looking at the Groups collection in each, or walk through the groups, looking at the Users collection in each. This example walks through the workspace's Users collection, one at a time, iterating the Groups collection for each user.) The following code loops through every item in the user's Groups collection, finding the matching name in tblGroups and then adding a row to tblUserGroups containing both the user's UserID field (from tblUsers) and the GroupID field (from tblGroups). This way, tblUserGroups contains a single row for every user/group pair.

```
' Now loop through all the groups
' that user belongs to, hooking up the rows
' in tblUserGroups.
For intJ = 0 To usr.Groups.Count - 1
    rstGroups.Index = "Group"
    rstGroups.Seek "=", usr.Groups(intJ).Name
    With rstUserGroups
```

continued on next page

continued from previous page

```
            If Not .NoMatch Then
                .AddNew
                    !UserID = rstUsers!UserID
                    !GroupID = rstGroups!GroupID
                .Update
            End If
        End With
    Next intJ
```

Once the code has looped through all the users and, for each user, all the groups to which he or she belongs, it closes all the objects.

```
rstUsers.Close
rstGroups.Close
rstUserGroups.Close
```

Now tblUsers, tblGroups, and tblUserGroups contain information about each user and the groups to which he or she belongs. Figure 10-20 shows the three tables, filled in for the sample workgroup.

Comments

Once you've filled the three tables, you can easily perform lookups in your VBA code or create reports like the one you get with the Tools|Security|Print Security command. You could also lift pieces of the code from ahtListUsers, once you understand it, for use in your own applications. The next How-To shows a much simpler function, ahtAmMemberOfGroup, that uses a similar technique to query on the fly if the current user is a member of a specific group.

The ahtListUsers procedure is not production quality code. To keep it simple, we left out the error-handling code. Certainly, any procedure of this nature that

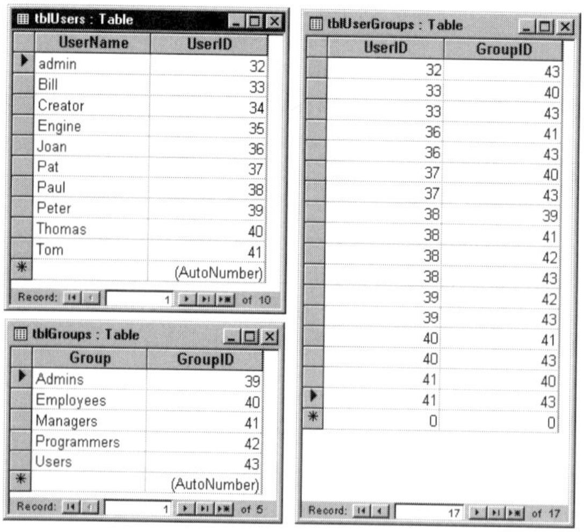

tblUsers : Table

UserName	UserID
▶ admin	32
Bill	33
Creator	34
Engine	35
Joan	36
Pat	37
Paul	38
Peter	39
Thomas	40
Tom	41
✱	(AutoNumber)

Record: ⏮ ◀ 1 ▶ ▶▶ ▶✱ of 10

tblGroups : Table

Group	GroupID
▶ Admins	39
Employees	40
Managers	41
Programmers	42
Users	43
✱	(AutoNumber)

Record: ⏮ ◀ 1 ▶ ▶▶ ▶✱ of 5

tblUserGroups : Table

UserID	GroupID
32	43
33	40
33	43
36	41
36	43
37	40
37	43
38	39
38	41
38	42
38	43
39	42
39	43
40	41
40	43
▶ 41	40
41	43
✱ 0	0

Record: ⏮ ◀ 17 ▶ ▶▶ ▶✱ of 17

Figure 10-20 The three user/group tables, filled in with data

manipulates tables must include sufficient error handling. Though it's not likely, some other user may have locked the output tables or, worse, deleted them; or you may not have permissions for the system tables you need to gather this information. In a production environment, it's best to trap errors and handle them.

In the list of users in Figure 10-20, there are two users that you might never have seen before: Creator and Engine. These two users are created by the Jet Engine itself and cannot be used or manipulated by VBA code. As you'll see in How-To 10.7, you can create a workspace object for any normal user, allowing that user to log into a new session of the Jet Engine, but you can't use Creator or Engine to create new workspace objects or log onto a session of Access using the UI. It's a good thing, too! Because neither can have a password (their passwords are always blank), this would otherwise provide a security breach.

Once you know how to enumerate through collections, as shown in this How-To, you should be able to apply the same techniques to other database collections and their objects. For more information, see Chapter 4.

COMPLEXITY:
ADVANCED

10.6 How do I... Adjust my application based on who's logged in?

Problem

I've secured my database so that certain classes of users, for example, can't edit data using a particular form or can't run a specific report, but this doesn't prevent them from trying to open the form or report and receiving a permission error. I'd like my application to adjust itself based on the current user's security level. Is there any way to accomplish this?

Technique

Using VBA code, you can create a function that determines if the current user is a member of a security group. Based on the value this function returns, you can change any runtime property of any form or control, thus adapting your application to the user's security level.

Steps

Because this How-To makes use of Access Security, before you can try the sample database, you'll need to join the supplied workgroup. Exit Access if you are running it and run the Access Workgroup Administrator program (WRKGADM.EXE) that was installed in your Access program directory. (Unfortunately, the Access install routine does not add a menu item for this essential program to your Start menu.) Click the Join… button on the first screen and the Browse… button in the second dialog box. Locate the supplied AHTSYS.MDW file (the same security database used in How-To 10.1) and join it. Exit from the Workgroup Administrator after you acknowledge the confirmation message.

Now start Access. You will be prompted for a user name and password. Enter the name of a user from Table 10-1 (from How-To 10.1). With the exception of the Paul and Admin accounts, the account passwords are blank. (The passwords for the built-in Admin account and the Paul account are both "password." Note that case *is* significant for passwords.)

Load 10-06.MDB. Open the frmSwitchboard form. Depending on which user you logged in as, you will see a Manager, Programmer, or default form. For example, Manager-level users will have see two Manager buttons and a close button (see Figure 10-21). In addition, a Close menu item will be included in the File menu. In contrast, a member of the Programmers group will see two Programmer buttons, no Close button, and no File|Close menu item (see Figure 10-22).

To implement this system in your own database, follow these steps:

1. Import the basGroupMember module into your database.

2. For each form that you wish to customize at runtime based on the user's group membership, you'll need to attach an event procedure to the form's Open event that calls the ahtAmMemberOfGroup function one or more times within an If…Then statement. Because users can be members of more than one group, you need to check for membership in the "highest"-level groups first, in decreasing order of security.

3. Once you have determined the security level for the currently logged-in user, selectively hide and unhide controls on the form to suit your application's needs. You might also wish to alter the caption of labels or other controls or to customize other aspects of the form's look and feel. You can also customize the menus for the form by changing the form's MenuBar property to point to different sets of menu macros. We have done all of this in the sample

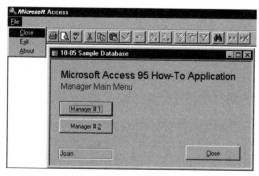

Figure 10-21 Database for user Joan—a member of Managers

Figure 10-22 Database for user Peter—a member of Programmers

frmSwitchboard form. The runtime customizations to frmSwitchboard are summarized in Table 10-15.

GROUP	VISIBLE BUTTONS	LBLMENU CAPTION	FILE|CLOSE MENU AVAILABLE?
Managers	Manager #1	Manager Main Menu	Yes
	Manager #2		
	Close		
Programmers	Programmer #1	Programmer Main Menu	No
	Programmer #2		
(default)	Default #1	Default Main Menu	No
	Default #2		

Table 10-15 The customizations made to frmSwitchboard

The code that drives this customization process for frmSwitchboard is shown here.

```
Private Sub Form_Open(Cancel As Integer)

    ' Adapt switchboard to match level of logged-in user.

    ' Because users can be members of more than one group,
    ' you need to check membership in decreasing order
    ' starting with the highest-level group.
    If ahtAmMemberOfGroup("Managers") Then
        With Me
            .MenuBar = "ManagerMenu"
            !cmdManager1.Visible = True
            !cmdManager2.Visible = True
            !cmdProgrammer1.Visible = False
            !cmdProgrammer2.Visible = False
            !cmdDefault1.Visible = False
            !cmdDefault2.Visible = False
```

continued on next page

continued from previous page

```
                    !cmdClose.Visible = True
                    !lblMenu.Caption = "Manager Main Menu"
                End With
            ElseIf ahtAmMemberOfGroup("Programmers") Then
                With Me
                    .MenuBar = "UserMenu"
                    !cmdManager1.Visible = False
                    !cmdManager2.Visible = False
                    !cmdProgrammer1.Visible = True
                    !cmdProgrammer2.Visible = True
                    !cmdDefault1.Visible = False
                    !cmdDefault2.Visible = False
                    !cmdClose.Visible = False
                    !lblMenu.Caption = "Programmer Main Menu"
                End With
            Else
                With Me
                    .MenuBar = "UserMenu"
                    !cmdManager1.Visible = False
                    !cmdManager2.Visible = False
                    !cmdProgrammer1.Visible = False
                    !cmdProgrammer2.Visible = False
                    !cmdDefault1.Visible = True
                    !cmdDefault2.Visible = True
                    !cmdClose.Visible = False
                    !lblMenu.Caption = "Default Main Menu"
                End With
            End If

End Sub
```

How It Works

By default, the form is saved with the least secure options set; if anything goes wrong, this provides a little extra insurance. When any user opens frmSwitchboard, the Load event procedure is called and the form's look and feel are customized on the fly. Group membership is determined using the ahtAmMemberOfGroup function found in basGroupMember.

```
Function ahtAmMemberOfGroup(strGroup As String)

    Dim wrk As Workspace
    Dim usr As User
    Dim strTest As String

    Set wrk = DBEngine.Workspaces(0)

    ' Refresh collections to stay in synch with
    ' Access UI
    wrk.Users.Refresh
    wrk.Groups.Refresh

    ' Set up pointer to current user
    Set usr = wrk.Users(CurrentUser())
```

```
' Handle errors in line
On Error Resume Next
' If any property of the Groups collection
' using the passed-in group works then user is
' a member. Otherwise an error will occur
' and you can assume user is not a member.
strTest = usr.Groups(strGroup).Name
ahtAmMemberOfGroup = (Err = 0)

End Function
```

This function is very simple. It determines if a user is a member of a group by setting a pointer to the Users collection of the current user and then attempting to get the name of group in the Groups collection of that user. If this fails, then the user is not a member of the group in question. If it succeeds, then the user must be a member of the group. See How-To 10.5 for more details on the programmatic manipulation of the Users and Groups collections.

Comments

We could have based the form customizations on the name of the current user using the built-in CurrentUser function, but this requires the consideration of each user individually, which should be avoided if at all possible. It's much easier to manage groups of users rather than individual users. Still, you could add additional user tests to the If…Then statement in the Load event procedure to handle exceptional users.

Note

Prior versions of Access did not allow a user to check group membership unless the user was also a member of the Admins group. This restriction is lifted in Access 95.

It's important that you include an Else clause in the If…Then statement of the Load event procedure to handle users who are not members of any of the groups you have tested for. In the sample event procedure, we only tested for membership in the Managers and Programmers groups. Any users who are not members of these two groups are handled by the Else clause.

You can use this technique to alter any runtime property in response to the user's group membership, including the following:

- Whether certain menu items appear

- Whether certain controls are visible and therefore active

- What query a form is based on—some users can see more records than others

What data entry controls are visible—some users can enter more fields than others

Which toolbars are shown

COMPLEXITY:
ADVANCED

10.7 How do I... List all users with blank passwords?

Problem

As database administrator, I need to ensure that every member of my workgroup has a password. I can use the NewPassword method to create a new password, and I understand why I can't retrieve the value of a user's password, but I need a way to find out if a user hasn't yet established a password. I'd like to create a list of all users, indicating which ones don't have a password. How can I do this?

Technique

You can't retrieve users' passwords. There's an easy way, however, for you to find out if a user has a blank password: Try logging onto the user's account using a blank password. If you succeed, then you know the user has no password. Unfortunately, this could be a tiresome process if there are a lot of users. Fortunately, you can automate it using DAO and the CreateWorkspace method.

Steps

The sample form, frmUserPasswords in 10-07.MDB, fills a table with a list of users and whether any of them have blank passwords and then presents this information to you in a list box. To test it out, open and run frmUserPasswords. Figure 10-23 shows the form in use for a sample workgroup.

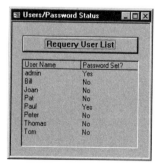

Figure 10-23 frmUserPasswords shows users and their password status for a sample workgroup

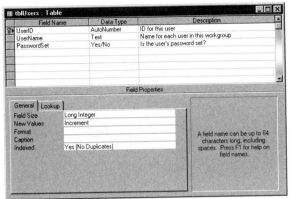

Figure 10-24 The table tblUsers in design
mode

To use this information in your own applications, follow these steps:

1. Create a table you'll need to hold the information. Import tblUsers from
10-07.MDB or use the information in Table 10-16 to create your own.
Figure 10-24 shows the table in design mode.

FIELD NAME	FIELD TYPE	PRIMARY KEY?
UserID	AutoNumber	Yes
UserName	Text	No
PasswordSet	Yes/No	No

 Table 10-16 Table layouts for gathering user/group information

2. Import the module basFindBlank from 10-07.MDB or enter the following
code into a global module. This is the code you'll use to fill the table you just
created.

```
Sub ahtFindBlankPasswords()

    ' Fill tblUsers with list of users, and
    ' whether or not their password is blank.

    Dim intI As Integer
    Dim usr As User
    Dim db As Database
    Dim wrk As Workspace
    Dim wrkTest As Workspace
    Dim rst As Recordset
    Dim fPwdUsed As Boolean
    Dim strUser As String

    Const ahtcErrInvalidPassword = 3029
```

continued on next page

551

continued from previous page

```
    DoCmd.SetWarnings False
    DoCmd.RunSQL "Delete * From tblUsers"
    DoCmd.SetWarnings True

    ' Set up object variables.
    Set wrk = DBEngine.Workspaces(0)
    Set db = wrk.Databases(0)
    Set rst = db.OpenRecordset("tblUsers")
    On Error Resume Next

    ' Loop through all the users.
    For intI = 0 To wrk.Users.Count - 1
        Set usr = wrk.Users(intI)
        strUser = usr.Name

        ' Skip the two special users, since you can't log in
        ' as either of them via CreateWorkspace().
        If strUser <> "Creator" And strUser <> "Engine" Then
            ' Try to log in with a blank password. If this
            ' doesn't fail, the user has a blank password.
            Set wrkTest = DBEngine. _
              CreateWorkspace("Test", strUser, "")
            fPwdUsed = (Err = ahtcErrInvalidPassword)

            ' Add a new row to tblUsers, storing the user's
            ' name and whether or not they have a password.
            With rst
                .AddNew
                    !UserName = strUser
                    !PasswordSet = fPwdUsed
                .Update
            End With
            wrkTest.Close
        End If
    Next intI

    rst.Close
    On Error GoTo 0
End Sub
```

3. To produce the list of all users whose passwords are blank, execute the code in
ahtFindBlankPasswords. You can call it from the Debug Window or from an
event procedure, as in the sample form, frmUserPasswords. (If you decide to
use frmUserPasswords, you must also create a query, qryUserPasswords, that
sorts the rows in tblUsers ascending on the UserName field. This query fills
the list box on the sample form.) You could create a report that pulls its rows
from tblUsers, as well, allowing you to prepare a report listing all users with
blank passwords.

How It Works

AhtFindBlankPasswords uses DAO to do most of its work. It starts by clearing out the previous contents of tblUsers so later code can fill the table in with the current list of users and their password status.

```
DoCmd.SetWarnings False
DoCmd.RunSQL "Delete * From tblUsers"
DoCmd.SetWarnings True
```

Next, the function sets up the object variables it will need to retrieve and store the password information. It uses the workspace object to loop through all the users (because the workspace object provides the Users collection that you'll use) and the recordset object to refer to the table into which you'll write the new data.

```
Set wrk = DBEngine.Workspaces(0)
Set db = wrk.Databases(0)
Set rst = db.OpenRecordset("tblUsers")
```

The next step is to loop through the Users collection of the default workspace object. For each user, the code attempts to create a new workspace, as shown here.

```
For intI = 0 To wrk.Users.Count - 1
    Set usr = wrk.Users(intI)
    '
    ' See the next code sample
    '
Next intI
```

Finally, the important step: For each user, the code calls the CreateWorkspace method of the DBEngine object. To call this method, you must supply three parameters: the name for the new workspace (because you only need the results of attempting to create the workspace, you don't really care about its name but you still must give it a name), the user's name, and the user's password. An empty string ("") is passed for the password. If an error occurs, that indicates that the current user has a password because the attempt to create a new workspace as that user failed. If there is no error, then that user does not have a password. The code checks whether an error occurred, comparing the Access built-in Err value with the known error value that occurs when you attempt to create a workspace with an invalid password. Regardless of whether an error occurred, the code adds a new row to tblUsers and stores the user name, along with the password status, in the table. Here is the code for these steps.

```
' Skip the two special users, since you can't log in
' as either of them via CreateWorkspace().
If strUser <> "Creator" And strUser <> "Engine" Then
    ' Try to log in with a blank password. If this
    ' doesn't fail, the user has a blank password.
    Set wrkTest = DBEngine. _
    CreateWorkspace("Test", strUser, "")
    fPwdUsed = (Err = ahtcErrInvalidPassword)
```

continued on next page

continued from previous page

```
' Add a new row to tblUsers, storing the user's
' name and whether or not they have a password.
With rst
   .AddNew
         !UserName = strUser
         !PasswordSet = fPwdUsed
   .Update
End With
wrkTest.Close
End If
```

As discussed in How-To 10.5, the Users collection contains two users that are not actually part of your workgroup: Creator and Engine. Access creates these two users but doesn't allow you to log on as either one, from the command line or by creating a new workspace. The code just skips these special users, because it doesn't really care whether their passwords are blank.

Comments

If you intend to use ahtFindBlankPasswords in a production environment, you may wish to add some error-handling code to the procedure. Anytime you write to tables, you should include some method of dealing with errors. At the very least, alert the user (which could very well be yourself) that an error has occurred and supply information about the error.

COMPLEXITY:
ADVANCED

10.8   How do I...
Implement a password aging system?

Problem

I'm using Access security to secure my database. I'd like to tighten up security further by making sure that users change their passwords on a regular basis. I'd also like to disallow passwords that are shorter than some minimum length. How can I add these features to my database?

Technique

This How-To shows how to maintain a table of users and a record of when they last changed their password. When a user logs onto the system, a routine checks to see if the password is too old; if so, the routine requires the password to be changed immediately via a custom form. By changing passwords through a form instead of through the Access Security menus, you gain the opportunity to enforce minimum-length restrictions on new passwords.

Steps

You can use this How-To database with any workgroup, but the supplied AHTSYS.MDW workgroup works best. If you decide to use the supplied workgroup, you'll need to exit Access if you are running it and run the Access Workgroup Administrator program (WRKGADM.EXE) that was installed in your Access program directory. (Unfortunately, the Access install routine does not add a menu item for this essential program to your Start menu.) Click the Join… button on the first screen and the Browse… button in the second dialog box. Locate the supplied AHTSYS.MDW file (the same security database used in How-To 10.1) and join it. Exit from the Workgroup Administrator after you acknowledge the confirmation message.

Now start Access. You will be prompted for a user name and password. Enter the name of a user from Table 10-1 (from How-To 10.1). With the exception of the Paul and Admin accounts, the account passwords are blank. (The passwords for the built-in Admin account and the Paul account are both "password." Note that case is significant for passwords.)

Open 10-08.MDB and run the macro mcrSampleAutoExec. If you have logged into Access using the Admin account or one of the accounts from Table 10-1 (see How-To 10.1), you'll see the warning shown in Figure 10-25 because the passwords for each of these users should have expired.

When you dismiss this dialog box, the Change Password form shown in Figure 10-26 opens and asks for a new password. If you enter an incorrect old password, neglect to change the password, don't type the new password the same way twice, or use a new password that's too short, you'll get an error message when you click the Change button. Otherwise, your password will be changed.

Caution

If you do this with your original SYSTEM.MDW file, you'll change your default Admin password. Make sure you immediately change it back to an empty password (using the Tools|Security|User and Group Accounts menu option) or note the new password.

Figure 10-25 Password
expiration message

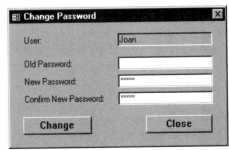

Figure 10-26 Password change form

To implement a password aging system in your own application, follow these steps:

1. Create a new table with the fields shown in Table 10-17 (or import the existing tblPasswordAging table from 10-08.MDB).

FIELD NAME	DATA TYPE	COMMENTS
UserName	Text	Primary Key
PasswordAge	Number—Integer	
PasswordChanged	Date/Time	

Table 10-17 tblPasswordAging fields

Save this table as tblPasswordAging.

2. Switch to datasheet view and enter one record for each user in your database, with the user's name, the maximum number of days you wish to elapse before forcing the user to change his or her password, and the date of last password change. The last two fields have default values of 60 days and the current system date, respectively. (Alternately, you can import frmPasswordAgingSetup from 10-08.MDB. When you run this form and press the "Generate rows for new users" button, an event procedure executes, walking through the Users collection of the current workgroup and generating a row for each user it finds.)

3. Create a new form with the properties shown in Table 10-18 (or import the existing frmChangePassword from 10-08.MDB).

PROPERTY	VALUE
Caption	Change Password
Default View	Single Form
Scroll Bars	Neither
Record Selectors	No
Navigation Buttons	No

Table 10-18 Properties of frmChangePassword

4. Place four unbound text boxes, named txtUser, txtOldPassword, txtNewPassword, and txtConfirmPassword, on the form. Set the ControlSource property of txtUser to:

```
=CurrentUser()
```

Leave the ControlSource property of the txtOldPassword, txtNewPassword, and txtConfirmPassword fields blank and set the Input Mask property of these fields to Password, so that the text typed by the user appears as asterisks.

5. Add two command buttons to the form. Name the first command button cmdChange, with a caption of "Change." Set its OnClick property to:

```
=ahtChangePassword()
```

Name the second command button cmdClose, with a caption of "Close." Create an event procedure attached to the OnClick property of cmdClose containing the following code.

```
DoCmd.Close
```

Save the form as frmChangePassword.

6. Create a new macro with a single RunCode action or add the action to your existing AutoExec macro. The RunCode action should call the function.

```
=ahtCheckPasswordAge()
```

7. Import the basChangePassword module from 10-08.MDB.

How It Works

The password aging checking function called from the macro you created in step 6 is shown here.

```
Function ahtCheckPasswordAge() As Boolean

    ' Check to make sure password isn't expired

    On Error GoTo ahtCheckPasswordAge_Err

    Dim db As DATABASE
    Dim rstAges As Recordset
    Dim strCriteria As String

    ahtCheckPasswordAge = True

    Set db = DBEngine.Workspaces(0).Databases(0)
    Set rstAges = db.OpenRecordset("tblPasswordAging", _
     dbOpenDynaset)

    fPasswordOK = False
    strCriteria = "UserName='" & CurrentUser() & "'"

    With rstAges
        ' Search for this user
        .FindFirst strCriteria
        ' Check if password has expired
        If Not .NoMatch Then
            If (Date - (!PasswordChanged + !PasswordAge)) _
             >= 0 Then
                MsgBox "Password Expired!", vbCritical, _
                 "Change Password"
                ahtCheckPasswordAge = False
                DoCmd.OpenForm "frmChangePassword", _
                 acNormal, , , acEdit, acDialog
```

continued on next page

continued from previous page

```
                Else
                    fPasswordOK = True
                End If
            End If
        End With

    ahtCheckPasswordAge_Exit:
        On Error GoTo 0
        Exit Function

    ahtCheckPasswordAge_Err:
        MsgBox "Error" & Err.Number & ":" & Err.Description, _
          vbCritical, "ahtCheckPasswordAge()"
        Resume ahtCheckPasswordAge_Exit

    End Function
```

This function works by first locating the row in tblPasswordAging that matches the name of the current user. It then checks to see if the following expression is greater than or equal to zero.

```
(Date - (rstAges!PasswordChanged + rstAges!PasswordAge))
```

If this expression is greater than or equal to zero, then the password has expired and the change form is opened in dialog box mode (the user must deal with this form before the rest of your application can proceed).

The ahtChangePassword function does the actual work of changing the password, making six separate checks of the data the user entered.

First, the function confirms that the old password was entered correctly by using it to open a new workspace for the current user (we used this trick in How-To 10.7):

```
' Check for correct old password
If IsNull(frmPW!txtOldPassword) Then
    strPassword = ""
Else
    strPassword = frmPW!txtOldPassword
End If
' Make sure it works!
Set wrkCheck = DBEngine.
 CreateWorkspace("Check", strUserName, strPassword)
If Err Then
    MsgBox "Invalid old password!", vbCritical, "Change Password"
    Exit Function
End If
```

Second, it confirms that the new password differs from the old.

```
' Make sure new password is not the same as the old one
If Nz(frmPW!txtOldPassword) = Nz(frmPW!txtNewPassword) Then
    MsgBox "New password can't be the same as old password!", _
        vbCritical, "Change Password"
    Exit Function
End If
```

The built-in Nz function (new for Access 95) converts any Nulls to zero-length strings for the sake of the comparison. This function is useful when comparing variant values that may be null.

Third, it confirms that the new password is longer than the ahtcPWMinLength constant (which we have set to 4).

```
' Make sure new password is long enough
If Len(Nz(frmPW!txtNewPassword)) < ahtcPWMinLength Then
    MsgBox "New password is too short!", vbCritical, _
     "Change Password"
    Exit Function
End If
```

Fourth, it confirms that the new password isn't the same as the user name.

```
' Make sure new password is not the same as the user name
If frmPW!txtNewPassword = strUserName Then
    MsgBox "New password ('" & strUserName & _
     "') can't be the same as user name!", _
     vbCritical, "Change Password"
    Exit Function
End If
```

Fifth, it confirms that the new password isn't the string "password."

```
' Make sure new password is not 'password'
If frmPW!txtNewPassword = "password" Then
    MsgBox "New password ('password') is illegal!", vbCritical, _
     "Change Password"
    Exit Function
End If
```

Sixth, it confirms that the new password was entered the same way twice to guard against an unintentional typographic error.

```
' Make sure new password was entered twice the same
' and is not null
If (frmPW!txtNewPassword <> frmPW!txtConfirmNewPassword) Then
    MsgBox "New Password Entered Incorrectly!", vbCritical, _
     "Change Password"
    Exit Function
End If
```

If the new password passes all of these tests, the function uses the NewPassword method of the User object to assign the new password to the user. The function checks for an error here, because it would still be possible to enter a password that was unacceptable to the Access security system.

```
' OK, change the password
wrk.Users(strUserName).NewPassword strPassword, _
 frmPW!txtNewPassword
If Err Then
    MsgBox "Invalid Password!", vbCritical, "Change Password"
    Exit Function
Else
```

continued on next page

continued from previous page

```
     ' Change global var
     fPasswordOK = True
     MsgBox "Password has been changed!", vbInformation, _
      "Change Password"
     ' And update the PasswordChanged date to today
     fRet = ahtUpdateChangedDate()
   End If
```

Once the password has been successfully changed, the appropriate record in tblPasswordAging is updated using the ahtUpdateChangedDate function. The complete ahtChangePassword function, as well as ahtUpdateChangedDate, are included here.

```
Global fPasswordOK As Boolean

Const ahtcPWMinLength = 4

Function ahtChangePassword() As Integer

   ' Change the user password
   ' Uses data entered on frmChangePassword

   On Error Resume Next

   Dim wrk As Workspace
   Dim wrkCheck As Workspace
   Dim strUserName As String
   Dim strPassword As String
   Dim frmPW As Form
   Dim fRet As Boolean

   Set wrk = DBEngine.Workspaces(0)
   strUserName = CurrentUser()
   Set frmPW = Forms!frmChangePassword

   ' Check for correct old password
   If IsNull(frmPW!txtOldPassword) Then
      strPassword = ""
   Else
      strPassword = frmPW!txtOldPassword
   End If
   ' Make sure it works!
   Set wrkCheck = DBEngine.
    CreateWorkspace("Check", strUserName, strPassword)
   If Err Then
      MsgBox "Invalid old password!", vbCritical, _
       "Change Password"
      Exit Function
   End If

   ' Make sure new password is not the same as the old one
   If Nz(frmPW!txtOldPassword) = Nz(frmPW!txtNewPassword) Then
      MsgBox "New password can't be the same as old password!", _
       vbCritical, "Change Password"
      Exit Function
   End If
```

```
    ' Make sure new password is long enough
    If Len(Nz(frmPW!txtNewPassword)) < ahtcPWMinLength Then
        MsgBox "New password is too short!", vbCritical, _
        "Change Password"
        Exit Function
    End If

    ' Make sure new password is not the same as the user name
    If frmPW!txtNewPassword = strUserName Then
        MsgBox "New password ('" & strUserName & _
        "') can't be the same as user name!", _
        vbCritical, "Change Password"
        Exit Function
    End If

    ' Make sure new password is not 'password'
    If frmPW!txtNewPassword = "password" Then
        MsgBox "New password ('password') is illegal!", vbCritical, _
        "Change Password"
        Exit Function
    End If

    ' Make sure new password was entered twice the same and
    ' is not null
    If (frmPW!txtNewPassword <> frmPW!txtConfirmNewPassword) Then
        MsgBox "New Password Entered Incorrectly!", vbCritical, _
        "Change Password"
        Exit Function
    End If

    ' OK, change the password
    wrk.Users(strUserName).NewPassword strPassword, _
    frmPW!txtNewPassword
    If Err Then
        MsgBox "Invalid Password!", vbCritical, "Change Password"
        Exit Function
    Else
        ' Change global var
        fPasswordOK = True
        MsgBox "Password has been changed!", vbInformation, _
        "Change Password"
        ' And update the PasswordChanged date to today
        fRet = ahtUpdateChangedDate()
    End If

ahtChangePassword_Exit:
    On Error GoTo 0
    If Not wrkCheck Is Nothing Then wrkCheck.Close
    Exit Function

ahtChangePassword_Err:
    MsgBox "Error" & Err.Number & ":" & Err.Description, _
        vbCritical, "ahtChangePassword()"
    Resume ahtChangePassword_Exit

End Function
```

continued on next page

continued from previous page

```
Function ahtUpdateChangedDate() As Boolean

    ' Update password changed date

    On Error GoTo ahtUpdateChangedDate_Err

    Dim db As Database
    Dim rstAges As Recordset
    Dim strCriteria As String

    ahtUpdateChangedDate = False

    Set db = DBEngine.Workspaces(0).Databases(0)
    Set rstAges = db.OpenRecordset("tblPasswordAging", _
      dbOpenDynaset)

    fPasswordOK = False
    strCriteria = "UserName='" & CurrentUser() & "'"

    With rstAges
        .FindFirst strCriteria
        If Not .NoMatch Then
            .Edit
                !PasswordChanged = Date
            .Update
        Else
            MsgBox "Error: Password aging record has " & _
              "been deleted!", _
              vbCritical, "ahtUpdateChangedDate()"
        End If
    End With

ahtUpdateChangedDate_Exit:
    On Error GoTo 0
    Exit Function

ahtUpdateChangedDate_Err:
    MsgBox "Error" & Err.Number & ":" & Err.Description, _
      vbCritical, "ahtUpdateChangedDate()"
    Resume ahtUpdateChangedDate_Exit

End Function
```

Comments

You may wish to add additional checks to ahtChangePassword that search for other
commonly used (and commonly discovered) passwords, such as the name of your
business.

In the sample database, the password change is not forced. The user can close the
Change Password form without entering anything or clicking the Change button. You
can prevent this behavior (which we recommend doing), and actually force a password change, by checking the value of the global constant fPasswordOK in the On

Close event of the password change form. The code sets this flag variable to True if the password is successfully changed and False otherwise.

A user might still fool this password aging system by setting the system clock to a date occurring after the current date. To prevent this, your best bet may be to take advantage of whatever features your network offers for time synchronization between the server and the individual workstations.

COMPLEXITY:
ADVANCED

10.9 How do I...
Track and limit users that have a shared database open?

Problem

I need better control over a networked Access application. Sometimes users log in and leave a form open while they go to lunch, locking other users out. Also, some users have a habit of logging in from multiple workstations at the same time. How can I keep track of who is logged into an Access database and set limits on the number of simultaneous connections they can have?

Technique

Although Access keeps track of who has which pages of records locked—storing this information in the LDB file associated with the database—this information is off limits to you. In addition, Access has no built-in tools to limit logins. You can work around both of these shortcomings by constructing your own table of active users in the shared database and maintaining its contents as users open and close your application.

Steps

This How-To employs two files, 10-09FE.MDB and 10-09BE.MDB. Before you can try it, you'll need to link the data tables from 10-09BE.MDB to 10-09FE.MDB. Load 10-09FE.MDB while holding down the SHIFT key to prevent the AutoExec macro from executing. Now use File|Get External Data|Link Tables to link both tblCurrentUsers and tblUserLimits from 10-09BE.MDB to this database. Close and reopen the database, this time letting the AutoExec macro execute. Open frmCurrentConnection; you should be the only connected user, as shown in Figure 10-27.

To see the login limiting process, open tblUserLimits and change the LoginLimit for Admin from 1 to 0. Close the table and then close and reopen the database. This time you'll see an error dialog box form (see Figure 10-28). Click on OK and Access will unload. You can get back in by reopening the database with the SHIFT key depressed.

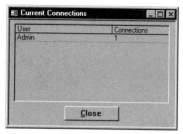

Figure 10-27 Current users

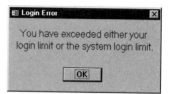

Figure 10-28 Login limit
message

To add login tracking to your own project, follow these steps:

1. Create two new tables in your shared database, with the field definitions
shown in Tables 10-19 and 10-20 (or import the existing tables from
10-09BE.MDB).

FIELD NAME	DATA TYPE	COMMENTS
UserName	Text	Primary Key
NumberOfLogins	Number	Integer

Table 10-19 Fields in tblCurrentUsers

FIELD NAME	DATA TYPE	COMMENTS
UserName	Text	Primary Key
LoginLimit	Number	Integer

Table 10-20 Fields in tblUserLimits

2. Open tblUserLimits and add a new record for each user of your workgroup.
Enter the user's name and the maximum number of simultaneous logins for that
user. (Alternately, you can import frmUserLimitsSetup from 10-09FE.MDB.
When you run this form and press the "Generate rows for new users" button,
an event procedure executes, walking through the Users collection of the current workgroup and generating a row for each user it finds.)

3. Close your shared database and open the database that will be used to access
the shared data. To this database, link both new tables from the shared database.

4. Create a new macro named AutoExec or add to your existing AutoExec macro
a RunCode action that calls the function:

```
=ahtAddLogin()
```

5. Create a new query based on tblCurrentUsers (or import qryCurrentConnections
from 10-09FE.MDB). Add the fields shown in Table 10-21 to the query grid.

FIELD	SORT
User: UserName	Ascending
Connections: NumberOfLogins	(not sorted)

 Table 10-21 The fields in qryCurrentConnections

Save this query as qryCurrentConnections.

6. Create a new form with the properties shown in Table 10-22 (or import frmCurrentConnections from 10-09FE.MDB and skip steps 6 through 9 of this How-To).

PROPERTY	VALUE
Caption	Current Connections
Default View	Single Form
Scroll Bars	Neither
Record Selectors	No
Navigation Buttons	No

 Table 10-22 frmCurrentConnections properties

7. Place an unbound list box control on the form, with the properties shown in Table 10-23.

PROPERTY	VALUE
Name	lboConnections
Row Source Type	Table/Query
Row Source	qryCurrentConnections
Column Count	2
Column Heads	Yes
Column Widths	1.75 in; 1 in

 Table 10-23 lboConnections properties

8. Place a command button on the form. Name it cmdClose and enter this event procedure for its On Click property:

```
Sub cmdClose_Click ()
    DoCmd.Close
End Sub
```

9. Save this form as frmCurrentConnections.

10. Create another new form. Set its On Unload property to:

```
=ahtRemoveLogin()
```

Place a single button on this form, name the button cmdClose, and enter this event procedure for its On Click property:

```
Sub cmdClose_Click ()
    DoCmd.Close
End Sub
```

Save this form as zsfrmCloseProcessing. You don't have to worry about any of the form's other properties because it will never be seen by the user.

11. Create another new form with the properties shown in Table 10-24 (or import zsfrmLoginError from 10-09FE.MDB).

PROPERTY	VALUE
Caption	Login Error
Default View	Single Form
Scroll Bars	Neither
Record Selectors	No
Navigation Buttons	No
Auto Center	Yes
Border Style	Dialog Box
On Close	=ahtQuitApplication()

 Table 10-24 zsfrmLoginError properties

Save this form as zsfrmLoginError.

12. Import the basUserLog module from 10-09FE.MDB.

How It Works

To track logins, this How-To runs one function whenever a user starts the database and another when the user quits the database. The startup function, ahtAddLogin, is called by the AutoExec macro, which runs whenever the database is opened. In a production database, you might use the Startup properties of the database to create a system where users could not override this macro with the (SHIFT) key.

The ahtAddLogin first determines whether there are any records in the login table matching the user name. If not, then the current user can't be exceeding his or her limit, so a record is added for this user.

```
strSQL = "SELECT * FROM tblCurrentUsers "
strSQL = strSQL & "WHERE UserName="
strSQL = strSQL & ahtcQuote & CurrentUser() & ahtcQuote
Set rstUsers = db.OpenRecordset(strSQL, dbOpenDynaset, _
    dbDenyWrite)
```

TRACK AND LIMIT USERS THAT HAVE A SHARED DATABASE OPEN?

```
' Does a record for this user appear in the users table?
' If not, then user can't already be logged in, so
' add a record for this user with a default NumberofLogins = 1
If rstUsers.EOF Then
    With rstUsers
        .AddNew
            ![UserName] = CurrentUser()
            ![NumberofLogins] = 1
            intRet = 1
        .Update
    End With
Else
```

For users already listed in the login table, the function compares the user's existing login count (if any) with the user's limit from tblUserLimits. If this login will not put the user over that limit, then the login count is increased. Otherwise the count is left unchanged.

```
Else
    ' Check to see whether this login would exceed the
    ' user's login limit
    strSQL = "SELECT * FROM tblUserLimits "
    strSQL = strSQL & "WHERE UserName="
    strSQL = strSQL & ahtcQuote & CurrentUser() & ahtcQuote    Set
rstLimits = db.OpenRecordset(strSQL, dbOpenDynaset)
    If Not rstLimits.EOF Then
      If rstUsers![NumberofLogins] >= rstLimits![LoginLimit] _
        Then
            intRet = -1
        Else
            intRet = ChangeUserCount(rstUsers, 1)
        End If
    Else
        intRet = ChangeUserCount(rstUsers, 1)
    End If
    rstLimits.Close
End If

rstUsers.Close
```

Depending on whether this is a legal login, the ahtAddLogin function opens one of two forms.

```
' Quit if individual user count or total user count exceeded
If intRet < 0 Or intTotalUsers > ahtcTotalUserLimit Then
    DoCmd.OpenForm "zsfrmLoginError", _
      acNormal, , , acEdit, acDialog
Else
    DoCmd.OpenForm "zsfrmCloseProcessing", _
      acNormal, , , acEdit, acHidden
End If
```

If the login is disallowed, the zsfrmLoginError form displays an error message and waits for a user response. Otherwise, the zsfrmCloseProcessing form opens in hidden mode and remains loaded while the rest of the application proceeds.

If the user is not allowed to log on, his or her only possible action is to close the error dialog box form. Whether this is done with its control menu or the form's OK button, the ahtQuitApplication function runs and uses the Quit method of the Application object to force this instance of Access to unload.

Whenever the user unloads Access in any fashion, the last form to close will be the hidden zsfrmCloseProcessing form that was opened during the startup processing. This automatically runs the ahtRemoveLogin function to decrease the user's count of active logins, with the code shown here.

```
strSQL = "SELECT * FROM tblCurrentUsers "
strSQL = strSQL & "WHERE UserName="
strSQL = strSQL & ahtcQuote & CurrentUser() & ahtcQuote
Set rstUsers = db.OpenRecordset(strSQL, dbOpenDynaset, _
 dbDenyWrite)

ahtRemoveLogin = ChangeUserCount(rstUsers, -1)

rstUsers.Close
```

The ahtAddLogin, ahtRemoveLogin, ahtQuitApplication, and ChangeUserCount functions are included here.

```
Const ahtcQuote = """"
Const ahtcTotalUserLimit = 5

Function ahtAddLogin() As Integer

   ' Increase the current user's login count.

   On Error GoTo ahtAddLogin_Err

   Dim db As Database
   Dim rstUsers As Recordset
   Dim rstLimits As Recordset
   Dim strSQL As String
   Dim intRet As Integer
   Dim intTotalUsers As Integer

   Set db = CurrentDb()
   strSQL = "SELECT * FROM tblCurrentUsers "
   strSQL = strSQL & "WHERE UserName="
   strSQL = strSQL & ahtcQuote & CurrentUser() & ahtcQuote
   Set rstUsers = db.OpenRecordset(strSQL, dbOpenDynaset, _
    dbDenyWrite)

   ' Does a record for this user appear in the users table?
   ' If not, then user can't already be logged in, so
   ' add a record for this user with a default NumberofLogins = 1
   If rstUsers.EOF Then
     With rstUsers
        .AddNew
           ![UserName] = CurrentUser()
           ![NumberofLogins] = 1
           intRet = 1
```

```
            .Update
        End With
    Else
        ' Check to see whether this login would exceed the
        ' user's login limit
        strSQL = "SELECT * FROM tblUserLimits "
        strSQL = strSQL & "WHERE UserName="
        strSQL = strSQL & ahtcQuote & CurrentUser() & ahtcQuote
        Set rstLimits = db.OpenRecordset(strSQL, dbOpenDynaset)
        If Not rstLimits.EOF Then
          If rstUsers![NumberofLogins] >= rstLimits![LoginLimit] _
            Then
                intRet = -1
            Else
                intRet = ChangeUserCount(rstUsers, 1)
            End If
        Else
            intRet = ChangeUserCount(rstUsers, 1)
        End If
        rstLimits.Close
    End If

    rstUsers.Close

    ' Also count the total number of logged-in users
    intTotalUsers = DSum("[NumberofLogins]", "tblCurrentUsers")

    ahtAddLogin = intRet

    ' Quit if individual user count or total user count exceeded
    If intRet < 0 Or intTotalUsers > ahtTotalUserLimit Then
        DoCmd.OpenForm "zsfrmLoginError", _
          acNormal, , , acEdit, acDialog
    Else
        DoCmd.OpenForm "zsfrmCloseProcessing", _
          acNormal, , , acEdit, acHidden
    End If

ahtAddLogin_Exit:
    On Error GoTo 0
    Exit Function

ahtAddLogin_Err:
    MsgBox "Error " & Err.Number & ": " & Err.Description, _
      vbCritical, "ahtAddLogin()"
    Resume ahtAddLogin_Exit

End Function

Function ahtQuitApplication() As Integer

    ' Quit Access

    On Error GoTo ahtQuitApplication_Err

    Application.Quit
```

continued on next page

continued from previous page

```
    ahtQuitApplication_Exit:
        On Error GoTo 0
        Exit Function

    ahtQuitApplication_Err:
        MsgBox "Error " & Err.Number & ": " & Err.Description, _
          vbCritical, "ahtQuitApplication()"
        Resume ahtQuitApplication_Exit

End Function

Function ahtRemoveLogin() As Integer

    ' Decrease the login count for the current user.
    ' Returns the new login count.

    On Error GoTo ahtRemoveLogin_Err

    Dim db As Database
    Dim rstUsers As Recordset
    Dim strSQL As String

    Set db = CurrentDb()
    strSQL = "SELECT * FROM tblCurrentUsers "
    strSQL = strSQL & "WHERE UserName="
    strSQL = strSQL & ahtcQuote & CurrentUser() & ahtcQuote
    Set rstUsers = db.OpenRecordset(strSQL, dbOpenDynaset, _
      dbDenyWrite)

    ahtRemoveLogin = ChangeUserCount(rstUsers, -1)

    rstUsers.Close

ahtRemoveLogin_Exit:
    On Error GoTo 0
    Exit Function

ahtRemoveLogin_Err:
    MsgBox "Error " & Err.Number & ": " & Err.Description, _
      vbCritical, "ahtRemoveLogin()"
    Resume ahtRemoveLogin_Exit

End Function

Function ChangeUserCount(rstUsers As Recordset, _
  intMod As Integer)
    With rstUsers
        .Edit
            ![NumberofLogins] = ![NumberofLogins] + intMod
        .Update
        ChangeUserCount = ![NumberofLogins]
    End With
End Function
```

Comments

In addition to the per user login limit that you specify in tblUserLimits, ahtAddLogin checks the total number of logged-in users against the ahtcTotalUserLimit constant in basUserLog, which we set to 5. You'll find this constant useful if you need to limit the number of concurrent users of an application because of performance or licensing concerns. If you don't want to limit the total number of users of your application, set ahtcTotalUserLimit to some large value, such as 99.

If you try to streamline the ahtAddLogin function by dropping the error message form and automatically closing the application if the login count is exceeded, you will find that the Application.Quit statement is not legal in any function that runs while your AutoExec macro is still processing. The sample database works around this limitation by opening a form and placing code that executes this method in the form's On Close processing. This works because form processing and module processing are asynchronous with regard to one another. When you open a form, the module continues processing without waiting for the form, and in this case finishes the login procedure before the user could possibly click the OK button.

If you do want to close the database without user intervention, you can modify the error form to unload itself in response to a Timer event, and open it in hidden mode.

If you have sufficient memory (at least 16 megabytes), you can test the login limit feature of this sample without having a second machine. Open two copies of Access and load the same database onto each copy. When you load the database, make sure to load it in shared mode by leaving the Exclusive box unchecked on the file open dialog box.

An Alternative Solution

During the fourth quarter of 1995, Microsoft released an unsupported dynamic link library, MSLDBUSR.DLL, that you can call to determine the machine names of all users logged into a database. You can use this DLL to provide functionality that's similar to this How-To.

COMPLEXITY:
ADVANCED

10.10   How do I...
Determine if a record is locked and by whom?

Problem

When I use pessimistic locking in my applications, Access informs me that a record has been locked by another user with the slash icon in the record selector of the form's Detail section (see Figure 10-29). Although this is nice, I often would like to know who specifically has the record locked so in urgent situations, for example, I could request the user to release the lock. Is there any way to determine who has a record locked?

Technique

There is no built-in menu command or toolbar button that tells you who has a record locked, but you can create a VBA function that returns the user name and machine name of the user who has the current record locked. This How-To shows how to create such a function you can call from any form.

Steps

Start Access and load the same copy of the 10-10.MDB database on at least two machines on your network. (If you don't have a network but have sufficient memory—at least 16 megabytes—you can test the sample database using two instances of Access on a single machine.)

Customizing the Record Locking Method

To change the method of locking for a form, open the form in design mode and modify the value of the form's RecordLocks property. If this property is set to EditedRecord, then Access uses pessimistic locking for the form, which means that Access locks the page of records as soon as you change any data on the form (when the pencil icon appears in the form's record selector). If this property is set to NoLocks, then Access uses optimistic locking for this form, which means that Access locks the page of records only at the moment you save your changes. For most forms, optimistic locking is the preferable setting because it keeps records locked for a much shorter period of time. Sometimes, however, you'll need to employ pessimistic locking if you need to ensure that no more than one user is editing a record at the same time.

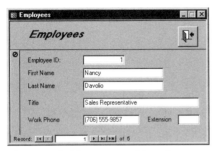

Figure 10-29 A record has been locked, but by whom?

Figure 10-30 The user and machine name of the user who has locked the current record

Open the frmEmployees form on the first machine (or instance), changing the data in any control of the form so that the pencil icon appears in the form's record selector. Don't release the lock and open the same form with the same record loaded on the second machine. On the second machine, click the button with the image of a padlock. A message box should appear displaying the user and machine name of the user who locked the record on the first machine (see Figure 10-30). (To get an accurate user name, both machines should share the same system database file with security enabled. For more information on enabling security, see How-To 10.1.)

To add a lock identification button to your own forms, follow these steps:

1. Import the basRecordLock module from 10-10.MDB into your database.

2. Add a command button to each form with the following in the command button's OnClick property.

```
=ahtWhoHasLockedRecord([Form])
```

How It Works

The ahtWhoHasLockedRecord function is shown here.

```
Function ahtWhoHasLockedRecord(frm As Form)

    On Error GoTo ahtWhoHasLockedRecord_Err

    ' Display a message box that says either:
    '   -No user has the current record locked, or
    '   -The user & machine name of the user who
    '    who has locked the current record.

    Dim rst As Recordset
    Dim fMUError As Boolean
    Dim varUser As Variant
    Dim varMachine As Variant
    Dim strMsg As String
```

continued on next page

continued from previous page

```
     ' Default message
     strMsg = "Record is not locked by another user."

     ' Clone the form's recordset and synch up to the
     ' form's current record
     Set rst = frm.RecordsetClone
     rst.Bookmark = frm.Bookmark

     ' If the current record is locked, then the next
     ' statement should produce an error that we will trap
     rst.Edit

ahtWhoHasLockedRecord_Exit:
     ' Display either the default message or one specifying
     ' the user and machine who has locked the current record.
     MsgBox strMsg, vbOKOnly + vbInformation, "Locking Status"
     Exit Function
ahtWhoHasLockedRecord_Err:
          ' Pass the error to ahtGetUserAndMachine which will attempt
          ' to parse out the user and machine from the error message
          fMUError = ahtGetUserAndMachine(Err.Description, varUser, _
           varMachine)
          ' If the return value is True, then ahtGetUserAndMachine
          ' was able to return the user and machine name of the user.
          ' Otherwise, assume the record was not locked.
          If fMUError Then
              strMsg = "Record is locked by user: " & varUser & _
               vbCrLf & "on machine: " & varMachine & "."
          End If
     End If

     Resume ahtWhoHasLockedRecord_Exit

End Function
```

This function accepts a single parameter: a pointer to a form. Using this form object, ahtWhoHasLockedRecord clones the form's recordset, synchronizes the clone's current record with that of the form, and attempts to lock the current record. Two things can happen as a result of this locking attempt:

- the attempt will succeed, which will tell you that the record was not locked by another user; or

- the attempt will fail with an error message stating who has locked the record.

By parsing this error message, you can determine who has locked the record. Parsing of the error message is accomplished by the ahtGetUserAndMachine function, which is shown here.

```
Function ahtGetUserAndMachine(ByVal strErrorMsg As String, _
    varUser As Variant, varMachine As Variant) As Boolean

     On Error Resume Next
```

```
' Parse out the passed error message, returning
'   -True and the user and machine name
'    if the record is locked, or
'   -False if the record is not locked.

Dim intUser As Integer
Dim intMachine As Integer
Dim strUser As String
Dim strMachine As String

Const ahtcUserStringLen = 16
Const ahtcMachineStringLen = 12

ahtGetUserAndMachine = False

intUser = InStr(strErrorMsg, " locked by user ")
If intUser > 0 Then
    intMachine = InStr(strErrorMsg, " on machine ")
    If intMachine > 0 Then
        strUser = Mid$(strErrorMsg, _
          intUser + ahtcUserStringLen, _
          intMachine - (intUser + ahtcUserStringLen - 1))
        strMachine = Mid$(strErrorMsg, _
          intMachine + ahtcMachineStringLen, _
          (Len(strErrorMsg) - intMachine - _
          ahtcMachineStringLen))
    End If
    varUser = strUser
    varMachine = strMachine
    ahtGetUserAndMachine = True
End If

End Function
```

This function accepts as its argument the description property of the Err object, which was generated by ahtWhoHasLockedRecord. If it can successfully parse the error message, determining at least the user name (and possibly the machine name), then it returns a True value to the calling routine with the name of the user and machine as the second and third parameters of the function call. There's nothing magic about this function—it uses the Instr function to locate certain landmarks in the parsed error message.

Comments

These functions will be much more useful if you've implemented security. If you haven't and try to use the ahtWhoHasLockedRecord function, you'll find that everyone is named Admin, which doesn't help much when trying to track down who has locked a particular record.

COMPLEXITY:
ADVANCED

10.11 How do I...
Stop a user from locking a record for an excessive period of time?

Problem

I've employed pessimistic locking on my application's forms to prevent two users from making changes to the same record at the same time. Sometimes users will lock a record for an excessive period of time. For example, a user might start to edit a record and then get a long phone call or leave for lunch without committing his or her edits. Is there any way to limit how long a user can lock a record and "time-out" the user when he or she has exceeded the locking time limit?

Technique

There's no built-in database or form option for "maximum record lock interval," but you can create your own record lock time-out feature by making use of the form's Timer event. This How-To shows how to create such a facility using an event procedure attached to the form's Timer event.

Steps

Load the 10-11.MDB database. Open the frmEmployees sample form to test the record lock time-out feature. Make a change to an existing record and leave the record in an unsaved state. After a brief delay, a message will appear in the form's footer (see Figure 10-31) informing you that you have so many seconds of edit time remaining. The

Figure 10-31 The unsaved edits will be timed-out in 43 seconds unless they are saved

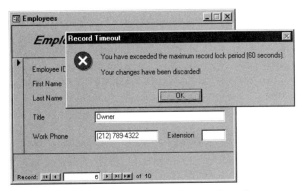

Figure 10-32 The edits have been timed-out

number will count down second by second; the message color will change to red when a few seconds remain. If you haven't either saved or undone your changes during the specified time interval, your edits will be undone and a confirming dialog box will inform you of the event (see Figure 10-32).

To add a record lock time-out feature to your own application, follow these steps for each form for which you wish to enable this feature:

1. Open the form in design mode and add an unbound text box to the form named txtMessage that will be used to display the countdown message. This control should be at least 3.45" wide and 0.1667" high. On the sample form, we placed txtMessage in the form's footer, but you can place it anywhere you'd like.

2. Change the form's TimerInterval property to 1,000. This will cause any code attached to the form's Timer event to be executed every 1,000 milliseconds (every second).

3. Create an event procedure attached to the form's Timer event. Figure 10-33 shows how the properties sheet for the form should look after completing these first two steps.

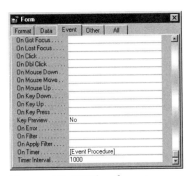

Figure 10-33 The form's
properties sheet

4. Add the following code to the form's Timer event procedure. (Alternately, you can import the frmEmployees sample form from 10-11.MDB, open frmEmployees in design mode, pull up the Timer event procedure code, and copy all the lines between "Private Sub Form_Timer()" and "End Sub" to the clipboard. Close the sample form, open *your* form's Timer event procedure, and paste the code from the sample form into your event procedure. Now delete frmEmployees from your database.)

```
' Record lock timeout time in seconds
Const ahtMaxLockSeconds = 60

Private Sub Form_Timer()

    Dim intElapsed As Integer
    Dim strMsg As String
    Dim ctlmsg As Control

    Static sfDirty As Boolean
    Static sdatTimerStart As Date

    Const ahtcBlack = 0
    Const ahtcRed = 255

    Set ctlmsg = Me!txtMessage

    If Me.NewRecord Then
      Exit Sub
    End If

    Select Case Me.Dirty

    ' Record has been modified since last save
    Case True

        If sfDirty Then
            ' Elapsed time may be over one minute, so
            ' grab both the minutes and seconds portion
            ' of the elapsed time
            intElapsed = Minute(Now() - sdatTimerStart) * 60 _
            + Second(Now() - sdatTimerStart)
        If intElapsed < ahtMaxLockSeconds Then
                ' Update message control with remaining time
                strMsg = "Edit time remaining: " _
                & (ahtMaxLockSeconds - intElapsed) & " seconds."
                ctlmsg = strMsg
                If intElapsed > (0.9 * ahtMaxLockSeconds) Then
                    ctlmsg.ForeColor = ahtcRed
                End If
            Else
                ' Timeout user and undo changes
                ctlmsg = ""
                ctlmsg.ForeColor = ahtcBlack
                ' Undo changes. One of these DoCmd statements
                ' might generate an error, so ignore errors
```

```
                           On Error Resume Next
                           DoCmd.DoMenuItem acFormBar, acEditMenu, _
                             acUndo, 0, acMenuVer70
                           DoCmd.DoMenuItem acFormBar, acEditMenu, _
                             acUndo, 0, acMenuVer70
                           On Error GoTo 0
                           sfDirty = False
                           MsgBox "You have exceeded the maximum record " _
                             & "lock period ("  & ahtMaxLockSeconds _
                             & " seconds). " & vbCrLf & vbCrLf _
                             & "Your changes have been discarded!", _
                             vbCritical + vbOKOnly, "Record Timeout"
                   End If
              Else
                   ' Start timing the edits
                   sdatTimerStart = Now()
                   sfDirty = True
              End If

        ' Record has not been modified since last save
        Case False

              If sfDirty Then
                   ' User has saved changes, so stop timer
                   sfDirty = False
                   ctlmsg = ""
              End If

        End Select

    End Sub
```

5. Save your form and open and test it.

How It Works

The technique in this How-To makes use of the form's Timer event, the form's Dirty property, and a couple of static variables to check repeatedly to see if a form has had unsaved changes for an extended period of time.

The timer subprocedure begins by declaring several variables, including the two static variables:

    sfDirty, a Boolean variable that is set to True if the form is dirty—that is, has unsaved changes

    sdatTimerStart, which stores the date and time the record was first dirtied

In addition, the code checks to see if the user is at a new record using the NewRecord property, and exits if this is the case. Because a user adding a new record can't lock the records of other users and likely will need additional time to complete the new record, we decided not to subject record additions to the time-out process. Here's the initial code of the event procedure.

```
Dim intElapsed As Integer
Dim strMsg As String
Dim ctlmsg As Control

Static sfDirty As Boolean
Static sdatTimerStart As Date

Const ahtcBlack = 0
Const ahtcRed = 255

Set ctlmsg = Me!txtMessage

If Me.NewRecord Then
   Exit Sub
End If
```

The remainder of the event procedure uses a Select Case…End Select statement to branch on the value of the form's Dirty property and compare it against sfDirty (the value of the form's Dirty property the last time it was checked). The process can be summarized using a state table (see Table 10-25).

CURRENT DIRTY VALUE	VALUE OF SFDIRTY	ACTION NEEDED
True	True	Form remains dirty. Need to check if time limit has been exceeded and undo edits if so.
True	False	Form has just been dirtied, so need to set sfDirty to True and sdatTimerStart to Now().
False	True	User has saved changes, so set sfDirty to False.
False	False	Nothing to do.

Table 10-25 The state table for the Form_Timer event procedure

If the form is currently dirty (Me.Dirty = True), it was previously dirty (sfDirty = True), and the elapsed time is less than ahtMaxLockSeconds, then the following piece of code is executed.

```
' Elapsed time may be over one minute, so
' grab both the minutes and seconds portion
' of the elapsed time
intElapsed = Minute(Now() - sdatTimerStart) * 60 _
 + Second(Now() - sdatTimerStart)
If intElapsed < ahtMaxLockSeconds Then
    ' Update message control with remaining time
    strMsg = "Edit time remaining: " _
     & (ahtMaxLockSeconds - intElapsed) & " seconds."
    ctlmsg = strMsg
    If intElapsed > (0.9 * ahtMaxLockSeconds) Then
        ctlmsg.ForeColor = ahtcRed
```

```
     End If
Else
     '...see below...
End If
```

This code updates the txtMessage control with the countdown message, changing the color of the text to red if the elapsed time is greater than 90% of ahtMaxLockSeconds to call extra attention to an impending time-out.

If the form is currently dirty (Me.Dirty = True), it was previously dirty (sfDirty = True), and the elapsed time is greater than or equal to ahtMaxLockSeconds, then the following piece of code is executed.

```
' Timeout user and undo changes
ctlmsg = ""
ctlmsg.ForeColor = ahtcBlack
' Undo changes. One of these DoCmd statements
' might generate an error, so ignore errors
On Error Resume Next
DoCmd.DoMenuItem acFormBar, acEditMenu, _
 acUndo, 0, acMenuVer70
DoCmd.DoMenuItem acFormBar, acEditMenu, _
 acUndo, 0, acMenuVer70
On Error GoTo 0
sfDirty = False
MsgBox "You have exceeded the maximum record " _
 & "lock period ("  & ahtMaxLockSeconds _
 & " seconds). " & vbCrLf & vbCrLf _
 & "Your changes have been discarded!", _
 vbCritical + vbOKOnly, "Record Timeout"
```

The edits to the record are undone by using DoCmd.DoMenuItem to simulate the user selecting Edit|Undo using the menus. Access has a two-level undo buffer (one for the current control, a second for the current record), so you must issue the undo command twice, ignoring any errors that may have occurred if only one undo was necessary. The code then puts up a message box to inform the user that he or she has lost the edits.

If the form is currently dirty (Me.Dirty = True) and it wasn't previously dirty (sfDirty = False), then sfDirty is set to True and the starting time is stored away in sdatTimerStart.

```
' Start timing the edits
sdatTimerStart = Now()
sfDirty = True
```

If the form is not currently dirty (Me.Dirty = True) and it was previously dirty (sfDirty = True), then the timer is stopped by setting sfDirty to False and clearing txtMessage.

```
' User has saved changes, so stop timer
sfDirty = False
ctlmsg = ""
```

Finally, if the form is not currently dirty (Me.Dirty = True) and it wasn't previously dirty (sfDirty = False), then nothing needs to be done.

Comments

Although the code for this How-To could have been placed in a global module, we chose not to because it uses two static variables that must be maintained between calls to the event procedure. Because this code could be used in multiple forms within the application, we chose to encapsulate it within each form's event procedure. You may wish to split the code into two parts: one part that maintains the static variables in the form's Timer event procedure, and a second common component that lives in a global module. To accomplish this, you would have to pass three variables (by reference) to the common function: a form variable referencing the form and the two static variables sfDirty and sdatTimerStart.

You could use a variation of the technique presented in this How-to to automatically log users off of a database at a certain time of day to perform maintenance procedures such as compacting or backing up the database.

10.12 How do I...
Automatically update objects at login?

COMPLEXITY:
ADVANCED

Problem

To improve multiuser performance of an application, I've split my database into a database that's stored on the central file server and multiple copies of an application database that are stored on each user's desktop. Although this scenario has improved the performance of my application, it's also created a lot of extra work when I need to upgrade the application database because numerous copies are distributed on desktops throughout my organization. I'd like somehow to automate the application upgrade process. Is this possible without my having to travel from desk to desk with update disks?

Technique

This How-To demonstrates a generic strategy for automatically upgrading multiple copies of a distributed application database using a third "upgrade" database that contains all of the objects you'd like to upgrade. It's safe because it copies over only objects that have version stamps older than the upgrade object and it includes provisions for deleting objects that are no longer needed in the application database.

Steps

This How-To will employ three files, 10-12FE.MDB, 10-12BE.MDB, and 10-12UPGRADE.MDB, that contain both objects that drive the upgrade process and sample objects used for demonstration purposes.

Trying Out the Sample Upgrade Application

Before you can try this How-To, you'll need to follow these steps to set up and demonstrate the upgrade process:

1. Copy 10-12FE.MDB to your local workstation.

2. Copy 10-12BE.MDB and 10-12UPGRADE.MDB to either your network file server or your local workstation.

3. Load 10-12FE.MDB and dismiss the opening error dialog box. Select File|Get External Data|Link Tables, and then select 10-12BE.MDB as the Access link database at the subsequent common file dialog box. At the Link tables dialog box, select zstblServerVersion and click OK.

4. Open the newly attached zstblServerVersion in datasheet mode and change the ServerVersion field to "95.1" and the UpgradeDB field so that it correctly points to the location of the 10-12UPGRADE.MDB file, as shown in Figure 10-34. You'll need to include the correct path to 10-12UPGRADE.MDB in the Upgrade field, even if it's in the same folder as 10-12FE.MDB. Close the database.

5. Load 10-12UPGRADE.MDB. Open the zsmcrTransferModules macro and change the Database Name argument of the TransferDatabase action so that it correctly points to the location of the 10-12UPGRADE.MDB file, as shown in Figure 10-35.

6. Reload 10-12FE.MDB. The AutoExec macro will execute, detecting that the database needs to be upgraded, and you will be briefed on the situation via the dialog box shown in Figure 10-36.

7. After selecting OK, the application upgrade process will proceed. A progress form will be displayed during the process (see Figure 10-37). When the process is complete, a message box will appear, as shown in Figure 10-38.

Figure 10-34 Editing the fields in the linked zstblServerVersion table

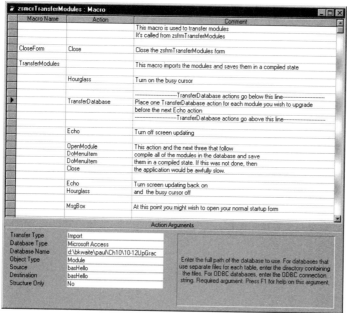

Figure 10-35 Editing 10-12UPGRADE.MDB's
zsmcrTransferModules macro

Adding the Upgrade Utility to Your Application

Follow these steps to implement this upgrade utility in your own application:

1. Create a database application that has been split into front-end and back-end MDB files. In the sample application, these components are 10-12FE.MDB and 10-12BE.MDB.

2. Create a third database that will hold the objects that you'd like to upgrade. You could easily create this database by using the backup utility from How-To 6.8, using as the input your recently updated development database. In the sample application, we called this upgrade database 10-12UPGRADE.MDB.

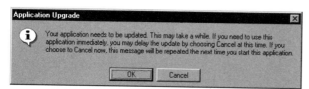

Figure 10-36 The application upgrade dialog
box

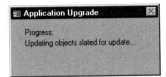

Figure 10-37 The upgrade progress dialog box

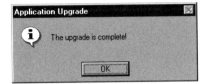

Figure 10-38 The upgrade completion dialog box

3. Import the objects listed in Table 10-26 into the listed database.

FROM DATABASE	TO DATABASE	OBJECT TYPE	OBJECT
10-12FE.MDB	Your front-end MDB	Table	zstblLocalVersion
		Form	zsfrmDatabaseUpdate
		Form	zsfrmTransferModules
		Module	zsbasUpdateObjects
10-12BE.MDB	Your back-end MDB	Table	zstblServerVersion
10-12UPGRADE.MDB	Your upgrade MDB	Table	zstblDeleteObjects
		Macro	zsmcrTransferModules

Table 10-26 The objects that make up the upgrade utility

4. Open your front-end database and select File|Get External Data|Link Tables to link the zstblServerVersion table from your back-end database.

5. Open the zstblLocalVersion table in your front-end database and change the LocalVersion field to some number designating your last application version.

6. Open the linked zstblServerVersion table in your front-end database and change the ServerVersion field to a number that is larger than the number entered in step 5. Also change the UpgradeDB field so that it correctly points to the location of your upgrade database. Close your front-end database.

7. Open your upgrade database. Open the zstblDeleteObjects table in datasheet mode. Delete all of the existing rows and add one record for each object in the front-end database that you'd like to delete during the upgrade process. Note: You don't need to list any objects in this table that you plan on replacing with newer versions, only those you wish to delete without replacing. Exception: You must include all modules that you plan on replacing in this table.

8. Open the zsmcrTransferModules macro in design mode (see Figure 10-35). You'll need to add TransferDatabase action for each module that you wish to upgrade (make sure each of these modules is also listed in the zstblDeleteObjects table). Delete the existing TransferDatabase action and add your TransferDatabase actions between the following macro comment lines.

```
---------------TransferDatabase actions go below this line--------------
```

```
---------------TransferDatabase actions go above this line--------------
```

Enter the action arguments from Table 10-27 into each TransferDatabase action.

ACTION ARGUMENT	VALUE
Transfer Type	Import
Database Type	Microsoft Access
Database Name	(complete path and database name of your upgrade database)
Object Type	Module
Source	(name of object)
Destination	(name of object)
Structure Only	No

Table 10-27 The action arguments for Transfer Database actions in zsmcrTransferModules

9. Reload your front-end database and add an AutoExec macro (or modify your existing AutoExec macro) with the following RunCode action.

```
=ahtCheckforUpdate()
```

10. Distribute copies of your front-end database to users' desktops. When a user opens the front-end database, the update process should start.

Upgrading a Database

After you have added the upgrade utility to your database for the first time, you need only make minor edits to roll out a new upgrade. When you wish to upgrade the users' front-end databases, you'll need to prepare your databases by following these steps:

1. Load your upgrade database. Clear out all of the existing objects except for zstblDeleteObjects and zsmcrTransferModules. Import all of the objects you wish to upgrade into this database. Once again, you may find the backup utility from How-To 6.8 useful.

2. Modify the zstblDeleteObjects and zsmcrTransferModules objects to coincide with the new upgrade. If you don't wish to delete existing objects, leave the zstblDeleteObjects table empty. If you don't wish to upgrade any modules, delete the zsmcrTransferModules macro. (But keep a backup copy somewhere for the next time you do need to upgrade modules.)

3. Test out the upgrade process by opening a copy of the old application front-end database and modifying the LocalVersion field in zstblLocalVersion so that it is a version less than the current server version. (We suggest doing this instead of changing the ServerVersion field in zstblServerVersion so that you can test out the process without causing the upgrade process to start on other users' desktops.)

4. When you are satisfied that the upgrade process ran smoothly on your test machine, you can then increment the version number of the ServerVersion field in the zstblServerVersion table, located on your back-end database.

How It Works

The ahtCheckforUpdate() function is called from the AutoExec macro. It compares the version number in zstblLocalVersion to that in zstblServerVersion. If the former table's version number is less than the latter's, the upgrade process is initiated by calling ahtUpgradeDatabase and passing it the name of the upgrade database and the server version (both of which it extracted from zstblServerVersion) after a confirming dialog box. AhtCheckforUpdate is shown here.

```
Const ahtcQuote = """"
Const ahtcErrCouldntFindObject = 3011
Const ahtcErrCouldntFindInputTable = 3078
Const ahtcFormProgress = "zsfrmDatabaseUpdate"

Function ahtCheckforUpdate() As Integer

    ' Check if need to update the database

    On Error GoTo ahtCheckforUpdate_Err

    Dim varLocalVer As Variant
    Dim varServerVer As Variant
    Dim varUpgradeDB As Variant
    Dim strMsg As String
    Dim intRet As Integer

    ahtCheckforUpdate = False

    ' Compare versions
    varLocalVer = DMax("LocalVersion", "zstblLocalVersion")
    varServerVer = DMax("ServerVersion", "zstblServerVersion")

    If varLocalVer < varServerVer Then
        varUpgradeDB = DLookup("UpgradeDB", "zstblServerVersion", _
        "[ServerVersion] = " & ahtcQuote & varServerVer & ahtcQuote)

        strMsg = "Your application needs to be updated. This may "
        strMsg = strMsg & "take a while. If you need to use this "
        strMsg = strMsg & "application immediately, you may delay "
        strMsg = strMsg & "the update by choosing Cancel at this time. "
        strMsg = strMsg & "If you choose to Cancel now, this message "
        strMsg = strMsg & "will be repeated the next time you start "
        strMsg = strMsg & "this application."
```

continued on next page

continued from previous page

```
        intRet = MsgBox(strMsg, vbOKCancel + vbInformation, _
         "Application Upgrade")
        If intRet = vbOK Then
            Call ahtUpgradeDatabase(varUpgradeDB, varServerVer)
            ahtCheckforUpdate = True
        End If
    End If

ahtCheckforUpdate_Exit:
    On Error GoTo 0
    Exit Function

ahtCheckforUpdate_Err:
    MsgBox "Error " & Err & ": " & Error$, _
     vbCritical, "ahtCheckforUpdate()"
    Resume ahtCheckforUpdate_Exit

End Function
```

The ahtUpgradeDatabase function then begins. This subroutine, which drives the entire upgrade process, is shown in its entirety here.

```
Sub ahtUpgradeDatabase(ByVal strUpgradeDB As String, _
 ByVal varServerVer As Variant)

    ' Upgrade the current database to using
    ' the strUpgrade database to drive the process

    On Error GoTo ahtUpgradeDatabase_Err

    Dim fRet As Boolean
    Dim db As Database
    Dim qdfApp As QueryDef
    Dim fTrans As Boolean
    Dim frmProgress As Form
    Dim varScrap As Variant

    DoCmd.SetWarnings False
    DoCmd.Hourglass True

    DoCmd.OpenForm ahtcFormProgress
    Set frmProgress = Forms(ahtcFormProgress)
    frmProgress.Repaint

    ' Create lists of objects in the current and upgrade databases
    fRet = ahtListObjects("zstblUpdateObjects", strUpgradeDB)
    fRet = ahtListObjects("zstblLocalObjects")

    frmProgress!txtProgress = "Preparing update..."
    frmProgress.Repaint

    ' Clear out any lingering zstblChangedObjects table
    fRet = ahtClearObjTable("zstblChangedObjects")
    If Not fRet Then
        MsgBox "Could not clear or create table zstblChangedObjects.", _
         vbCritical, "ahtUpgradeDatabase()"
        GoTo ahtUpgradeDatabase_Exit
    End If
```

```
' Compare the two lists of objects, populating
' zstblChangedObjects with a list of changed objects
' using an append query
Set db = CurrentDb()
Set qdfApp = db.CreateQueryDef("")
qdfApp.SQL = "INSERT INTO zstblChangedObjects " _
 & "SELECT zstblUpdateObjects.ObjectName, " _
 & "zstblUpdateObjects.ObjectType, zstblLocalObjects.LastUpdated " _
 & "FROM zstblUpdateObjects LEFT JOIN zstblLocalObjects ON " _
 & "(zstblUpdateObjects.ObjectType = zstblLocalObjects.ObjectType) AND " _
 & "(zstblUpdateObjects.ObjectName = zstblLocalObjects.ObjectName) " _
 & "WHERE (((zstblLocalObjects.LastUpdated) Is Null Or " _
 & "(zstblLocalObjects.LastUpdated)< zstblUpdateObjects.LastUpdated));"
qdfApp.Execute

' Delete the to-be-updated objects
frmProgress!txtProgress = "Removing objects slated for update..."
frmProgress.Repaint
If Not ahtDeleteObjects("zstblChangedObjects") Then
    GoTo ahtUpgradeDatabase_Exit
End If

' Import the to-be-updated objects
frmProgress!txtProgress = "Updating objects slated for update..."
frmProgress.Repaint
If Not ahtImportObjects(strUpgradeDB, "zstblChangedObjects") Then
    GoTo ahtUpgradeDatabase_Exit
End If

' Delete the to-be-deleted objects using zstblDeleteObjects,
' which should have been imported in the last step.
' First check if the zstblDeleteObjects table exists.
On Error Resume Next
varScrap = db.TableDefs("zstblDeleteObjects").Name
If Err.Number = 0 Then
    frmProgress!txtProgress = "Removing objects slated for deletion..."
    frmProgress.Repaint
    If Not ahtDeleteObjects("zstblDeleteObjects") Then
        GoTo ahtUpgradeDatabase_Exit
    End If
End If
On Error GoTo ahtUpgradeDatabase_Err

' Modules require special consideration, because Access
' won't let you import a new module using VBA code.

' Run the zsmcrTransferModules macro to import the modules
' This macro should have been imported during the import process.
' First check if zsmcrTransferModules exists.
On Error Resume Next
varScrap = db.Containers!Scripts. _
 Documents("zsmcrTransferModules").Name
If Err.Number = 0 Then
    On Error GoTo ahtUpgradeDatabase_Err
    frmProgress!txtProgress = "Importing updated modules..." _
      & "Please wait until the Update Complete dialog appears..."
    frmProgress.Repaint
```

continued on next page

continued from previous page

```
                ' This form opens a form, that, after a 10 second delay,
                ' runs a macro that imports the modules into the database.
                ' The delay ensures that this function is no longer
                ' executing when the macro begins the module import process.
                DoCmd.OpenForm FormName:="zsfrmTransferModules"
            Else
                ' There's no zsmcrTransferModules macro, so it's done
                frmProgress!txtProgress = "Complete!"
                frmProgress.Repaint
                DoCmd.Hourglass False
            End If

            DoCmd.RunSQL "UPDATE zstblLocalVersion SET LocalVersion =" _
                & ahtcQuote & varServerVer & ahtcQuote

    ahtUpgradeDatabase_Exit:
        DoCmd.SetWarnings True
        DoCmd.Close acForm, ahtcFormProgress
        On Error GoTo 0
        Exit Sub

    ahtUpgradeDatabase_Err:
        MsgBox "Error " & Err.Number & ": " & Err.Description, _
            vbCritical, "ahtUpgradeDatabase()"
        Resume ahtUpgradeDatabase_Exit

    End Sub
```

After declaring a bunch of local variables, ahtUpgradeDatabase sets warnings off, turns the busy cursor on, and opens the progress form.

```
DoCmd.SetWarnings False
DoCmd.Hourglass True

DoCmd.OpenForm ahtcFormProgress
Set frmProgress = Forms(ahtcFormProgress)
frmProgress.Repaint
```

The Repaint method is used throughout the subroutine to force screen updating of the progress form.

Next, the ahtListObjects function is called twice to list all of the objects in the upgrade and local databases (not including system objects and modules) in two local tables, called zstblUpdateObjects and zstblLocalObjects, respectively. You'll find this function along with several other helper functions in the zsbasUpdatedObjects module.

Following a progress update, the two tables' objects are compared using an append query that places a row in zstblChangedObjects only if:

- an object in zstblUpdateObjects is absent from zstblLocalObjects; or

- an object in zstblUpdateObjects has a LastUpdated date that is later than the date in zstblLocalObjects.

This section of code is shown here.

```
' Clear out any lingering zstblChangedObjects table
fRet = ahtClearObjTable("zstblChangedObjects")
If Not fRet Then
    MsgBox "Could not clear or create table zstblChangedObjects.", _
        vbCritical, "ahtUpgradeDatabase()"
    GoTo ahtUpgradeDatabase_Exit
End If

' Compare the two lists of objects, populating
' zstblChangedObjects with a list of changed objects
' using an append query
Set db = CurrentDb()
Set qdfApp = db.CreateQueryDef("")
qdfApp.SQL = "INSERT INTO zstblChangedObjects " _
  & "SELECT zstblUpdateObjects.ObjectName, " _
  & "zstblUpdateObjects.ObjectType, zstblLocalObjects.LastUpdated " _
  & "FROM zstblUpdateObjects LEFT JOIN zstblLocalObjects ON " _
  & "(zstblUpdateObjects.ObjectType = zstblLocalObjects.ObjectType) AND " _
  & "(zstblUpdateObjects.ObjectName = zstblLocalObjects.ObjectName) " _
  & "WHERE (((zstblLocalObjects.LastUpdated) Is Null Or " _
  & "(zstblLocalObjects.LastUpdated)< zstblUpdateObjects.LastUpdated));"
qdfApp.Execute
```

Next, the function uses two helper functions, ahtDeleteObjects and ahtImportObjects, to delete the existing copies of the to-be-updated objects and then imports the newer copies from the upgraded database.

```
' Delete the to-be-updated objects
frmProgress!txtProgress = "Removing objects slated for update..."
frmProgress.Repaint
If Not ahtDeleteObjects("zstblChangedObjects") Then
    GoTo ahtUpgradeDatabase_Exit
End If

' Import the to-be-updated objects
frmProgress!txtProgress = "Updating objects slated for update..."
frmProgress.Repaint
If Not ahtImportObjects(strUpgradeDB, "zstblChangedObjects") Then
    GoTo ahtUpgradeDatabase_Exit
End If
```

The objects that were marked for deletion in zstblDeleteObjects are then deleted from the local database. The TableDefs collection of the local database is first checked for the presence of zstblDeleteObjects; if it is missing, this step is skipped.

```
' Delete the to-be-deleted objects using zstblDeleteObjects,
' which should have been imported in the last step.
' First check if the zstblDeleteObjects table exists.
On Error Resume Next
varScrap = db.TableDefs("zstblDeleteObjects").Name
If Err.Number = 0 Then
    frmProgress!txtProgress = "Removing objects slated for deletion..."
    frmProgress.Repaint
    If Not ahtDeleteObjects("zstblDeleteObjects") Then
```

continued on next page

continued from previous page

```
        GoTo ahtUpgradeDatabase_Exit
     End If
  End If
On Error GoTo ahtUpgradeDatabase_Err
```

The trickiest part of ahtUpgradeDatabase comes next. Access has an annoying limitation that you can't import a global module into a database while VBA code is executing. After trying several failed workarounds, we came up with the following method to trick Access into importing the upgraded modules.

Open a form, zsfrmTransferModules, that has its TimerInterval property set to 10,000 and a macro, zsmcrTransferModules.CloseForm, attached to its OnTimer property that closes the form. This will cause the form to close 10 seconds after it has been opened.

Attach another macro, zsmcrTransferModules.TransferModules, to the OnClose property of the form that executes when the Timer macro attempts to close the form. This macro performs the module import.

The event properties sheet for zsfrmTransferModules is shown in Figure 10-39. None of these actions can be implemented using VBA code; only macros can be used. The 10-second delay ensures that ahtUpgradeDatabase will have completed its execution before the TransferDatabase macro imports the modules. If any VBA code is running, the TransferDatabase actions will not work. Figure 10-40 shows the zsfrmTransferModules form in action.

The final piece of code that calls the zsfrmTransferModules form updates the zstblLocalVersion table with the new version number and is shown here.

```
' Modules require special consideration, because Access won't let
' you import a new module using VBA code.

' Run the zsmcrTransferModules macro to import the modules
' This macro should have been imported during the import process.
' First check if zsmcrTransferModules exists.
On Error Resume Next
varScrap = db.Containers!Scripts. _
 Documents("zsmcrTransferModules").Name
If Err.Number = 0 Then
    On Error GoTo ahtUpgradeDatabase_Err
    frmProgress!txtProgress = "Importing updated modules..." _
     & "Please wait until the Update Complete dialog appears..."
    frmProgress.Repaint

    ' This form opens a form, that, after a 10 second delay,
    ' runs a macro that imports the modules into the database.
    ' The delay ensures that this function is no longer
    ' executing when the macro begins the module import process.
    DoCmd.OpenForm FormName:="zsfrmTransferModules"
Else
```

```
    ' There's no zsmcrTransferModules macro, so we're done
    frmProgress!txtProgress = "Complete!"
    frmProgress.Repaint
    DoCmd.Hourglass False
End If

DoCmd.RunSQL "UPDATE zstblLocalVersion SET LocalVersion =" _
    & ahtcQuote & varServerVer & ahtcQuote
```

Although this may seem like a rather long and arduous process, it works.

Comments

Except for the AutoExec macro, we have prefixed all objects that are part of the upgrade utility with "zs," which stands for system object (the "z" is used to force the objects to sort to the bottom of the database container). We have left these objects visible, but you may wish to hide them. You can hide an object by right-clicking on an object in the database container and choosing Properties at the shortcut menu. When the properties sheet is displayed, check the Hidden attribute check box and press OK.

An Alternate Solution

Another way to approach the problem addressed in this How-To is to use replication. Simply replicate the application database, and place a replica of the application database on each user's desktop. Then synchronize the replicas when you need to roll out a new version of the application. The major downside of this alternative is that using replication adds overhead and additional complexity to your database. You'll have to decide which option works best for you.

Figure 10-39 The properties sheet for zsfrmTransferModules

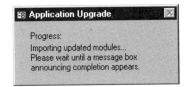

Figure 10-40 The zsfrmTransferModules form waits 10 seconds before attempting to close itself

MAKING THE MOST OF
THE WINDOWS API

11

MAKING THE MOST OF THE WINDOWS API

How do I...

597

11.13 Collect and display information on the system and the Access installation?

11.14 Create and cancel network connections programmatically?

The Windows API has a "bad rap" among many Access programmers who think it's too hard to figure out, too hard to call, or just plain "mysterious." We're here to prove that none of these ideas are correct—even if you've never seen the Windows API programmer's reference, you can use the Windows API, given some help. In this chapter, we'll present some interesting uses of the Windows API from within Access, with example forms and modules for each How-To. In most cases, using these in your own applications takes little more work than simply importing a module or two and then calling the functions. We've divided the How-To's in this chapter into three broad categories: Windows user interface, Windows shell, and hardware information.

User Interface Issues: You'll learn how to remove a form's system menu; how to maximize and minimize buttons at runtime; and how to draw attention to a specific form by flashing its title bar or icon. We'll discuss language-independent classification of keypresses, so you can monitor exactly what keys have been pressed. We'll also show how to restrict the mouse movement to a specific area on the screen.

The Windows Shell: You'll learn how to have code (which runs asynchronously) run another program and pause until the other program is done before continuing. We'll demonstrate a method for shutting down Windows under program control and all the options of the associated API functions. You'll learn to find and run an application, given an associated data file, and how to determine if the application is already running. You'll see how to retrieve a list of all the open top-level windows (generally, one per application) and how to close a window from your VBA code.

Files, Drives, and Hardware: You'll learn how to set file date and time stamp information, useful if you're moving files around from within applications or making backups based on dates. You'll learn how to retrieve information about your disk drives, and see how to retrieve information about your hardware and the current Windows environment. In addition, you'll see how to connect and disconnect from remote network devices under program control or using standard dialog boxes.

> **Note**
>
> Most of the How-To's in this chapter instruct you to import one or more modules from the example databases. In each case, the module contains the Windows API user-defined types and function declarations you need for the example. If you've already imported a module with the specified name for a previous How-To, you can skip it, as all modules with matching names contain the same code.

11.1   Remove a Form's System Menu and the Maximize and Minimize Buttons

Access 95 makes it trivial to remove a specific form's system menu and its maximize and minimize buttons. You have to make these changes at design time, however. The code in this How-To also will let you remove and replace these items while your application is running.

11.2   Flash a Window's Title Bar or Icon

You may have a need in your application to draw attention to a specific form. This How-To will demonstrate a method for flashing the title bar or icon for any form. This technique can easily be extended to work with any application window as well.

11.3   Classify Keypresses in a Language-Independent Manner

The Windows API includes a number of functions you can call to categorize characters. The isCharAlpha and isCharAlphaNumeric functions are both faster than the built-in VBA functions and are able to deal with international issues. This How-To will demonstrate how you can use these functions to classify characters.

11.4   Restrict Mouse Movement to a Specific Region

You may find that you need to have strict control over the mouse movement in your application. This How-To will demonstrate using the ClipCursor API call to limit the region available to the mouse.

11.5   Run Another Program and Pause Until It's Done

You may need to run another program as part of an application. Because VBA runs asynchronously, it keeps on going while your program is running. If you need to stop and wait until the other program has finished its work, investigate this How-To, which will show a method for pausing VBA until the application has finished.

11.6   Exit Windows under Program Control

The Windows API allows you to call a function and shut down Windows, log out of Windows, and wait for a new log-in or reboot your machine. This How-To will explain the steps necessary to call this Windows API.

11.7 Run an Application, Given a Data File Associated with That Application

In Windows, many file name extensions are associated with the application that created them. Use the information in this How-To to locate the particular application associated with a given data file, if such an association exists.

11.8 Check to See If an Application Is Already Running

You can use the Shell function to start up a foreign application, such as Excel, but there's no built-in function to determine whether Excel is already running. This How-To will show how to detect whether Excel (or any other application) is already running to avoid starting up a second copy.

11.9 Retrieve a List of All the Top-Level Windows

When you need to know what other applications are also running, this How-To will demonstrate walking through the list of windows, starting with the Windows desktop, to fill an array with information about each running application's main window.

11.10 Close a Running Windows Application

If you start an application from VBA code, most likely you'll also want to shut it down when your program terminates. This How-To will use the PostMessage Windows API function to close the other application's main window.

11.11 Set File Date and Time Stamps

Visual Basic for Applications supplies a function to retrieve the time and date of the last modification for a file, but it doesn't supply a way to set the values. If you're performing automated backups or need to compare the dates of two files, it may be important to be able to change a file's time/date stamp. In this How-To, you'll use the Windows API to set the time and date stamp information for the file you specify.

11.12 Retrieve Information about the Disk Drives in My Computer

If you need to know how much space is free on a disk drive or how much total space is available on that drive, you'll need some external help. Access itself doesn't include such a function. This How-To shows how you can call the Windows API to retrieve disk information, including whether a disk drive is local, remote, removable, or a CD-ROM.

11.13 Collect and Display Information on the System and the Access Installation

The Windows API and Access itself include a number of function calls you can use to retrieve information about your application's environment (the version of Windows that's running, the amount of memory, etc.). This How-To will show you how to gather this information for your own About… box or other information display.

11.14   Create and Cancel Network Connections Programmatically

Windows provides strong support for networks, but Access has no built-in interface for connecting and disconnecting from remote resources. This How-To will show how you can use common dialog boxes to connect and disconnect from remote drives and printers from within your Access application. It'll also show how you can do the same things with no user interference, and how to retrieve the current user and machine names.

COMPLEXITY:
ADVANCED

11.1   How do I...
Remove a form's system menu and the maximize and minimize buttons?

Problem

Access makes it easy to remove the control box (often called the system menu) and the minimize and the maximize buttons when I design forms, but there doesn't seem to be a way to do this for forms at runtime. I have an application for which I'd like to be able to remove these buttons to control how users interact with the application. Is there a way to remove these items and then replace them later?

Technique

Removing or replacing these window controls requires changing the style bits for the particular window. That is, every window maintains a 32-bit value that describes its physical characteristics: its border type and the existence of scroll bars, a system menu, and the minimize and maximize buttons, for example. The values are stored as bit flags, in which the state of a single bit in the 32-bit value indicates the value of some characteristic of the window. In general, you can't change the state of many of these flags without re-creating the window; by setting or clearing the bits in the window's style value, however, you can force the system menu and the minimize/maximize buttons to appear or disappear.

Steps

Load and run frmSystemItems in 11-01.MDB. This form, shown in Figure 11-1, allows you to add or remove the control menu, the minimize button, and/or the maximize button from the current form. Select items on the form to make the corresponding items visible, or deselect to remove them. Once you've made your choices, click on the Execute button, and the code will remove or replace the items you've chosen.

To include this functionality in your own applications, follow these steps:

1. Import the module basControl from 11-01.MDB.

2. To remove or replace a form's system items, call the subroutine ahtFormSystemItems, passing to it four parameters, as shown in Table 11-1.

PARAMETER	TYPE	VALUE
frm	Form	Reference to the current form
fSystemMenu	Integer	True = Show system menu; False = Hide
fMaxButton	Integer	True = Show maximize button, False = Hide
fMinButton	Integer	True = Show minimize button, False = Hide

Table 11-1 Parameters for ahtFormSystemItems

For example, the following statement, called from a button's Click event in a form's module, will show the system menu, but will hide the minimize and maximize buttons.

```
ahtFormSystemItems Me, True, False, False
```

Though Access does provide the ControlBox, MaxButton, and MinButton properties for forms, they're read-only once the form's in use; if you need to alter these properties at runtime, you'll need to use ahtFormSystemItems to do your work, rather than changing the properties directly.

Windows 95 vs. Windows NT

Because of Windows 95's new interface, the behavior of the control box and minimize and maximize buttons is different than it is under the standard Windows NT interface. Under Windows 95, using ahtFormSystemItems to remove one of the minimize or maximize buttons leaves them both visible, but disables the one you've requested to hide. Removing them both with ahtFormSystemItems makes them both invisible. Under Windows NT, these buttons are independent, and using the subroutine to remove one makes it invisible. Under Windows 95, removing the control box also removes the minimize and maximize buttons. Under Windows NT, these items are independent.

How It Works

The bulk of the work in controlling these system items takes place in the private function, HandleStyles, in the module basControl. This function accepts a window handle (the hWnd property of a form) and three True/False values indicating which

1 1 . 1

REMOVE A FORM'S SYSTEM MENU AND THE MAXIMIZE AND MINIMIZE BUTTONS?

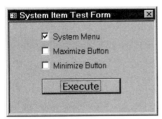

Figure 11-1 The sample form, frmSystemItems, allows you to remove or replace any of the system items

options you'd like to see and which you'd like removed. Like every window, the window you want to alter maintains a 32-bit value, its style value. Within that long integer, each of the 32 positions represents one of the possible styles for the window. If the bit is 1, the style is set on; if it's 0, the style is set off. HandleStyle builds up two long integers, each containing a series of 32 bits. The first, lngStylesOn, contains all 0s, except for the bits representing the styles you want turned on, which contain 1s. The other, lngStylesOff, contains all 1s, except the bits representing the styles you want turned off, which contain 0s.

Using the AND operator to combine the current window style with lngStylesOff sets each style whose bit contains 0 in lngStylesOff to be 0. Using the OR operator to combine the current window style with lngStylesOn sets each style whose bit contains 1 in lngStylesOn to be 1. For example, suppose the current window style value is this:

```
10001000  10001010  10101011  01101101
```

The value in lngStylesOff contains 1s in all positions except the ones you want turned off, which contain 0s. If the value of lngStylesOff is this:

```
11111111  11111111  11111111  11111011
```

the result of using the AND operator with the original style and lngStylesOff will be this:

```
10001000  10001010  10101011  01101001
```

The value in lngStylesOn contains 0s in all positions except the ones you want turned on, which contain 1s. If the value of lngStylesOn is this:

```
00000000  00000000  00010000  10000000
```

the result of using the OR operator with lngStylesOn and the result of ANDing the original style with lngStylesOff will be this:

```
10001000  10001010  10111011  11101001
```

This final result will have three changed values: One bit that was 1 is now 0 due to the settings in lngStylesOff, and 2 bits that were 0 are 1 due to the settings in lnStylesOn.

To retrieve and replace the window's style information, the code uses the GetWindowLong and SetWindowLong API functions. Given a window handle and a flag (GWL_STYLE) indicating which 32-bit value to retrieve or set about the window, these functions allow you to get the current value, do your work with it, and then set it back. This is the line of code that does all the work:

```
HandleStyles = aht_apiSetWindowLong(hWnd, GWL_STYLE, _
   (aht_apiGetWindowLong(hWnd, GWL_STYLE) And lngStylesOff) _
   Or lngStylesOn)
```

It sets the window style to be the value GetWindowLong retrieved, combined with the two style flags the code previously built up based on your choices.

The entire procedure looks like this:

```
Private Function HandleStyles(ByVal hWnd As Long, fSystemMenu As Boolean, _
   fMaxButton As Boolean, fMinButton As Boolean) As Long

   Dim lngStylesOn As Long
   Dim lngStylesOff As Long

   On Error GoTo HandleStylesExit

   ' Set all bits off.
   lngStylesOn = 0

   ' Set all bits on.
   lngStylesOff = &HFFFFFFFF

   ' Turn ON bits to set attribute, turn them OFF to turn attribute off.
   If fSystemMenu Then
      lngStylesOn = lngStylesOn Or WS_SYSMENU
   Else
      lngStylesOff = lngStylesOff And Not WS_SYSMENU
   End If
   If fMinButton Then
      lngStylesOn = lngStylesOn Or WS_MINIMIZEBOX
   Else
      lngStylesOff = lngStylesOff And Not WS_MINIMIZEBOX
   End If
   If fMaxButton Then
      lngStylesOn = lngStylesOn Or WS_MAXIMIZEBOX
   Else
      lngStylesOff = lngStylesOff And Not WS_MAXIMIZEBOX
   End If

   ' Set the attributes as necessary.
   HandleStyles = aht_apiSetWindowLong(hWnd, GWL_STYLE, _
      (aht_apiGetWindowLong(hWnd, GWL_STYLE) And lngStylesOff) _
      Or lngStylesOn)

HandleStylesExit:
   Exit Function
End Function
```

Comments

After the style bits are set, there's still one issue left: You must coerce the window into repainting itself so the changes become visible. Simply changing the styles isn't enough, because they don't become visible until the next time the window repaints its border.

All you need to do is turn off the form's Painting property before you make the changes, and then turn it on again once you're done. This forces the entire form, including its border, to repaint. The ahtFormSystemItems subroutine does exactly that.

```
Sub ahtFormSystemItems(frm As Form, ByVal fSystemMenu As Boolean, _
  ByVal fMaxButton As Boolean, ByVal fMinButton As Boolean)
    Dim hWnd As Long
    Dim intRetval As Integer

    hWnd = frm.hWnd
    frm.Painting = False
    HandleStyles hWnd, fSystemMenu, fMaxButton, fMinButton
    frm.Painting = True
End Sub
```

The previous edition of this book extended this technique to also allow you to change the corresponding settings for the Access main window (actually, for any window). Due to changes in the way Microsoft Office products display their title bars, this technique no longer works for the Microsoft Access main window. Therefore, we've removed the code from the book.

COMPLEXITY:
INTERMEDIATE

11.2 How do I...
Flash a window's title bar or icon?

Problem

With so many windows open at once in my Access applications, it's often difficult to force my user's attention to a specific form. Is there something I can do to make one of the forms really stand out? I'd like to be able to make the title bar flash.

Technique

Windows supplies a simple API call, FlashWindow, that allows you to flash the title bar of a form or its icon (if it's iconized) on and off. This How-To will demonstrate how you can use the FlashWindow API call to make a specific form very visible.

Steps

Load and run frmControlFlash from 11-02.MDB. When you load that form, it loads a second form, frmFlash. By clicking on the Flash button on frmControlFlash, you can

Figure 11-2 FlashWindow has caused the subsidiary form's caption bar to invert

turn on or off the flashing of frmFlash's caption bar (see Figure 11-2). If you iconize frmFlash, it will still be flashing.

To include this functionality in your own applications, follow these steps:

1. Add this API declaration to your code in the Declarations area of the form's module.

```
Private Declare Function FlashWindow Lib "User32" _
(ByVal hWnd As Long, ByVal lngInvert As Long) As Long
```

In the sample, it's in the module for frmControlFlash.

2. Create a module-level variable (mhWnd in the example) to hold the flashed form's window handle.

```
Dim mhWnd As Long
```

3. Create a procedure attached to your controlling form's Timer event, causing the flashing form to do its flashing.

```
Private Sub Form_Timer()
    Static fFlash As Boolean

    FlashWindow mhWnd, fFlash
    fFlash = Not fFlash
End Sub
```

4. To turn the flashing on and off, add code like this to react to some event (on the sample form, you trigger the code in reaction to the Click event of the Flash button):

```
Private Sub cmdFlash_Click()
    Dim strCaption As String
    Dim ctl As Control

    Set ctl = Me!cmdFlash
    strCaption = ctl.Caption
    If strCaption = "Flash" Then
        ' If the form's already open, this will just
        ' set the focus to that form.
        DoCmd.OpenForm "frmFlash"
        mhWnd = Forms!frmFlash.hWnd
        ' Change the button's caption to
        ' indicate its state.
        ctl.Caption = "Stop Flashing"
        Me.TimerInterval = 250
```

```
    Else
        ctl.Caption = "Flash"
        Me.TimerInterval = 0
        FlashWindow mhWnd, False
    End If
End Sub
```

How It Works

The FlashWindow API call takes two values as its parameters: the handle to a window and a logical value. When Windows creates a new window (as it does when you open a form in Access), it supplies it with a unique 32-bit value, its handle, that any program can use to work directly with that window. Access gives you a form's handle in its hWnd property. Given that handle and a Boolean value (True or False) indicating whether you want the window to invert or not, FlashWindow takes the requested action with the window you've indicated. For example:

```
FlashWindow Forms!frmFlash.hWnd, True
```

would make the title bar of frmFlash look like it is selected, even if it isn't the currently active form. Sending a False for the second parameter would make it look as if it isn't selected. Alternating between these two calls is what makes the window look like it's flashing; this is where the Timer event comes in.

By reacting to a form's Timer event, you can have your code take effect at a set interval. In this case, you set the timer interval to be 250, or 1/4 second (the TimerInterval property measures time in milliseconds—1/1000 second).

```
Me.TimerInterval = 250
```

To make it so that the code attached to the Timer event doesn't ever run, set the TimerInterval property to be 0. That's how you control the flashing in this example. To turn flashing on, set the TimerInterval property to be the rate at which you'd like the flashing to occur. To turn it off, just set the TimerInterval property to 0.

The code called from the main form's Timer event uses a static variable to keep track of the state of the flashing. Static variables are local to the procedure in which they're declared, but maintain their value between calls to the procedure. This way, the first time the form's Timer event occurs, the static variable fFlash contains False (because Access initializes variables to 0 [False] for you). Once the routine has done its work, it toggles the state of that variable using this statement:

```
fFlash = Not fFlash
```

If fFlash was False, it becomes True; if it was True, it becomes False. The next time Access calls that procedure (after 250 milliseconds in the example), the variable is still available, containing the value it held last time it was used.

Comments

This example takes one extra step: When it turns off the flashing, it also makes sure that the caption bar of the flashed form is no longer inverted. That is, it calls FlashWindow one more time, forcing the flashing off.

```
Me.TimerInterval = 0
FlashWindow mhWnd, False
```

This ensures that no matter where in the cycle you turn off the flashing, the flashed form reverts to its normal appearance.

You can control the speed of the flashing by changing the TimerInterval property value. Currently, it's set at 250 (1/4 second). You may want to speed that up, but beware that flashing is not a normal Windows mechanism; it goes against the Windows design standards, and should only be used for brief periods of time and only in special circumstances.

Because FlashWindow accepts the handle to any window as its parameter, you could use this same technique to cause any application's main window to flash as well. How-To 11.9 shows how to retrieve a list of all open top-level windows. You could use the hWnd properties from that list with FlashWindow as well.

Note that even though the form's Timer event is set to do its work every 250 milliseconds, it may take longer for your flashing form to start flashing. The code in the form's Timer event sends a message to Windows, telling it to flash the other form's title bar, but that doesn't guarantee when the form gets or processes the message. This may take a few milliseconds on a slower machine.

COMPLEXITY:
INTERMEDIATE

11.3   How do I...
Classify keypresses in a language-independent manner?

Problem

I need to be able to classify a keypress as a character, a digit, or neither. I also need to know if a character is uppercase or lowercase. I know I can write code to handle this, but if I do that, I'm limiting myself to a single national language, and languages classify their characters differently. Because Windows knows all these things about various character sets, is there some way I can use Windows to do this work for me?

Technique

You could write VBA code to classify characters, but it certainly wouldn't be language independent. For example, the ANSI character 65 is an uppercase character in the standard multinational character set, but that doesn't guarantee anything about any other character set. If you want your applications to work in various languages, you must not assume specific character ranges. Windows provides a set of simple functions that will classify characters for you based on their ANSI values. Luckily, this is exactly what the KeyPress event procedure in Access sends you, so you can use these functions from within KeyPress event procedures that you write.

Steps

In addition to the necessary function declarations, the sample database 11-03.MDB includes a demonstration form showing all the ANSI characters and their classifications. Load and run frmCharClasses from 11-03.MDB, and you'll see a display like that in Figure 11-3. By scrolling through the form, you'll be able to see all 255 ANSI characters (in the Arial font) and their classifications.

To use this functionality in your own applications, follow these steps:

1. Import the module basClassifyChars from 11-03.MDB into your application.

2. To classify an ANSI value, call one or more of the functions in Table 11-2. Each of these functions takes as its parameter a value between 1 and 255. Each function returns a nonzero value if the character code you passed is a member of the function's tested group, or 0 if it's not. (As you can see from Table 11-2, some of the functions come directly from the Windows API and others return values based on those functions.) These functions will return correct values no matter which language version of Windows is running.

FUNCTION	API?	INCLUSION CLASS
aht_apiIsCharAlphaNumeric	Yes	Language-defined alphabetic or numeric characters
aht_apiIsCharAlpha	Yes	Language-defined alphabetic characters
ahtIsCharNumeric	No	Alphanumeric, but not alpha
ahtIsSymbol	No	Not alphanumeric
aht_apiIsCharUpper	Yes	Language-defined uppercase characters
aht_apiIsCharLower	Yes	Language-defined lowercase characters

Table 11-2 The character classification functions in basClassifyChars

For example, imagine that you need to limit the number of characters typed into a text box, and the number of allowable characters isn't known until runtime. In addition, you want to allow only alphabetic or numeric values, and that choice, too, isn't known until runtime. Although you could programmatically control the input masks (creating a new one each time conditions change), it is simpler to handle this problem using the KeyPress event and some code that checks the state of the current keypress. The sample form, frmInputTest (Figure 11-4), shows a simple test form. The text box labeled "Enter some characters" allows you to enter up to as many characters as shown in the "Maximum number of characters" text box, and you can only enters characters whose type you've chosen in the character type option group.

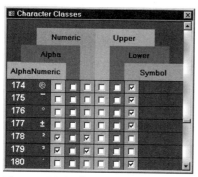

Figure 11-4 The sample input form, frmInputTest, uses character classifications to disallow

Figure 11-3 The sample form, frmCharClasses, shows all the ANSI characters and their classifications

The code attached to txtCharTest's KeyPress event looks like this:

```
Sub txtCharTest_KeyPress (KeyAscii As Integer)

    ' Always allow a backspace.
    If KeyAscii = vbKeyBack Then Exit Sub

    ' If txtChars is nonnull and greater than 0,
    ' and txtCharTest is nonnull and has too many
    ' characters, then set KeyAscii to 0.
    If Not IsNull(Me!txtChars) Then
        If Me!txtChars > 0 Then
            If Not IsNull(Me!txtCharTest.Text) Then
                If Len(Me!txtCharTest.Text) >= Me!txtChars Then
                    KeyAscii = 0
                End If
            End If
        End If
    End If
    ' In any case, if the keypress isn't the correct
    ' type, set KeyAscii to 0.
    If Me!grpCharType = 1 Then
        If (aht_apiIsCharAlpha(KeyAscii) = 0) Then KeyAscii = 0
    Else
        If (ahtIsCharNumeric(KeyAscii) = 0) Then KeyAscii = 0
    End If
End Sub
```

In the KeyPress event, Access sends you a parameter, KeyAscii, that contains the ANSI value of the key that was just pressed. To tell Access to disregard this key, modify its value to 0 during the event procedure. In this case, if there's no room left in the field (based on the number in Me!txtChars) or if the character's not the right type (based on calls to aht_apiIsCharAlpha and ahtIsCharNumeric), the code sets the value of KeyAscii to 0, causing Access to disregard the keypress. Play with the sample form, changing the values, to see how the code works.

How It Works

Windows internally maintains information about the currently selected language and character set. For each language, certain characters are treated as uppercase and others aren't. Some characters in the character set represent alphabetic characters and others don't. It would be impractical to maintain this information for each language your application might use. Luckily, you don't have to manage this. The Access functions UCase and LCase handle case conversions for you, but Access doesn't include case-testing functions. That's the role of the functions introduced in this How-To—they allow you to test the classification of characters, no matter what the language. Attempting to perform this task in VBA will cause you trouble sooner or later if you plan on working internationally.

Comments

You may not need these routines often, but when you do, the API versions are both faster and more reliable than handwritten code would be. Don't count on specific ANSI values to be certain characters, uppercase or lowercase, because these values change from version to version of internationalized Windows.

COMPLEXITY:
INTERMEDIATE

11.4 How do I...
Restrict mouse movement to a specific region?

Problem

I'd like to be able to restrict mouse cursor movement to certain areas of the current form. I think I can help users of my application by making sure the mouse stays where it needs to be until I'm done with it. How can I limit the mouse movement in Access?

Technique

The Windows API's ClipCursor subroutine will limit the movement of the mouse, just as you require, to a single form or region on a form, as you'll see in this How-To.

Steps

To try out this technique, load and run the form frmClip, in 11-04.MDB. This form, shown in Figure 11-5, limits the mouse movement to the area of the form once you click the large button. If you click the button again or close the form, code attached to either event frees the mouse cursor to move anywhere on the screen. If you move the form, Windows frees the mouse cursor for you.

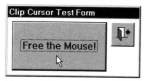

Figure 11-5 The sample form, frmClip, limits the mouse movement to the area of the form

To use this technique in your own applications, follow these steps:

1. Import the module basClipCursor from 11-04.MDB. This module contains the function declarations and user-defined types that you'll need.

2. To limit the mouse to a single form, you'll need to get the form coordinates, and then tell Windows to use those coordinates as limits for the mouse. To do this, you'll need code something like this (because this code fragment uses "Me," it must be in a form's module, not a global module):

```
Dim typRect as aht_tagRect

Call aht_apiGetWindowRect (Me.Hwnd, typRect)
Call aht_apiClipCursor(typRect)
```

3. To free the mouse cursor, use code like this:

```
Call aht_apiClipCursor(ByVal vbNullString)
```

See the How It Works section for an example.

How It Works

The ClipCursor API routine (aliased as aht_apiClipCursor in the code) expects as its only parameter a user-defined data type consisting of four long integers representing coordinates of a rectangle. This data type has been declared for you in basClipCursor as aht_tagRect. This is a very common data structure, used often with API routines that interact with the screen or printer.

```
Type aht_tagRect
    lngLeft As Long
    lngTop As Long
    lngRight As Long
    lngBottom As Long
End Type
```

When you want to restrict the mouse movement, you'll need to retrieve the coordinates of the current form. You can accomplish this by calling the GetWindowRect API function, (aliased as aht_apiGetWindowRect in the code) which will fill in an aht_tagRect structure with the left, top, right, and bottom coordinates of the window whose handle you pass it. Therefore, by calling aht_apiGetWindowRect with the handle of the current form, you'll retrieve the coordinates of that form in pixels.

```
Dim typRect as aht_tagRect
Call aht_apiGetWindowRect (Me.hWnd, typRect)
```

Once you've got a structure containing the coordinates of the current form, you can call ClipCursor and pass to it that filled-in structure. The sample form combines these API calls, as shown below.

```
Private Sub cmdClip_Click()
    Dim typRect As aht_tagRect
    Static sstrCaption As String

    ' Static variable to keep track of
    ' clipping.
    Static fClip As Boolean

    If fClip Then
        Me!cmdClip.Caption = sstrCaption
        Call aht_apiClipCursor(ByVal vbNullString)
    Else
        sstrCaption = Me!cmdClip.Caption
        Me!cmdClip.Caption = "Free the Mouse!"
        Call aht_apiGetWindowRect(Me.hWnd, typRect)
        Call aht_apiClipCursor(typRect)
    End If
    fClip = Not fClip
End Sub
```

In the sample routine, which is executed each time you click the large button on frmClip, fClip alternates between True and False, keeping track of whether mouse clipping is currently in effect. If it is, the routine calls aht_apiClipCursor to disable clipping and resets the button's caption. If clipping is not in effect, the routine stores away the original caption, sets a new one ("Free the Mouse!"), retrieves the form's coordinates, and finally calls aht_apiClipCursor to restrict the cursor's movement.

To end the mouse cursor restrictions, send a null value to aht_apiClipCursor. To do that, use the intrinsic constant, vbNullString, passed by value. Because the aht_apiClipCursor procedure has been declared to accept any type of parameter, you can send it a structure in one call, and a null value in another.

Comments

The method presented in this How-To is not foolproof in Access. You're taking control of a feature that Access normally controls itself, and sometimes the interaction may be unpredictable. In this case, if you restrict the mouse movement to a single form, but you use the mouse to move or resize the form, Access will free the mouse for you. So if you're using this technique to *force* users to stay on a single form, you're better off using a modal form instead. If, on the other hand, you're just trying to ensure that the mouse remains in the area of the form where the users need it to be, the method described here is appropriate. Restricting the mouse movement is not meant for every application, but if you want to help your users out a little, try it.

Don't forget that the mouse is a shared resource: If you limit its use in Access, it's limited in every other application, too. Therefore, keep the mouse restricted for the shortest possible periods. You should make sure that any event that closes your form releases the mouse as well. If an error occurs while the mouse movement is limited, you'll need to execute code that frees it, or reboot your computer, to regain the full control of the mouse. Certainly, if you're going to limit the mouse movement, make sure that your error handler knows to free the mouse should any error occur.

COMPLEXITY:
INTERMEDIATE

11.5 How do I...
Run another program and pause until it's done?

Problem

From within my application, sometimes I need to run a DOS batch file or utility program that requires some time to do its job. Sometimes I'd like to run another Windows application. In both cases, I'd like my Access application to pause until the other program has finished its work. Every time I try this, the code starts up the other application but then keeps on going. Is there a way to make Access wait until the other application has completed before moving on?

Technique

The Shell function in VBA (and the ShellExecute function mentioned in How-To 11.7) returns a unique long integer value representing the running task. You can use this value, the *instance handle* for the running application, to track the state of the application. Given an instance handle, you can use the OpenProcess API function to retrieve the process handle for the process. Armed with that process handle, you can call the GetExitCodeProcess function continually until it sees that the process has shut down. Because this happens automatically once a DOS application has finished running, you can use this technique to wait until a DOS window has closed before moving on in your application.

Steps

The sample form, frmTestWait in 11-05.MDB, allows you to try starting both a DOS application and a Windows application, and wait for either to complete. There's also a button that allows you to start a DOS application, but continue the attached code. In any of these three cases (see Figure 11-6), the sample code attempts to load the text

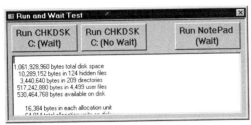

Figure 11-6 The sample form, frmTestWait, after it has run an application

file C:\AHTTEST.TXT (choosing either of the first two buttons sends the output of CHKDSK to C:\AHTTEST.TXT for you) into a text box on the form once the application you've started finishes its work. (In the case where the code doesn't wait for the other application, of course, there's nothing to load.) Use frmTestWait, trying each of the command buttons to test the functionality demonstrated in this How-To. The first button runs CHKDSK, waits until it's written its output to C:\AHTTEST.TXT, and then loads the text file. The second button runs CHKDSK, and immediately loads the text file. The final button, Run Notepad, loads a Windows application, Notepad, and waits until you've closed it before loading the text file.

To use this functionality in your own applications, follow these steps:

1. Import the module basRunApp from 11-05.MDB into your application.

2. To run another application, waiting for it to finish before going on with your code, call the ahtRunAppWait subroutine, passing it two parameters: a command string telling it what to run and an integer designating the window mode you'd like to use (see Table 11-3). These are essentially the same values you use when calling the ShellExecute Windows API function, as shown in How-To 11.7.

VALUE	VBA CONSTANT	DESCRIPTION
0	vbHide	Hidden.
1	vbNormalFocus	Restored to its previous state (neither minimized nor maximized).
2	vbMinimizedFocus	Made visible and minimized.
3	vbMaximizedFocus	Made visible and maximized.
4	vbNormalNoFocus	Displayed, but doesn't gain the input focus.
6	vbMinimizedNoFocus	Minimized (as an icon) when started.

Table 11-3 Window display options, using Shell

For example, to start the Windows calculator maximized, use a statement like this:

```
ahtRunAppWait "CALC.EXE", vbMaximizedFocus
MsgBox "Done with the calculator."
```

You won't see the message box until you finish with the calculator.

How It Works

The secret to the ahtRunAppWait subroutine is its use of the Windows API function GetExitCodeProcess. This function takes as a parameter the process handle of an application, which you can retrieve by calling the OpenProcess API function, given the instance handle returned by the call to Shell. GetExitCodeProcess monitors a running process and retrieves that process's exit code. As long as the process continues to run, GetExitCodeProcess retrieves the value STILL_ACTIVE (defined in basRunApp).

Consider the following code, which will check for the existence of a running application:

```
Do
    ' Attempt to retrieve the exit code, which will
    ' not exist until the application has quit.
    lngRetval = GetExitCodeProcess(hProcess, lngExitCode)
Loop Until lngExitCode <> STILL_ACTIVE
```

Though this will almost do what you need, it won't quite succeed. You've left Access running a tight loop, waiting for the new application to finish. Unfortunately, this loop is grabbing all of Access' clock cycles, looping and waiting for the other application to be done. While this loop is active, Access is effectively dead. All the rest of Windows continues to work perfectly, but Access' only thread of execution is completely tied up. You'll see that Access simply can't update its screen, for example, while you're running Notepad.

The solution, then, is to be a good citizen, allowing Access its processing time. To do this, you must add a DoEvents statement inside the loop. This allows Access to continue executing while this code loops, waiting for the application you started to be finished. (See How-To 7.4 for more information on DoEvents.) Thus, the ahtRunAppWait subroutine looks like this:

```
Sub ahtRunAppWait(strCommand As String, intMode As Integer)
    ' Run an application, waiting for its completion
    ' before returning to the caller.

    Dim hInstance As Long
    Dim hProcess As Long
    Dim lngRetval As Long
    Dim lngExitCode As Long

    On Error GoTo ahtRunAppWait_Err
    ' Start up the application.
    hInstance = Shell(strCommand, intMode)
    hProcess = OpenProcess(PROCESS_QUERY_INFORMATION Or SYNCHRONIZE, _
        True, hInstance)
    Do
        ' Attempt to retrieve the exit code, which will
```

```
        ' not exist until the application has quit.
        lngRetval = GetExitCodeProcess(hProcess, lngExitCode)
        DoEvents
    Loop Until lngExitCode <> STILL_ACTIVE

ahtRunAppWait_Exit:
    Exit Sub

ahtRunAppWait_Err:
    Select Case Err.Number
        Case ahtcErrFileNotFound
            MsgBox "Unable to find '" & strCommand & "'"
        Case Else
            MsgBox Err.Description
    End Select
    Resume ahtRunAppWait_Exit
End Sub
```

Comments

To use the Shell command, you must specify an executable file. If you need to run a DOS internal command, or if you need to redirect the output from a program to a text file, you'll need to load a copy of COMMAND.COM to do your work. In addition, you'll need to use the /C parameter, indicating to COMMAND.COM that you just want a temporary instance and that it should quit when the program you run finishes. For example, to run the CHKDSK.EXE program directly, you could use the following function call. (All these examples assume that the necessary programs are available in the DOS PATH.)

```
hInstance = Shell("CHKDSK.EXE", 6)
```

To run DIR, on the other hand, you'll need to start COMMAND.COM first.

```
hInstance = Shell("COMMAND.COM /C DIR C:\*.BAT", 6)
```

To redirect the output from a program to a text file, you'll also need to use COMMAND.COM:

```
hInstance = Shell("COMMAND.COM /C CHKDSK C: > C:\AHTTEST.TXT", 6)
```

> **Note**
> You also may want to study the FileRead subroutine in the sample form's module, which demonstrates how to open a text file and read its contents directly into a control on a form.

617

11.6   How do I... Exit Windows under program control?

Problem

I'd like to be able to control what happens once I quit my applications. That is, sometimes I want to shut down Windows at the same time, or even perhaps reboot the machine. How can I do that from within Access?

Technique

The Windows API provides the ExitWindowsEx function that grants you control over exiting Windows, and you have a choice of three different things you can do: log off and await a new log-in; shut down to the point at which it's safe to turn off the computer's power; or reboot the computer. This How-To demonstrates these simple functions.

Steps

To try closing Windows under program control, load and run frmExitWindows in 11-06.MDB. This sample form, shown in Figure 11-7, allows you to choose from the three options. Make your choice and click on the ! button, which will execute the code necessary to quit in the manner you've specified.

To use this functionality within your own applications, follow these steps:

1. Import the module basExitWindows from 11-06.MDB.

2. Call the function, chosen from Table 11-4, that best suits your needs. In each case, if the function returns at all, it indicates that some Windows process wasn't able to shut down and your function call failed. This won't happen often.

For example, to reboot your computer:

Figure 11-7 The sample form, frmExitWindows

```
intRetval = ahtReboot()
```

FUNCTION	DESCRIPTION
ahtLogOff	Shuts down all processes running in the security context of the process that called the function. Then it logs the user off. Under Windows 95, all applications get the shutdown message EXCEPT the one that called this function. Under Windows NT, all applications get shut down automatically.
ahtReboot	Reboots the computer.
ahtShutDown	Shuts down the system to a point at which it is safe to turn off the power. All file buffers have been flushed to disk, and all running processes have stopped.

Table 11-4 Available functions for exiting Windows

How It Works

When you shut down Windows by your normal means, it sends a message to check with every running application before shutting down. If other applications have any unsaved data files that require user intervention, you'll usually be asked if it's OK to save the files. Once all the applications have agreed to shut down, Windows shuts itself down.

Windows will follow the same shutdown procedures when you use any of the functions listed in Table 11-4. The only difference between the functions listed in the table is what happens after Windows shuts down.

Comments

Each of the functions listed in Table 11-4 has its own role. You're most likely to use ahtShutDown in a situation where your application is meant for users who *only* use Access. When they're done with your application, they're done with Windows! The other functions have more usefulness in utility applications other than Access; use your imagination! There may be reasons why you'd need to reboot; perhaps you've changed a setting in the Windows registry for the user, and you'd like it to take effect now.

Certainly, these are not functions that every application will need or that you will use every day. But if you need to control what happens once your application has done its work, there's no replacing them!

11.7   How do I...
Run an application, given a data file associated with that application?

Problem

I'd like to find a way to provide a list of existing files and allow users to select a file and run the appropriate application to edit that file. Windows knows how to do this—for instance, when I double-click on a file with a .TXT extension in Explorer, Windows runs Notepad with that file. How can I provide this sort of functionality in my own applications?

Technique

Windows provides two API functions, FindExecutable and ShellExecute, which make running a related application possible from within an Access application. They both rely heavily on the Windows registry, which tracks the relationships between file name extensions and related executable programs. Figure 11-8 shows the results of running the REGEDIT.EXE program, which ships as part of Windows. REGEDIT allows

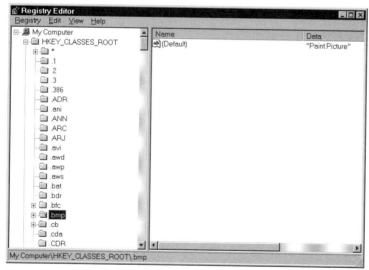

Figure 11-8 REGEDIT.EXE, showing file types registered on a typical system

you to add, edit, modify, or delete file associations. (The registry editor is named REGEDT32.EXE under Windows NT, and, though it looks different, it functions in a very similar manner.)

Tracing File Associations in REGEDIT

You can follow the paths of file associations in REGEDIT.EXE if you care to. Starting from the HKEY_CLASSES_ROOT item, open the folder (by double-clicking) and look for the .TXT entry. Selecting that item, you'll see that the default value (on the right side of REGEDIT's display) says "txtfile". This indicates what type of file should be associated with the .TXT file extension. To find what command to execute when you double-click on a txtfile type of file, keep searching (the items are listed alphabetically) until you find the txtFile entry (see Figure 11.8). If you continue to open subfolders until you find the command entry under the open entry, REGEDIT will show you the command to execute when you attempt to open a text file, on the right side of the display.

Be sure not to change any of the entries in the registry when looking through REGEDIT.

In this How-To, you use the FindExecutable function to get the name of the executable file associated with a selected data file. You also use the ShellExecute function to run the executable file, with the selected data file opened and ready to edit.

Steps

Load and run frmTestExecute, shown in Figure 11-9, from 11-07.MDB. To use this form, select a path (it defaults to your Windows directory when it first loads). Once the list box has been filled with all the files in the specified directory, click on one with

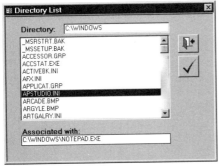

Figure 11-9 The sample form, frmTestExecute, from 11-07.MDB

the mouse. If there's an active file association for the selected file, the form will display that executable file name in a text box. If there's an associated executable file, you can run it and load your chosen file by double-clicking on the list box or clicking on the check mark button.

To use this functionality in your own applications, follow these steps:

1. Import the module basShellAPI from 11-07.MDB into your application.

2. To find the executable file associated with a given document, use the FindExecutable API function (aliased as aht_apiFindExecutable in the code). Call it with three parameters, as described in Table 11-5.

PARAMETER	TYPE	DESCRIPTION
strFile	String	The file name that has an association in the registration database.
strDir	String	The drive letter and path for the default directory (you can use "." to indicate the current directory).
strResult	String	A buffer to contain the returned executable name.

Table 11-5 Parameters for the FindExecutable API function

The FindExecutable function returns an integer error code. If the value is greater than 32, the function succeeded. Otherwise, it returns one of the error codes in Table 11-6 (note that these error codes are shared by several functions). If the function succeeded, strResult will be a null-terminated string containing the associated executable file. You'll need to trim off that trailing null character; one easy way to do this is by using the TrimNull function in basShellAPI.

```
Private Function TrimNull (strValue As String)

    ' Trim strValue at the first
    ' null character you find.

    Dim intPos As Integer
    intPos = InStr(strValue, vbNullChar)
    If intPos > 0 Then
        TrimNull = Left$(strValue, intPos - 1)
    Else
        TrimNull = strValue
    End If
End Function
```

VALUE	MEANING
0	System error occurred.
2	File not found.
3	Path not found.

VALUE	MEANING
5	Sharing violation occurred.
8	Not enough memory to start the task.
27	Association incomplete.
31	No association in the Registration Database for the file extension.
32	DLL not found.

Table 11-6 Some of the shared error codes for FindExecutable and ShellExecute

For example, the following code will find the executable file associated with MyFile.OOG.

```
Dim strBuffer As String
Dim strResult As String

strBuffer = Space(128)
strResult = ""

intRetval = aht_apiFindExecutable("MyFile.OOG", ".", strBuffer)
If intRetval > ahtcHinstanceErr Then
    ' Use the TrimNull() function, in basShellAPI,
    ' to remove the trailing null character
    strResult = TrimNull(strBuffer)
End If
' Now, strResult holds either "" or the
' name of the executable you need.
```

To make this simpler, basShellAPI includes the ahtFindExecutable function. This function requires the same parameters and returns the same values as aht_apiFindExecutable, but it handles the details of initializing the string buffer and trimming off the trailing null for you. You'll want to use this function, rather than calling the Windows API directly, because it will ensure that you use the correct methods for sending and receiving strings.

Once you know the name of the executable file associated with the selected document, you'll want to execute it with the ShellExecute API function. You could, of course, use the Shell command, but ShellExecute gives you a bit more flexibility.

ShellExecute returns an error code if something goes wrong, but Shell requires that you write error-handling code to trap and deal with errors. Using ShellExecute is simpler, in the long run.

ShellExecute allows you to specify the default drive/directory for your application. Shell does not.

ShellExecute provides a few more options than does Shell: See Table 11-8 for details.

623

Not that you'll use it often, but ShellExecute allows you to specify the action to take on opening a file. If you want to print the file rather than open it, specify the "print" operation for the second parameter.

To use this function, call it with six parameters, as shown in Table 11-7.

PARAMETER	TYPE	DESCRIPTION
hWnd	Integer	The handle of the window to be used as the parent for message boxes that may appear.
StrOp	String	The operation to perform. Normally, can only be "open" or "print."
StrFile	String	Name of the program to start.
StrParams	String	Command line arguments for the executable program. Normally, the name of the file to load into the application.
StrDir	String	The default drive/directory for the application when it starts up.
IntShowCmd	Integer	Specification of how to show the new window when the application starts up. For a list of values, see Table 11-8.

Table 11-7 Parameters for the ShellExecute API function

Table 11-8 lists all the possible values you can use for the intShowCmd parameter. These values control how the new application's window appears on the Windows desktop.

CONSTANT	VALUE	MEANING
ahtSW_HIDE	0	The window is hidden when started.
ahtSW_SHOWNORMAL	1	The window is restored to its previous state (neither minimized nor maximized).
ahtSW_SHOWMINIMIZED	2	The window is made visible and minimized.
ahtSW_SHOWMAXIMIZED	3	The window is made visible and maximized.
ahtSW_SHOWNOACTIVATE	4	The window is displayed, but doesn't gain the input focus.
ahtSW_MINIMIZE	6	The window is minimized (as an icon) when started.
ahtSW_SHOWMINNOACTIVE	7	The window is made visible and minimized, but doesn't receive the input focus.
ahtSW_SHOWNA	8	The window is displayed without any change to the window's state (remains minimized, normal, or maximized).
ahtSW_RESTORE	9	The window is restored to its previous state (neither minimized nor maximized) (same as ahtSW_SHOWNORMAL).

Table 11-8 Window display options for the intShowCmd parameter to ShellExecute

For example, to run the program C:\OOGLY\MKOOGLE.EXE, which created MyFile.OOG, maximized on the screen, you could run code like this from a form's module:

```
intRetval = aht_apiShellExecute(Me.hWnd, "open", _
    "C:\OOGLY\MKOOGLE.EXE", "MyFile.OOG", "C:\OOGLY", _
    ahtSW_SHOWMAXIMIZED)
```

How It Works

Normally, you'll use the FindExecutable function to retrieve an associated executable file for a given document, and then you'll pass both the executable name and the document name to ShellExecute to load them. For example, you might use code like this in your application:

```
Dim intRetval As Integer
Dim strBuffer As String

intRetval = aht_apiFindExecutable("MyFile.XXX", ".", strBuffer)
If intRetval <= HINSTANCE_ERR Then
    MsgBox "Unable to find executable. Error " & intRetval & "."
Else
    ' You're only here if you found the executable.
    intRetval = aht_apiShellExecute(Me.hWnd, "open", strBuffer, _
        "MyFile.XXX", "C:\NewDocs", ahtSW_SHOWMAXIMIZED)
    If intRetval <= HINSTANCE_ERR Then
        MsgBox "Unable to load application. Error " & intRetval & "."
    End If
End If
```

Comments

You may find it interesting to work your way through the sample form frmTestExecute. It borrows code presented in other chapters to provide the list of files, but once you've selected one, it uses code similar to the previous code sample to find and load the associated executable.

The methods presented in this How-To rely heavily on the Windows registry. You may find it useful to dig through the file associations in the registry (as discussed in the note above) and see how Windows finds applications itself when you double-click on data files.

11.8 How do I...
Check to see if an application is already running?

Problem

I need to startup other Windows programs from within my Access application—for instance, to send data to Excel or to format a report in Word for Windows. If I just use the Shell command to start these programs up, it's possible I'll end up with multiple instances of the application. How can I tell if an application is already running before I attempt to start it up?

Technique

There are a number of solutions to this problem, and none, unfortunately, are as easy as you'd like. To ask Windows, "Is Excel currently running?" and get an answer, you must know the Windows class name for the main window of the application. This How-To explains the format of the question and how to ask it. In addition, this How-To will demonstrate how to switch to a running application from your Access application.

Steps

Normally, you need to know whether a specific application is currently running so that you can either activate that application or use it as part of a DDE or OLE conversation (see Chapter 12 for more information on DDE and OLE). The sample form, frmAppsRunning (Figure 11-10), asks Windows the question, "Is this app running?"

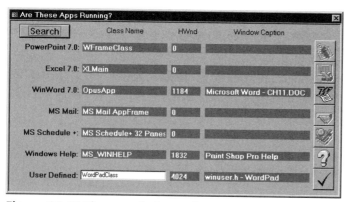

Figure 11-10 The sample form, frmAppsRunning, shows the state of certain applications

for each of six predefined window classes, and you can add one more of your own. For each application that frmAppsRunning finds, it fills in the window handle (hWnd) column and window caption column on the form. The AppActivate command in Access requires that you know the exact title of the window, and so the form uses code from Chapter 4 (in basAccessCaption) to retrieve the caption for each running application. Finally, you can click on any of the enabled buttons in the right-hand column to switch to the running application.

Try the sample form with Microsoft applications you have installed. Press F1 to bring up Help, and then switch back to Access and click on the Search button on the sample form. This will reinitiate the search for active applications, and it will find WIN-HELP.EXE running. Click on the question-mark icon to switch back to WinHelp.

Follow these steps to include this functionality in your own applications:

1. Import the modules listed in Table 11-9 from 11-08.MDB into your application.

MODULE	CONTAINS
basCaption	ahtGetAccessCaption, ahtGetWindowCaption, ahtSetAccessCaption
basUsage	ahtIsAppLoaded

Table 11-9 Modules to import from 11-08.MDB

2. To be able to ask Windows the question, "Is some application running?" you'll need to know the Windows class name for the main window of the application. Table 11-10 lists the names for several Windows applications. As you can see the class names appear somewhat arbitrary. Because they're assigned not by the marketing or documentation departments, but by the development staff, class names often reflect the project's code name or the state of mind of the developer.

Finding Class Names

There are many ways to find the class names for applications' main windows. The simplest is to use the sample form for How-To 11.9, which displays a list of open windows and their class names. If you want to know the class name for a specific application, open it, then run the sample form. The second column will list the class name for you.

APPLICATION	CLASS NAME
Access	OMain
Calculator	SciCalc
Excel	XLMain

continued on next page

continued from previous page

APPLICATION	CLASS NAME
Explorer	ExploreWClass
File Manager	WFS_Frame
MS Exchange Inbox	Microsoft Exchange 4.0 Viewer
MS Schedule +	MS Schedule+ 32 Panesdi
Notepad	Notepad
Paintbrush	MSPaintApp
PowerPoint	WFrameClass
Windows Help	MS_WINHELP
WordPad	WordPadClass
Word for Windows	OpusApp

Table 11-10 Class names for some Windows applications

3. To check to see whether a given application is currently running, use the ahtIsAppLoaded function in basUsage. Pass a class name to this function as a parameter, and it returns the window handle of the application if it's running, or 0 if it's not. For example:

```
hWnd = ahtIsAppLoaded("ms_winhelp")
```

will return a nonzero value if Windows Help is currently running. (Note that the class names are not case sensitive.)

4. Once you know the window handle for the application, if you want to make that application active, you can use the AppActivate command in Access. To switch to the application, though, you'll need to know the exact window caption. To make that easier, you can call the ahtGetWindowCaption function in basCaption *before* attempting to activate the application. For example, this code will switch to Excel, if it's running:

```
Dim hWnd as Integer

hWnd = ahtIsAppLoaded("XLMain")
If hWnd <> 0 Then
    AppActivate ahtGetWindowCaption(hWnd)
End If
```

5. If the application you want to activate isn't currently running (ahtIsAppLoaded returned 0), use the Shell command. In this case, you'll need to know the DOS executable file name for the given application (EXCEL.EXE, for example). The example form doesn't attempt to load the applications if they aren't already loaded, but your own application could load the program as needed.

How It Works

The ahtIsAppLoaded function couldn't be simpler: It calls a single Windows API function. The entire routine looks like this:

```
Function ahtIsAppLoaded (ByVal varClassName As Variant) As Long
    If IsNull(varClassName) Then
        ahtIsAppLoaded = 0
    Else
        ahtIsAppLoaded = aht_apiFindWindow(CStr(varClassName), 0&)
    End If
End Function
```

It allows you to pass in a class name. If the class name isn't null, the function calls the FindWindow (aliased as aht_apiFindWindow) API function, which takes a class name and returns the window handle of the first instance of that class it finds. AhtIsAppLoaded returns that handle to its caller.

Comments

Don't expect ahtIsAppLoaded to distinguish between multiple copies of the same application. That is, if you have two copies of Notepad running, you can't count on ahtIsAppLoaded to return the handle to a specific instance of Notepad. It will return the handle of the first one it comes across. But that shouldn't bother you, if all you're looking to find out is if *any* copy of the application is currently running.

COMPLEXITY:
INTERMEDIATE

11.9 How do I...
Retrieve a list of all the top-level windows?

Problem

I know I can determine if specific applications are currently running (I learned how to do that in How-To 11.8), but I'd like to obtain a list of all the running applications. That way, I could decide, as part of my application, what to present to my users. Is there a way to walk through all the open main windows and build up a list?

Technique

Windows is nothing if not hierarchical: It includes API functions that allow you to walk down and around the tree of open windows, starting with the main desktop window. This How-To provides a function that will do that for you, filling an array with information on each top-level window. You can then use that array to list applications, switch to them, or close them (see How-To 11.10 for information on closing other windows).

Steps

Load and run frmListWindows from 11-09.MDB. This sample form fills a list box with all the top-level windows and provides a button that will use the VBA AppActivate command to display the selected window. In addition, the Show visible windows only check box allows you to add invisible windows to the list. Of course, attempting to use AppActivate to switch to an invisible window will fail. Figure 11-11 shows the sample form in action.

To include this functionality in your own applications, follow these steps:

1. Import the module basWindowList from 11-09.MDB. This module includes the API declarations, constants, and wrapper functions you'll need to list and select top-level windows.

2. In your code, declare an array of type aht_tagWindowInfo to hold the list of open windows, like this:

```
Dim atypWindowList() As aht_tagWindowInfo
```

3. Call ahtWindowList, passing your array to be filled in and a Boolean value indicating whether to show visible windows only. The function returns the number of windows it found. After the function call, your array will have *intCount* rows, with each row containing information about a specific top-level window. For example, the following call will fill the array with information about all the visible top-level windows.

```
intCount = ahtWindowList(atypWindowList(), True)
```

4. In your application, decide which (if any) window you'd like to display, perhaps by looping through all the elements of the array. Use the AppActivate command, along with the window name, to activate the selected window:

```
AppActivate atypWindowList(intI).strCaption
```

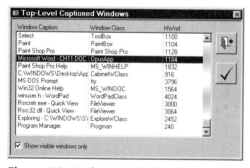

Figure 11-11 The sample form, frmListWindows, allowing you to select and display any of the top-level windows

How It Works

This example uses two functions for navigating through the hierarchy of windows. Table 11-11 describes the functions (both are aliased with the "aht_api" tag in the code).

FUNCTION	PURPOSE
GetDesktopHWnd	Retrieve the window handle for the main desktop window. All applications are children of this window.
GetWindow	Find a window, in a specified relation to a specified window. In this case, you'll be looking for the first child window of the desktop window.
GetWindowLong	Retrieve one of the 32-bit pieces of information stored with a window's structure in memory. You'll need to retrieve the style information (using the GWL_STYLE constant) so you can tell if a window is visible or not.
GetClassName	Retrieve the window class name for the specified window.

Table 11-11 Windows API navigation functions

The ahtWindowList function first retrieves a handle to the main desktop window, using GetDesktopHWnd. Once it knows that, it can find the handle for the desktop's first child window, using GetWindow. From then on, as long as the handle for the current window isn't 0, the code loops, filling in the array with information about the current window and then moving on to the next window with the GetWindow function. You'll note that the loop skips windows without captions (of which there are quite a few). Windows maintains a number of top-level hidden windows without captions for its own use. In addition, by specifying the fVisibleOnly parameter for ahtWindowList, you can include or exclude invisible windows. Windows 95 and OLE both set up a number of invisible windows to do their work, and most likely you won't want them to show up in your list. If you're interested, however, pass a False in for this parameter to add all the hidden windows to your list.

```
Type aht_tagWindowInfo
    strCaption As String
    hWnd As Long
    strClass As String
End Type

Function ahtWindowList(aWI() As aht_tagWindowInfo, _
    ByVal fVisibleOnly As Boolean) As Integer

    ' Fill an array with a list of all the currently
    ' open top-level windows.

    Dim hWnd As Long
    Dim strCaption As String
    Dim intCount As Integer
    Dim lngStyle As Long

    ' Get the desktop window, and from there,
```

```
' the first top-level window.
hWnd = aht_apiGetDesktopWindow()
hWnd = aht_apiGetWindow(hWnd, GW_CHILD)

' Loop through all the top-level windows.
Do While hWnd <> 0
    strCaption = ahtGetCaption(hWnd)
    If Len(strCaption) > 0 Then
        ' If you got a caption, add one element
        ' to the output array, and fill in the
        ' information (name and hWnd).
        lngStyle = aht_apiGetWindowLong(hWnd, GWL_STYLE)
        ' The Imp operator (Implies) returns True unless
        ' the first condition is True and the second is False.
        ' So this condition will be true unless you're
        ' showing visible only, and the window is not visible.
        If fVisibleOnly Imp (WS_VISIBLE And lngStyle) Then
            ReDim Preserve aWI(0 To intCount)
            aWI(intCount).strCaption = strCaption
            aWI(intCount).hWnd = hWnd
            aWI(intCount).strClass = GetClassName(hWnd)
            intCount = intCount + 1
        End If
    End If
    ' Move to the next top-level window.
    hWnd = aht_apiGetWindow(hWnd, GW_HWNDNEXT)
Loop

' Return the number of windows.
ahtWindowList = intCount
End Function
```

Comments

You may find it instructive to study the code in the sample form's module. It calls ahtWindowList, and then uses a list-filling callback function to fill the list box on the form with the window captions, classes, and handles. This is a perfect example of when you'd use such a function: when you need to fill a control with data from an array that couldn't be gathered until the application is running.

Some of the windows on the list exist at the time the form is filling its list, but aren't available (the Access Immediate window, for example). You can attempt to switch to them, but the attempt will fail. The code attached to the check mark button's Click event disregards errors, so it just keeps going if an error occurs when it tries to switch the active window. See How-To 11.10 for information on deleting windows in this list.

COMPLEXITY:
INTERMEDIATE

11.10 How do I...
Close a running Windows application?

Problem

As part of some of my large Access applications, I often allow users to start other Windows tools (notepad, calculator, calendar, etc.); once those tools are open, my application doesn't touch them. Some users have been complaining about all the "junk" left over once my application closes. Is there some way I can close another window from my Access application? That way, on the way out, I can attempt to close any tools my application has opened.

Technique

How-To 11.9 demonstrates retrieval of a list of all the running Windows applications' captions, class names, and window handles. Once you know that information, it's trivial to close an application: Given a window handle, tell it to close. Using the Windows API PostMessage function, you can close any window at any time. Of course, newer applications such as Excel 7.0 and Word for Windows 7.0 support OLE Automation to the extent that you can close them without using the Windows API. Other applications that don't support OLE Automation will require either the API method described here or SendKeys, which is, at best, unreliable.

Steps

Load and run frmListWindows from 11-10.MDB. This form, shown in Figure 11-12, is similar to the sample form in How-To 11.9, with the addition of the Close (stop sign) button, which lets you close the selected window. Try a few (you can even close Access this way, if you want).

> **Don't Try This at Home**
>
> Some top-level windows shouldn't be closed—you should never include a form like this as part of an end-user application. On the other hand, given an array of window captions and handles, you could programmatically decide which window to close and close it yourself from within your application. This form is a demonstration of the power of the method, not a tool you'd actually use.

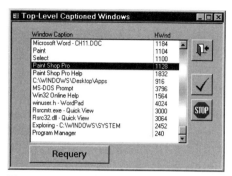

Figure 11-12 The demonstration form, frmListWindows, including a "kill" button to close top-level windows

To use this functionality in your own applications, follow these steps:

1. Import the modules basWindowList (if you didn't do so for How-To 11.9) and basCloseWindows.

2. Follow the steps listed in How-To 11.9 to create and fill in the array of top-level windows.

3. Decide which window you want to close, if any. Because Windows sometimes appends document names to the application name (such as "Microsoft Word 11-10.DOC"), you'll need to check against just the first portion of the window name in your array. For example:

```
For intI = 0 To intCount - 1
    If Left$(atypWindowList(0).strCaption, 14) = _
        "Microsoft Word" Then
            ' You found a match. Do something.
    End If
Next intI
```

4. When you've found the item you want to close, use the ahtCloseWindow function, passing to it the handle of the window you care about.

```
If ahtCloseWindow(atypWindowList(intI).hWnd) = 0 Then
    ' If you got 0 back, it got the message!
End If
```

How It Works

The ahtCloseWindow function calls the PostMessage API function. By posting a message to a particular window, you send it a message telling it to do something, but you don't bother waiting for a response. (The corresponding API function, SendMessage, *does* cause you to wait for a response. You can use SendMessage if you want to stop and wait for the other application to close, but we don't recommend it.) The ahtCloseWindow function sends the WM_CLOSE message to your chosen window, telling it to shut down. It's as if you quit your Windows shell program with some applications running. Your shell sends a message to each main application window to shut down because Windows is shutting down. The ahtCloseWindow function, then, looks like this:

```
Function ahtCloseWindow (ByVal hWnd As Long)

    Const WM_CLOSE = &H10

    ahtCloseWindow = PostMessage(hWnd, WM_CLOSE, 0, vbNullString)
End Function
```

The purpose of this wrapper function that calls PostMessage is to shield you from having to remember how to post a message to a window. It's a lot simpler to call ahtCloseWindow than to call PostMessage directly.

Comments

Sending a WM_CLOSE message to a window doesn't necessarily close it. If that application has an unsaved document that needs saving, it will pop up its own dialog box asking what you want to do with that unsaved document. In the sample form, if this happens, the list box won't be updated correctly. Once you return from your duties with the foreign application, press the Requery button on the form to force it to search again for all open applications.

COMPLEXITY:
ADVANCED

11.11 How do I...
Set file date and time stamps?

Problem

Access makes it easy to retrieve the modification date and time for files on disk, using the FileDateTime function. In one application, though, I need to be able to reset the last-modification date of files manually: The Access FileCopy function doesn't reset file date and time stamps, and I'd like copied files to have the current time. Is there a Windows API call to allow me to set file date and time stamps?

Technique

Windows provides the GetFileTime and SetFileTime API functions. Both work with three different date/time values: date of creation, date of last access, and date of last write. You want to preserve the date of creation and update the date of last access and update. The code shown in this example will allow you to do this.

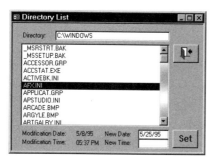

Figure 11-13 The sample form, frmTimeStamp, showing a selected file's modification date and time

Steps

The sample form, frmTimeStamp, allows you to select a file name. Then the function displays the date and time of last modification for the file, as shown in Figure 11-13. In addition, you can set a new file date, time, or both (it'll retain whichever setting you don't change, if you just change one).

To set file date and time information in your own applications, follow these steps:

1. Import the module basTimeStamp from 11-11.MDB. This module includes the type definitions and Windows API declarations you'll need. It also includes a VBA function to convert dates and times as retrieved from the API call into a date/time value that Access can understand. If you want to use the sample form as is in your own applications, you'll also need to import basFillList and basSortArray, which include functions to retrieve the list of files and sort that list.

2. To set the modification date information about a specific file, call the ahtSetFileDateTime function, passing it a file name and a date/time value as parameters. For example, the following code will change the last modification time and date for C:\AUTOEXEC.BAT to the current date and time:

```
fOK = ahtSetFileDateTime("C:\AUTOEXEC.BAT", Now)
```

How It Works

The ahtSetFileDateTime function, shown below, consists of three basic steps.

```
Function ahtSetFileDateTime(strFileName As String, varDate As Date) ⇒
As Boolean
    Dim hFile As Long
    Dim of As OFSTRUCT
    Dim st As SYSTEMTIME
    Dim ftCreation As FILETIME
    Dim ftLastAccess As FILETIME
```

```
    Dim ftLastWrite As FILETIME
    Dim ftLocal As FILETIME
    Dim fOK As Boolean

    st.wYear = Year(varDate)
    st.wMonth = Month(varDate)
    st.wDay = Day(varDate)
    st.wHour = Hour(varDate)
    st.wMinute = Minute(varDate)
    st.wSecond = Second(varDate)

    hFile = OpenFile(strFileName, of, OF_READWRITE)
    If hFile > 0 Then
        fOK = GetFileTime(hFile, ftCreation, ftLastAccess, ftLastWrite)
        If fOK Then fOK = SystemTimeToFileTime(st, ftLastWrite)
        If fOK Then fOK = LocalFileTimeToFileTime(ftLastWrite, ftLocal)
        If fOK Then fOK = SetFileTime(hFile, ftCreation, ftLocal,
ftLocal)
        CloseHandle hFile
    End If
    ahtSetFileDateTime = fOK
End Function
```

The first step the function takes is to copy the date information from the Access Date-type variable into a structure that the API can use.

```
' In the Declarations area:
Private Type SYSTEMTIME
    wYear As Integer
    wMonth As Integer
    wDayOfWeek As Integer
    wDay As Integer
    wHour As Integer
    wMinute As Integer
    wSecond As Integer
    wMilliseconds As Integer
End Type

Dim st As SYSTEMTIME

' In the function:
st.wYear = Year(varDate)
st.wMonth = Month(varDate)
st.wDay = Day(varDate)
st.wHour = Hour(varDate)
st.wMinute = Minute(varDate)
st.wSecond = Second(varDate)
```

Next, the function must open the requested file with read/write access, so it can write to the file's time stamp.

```
hFile = OpenFile(strFileName, of, OF_READWRITE)
```

If this succeeds, the function then retrieves the current time stamps, converts the system time structure to a file time structure, converts that time from local time to the internal generalized time that Windows uses, and then sets the file time.

```
fOK = GetFileTime(hFile, ftCreation, ftLastAccess, ftLastWrite)
If fOK Then fOK = SystemTimeToFileTime(st, ftLastWrite)
If fOK Then fOK = LocalFileTimeToFileTime(ftLastWrite, ftLocal)
If fOK Then fOK = SetFileTime(hFile, ftCreation, ftLocal, ftLocal)
CloseFileHandle hFile
```

The function sets both the time of last access and the time of last write to be the date and time you've specified.

When you select the Set button on the sample form, it executes the following procedure.

```
Private Sub cmdSetTime_Click()
    Dim varDate As Date
    Dim strDate As String
    Dim strTime As String

    strDate = IIf(IsNull(Me!txtNewDate), Me!txtDate, Me!txtNewDate)
    strTime = IIf(IsNull(Me!txtNewTime), Me!txtTime, Me!txtNewTime)
    varDate = CVDate(strDate & " " & strTime)
    If Not ahtSetFileDateTime(GetPath(), varDate) Then
        MsgBox "Unable to set the file date!"
    Else
        Me!txtDate = Format(varDate, "Short Date")
        Me!txtTime = Format(varDate, "Short Time")
    End If
End Sub
```

This procedure retrieves the dates you've typed on the form, converts them to an Access date/time value, and then sets the date for the file you've selected. Note that the example uses the existing date or time for any value you didn't enter. Because the Set button won't be enabled unless you enter at least the date or the time, there's no need to worry about when they're both null.

Comments

Unless you take the extra step of converting the passed-in date/time value from local time to the internal time Windows uses (Greenwich mean time), the time you set will be off by the difference in time zones between your time and the standardized time. The call to LocalTimeToFileTime takes care of this for you. This does, of course, count on the local time having been set correctly when you installed Windows.

COMPLEXITY:
INTERMEDIATE

11.12 How do I...
Retrieve information about the
disk drives in my computer?

Problem

I'd like to be able to gather specific information about the disk drives in my computer: for example, how large they are, how much space is free, whether they're local or remote, and whether they're removable or not. Certainly, Access doesn't provide this information. Is it available using a Windows API function?

Technique

The Windows API provides three functions that you can use to extract information about the drives in your computer: GetLogicalDriveStrings, which returns a string containing a list of all the logical drives; GetDriveType, which returns information about the specified drive; and GetDiskFreeSpace, which returns information about the total and free disk space for a specified drive.

Steps

Load and run frmDiskSpace from 11-12.MDB. This form, shown in Figure 11-14, contains a list box with information on all the logical drives in your system. To fill the list box, the example code walks through all the drives returned from a call to GetLogicalDriveStrings, calling the other functions mentioned above for each drive.

To use these functions in your own applications, follow these steps:

1. Import the modules basDiskInfo and basToken from 11-12.MDB.

2. To call the functions, use the information in Table 11-12. Each function takes only a single parameter, the drive to be interrogated.

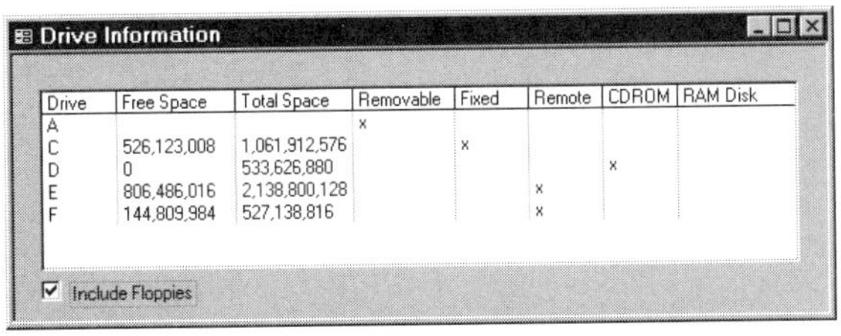

Drive	Free Space	Total Space	Removable	Fixed	Remote	CDROM	RAM Disk
A			x				
C	526,123,008	1,061,912,576		x			
D	0	533,626,880				x	
E	806,486,016	2,138,800,128		x			
F	144,809,984	527,138,816		x			

☑ Include Floppies

Figure 11-14 The sample form, frmDiskSpace, showing information on all the installed drives

639

FUNCTION	PURPOSE	RETURN VALUE	EXAMPLE
ahtGetFreeSpace	Retrieve the amount of free space on the specified drive.	Variant (the amount of free disk space, in bytes), or Null, if the function failed.	lngFree = ahtGetFreeSpace("C")
ahtGetTotalSpace	Retrieve the total amount of space on the specified drive.	Variant (the amount of total disk space, in bytes) or Null, if the function failed.	lngTotal = ahtGetTotalSpace("C")
ahtIsDriveCDROM	Verify that a drive is a CD-ROM.	True if CD-ROM, False otherwise.	fCD = ahtIsDriveCDROM("D")
ahtIsDriveFixed	Verify that a drive is a hard disk.	True if a hard disk, False otherwise.	fFixed = ahtIsDriveFixed("C")
ahtIsDriveLocal	Verify that the specified drive is local.	True if local, False if remote.	fLocal = ahtIsDriveLocal("C")
ahtIsDriveRAMDisk	Verify that a drive is a RAM disk.	True if RAM disk, False otherwise.	fRAM = ahtIsDriveRAMDisk("F")
ahtIsDriveRemote	Verify that the specified drive is a network drive.	True if remote, False if local.	fNetwork = ahtIsDriveRemote("E")
ahtIsDriveRemovable	Verify that the specified drive is for removable media.	True if removable, False otherwise.	fRemovable = ahtIsDriveRemovable("A")

Table 11-12 The functions in basDiskInfo

How It Works

The sample form doesn't actually use any of the ahtIs… functions; they're supplied only for your own applications. Instead, it calls the ahtGetDrives function in basDiskInfo, which fills an array of aht_tagDriveInfo structures directly with information about each of the installed drives, physical or logical. The structure looks like this:

```
Type aht_tagDriveInfo
    strDrive As String
    varFreeSpace As Variant
    varTotalSpace As Variant
    fRemovable As Boolean
    fFixed As Boolean
    fRemote As Boolean
    fCDROM As Boolean
    fRamDisk As Boolean
End Type
```

and it stores all the information that the sample form displays. The sample form then uses a list-filling callback function to display the information in a list box. (For more information on using list-filling callback functions, see Chapter 7.)

The ahtGetDrives function, shown below, starts out by calling the Windows API function GetLogicalDriveStrings. This function returns a string containing all the logical drives on your machine, in this format:

```
C:0D:0G:0H:0
```

where the 0s indicate null characters, Chr$(0) (Access provides the vbNullChar constant that's equivalent to Chr$(0)). The ahtGetDrives function loops through this string, using the ahtGetToken function in basTokens to pull out the drive names, one at a time, and then gathering information about each.

```
Function ahtGetDrives(astrDrives() As aht_tagDriveInfo, _
    fIncludeFloppies As Boolean)
    ' Fill astrDrives() with all the available logical drive letters.

    Dim strBuffer As String
    Dim intCount As Integer
    Dim intI As Integer
    Dim varTemp As Variant
    Dim lngType As Long

Const ahtcMaxSpace = 1024

    strBuffer = Space(ahtcMaxSpace)

    intCount = GetLogicalDriveStrings(ahtcMaxSpace - 1, strBuffer)
    strBuffer = Left(strBuffer, intCount)
    intI = 1
    intCount = 0
    Do
        varTemp = ahtGetToken(strBuffer, vbNullChar, intI)
        If Len(varTemp & "") > 0 Then
            ' The next statement will be true except in the
            ' case where the drive < C and you DON'T want
            ' to include floppies. Then it'll skip the drive.
            If (UCase(Left(varTemp, 1) < "C")) Imp fIncludeFloppies Then
                intCount = intCount + 1
                ' Get the drive name.
                astrDrives(intCount).strDrive = varTemp

                ' Get the drive type, and set the flags accordingly.
                lngType = GetDriveType(varTemp)
                Select Case lngType
                    Case DRIVE_REMOVABLE
                        astrDrives(intCount).fRemovable = True
                    Case DRIVE_FIXED
                        astrDrives(intCount).fFixed = True
                    Case DRIVE_REMOTE
                        astrDrives(intCount).fRemote = True
                    Case DRIVE_CDROM
                        astrDrives(intCount).fCDROM = True
                    Case DRIVE_RAMDISK
                        astrDrives(intCount).fRamDisk = True
                End Select
```

continued on next page

641

continued from previous page

```
                         ' Get the drive space information.
                         astrDrives(intCount).varTotalSpace =
                           ahtGetTotalSpace(varTemp)
                         astrDrives(intCount).varFreeSpace =
                           ahtGetFreeSpace(varTemp)
                    End If
                    intI = intI + 1
                End If
            Loop Until Len(varTemp & "") = 0
            ahtGetDrives = intCount
        End Function
```

The ahtGetTotalSpace and ahtGetFreeSpace functions both call the private GetDiskSpace function, which in turn calls the GetDiskFreeSpace API function. The GetDiskSpace function, shown below, takes the four pieces of information returned from GetDiskFreeSpace—sectors per cluster, bytes per sector, free clusters, and total clusters—and returns the calculated value that you've requested.

```
Private Function GetDiskSpace(ByVal strDrive As String, _
    fTotal As Boolean) As Variant

    ' Input:
    '     strDrive: string representing drive letter
    '     fTotal: True for total space on drive, False for free space on drive
    ' Output:
    '     Free or Total space, if no error.
    '     Null, otherwise.

    Dim lngSectorsPerCluster As Long
    Dim lngBytesPerSector As Long
    Dim lngFreeClusters As Long
    Dim lngTotalClusters As Long

    ' Force the string into the correct format
    strDrive = Left(strDrive, 1) & ":\"
    If GetDiskFreeSpace(strDrive, lngSectorsPerCluster, lngBytesPerSector, _
        lngFreeClusters, lngTotalClusters) Then
        GetDiskSpace = lngSectorsPerCluster * lngBytesPerSector * IIf(fTotal, _
            lngTotalClusters, lngFreeClusters)
    Else
        GetDiskSpace = Null
    End If
End Function
```

Comments

If you're interested in digging in a bit further, you might investigate the GetVolumeInformation API function. This function retrieves even more information about the specified drive, including its volume name, serial number, whether or not compression is enabled, the file system (FAT, HPFS, NTFS), and other information about how data is stored on that drive. This information is of less importance to Access developers than to system application developers, so we've left the extra material out of this topic.

COMPLEXITY:
ADVANCED

11.13 How do I... Collect and display information on the system and the Access installation?

Problem

My application really needs to know some information about the computer it's running on. In addition, I'd like to add some professional polish and an About... box that shows information about the computer, the resources, and the user. Access doesn't provide any way to find these things. How can I gather this information?

Technique

You can use the Windows API to retrieve information about the system on which your program is running. By using these various functions as the control sources for unbound controls, you can present a selection of system information to your user.

Steps

Load 11-13.MDB and open frmSystemInfo in regular form view. This form includes five "pages" of information about the current computer and its resources. The values shown on your screen will, of course, differ from those shown in Figure 11-15, depending on your hardware and the other software you have running. If you like the look of this form, use it as is in your own applications. (You'll still need to import the form, frmSystemInfo; its subform, fsubInfo; and the module, basSystemInfo, into your

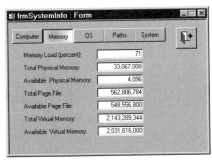

Figure 11-15 The demo form, frmSystemInfo, showing memory status information

application, as directed in step 1, below.) To create a similar form in your own application, follow these steps:

1. Import the module basSystemInfo from 11-13.MDB to your own application. This module contains all the constants, API declarations, and wrapper functions that you'll need.

2. Create a new form. Place an unbound text box (or check box or option group—see fsubInfo for hints) on the form for each piece of information you wish to display. Set the Control Source of control as shown in Table 11-13. The sample form, frmSystemInfo, uses an option group letting you choose which page of the subform, fsubInfo, you'd like to see. This has nothing to do with the functionality of the sample beyond cosmetics, and just makes it easier to group the information.

ITEM	CONTROL SOURCE
Screen Resolution	=ahtGetScreenX() & " x " & ahtGetScreenY()
Mouse Installed	=ahtMouseInstalled()
Keyboard Type	=ahtKeyboardType()
Memory Load	=ahtGetMemoryStatus(0)
Total Physical Memory	=ahtGetMemoryStatus(1)
Available Physical Memory	=ahtGetMemoryStatus(2)
Total Page File	=ahtGetMemoryStatus(3)
Available Page File	=ahtGetMemoryStatus(4)
Total Virtual Memory	=ahtGetMemoryStatus(5)
Available Virtual Memory	=ahtGetMemoryStatus(6)
Operating System Version	=ahtGetOSInfo(0) & "." & ahtGetOSInfo(1)
Build Number	=ahtGetOSInfo(2)
Platform	=ahtGetOSInfo(3)
Windows Directory	=ahtWindowsDirectory()
System Directory	=ahtSystemDirectory()
Temp Path	=ahtTempPath()
Access Directory	=ahtAccessDirectory()
OEM ID	=ahtGetSystemStatus(0)
Page Size	=ahtGetSystemStatus(1)
Lowest Memory Address	=ahtGetSystemStatus(2)
Highest Memory Address	=ahtGetSystemStatus(3)
Active Processor Mask	=ahtGetSystemStatus(4)
Number of Processors	=ahtGetSystemStatus(5)
Processor Type	=ahtGetSystemStatus(6)

Table 11-13 Control sources used for text boxes on frmSystemInfo

How It Works

The functions used here employ a variety of techniques to return the requested information. In general, they query the low-level Windows API to retrieve hardware and Windows environment information. We've wrapped each low-level function in an Access function to handle data type conversions from the DLLs used by Windows into the format that Access can understand.

Retrieving Information about the Computer

The example form uses several functions to return information about the current computer.

 Screen resolution: The ahtGetScreenX and ahtGetScreenY use the GetSystemMetrics API function to return the size of the screen in pixels. This API function can return many other pieces of information about your system, including the width of the window borders, the size of icons, and whether or not a mouse is installed. You can use this function to retrieve a great number of details about the current Windows installation. To call it, just pass it one of the constants in Table 11-14, and it returns the requested value to you. For example:

```
Function ahtGetScreenX()
    ' Retrieve the screen width in pixels.
    ahtGetScreenX = GetSystemMetrics(SM_CXSCREEN)
End Function
```

 Mouse installed: Again, the GetSystemMetrics function does the work.

Keyboard type: The GetKeyboardType function provides the answers.

```
Function ahtKeyboardType()
    ' Retrieve information about the keyboard.
    ' Call GetKeyboardType with
    '   0    Keyboard Type
    '   1    Keyboard SubType (depends on the manufacturer)
    '   2    Number of function keys
    ahtKeyboardType = GetKeyboardType(0)
End Function
```

 Memory information: The GlobalMemoryStatus function fills in a user-defined data structure with information about the current memory load, available and total real and virtual memory, and paging space. We've wrapped all this information up in the ahtGetMemoryStatus function:

```
Function ahtGetMemoryStatus(intItem As Integer) As Variant

    ' Retrieve system memory information
    ' In:
```

continued on next page

continued from previous page

```
'       intItem: which piece of information to retrieve
'           0: Memory Load (0 to 100)
'           1: Total physical memory in bytes
'           2: Available physical memory in bytes
'           3: Total size in page file in bytes
'           4: Available page file in bytes
'           5: Total virtual memory in bytes
'           6: Available virtual memory in bytes
' Out:
'     Return Value: the requested information

Dim MS As MEMORYSTATUS

' Set the length member before you call GlobalMemoryStatus
MS.dwLength = Len(MS)
GlobalMemoryStatus MS
Select Case intItem
    Case 0
        ahtGetMemoryStatus = MS.dwMemoryLoad
    Case 1
        ahtGetMemoryStatus = MS.dwTotalPhys
    Case 2
        ahtGetMemoryStatus = MS.dwAvailPhys
    Case 3
        ahtGetMemoryStatus = MS.dwTotalPageFile
    Case 4
        ahtGetMemoryStatus = MS.dwAvailPageFile
    Case 5
        ahtGetMemoryStatus = MS.dwTotalVirtual
    Case 6
        ahtGetMemoryStatus = MS.dwAvailVirtual
    Case Else
        ahtGetMemoryStatus = 0
End Select
End Function
```

Operating system information: The GetVersionEx API function does the work here. To simplify its use, we've provided the ahtGetOSInfo function, shown below.

```
Function ahtGetOSInfo(intItem As Integer) As Variant

' Retrieve operating system information
' In:
'     intItem: which piece of information to retrieve
'         0: Major Version
'         1: Minor version
'         2: Build Number
'         3: Platform ID
'             0 = Win32s (not going to happen!)
'             1 = Win95
'             2 = WinNT
' Out:
'     Return Value: the requested information
```

```
    Dim OSInfo As OSVERSIONINFO

    ' Set the length member before you call GetVersionEx
    OSInfo.dwOSVersionInfoSize = Len(OSInfo)
    If GetVersionEx(OSInfo) Then
        Select Case intItem
            Case 0
                ahtGetOSInfo = OSInfo.dwMajorVersion
            Case 1
                ahtGetOSInfo = OSInfo.dwMinorVersion
            Case 2
                ' Get just the low word of the result
                ahtGetOSInfo = OSInfo.dwBuildNumber And &HFFFF&
            Case 3
                ahtGetOSInfo = OSInfo.dwPlatformId
        End Select
    Else
        ahtGetOSInfo = 0
    End If
End Function
```

Directories: To retrieve the Windows directory, call ahtWindowsDirectory, shown below. For the Windows System directory, call ahtSystemDirectory; for the temporary storage path, call ahtTempPath; and to find out which directory Access is running from, call ahtAccessDirectory. (Note that ahtAccessDirectory doesn't actually use the Windows API to find the location of Access; the SysCmd function in Access makes that information available.)

```
Function ahtWindowsDirectory()
    ' Retrieve the Windows directory
    Dim strBuffer As String
    Dim intCount As Integer

    strBuffer = Space(MAX_PATH)
    intCount = GetWindowsDirectory(strBuffer, MAX_PATH)
    ahtWindowsDirectory = CleanPath(Left(strBuffer, intCount))
End Function
```

System information: The GetSystemInfo API function provides all the information. To make this easier for you, we've provided the ahtGetSystemStatus function, shown below. Call this function with a number representing the piece of information you want.

```
Function ahtGetSystemStatus(intItem As Integer) As Variant

    ' Retrieve system status information
    ' In:
    '     intItem: which piece of information to retrieve
    '         0: Computer identifer, specific to OEM
    '         1: Returns page size and specifies the granularity of page
    '             protection and commitment
```

continued on next page

continued from previous page

```
'                  2: Lowest memory address accessible to applications and
'                     dynamic-link libraries (DLLs)
'                  3: Highest memory address accessible to applications and DLLs
'                  4: Mask representing the set of processors configured into
'                     the system
'                     Bit 0 is processor 0; bit 31 is processor 31
'                  5: Returns the number of processors in the system
'                  6: Type of the current processors in the system
'                  7: Allocation granularity in which memory will be allocated
'                     on (usually 64K)
' Out:
'     Return Value: the requested information

Dim SI As SYSTEM_INFO

GetSystemInfo SI
Select Case intItem
    Case 0
        ahtGetSystemStatus = SI.dwOemID
    Case 1
        ahtGetSystemStatus = SI.dwPageSize
    Case 2
        ahtGetSystemStatus = SI.lpMinimumApplicationAddress
    Case 3
        ahtGetSystemStatus = SI.lpMaximumApplicationAddress
    Case 4
        ahtGetSystemStatus = SI.dwActiveProcessorMask
    Case 5
        ahtGetSystemStatus = SI.dwNumberOrfProcessors
    Case 6
        ahtGetSystemStatus = SI.dwProcessorType
    Case 7
        ahtGetSystemStatus = SI.dwAllocationGranularity
    Case Else
        ahtGetSystemStatus = 0
    End Select
End Function
```

CONSTANT NAME	VALUE	MEANING
SM_CXSCREEN	0	Width of screen.
SM_CYSCREEN	1	Height of screen.
SM_CXVSCROLL	2	Width of arrow bitmap on a vertical scroll bar.
SM_CYHSCROLL	3	Height of arrow bitmap on a horizontal scroll bar.
SM_CYCAPTION	4	Height of window title. This is the title height plus the height of the window frame that cannot be sized (SM_CYBORDER).
SM_CXBORDER	5	Windows NT only: Width of window border.
		Windows 95 only: Dimensions of a single border, in pixels.
SM_CYBORDER	6	Windows NT only: Height of window border.
		Windows 95 only: Dimensions of a single border, in pixels.

CONSTANT NAME	VALUE	MEANING
SM_CXFIXEDFRAME	7	Width of frame when window has the WS_DLGFRAME style.
SM_CYFIXEDFRAME	8	Height of frame when window has the WS_DLGFRAME style.
SM_CYVTHUMB	9	Height of scroll box on vertical scroll bar.
SM_CXHTHUMB	10	Width of scroll box (thumb) on horizontal scroll bar.
SM_CXICON	11	Width of icon.
SM_CYICON	12	Height of icon.
SM_CXCURSOR	13	Windows NT only: Width of cursor.
		Windows 95 only: Width of standard cursor bitmaps, in pixels.
SM_CYCURSOR	14	Windows NT only: Height of cursor.
		Windows 95 only: Height of standard cursor bitmaps, in pixels.
SM_CYMENU	15	Height of single-line menu bar.
SM_CXFULLSCREEN	16	Width of window client area for a full-screen window.
SM_CYFULLSCREEN	17	Height of window client area for a full-screen window (equivalent to the height of the screen minus the height of the window title).
SM_CYKANJIWINDOW	18	Height of Kanji window.
SM_MOUSEPRESENT	19	Nonzero if the mouse hardware is installed.
SM_CYVSCROLL	20	Height of arrow bitmap on a vertical scroll bar.
SM_CXHSCROLL	21	Width of arrow bitmap on a horizontal scroll bar.
SM_DEBUG	22	Nonzero if the Windows version is a debugging version.
SM_SWAPBUTTON	23	Nonzero if the left and right mouse buttons are swapped.
SM_CXMIN	28	Minimum width of window.
SM_CYMIN	29	Minimum height of window.
SM_CXSIZE	30	Width of bitmaps contained in the title bar.
SM_CYSIZE	31	Height of bitmaps contained in the title bar.
SM_CXFRAME	32	Width of window frame for a window that can be resized.
		Windows 95 only: Obsolete; use SM_CXFIXEDFRAME and SM_CYFIXEDFRAME instead.
SM_CYFRAME	33	See SM_CXFRAME (height, instead).
SM_CXMINTRACK	34	Minimum tracking width of window.
SM_CYMINTRACK	35	Minimum tracking height of window.
SM_CXDOUBLECLK	36	Width of the rectangle around the location of the first click in a double-click sequence. The second click must occur within this rectangle for the system to consider the two clicks a double-click.
SM_CYDOUBLECLK	37	Height of the rectangle around the location of the first click in a double-click sequence. The second click must occur within this rectangle for the system to consider the two clicks a double-click.

continued on next page

continued from previous page

CONSTANT NAME	VALUE	MEANING
SM_CXICONSPACING	38	Width of rectangles the system uses to position tiled icons.
SM_CYICONSPACING	39	Height of rectangles the system uses to position tiled icons.
SM_MENUDROPALIGNMENT	40	Alignment of pop-up menus. If this value is zero, the left side of a pop-up menu is aligned with the left side of the corresponding menu-bar item. If this value is nonzero, the left side of a pop-up menu is aligned with the right side of the corresponding menu-bar item.
SM_PENWINDOWS	41	Handle of the Pen Windows dynamic-link library (DLL) if Pen Windows is installed.
SM_DBCSENABLED	42	Nonzero if current version of Windows uses double-byte characters; otherwise, this value returns zero.
SM_CMOUSEBUTTONS	43	Number of buttons on the mouse, or zero if no mouse is present.
SM_SECURE	44	Windows 95 only: nonzero if security is present, zero otherwise.
SM_CXMINSPACING	47	Windows 95 only: Along with SM_CYMINSPACING, dimensions of a grid cell for minimized windows, in pixels. Each minimized window fits into a rectangle this size when arranged. These values are always greater than or equal to SM_CXMINIMIZED and SM_CYMINIMIZED.
SM_CYMINSPACING	48	See SM_CXMINSPACING.
SM_CXSMICON	49	Windows 95 only: With SM_CYSMICON, recommended dimensions of a small icon, in pixels. Small icons typically appear in window captions and in small icon view.
SM_CYSMICON	50	See SM_CXSMICON.
SM_CXSMSIZE	52	Windows 95 only: With SM_CYSMSIZE, dimension of small caption buttons, in pixels.
SM_CYSMSIZE	53	See SM_CXSMSIZE.
SM_CXMENUSIZE	54	Windows 95 only: Width of menu bar buttons (such as multiple document (MDI) child Close), in pixels.
SM_CYMENUSIZE	55	Windows 95 only: Height of menu bar buttons (such as multiple document (MDI) child Close), in pixels.
SM_ARRANGE	56	Windows 95 only: Flags specifying how the system arranged minimized windows.
SM_CXMINIMIZED	57	Windows 95 only: Width of a normal minimized window, in pixels.
SM_CYMINIMIZED	58	Windows 95 only: Height of a normal minimized window, in pixels.
SM_CXMAXTRACK	59	Windows 95 only: Default maximum width of a window that has a caption and sizing borders. The user cannot drag the window frame to a size larger than these dimensions.
SM_CYMAXTRACK	60	See SM_CXMAXTRACK (height, instead).
SM_CXMAXIMIZED	61	Windows 95 only: Default width of a maximized top-level window, in pixels.
SM_CYMAXIMIZED	62	Windows 95 only: Default height of a maximized top-level window, in pixels.

CONSTANT NAME	VALUE	MEANING
SM_NETWORK	63	Windows 95 only: The least significant bit is set if a network is present; otherwise, it is cleared. The other bits are reserved for future use.
SM_CLEANBOOT	67	Windows 95 only: Value that specifies how the system was started: 0 (Normal boot), 1 (Fail-safe boot), 2 (Fail-safe with network boot). Fail-safe boot (also called SafeBoot) bypasses the user's startup files.
SM_SHOWSOUNDS	70	Nonzero if the user requires an application to present information visually in situations where it would otherwise present the information only in audible form; zero otherwise.
SM_CXMENUCHECK	71	Windows 95 only: Width of the default menu check mark bitmap, in pixels.
SM_CYMENUCHECK	72	Windows 95 only: Height of the default menu check mark bitmap, in pixels.
SM_SLOWMACHINE	73	Windows 95 only: Nonzero if the computer has a low-end (slow) processor, zero otherwise.
SM_CMETRICS	75	Windows 95 only: Number of system metrics and flags.

Table 11-14 Subset of the options for GetSystemMetrics

Comments

In addition to the functions listed here, you may find the SystemParametersInfo API function to be of use. It allows you to set and retrieve many system parameters, but calling it is a bit more difficult than calling GetSystemMetrics. If you have access to a Windows API reference, you'll find it interesting to dig into this useful function.

COMPLEXITY:
ADVANCED

11.14 How do I....
Create and cancel network connections programmatically?

Problem

I'd like to be able to connect to remote network devices from within my own Access applications. I know that I could do this manually, using Explorer or File Manager, but there must be some internal API for controlling these connections. Is there some way I can manage connections from within Access?

Technique

Windows provides a very rich interface to its networking subsystem through its API. Many of the function calls are difficult, if not impossible, to call from Basic, because

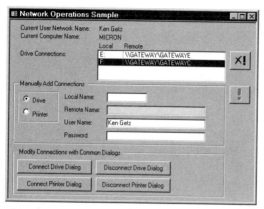

Figure 11-16 The sample form, frmNetworkSample, allows you to add and cancel connections manually or by using the common dialog boxes

of the language's lack of pointer variable types. Some important calls, however, are quite simple to use, as you'll see in this How-To. The example form will demonstrate connecting and disconnecting from remote devices (printers and drives) using common dialog boxes, or using just code with no user-interface.

Steps

Load and run frmNetworkSample from 11-14.MDB. Figure 11-16 shows the form in use on a small Windows NT network. This sample form, which demonstrates all the capabilities covered in this How-To:

- Retrieves the current user name and computer name

- Walks through all 26 possible drive letters, and displays any drive mappings connected to those drives

- Allows you to delete any of the displayed drive connections

- Provides a method for adding new connections, where you supply the four necessary parameters

- Uses the common dialog boxes for adding and canceling drive and printer connections. Figure 11-17 shows the Disconnect Network Drive dialog box.

Though you would never use this exact form in any application, it allows you to experiment with all the functionality that's covered in this How-To. To use these API calls in your own applications, follow these steps:

1. Import the module basNetwork from 11-14.MDB. This module contains all the API function declarations, wrapper functions, data type declarations, and error constants that you'll need.

2. The sample form displays the current user name. To retrieve this information in your own code, call the ahtGetUser function, from basNetwork. Its return value is the name of the current logged-in user. For example:

```
Debug.Print ahtGetUser()
```

3. The sample form also displays the name of the current computer. To retrieve this information yourself, call the ahtGetComputerName function, from basNetwork. This function returns the name of the current computer. For example:

```
Debug.Print ahtGetComputerName()
```

4. The list box on the form displays all the current connections. You can choose one, and delete it (see the next step). To retrieve a list of all 26 possible drives and their connections in your own application, call ahtListDriveConnections, a function which takes as a parameter an array of 26 ahtConnectionInfo structures. The following example will fill the list with drive information, and then will print it out to the immediate window.

```
Dim aci(0 To 25) As ahtConnectionInfo
intCount = ahtListDriveConnections(aci())
For intI = 0 To intCount
    Debug.Print aci(intCount).strDrive, aci(intCount).strConnection
Next intI
```

5. To delete a drive connection once you've selected a drive from the list box, click on the delete button to the right of the drive list box. When you do, the code will call the ahtCancelConnection function:

```
fOK = (ahtCancelConnection(Me!lstConnections.Column(0), True) = 0)
```

deleting the connection for the drive you had selected in the list box.

Figure 11-17 The Disconnect Network Drive dialog box is simple to use, and allows users to disconnect drives from your applications

6. To manually add a new printer or drive connection, first select Printer or Drive from the option group on the form, and then enter the four pieces of information the ahtAddDriveConnection and ahtAddPrintConnection functions need: local name ("LPT1:", for example), remote name ("\\GATEWAY\HPLJ4", for example), user name and password. The only one of these values that's required is the remote name. Once you've entered the values, click on the Add Connection button to the right of the text boxes. This will call the following code:

```
If Me!grpDeviceType = 1 Then
    ' The '& ""' below convert from Null values to strings.
    '
    ' Drive
    fOK = (ahtAddDriveConnection(Me!txtLocalName & "", _
        Me!txtRemoteName & "", Me!txtUserName & "", Me!txtPassword ⇒
            & "") = 0)
Else
    ' Printer
    fOK = (ahtAddPrintConnection(Me!txtLocalName & "", _
        Me!txtRemoteName & "", Me!txtUserName & "", Me!txtPassword ⇒
            & "") = 0)
End If
End If
```

7. To use the common dialog boxes for adding or canceling connections, click on any of the four buttons at the bottom of the form. Each calls a single line of Windows API code that pops up the appropriate dialog box. The How It Works section, below, will describe these function calls in detail.

How It Works

The following sections describe all you need to know to use the networking functionality demonstrated on the sample form. Though you could call the API functions directly, in each case we've provided a "wrapper" function, shielding you from as much of the detail as possible. This section will describe, for each of the various wrapper functions, information on how to call them, what parameters to send, and what values to expect back.

Most of the functions either return, or set, an error value, indicating the outcome of the function call. Though there are too many possible errors to list them all here, Table 11-15 lists most of the common errors that you'll be receiving when making these function calls.

VALUE	DESCRIPTION	CONSTANT
0	No error occurred	NO_ERROR
5	Access is denied.	ERROR_ACCESS_DENIED
66	The network resource type is not correct.	ERROR_BAD_DEV_TYPE
67	The network name cannot be found.	ERROR_BAD_NET_NAME

VALUE	DESCRIPTION	CONSTANT
85	The local device name is already in use.	ERROR_ALREADY_ASSIGNED
86	The specified network password is not correct.	ERROR_INVALID_PASSWORD
170	The requested resource is in use.	ERROR_BUSY
234	More data is available.	ERROR_MORE_DATA
1200	The specified device name is invalid.	ERROR_BAD_DEVICE
1201	The device is not currently connected but it is a remembered connection.	ERROR_CONNECTION_UNAVAIL
1202	An attempt was made to remember a device that had previously been remembered.	ERROR_DEVICE_ALREADY_REMEMBERED
1203	No network provider accepted the given network path.	ERROR_NO_NET_OR_BAD_PATH
1204	The specified network provider name is invalid.	ERROR_BAD_PROVIDER
1205	Unable to open the network connection profile.	ERROR_CANNOT_OPEN_PROFILE
1206	The network connection profile is corrupt.	ERROR_BAD_PROFILE
1208	An extended error has occurred.	ERROR_EXTENDED_ERROR
1222	The network is not present or not started.	ERROR_NO_NETWORK
1223	User canceled a dialog box.	ERROR_CANCELED
2250	This network connection does not exist.	ERROR_NOT_CONNECTED

Table 11-15 Common networking errors

Retrieving Information

To retrieve the current user name, call the ahtGetUser function, shown below:

```
Function ahtGetUser(Optional varErr As Variant) As String

    Dim strBuffer As String
    Dim lngRetval As Long
    Dim lngSize As Long

    lngSize = ahtcMaxPath
    Do
        strBuffer = Space(lngSize)
        lngRetval = WNetGetUser(0&, strBuffer, lngSize)
    Loop Until lngRetval <> ERROR_MORE_DATA
    If lngRetval <> NO_ERROR Then
        ahtGetUser = ""
    Else
        ahtGetUser = TrimNull(strBuffer)
    End If
    varErr = lngRetval
End Function
```

The ahtGetUser function calls the Windows API to retrieve the current logged-in user's name. It's interesting to note here that there are several ways to communicate the length of data to be returned, between the Windows API and Access. In this case, the code sets up a buffer of arbitrary length, and calls the Windows API. If the buffer was large enough, it fills it in with the requested name. If not, it returns the value ERROR_MORE_DATA, indicating that it needs more space. If it returns that value, it passes back, in the lngSize variable, the actual number of characters it does need, and the code loops around, trying again with the specified size.

If you're interested in knowing the exact error code that occurred in the attempt to retrieve the current user name, you can pass a variant variable in as a parameter to ahtGetUser. It's optional, but if you supply the value, the function will pass back to you in that variable the error code. For example:

```
Dim varErr as Variant
' If you care about the error:
Debug.Print ahtGetUser(varErr)
Debug.Print "The error was: "; varError
' If you don't care about any errors:
Debug.Print ahtGetUser()
```

To retrieve the current computer name, call the ahtGetComputerName wrapper function. Windows stores the current computer name in the registry database, and reads it from there when necessary. To shield your code from having to know exactly where that piece of information is stored, Windows provides the GetComputerName API function. The following function, ahtGetComputerName, handles the passing of data between Access and Windows for you:

```
Function ahtGetComputerName() As String

    ' Retrieve the network name of the current computer.

    Dim strBuffer As String
    Dim lngSize As Long
    Dim fOK As Integer

    lngSize = ahtcMaxComputerNameLength+ 1
    strBuffer = Space(lngSize)

    fOK = GetComputerName(strBuffer, lngSize)
    ahtGetComputerName = Left$(strBuffer, lngSize)
End Function
```

It's interesting to note that in this case, the API function gives you no second chance. If the buffer wasn't large enough, it just returns as much as it could fit into the buffer you passed.

To retrieve the name of the remote device connected to a named local device, call the ahtGetConnection function. Pass to it the local device name, and an optional variable in which to receive the error code. It will return back to you the remote device name connected to the requested local name. For example:

```
Debug.Print ahtGetConnection("LPT1:")
```

might return a value like this (a \\server\share name):

```
\\WOMBAT\HPLJ4
```

The function works just the same way for drive connections.

The ahtGetConnection function, shown below, works the same way as the ahtGetUser function: It calls the API function once with an arbitrarily sized buffer. If that wasn't enough room, it'll try again, with the buffer resized to fit.

```
Function ahtGetConnection(strLocalName As String, Optional varErr ⇒
As Variant) _
  As String

    Dim strBuffer As String
    Dim lngRetval As Long
    Dim lngSize As Long

    lngSize = ahtcMaxPath

    Do
        strBuffer = Space(lngSize)
        lngRetval = WNetGetConnection(strLocalName, strBuffer, lngSize)
    Loop Until lngRetval <> ERROR_MORE_DATA

    If lngRetval <> NO_ERROR Then
        ahtGetConnection = ""
    Else
        ahtGetConnection = TrimNull(strBuffer)
    End If
    varErr = lngRetval
End Function
```

Adding and Canceling Connections Using Common Dialog Boxes

Windows makes this incredibly easy. To add or cancel a connection, just make a single function call, as shown in Table 11-16. Each of the wrapper functions expects a single parameter: a window handle for the parent of the dialog box window. Most of the time, this will just be Me.hWnd, or Screen.ActiveForm.hWnd.

TO	CALL THIS WRAPPER FUNCTION
Add a drive connection	ahtConnectDriveDialog
Cancel a drive connection	ahtDisconnectDriveDialog
Add a printer connection	ahtConnectPrintDialog
Cancel a printer connection	ahtDisconnectPrintDialog

Table 11-16 Wrapper functions for common dialog box connections

For example, to pop up the common drive connection dialog box, you'd call

```
fOK = ahtConnectDriveDialog(Me.hWnd)
```

The code in each of the wrapper functions is similar, and is quite trivial. In each case, it just calls a single Windows API function. We've provided the wrappers only to provide a consistent interface for all the API functions: There's no real reason for you not to call the API functions directly, except for a tiny bit of convenience. For example, the ahtConnectPrintDialog function looks like this:

```
Function ahtConnectPrintDialog(hWnd As Long) As Long
    ' Use the common print connection dialog to create a new connection
    ahtConnectPrintDialog = WNetConnectionDialog(hWnd, RESOURCETYPE_PRINT)
End Function
```

Adding and Canceling Connections with No User Intervention

Adding or canceling a connection "silently" requires a bit more work, but it's not a problem. Table 11-17 lists the available wrapper functions, and what information they require.

ACTION	FUNCTION NAME	PARAMETERS	DESCRIPTION
Add drive connection	ahtAddDriveConnection	strLocalName As String	Local name, like "LPT1:" or "G:".
		strRemoteName As String	Remote name, like "\\SERVER\SHARE".
		strUserName As String	User name to be used. If empty, uses default user name.
		strPassword As String	Password for the user specified. If Null, uses the default user's password.
Add printer connection	ahtAddPrintConnection	strLocalName As String,	See parameters for
		strRemoteName As String,	ahtAddDriveConnection.
		strUserName As String,	
		strPassword As String	
Cancel any connection	ahtCancelConnection	strLocalName as String	Local name of resource to disconnect.
		fForce as Boolean	If True, forces disconnection, even if the device is in use. If False, the function returns an error if it tries to disconnect an active device.

Table 11-17 Functions to manually add and cancel connections

For example, the following code fragment will add a new printer connection for LPT2: to the CanonColor printer on server Bart, set up for the current user and password:

```
fOK = ahtAddPrintConnection("LPT2:", "\\BART\CanonColor", "", "")
```

Each of these functions will return an error value (NO_ERROR (0)) if there was no error, or some other error from Table 11-15 if an error occurs. Each of the functions that add connections calls the private function, AddConnection, which in turn calls the Windows API to create that connection, as shown below:

```
Function ahtAddDriveConnection(strLocalName As String, _
 strRemoteName As String, strUserName As String, strPassword As String)

    ahtAddDriveConnection = AddConnection(RESOURCETYPE_DISK, strLocalName, _
      strRemoteName, strUserName, strPassword)
End Function

Private Function AddConnection(intType As Integer, strLocalName ⇒
As String, _
 strRemoteName As String, strUserName As String, strPassword As String)

    ' Internal function, provided for adding new connections.
    ' Call ahtAddPrintConnection or ahtAddDriveConnection instead.

    Dim nr As NETRESOURCE
    Dim lngRetval As Long

    nr.lpLocalName = strLocalName
    nr.lpRemoteName = strRemoteName
    nr.dwType = intType
    lngRetval = WNetAddConnection2(nr, strPassword, strUserName, _
      CONNECT_UPDATE_PROFILE)
    AddConnection = lngRetval
End Function
```

The ahtCancelConnection function is very simple. It just calls directly to the Windows API, canceling the connection for the named local device.

```
Function ahtCancelConnection(strName As String, fForce As Boolean) As Long
    ahtCancelConnection = WNetCancelConnection2(strName, _
      CONNECT_UPDATE_PROFILE, fForce)
End Function
```

Comments

You may find it interesting to work through all the code in basNetwork. There are some interesting twists involved in transferring information between Access and the Windows API, especially since it seems that every API function that involves strings uses a different mechanism for indicating how much space it needs.

It would be very useful to have a function that could enumerate all network resources, and Windows itself, of course, provides functions to do this. Unfortunately, calling these functions from Access is beyond the scope of this book. Calling these functions requires a great deal of effort, since Basic just doesn't support the necessary mechanisms (pointers, in specific) to make it possible. It's possible, but it's just a great deal of work.

CHAPTER 12

USING OLE (AND DDE) TO EXTEND YOUR APPLICATIONS

12

USING OLE (AND DDE) TO EXTEND YOUR APPLICATIONS

How do I...

No Access application exists on its own. Because Windows is a multitasking operating system, you'll want to be able to link Access and other Windows applications. Windows provides two mechanisms for communicating between applications: Object Linking and Embedding (OLE) and Dynamic Data Exchange (DDE). OLE is easy for users and application programmers to work with and allows for the creation of custom controls. It also accommodates OLE Automation, making it possible for Access to control various applications using VBA. Because OLE is a new technology, many mainstream Windows applications don't yet (or perhaps will never) include support for it. DDE is more manageable for developers who create the tools you use, but it's far more limited in scope and can be "cranky" to control. It's also interesting to note that Microsoft did not update their DDE support in any of the Office for Windows 95 products, and there's no indication that this technology will ever be updated. On the other hand, OLE support continues to grow and change.

This chapter presents examples of using OLE with each of the Microsoft Office products. You'll also find an example of using DDE with an application that doesn't yet offer OLE Automation for VBA programmers: the Windows shell. You'll learn to activate an embedded OLE object (a sound file). You'll learn how to control Access itself via OLE Automation. You'll get a chance to use the statistical, analytical, and financial prowess of the Excel function libraries directly from Access, as well as to retrieve Word for Windows Summary Info for any selected document. You'll dig into OLE Automation, creating a form that allows you to alter properties of Microsoft Graph objects on a form. The final two topics will delve into applications which in previous incarnations didn't support OLE Automation: PowerPoint and Schedule+. These examples will show how you can manipulate and create objects in those applications directly from Access.

What You'll Need

To take full advantage of this chapter, you'll need to own a copy of Microsoft Office for Windows 95. You're welcome to read all the examples even if you don't have a copy of Microsoft Office, but each example in this chapter, except the first, requires at least one other Office product in addition to Access 95. In most cases, you can duplicate the Excel and Word functionality with previous versions of those products, but PowerPoint and Schedule+ must be from Office for Windows 95 in order to perform for you.

12.1 Play an Embedded Sound File from within My Application

Sound capability has become an integral part of the Windows environment. This How-To will show how to use the Windows API to play WAV files at any time throughout your applications. It will demonstrate how to activate any embedded OLE object programmatically.

12.2   Print an Access Report from Excel

Access 95 is an OLE automation server, so you can now use many of the powerful features of Access from other applications. This How-To will demonstrate how you can print an Access report from Excel while in Microsoft.

12.3   Use Excel's Functions from within Access

Through the power of the OLE Automation, you can harness Excel's function library from within Access. This How-To will show the basics of retrieving values from Excel's exhaustive repertoire of financial and statistical functions.

12.4   Retrieve and Set Word Documents' Summary Info from Access

OLE Automation allows you to modify Word documents on the fly from within Access. This How-To will demonstrate how you can retrieve and set the Summary Info for a Word document without ever leaving Access using OLE Automation.

12.5   Add an Item to the Startup Group

The Windows shell supports a full command set, available from any application that supports DDE. It is the vehicle by which every installation program adds groups and items to the Startup menu. This How-To will show how you can use that same capability from within your own programs.

12.6   Modify Microsoft Graph Settings Programmatically

Microsoft Graph, shared between Access and several other Windows applications, allows you to create sophisticated charts from your Access data. This How-To offers a striking demonstration of manipulating the objects created with Microsoft Graph from VBA code.

12.7   Create a PowerPoint Presentation from Access Data

PowerPoint for Windows 95 includes a rich and extensive object model. This How-To will demonstrate a method you can use for creating slide presentations programmatically, storing data in Access.

12.8   Edit Schedule Plus Contact Data from Access

One admirable goal when designing applications is to store data in one place only. Why store contact information in Access and in your contact management program? Schedule Plus cannot read Access data directly, but Access can read and write data in Schedule Plus, using OLE Automation. This How-To will demonstrate a front end for Schedule Plus' contact management, allowing you to add, edit, or delete contacts directly from an Access application.

Where's the Documentation?

At this time, there's no complete documentation on the object models, events, and properties for the different OLE Automation servers that we discuss in this chapter. This chapter does not intend to be a reference, but rather a demonstration of the kinds of things you can do. For more information, use the Object Browser that's part of Access (that's how we retrieved our information). You can also refer to the *Office Object Model Guide,* a booklet that's part of the Access for Windows 95 Developer's Toolkit. Other than that, we'll all have to wait until Microsoft releases complete documentation.

COMPLEXITY:
INTERMEDIATE

12.1 How do I...
Play an embedded sound file from within my application?

Problem

My application stores WAV files as OLE objects within a table. I'd like to be able to play them on demand. I know that users can double-click on the icon in a form to play the sounds, but I'd like some control over this. Is there some method to play one of these embedded sounds when I need to?

Technique

Access gives you substantial control over the use of OLE objects. Using the Action property of the control that's displaying the OLE object, you can tell the object to activate itself, copy to or paste from the Windows Clipboard, update its data, close, or delete itself. (The Action property pertains to bound or unbound OLE objects and graphs, too.) You can also call up the Insert Object or Paste Special dialog box to place data into the control. This How-To uses a bound OLE field, but it works just as well with an unbound object on a form.

Steps

Load and run frmOLE from 12-01.MDB. This sample form, shown in Figure 12-1, is a continuous form, pulling the data from the table tblOLE. If you click on an Activate button, the form will activate that OLE object, stored in the OLEObject field of the table. The sample table includes a few WAV files, one Microsoft Graph object, and a

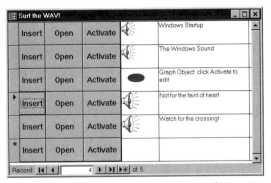

Figure 12-1 The OLE sample form, frmOLE, allows you to play or insert OLE objects

MIDI file. Clicking on the Activate button will either play the sound or activate Microsoft Graph so you can edit the tiny graph object. Click on the Insert button to call up the Insert Object dialog box, which allows you to insert any OLE object you like into the table. Click on the Open button to open the object in its own editing window, rather than activating in place.

Follow these simple steps to create such a form:

1. Create a new table or modify an existing table, adding a column (named OLEObject in the sample) with its Data Type set to OLE object. (Note that you cannot index on an OLE field and, therefore, it can't be your Primary Key for the table.)

2. Create a new form. To emulate the sample form, the only property you need to set is the DefaultView property. Set it to Continuous Forms so that you'll see multiple rows at the same time. This isn't necessary, but it will make your form look like the sample.

3. Create a bound OLE object (the cactus picture with the XYZ across the top on the toolbar) on the form. The code in this example is based on an a control named objOLE. You'll need to adjust the code appropriately if you name your control something else. The sample form includes the description field from tblOLE, as a text box, but this isn't used in the sample code.

4. Add three buttons, named cmdOpen, cmdActivate, and cmdInsert, captioned Open, Activate and Insert. Attach the following code to the Activate button's Click event (see the book's Introduction for more information on creating event procedures).

```
Private Sub cmdActivate_Click()
    Dim ctl As Control

    On Error Resume Next
    Set ctl = Me!objOLE
    ctl.Verb = acOLEVerbPrimary
    ctl.Action = acOLEActivate
```

continued on next page

continued from previous page

```
        On Error GoTo 0
    End Sub
```

Attach the following code to the Insert button's Click event.

```
Private Sub cmdInsert_Click()
    On Error Resume Next
    Me!objOLE.Action = acOLEInsertObjDlg
    On Error GoTo 0
End Sub
```

Attach the following code to the Open button's Click event.

```
Private Sub cmdOpen_Click()
    Dim ctl As Control

    On Error Resume Next
    Set ctl = Me!objOLE
    ' Open, rather than just activate in place.
    ctl.Verb = acOLEVerbOpen
    ctl.Action = acOLEActivate
    On Error GoTo 0
End Sub
```

5. Save your form and run it. When you click on the Insert button, you'll see the Insert Object dialog box (Figure 12-2). This dialog box allows you to create a new object or to insert one from an existing file. Once you make your choice, Access will place the object into the table and display it on the form. When you want to activate the object, click on the Activate button. For a WAV or MIDI file, this will cause your sound to play. For a Microsoft Graph object, it'll activate Microsoft Graph. The same goes for any other object you insert;

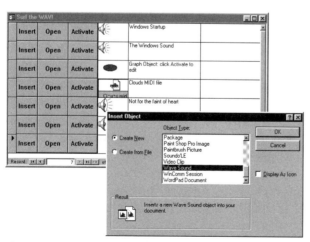

Figure 12-2 The Insert Object dialog box allows you to insert any OLE object into the form

clicking the Activate button will activate the object you've inserted. To open an editing window for the object, click on the Open button.

How It Works

The Action property for OLE objects in Access is different from almost any other property, in that setting its value causes an action to take place. Normally, properties describe characteristics of an object and methods cause actions to take place. In this case, however, when you set the Action property to the constant acOLEActivate, Access activates the control at the time you set the property. If you set the Action property to the constant acOLEInsertObjDlg, Access displays the modal Insert Object dialog box at the time you change the property. By changing the OLE control's Action property, the code tells Access what action to take at that point. By changing the Verb property from acOleVerbPrimary (to activate the object) to acOleVerbOpen, you control how the object is opened: in place, or in its own window.

Table 12-1 lists the values for the Action property that you're likely to use. Others are available, but this list will get you started. For more information, see the Online help topics on the Action and Verb properties.

CONSTANT	VALUE	DESCRIPTION
acOLECopy	4	Same as choosing the Edit|Copy menu item. Copies the OLE object onto the Windows Clipboard.
acOLEPaste	5	Same as choosing the Edit|Paste menu item. Pastes the OLE object from the Clipboard into your control.
acOLEUpdate	6	Retrieves the most current data for the OLE object from the application that created the object, and displays it as a graphic.
acOLEActivate	7	Same as double-clicking the control. You must set the control's Verb property before you can use this Action.
acOLEClose	9	Closes the OLE object and ends the active connection with the application that provided the object.
acOLEInsertObjDlg	14	Displays the Insert Object modal dialog, allowing the user to insert an object.

Table 12-1 Some of the Action property's possible values and their descriptions

Comments

This technique works just as well for unbound objects on forms. For example, if you have an embedded Word document, you could use code to activate the OLE object (named Embedded0 in the following example), set its first paragraph to bold, and then close the object.

```
Dim objWord As Object
' Activate the OLE object, using the primary verb
Me!Embedded0.Verb = acOLEVerbPrimary
Me!Embedded0.Action = acOLEActivate
Set objWord = Me!Embedded0.Object.Application.WordBasic

objWord.StartOfDocument
objWord.ParaDown 1, 1
objWord.Bold 1
Set objWord = Nothing
' Close the OLE object
Me!Embedded0.Action = acOLEClose
```

By the way, if you need to play a WAV file but don't want to embed an OLE object or use OLE at all, you can use the Windows API sndPlaySound function to do your work. (This function is aliased as aht_apiSndPlaySound.) Just insert the following declarations and constants in a form's module.

```
Private Declare Function aht_apiSndPlaySound Lib "winmm.dll" _
  Alias "sndPlaySoundA" (ByVal lpszSoundName As String, _
  ByVal uFlags As Long) As Long
Const ahtcSND_SYNC = &H0
Const ahtcSND_ASYNC = &H1
Const ahtcSND_NODEFAULT = &H2
Const ahtcSND_LOOP = &H8
Const ahtcSND_NOSTOP = &H10
```

Table 12-2 describes the possible flag values for the sndPlaySound function call.

CONSTANT	VALUE	DESCRIPTION
ahtcSND_SYNC	0	Plays the sound synchronously and does not return from the function until the sound ends.
ahtcSND_ASYNC	1	Plays the sound asynchronously and returns from the function immediately after beginning the sound. To terminate a sound once it's started, call aht_apiSndPlaySound, passing vbNullChar as the first parameter.
ahtcSND_NODEFAULT	2	Doesn't play the default sound if the requested sound can't be found.
ahtcSND_LOOP	8	The sound continues to play repeatedly until you call aht_apisndPlaySound with the first parameter set to vbNullChar. You must also specify the SND_ASYNC flag to loop sounds.
ahtcSND_NOSTOP	16	Returns immediately with a value of FALSE without playing the requested sound if a sound is currently playing.

Table 12-2 Possible values for the intFlags parameter to sndPlaySound

Normally, you'll call the aht_apiSndPlaySound function to play the WAV file. If you use the SND_ASYNC or SND_LOOP flags, you'll need to call the aht_apiSndPlaySound function again, passing the vbNullChar constant as the first parameter. The following code example is the simplest way to play a WAV file using the Windows API. You can try this out by loading the form frmSndPlaySound from 12-01.MDB and pressing the button on the form, which executes the following code.

```
Private Sub Button0_Click()
    Dim varSound As Variant
    Dim intFlags As Integer
    Dim intResult As Integer
    Dim strWinDir As String
    Dim intCount As Integer

Const ahtcMaxLen = 255

    ' Find the Windows directory.
    strWinDir = Space(ahtcMaxLen)
    intCount = aht_apiGetWindowsDirectory(strWinDir, ahtcMaxLen)
    strWinDir = Left(strWinDir, intCount)

    ' Get the file name, using the common file open dialog.
    varSound = ahtCommonFileOpenSave(InitialDir:=strWinDir, _
     Filter:=ahtAddFilterItem("", "WAV Files", "*.WAV"), _
     DialogTitle:="Choose a WAV File")
    If Not IsNull(varSound) Then
        intFlags = ahtcSND_ASYNC Or ahtcSND_NODEFAULT
        intResult = aht_apiSndPlaySound(varSound, intFlags)
        If intResult = 0 Then
            MsgBox "Unable to play sound."
        End If
    End If
End Sub
```

This example is complicated by the fact that it uses the Windows common file open dialog box to request the name of the WAV file that you'd like to play, but the heart of the routine is quite simple. In addition, you can play Windows system sounds by specifying their names as the name of the file to play. To demonstrate this, frmAPI also retrieves, from the system registry, a list of all the system sounds and offers them to you in a combo box. This code is far beyond the scope of this How-To, but you may find it interesting to play with this combo, trying out your system sounds and then working through the rather complex code that fills the combo box. The code must read from the registry in a number of places to build up the list of "user-friendly" sound names and involves a number of Windows API calls. (Look in basFriendlyName for the code that reads from the system registry.)

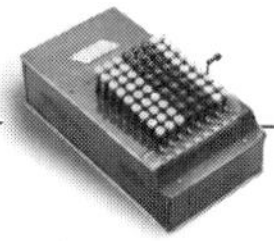

COMPLEXITY:
INTERMEDIATE

12.2 How do I... Print an Access report from Excel?

Problem

I keep my data in Excel and I need to work with it there, but I'd like to print reports using Access. I know I can use the Access Report Wizard directly from Excel for Windows 95, but I'd like more control over the process. Can I do this using VBA?

Technique

Access allows you to control its actions using OLE Automation. Anything you can do directly from Access, you can do from Excel. This How-To uses OLE Automation to link your Excel worksheet to an Access database, to use that data as the data source for a report, and then to remove the linked table. Because you can now directly link to an Excel worksheet from Access, this process doesn't need to involve importing the data—you can use it as is, live, in your Excel environment.

Steps

To try out the sample database, first load 12-02.XLS into Excel 95. This workbook includes two pages, one with the data (shown in Figure 12-3) and one with the VBA code that controls the sample. Next, click the Print Access Report button, causing Excel to load a copy of Access; load 12-02.MDB; link the current data to that database; print the report; remove the link; and close the database.

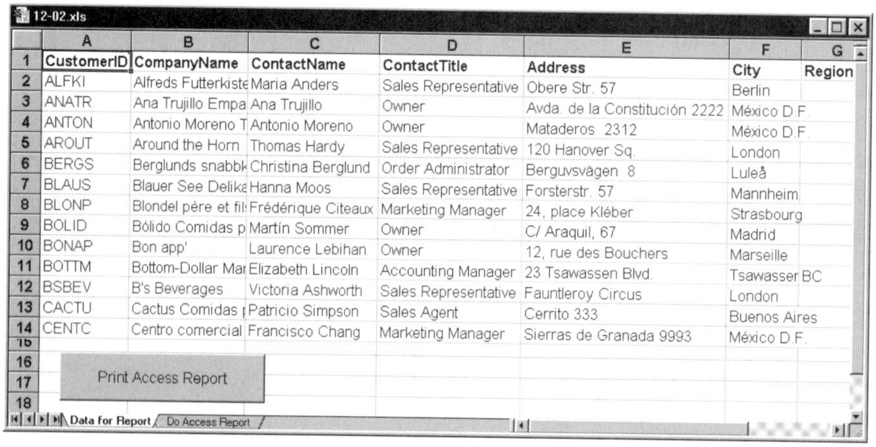

	A	B	C	D	E	F	G
1	CustomerID	CompanyName	ContactName	ContactTitle	Address	City	Region
2	ALFKI	Alfreds Futterkiste	Maria Anders	Sales Representative	Obere Str. 57	Berlin	
3	ANATR	Ana Trujillo Empa	Ana Trujillo	Owner	Avda. de la Constitución 2222	México D.F.	
4	ANTON	Antonio Moreno T	Antonio Moreno	Owner	Mataderos 2312	México D.F.	
5	AROUT	Around the Horn	Thomas Hardy	Sales Representative	120 Hanover Sq.	London	
6	BERGS	Berglunds snabbk	Christina Berglund	Order Administrator	Berguvsvägen 8	Luleå	
7	BLAUS	Blauer See Delika	Hanna Moos	Sales Representative	Forsterstr. 57	Mannheim	
8	BLONP	Blondel père et fil	Frédérique Citeaux	Marketing Manager	24, place Kléber	Strasbourg	
9	BOLID	Bólido Comidas p	Martín Sommer	Owner	C/ Araquil, 67	Madrid	
10	BONAP	Bon app'	Laurence Lebihan	Owner	12, rue des Bouchers	Marseille	
11	BOTTM	Bottom-Dollar Mar	Elizabeth Lincoln	Accounting Manager	23 Tsawassen Blvd.	Tsawassen	BC
12	BSBEV	B's Beverages	Victoria Ashworth	Sales Representative	Fauntleroy Circus	London	
13	CACTU	Cactus Comidas p	Patricio Simpson	Sales Agent	Cerrito 333	Buenos Aires	
14	CENTC	Centro comercial	Francisco Chang	Marketing Manager	Sierras de Granada 9993	México D.F.	

Figure 12-3 Use data in Excel to print a report in Access

PRINT AN ACCESS REPORT FROM EXCEL?

To use this technique in your own applications, follow these steps:

1. Create a database, including a report that you'd like to print. You may want to link the Excel data that's going to be the data source now, so that it's easier to create the report. You can leave it linked (in which case you'll want to modify the example code in your spreadsheet to not bother relinking the table) or you can delete the link once you've created the report.

2. In Excel, create a new workbook or use an existing one. Add a new module (choose the Insert|Macro|Module menu item) and enter the following code (or copy it from 12-02.XLS).

```
' The Access typelib doesn't include this constant.
Const acExcel5 = 5

' Constants for the file names, just to be neat.
Const ahtcXLS = "12-02.xls"
Const ahtcMDB = "12-02.mdb"
Const ahtcTableName = "CustomersXLS"
Const ahtcReportName = "Customers"

Sub DoAccessReport()

    ' Attach the data from "Data for Report" to 12-02.mdb,
    ' and then print a report based on that data.
    Dim strPath As String

    ' Find out where these files are.
    strPath = Application.ActiveWorkbook.Path

    Call HandleAccessReport( _
      strDatabase:=strPath & "\" & ahtcMDB, _
      strXLS:=strPath & "\" & ahtcXLS, _
      strTableName:=ahtcTableName, _
      strReportName:=ahtcReportName)
End Sub

Private Sub HandleAccessReport(strDatabase As String, strXLS As String, _
  strTableName As String, strReportName As String)
    ' This sample assumes that the database and
    ' the spreadsheet are in the same directory.
    ' It doesn't HAVE to be that way, of course,
    ' but makes this simple example a lot
    ' simpler! (It also assumes the files are NOT
    ' in the root directory of a drive, because it's
    ' appending a "\" to the path name.)

    Dim obj As Object

    Set obj = CreateObject("Access.Application")

    With obj
        .OpenCurrentDatabase strDatabase
        With .DoCmd
            ' Attach the spreadsheet from here.
```

continued on next page

continued from previous page

```
                .TransferSpreadsheet TransferType:=acLink, _
                SpreadSheetType:=acExcel5, _
                TableName:=strTableName, _
                FileName:=strXLS, _
                HasFieldNames:=True
                ' Open the report (print it)
                .OpenReport strReportName
                ' Delete the attached table
                .DeleteObject acTable, strTableName
            End With
            ' This isn't necessary, but it's neat.
            .CloseCurrentDatabase
            ' Quit Access now.
            .Quit
        End With
        Set obj = Nothing
    End Sub
```

3. Choose the Tools|References… menu item and, from the list of references, check the Microsoft Access for Windows 95 item. This will add an explicit reference to the Access 95 type library to your project, making Access' object model and constants available to your code.

4. In the code you've just entered, modify the constants ahtcXLS and ahtcMDB to match the names of your spreadsheet and database, respectively. Also modify the ahtcTableName and ahtcReportName constants to match the data source for your report (its RecordSource property) and the name of the report itself.

5. The example code expects three details to all be true:

    The spreadsheet and the database are in the same directory.

    The spreadsheet data includes the field names in the first row.

    The path that contains the files is not the root directory.

Make sure that all these assumptions are met. You could code around all three of these, but these reflect the way the example was set up.

6. Click the Drawing toolbar button or use View|Toolbars to make sure the Drawing toolbar is visible. Choose the Create Button option on the toolbar to create a button on your spreadsheet. When it asks you for the Macro Name/Reference to attach to the button, choose DoAccessReport. This will cause a button click to run that procedure. Give your button whatever caption you like.

7. Save your spreadsheet. Now when you click the button you've created, it will start Access, link the table, print the report, delete the link, close the database, and quit Access.

How It Works

This example uses OLE Automation to control Access directly from Excel. The process of printing the report can be broken down into four steps:

- Get the reference to Access and open the database.
- Link the Excel worksheet to the database.
- Print the report.
- Clean up.

The next few paragraphs discuss these items. The procedure HandleAccessReport, in step 2, includes all the code for this process.

To retrieve a reference to Access, you can use either CreateObject, which will always start a new copy of Access, or GetObject, which will attempt to get a reference to a running copy of Access. We opted for CreateObject in this example because the intent is to get in, print the report, and get out. Because Access can maintain only a single open database, using GetObject would be more disruptive: You would have to close any open database, open the one you want, and then reopen the original database. CreateObject consumes a bit more memory but is simpler, in this case. The line of code that does the work looks like this:

```
Set obj = CreateObject("Access.Application")
```

To open the database, use the OpenCurrentDatabase method of the Application object.

```
With obj
   .OpenCurrentDatabase strDatabase
```

Access provides three methods that work with the current database from OLE Automation. OpenCurrentDatabase (not to be confused with the DAO method, OpenDatabase) opens a database in the Access user interface. If a database is already open, you'll get a runtime error. Use the CloseCurrentDatabase method to close the current database. This method will generate a runtime error if there's no current database. Finally, you can use the NewCurrentDatabase method to create a new database altogether. Once you've done this, you can use OLE Automation to create all the objects you need in that database as well.

In addition to these three methods, the Access Application object provides two useful properties: UserControl and Visible. The UserControl property returns True if you opened Access under your own power or False if OLE Automation started Access. The property is read-only and lets your code work differently, depending on how the database was loaded (by hand or by OLE Automation). The Visible property allows you to control whether or not an instance of Access started via OLE Automation is visible or not. If UserControl is True, you cannot change the Visible property. If

UserControl is False, the default value for Visible is False, but you can set it to be True with code like this:

```
' Set the Application's Visible property to True
' if OLE Automation initiated the session.
With Application
    If Not .UserControl Then
        .Visible = True
    End If
End With
```

To link the Excel spreadsheet to the Access database, use the TransferSpreadsheet method of the DoCmd object. This method allows you to import or link (Excel only) a spreadsheet to the database depending on the parameters you set. In this example, the code specifies that the type of spreadsheet is Excel5, it includes field names in the top row, and it indicates that it is to be linked, not imported. (The Access type library, to which you added an explicit reference in step 3, includes the acLink constant. It doesn't include the acExcel5 constant, so the code had to declare it locally.) Once you've executed the TransferSpreadsheet method, your database will include an attached table, with the name stored in strTableName, retrieving data from the spreadsheet whose name is in strXLS.

```
With .DoCmd
    ' Attach the spreadsheet from here.
    .TransferSpreadsheet TransferType:=acLink, _
      SpreadSheetType:=acExcel5, _
      TableName:=strTableName, _
      FileName:=strXLS, _
      HasFieldNames:=True
    ' Open the report (print it)
    .OpenReport strReportName
    ' Delete the attached table
    .DeleteObject acTable, strTableName
End With
```

To print the report, use the OpenReport method of the DoCmd object, as shown in the previous code fragment.

When Did DoCmd Become an Object?

In Access 2.0, DoCmd was a statement. Now it's an object, with methods. Why? To allow for OLE Automation, the Access design team had to find a way for you to execute macro actions from outside Access. The only way to execute actions remotely, based on the OLE Automation model, is to use methods of objects. The simplest solution, therefore, was to maintain the same syntax but change DoCmd into an object. Everywhere you would have seen DoCmd Action in Access 2.0, you'll see DoCmd.Method in Access 95.

To clean up once your report has finished printing, the code first deletes the linked table, then closes the database, and finally shuts down the instance of Access that it initiated. To close the table, it uses the DeleteObject method of the DoCmd object. To close the current database, it uses the CloseCurrentDatabase method of the Application object. Finally, to shut down Access, it uses the Quit method of the Application object.

```
With DoCmd
    ' Do all the work here...
    .DeleteObject acTable, strTableName
End With
' This isn't necessary, but it's neat.
.CloseCurrentDatabase
' Quit Access now.
.Quit
End With
Set obj = Nothing
```

Comments

You aren't limited to running Access from Excel. You could have any OLE Automation client (including Access itself) start up a new copy of Access to accomplish Access tasks from that host. For example, you might use OLE Automation between Access and another copy of itself to allow your application to compact/repair a database from within your application. Or, because you can't programmatically insert global modules into the current database, you could use OLE Automation to start a new copy of Access and perform the insertions into a database that isn't currently executing code. The possibilities are endless. Just remember: If you can do it in Access, you can do it from anywhere, as long as the application supports OLE Automation as a client. At this point, Word for Windows 95 cannot be an OLE Automation client, but Excel and Project can, as can Visual Basic and Access itself.

It's also interesting to note that this example works fine with Excel 5.0, as well. There's no problem using a 16-bit OLE Automation client with a 32-bit server. Windows takes care of the differences, and it works just fine. Because the Excel file format has not changed between the last two versions, you should be able to use this example as is with Excel 5.0.

COMPLEXITY:
INTERMEDIATE

12.3 How do I...
Use Excel's functions from within Access?

Problem

Excel offers an amazing array of statistical, analytical, and financial functions that I'd like to be able to use in Access. I know I can control embedded Excel worksheets, but is there some way to call Excel functions from within Access?

Technique

Access users often ask how they can use Excel functions directly from Access. Using OLE Automation, you can actually request Excel to use its built-in functions to perform calculations and return a value back to your Access application. This requires starting Excel, however, and that can take some time, so you wouldn't normally do this just for a single calculation. But for a number of calculated values or a single calculation that would be too difficult or take too much time in Access, it's worth tapping into the OLE connections between Access and Excel.

There are many ways to use OLE to link Excel and Access. You can embed an Excel spreadsheet or chart object into an Access form and control the Excel objects programmatically. In that situation, your interaction with Excel would be very similar to the example shown in How-To 12.6, for example, when you will control a Microsoft Graph object from Access. You can also use OLE Automation from Access to create and manipulate Excel objects *without* using an embedded spreadsheet or chart. These methods are detailed in both the Access and the Excel manuals. This How-To, however, just uses the Excel engine without creating any specific Excel object; this technique isn't usually mentioned anywhere.

Steps

To test the OLE communication between Access and Excel, load frmTestExcel from 12-03.MDB. To start the test, click the button on the form. The code attached to the button will start up Excel and run a series of tests, calling Excel to retrieve the results for a number of function calls. After all the tests, the sample looks like Figure 12-4.

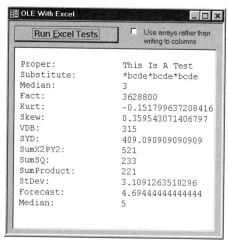

Figure 12-4 The sample form, frmTestExcel, once its function calls are completed

You can try the tests either writing directly to spreadsheet cells to test the multiple-value functions or using arrays. The check box on the form lets you try both methods.

The sample form tests two different types of function calls you can make to Excel from Access: functions that accept simple parameters and functions that require multiple values (ranges) as parameters.

The following steps describe how set up the example form; How It Works explains how to call the two types of Excel functions:

1. Create a new form containing a single text box (named txtResults on the sample form) and a command button to run the Excel tests (Figure 12-4).

2. Import the module basExcel from 12-03.MDB. This module contains the function you need to copy data from a column in Access to a spreadsheet column in Excel. The module also includes a function to copy data from a column in Access to an array, which OLE Automation can use in place of a range.

3. Enter the following code into the form's module (click on the Build button on the toolbar or choose View|Code).

```
Private Sub AddLine(strLabel As String, varValue As Variant)
    Me!txtResults = Me!txtResults & vbCrLf & _
    " " & Left(strLabel & Space(20), 20) & varValue
    DoEvents
End Sub

Private Function TestExcel()
    Dim obj As Object
    Dim intCount As Integer
    Dim fUseArrays As Boolean

    Me!txtResults = Null
    fUseArrays = Nz(Me!chkUseArrays)

    DoEvents
    AddLine "Starting Excel:", "Please wait..."

    ' If you know Excel is open, you could use GetObject()
    Set obj = CreateObject("Excel.Application")

    ' Clear out the results text box.
    Me!txtResults = Null
    DoEvents

    ' String functions
    AddLine "Proper:", obj.Proper("this is a test")
    AddLine "Substitute:", obj.Substitute("abcdeabcdeabcde", "a", "*")

    ' Simple math functions
    AddLine "Median:", obj.Median(1, 2, 3, 4, 5)
    AddLine "Fact:", obj.Fact(10)

    ' Analytical functions
    AddLine "Kurt:", obj.Kurt(3, 4, 5, 2, 3, 4, 5, 6, 4, 7)
    AddLine "Skew:", obj.Skew(3, 4, 5, 2, 3, 4, 5, 6, 4, 7)
    AddLine "VDB:", obj.VDB(2400, 300, 10, 0, 0.875, 1.5)
    AddLine "SYD:", obj.SYD(30000, 7500, 10, 10)
```

continued on next page

continued from previous page

```
        If Not fUseArrays Then
            ' Using ranges
            Dim objBook As Workbook
            Dim objSheet As Worksheet

            Dim objRange1 As Range
            Dim objRange2 As Range

            ' Create the workbook.
            Set objBook = obj.Workbooks.Add
            Set objSheet = objBook.WorkSheets(1)

            ' Copy two fields to columns
            intCount = ahtCopyColumnToSheet(objSheet, "tblNumbers", "Number1", 1)
            intCount = ahtCopyColumnToSheet(objSheet, "tblNumbers", "Number2", 2)

            ' Create ranges
            Set objRange1 = objSheet.Range("A1:A" & intCount)
            Set objRange2 = objSheet.Range("B1:B" & intCount)

            ' Print out calculations based on those ranges
            AddLine "SumX2PY2:", obj.SumX2PY2(objRange1, objRange2)
            AddLine "SumSQ:", obj.SumSQ(objRange1)
            AddLine "SumProduct:", obj.SumProduct(objRange1, objRange2)
            AddLine "StDev:", obj.STDEV(objRange1)
            AddLine "Forecast:", obj.ForeCast(5, objRange1, objRange2)
            AddLine "Median:", obj.Median(objRange1)
            ' Convince Excel that it needn't save that
            ' workbook you created.
            obj.ActiveWorkbook.Saved = True
            Set objRange1 = Nothing
            Set objRange2 = Nothing
            Set objSheet = Nothing

        Else
            ' Using arrays
            Dim varCol1 As Variant
            Dim varCol2 As Variant

            ' Copy two fields to columns
            Call ahtCopyColumnToArray(varCol1, "tblNumbers", "Number1")
            Call ahtCopyColumnToArray(varCol2, "tblNumbers", "Number2")

            ' Print out calculations based on those ranges
            AddLine "SumX2PY2:", obj.SumX2PY2(varCol1, varCol2)
            AddLine "SumSQ:", obj.SumSQ(varCol1)
            AddLine "SumProduct:", obj.SumProduct(varCol1, varCol2)
            AddLine "StDev:", obj.STDEV(varCol1)
            AddLine "Forecast:", obj.ForeCast(5, varCol1, varCol2)
            AddLine "Median:", obj.Median(varCol1)
        End If

TestExcel_Exit:
    ' Quit and clean up.
    obj.Quit
    Set obj = Nothing
End Function
```

4. In the properties sheet for the command button, enter the value

```
=TestExcel()
```

in the OnClick event property.

5. With a module open in design mode, choose the Tools|References... menu item. Choose Microsoft Excel 5.0 Object Library from the list of choices (if you installed Excel correctly, this item will be on the list). This provides your VBA code with information about the Excel object library, properties, methods, and constants.

6. Open the form in Run mode and click the command button. This will call the TestExcel function and fill the text box with the results.

How It Works

Excel obligingly exposes all of its internal functions to external callers via the Application object. The following sections describe each of the steps necessary to call Excel functions directly from Access.

All the World's a Variant

No matter which Excel function you call, the return value will be a variant. Declare a variable as a variant if it will contain the return value from an Excel function. In the examples, the return values went directly to a text box, so the issue didn't come up.

Setting Up to Communicate with Excel

Before you can call any Excel function, you must start Excel and create an object variable in Access to link the two applications. You'll always use code like this to create this linkage:

```
Dim objExcel As Object
Set objExcel = CreateObject("Excel.Application")
```

By linking with Excel's Application object, you can request Excel to evaluate any of its internal functions for you. Creating the object will take a few seconds, because Excel must be started. Calling CreateObject will start a new instance of Excel, hidden, even if it's already running.

You have two other choices. If you know Excel is already running, you can use GetObject to retrieve a reference to an object within Excel or to the Excel aApplication object. The following code will retrieve a reference to the aApplication object if Excel is already running.

```
Set objExcel = GetObject(, "Excel.Application")
```

If you've set up a reference to Excel using the Tools|References... menu item (and you must have for this example to run), you should be able to use the following code to retrieve a reference to the Excel Application object.

```
Set objExcel = Excel.Application
```

In actual experimentation, this caused an OLE Automation error if we ran the example several times in succession. The object model guide in the Developer's Toolkit does not use this syntax (no explanation given), so you'll need to try it out before using this syntax. There doesn't appear to be an obvious advantage, besides simplicity, in choosing this option.

If you need an actual sheet within Excel (and you will, if you decide to use a spreadsheet region for functions that require a range of values as input), you must also set up an object in Access that refers to that sheet. To do that, you'll need code that looks like this:

```
Dim objSheet As Object
Set objSheet = CreateObject("Excel.Sheet")
```

This code starts Excel if it's not already running and instructs Excel to create a new sheet. You can manipulate this sheet directly from Access; you'll do that later in this How-To when you copy data from a table column into a spreadsheet column, but that's not the real intent of this How-To. Of course, Excel must be registered correctly in your Windows registration database for CreateObject to be able to start Excel. If you installed Excel correctly and your registration database is not corrupted, there shouldn't be any problems.

Calling Simple Excel Functions

Once you've created your Access object that refers to the Excel Application object, you can ask Excel to perform simple calculations for you. For example, to use the Excel Product function, use code like this:

```
Dim varProd As Variant
varProd = obj.Product(5, 6)
```

After this call, the variable varProd will contain the value 30.

For example, TestExcel, in frmTestExcel's module, uses the following code fragment to call four Excel functions (Proper, Substitute, Median, and Fact). Each of these functions requires one or more simple parameters and returns a single value. (The AddLine statement just adds the output of the function call to the text box on the sample form. These four functions are the first four in the output text box.)

```
' String functions
AddLine "Proper:", obj.Proper("this is a test")
AddLine "Substitute:", obj.Substitute("abcdeabcdeabcde", "a", "*")

' Simple math functions
AddLine "Median:", obj.Median(1, 2, 3, 4, 5)
AddLine "Fact:", obj.Fact(10)
```

Excel supplies many simple functions like these that Access doesn't have. (You'll need the Excel spreadsheet function reference, available separately from Microsoft Press, to be able to take advantage of any of these functions.) Some of these functions (Proper, for example) are easy enough to replicate in VBA (the StrConv function will convert strings to proper case), but if you've already got the connection to Excel working, it makes perfect sense to use Excel to retrieve these sorts of values rather than writing the code yourself.

To call analytical or statistical functions in Excel, use the same technique shown above. With the reference to the Excel.Application object, call any function that takes simple parameters and returns a single value. The next four examples on the sample form call the Kurt, Skew, VDB, and SYD functions.

```
' Analytical functions
AddLine "Kurt:", obj.Kurt(3, 4, 5, 2, 3, 4, 5, 6, 4, 7)
AddLine "Skew:", obj.Skew(3, 4, 5, 2, 3, 4, 5, 6, 4, 7)
AddLine "VDB:", obj.VDB(2400, 300, 10, 0, 0.875, 1.5)
AddLine "SYD:", obj.SYD(30000, 7500, 10, 10)
```

Sometimes you'll need to call Excel functions that require a variable number of values or you'll want to use the data in a table as the input to an Excel function. In that case, you have two choices: You can either call the Excel function using a spreadsheet range as the input or you can pass a VBA array directly to the function; it'll convert it and treat it as a built-in range of values. In either case, you'll need some method of getting the Access data into the spreadsheet or into an array so you can use that data as input to the function.

Calling Excel Functions Using Ranges

To copy a column of data from an Access table or query into an Excel spreadsheet column, call the ahtCopyColumnToSheet function, found in basExcel (in 12-03.MDB).

```
Function ahtCopyColumnToSheet(objSheet As Object, _
 strTable As String, strField As String, intColumn As Integer)

   ' Copy a column from a table to a spreadsheet.
   ' Place the data from the given field (strField) in
   ' the given table/query (strField) in the specified
   ' column (intColumn) in the specified worksheet object
   ' (objSheet).
   ' Return the number of items in the column.

   Dim rst As Recordset
   Dim intRows As Integer
   Dim db As Database
   Dim varData As Variant

   Set db = CurrentDb()
   Set rst = db.OpenRecordset(strTable)
   Do While Not rst.EOF
      intRows = intRows + 1
      ' Small bug in Jet, or OLE, at the moment.
      ' You can't copy data directly from a field to
```

continued on next page

continued from previous page

```
        ' Excel. You've got to force a conversion to
        ' a value first, by placing it in parentheses.
        ' This is equivalent to passing an item by value.
        objSheet.Cells(intRows, intColumn).Value = (rst(strField))
        rst.MoveNext
    Loop
    rst.Close
    ahtCopyColumnToSheet = intRows
End Function
```

Note

There is a small bug in the mixing of Jet and OLE Automation: You should be able to send a value from a recordset through OLE without problems, but it appears, at least at the time of this writing, that there's a problem. If you attempt to assign a value from a recordset directly to the Value property of a cell, you won't see a runtime error, but the cell will contain #N/A in Excel. You'll find similar behavior from other OLE servers. The trick is to surround the value with parentheses, forcing VBA to convert it to a value rather than passing the expression directly to OLE to evaluate. If you don't enclose the value in parentheses, VBA passes the expression (rst(strField) in this case) off to OLE to handle, and it doesn't do it correctly.

Given a reference to an Excel sheet, a table or query name, a field name, and a column number for the Excel sheet, ahtCopyColumnToSheet will walk down all the rows of Access data, copying them over to the Excel sheet. The function returns the number of rows that it copied over to Excel. For example, to copy the Unit Price field values from the tblProducts table to the first column of the opened spreadsheet in Excel, use

```
intCount = ahtCopyColumnToSheet(objSheet, "tblProducts", "Unit Price", 1)
```

Note

To keep it simple, this version of the ahtCopyColumnToSheet function doesn't include error checking, but any code used in real applications would need to check for errors that might occur as you move data from Access to Excel.

Once you've copied the data to Excel, you can create an object that refers to that range of data as a single entity. Most Excel functions accept a range as a parameter if they'll accept a group of values as input. For example, the Median function, used above, accepts either a list of numbers or a range.

To create a range object in Access, use the Range function, passing a string that represents the range you want. The following example, used after the form copies the data from a table over to Excel, calculates the median of all the items in the column.

```
Dim objRange1 As Object

Set objRange1 = objSheet.Range("A1:A" & intCount)
AddLine "Median:", obj.Median(objRange1)
```

Some Excel functions require two or more ranges as input. For example, the SumX2PY2 function, which returns the sum of the squares of all the values in two columns (that is, the sum of $x^2 + y^2$), takes two ranges as its parameters. The following code fragment, also from the sample form, copies two columns from tblNumbers to the open sheet in Excel and then performs a number of calculations based on those columns.

```
' Copy two fields to columns
intCount = ahtCopyColumnToSheet(objSheet, "tblNumbers", "Number1", 1)
intCount = ahtCopyColumnToSheet(objSheet, "tblNumbers", "Number2", 2)

' Create ranges
Set objRange1 = objSheet.Range("A1:A" & intCount)
Set objRange2 = objSheet.Range("B1:B" & intCount)

' Print out calculations based on those ranges
AddLine "SumX2PY2:", obj.SumX2PY2(objRange1, objRange2)
AddLine "SumSQ:", obj.SumSQ(objRange1)
AddLine "SumProduct:", obj.SumProduct(objRange1, objRange2)
AddLine "StDev:", obj.STDEV(objRange1)
AddLine "Forecast:", obj.ForeCast(5, objRange1, objRange2)
AddLine "Median:", obj.Median(objRange1)
```

Calling Excel Functions Using Arrays

Rather than writing to a spreadsheet directly, you might find your work faster if you load a column of data into an array and send it to Excel that way. This avoids multiple OLE calls to Excel (each time you place a value into a cell in Excel, you're going through a *lot* of internal OLE code). The drawback, of course, is that you're loading all your data into memory. On the other hand, if you're working with so much data that it won't fit into memory, OLE will be too slow to be of much use, anyway!

To copy a column of data to an array, call the ahtCopyColumnToArray function (from basExcel in 12-03.MDB), shown below. Pass a variant variable (variants can hold entire arrays in VBA), a table name, and a field name to the function and it will return the number of rows it placed into the array. This function walks through all the rows in your recordset, copying the values from the specified column into the array.

```
Function ahtCopyColumnToArray(varArray As Variant, _
  strTable As String, strField As String)

    ' Copy the data from the given field (strField) of the
    ' given table/query (strTable) into a dynamic array (varArray)

    ' Return the number of rows.
```

continued on next page

```
    Dim db As Database
    Dim rst As Recordset
    Dim intRows As Integer

    Set db = CurrentDb()
    Set rst = db.OpenRecordset(strTable)
    rst.MoveLast
    ReDim varArray(1 To rst.RecordCount)
    rst.MoveFirst
    Do While Not rst.EOF
        intRows = intRows + 1
        varArray(intRows) = rst(strField)
        rst.MoveNext
    Loop
    rst.Close
    ahtCopyColumnToArray = intRows
End Function

' Using arrays
Dim varCol1 As Variant
Dim varCol2 As Variant
```

Once you've copied the data into arrays, you can call functions in Excel, passing those arrays as if they were ranges. Excel understands that it's receiving multiple values and returns the same results as the tests involving ranges.

```
' Copy two fields to columns
Call ahtCopyColumnToArray(varCol1, "tblNumbers", "Number1")
Call ahtCopyColumnToArray(varCol2, "tblNumbers", "Number2")

' Print out calculations based on those ranges
AddLine "SumX2PY2:", obj.SumX2PY2(varCol1, varCol2)
AddLine "SumSQ:", obj.SumSQ(varCol1)
AddLine "SumProduct:", obj.SumProduct(varCol1, varCol2)
AddLine "StDev:", obj.STDEV(varCol1)
AddLine "Forecast:", obj.ForeCast(5, varCol1, varCol2)
AddLine "Median:", obj.Median(varCol1)
```

This method is both simpler and faster than writing to a spreadsheet. On the other hand, if you're working with large volumes of data, you won't want to copy all the data to an array, but will need to copy it to a spreadsheet for Excel to process.

Closing Excel

Once you're done with your Access/Excel session, you must close the Excel application. If you don't, OLE will continue to start new instances of Excel every time you attempt to connect with Excel.Application (using CreateObject), eating up system resources each time.

To close Excel, use its Quit action.

```
obj.Quit
```

> **Warning**
>
> In Access 2.0, you were required to surround the Quit method with square brackets because Access itself included a Quit method and it got confused when it saw the Quit method of the Excel Application object. Access 2.0 would then allow this instruction to pass on through to Excel, which would shut itself down. In the current versions of the two products, this method is doomed to failure. Excel won't complain about the [Quit], but it won't honor it either. If you don't remove the square brackets from existing OLE Automation code, the statement will fail silently and you'll end up with multiple copies of Excel running in the background. We found that after about 16 iterations of this, Windows 95 wasn't very happy.

Finally, release any memory used by Access in maintaining the link between itself and Excel. To do this, use code like the following, which "closes" the object variables and releases any memory Excel might have been using.

```
Set obj = Nothing
```

Comments

Each application reacts differently to the CreateObject function. Excel starts a new hidden instance of itself when you call CreateObject, using the Excel.Application value, but uses the current instance if you call CreateObject with the Excel.Sheet value. Microsoft Word, on the other hand, uses the running copy of itself, if possible, when you create an object linked to the Word.Basic object (that's the only object that Microsoft Word exposes, as you'll see in How-To 12.4). If a copy of Word running is not running, CreateObject will start one up, but it won't be hidden.

Because it takes time to start Excel once you call the CreateObject function, build your applications so that all work with Excel is isolated to as few locations in your code as possible. Start Excel, then do all your work. Another alternative is to make your object variables global and have your application start Excel if it needs to, and then leave it open until it's done. Don't forget to close Excel, however, so that you don't reduce your system memory and resources.

When you're done with the OLE application, you'll need some way of closing down. As with the CreateObject command, each application reacts differently to your attempts to shut it down. Excel won't quit unless you explicitly order it to, using the Quit action. If you just set the object variable that refers to Excel.Application to the value Nothing without executing the Quit action, the hidden copy of Excel will continue running, chewing up memory and resources. If CreateObject started Word, setting the object referring to the Word.Basic object equal to Nothing will automatically shut down Word. You'll need to be aware of how each application you use expects to be closed.

Excel exposes rich and varied inner workings via OLE. Taking advantage of Excel's capabilities is nearly impossible without reference materials. This How-To topic barely scratches the surface of what's available to you in Access from Excel. If you need to use the two products together, invest in the reference materials on Excel's Visual Basic for Applications from Microsoft Press and/or any other Microsoft Office-specific information available from Microsoft.

COMPLEXITY:
INTERMEDIATE

12.4 How do I...
Retrieve and set Word documents' Summary Info from Access?

Problem

As part of a document management system that I'm developing, I need to be able to retrieve and set the Summary Info for Microsoft Word documents. I just can't figure out how to communicate with Word to retrieve the information I need.

Technique

Unlike Excel, which exposes almost all of itself via OLE, Word exposes very little. The only object you can refer to from Access is the WordBasic object. However, using this object, you can do anything that Word Basic can do, and that's a lot. This How-To shows how to use Word Basic to retrieve the information you need and how to communicate with Word for Windows in general.

Steps

To retrieve Summary Info for any Word for Windows document with the .DOC extension, open frmDocInfo in 12-04.MDB. This sample form, shown in Figure 12-5, allows you to view and/or change the Summary Info for Word documents.

To use the sample form, follow these steps:

1. Import the form frmDocInfo and the module basSortArray from 12-04.MDB.

2. Run frmDocInfo and type a path name into the text box. Click the Find Files button to retrieve a sorted list of the DOC files in the specified location.

3. To view the Summary Info for your chosen document, double-click on its name in the list box. This will start Word, load the specified document, retrieve the Summary Info, and then close the document.

4. To change the Summary Info, enter the data in the enabled text boxes on frmDocInfo and click the Save Summary button to store the information.

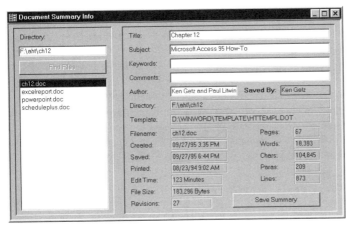

Figure 12-5 The sample form, frmDocInfo, showing a document's Summary Info

How It Works

Microsoft Word for Windows exposes only a single object, the Basic object. Once you've established a link between Access and this object, you can use all its capabilities from your Access application. The next few sections outline the steps involved in communicating with Word via OLE.

Starting the Connection with Word for Windows

To be able to retrieve or set Summary Info from Access, you must create an object variable to refer to the WordBasic object. (If you make it a module global variable, it'll be easier to close later on.) For working with a specific form, consider using a module global variable for the form's module—this is how the sample form works:

```
Dim objWord As Object
```

To start the conversation with Microsoft Word, use the CreateObject function to obtain a reference to the Word.Basic object. If Word isn't running, this function will start a nonhidden instance of it. If Word is running, this function will obtain a reference to the currently running instance. In either case, because you can't control how Word starts up, you may want to minimize it (using Word Basic's AppMinimize command) so that it's out of the way visually. The DoEvents command gives Windows a time slice before going on so it can make sure the screen gets repainted after minimizing the Word window.

```
Set objWord = CreateObject("Word.Basic")
objWord.AppMinimize
DoEvents
```

See the OpenWord function in frmDocInfo's module for an example using this code.

Retrieving the Summary Info

To retrieve the Summary Info for a given document, open the document, using Word Basic's FileOpen command.

```
objWord.FileOpen "C:\TESTFILE.DOC"
```

Once the file's open, use the Word Basic CurValues object, which maintains the current values of all the dialog boxes in Word, to retrieve the information you want. Set an Access object variable to refer to a Word Basic data structure, a "record" of values from the File Summary dialog box in Word.

```
Dim fsi As Object
objWord.FileOpen "C:\TESTFILE.DOC"
Set fsi = objWord.CurValues.FileSummaryInfo
```

See the lstAvailable_DblClick event procedure in frmDocInfo's module for an example of using this technique.

The object variable, fsi, now refers to a live data structure in Word. It acts as a user-defined type in Access and contains members that each contain data. Table 12-3 describes the members of the FileSummaryInfo data structure. All elements are strings except for the Update member, which is only used when executing the FileSummaryInfo statement.

MEMBER	DESCRIPTION
Title	Title of the document.
Subject	Subject of the document.
Author	Author of the document.
Keywords	Identifying keywords.
Comments	Comments about the document.
FileName	File name of the document, without its path.
Directory	Directory location of the file (read-only).
Template	Document's template (read-only).
CreateDate	Creation date for the document (read-only).
LastSavedDate	Date the document was last saved (read-only).
LastSavedBy	Name of the last person who saved the document (read-only).
RevisionNumber	Number of times the document has been saved (including changes to the summary information by this program; read-only).
EditTime	Cumulative time the document has been open, in minutes.
LastPrintedDate	Date the document was last printed (read-only).
NumPages	Number of pages in the document (read-only).
NumWords	Number of words in the document (read-only).
NumChars	Number of characters in the document (read-only).
NumParas	Number of paragraphs in the document (read-only).

MEMBER	DESCRIPTION
NumLines	Number of lines in the document (read-only).
Update	Used only when executing the FileSummaryInfo statement, ensures that the summary information is current.
FileSize	Size of the document, in the form "12,345 Bytes" (read-only).

Table 12-3 Members of the FileSummaryInfo data structure

To use the members of fsi, treat them as any other user-defined type except that you can only read the values (you'll need to use the FileSummaryInfo statement to change the values). For example, to retrieve a document's keywords, you could use code like this:

```
Set fsi = objWord.CurValues.FileSummaryInfo
Debug.Print fsi.Keywords
Set fsi = Nothing
objWord.FileClose 2
```

This code retrieves the summary information it needs, then "unlinks" the fsi variable from the Word FileSummaryInfo structure by setting it equal to Nothing. Finally, it closes the file you opened, using the FileClose WordBasic action. The 2 on the FileClose statement tells Word not to save the file, whether it's been changed or not. See the DisplayFileSummaryInfo subroutine in frmDocInfo's module for more information.

Changing the Summary Info

To write information to a document's FileSummaryInfo structure, use the Word Basic FileSummaryInfo statement. This statement takes as many parameters as there are rows in Table 12-3, and you can use whichever parameters you need. Unless you name the parameters (using VBA's capability to pass named parameters), the parameters are position sensitive—you must use commas as placeholders for any parameters you don't specify. You needn't put trailing commas after the last value you specify, however. (If you want to set Summary Info for a document that's currently open in Word but you're not sure if it's the current document, you must specify the FileName parameter to identify the document.) Note that most of the FileSummaryInfo values are read-only.

The example uses code like this to set the FileSummaryInfo values for the selected document:

```
Private Sub cmdSaveSummary_Click()

    ' Save the file summary information.

    On Error GoTo SaveSummaryError
    If OpenWord() Then
        ' Open the selected file, call the FileSummary
        ' statement in Word, and then close the file, saving it.
        objWord.FileOpen mvarDir & avarFiles(Me!lstAvailable.ListIndex)
        objWord.FileSummaryInfo _
```

continued on next page

continued from previous page

```
            Title:=Me!txtTitle & "", _
            Subject:=Me!txtSubject & "", _
            Author:=Me!txtAuthor & "", _
            Keywords:=Me!txtKeywords & "", _
            Comments:=Me!txtComments & "", _
            FileName:= mvarDir & Me!txtFileName & ""
        objWord.FileClose 1
    End If

SaveSummaryExit:
    Exit Sub

SaveSummaryError:
    MsgBox "Error: " & Err.Description & " (" & Err.Value & ")", _
      vbExclamation, "cmdSaveSummary_Click"
    Resume SaveSummaryExit
End Sub
```

On the sample form, frmDocInfo, you can enter new data into the read/write fields only. To set new Title and Keyword values, you could use code like this:

```
objWord.FileOpen "C:\TESTFILE.DOC"
objWord.FileSummaryInfo Title:="New Title", Keywords:="New Keywords"
objWord.FileClose 1
```

Note the parameter names, making it unnecessary to use commas as placeholders for the Subject and Author fields, which this code is not changing.

Closing Word for Windows

Once you're done, sever the connection by setting the object variable that refers to the Word Basic object to be Nothing, as shown here.

```
Set objWord = Nothing
```

This will close Word if you opened it with the call to CreateObject and release any memory used by the OLE connection between Access and Word. If Word was previously open, it will stay open.

Comments

To refer to an embedded Word document, rather than loading Word and the file explicitly, you must first activate the object and then you can take whatever action you need. For example, if you want to set the first paragraph of your document to be bold, you could use code like the following, attached to the Click event of a command button. This code fragment assumes that the name of your OLE control is Embedded0. See the Word Basic documentation for explanations of the StartOfDocument, ParaDown, and Bold actions.

```
Dim objWord As Object
' Activate the OLE object, using the primary verb
Me!Embedded0.Verb = acOLEVerbPrimary
Me!Embedded0.Action = acOLEActivate
Set objWord = Me!Embedded0.Object.Application.WordBasic
```

```
objWord.StartOfDocument
objWord.ParaDown 1, 1
objWord.Bold 1
Set objWord = Nothing
' Close the OLE object
Me!EmbeddedO.Action = acOLEClose
```

When you use the CreateObject function to start Word for Windows, you have no control over how or where it loads. If it was last used full-screen, it will start up full-screen. If the aesthetics are important to you, take matters into your own hands: Use the Shell function to start Word minimized. You can use the information in How-To 11.8 to check to see if Word is running first. You can use the information in How-To 11.10 to close Word when you're done, because there's no automated way to shut it down if you started it yourself.

Word 95 has replaced the FileSummaryInfo with a new method of retrieving document properties, the GetDocumentProperty function. Though we could have adopted this new method, it requires a separate call to Word to retrieve each and every document property. Retrieving the settings through the FileSummaryInfo structure is faster and is included in Word 95 for backwards compatability. If you're retrieving a single item, you might want to investigate GetDocumentProperty: For this example, it didn't make sense.

COMPLEXITY:
ADVANCED

12.5 How do I...
Add an item to the Startup Group?

Problem

As part of my application, I would like to allow users to add an application to the Startup menu so that my application will start up when Windows does. I just can't figure out how to put the information into the Startup Group. Is there a way to communicate between Access and the Windows shell so I can do this?

Technique

The Windows shell accepts commands using DDE that allow you to create and delete groups and create and delete items. You can also retrieve lists of existing groups and items within those groups. This How-To answers the "How do I..." question by explaining most of the the Windows shell's DDE interface.

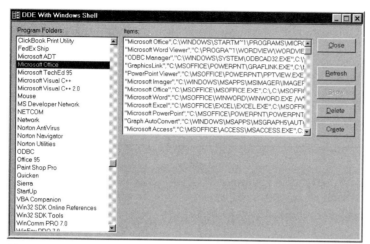

Figure 12-6 The sample form, frmShell, allows you to communicate with the Windows shell via DDE

Steps

To test out the DDE interface, load and run the form frmShell from 12-05.MDB. This form, shown in Figure 12-6, allows you to view groups and their items, create and delete groups and items, and show a particular group. It will decide whether to use the "groups" and "items" or the "folders" and "shortcuts" terminology after determining whether you are using the Windows 95 shell or the Windows NT Program Manager.

> **Note**
>
> You'll find several references to Program Manager and ProgMan throughout this How-To (as well as the use of the group/item notation rather than folder/shortcut), but the effect is the same either way: You can create groups and items in Program Manager or in the Windows shell, depending on your environment.

Once you select a group from the list on the left in Figure 12-6, the form will display the group's items in the list on the right. If you select the first item in the right-hand list—the group itself—the form will display the information Windows stored about that group. (Figure 12-7 shows frmShell with a group selected.) Once you've selected a group in the right-hand list box, you can click the Show button to have Windows display that group. The code attached to the Show button requests Windows to open the group window using style 3 (see Table 12-9 for a list of window styles). As described in the box Switching Focus, Windows may grab the focus, depending on the previous state of the group window you've selected.

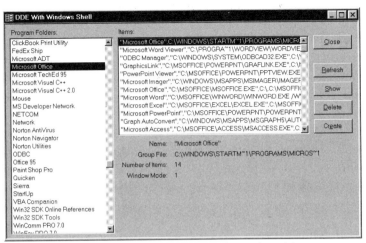

Figure 12-7 frmShell with a group selected and its information displayed

---

Note

The Shell DDE interface does not support long file names, and attempts to enter long file names will fail with an error. The example form displays long file names using the 8.3 short version of the name, usually 6 characters, followed by a "~1" (or a higher digit).

Select an item in the group (one of the rows below the first in the right-hand list box), and the form will display all the information that Windows stores about that item. Figure 12-8 shows frmShell with an item selected.

With either a group or an item selected, you can create or delete a group or an item. If you've selected a group, pressing the Delete button will instruct Windows to delete that group. If you've selected an item, frmShell will instruct Windows to delete the item from within its group. No matter what's selected, pressing the Create button will pop up a dialog box asking you whether you want to create a new item or a new group. Either choice will pop up the appropriate dialog box requesting the necessary information.

The following steps first describe how to use the sample forms in your own applications and then explain most of the DDE interface to the Windows shell. Although more DDE options are available, the most useful tasks can be accomplished with the tools provided here.

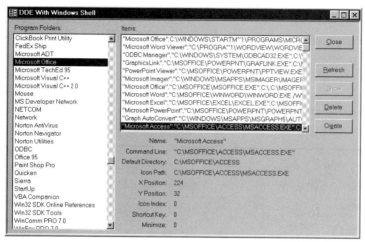

Figure 12-8 frmShell with an item selected and its
information displayed

Using the Sample Forms

To include the sample forms from 12-05.MDB into your own applications, follow
these steps:

1. Import the items shown in Table 12-4 from 12-05.MDB into your own
application.

OBJECT	NAME	PURPOSE
Form	frmNew	Choose new group vs. new item.
Form	frmNewGroup	Enter new group information.
Form	frmNewItem	Enter new item information.
Form	frmShell	Main form.
Module	basShell	Perform DDE conversations with Windows shell.
Module	basSortArray	Sort arrays (list of program groups).
Module	basToken	Pull apart strings (item and group information on frmShell).

Table 12-4 Objects to import from 12-05.MDB

2. Load and run frmShell.

As described above, you can use the form to manipulate shell groups and
items from your Access application. If you want to use pieces of frmShell in
your application but not the whole thing, that's fine, too. If you use the group
list (lstGroups), you'll also need to include the function that fills it, FillGroups.
If you want the item list (lstItems) from frmShell, you'll also need its list-filling

function, FillItems. In addition, place code in lstGroup's AfterUpdate event that requeries lstItems once you've made a selection in lstGroups. You'll end up with an event procedure like this:

```
Sub lstGroups_AfterUpdate ()
    Me!lstItems.Requery
End Sub
```

To use other bits and pieces of the functionality of frmShell, you'll need to investigate its form module.

Using DDE with the Windows Shell

If your main interest is just using DDE to control the Windows shell, follow these steps:

1. Import the module basShell from 12-05.MDB into your own application. This module is completely self-contained and includes a number of functions that will set up the DDE conversation, do the work, or retrieve the information you need and then terminate the conversation. Because we've hidden all the details of the DDE, you needn't worry about getting all the syntax and parameters correct.

2. Depending on your needs, call one or more of the wrapper procedures described in Table 12-5. All of these functions are discussed in detail (Table 12-10) in How It Works.

PROCEDURE	PURPOSE
ahtPMCreateGroup	Create a group, given a group name and a path name for the group file.
ahtPMCreateItem	Create a new item, given the group name, the item name, the command line, the default directory, and whether or not to run the application minimized.
ahtPMDeleteGroup	Delete a group, given the name of the group to delete.
ahtPMDeleteItem	Delete an item from a group, given the name of the group and the name of the item.
ahtPMGetGroups	Fill a dynamic array with all the groups.
ahtPMGetItems	Fill a dynamic array with all the items for a particular group.
ahtPMShowGroup	Show a particular group, given the name of the group and the window mode to use.
ahtPMShowMessages	Allow callers outside this module to set the status of message showing/hiding. Send in True to show messages, False to hide them (no DDE involved).

Table 12-5 Procedures in basShell to aid in using DDE between Access and Windows shell

How It Works

The Windows shell supports two operations: You can either request information using the DDERequest function (Table 12-6 lists the DDERequest items) or execute actions using the DDEExecute subroutine (Table 12-7 lists the most useful subset of the shell's

DDEExecute command-string interface). DDE conversations between Access and the shell involve three steps:

1. Initiate the conversation.

2. Perform the necessary tasks.

3. Terminate the conversation.

Retrieving Information from the Windows Shell

Table 12-6 describes the two groups of information you can request from Windows. The sample form, frmShell in 12-05.MDB, uses both these requests to fill its two list boxes.

TO RETRIEVE	PROGRAM	TOPIC	ITEM	RETURNS
List of groups	ProgMan, or Folders	ProgMan, or AppProperties	ProgMan	List of existing groups, separated with CR/LF pair.
List of items in a group	ProgMan, or Folders	ProgMan, or AppProperties	<Group Name>	List of items in the specified group, separated with CR/LF pair.

Table 12-6 DDERequest topics for the Windows shell

To retrieve a list of groups from Windows using the Access DDERequest function, you must first initiate a conversation with the ProgMan program on the ProgMan topic requesting information on the ProgMan item (the shell's DDE is a bit single minded); even if you use the undocumented "Folders" program name and "AppProperties" topic, it still expects you to request information on the ProgMan item. The DDERequest call returns a carriage-return/line-feed delimited string of group names. It's up to your code to pull apart the list of groups and place them into whatever data structure is most convenient for you. To simplify this task, you can use the ahtPMGetGroups function in basShell. It accepts, as a parameter, a dynamic array to fill in with the list of groups. This function, shown below, performs the DDERequest for you and calls the private CopyToArray function to break apart the returned stream of groups and fill the array you've sent it. It returns the number of items in the array.

```
Function ahtPMGetGroups(avarGroups() As Variant)

    ' Fill a dynamic array with all the groups.

    Dim lngChannel As Long
    Dim strGroups As String
    Dim intCount As Integer

    On Error GoTo GetProgmanGroupsError
    ' Most replacement shells will start progman for you
    ' if you attempt to start up a DDE conversation with it.
    ' That is, you won't need to Shell() ProgMan if you're using
    ' a replacement shell.
    lngChannel = DDEInitiate("PROGMAN", "PROGMAN")
```

```
    strGroups = DDERequest(lngChannel, "PROGMAN")
    intCount = CopyToArray(strGroups, avarGroups())

GetProgmanGroupsExit:
    ahtPMGetGroups = intCount
    On Error Resume Next
    DDETerminate lngChannel
    On Error GoTo 0
    Exit Function

GetProgmanGroupsError:
    MsgBox "Error: " & Err.Description & " (" & Err.Number & ")", _
      vbExclamation, "ahtGetProgmanItems"
    Resume GetProgmanGroupsExit
End Function
```

To call this function from your own code, use code like this:

```
Dim avarGroups() as Variant
Dim intCount as Integer

intCount = ahtPMGetGroups(avarGroups())
' If you want the list sorted, call
' ahtSortArray, in basSortArray
ahtSortArray avarGroups()
```

To retrieve a list of items within a selected group, use the ahtPMGetItems function, which works almost exactly as ahtPMGetGroups does. This time, however, you pass in a group name along with the dynamic array to be filled in; the function uses the group name as the topic rather than ProgMan (see Table 12-6). It calls the CopyToArray function to move the items into the dynamic array. You generally won't sort the array, however, unless you store the first item; this first item returns information about the group window itself. All the rest of the rows contain information about the individual items. To use ahtPMGetItems, you might use code like this:

```
Dim avarGroups() as Variant
Dim avarItems() as Variant
Dim intCount as Integer

intCount = ahtPMGetGroups(avarGroups())
' If you want the list sorted, call
' ahtSortArray, in basSortArray
ahtSortArray avarGroups()
intCount = ahtPMGetItems(avarGroups(0), avarItems())
' List all the item information for the specified group
For intI = 0 To intCount - 1
    Debug.Print avarItems(intI)
Next intI
```

Executing Tasks

The Windows shell includes a command-string interface that you can access via DDE allowing you to execute tasks involving groups and items within those groups. Table 12-7 lists the commands that are addressed in this How-To. Other commands are available (they're documented in the Windows SDK documentation) but they're not as useful for Access programmers.

FUNCTION	PARAMETERS	COMMENTS
AddItem	See Table 12-8	Uses CreateGroup first to select the group.
CreateGroup	*GroupName* [, *GroupPath*]	Selects the group if it exists; otherwise creates it.
DeleteGroup	*GroupName*	
DeleteItem	*ItemName*	Uses CreateGroup first to select the group.
ShowGroup	*GroupName, ShowCommand*	See Table 12-9 for ShowCommand values.

Table 12-7 DDEExecute command-string interface for the Windows shell

In each case, you use the Access DDEExecute procedure to communicate with the shell. You must construct a string containing the function name, parentheses, and any arguments for the function. For example, to create a group from within Access, you can use code like this:

```
Dim intChannel as Integer
intChannel = DDEInitiate("PROGMAN", "PROGMAN")
DDEExecute intChannel, "[CreateGroup(My Group, MYGROUP.GRP)]"
```

The command string must be surrounded by square bracket delimiters ([ ]). Luckily, the Windows shell is far more relaxed about the use of embedded quotes than almost any other DDE-enabled application. For example, WinFax Pro's implementation of DDE requires quotes embedded in command strings you send to it. The Windows shell will accept embedded quotes but doesn't require them.

Some functions, such as AddItem, allow quite a few parameters, almost all of which can be left blank (Table 12-8). To use the AddItem command to add a new item, you must first select a group in which to add the item. To select the group, use the CreateGroup command, which creates a group if necessary or selects it if it already exists. The only AddItem parameter that's required is the command line; if you specify the coordinates for the icon, you must specify them both. For example, to create a new icon to run C:\EDIT\MYEDIT.EXE with the description My Editor minimized in the My New Group group, use code like this (you'd normally include error-handling code, too):

```
Dim intChan As Integer
intChan = DDEInitiate("PROGMAN", "PROGMAN")
' First select the group (or create it)
DDEExecute intChan, "[CreateGroup(My New Group)]"
' Use commas to delimit parameters, even missing ones
DDEExecute intChan, "[AddItem(C:\EDIT\MYEDIT,My Editor,,,,,,1)]"
```

PARAMETER	DESCRIPTION	REQUIRED?	USED IN SAMPLE?
CmdLine	Command line to run the application. Must be at least the executable file name, but it can also include parameters as necessary.	Yes	Yes
Name	Name that appears below the icon in the group.	No	Yes
IconPath	Name and path of the icon file to use. If executable file specified, use the first icon in that file. If left blank, use the first icon in the executable file specified in the CmdLine parameter.	No	No
IconIndex	Index of the icon in the specified IconPath file (or the specified executable). Use the first icon specified otherwise.	No	No
Xpos	X-position of the icon within the group, as an integer. Both this and YPos required to set the specific position. If left blank, use the next available position.	No	No
Ypos	Y-position of the icon within the group, as an integer.	No	No
DefDir	Default (or working) directory for the application.	No	Yes
HotKey	Hot key for this application (stored as an integer).	No	No
fMinimize	Run Minimized (1 = True, 0 = False).	No	Yes
fSeparateMemSpace	In Windows NT only, run the application in a separate memory space (applies to 16-bit applications only).	No	No

Table 12-8 Parameters for the AddItem function

Switching Focus

Using the ShowGroup command sometimes moves the focus to the shell, but most often does not. Whether or not the focus switches depends on the state you request for the program group and on its current state. Though you could make a matrix of options, comparing current states (minimized, normal, or maximized) against the new window state (1 through 8, as in Table 12-9), the rules are quite simple. If you change the state of a group that's currently minimized, the focus will switch to the shell. That means that if you choose actions 1, 3, or 4 for a group that is currently minimized, the shell will grab the focus. You can try this yourself, calling the ahtPMShowGroup function and passing it the name of a group and a new window style.

WINDOW STYLE	ACTION
1	Activate and display the group window. If it was minimized or maximized, restore it to its original position (normalized).
2	Activate the group window, and display it as an icon.
3	Activate the group window, and display it maximized.
4	Display the group window normalized, and leave the current group selected.
5	Activate the group window, and display it in its current placement.
6	Minimize the group window.
7	Minimize the group window, and leave the current group selected.
8	Display the group window in its current placement, and leave the current group selected.

Table 12-9 Command values for the ShowGroup function

Using the Wrapper Procedures

To make your DDE programming simpler, the module basShell includes wrapper procedures (Tables 12-5 and 12-10) that handle all the details for you. (Table 12-5 provides a description of each of the wrapper procedures; Table 12-10 describes each procedure's parameters.) The module provides functions that handle each of the commands described in Table 12-7. In some cases (AddItem, for example), the wrapper functions don't allow you to specify all the possible parameters for the command string. If you find these wrapper functions too limiting, you can modify them so they allow you to pass in whatever parameters you like.

All of the wrapper procedures (except ahtPMShowMessages) in Table 12-10 end up performing the same set of steps to communicate with the Windows shell. To simplify the code and to centralize error handling, those steps have been pulled out into the single private procedure in basShell, DDEExecutePM, shown in the following code example.

```
Private Function DDEExecutePM(strCommand As String)

    ' DDEExecute to Windows shell with the passed-in
    ' command. If it succeeds, return True. If it fails,
    ' return False.

    ' At this point, this function handles error messages
    ' itself. You could move this out of here to a higher
    ' level, if you want, by setting the SHOW_MESSAGES constant
    ' to False.

    Dim lngChannel As Long

    On Error GoTo DDEExecutePMError

    lngChannel = DDEInitiate("PROGMAN", "PROGMAN")
    DDEExecute lngChannel, strCommand
    DDEExecutePM = True

DDEExecutePMExit:
    On Error Resume Next
    DDETerminate lngChannel
    On Error GoTo 0
    Exit Function

DDEExecutePMError:
    If Not mfHideMessages Then
        Dim strError As String

        strError = "Error: " & Error & " (" & Err & ")" & vbCrLf
        strError = strError & "DDEExecute Failed: " & strCommand
        MsgBox strError, vbExclamation, "DDEExecutePM"
    End If

    DDEExecutePM = False
    Resume DDEExecutePMExit
End Function
```

This code, given a string to execute, initiates the DDE channel, uses DDEExecute to execute the command, and then terminates the connection. If all goes according to plan, the procedure returns a True value. If an error occurs, it displays a message box (unless you've used the ahtPMShowMessages procedure to disable warning messages), and then returns False.

Table 12-10 lists the parameters for the wrapper procedures in basShell. Each of these procedures (except ahtPMShowMessages) returns True if the function succeeded or False if it failed. Unless you've called the ahtPMShowMessages subroutine to disable messages, you'll be warned with a message box before deleting a group or an item or if any error occurs.

PROCEDURE	PARAMETER	DATA TYPE	PARAMETER DESCRIPTION
ahtPMCreateGroup	varName	Variant	Name of new group.
	varGroupPath	Variant	Name of group file (can be Null, in which case Windows uses a name of its own choosing).
ahtPMCreateItem	varGroup	Variant	Name of the group in which to create the new item.
	varName	Variant	Descriptive name for the new item, appears under the icon.
	varCommandLine	Variant	Command line to execute when this icon is chosen. Cannot be Null.
	varDirectory	Variant	Default (working) directory when the application starts up.
	varMinimized	Variant	Logical value: Run the app minimized?
ahtPMDeleteGroup	varName	Variant	Group to delete.
ahtPMDeleteItem	varGroup	Variant	Group from which to delete item.
	varName	Variant	Name of the item to delete.
ahtPMShowGroup	varName	Variant	Name of the group to show.
	intMode	Integer	Window mode, as listed in Table 12-9.
ahtPMShowMessages	fShow	Integer	Logical value: display messages during DDE wrapper functions? If True, functions use message box if errors occur and when deleting items. This subroutine sets a module global variable, so you only need to call it once per session.

Table 12-10 Wrapper functions in basShell

For example, to use the wrapper functions to add an icon to the My Group group that will run C:\EDIT\MYEDIT.EXE minimized with the description My Editor (as in the example above that called AddItem directly) you could use code like this:

```
Dim fSuccess As Boolean

' Disable error messages
ahtPMShowMessages False
fSuccess = ahtPMCreateItem("My Group", "My Editor", _
  "C:\EDIT\MYEDIT.EXE", Null, True)
If Not fSuccess Then MsgBox "Unable to create new item!"
```

This example also calls ahtPMShowMessages to disable error messages from within ahtPMCreateItem so the code fragment itself can handle them.

For examples of each of the wrapper functions, check out the code in frmShell's module.

Comments

Though this How-To covers a great deal more than the original question, all of the information here will be of use to Access programmers working with the DDE interface to the Windows shell.

The sample form, frmShell, is not only a good example of using DDE to converse with Windows, it's also a useful tool on its own. Because you can see what's in each group without having to open and close each group's window, it's a quick and easy way to clean out your groups. For it to be a really useful tool, though, some extra work would be required. But it's a good start.

In 16-bit applications, DDEInitiate returns a short integer (16 bits) handle. In Access 95 (and other 32-bit applications), this function returns a long integer (32 bits). If you have existing code that uses DDE, you'll want to convert the variables containing the return values into long integers.

The Windows 95 shell has an undocumented DDE Application|Topic pair which is not supported by the original Program Manager or any of the major third-party shell substitutes: Folders|AppProperties. Presumably the Windows NT version of the new shell will also have this feature. This syntax seems to be just an alias for the regularly documented DDE interface, because the item name syntax and all the operations you use are identical to when using the documented application|topic pair.

This undocumented syntax can be of some benefit. If you are going to add the functionality to interact with the shell, you can use code such as the following to determine whether your user is using the Windows 95 shell or not:

```
Function ahtNewShell () as Boolean
    Dim lngChannel as Long
    On Error Resume Next
    lngChannel = DDEInitiate("Folders","AppProperties")
    ahtNewShell = (lngChannel <> 0)
    DDETerminate lngChannel
End Function
```

You'll notice that the example uses this function (as well as a public flag) to decide whether to call the various Shell objects "groups" and "items" (as they are called in the Windows NT Program Manager) or "folders" and "shortcuts" (as they are called in the Windows 95 shell).

To shield you from the details of the DDE conversation and to isolate the DDE code in one routine, each of the command-string replacement functions calls the DDEExecutePM function. This makes the code neat and easy to understand, but it does introduce an issue to consider: By calling DDEInitiate and DDETerminate each and every time you call one of the wrapper functions, you're adding substantial time and overhead to your application. If you make many calls to Window via DDE, you'll want to reconsider this design. For most applications, though, this shouldn't be a problem.

COMPLEXITY:
ADVANCED

12.6 How do I...
Modify Microsoft Graph settings programmatically?

Problem

I need to be able to alter Microsoft Graph objects programmatically. Sometimes I'd like my users to be able to modify some of the attributes of a graph before printing it. Other times I'd like to be able to modify the title or the size of a graph's title. Is there a programmatic interface to Graph objects?

Technique

When you create a graph object (using the form design toolbox), you actually embed an OLE object onto your form. The parent application for this object is GRAPH5.EXE, which is normally installed in the Program Files\Common Files\Msgraph5 folder. Graphs created by GRAPH5 expose a rich and powerful set of objects and properties that you can control programmatically from Access. The only current documentation for these objects and properties is in the Microsoft Excel help file; a discussion of all of them is far beyond the scope of this How-To. The goal here is to demonstrate some simple manipulations involving pie charts. Once you understand the concepts behind setting and retrieving graph object properties, you will be able to expand on the sample provided here to create your own masterpieces.

Steps

Load and run frmGraph in 12-06.MDB. This form, shown in Figure 12-9, includes a simple 3D pie graph and controls that allow you to alter its properties. All of these operations are performed by manipulating the graph object's properties using OLE Automation. For example, with the Rotation and Elevation group of controls, you can rotate the pie graph around the horizontal axis (change its elevation) and around the vertical axis (change its rotation). You can change the location or size of the title, the legend, or the plot area. You can explode one or more pie slices a specified percentage by checking one of the items in the list on the right side of the form.

Because the topic of OLE Automation control over graph objects is so immense, this How-To focuses on creating a simple form like frmGraph. Once you've walked through the steps involved in this form, and armed yourself with the Microsoft Graph help file, you should be able to work wonders with Microsoft Graph and Access.

The following steps document all you need to do to create a form similar to the sample form, frmGraph. You might start by creating this form and then expanding on it,

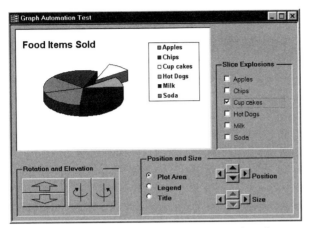

Figure 12-9 The sample form, frmGraph, allows you to alter properties of the 3D pie graph

adding your own features once you've got it all working. We won't specify exact locations or properties for the controls on your form, as you may want to modify the look of the sample form as you create it. On the other hand, we will specify control event procedures because these determine how the form operates.

Setting Up the Form

1. Create the table that will hold your data. In the sample database, you'll find tblFoods, which is the example that will be used throughout this How-To. If you use a different table for your example, you'll need to substitute field names to match those in tblFoods. Table 12-11 lists the structure for tblFoods. Any field properties not mentioned in the table have no bearing on the example and can be set any way you'd like.

FIELD NAME	FIELD TYPE	OTHER DETAILS	COMMENTS
ID	AutoNumber	Primary Key	
Item	Text		The food item name.
Quantity	Number	Integer	The number sold for the given item.
IsExploded	Yes/No		Is this item exploded on the graph?

Table 12-11 The structure for the sample table, tblFoods

2. Create a query, based on tblFoods, named qryItems. This query will be the basis for the graph itself and for the list box showing the list of pie slices. Figure 12-10 shows the query design surface for qryItems. Your own version of this query must contain all the fields you want graphed as well as the

Yes/No field, IsExploded, which controls the subform showing which slices are exploded.

3. Create an unbound form (named frmGraph in the example, but this name can be changed to whatever you like). Set its properties as shown in Table 12-12; these are the standard settings you'd use for any unbound form. Other properties can be set as you like.

PROPERTY	VALUE
RecordSource	<Blank>
DefaultView	Single Form
ScrollBars	Neither
RecordSelectors	No
NavigationButtons	No
AutoResize	Yes

Table 12-12 Property settings for the unbound sample form

4. Choose the Insert|Chart menu item and drag the cursor to create a graph on the empty form. Then follow the steps in Table 12-13 for creating a pie chart. Your form will look something like the one shown in Figure 12-11.

QUESTION	CHOICE
What table or query would you like to use to create your chart?	qryItems (Click on the Queries button to see the queries list).
Which fields contain the data you want for the chart?	Item, Quantity.
What type of graph do you want?	Three-Dimensional Pie Chart (3rd row, 2nd column).
How do you want to lay out the data in your chart?	Accept the default choices.
What title do you want for your chart?	Food Items Sold (or anything else you like).
Do you want the chart to display a legend?	Yes, display a legend.

Table 12-13 Steps to take through the Graph Wizard

5. With the graph control selected, change the control's Name property in the properties sheet from Graph0 (the default name that Access gave it) to objGraph. That's the control name expected by prewritten code later in this How-To.

6. With your form still in design mode, double-click on the graph control. Access will send you to the Microsoft Graph application so you can modify any and all portions of your graph's display. For frmGraph, we moved the legend, title, and plot area around within the graph area. Make any changes you like.

7. Go back to Access using the File|Exit and Return… menu option and make sure to save your form.

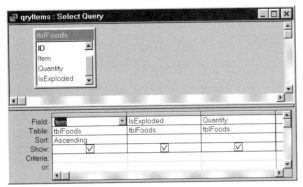

Figure 12-10 The sample query, qryItems, in design mode

Creating the Controls

The following steps outline how to create the controls that will be used later to manipulate the graph object. The sample form, frmGraph, lays them out in very specific groups but you can place them any way you like. For the controls with bitmaps, you may find it easiest to copy them from frmGraph if you want to use the bitmaps. Otherwise, you can supply your own or use text captions.

8. Create four command buttons on the form to control the graph's rotation and elevation (see Figure 12-12). Name them (from top to bottom and left to right in the figure) cmdElevationUp, cmdElevationDown, cmdRotateLeft, and cmdRotateRight. If you like the bitmaps as displayed, just copy the buttons from frmGraph rather than creating your own.

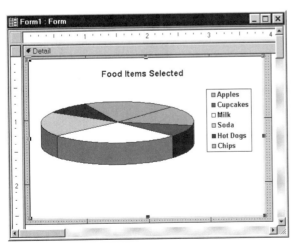

Figure 12-11 The initial pie chart will look something like this

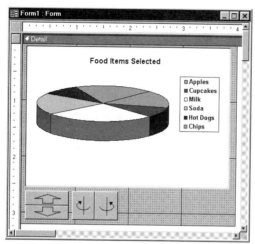

Figure 12-12 The sample form with the four rotation buttons added

9. Create an option group named grpPosSize. Set its DefaultValue property to 1. Inside it, create three option buttons, labeled Plot Area, Legend, and Title, with values 1, 2, and 3, respectively. This option group will indicate to the form whether you want to move and size the plot area, the legends, or the graph title.

10. Create two "clumps" of buttons, as shown in Figure 12-13, to control the movement and resizing of the graph. You'll probably just want to copy these from frmGraph, but if you create your own, name them as follows: cmdLeft, cmdUp, cmdRight, cmdDown for the top group; and cmdSizeLeft, cmdSizeUp, cmdSizeRight, and cmdSizeDown for the bottom group. Lay them out in any fashion you like or use the configuration in Figure 12-13. You may also find it useful to create labels for the groups of buttons, as shown in the figure.

11. Create a new form (it will become the subform showing the list of exploded items). Place a check box and a text box on the form, as shown in Figure 12-14. (The check box's label overlays the text box exactly.) Set form and control properties as shown in Table 12-14.

OBJECT	PROPERTY	VALUE
Form	RecordSource	Select [IsExploded],[Item] from qryItems;
Form	DefaultView	Continuous Forms
Form	Scrollbars	Neither
Form	RecordSelectors	No
Form	NavigationButtons	No

OBJECT	PROPERTY	VALUE
Form	DividingLines	No
Form	AutoResize	Yes
Form	AllowAdditions	No
CheckBox	Name	chkExploded
CheckBox	ControlSource	IsExploded
CheckBox	AfterUpdate	[Event Procedure]
TextBox	Name	txtItem
TextBox	ControlSource	Item

Table 12-14 Form and control properties for the subform

12. Create an event procedure in the new form's module (see this book's Introduction for more information on creating event procedures).

```
Private Sub chkExploded_AfterUpdate()
    ExplodeIt Me.Parent, Me.CurrentRecord, Me!chkExploded
End Sub
```

13. Save the new form and give it the name fsubExplode.

14. With your original form open in design view, click and drag fsubExplode from the Database Explorer to your form (Form1). (You can also choose the Subform/Subreport tool from the toolbox and set its properties so that it displays fsubExplode.) Size the subform control so it's about the same size as the subform in Figure 12-14, which shows the new form with all its controls in place.

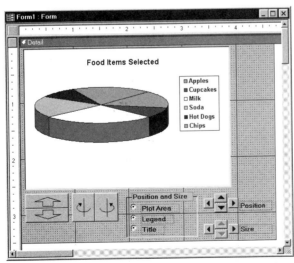

Figure 12-13 The sample form after adding the option group and command buttons for moving and resizing objects

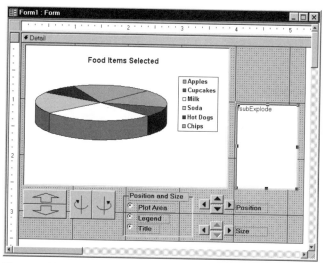

Figure 12-14 The new sample form with all its controls created

15. Select all the controls on your form besides objGraph. (To do this, drag the mouse in the left vertical ruler until you've selected all the objects. Then [SHIFT]-[CLICK] on objGraph to *remove* it from the selection. Neat trick!) Once you've got them all selected, set their collective DisplayWhen properties to Screen Only.

Creating and Attaching the Code

The following steps create the form module that controls the elements of the graph:

16. Import the module basHandleGraph from 12-07.MDB. This module contains the general-purpose routines that move, size, rotate, and elevate the chart objects. Table 12-15 describes each of the properties used in the example, along with the procedure from basHandleGraph that does the work.

17. Open the form's module and enter the following fragment in the Declarations area. This creates the constants used in determining how fast things move and rotate on the screen. Altering these constants can change the apparent speed at which parts move.

```
Const ahtcMoveDelta = 5
Const ahtcElevateDelta = 5
Const ahtcRotateDelta = 15
Const ahtcSizeDelta = 5
```

18. Table 12-15 lists the events to which you'll need to attach code. For each object in Table 12-15, set the appropriate property to [Event Procedure]. Then enter the procedures shown below. These are the routines that react to your mouse clicks on the form to move the various pieces of the graph. (You can copy each of these from frmGraph's module if you'd like.) Most of these subroutines just call directly to the procedures imported in step 15. A few of them, though, actually do substantial work. See the How It Works section for details.

OBJECT	EVENT PROPERTY
cmdDown	On Click
cmdElevationDown	On Click
cmdElevationUp	On Click
cmdLeft	On Click
cmdRight	On Click
cmdRotateLeft	On Click
cmdRotateRight	On Click
cmdSizeDown	On Click
cmdSizeLeft	On Click
cmdSizeRight	On Click
cmdSizeUp	On Click
cmdUp	On Click
Form	On Load
Form	On Close
grpPosSize	After Update
lstItems	On Dbl Click

Table 12-15 Objects and their properties that include event procedures

```
Private Sub cmdDown_Click()
    MoveIt Me, ahtcMoveDelta, 0
End Sub

Private Sub cmdElevationDown_Click()
    ElevateIt Me, ahtcElevateDelta
End Sub

Private Sub cmdElevationUp_Click()
    ElevateIt Me, -ahtcElevateDelta
End Sub

Private Sub cmdLeft_Click()
    MoveIt Me, 0, -ahtcMoveDelta
End Sub

Private Sub cmdRight_Click()
    MoveIt Me, 0, ahtcMoveDelta
End Sub
```

continued on next page

continued from previous page

```
Private Sub cmdRotateLeft_Click()
    RotateIt Me, ahtcRotateDelta
End Sub

Private Sub cmdRotateRight_Click()
    RotateIt Me, -ahtcRotateDelta
End Sub

Private Sub cmdSizeDown_Click()
    SizeIt Me, 0, ahtcSizeDelta
End Sub

Private Sub cmdSizeLeft_Click()
    SizeIt Me, -ahtcSizeDelta, 0
End Sub

Private Sub cmdSizeRight_Click()
    SizeIt Me, ahtcSizeDelta, 0
End Sub

Private Sub cmdSizeUp_Click()
    SizeIt Me, 0, -ahtcSizeDelta
End Sub

Private Sub cmdUp_Click()
    MoveIt Me, -ahtcMoveDelta, 0
End Sub

Private Sub Form_Close()
    CloseObj
End Sub

Private Sub Form_Load()
    DoCmd.SetWarnings False
    DoCmd.RunSQL "UPDATE tblFoods SET IsExploded = False;"
    DoCmd.SetWarnings True
End Sub

Private Sub grpPosSize_AfterUpdate()

    ' After choosing one of Plot Area, Legend, Title,
    ' make sure the appropriate sizing buttons
    ' are available.

    Dim fEnabled As Integer

    ' Only enable the Up and Down sizing arrows
    ' if the Legends are selected (item 2).
    fEnabled = (Me!grpPosSize = 2)
    Me!cmdSizeUp.Enabled = fEnabled
    Me!cmdSizeDown.Enabled = fEnabled
End Sub
```

19. That's it. Save your form and then run it. You should be able to manipulate its pieces just like you could on the original frmGraph.

How It Works

This section first discusses the generic routines imported in step 16 and then covers the more specific event procedures that call the generic routines (described in step 18).

Referring to Objects

The first step in manipulating an OLE object is referring to it. The SetObject function (in basHandleGraph) sets the global variable, obj, to refer to the graph object on your form. The main portion of this simple function boils down to this statement:

```
If obj Is Nothing Then
    Set obj = frm(ahtcGraphControl).Object
End If
```

This fragment uses a variable of type Object. This data type, used only when referencing OLE objects, allows you to refer to any part of an OLE object. As you'll see, you can set an object variable to point to a section of a graph, or a point, or the legend, or the whole graph itself.

SetObject first checks to see whether obj (a module global variable of type Object) is currently referring to an object. If not, its value is the predefined constant Nothing and you need to initialize it. Otherwise, just use it as it is. (This check can save you some time, as it takes a fraction of a second to initialize the variable. When you're trying to rotate pie charts, every millisecond counts.) If you must assign obj to refer to the graph object, set it equal to the graph control's Object property. The graph control exposes many properties, just like any other control, and its Object property is one of them. A graph control's Object property is a reference to the OLE object itself. Once you have that reference, you can treat it as an entity with properties and methods. The rest of this How-To focuses on using the graph object's properties and methods to force it to do what you want.

Manipulating Objects and Their Properties

The generic routines imported in step 16 deal with properties of the graph object—in this case, a 3D pie chart. Table 12-16 lists the properties of the graph objects managed with the code here. Each of the procedures in basHandleGraph uses these properties to change the appearance of the pie chart on the sample form.

PROPERTY	DESCRIPTION	VALUES	EXAMPLE	USED IN
Elevation	Front-to-back rotation, or the viewing angle for the graph.	From 10° to 80° (though documented as accepting −90° to 90°)	obj.Elevation = 25	Elevatelt

continued on next page

continued from previous page

PROPERTY	DESCRIPTION	VALUES	EXAMPLE	USED IN
Explosion	Percentage explosion of a single pie slice. [1]	0% (the pie slice point is in the center of the pie) to 100% (the point is at the outer rim of the pie)	obj.SeriesCollection(1).Points(1).Explosion = 50	ExplodeIt
Left and Top	Position of the left and top edges of an object (in points). [2]	0 to the size of the graph area	obj.PlotArea.Left = 0 or obj.Legend.Left = 0 or obj.ChartTitle.Left = 0	MoveIt
Rotation	Rotation of an object around its vertical (z) axis.	0° to 360° (except for 3-D bar charts, where the value must be between 0° and 44°)	obj.Rotation = 300	RotateIt
Width and Height	Width and height of a graph object, in points.	0 to the size of the graph area.	obj.PlotArea.Width = 100 or obj.Legend.Height = 300	SizeIt
Size	Point size of a specific font object[3]	A reasonable font size, in points.	obj.ChartTitle.Font.Size = 12	SizeIt

[1] Not a property of the graph, but of a specific point within a specific collection of points within the graph.

[2] Note that Access uses twips (1/20 point), but Graph uses points. The examples use the PlotArea, Legend, and ChartTitle objects.

[3] The Size property is a property of a Font object, which is itself a property of a graph object that displays text.

Table 12-16 Sample graph object properties and their uses

For example, clicking the Rotate Right button calls the RotateIt procedure, shown below. This procedure adds ahtcRotateDelta degrees to the current rotation property, then works with it to ensure that it's between 0 and 360 degrees. (For information on the fInHere flag, see the next section.)

```
Sub RotateIt(frm As Form, intAmount As Integer)

    ' Rotate the pie chart about its z-axis

    Static fInHere As Boolean

    ' Avoid recursive calls into here.
    If fInHere Then Exit Sub
    fInHere = True
```

```
    If SetObject(frm) Then
        ' Convert all values to be between 0 and 360
        obj.Rotation = ((obj.Rotation + intAmount) + 360) Mod 360
        DoEvents
    End If
    fInHere = False
End Sub
```

Avoiding Overlapping Procedure Calls

Because of display anomalies, we did not instruct you to set the AutoRepeat property of the command buttons in this example. (Doing so caused a great deal of flicker on the screen in our test cases, but you're welcome to try in your own environment.) If you do enable AutoRepeat, there's nothing to keep you from holding the button down and calling the procedure attached to the button's Click event over and over, perhaps even before the previous invocation has completed. This overlapping calling can cause you trouble, because Access supports only limited space on its internal stack for procedure calls. To avoid this problem, each of the generic procedures includes code to ensure that it doesn't get called until the previous call is completed. To do this, each uses a static variable, fInHere, as a flag that the routine checks as soon as it starts.

```
Static fInHere As Boolean

' Avoid recursive calls into here.
If fInHere Then Exit Sub
fInHere = True


'
' Do the work here
'
' Let Windows catch up
DoEvents

' Clear the flag
fInHere = False
```

If the flag is true, exit from the routine. If not, the routine sets the flag to True, does its work, calls DoEvents to allow Windows to catch up, and then clears the flag once it's done. Using this framework ensures that you won't run out of Windows stack space while holding down a particular button. (For more information, see How-To 7.4.)

Handling Specific Events

In addition to all the moving and sizing done in response to button clicks, two more events require discussion. When you first load the form, code attached to the OnLoad event property clears all pie-slice explosions. When you choose one of the slices on the subform, code attached to the AfterUpdate event property for the check box finds the correct pie slice and explodes it if it wasn't exploded or sets its explosion back to 0 if it was. The AfterUpdate event calls the ExplodeIt procedure from basHandleGraph. This routine sets the Explosion property of the specific point within the SeriesCollection collection (you're only displaying a single series, so you'll work with SeriesCollection(1)).

```
Sub ExplodeIt(frm As Form, ByVal intSlice As Integer, _
ByVal fExploded As Variant)

    ' Explode the specified pie slice.

    ' There's only one collection of points on this graph,
    ' so use SeriesCollection(1)
    ' The Points collection is 1-based, as well.
    On Error Resume Next
    If SetObject(frm) Then
        obj.SeriesCollection(1).Points(intSlice).Explosion = _
        IIf(fExploded, ahtcExplode, 0)
    End If
    On Error GoTo 0
End Sub
```

Comments

The examples shown here barely scratch the surface of the capabilities of OLE Automation with Microsoft Graph. You can take these examples and build on them using the help file as a guide. You may find it useful to add a reference to the Graph 5.0 type library (choose Microsoft Graph 5.0 Object Library from the Tools|References… dialog box). We decided not to require a reference to that library in this example because the information it provided would not have made the example work any better. You may find the hierarchy information provided there to be of use if you want to modify this example.

Graph 5: Not Just Useful in Access

Access and Excel share the same graphing engine, and therefore, the object model for graphs is the same whether you're working in Access or Excel. (This explains why the Microsoft Graph help file is geared toward Excel programmers—the Excel group put together the help file.) In any case, code you write for graphs in Access should work almost unmodified in Excel and much of the Excel code in the help file should work just fine in Access. Certainly, learning to program Microsoft Graph in Access is a worthwhile use of your time if you ever intend to also write applications in Excel.

The sample form, frmGraph in 12-06.MDB, has been set up so that only the graph itself will print (every other control on the form has its DisplayWhen property set to Screen Only), so it does serve a real purpose. You could supply a form like this to end users, perhaps allowing them to specify a row source for the graph on a previous form. Using this graph form, they could alter the characteristics of the graph before printing it. Only the altered graph would print; all the other controls on frmGraph are hidden when you print the form.

One useful addition to the sample form presented here would be to allow for different graph types. Although the mechanics of changing the graph type are simple (it only requires changing the object's Type property), the ramifications for this example are complex, because it would require changing all the limits for the various movement and rotation values. It's a good project for you to take on.

Simpler additions include:

- Allowing the title to be toggled on and off (using the chart's HasTitle property)

- Allowing the legend to be toggled on and off (using the chart's HasLegend property)

- Changing the font style for the legend items—for instance, changing obj.Legend.LegendEntries(n).Font.FontStyle to Bold Italic

There are many other variations on item visibility (axis titles, point markers for non-pie graphs, etc.) and font/style changes. Have fun with Microsoft Graph! It allows more flexibility than any built-in Access component and is guaranteed to give you hours of tinkering pleasure.

COMPLEXITY:
ADVANCED

12.7 How do I... Create a PowerPoint presentation from Access data?

Problem

I need to create similar Microsoft PowerPoint presentations over and over. I currently take an existing presentation, copy it to a new location, and modify it as necessary. That way, I have a number of iterations of the same text littering my hard disk. It seems that I could just store all the text and its formatting information in an Access table and then create the presentation programmatically when necessary. This way, I could choose just the slides I need, make modifications as needed, and only have one place where I store the data. Is this possible?

Technique

Microsoft PowerPoint for Windows 95 (part of Microsoft Office for Windows 95) offers an amazingly rich set of objects, methods, and properties, considering its place in the Office world. It's not a developer's tool, yet its object model is spectacularly deep, especially in comparison to Access'. It appears that you can do anything programmatically from an OLE client (like Access) that you can do manually, using PowerPoint as an

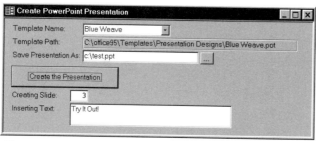

Figure 12-15 Use frmPowerPoint to create
PowerPoint presentations from within Access

OLE Automation server. The answer, then, to the original question is "Yes!" You can
definitely create presentations programmatically from Access using tables to store all
the information about your presentation.

Steps

Two major areas are involved in this How-To: setting up the data in its tables and using
the interface to create your presentation. This section includes two sets of steps, one
for each area.

To try out the sample application, load and run frmPowerPoint from 12-07.MDB.
First choose a template from the combo box's list of templates; then enter a file name
to which to save your presentation (click on the "…" button to use the common File
Open/Save dialog boxes). Click the Create Presentation button to start PowerPoint and
create the presentation (taken from a lecture based on How-To 12-4). Figure 12-15
shows the sample form in action.

To use this technique to create your own presentations, follow these steps (or you
can use 12-07.MDB as is and skip these steps):

Setting Up Your Database

1. Import the four tables from 12-07.MDB (tblParagraphs, tblSlides, tlkpLayouts,
and tlkpOptions).

2. Import the three forms frmPowerPoint, zfrmParagraphs, and zsfrmSlides (the
last two are for setting up your slides only and are not part of the sample's user
interface).

3. Import the four modules basCommonFile, basGetTemplate, basPowerPoint,
and basRegistry.

4. Open one of the modules in design mode and choose the Tools|References…
menu item. For the code to work, your database must include an explicit reference to the PowerPoint type library. Find the option labeled PowerPoint 7.0
Object Library, and make sure it's checked. Figure 12-16 shows the References
dialog box as it might appear on your machine once you've found and selected the reference.

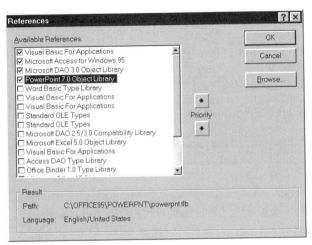

Figure 12-16 Use the Tools|References... dialog box to add a new library reference

Adding Data to Your Tables

5. Plan your presentation carefully. You may want to play in PowerPoint for a while, choosing slide layouts first, before you begin adding data to tables. Or you may want to take an existing presentation and enter it into Access (this is how we created this example set of data).

6. Delete all the rows from tblSlides and tblParagraphs, the two tables containing the presentation information (you might make copies of the originals first, in case you want to refer to them). Leave the two tables whose names start with tlkp alone: These tables are necessary for the application to run.

7. Using zsfrmSlides or editing the table directly add one row to tblSlides for each slide in your presentation. The SlideNumber field will be used for sorting the slides in the presentation (you can enter them in any order you like). The SlideLayout field tells PowerPoint which of its layouts you want to use for the slide: Choose its value from the combo box, which pulls its values from tlkpLayouts. It may take some experimentation to find the layout you want. The Include field tells this application whether or not to create a slide in PowerPoint. This way, you can create all your slides in Access but export only selected slides to PowerPoint. Figure 12-17 shows zsfrmSlides gathering slide information.

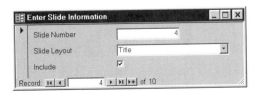

Figure 12-17 Use zfrmSlides to add new slides to your presentation

8. Using zsfrmParagraphs or editing the table directly add one row to tblParagraphs for each paragraph on each slide in your presentation. Table 12-17 lists the fields with comments about each. This table is linked to tblSlides on the SlideNumber field and should include one row for each output paragraph that you need. The three fields, SlideNumber, ObjectNumber, and ParagraphNumber, together make up the primary key; the combination of the three must be unique (none of these fields can be left blank for a given paragraph). Figure 12-18 shows zsfrmParagraphs gathering paragraph information.

FIELD	DESCRIPTION	VALUES
SlideNumber	Slide number for this paragraph.	Any valid slide number.
ObjectNumber	Object number on the selected slide. All text boxes and other items count as objects.	Any valid object number, depending on the slide layout. This example app does not support adding new objects.
ParagraphNumber	Paragraph within the object.	A contiguous, incrementing number, based on previous paragraphs in the selected object.
IndentLevel	How many levels to indent this paragraph?	An integer between 1 (no indent) and 5.
Text	The text for the selected paragraph.	Any text, up to a reasonable length (6 or 7 words).
FontName	Name of the font for this paragraph.	Any valid installed font. Leave blank to use the default font for the style you've selected.
FontSize	Font size for this paragraph.	Any valid font size (1 to 127). 0 indicates that you want to use the default font size for the style you've selected.
Color	Color for this paragraph.	Numeric value representing the color you want to use for your paragraph. 0 indicates that you want to use the default color for the style you've selected.
Shadow	Shadow for this paragraph?	Select from Yes (−1), No (0), or Use Slide Default (1).
Bold	Make this paragraph bold?	Select from Yes (−1), No (0), or Use Slide Default (1).
Italic	Make this paragraph italicized?	Select from Yes (−1), No (0), or Use Slide Default (1).
Underline	Underline this paragraph?	Select from Yes (−1), No (0), or Use Slide Default (1).
Bullet	Precede this paragraph with a bullet?	Select from Yes (−1), No (0), or Use Slide Default (1).

Table 12-17 Field values allowed in tblParagraphs

9. Before creating your presentation, peruse the data in tblSlides, making sure that the Include field is set the way you want it (to include or exclude each slide).

10. Using frmPowerPoint as described above, create your presentation in PowerPoint.

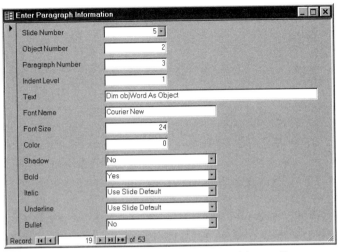

Figure 12-18 Use zsfrmParagraphs to add or edit
paragraph text and properties

How It Works

Creating the presentation boils down to four basic steps:

- Start PowerPoint (and shut it down once you're finished).

- Create the presentation.

- Loop through tblSlides, creating the slides one at a time.

- For each slide, loop through the appropriate rows of tblParagraphs, placing text and formatting it.

You'll find all the necessary code in basPowerPoint in 12-07.MDB. The following sections describe, in detail, how each of these steps works.

Starting and Stopping PowerPoint

To create the presentation, you must first retrieve a reference to the PowerPoint Application object. If PowerPoint is already running, the GetObject function will be able to retrieve the object reference. If not, the code will jump to an error handler, which will try the CreateObject method. Once the procedure has done its work, created the slide presentation, and saved it, if the code started PowerPoint, it will try to close PowerPoint. If not, it will leave the application running. The following skeleton version of the CreatePresentation function (shown in its entirety below) handles the application startup and shutdown.

```
Function CreatePresentation(fShowIt As Boolean, _
  ByVal varTemplate As Variant, varFileName As Variant)

    Dim app As Object
    Dim fAlreadyRunning As Boolean

    On Error GoTo CreatePresentation_Err

    ' Assume that PowerPoint was already running.
    fAlreadyRunning = True

    Set app = GetObject(, "PowerPoint.Application")
    '
    ' Do the work, creating the presentation.
    '
    If Not fAlreadyRunning Then
        app.Quit
    End If
    Set app = Nothing

CreatePresentation_Exit:
    Exit Function

CreatePresentation_Err:
    Select Case Err.Number
        Case ahtcErrCantStart
            Set app = CreateObject("PowerPoint.Application")
            fAlreadyRunning = False
            Resume Next

        ' Handle other errors...
    End Select
    Resume CreatePresentation_Exit
End Function
```

Creating the Presentation

To create the presentation, you must add a new presentation to the application's collection of open presentations (that is, even if PowerPoint had been running when you started your slide-creation application, you would want to create a new presentation and not work with any existing, open presentations). To add a new item to the collection, use the Add method of the Presentations collection of the Application object.

```
' Get a reference to that new presentation.
Set objPresent = app.Presentations.Add(WithWindow:=False)
```

> **Note**
>
> The Add method of the Presentations collections allows you to create the new presentation with or without a window. If you want PowerPoint to be visible while it's creating the presentation, you might want to set this parameter to True instead of False. On the other hand, if you set it to True, the code that creates the slides runs noticeably slower and you'll have to contend with other user-interface issues as well (PowerPoint will request confirmation on overwriting existing presentations when you save this one, for example). We suggest leaving this parameter set to False, unless you have some overriding reason to change it.

Once you've created the presentation, the code uses the ApplyTemplate method of the new Presentation object, given the name of the template you've chosen from frmPowerPoint.

```
If Len(varTemplate & "") > 0 Then
    objPresent.ApplyTemplate varTemplate
End If
```

At this point, the code calls the user-defined CreateSlides function, passing to it the new Presentation object, to create all the slides for the presentation.

This section and the previous one draw their code from the CreatePresentation function in basPowerPoint. Here's the function in its entirety.

```
Function CreatePresentation(fShowIt As Boolean, _
 ByVal varTemplate As Variant, varFileName As Variant)

    ' Highest level routine. Actually create the
    ' presentation, and set up the slides.

    Dim objPresent As Presentation
    Dim lngResult As Long
    Dim app As Object
    Dim fAlreadyRunning As Boolean

    On Error GoTo CreatePresentation_Err

    ' Assume that PowerPoint was already running.
    fAlreadyRunning = True

    Set app = GetObject(, "PowerPoint.Application")
    ' If the caller wants to see this happening, make the
    ' application window visible, and set the focus there.
    If fShowIt Then
        app.AppWindow.Visible = True
        AppActivate "Microsoft PowerPoint"
    End If
    ' Get a reference to that new presentation.
```

continued on next page

continued from previous page

```
        Set objPresent = app.Presentations.Add(WithWindow:=False)
        If Len(varTemplate & "") > 0 Then
            objPresent.ApplyTemplate varTemplate
        End If
        lngResult = CreateSlides(objPresent)
        objPresent.SaveAs fileName:=varFileName, FileType:=0, SaveCopy:=False
        objPresent.Delete
        If Not fAlreadyRunning Then
            app.Quit
        End If
        Set app = Nothing

CreatePresentation_Exit:
    Exit Function

CreatePresentation_Err:
    Select Case Err.Number
        Case ahtcErrCantStart
            Set app = CreateObject("PowerPoint.Application")
            fAlreadyRunning = False
            Resume Next

        Case ahtcErrFileInUse
            MsgBox "The output file name is in use." & vbCrLf & _
                "Switch to PowerPoint and save the file manually.", _
                vbExclamation, "Create Presentation"

        Case Else
            MsgBox "Error: " & Err.Description & " (" & _
                Err.Number & ")", vbExclamation, "Create Presentation"

    End Select
    Resume CreatePresentation_Exit
End Function
```

Creating Each Slide

Once you've created the presentation, the next step is to loop through all the rows in tblSlides, creating the slide described by each row. The code in CreateSlides, shown below, does the work. The work done here boils down to a single line of code: You must call the Add method of the Slides collection for the current presentation to add each of the slides.

```
Set objSlide = obj.Slides.Add(intCount, rstSlides![SlideLayout])
```

As you can see, you must provide the Add method with the index of the slide you're creating and the layout type for the slide. (See the table tlkpLayouts for all the possible layouts and the associated code for each.) The CreateSlides function walks through tblSlides one row at a time (including the slides where the Include flag is set to True), creating the slide and then calling the user-defined CreateSlideText function for each.

```
Function CreateSlides(obj As Presentation)
    ' obj is the PowerPoint presentation object.
    ' If contains slide objects.
```

```
    On Error GoTo CreateSlidesErr

    Const ahtcDataSource = "qrySlideInfo"

    Dim rstSlides As Recordset
    Dim db As Database
    Dim objSlide As Slide

    Dim intSlide As Integer
    Dim intObject As Integer
    Dim intParagraph As Integer
    Dim intCount As Integer
    Dim strText As String
    Dim fDone As Boolean

    Set db = CurrentDb()
    Set rstSlides = db.OpenRecordset( _
     "Select * from [tblSlides] Where [Include] Order By [SlideNumber]")
    fDone = False
    Do While Not rstSlides.EOF And Not fDone
        If rstSlides![Include] Then
            intCount = intCount + 1
            ' Add the next slide.
            Set objSlide = obj.Slides.Add(intCount, rstSlides![SlideLayout])
            If Not CreateSlideText(objSlide, rstSlides![SlideNumber]) Then
                fDone = True
            End If
        End If
        rstSlides.MoveNext
    Loop

CreateSlidesExit:
    If Not rstSlides Is Nothing Then rstSlides.Close
    Exit Function

CreateSlidesErr:
    Select Case Err.Number
        Case Else
            MsgBox "Error: " & Err.Description & " (" & _
            Err.Number & ")", vbExclamation, "Create Slides"

    End Select
    Resume CreateSlidesExit

End Function
```

Creating the Text

Creating the slide text can be broken down into a number of smaller substeps:

Retrieve the list of pertinent paragraphs from tblParagraphs.

Loop through all the rows, adding a paragraph to the specified object for each.

Set the formatting for each paragraph.

The following paragraphs describe each step from the CreateSlideText function, shown in its entirety below.

To retrieve the list of paragraphs that apply to the current slide, CreateSlides has passed to CreateSlideText the slide object and its index. Given that index, CreateSlideText can request just the paragraphs associated with that slide from tblParagraphs.

```
' objSlide is a slide object, to which you're going to add text.
Set db = CurrentDb()

' Go get the text that applies to this slide.
Set rst = db.OpenRecordset( _
  "Select * from tblParagraphs Where [SlideNumber] = " & intSlideNumber & _
  " Order By [ObjectNumber], [ParagraphNumber]")
```

For each of the rows in the recordset, CreateSlideText must retrieve a reference to the specified slide object. Each of the objects on the slide that can contain text is numbered and the recordset contains an index (intObject) indicating which object you want to place your text into. If the value of the index in the recordset equals the current object index on the slide, then the code appends the paragraph to that object. If not, the code retrieves an object that refers to the object using the Objects collection of the current slide.

```
If intObject = rst!ObjectNumber Then
    obj.Text.Append vbCrLf & rst![Text]
    intParagraph = intParagraph + 1
Else
    intObject = rst!ObjectNumber
    Set obj = objSlide.Objects(intObject)
    obj.Text = rst![Text] & ""
    intParagraph = 1
End If
```

The code next needs to retrieve object references to the paragraph itself (a TextRange object), to the paragraph's bullet (using the Bullet property of the text range's ParaFormat object), and to the character formatting object (the CharFormat property of the text range). Given those object references, the code can set all the necessary properties.

```
' Get a reference to the paragraph in question,
' and then set its paragraph properties.
Set objTextRange = obj.Text.Paragraphs(intParagraph, 1)
Set objBullet = objTextRange.ParaFormat.Bullet
Set objFormat = objTextRange.CharFormat
```

Setting the indent level is a bit tricky, because attempting to set the indent level of certain objects (slide headers, for example) triggers a runtime error. To avoid dealing with this problem, the code avoids errors for this small fragment.

```
' Setting the indent level of certain
' objects triggers a runtime error, which would
' skip the other property settings in this
' construction. Therefore, disregard errors
' when trying to set the indent level.
On Error Resume Next
If Not IsNull(rst![IndentLevel]) Then
```

```
    objTextRange.IndentLevel = rst![IndentLevel]
End If
On Error GoTo CreateSlideTextErr
```

Next, CreateSlideText sets the properties that aren't dependent on the tlkpOptions table.

```
If Not IsNull(rst![FontName]) Then
    objFormat.Font = rst![FontName]
End If
If rst![FontSize] > 0 Then
    objFormat.Points = rst![FontSize]
End If
If rst![Color] > 0 Then
    objFormat.Color.RGB = rst![Color]
End If
```

Finally, the code sets all the properties whose value can be either True or False, or can use the slide formatting defaults.

```
' Set Yes/No/Use Default properties
If rst![Shadow] <> ahtcUseDefault Then
    objFormat.Shadow = rst![Shadow]
End If
If rst![Bold] <> ahtcUseDefault Then
    objFormat.Bold = rst![Bold]
End If
If rst![Italic] <> ahtcUseDefault Then
    objFormat.Italic = rst![Italic]
End If
If rst![Underline] <> ahtcUseDefault Then
    objFormat.Underline = rst![Underline]
End If
If rst![Bullet] <> ahtcUseDefault Then
    objBullet.Exists = rst![Bullet]
End If
```

Once CreateSlideText has set all the necessary properties, it moves on to the next row. If at any point it encounters an error setting the properties of a given paragraph, it moves on to the next paragraph. (You might consider beefing up this error handling, but for the most part, it works fine.) Here, then, is the complete source for CreateSlideText.

```
Function CreateSlideText(objSlide As Slide, intSlideNumber As Integer)
    Dim db As Database
    Dim rst As Recordset
    Dim obj As SlideObject
    Dim intObject As Integer
    Dim intParagraph As Integer
    Dim objTextRange As TextRange
    Dim objFormat As CharFormat
    Dim objBullet As BulletFormat

    On Error GoTo CreateSlideTextErr
```

continued on next page

continued from previous page

```
' objSlide is a slide object, to which you're going to add text.
Set db = CurrentDb()

' Go get the text that applies to this slide.
Set rst = db.OpenRecordset( _
 "Select * from tblParagraphs Where [SlideNumber] = " & intSlideNumber & _
 " Order By [ObjectNumber], [ParagraphNumber]")

' Now walk through the list of text items,
' sticking them into the objects, and applying
' properties.
Do While Not rst.EOF
   With Forms!frmPowerPoint
      .UpdateDisplay rst![SlideNumber], rst![Text]
      .RepaintObject
   End With
   ' If the current object is the same as the object into
   ' which you're trying to insert text, then you've already
   ' created the object. Just append the text. Otherwise,
   ' create the object reference and insert the first
   ' paragraph.
   If intObject = rst!ObjectNumber Then
      obj.Text.Append vbCrLf & rst![Text]
      intParagraph = intParagraph + 1
   Else
      intObject = rst!ObjectNumber
      Set obj = objSlide.Objects(intObject)
      obj.Text = rst![Text] & ""
      intParagraph = 1
   End If
   ' Get a reference to the paragraph in question,
   ' and then set its paragraph properties.
   Set objTextRange = obj.Text.Paragraphs(intParagraph, 1)
   Set objBullet = objTextRange.ParaFormat.Bullet
   Set objFormat = objTextRange.CharFormat

   ' Setting the indent level of certain
   ' objects triggers a runtime error, which would
   ' skip the other property settings in this
   ' construction. Therefore, disregard errors
   ' when trying to set the indent level.
   On Error Resume Next
   If Not IsNull(rst![IndentLevel]) Then
      objTextRange.IndentLevel = rst![IndentLevel]
   End If
   On Error GoTo CreateSlideTextErr

   If Not IsNull(rst![FontName]) Then
      objFormat.Font = rst![FontName]
   End If
   If rst![FontSize] > 0 Then
      objFormat.Points = rst![FontSize]
   End If
   If rst![Color] > 0 Then
      objFormat.Color.RGB = rst![Color]
   End If
```

```
                ' Set Yes/No/Use Default properties
                If rst![Shadow] <> ahtcUseDefault Then
                    objFormat.Shadow = rst![Shadow]
                End If
                If rst![Bold] <> ahtcUseDefault Then
                    objFormat.Bold = rst![Bold]
                End If
                If rst![Italic] <> ahtcUseDefault Then
                    objFormat.Italic = rst![Italic]
                End If
                If rst![Underline] <> ahtcUseDefault Then
                    objFormat.Underline = rst![Underline]
                End If
                If rst![Bullet] <> ahtcUseDefault Then
                    objBullet.Exists = rst![Bullet]
                End If
CreateSlideTextNext:
            rst.MoveNext
        Loop
        CreateSlideText = True

CreateSlideTextExit:
    Exit Function
CreateSlideTextErr:
    Select Case Err.Number
        Case ahtcErrInvalidObjectIndex
            Resume CreateSlideTextNext

        Case Else
            MsgBox "Error: " & Err.Description & " (" & _
              Err.Number & ")", vbExclamation, "Create Slides Text"

    End Select
    CreateSlideText = False
    Resume CreateSlideTextExit

End Function
```

Comments

This How-To uses only a small subset of the PowerPoint OLE Automation interface. You actually have a great deal more functionality available to you if you care to dig deep enough to find it. For example, you might want to support more of the text attributes than we've chosen, or more bullet attributes. You might want to dig into slide transitions, builds, and animation. Use the Object Browser (press F2 in a module window), shown in Figure 12-19, to help dig through the PowerPoint object model. You can work your way down through the hierarchy in an orderly fashion. For example, find the Application object in the left window and then browse through the right window until you find the Presentations collections. On the left, find the Presentations collection, and on the right, find the Add method. That's how we wrote this How-To: by digging through the various objects, collections, methods, and properties that the Object Browser displays.

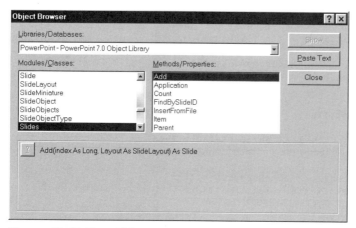

Figure 12-19 The Object Browser makes it possible to dig around in object models

Because PowerPoint exposes its entire object model in its type library (as opposed to Schedule Plus, which does not), the code in this example is able to use object types that are imported from PowerPoint. For example, rather than creating a variable that will refer to a presentation As Object, the code can dimension it As Presentation. Because of this, Access can perform compile-time checking of syntax and early binding to the PowerPoint library. This gets you faster running code and better syntax checking as you write your code.

You may also want to take a look at basGetTemplate, which includes a substantial amount of code dedicated to retrieving a list of all of its design templates. PowerPoint places the location of these templates in your registry as it's installed. Two issues are involved here that you might find of interest: finding the name of the directory where the templates have been installed and creating an array containing the names of the templates. Once the code creates the array, it uses the standard list-filling callback function mechanism, described in Chapter 7, to populate the combo box on the sample form. Though these topics are beyond the scope of this How-To, you may find it useful to dig into the code, which has comments to help you through it.

Have fun with PowerPoint! Its object model is a pleasure to work with. We were a bit surprised to find that each paragraph in a text box is not treated as a separate object, but despite that minor issue, working with PowerPoint was loads of fun. We hope that all of the Office product programmers (and other vendors) learn from the PowerPoint team and adopt the same type of full-featured object model that you'll find there.

COMPLEXITY:

ADVANCED

12.8 How do I...
Edit Schedule Plus contact data from Access?

Problem

I store all my contact data in Microsoft Schedule Plus. I'd like to be able to edit my contact data or add new contacts from within an Access application. Can I use OLE Automation to access that information directly from Access? It seems silly to maintain information both in Access and in Schedule Plus!

Technique

Again, OLE Automation can come to your rescue. Schedule Plus, part of Microsoft Office for Windows 95, exposes a rich and powerful set of objects, methods, and properties. Although the concepts for data handling clash a bit with the Access way of doing things, this How-To demonstrates what you can do to retrieve, edit, and save data directly from Access in your Schedule Plus contact list.

Steps

This example is almost completely self-contained, so implementing it in your own applications is simple. To try out frmSchedule, as shown in Figure 12-20, load and run the form from 12-08.MDB. (If you don't have Schedule Plus from Microsoft Office for Windows 95 installed on your machine, the rest of this example will not work correctly.)

Follow these steps to try out the sample form:

1. Create a new contact. Type in the information you want to store, choosing different pages by clicking on the buttons at the top of the form. Choose the Save button to save your new contact.

2. Load existing contacts. Choose the Load button. This will cause the application to loop through all the contacts in your schedule, placing them all in the combo box at the top of the form. Choose a contact from the combo box. Make any changes you like and then save the changes with the Save button.

3. Delete the selected contact. Click the Delete button.

4. Add a new contact to the list. Click the Add New button. This will suggest saving the current contact if you've made changes and will then clear out the data entry form, allowing you to enter data for a new contact.

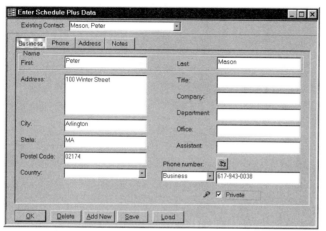

Figure 12-20 Edit Schedule Plus contact data from within Access using frmSchedule

To include this form in your own applications, follow these steps:

1. Import the modules basSchedule (the Schedule Plus information), basDial (handles the phone dialer), and basSortNameInfo (sorts the name list) into your database.

2. Import the form frmSchedule into your database.

How It Works

This example provides a great deal of functionality wrapped up in a single form. The following sections detail the steps involved in getting each feature working. To use this information best, load 12-08.MDB and open basSchedule so you can follow along.

Retrieving the Schedule Plus Schedule Reference

As with any other OLE server, you must retrieve a reference to the top-level object for the application before you can delve any deeper into the object's hierarchy. In this case, the Application object is on top, with the Schedule object right below. Because most activities in this example center on the schedule itself rather than on the Application object, all the code calls the GetSchedule function, listed below, to set a module-level object that will refer to the logged schedule. Any procedure that will need to access an object that's part of the schedule calls this function, which returns a reference to the logged schedule. GetSchedule first checks to see if objApp is Nothing. If so, it knows that it must use the CreateObject function to retrieve a reference to Schedule Plus. If not, it uses the existing reference.

Once GetSchedule has set objApp, it checks to see if any schedule is currently logged (by checking the LoggedOn property of the Application object). If not, the code must call the LogOn method of the Application object. Either way, if all succeeds, the function returns the ScheduleLogged property of the Application object—a reference to the current schedule. As you'll see in later paragraphs, almost every function in basSchedule that works with data must first retrieve a reference to the current schedule, using GetSchedule, before it can do its own work.

```
Private Function GetSchedule() As Object

    ' General purpose function, gets a reference to the
    ' logged schedule in Schedule Plus. Called from
    ' most of the routines here. If unable to retrieve
    ' the reference, returns Nothing.

    On Error GoTo GetSchedule_Err

    ' If the schedule is open already, just
    ' use it. We're assuming that the user
    ' has not changed the schedule logged in the
    ' UI. If so, just remove the check for Is Nothing
    ' in the code immediately following.
    If objApp Is Nothing Then
        Set objApp = CreateObject("SchedulePlus.Application")
        If objApp Is Nothing Then Exit Function
    End If
    If Not objApp.LoggedOn Then
        objApp.LogOn
    End If
    Set GetSchedule = objApp.ScheduleLogged

GetSchedule_Exit:
    Exit Function

GetSchedule_Err:
    Select Case Err.Number
        Case Else
            Call ahtGenericError(Err, "GetSchedule")
    End Select
    Set GetSchedule = Nothing
    Resume GetSchedule_Exit
End Function
```

Quitting Schedule Plus Gracefully

Unlike Access and Excel, Schedule Plus does not provide a Quit method. To exit Schedule Plus gracefully under program control, use the LogOff method of its Application object. The procedure ahtQuitSchedule, called from the sample form's Close event, uses this method to shut down Schedule Plus. If you neglect to use this method, you'll find part of Schedule Plus left in memory even after you've quit Access. (You can verify this by pressing CTRL-ALT-DEL to retrieve a task list.)

Adding a New Contact

The Schedule object provides, as subsidiary objects, tables of values. If you study the full Schedule Plus object model, you'll also find tables named Appointments, SingleAppointments, RecurringAppointments, Events, SingleEvents, Projects, Tasks, and RecurringTasks, among others, as tables within the schedule. This example will use only the Contacts and RecurringEvents tables.

When you choose the Add New button on the sample form, you're actually causing code to clear out the temporary table (tblSchedule) that the sample application uses to store a single contact's data, leaving you with an empty form on which to enter new data. Before it can delete the row, however, the code calls the CheckForSave procedure, which offers a chance to save the data if it's been changed.

```
Private Sub cmdAddNew_Click()

    ' Clear everything out in preparation for adding a new contact.
    ' This really just checks to make sure the existing
    ' contact doesn't need saving, and then clears out the
    ' underlying single-row table.

    On Error GoTo cmdAddNew_ClickErr

    If Not IsNull(frmData!ID) Then
        DoCmd.Hourglass True
        Me.Painting = False

        Call CheckForSave(Me!txtID, True)
        Call ClearContact

cmdAddNew_ClickErr:
        DoCmd.Hourglass False
        Me.Painting = True
    End If
End Sub

Private Sub CheckForSave(ByVal varID As Variant, ByVal fAsk As Boolean)
    Dim fSaveIt As Boolean

    ' If the data has changed, then either ask to save,
    ' or, if fAsk is True, just perform the save.
    If frmData.HasChanged Then
        If fAsk Then
            fSaveIt = (vbYes = MsgBox( _
              "You have changed the current contact's data." & _
              vbCrLf & "Do you want to save this contact?", _
              vbQuestion Or vbYesNo, "Contact Modified"))
        Else
            fSaveIt = True
        End If
        If fSaveIt Then
            Call ahtSaveContact(varID)
            frmData.HasChanged = False
        End If
```

```
    End If
End Sub

Private Sub ClearContact()
    ' Clear the form to accept a new contact.
    Call ahtClearTable
    Me!cboNames = Null
    Me!txtID = Null
    frmData.Requery
End Sub

Sub ahtClearTable()

    ' Clear the single row from the table that's
    ' temporarily holding the data.

    Dim qdf As QueryDef
    Dim db As Database

    On Error GoTo ahtClearTable_Err

    Set db = CurrentDb()
    Set qdf = db.CreateQueryDef("", "Delete * From " & ahtcTable)
    qdf.Execute

ahtClearTable_Exit:
    Exit Sub

ahtClearTable_Err:
    Select Case Err.Number
        Case Else
            Call ahtGenericError(Err, "ahtClearTable")
    End Select
    Resume ahtClearTable_Exit
End Sub
```

The code that actually creates the new contact uses the New method of the Contacts table. The NewContact function first calls the GetSchedule function, shown above, to retrieve a reference to the current schedule and then adds a new contact if it gets a good reference.

```
Private Function NewContact() As Object
    Dim objSched As Object

    ' Create a new contact object, and return that object.

    On Error GoTo NewContact_Err

    Set objSched = GetSchedule()
    If objSched Is Nothing Then
        Set NewContact = Nothing
    Else
        Set NewContact = objSched.Contacts.New
    End If
```

continued on next page

continued from previous page

```
NewContact_Exit:
    Set objSched = Nothing
    Exit Function

NewContact_Err:
    Select Case Err.Number
        Case Else
            Call ahtGenericError(Err, "NewContact")
    End Select
    Set NewContact = Nothing
    Resume NewContact_Exit
End Function
```

Saving Properties for a Contact

Of course, creating a new contact isn't very useful unless you also save the properties for that new contact. In this example, the SaveProps procedure saves all of the properties for a given contact to the appropriate row in your schedule. In addition, SaveProps must save information or add new items to the RecurringEvents table for the birthday and anniversary dates if you've entered values for those fields on the form.

SaveProps, shown below, counts on the fact that the names of the fields in tblSchedule match the names of the Schedule Plus contact properties. Therefore it's just a matter of walking through the list of fields in tblSchedule, using the name of each field as the name of a property in Schedule Plus and assigning each property the value of the field. The following fragment from SaveProps walks through the Fields collection of the recordset, copying the data to the corresponding property in Schedule Plus if the field contains some data.

```
Set db = CurrentDb()
Set rst = db.OpenRecordset(ahtcTable, dbOpenTable)

' Add the new row, and then fill in all the data.
' This works only because we cleverly named the fields in the
' table to exactly match the properties in Schedule Plus.
' If Microsoft  changes the property names, field names here will
' have to change as well.
For Each fld In rst.Fields
    If Len(fld.Value & "") > 0 Then
        varValue = fld.Value
        obj.Properties(fld.Name) = varValue
    End If
Next fld
```

Every record in the Schedule Plus database can be public or private; this privacy is controlled by the AccessActual property. Though no real documentation exists for this property at this time, experience has shown that private items have an AccessActual value of 5 (saclOwner) and public items have a value of 1 (saclReadMinimal). The following fragment sets that property, based on the Private field in tblSchedule.

```
obj.AccessActual = IIf(rst!Private, saclOwner, saclReadMinimal)
```

Saving the birthday and anniversary as recurring events is the final piece of the puzzle.

```
' So what about those two extra fields, Anniversary and Birthdate?
Call SaveRecurringEvents(obj, rst)
```

The SaveRecurringEvents procedure, too long to print here, does its work by adding recurring events for the birthday and anniversary to the RecurringEvents table if necessary or altering the values if they already exist. If SaveRecurringEvents must create the new events, it stores their ItemId values in the contact record along with the rest of the contact information.

The full code for SaveProps, shown below, accepts a reference to a contact object and saves all the non-null properties in tblSchedule to the object's Properties collection.

```
Private Sub SaveProps(obj As Object)
    Dim db As Database
    Dim rst As Recordset
    Dim fld As Field
    Dim varValue As Variant

    ' Save properties for the selected contact object.

    On Error GoTo SaveProps_Err

    ' Open up the recordset for additions.
    Set db = CurrentDb()
    Set rst = db.OpenRecordset(ahtcTable, dbOpenTable)

    ' Add the new row, and then fill in all the data.
    ' This works only because we cleverly named the fields in the
    ' table to exactly match the properties in Schedule Plus.
    ' If Microsoft changes the property names, field names here will
    ' have to change as well.
    For Each fld In rst.Fields
        If Len(fld.Value & "") > 0 Then
            varValue = fld.Value
            obj.Properties(fld.Name) = varValue
        End If
NextField:
    Next fld

    obj.AccessActual = IIf(rst!Private, saclOwner, saclReadMinimal)

    ' So what about those two extra fields, Anniversary and Birthdate?
    Call SaveRecurringEvents(obj, rst)

SaveProps_Exit:
    If Not rst Is Nothing Then rst.Close
    Exit Sub

SaveProps_Err:
    Select Case Err.Number
        Case ahtcErrCantSetProperty
            Resume NextField
        Case Else
            Call ahtGenericError(Err, "SaveProps")
    End Select
    Resume SaveProps_Exit
End Sub
```

Retrieving a List of All Contacts

To retrieve a list of all the available contacts, this sample loops through all the rows in your schedule's Contacts table until it hits the end. It loads the FirstName, LastName, and ItemId properties of each contact into an array of user-defined types named matypNames. The ahtGetNameList function does this work, returning the number of contacts it found. Along the way, it calls the AddToArray function, which places items in matypNames and adds rows to the array as necessary.

To retrieve all the names, ahtGetNameList walks through your schedule's Contacts table one row at a time. When walking through recordsets in Access, you use a loop like this:

```
Do While Not rst.EOF
    ' Work with the current row of data.
    rst.MoveNext
Loop
```

The Schedule Plus programmers decided on a different approach. The same sort of loop in Schedule Plus looks like this:

```
Do While Not objTable.IsEndOfTable
    ' Work with the current item in the table.
    objTable.Skip
Loop
```

To retrieve the list of contacts and place their names and ItemIDs into an array, ahtGetNameList includes the following code fragment, using the Item property of the selected table (Contacts, in this case) to retrieve a reference to the selected item.

```
intItem = 1
Do While Not objContacts.IsEndOfTable
    ' Get a reference to the specific contact
    Set objName = objContacts.Item
    intItem = AddToArray(objName, intItem)
    frm.Prompt "Loading: " & matypNames(intItem - 1).strName
    frm.Repaint
    objContacts.Skip
Loop
```

In the complete function, shown below, you'll note that the code redimensions matypNames after it has loaded all the data so that it's no larger than necessary. Then it calls ahtSortArray to sort the array based on the LastName field.

```
Function ahtGetNameList(frm As Form)
    Dim objSched As Object
    Dim objContacts As Object
    Dim objName As Object
    Dim intItem As Integer

    On Error GoTo ahtGetNameListErr
    DoCmd.Hourglass True

    frm.Prompt "Retrieving connection. Please wait..."
    Set objSched = GetSchedule()
```

```
        frm.Prompt ""
    If Not objSched Is Nothing Then
        Set objContacts = objSched.Contacts

        intItem = 1
        Do While Not objContacts.IsEndOfTable
            Set objName = objContacts.Item
            intItem = AddToArray(objName, intItem)
            frm.Prompt "Loading: " & matypNames(intItem - 1).strName
            frm.Repaint
            objContacts.Skip
        Loop
        mintItems = intItem - 1
        If intItem > 1 Then
            ReDim Preserve matypNames(1 To mintItems)
            If intItem > 0 Then
                ahtSortArray matypNames()
            End If
        End If
        frm.Prompt ""
    End If

ahtGetNameListExit:
    DoCmd.Hourglass False
    Set objName = Nothing
    Set objContacts = Nothing
    Set objSched = Nothing
    ahtGetNameList = intItem - 1
    Exit Function

ahtGetNameListErr:
    Select Case Err.Number
        Case Else
            Call ahtGenericError(Err, "Get Name List")
    End Select
    Resume ahtGetNameListExit
End Function
```

Loading an Existing Contact

Once you've chosen to load the full list of contacts, Access uses a list-filling callback function to display the information from the global array (matypNames) in the combo box on the form. (See Chapter 7 for more information on these list-filling functions.) When you choose an item from the list, the combo box's AfterUpdate event procedure calls the ahtLoadContactInfo function, the main portion of which is shown below.

```
Set objContact = ahtLoadContact(varID)
If Not objContact Is Nothing Then
    Call ahtClearTable
    Call LoadProps(objContact)
    ahtLoadContactInfo = True
End If
```

Schedule Plus needs some way to identify each row in its tables uniquely. That way, it can quickly find a row given that unique value. Because the data itself need not be unique, Schedule Plus must have some value that it can use as its own primary key value—the ItemId property of each piece of data fulfills this need. Although you won't ever have to look at the ItemId property for a contact or event, you'll need to use that value to identify the correct birthday and/or anniversary for a specific contact or to load a specific contact once you've stored the contact's ItemId in the combo box on your form. When you specify either of those date values for a contact, Schedule Plus stores only the ItemId for the corresponding row in the RecurringEvents table in the contact's row. When it needs to find the date information, it goes to the appropriate row in the RecurringEvents table and retrieves it.

The ahtLoadContact function is quite simple, as its main section below shows. It calls GetSchedule to retrieve a reference to the current schedule and then uses the ItemId value passed into the procedure to find the requested contact. The function returns a reference to the contact object or Nothing if it was unable to find the requested contact. The next subsection covers the LoadProps function, which retrieves all the contact information for the specified contact.

```
Set objSched = GetSchedule()
If objSched Is Nothing Then
    Set ahtLoadContact = Nothing
Else
    Set ahtLoadContact = objSched.Contacts.Item(varID)
End If
```

Retrieving the Properties for a Given Contact

The function shown previously, ahtGetNameList, fills the global array matypNames with the LastName, FirstName, and ItemID properties of the contact. Once you've chosen a name from the list of contacts and have retrieved an object from Schedule Plus that is the specific contact, you'll need to retrieve all the information about the contact. To display the rest of the fields, you must retrieve all the associated properties from Schedule Plus. Given a reference to an existing contact, LoadProps walks through tblSchedule, loading values into each of its fields from the matching property names for the contact.

Note

This procedure counts on the field names in tblSchedule matching the Schedule Plus contact property names exactly. A few fields in tblSchedule don't match properties—they're used for this example only—so the code is smart enough to skip over fields in the table that cause an error in attempting to retrieve a property value.

```
Private Sub LoadProps(obj As Object)
    ' Get all the properties for the given contact object
    ' from Schedule Plus.
    Dim db As Database
    Dim rst As Recordset
```

```
        Dim fld As Field
        Dim objProp As Object

        On Error GoTo LoadProps_Err

        ' Open up the recordset for additions.
        Set db = CurrentDb()
        Set rst = db.OpenRecordset(ahtcTable, dbOpenTable, dbAppendOnly)

        ' Add the new row, and then fill in all the data.
        ' This works only because we cleverly named the fields in the
        ' table to exactly match the properties in Schedule Plus.
        ' If Microsoft  changes the property names, field names here will
        ' have to change as well.
        rst.AddNew
           For Each fld In rst.Fields
              Set objProp = obj.Properties(fld.Name)
              If Len(objProp.Value & "") > 0 Then
                 fld = objProp.Value
              End If
NextField:
           Next fld
           ' Handle the Private check. If the AccessActual property
           ' is 5 (saclOwner) then it's private.
           rst!Private = (obj.Properties("AccessActual") = saclOwner)
        rst.Update
        rst.Move 0, rst.LastModified

        ' So what about those two extra fields, Anniversary and Birthdate?
        ' If there are values in BirthdayItemID and/or AnniversaryItemID,
        ' let's go get them!
        Call GetEventDate(rst, "BirthdayItemID", "BirthDate", _
        "CheckBirthdate")
        Call GetEventDate(rst, "AnniversaryItemID", "Anniversary", _
        "CheckAnniversary")

        ' Extra code missing here... See the sample database
        ' for the exact details.

LoadProps_Exit:
    Set objProp = Nothing
    Exit Sub

LoadProps_Err:
    Select Case Err.Number
        ' If you come across a property that Schedule Plus doesn't
        ' understand, just move on to the next field.
        Case ahtcErrPropertyNotSupported
           Resume NextField
        Case Else
           Call ahtGenericError(Err, "LoadProps")
    End Select
    Resume LoadProps_Exit
End Sub
```

Working with Recurring Events

If a contact record includes information on a birthday or anniversary, Schedule Plus stores the starting date and other pertinent information in the schedule's RecurringEvents table. In the contact record, it stores the ItemId of the event item as a reference to the real data. The following procedure, GetEventDate, accepts as parameters a record-set object (based on tblSchedule) and the names of three fields in the recordset: strIDField contains the name of the field containing the date's ItemId; strDateField contains the name of the field into which you'd like to place the event's annual date; and strCheckField contains the name of the field that indicates whether or not your contact stores this particular date field or not (see the sample form in action for more information on the check field).

The LoadProps procedure calls GetEventDate to gather information on the contact's birthday and anniversary, calling it like this:

```
Call GetEventDate(rst, "BirthdayItemID", "BirthDate", _
  "CheckBirthdate")
Call GetEventDate(rst, "AnniversaryItemID", "Anniversary", _
  "CheckAnniversary")
```

The GetEventDate subroutine, shown below, uses the ItemId for the date to retrieve a reference to it from the RecurringEvents table. With that object, it can add the appropriate date value to tblSchedule for display on the form. (It retrieves the StartRecurringDate property, which indicates on which date you want to start the annual event.) Note the use of the SchedToDate function, discussed in the next subsection.

```
Private Sub GetEventDate(rst As Recordset, strIDField As String, _
  strDateField As String, strCheckField As String)

    ' Given an event ID from Schedule Plus, go get
    ' that event record from the RecurringEvents
    ' table, and then send the StartRecurringDate
    ' property to the Access table.

    Dim objEvent As Object
    Dim varValue As Variant

    On Error GoTo GetEventDate_Err

    If Len(rst(strIDField) & "") > 0 Then
        Set objEvent = LoadEvent(rst(strIDField))
        varValue = objEvent.Properties("StartRecurringDate")
        If Len(varValue & "") > 0 Then
            rst.Edit
                rst(strDateField) = SchedToDate(varValue)
                rst(strCheckField) = True
            rst.Update
        End If
    End If

GetEventDate_Exit:
    Set objEvent = Nothing
```

```
    Exit Sub

GetEventDate_Err:
    Select Case Err.Number
        Case Else
            Call ahtGenericError(Err, "GetEventDate")
    End Select
    Resume GetEventDate_Exit

End Sub

Private Function LoadEvent(varID As Variant) As Object
    ' Given an Event ID, get an Access object
    ' that can refer to that event object in Schedule Plus.

    Dim objSched As Object

    On Error GoTo LoadEvent_Err

    Set objSched = GetSchedule()
    If objSched Is Nothing Then
        Set LoadEvent = Nothing
    Else
        Set LoadEvent = objSched.RecurringEvents.Item(varID)
    End If

LoadEvent_Exit:
    Set objSched = Nothing
    Exit Function

LoadEvent_Err:
    Select Case Err.Number
        Case Else
            Call ahtGenericError(Err, "LoadEvent")
    End Select
    Set LoadEvent = Nothing
    Resume LoadEvent_Exit
End Function
```

Handling Date Values

Although discussing bitmasking and shifting is beyond the scope of this book, you should be aware that Schedule Plus stores some (but not all) of its dates in a rather unusual format. Rather than storing text strings or serial dates (the number of days since some starting date), Schedule Plus uses a bitmapped format. That is, it stores dates in five hexadecimal digits, in this format (shown one bit at a time, with spaces between the hex digits):

YYYY YYYY YYYM MMMD DDDD

Converting this value to a readable date involves masking off the portion of interest (setting all the other bits to 0) and shifting the results until the portion you want sits on the right-hand edge of the number. The SchedToDate function, shown below, does just this. You needn't worry about how it does its work, just that you'll need to call it (and its inverse, DateToSched) when working with Schedule+ date fields.

```
Private Function SchedToDate(ByVal lngSched As Long) As Date
    Dim intYear As Integer
    Dim intMonth As Integer
    Dim intDay As Integer

    ' Schedule+' dates are stored in binary, with this
    ' format:
    ' YYYY YYYY YYYM MMMD DDDD
    ' This code uses bitmasks and shifting (dividing by
    ' powers of 2) to pull apart the various pieces.
    ' Figuring this out without documentation was LOADS
    ' of fun!

    intYear = (lngSched And ahtcYearMask) / ahtcYearShift
    intMonth = (lngSched And ahtcMonthMask) / ahtcMonthShift
    intDay = lngSched And ahtcDayMask
    SchedToDate = DateSerial(intYear, intMonth, intDay)
End Function

Private Function DateToSched(varDate As Variant) As Long
    ' Convert an Access date into a Schedule Plus date.
    ' See SchedToDate for more information.
    DateToSched = (Year(varDate) * ahtcYearShift) + _
        (Month(varDate) * ahtcMonthShift) + Day(varDate)
End Function
```

Schedule+ also stores dates and months for recurring events in an odd format. Within a long integer, it sets a single bit within the integer to represent which day or month you've selected. That is, it would represent the 12th of a month as a long integer with just the 12th bit set (counting from the right). To handle these conversions, you can call the MaskToDec and DecToMask functions in basSchedule.

```
Private Function MaskToDec(dblMask As Double)
    ' Convert from Schedule+ date and month masks
    ' back to decimal values. The values represent
    ' which bit within a 32-bit value is set, so
    ' all you need to do is find out the corresponding
    ' value. To do that, you need the base-2 log of the
    ' number, and to get that, just use Log(n)/Log(2).
    If dblMask > 0 Then
        MaskToDec = Log(dblMask) / Log(2) + 1
    Else
        MaskToDec = 1
    End If
End Function

Private Function DecToMask(intValue As Integer)
    ' Only allow values between 1 and 31.
    If intValue > 31 Or intValue < 0 Then
        intValue = 1
    End If
    DecToMask = 2 ^ (intValue - 1)
End Function
```

Deleting a Contact

Once you've asked frmSchedule to load all the contacts from Schedule Plus, you'll have the option to choose the Delete button on the form, allowing you to delete the selected contact. This operation is simple: The code first deletes the birthday and anniversary recurring events, if they exist, and then deletes the contact. Schedule Plus provides the Delete method of a table object; the ahtDeleteContact function, along with the DeleteEvent function, does the work.

```
Function ahtDeleteContact(varID As Variant) As Boolean
    ' Given an ItemID, delete the given contact.
    ' Also delete the recurring events.
    ' Not sure whether it's required or not, but it can't hurt.
    ' Those birthday and anniversary events can only be tied to a
    ' single contact!
    '
    ' We could have simplified this some, calling it from the
    ' form, because the form knows the AnniveraryID and the BirthdayID
    ' already. But this code is a bit more generic.

    Dim objContact As Object
    Dim objSched As Object

    On Error GoTo ahtDeleteContact_Err

    Set objContact = ahtLoadContact(varID)
    If Not objContact Is Nothing Then
        Call DeleteEvent(objContact.BirthdayItemID)
        Call DeleteEvent(objContact.AnniversaryItemID)
    End If
    Set objSched = GetSchedule()
    objSched.Contacts.DeleteItem varID
    ahtDeleteContact = True

ahtDeleteContact_Exit:
    Set objContact = Nothing
    Set objSched = Nothing
    Exit Function

ahtDeleteContact_Err:
    Select Case Err.Number
        Case Else
            Call ahtGenericError(Err, "ahtDeleteContact")
    End Select
    ahtDeleteContact = False
    Resume ahtDeleteContact_Exit

End Function

Private Sub DeleteEvent(varID As Variant)

    ' Delete a specified event.

    Dim objSched As Object
```

continued on next page

continued from previous page

```
        On Error GoTo DeleteEvent_Err

        If Len(varID & "") > 0 Then
           Set objSched = GetSchedule()
           If Not objSched Is Nothing Then
              objSched.RecurringEvents.DeleteItem varID
           End If
        End If

    DeleteEvent_Exit:
        Set objSched = Nothing
        Exit Sub

    DeleteEvent_Err:
        Set objSched = Nothing
        Select Case Err.Number
           Case Else
              Call ahtGenericError(Err, "DeleteEvent")
        End Select
        Resume DeleteEvent_Exit
    End Sub
```

Comments

This example is not nearly as simple as we would have liked. It took far too much code to emulate the Schedule Plus data card interface; much of the useful code is buried in supporting that interface. You'll find much of the important code discussed here; but your best bet, if you want to understand the complete example fully, is to set a breakpoint at the beginning of the ahtGetNameList function and work through it line by line.

This sample application, though moderately full featured, is just a starting point: It deals with only a small portion of the Schedule Plus functionality. You could expand this example to work with appointments, tasks, single events, or any other area of Schedule Plus that interests you.

If you'd like to modify this example to print reports based on your Schedule Plus data, you'll need to write code to retrieve all of the necessary contact properties and add multiple rows to tblSchedule. As it stands, the code reads only a few properties from Schedule Plus and fills a single row in tblSchedule when you choose a contact from the combo box. It should be easy to "borrow" the code from ahtGetNameList and write the full details of each contact to tblSchedule.

At the time of this writing, there is no documentation available on the properties and methods that Schedule Plus exposes. We gathered most of our information from two sources: Mike Gilbert's excellent white paper for Tech-Ed 95 (session EX206) and VBA Companion from Apex Software. This tool, available in retail outlets, makes it easier to gather information about many OLE Automation servers. There is no demo version available at this time, but the tool itself costs less than $100 and has saved us many, many hours of frustration. We also used the Object Browser that's built into Access, but VBA Companion gave more useful information than the Object Browser.

INDEX

& operator, 133
+ operator, 133
< > and sort order, 42, 44
@ characters, 466-467

A

About box, 643-651
Access Basic, xvi
Access caption, 221-225
access, query table, 54-56
Access type library, 674, 676
AccessActual property, 738
Action property, 666, 669-670
Add method, 113, 724-726, 731
add-in distribution, 241-247
add-in installation, 241-244, 247
Add-In Manager, 242, 244-246
AddItem method, 369-370
addresses, sorting, 19-22
Admin account, 517-518, 521
AfterUpdate event, 76-78, 81-83, 87
aging data, 32-35
AllowAdditions property, 537
AND operator, 229, 231, 425
animation, buttons, 483-488
apostrophes, as delimiters, 352-353
AppActivate, 628, 630

AppIcon property, 223
Application object, 207-208, 456, 568, 571,
    675, 677, 734
applications
    adjust for security level, 545-550
    client/server, 443-447, 527, 666
        See also DDE *and* OLE
    closing, 459, 633-635
    development, 182
    distribution, 182
    multiuser. *See* multiuser applications
    pausing, 614-617
    run by file association, 620-625
    run status, 626-632
    upgrade utility, 582-593
AppTitle property, 221, 223-224
arrays, objects, 338-341
arrays, passing, 378-382, 387
arrays, sorting, 383-387, 389-390
AutoKeys macro, 454-459
AutoNumber, flexible, 331-336
AutoRepeat property, 717
average (mean), 318, 322

B

BackColor property, 69, 72, 232, 234
background color, 67-68, 156, 232, 234

function *(continued)*
TrimNull, 622
UBound, 381-382
UCase, 611
UCaseArray, 379-381
WinHelp, 104-105
functions
callback, 370, 372-378, 387-391, 632
creating, xxiii-xxiv, xxvii
Excel, 322, 677-688
list-filling, 337-338, 370-378, 387-391, 632, 696-697, 741
names, xxiv

G

gauge (status meter), 501-507
Get/Let/Set property procedures, 103, 498-501, 506-507
GetOption method, 207-208, 457-458
global module, 27-29
GotoPage, 79, 82
GotoRecord, 84, 87
Graph, 666-667, 706-719
Graph 5.0 type library, 718
graphs
bar graph, 136-139
editing, 666-667
pie charts, 706-719
gray bar reports, 156-159
Group Interval property, 129
Group On property, 129
grouping, 127-129, 168-177
Groups collections, 542-543, 549
groups/users list, 538-545

H

handle
instance, 614, 616
process, 614
window, 207, 222, 224, 606-608
hardware requirements, xvii
headers, 135-136, 149-151
Help button, 466, 469
help file, 104-105, 469

I

icon, flashing, 605-608
icon, setting, 223

index properties, 539
indexes, table, 51-53
indexing fields, 422, 424-425, 427, 442
input box, 99-105
InputMask property, 556
installation, CD files, xxix-xxxiv
instance handle, 614, 616
integer division, 429, 436
interface, map, 462-465
interface, user, 451-452
interface, Windows, 598
international characters, 608-611
international text, 215-221
international versions, 210-215
inventory, objects, 187-194
ItemId property, 742

J

Jet engine, xxxi, 48, 57, 193, 423, 425, 432, 435, 545
join
equality, 36
inner, 46
nonequality, 35-38
outer, 46-47
properties, 46
self-join, 45, 47
tables, 23-25, 39-41

K

KeepTogether property, 164-165
key assignment, 454-459
KeyDown event, 73-74, 81
KeyPress event, 609-610
KeyPreview property, 73, 81
keys, shortcut, 454-459
keystrokes, classifying, 608-611
keystrokes, trapping, 73, 81

L

language translation, 215-221
language version, 210-215, 608-611
Layout, 126-128
layout, consistency, 195-205
layout settings, 265-272
Let/Get/Set property procedures, 103, 498-501, 506-507
Like operator, 442

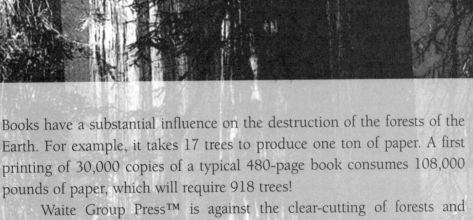

ENVIRONMENTAL AWARENESS

Books have a substantial influence on the destruction of the forests of the Earth. For example, it takes 17 trees to produce one ton of paper. A first printing of 30,000 copies of a typical 480-page book consumes 108,000 pounds of paper, which will require 918 trees!

Waite Group Press™ is against the clear-cutting of forests and supports reforestation of the Pacific Northwest of the United States and Canada, where most of this paper comes from. As a publisher with several hundred thousand books sold each year, we feel an obligation to give back to the planet. We will therefore support organizations which seek to preserve the forests of planet Earth.

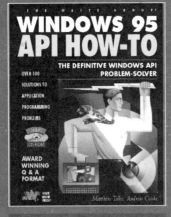

This is a legal agreement between you, the end user and purchaser, and The Waite Group®, Inc., and the authors of the programs contained in the disk. By opening the sealed disk package, you are agreeing to be bound by the terms of this Agreement. If you do not agree with the terms of this Agreement, promptly return the unopened disk package and the accompanying items (including the related book and other written material) to the place you obtained them for a refund.

SOFTWARE LICENSE

1. The Waite Group, Inc. grants you the right to use one copy of the enclosed software programs (the programs) on a single computer system (whether a single CPU, part of a licensed network, or a terminal connected to a single CPU). Each concurrent user of the program must have exclusive use of the related Waite Group, Inc. written materials.

2. The program, including the copyrights in each program, is owned by the respective author and the copyright in the entire work is owned by The Waite Group, Inc. and they are therefore protected under the copyright laws of the United States and other nations, under international treaties. You may make only one copy of the disk containing the programs exclusively for backup or archival purposes, or you may transfer the programs to one hard disk drive, using the original for backup or archival purposes. You may make no other copies of the programs, and you may make no copies of all or any part of the related Waite Group, Inc. written materials.

3. You may not rent or lease the programs, but you may transfer ownership of the programs and related written materials (including any and all updates and earlier versions) if you keep no copies of either, and if you make sure the transferee agrees to the terms of this license.

4. You may not decompile, reverse engineer, disassemble, copy, create a derivative work, or otherwise use the programs except as stated in this Agreement.

GOVERNING LAW

This Agreement is governed by the laws of the State of California.

LIMITED WARRANTY

The following warranties shall be effective for 90 days from the date of purchase: (i) The Waite Group, Inc. warrants the enclosed disk to be free of defects in materials and workmanship under normal use; and (ii) The Waite Group, Inc. warrants that the programs, unless modified by the purchaser, will substantially perform the functions described in the documentation provided by The Waite Group, Inc. when operated on the designated hardware and operating system. The Waite Group, Inc. does not warrant that the programs will meet purchaser's requirements or that operation of a program will be uninterrupted or error-free. The program warranty does not cover any program that has been altered or changed in any way by anyone other than The Waite Group, Inc. The Waite Group, Inc. is not responsible for problems caused by changes in the operating characteristics of computer hardware or computer operating systems that are made after the release of the programs, nor for problems in the interaction of the programs with each other or other software.

THESE WARRANTIES ARE EXCLUSIVE AND IN LIEU OF ALL OTHER WARRANTIES OF MERCHANTABILITY OR FITNESS FOR A PARTICULAR PURPOSE OR OF ANY OTHER WARRANTY, WHETHER EXPRESS OR IMPLIED.

EXCLUSIVE REMEDY

The Waite Group, Inc. will replace any defective disk without charge if the defective disk is returned to The Waite Group, Inc. within 90 days from date of purchase.

This is Purchaser's sole and exclusive remedy for any breach of warranty or claim for contract, tort, or damages.

LIMITATION OF LIABILITY

THE WAITE GROUP, INC. AND THE AUTHORS OF THE PROGRAMS SHALL NOT IN ANY CASE BE LIABLE FOR SPECIAL, INCIDENTAL, CONSEQUENTIAL, INDIRECT, OR OTHER SIMILAR DAMAGES ARISING FROM ANY BREACH OF THESE WARRANTIES EVEN IF THE WAITE GROUP, INC. OR ITS AGENT HAS BEEN ADVISED OF THE POSSIBILITY OF SUCH DAMAGES.

THE LIABILITY FOR DAMAGES OF THE WAITE GROUP, INC. AND THE AUTHORS OF THE PROGRAMS UNDER THIS AGREEMENT SHALL IN NO EVENT EXCEED THE PURCHASE PRICE PAID.

COMPLETE AGREEMENT

This Agreement constitutes the complete agreement between The Waite Group, Inc. and the authors of the programs, and you, the purchaser.

Some states do not allow the exclusion or limitation of implied warranties or liability for incidental or consequential damages, so the above exclusions or limitations may not apply to you. This limited warranty gives you specific legal rights; you may have others, which vary from state to state.

SATISFACTION REPORT CARD

Please fill out this card if you wish to know of future updates to
Microsoft Access 95 How-To or to receive our catalog.

First Name: _____   **Last Name:** _____

Address: _____

City: _____   **State:** _____   **Zip:** _____

Daytime Telephone: (_____) _____

E-mail Address: _____

Date product was acquired: Month _____ **Day** _____ **Year** _____   **Your Occupation:** _____

Overall, how would you rate *Microsoft Access 95 How-To?*

☐ Excellent   ☐ Very Good   ☐ Good
☐ Fair   ☐ Below Average   ☐ Poor

What did you like MOST about this book? _____
_____

What did you like LEAST about this book? _____
_____
_____

Please describe any problems you may have encountered with installing or using the disk: _____
_____

How did you use this book (problem-solver, tutorial, reference…)?
_____

What is your level of computer expertise?

☐ New   ☐ Dabbler   ☐ Hacker
☐ Power User   ☐ Programmer   ☐ Experienced Professional

What computer languages are you familiar with? _____
_____

Please describe your computer hardware:

Computer _____ Hard disk _____
Modem _____ 3.5" disk drives _____
Video card _____ Monitor _____
Printer _____ Peripherals _____
Sound board _____ CD-ROM _____

Where did you buy this book?

☐ Bookstore (name): _____
☐ Discount store (name): _____
☐ Computer store (name): _____
☐ Catalog (name): _____
☐ Direct from WGP   ☐ Other

What price did you pay for this book? _____

What influenced your purchase of this book?

☐ Recommendation   ☐ Advertisement
☐ Magazine review   ☐ Store display
☐ Mailing   ☐ Book's format
☐ Reputation of Waite Group Press   ☐ Other

How many computer books do you buy each year? _____

How many other Waite Group books do you own? _____

What is your favorite Waite Group book? _____
_____

Is there any program or subject you would like to see Waite Group Press cover in a similar approach? _____
_____

Additional comments? _____
_____
_____

Please send to: Waite Group Press
200 Tamal Plaza
Corte Madera, CA 94925

☐ **Check here for a free Waite Group catalog**

BEFORE YOU OPEN THE DISK OR CD-ROM PACKAGE ON THE FACING PAGE, CAREFULLY READ THE LICENSE AGREEMENT.

Opening this package indicates that you agree to abide by the license agreement found in the back of this book. If you do not agree with it, promptly return the unopened disk package (including the related book) to the place you obtained them for a refund.